GOLF

RECORDS
FACTS
AND
CHAMPIONS

DONALD STEEL

Acknowledgements

Bill Hodge (PGA European Tour)
Tony Greer (IMG)
Colonel A A Duncan
John Redmond
James Lindsay
The LPGA of America
John Bailey
The PGA American Tour
The WPGA
Karen Bednarski, United States Golf Association
Cecil Timms

British Library Cataloguing in Publication Data

Steel, Donald
    Guinness golf: record facts & champions.
    —3rd ed.
    1. Golf—Records
    I. Title   II. The Guinness book of golf
    facts and feats
    796.352'09   GV965

ISBN 0–85112–847–5

Editor: Beatrice Frei
Design and Layout: Geoffrey Hart Associates

© Donald Steel and Guinness Superlatives Ltd, 1987

Published in Great Britain by Guinness Superlatives Ltd,
33 London Road, Enfield, Middlesex

Typeset by Fakenham Photosetting Ltd,
Fakenham, Norfolk
Printed and bound in Great Britain by Redwood Burn Ltd

'Guinness' is a registered trade mark of
Guinness Superlatives Ltd

**The Golf Links at Pau, France—the first course on the
Continent of Europe. (BBC Hulton Picture Library)**

CONTENTS

History of Golf

Golfing countries

Golf history is an involved subject and the source of much argument. Nobody knows for certain where it was first played, except that it was on largely rough, uncharted territory with no defined limits such as the modern courses. Many games in various countries have had similarities with golf—hence the difficulty in the arguments over which of the rudimentary forms was actually golf.

In many countries, too, it has been established that recognized golf was introduced long before it became a regular and organized pursuit. For instance, incontrovertible evidence exists to show that golf was played in Charleston, North Carolina and in Virginia in the mid-18th century. Golf was also played in several islands in the West Indies between 1810 and 1860 and a start was made in New Zealand in 1871.

A group of golfers in Ceylon, now Sri Lanka. (Illustrated London News)

OLDEST CLUBS

Country	First Club	Country	First Club	Country	First Club
Scotland	1744	Australia	1891	Malawi	1911
England	1766	Spain	1891	Trinidad and Tobago	1914
India	1829	New Zealand	1891	Colombia	1917
France	1856	Singapore	1891	Uganda	1919
Pakistan	1857	Switzerland	1891	Republic of China	1919
Jamaica	1868	Germany	1893	Bermuda	1922
Indonesia	1872	Holland	1893	Norway	1924
Canada	1873	Turkey	1895	Morocco	1925
Sri Lanka	1879	Chile	1895	Swaziland	1928
Egypt	1880	Zimbabwe	1896	Tanzania	1929
Ireland	1881	Mexico	1897	Finland	1932
Italy	1885	Denmark	1898	Nigeria	1933
South Africa	1885	Brazil	1901	Ghana	1934
Wales	1888	Austria	1901	Iceland	1934
Belgium	1888	Sweden	1902	Luxembourg	1936
The United States of America	1888	Zambia	1902	Korea	1954
Malaysia	1888	Japan	1903	Botswana	1954
Hong Kong	1889	Philippines	1903	Barbados	1960
Argentina	1889	Czechoslovakia	1904	Israel	1961
Portugal	1890	Burma	1905	Greece	1963
Thailand	1890	Kenya	1907		

Footnote. *Before World War II, golf was played in Poland, Hungary, Russia, Yugoslavia and Romania. It has picked up again in Yugoslavia but no news exists of it in these other countries.*

This turned out to be a 'false dawn' as it did in Australia where golf was played around Sydney and Melbourne about 1850. This section deals, therefore, with the founding of golf in the various countries, based entirely on the date of the first Club which has been in continuous existence since that date.

A little bit of licence has been necessary where new countries have been formed (like Pakistan) or where others have gained independence and perhaps even changed their name. The Lahore Gymkhana Club is given as the oldest in Pakistan although the country was not born until 90 years later.

What constitutes a golfer? One who is a member of a Club? One who plays regularly on a public course? One who plays on high days and holidays? One who has a set of clubs in the attic?

In theory, they all qualify but, for the purposes of this

An unusual distraction: elephants crossing the Riverside Hole at Madras GC, 1894. (Illustrated London News)

exercise, the figures given are those supplied by the Golfing Unions or Federations or Associations of the various countries. They deal with what may be termed the official golfers and so some upward adjustment must be made in the case of the larger countries where there are plentiful public courses. In smaller golfing countries, the figures are probably very accurate and they give some fairly good idea of the number of golfers and courses in the world.

No attempt has been made to estimate the numbers of golfers in countries such as Libya, Lebanon and Afghanistan. Golf was played there but whether it has survived is another matter.

Golf in the rarefied atmosphere of the Himalayas in 1899. The golfers, it seems, have caddies and horses at Chakarta Hills. (Illustrated London News)

Above: The famous Swilcan bridge at St Andrews, showing Allan Robertson playing Tom Morris (left). (Author)

Right: Allan Robertson, golf's first great player. It was his death that led to the founding of the Open championship in order to find a worthy successor as champion. (Author)

TOTAL NUMBER OF COURSES AND GOLFERS

	Number of courses		*Total number*	*Oldest club with*
	Private	*Public*	*of golfers*	*continuous existence*
Argentina	129	2	25 000	Lomas, BA, 1890
Australia	1390	100	800 000	Royal Melbourne, 1891
Austria	25	—	6040	Golf Club Vienna, 1901
Barbados	3	—	300	Sandy Lane, 1960
Belgium	19	—	10 000	Royal Antwerp, 1888
Bermuda	5	3	3000	Riddell's Bay, 1922
Bolivia	9	0	1000	
Botswana	6	—	750	Lobatse, 1954
Brazil	46	—	6000	Sao Paolo, 1901
Burma	50	—	15 000	
Canada	750	850	1 500 000	Royal Montreal, 1873
Chile	31	—	7500	
Rep. of China	23	—	200 000	Taiwan G & CC, 1919
China	1	—	1000	Chung Shang, Hot Spring
Colombia	30	—	7500	
Czechoslovakia	0	8	1110	International Sporting Club, Karlovy Vary, 1904
Denmark	54	—	26 000	Copenhagen GC, 1898
Dominican Rep.	4	—	500	
Egypt	4	—	500	
England	1298	125	1 000 000	Royal Blackheath, 1766
Fiji	15 (only 2 18 holes)	—	5000	
Finland	18 (14 only 9 holes)	—	8500	Helsinki GC, 1932
France	139	31	100 000	Pau, 1856
Germany	197	4	80 000	Wiesbadener GC, 1893
Ghana	10	—	1000	Achimota GC, 1934
Greece	4	—	750	Glyfada, Athens, 1963
Guatemala	4	—	700	
Holland	30	4	30 000	Haagsche, 1893
Hong Kong	4	—	4200	Royal Hong Kong, 1889
Iceland	27	1	3500	Golfklubbur Reykjavikur, 1934
India	147	—	10 000	Royal Calcutta, 1829
Indonesia	50	10	50 000	Jakarta GC, 1872
Ireland	257	5	97 000	Royal Belfast, 1881
Israel	1	—	500	Caesarea, 1961
Italy	69	—	22 000	Roma, 1885
Ivory Coast	2	—	300	
Jamaica	11	—	1000	Manchester Club, 1868
Japan	1314	127	9 900 000	Kobe GC, 1903
Kenya	31	—	3000	Royal Nairobi, 1907
Korea	37	8	355 000	Seoul, 1954
Luxembourg	1	—	825	Grand Ducal De Luxembourg, 1936
Malawi	1	—	500	Lilongwe
Malaysia	50	—	12 000	Perak at Taiping, 1888
Mexico	45	—	10 000	Puebla, 1897
Morocco	14	—	500	
New Zealand	392	—	107 060	Christchurch, 1891. First Club Otago, 1871
Nigeria	17	—	1500	Ikoyi, Lagos, 1933
Norway	8	—	6265	Oslo, 1924
Pakistan	22	—	2000	Lahore Gymkhana, 1857
Peru	15	—	2000	
Philippines	57	—	100 000	Zamboanga, 1903
Portugal	21	—	4000	Oporto, 1890
Scotland	480	—	251 000	Honourable Company of Edinburgh Golfers, 1744
Singapore	9	—	10 000	Golf played since 1891
South Africa	385	6	69 000	Royal Cape, 1885
Spain	68	24	35 000	Las Palmas, 1891
Sri Lanka	2	—	500	Royal Colombo, 1879
Swaziland	6	3	550	Manzini, 1928
Sweden	170	5	150 000	Gothenburg, 1902
Switzerland	31	—	12 000	Samedan, 1891 (St Moritz GC)

TOTAL NUMBER OF COURSES AND GOLFERS

	Number of courses		Total number	Oldest club with
	Private	*Public*	*of golfers*	*continuous existence*
Thailand	45	—	40 000	Royal Bangkok, 1890
Trinidad	9	1	1200	St Andrews GC, 1914
Tanzania	5	0	400	Dar Es Salaam Gymkhana Club, 1929
Transkei	6	—	455	Umtata Country Club, 1931
Turkey	1	0	150	Istanbul GC, 1895
Uruguay	4	—	500	Uruguay GC, Montevideo
USA	12 300	9300 (2000 Municipal 7300 Daily fee)	21 300 000	St Andrews (Yonkers) NY, 1888
Venezuela	21	—	10 000	
Wales	118	1	29 718	Tenby, 1888
Zambia	20	—	3650	Chipata, 1902
Zimbabwe	70	—	4000	Bulawayo GC, 1896

	Number of courses		
	Private	*Public*	*Total number of golfers*
TOTALS	20 631	10 618	32 422 318

Picture of the finish of the first tournament held at St Andrews. The crowd are a little close by today's standards but they didn't seem to have bothered Mr Chambers. (Author)

By 1898, caddies had graduated to golf bags. Here, A J Balfour, the Prime Minister, opens the course at Broadstone, Dorset. He was a keen golfer but it was a Scottish caddie of his at St Andrews who, on seeing him miss his third short putt in a row commented 'and to think it is devils like that who are running the country'. (Illustrated London News)

Founding of early Golf Clubs and other interesting dates

1744 The Honourable Company of Edinburgh Golfers
1754 Golf Club of St Andrews
1766 Royal Blackheath
1773 The Royal Burgess Golfing Society of Edinburgh
1774 Royal Musselburgh
1780 Royal Aberdeen
1786 Crail Golfing Society, Fife
1787 Glasgow
     The Bruntsfield Links Golfing Society formed themselves into a Club
1797 Burntisland
1810 First evidence of a ladies competition. Held by the Musselburgh GC for local fisherwomen.
     Royal Albert, Montrose
1817 Scotscraig

1818 Manchester golfers (Old Manchester Club) started playing on Kersal Moor
1829 Royal Calcutta (first Club outside Britain)
1832 North Berwick
1834 William IV confers the title Royal and Ancient—previously the Golf Club of St Andrews
1842 (Royal) Bombay Golfing Society
1851 Prestwick
1856 Royal Curragh GC founded in Ireland
     Pau GC, France (first Club in Continental Europe)
1864 Royal North Devon (first English seaside links)
1873 Royal Montreal (first Golf Club in North American continent)
1878 First match between Oxford and Cambridge. It is the oldest surviving match between two Clubs.
1880 The Glasgow GC founded the Tennant Cup, the oldest surviving annual open competition
1898 Oxford and Cambridge Golfing Society formed, the oldest Society in the world without a course of its own

* Dates based on earliest written evidence.
Reference: *The History of Golf* by Robert Browning

History of equipment

CLUBS

1502 Earliest reference to bowmakers making clubs. King James IV of Scotland bought 'golf clubbes' from a bowmaker in Perth.

1787 Death of John Dickson of Leith, Edinburgh, member of first great family of clubmakers.

1800 Clubmaking became a recognized and thriving trade. The most famous names were the McEwans of Leith; Forgans of St Andrews; Patricks of Leven; Morrises of St Andrews; Parks of Musselburgh and Dunns of North Berwick. In addition, two individuals, Simon Cossar and Hugh Philp were well known.

However, by 1900, only the Patricks and Forgans were still trading. As the popularity of the game spread, mass production took over although individual clubmakers (notably Club professionals) continued; indeed, a few still do.

It is the clubs produced before about 1850 which attract increasingly large sums in sales at auction rooms.

1900 Until 1900, the head of a wooden club was fixed to the shaft by means of a long splice tightly bound with whipping. Before 1820, the shafts consisted largely of ash but hickory, a wood originating in North America, became fashionable.

Up until about 1850, a 'set' of clubs comprised all wooden clubs. The shafts were long, the heads were long (4–5 in), narrow and gracefully curved (concave). The face of the club was not more than about an inch deep.

The use of woods helped protect the feather balls which were liable to burst or cut. Since a ball was much more expensive than a club, this was quite a consideration but a single iron, a rut or track iron, was carried to help in 'tight corners'. The putters were also wood.

When the gutta-percha ball was introduced, the number of iron clubs increased. They had names (jigger, mashie, niblick, mid-iron) not numbers.

The 'modernized' look to wooden clubs began to develop in the latter part of the 19th century. Heads became shorter, squatter and the faces deeper. The concave look was also replaced by a more bulging, convex appearance; and the shafts became shorter (38–40 in standard).

1910 Persimmon had replaced ash for the manufacture of clubheads. Persimmon is another hard wood from North America. The method of fixing the head to the shaft altered.

However, a growing shortage of hickory led to the adoption of tubular steel shafts in the 1920s, although Bobby Jones remained loyal to hickory until he retired in 1930.

Experiments and research have led to aluminium, graphite, carbon fibre and all manner of other shafts as it has to metal headed woods but wood and steel still predominate.

The shape of the heads of iron clubs has taken various forms in recent years as marketing forces face increasing competition.

Above: Some nifty footwork by Willie Park, Jr, designer of the Old course at Sunningdale and one of the first golf course architects. (Illustrated London News)
Right: More sophisticated clubs on view at St Andrews in 1898 and a golf umbrella (one of the first) held by the umpire of a match involving Andrew Kirkaldy, A Simpson and Sandy Herd. Also seen are Old Tom Morris and Ben Sayers. (Illustrated London News)

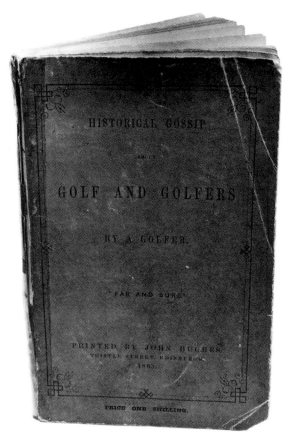

Above: Feathery balls were always expensive on account of all the hand work that went into their production but on 23 January 1987, a sale at Phillips, Chester realized £4500 for a mint condition Gourlay—a world record. At the same sale, the book in the picture fetched £11 200, having cost its first owner one shilling. (Phillips, Chester)

BALL AND ANCILLARY EQUIPMENT

c **1600–1850** Feathery ball in sole use. Consisted of an outer casement of cowhide stitched together to surround boiled chicken or goose feathers (enough to fill an old-fashioned top hat). It was then painted with a white lead paint to aid waterproofing. However, it did absorb water, became heavy, was liable to cut or even burst, and could be difficult to hit well.

1759 First mention of strokeplay golf.

c **1850** Gutta-percha balls introduced to replace the feathery. The dictionary defines gutta-percha as a tough, greyish-black plastic substance, got from the latex of various Malayan trees.

Its great advantage was that it was tougher, less absorbent and cheaper than the feathery. The cost factor resulted in the game becoming more a game for the people.

c **1857** Publication of first book on golf instruction, *The Golfer's Manual* by 'A Keen Hand' (H B Farnie).

c **1865** Introduction of score cards although it was some time before they printed details relating to length of hole etc.

c **1880** Production of first golf bag. J H Taylor always attributed the manufacture of the first golf bag to Andrews, the famous Steward at Westward Ho!

c **1900** Introduction of the Haskell (after Coburn Haskell) or rubber-cored ball. Strips of rubber were wrapped around a single core. First used by a winner of the Open championship in 1902 (Sandy Herd).

c **1920** Fitting of special spikes to shoes for golf. Also detachable hoods to golfbags.

c **1925** Introduction of waterproof clothing.

c **1930** Left-hand gloves became fashionable, largely due to the influence of Henry Cotton.

Introduction of larger golf bags to accommodate increasing number of clubs carried.

1932 Having intimated in May 1929 that they intended to adopt 'an easier and pleasanter ball for the average player', the United States Golf Association added the clause to the specification for the 1.68-in ball that the weight be increased to 1.62 oz.

1938 Limitation on the number of clubs to be carried imposed at fourteen by the Royal and Ancient and the United States Golf Association on 1 January 1938.

Use of tee pegs became popular.

1951 Abolition of the stymie.

c **1965** Golfing fashion changing. Traditional tweeds augmented by whole new range of sports shirts, trousers, caps etc.

c **1975–80** Solid golf balls and coloured balls became commonplace.

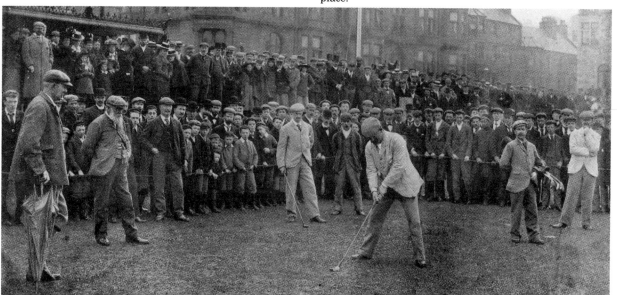

The Supreme Champions

Bobby Jones's assertion that 'there are tournament winners and major tournament winners' was a neat way of stressing the difference between the good and the great.

He, for his part, was the supreme champion, and this section is concerned solely with those men whose achievements have enriched the history of competitive golf: the legends like Jones, Hogan and Nicklaus.

It has become customary to measure success by the number of victories in the major championships, but such a measurement is not entirely fair. Before the start of the US Masters in 1934 and the USPGA championship in 1916, the only major championships were the British and American Opens; and, until the start of the jet age, it was very much the exception for anyone to play in both in the same year.

As a result, Harry Vardon, say, had far fewer chances than Jack Nicklaus who has taken part in all four major championships since first appearing as a professional in 1962. Inspired and influenced by Jones, however, he has always set his standards by the major championships and, by this insistence, has guaranteed their pre-eminence.

They remain the most cherished titles in the world of golf largely because they act as some means of comparison between the generations. In modern times, they have also become a passport to fortune, but the stunning thought today is that Jones was an amateur. His total of championship victories is, therefore, based on the Open and Amateur championships of Britain and America.

Any parallel between him and Hogan or Sarazen or Snead cannot be exact. If one includes Jones's Amateur championship successes, one has to include the two by Nicklaus and one by Arnold Palmer but, while it is impossible to argue with figures, the accompanying charts and tables illustrate what it is, by any reckoning, that sets a few golfers apart from the others.

Champion of the year

It is commonly believed that a 36-hole competition is a better test of a golfer's ability than a single round, and a 72-hole competition better still.

Frequently, we see a first or even second round leader in a major championship fading completely from the scene long before the end.

The man who shoots 67 today takes 77 tomorrow. Sometimes it may be due to luck averaging out or to an attack of nerves but sometimes, too, it is because tomorrow's share of putts are holed today.

If 72 holes is a surer test of ability than 18 or 36, it follows that 288 holes must be an even better test; and, if

the 288 holes are the aggregate of the four major championships, then the golfer with the lowest total for those 288 holes can fairly claim to be 'champion of the year'.

Until 1960, it was very rare for anyone to play in all four majors but since then it has become much more fashionable. The following is the roll of honour but it must be stressed that, in order to qualify, a player must have played in all four championships.

The name of Jack Nicklaus, as one would expect, features prominently, but in 1963 he was ineligible on account of failing to qualify in the US Open when defending champion although in the other three majors, he had two firsts and a third.

RESULTS

		British Open	US Open	US Masters	USPGA	Total
1960	Arnold Palmer	279(1)	280(1)	282(1)	286(7)	1127
1961	Arnold Palmer	284(1)	289(=14)	281(=2)	282(=5)	1136
1962	Arnold Palmer	276(1)	283(2)	280(1)	288(=17)	1127
1963	Gary Player	287(=7)	296(=8)	289(=5)	283(=13)	1155
1964	Jack Nicklaus	284(2)	295(=23)	282(=2)	274(=2)	1135
1965	Jack Nicklaus	294(=12)	299(=32)	271(1)	282(=2)	1146
1966	Arnold Palmer	288(=8)	278(2)	290(=4)	287(=6)	1143
1967	Doug Sanders	290(=18)	292(=34)	292(=16)	292(=28)	1166
1968	Billy Casper	292(4)	286(=9)	285(=16)	284(=6)	1147
1969	Miller Barber	288(10)	284(=6)	284(7)	280(=5)	1136
1970	Jack Nicklaus	283(1)	304(=51)	284(8)	283(6)	1154
1971	Jack Nicklaus	283(=5)	280(2)	281(=2)	281(1)	1125
1972	Jack Nicklaus	279(2)	290(1)	286(1)	287(=13)	1142
1973	Jack Nicklaus	280(4)	282(=4)	285(=3)	277(1)	1124
1974	Gary Player	282(1)	293(=8)	278(1)	280(7)	1133
1975	Jack Nicklaus	280(=3)	289(=7)	276(1)	276(1)	1121
1976	Raymond Floyd	286(4)	288(=13)	271(1)	282(=2)	1127
1977	Tom Watson	268(1)	284(=7)	278(1)	283(=6)	1114
1978	Tom Watson	287(=14)	289(=6)	278(=2)	276(=2)	1130
1979	Jack Nicklaus	286(=2)	291(=9)	281(4)	294(=65)	1152
1980	Jack Nicklaus	280(=4)	272(1)	291(=33)	274(1)	1117
1981	Jack Nicklaus	290(=23)	281(=6)	282(=2)	279(=4)	1132
	Bill Rogers	276(1)	276(=2)	295(=37)	285(=31)	1132
1982	Tom Watson	284(1)	282(1)	287(=5)	280(=9)	1133
1983	Tom Watson	275(1)	281(2)	285(=4)	290(=47)	1131
	Severiano Ballesteros	279(=6)	286(=4)	280(1)	286(=27)	1131
1984	Tom Watson	278(=2)	287(=11)	279(2)	291(=37)	1135
	Fred Couples	281(=4)	286(=9)	283(=10)	286(=20)	1136
1985	Payne Stewart	283(2)	281(=5)	292(=25)	285(=12)	1140
	Severiano Ballesteros	292(=39)	281(=24)	284(4)	289(=32)	1146
1986	Greg Norman	280(1)	285(=12)	280(=2)	278(2)	1123
	Bob Tway	298(=46)	284(=8)	284(=8)	276(1)	1142

Left: The immortal trio of champions (left to right), J H Taylor, James Braid and Harry Vardon shown with Sandy Herd, one of the few to break their dominance in the Open championship between 1894 and 1914. (BBC Hulton Picture Library)

Individual victories in the major championships

20—JACK WILLIAM NICKLAUS
US Open, 1962–67–72–80
British Open, 1966–70–78
US Masters, 1963–65–66–72–75–86
USPGA, 1963–71–73–75–80
US Amateur, 1959–61

13—ROBERT TYRE JONES, Jr
US Open, 1923–26–29–30
British Open, 1926–27–30
US Amateur, 1924–25–27–28–30
British Amateur, 1930

11—WALTER CHARLES HAGEN
US Open, 1914–19
British Open, 1922–24–28–29
US Masters, None
USPGA, 1921–24–25–26–27

9—BENJAMIN WILLIAM HOGAN
US Open, 1948–50–51–53
British Open, 1953
US Masters, 1951–53
USPGA, 1946–48

9—GARY PLAYER
US Open, 1965
British Open, 1959–68–74
US Masters, 1961–74–78
USPGA, 1962–72

8—ARNOLD DANIEL PALMER
US Open, 1960
British Open, 1961–62
US Masters, 1958–60–62–64
USPGA, None
US Amateur, 1954

8—TOM WATSON
US Open, 1982
British Open, 1975–77–80–82–83
US Masters, 1977–81
USPGA, None

7—HARRY VARDON
US Open, 1900
British Open, 1896–98–99–03–11–14

7—EUGENE (GENE) SARAZEN
US Open, 1922–32
British Open, 1932
US Masters, 1935
USPGA, 1922–23–33

7—SAMUEL JACKSON SNEAD
US Open, None
British Open, 1946
US Masters, 1949–52–54
USPGA, 1942–49–51

6—LEE TREVINO
US Open, 1968–71
British Open, 1971–72
US Masters, None
USPGA, 1974–84

5—BYRON NELSON
US Open, 1939
British Open, None
US Masters, 1937–42
USPGA, 1940–45

5—JOHN HENRY TAYLOR
British Open, 1894–95–1900–09–13

5—PETER THOMSON
British Open, 1954–55–56–58–65

5—JAMES BRAID
British Open, 1901–05–06–08–10

4—YOUNG TOM MORRIS
British Open, 1868–69–70–72

4—SEVERIANO BALLESTEROS
US Open, None
British Open, 1979–84
US Masters, 1980–83
USPGA, None

4—ARTHUR D'ARCY LOCKE
British Open, 1949–50–52–57

4—RAYMOND FLOYD
US Open, 1986
British Open, None
US Masters, 1976
USPGA, 1969–82

4—WILLIE ANDERSON
US Open, 1901–03–04–05

Major title winners

US Open, British Open, US Masters, USPGA, US Amateur

In same year None
In different years Jack Nicklaus

US Open, British Open, US Masters, US Amateur

In same year None
In different years Arnold Palmer, Jack Nicklaus

British Open, US Open, US Masters, USPGA

In same year None
In different years Gene Sarazen, Ben Hogan, Gary Player and Jack Nicklaus

British Open, US Open, British Amateur, US Amateur

In same year R T Jones, Jr (1930)
In different years None

British Open, US Open, US Masters

In same year Ben Hogan (1953)
In different years Gene Sarazen, Arnold Palmer, Gary Player, Jack Nicklaus and Tom Watson

British Open, US Open, USPGA

In same year None
In different years Walter Hagen, Jim Barnes, Gene Sarazen, Tommy Armour, Ben Hogan, Gary Player, Jack Nicklaus and Lee Trevino

British Open, USPGA, US Masters

In same year None
In different years Gene Sarazen, Ben Hogan, Sam Snead, Gary Player and Jack Nicklaus

US Open, USPGA, US Masters

In same year None
In different years Gene Sarazen, Byron Nelson, Ben Hogan, Gary Player, Jack Nicklaus and Raymond Floyd

British Open, US Open, US Amateur

In same year R T Jones, Jr (1930)
In different years R T Jones, Jr, Jack Nicklaus and Arnold Palmer

British Open, British Amateur, US Amateur

In same year R T Jones, Jr (1930)
In different years Harold Hilton

British Open, US Open, British Amateur

In same year R T Jones, Jr (1930)
In different years None

US Open, US Amateur, British Amateur

In same year R T Jones, Jr (1930)
In different years W Lawson Little

British Open, US Open

In same year R T Jones, Jr (1926 and 1930), Gene Sarazen (1932), Ben Hogan (1953), Lee Trevino (1971), Tom Watson (1982)
In different years Ted Ray, Harry Vardon, Walter Hagen, Jim Barnes, R T Jones, Jr, Tommy Armour, Arnold Palmer, Gary Player, Jack Nicklaus, Tony Jacklin, Lee Trevino and Johnny Miller

British Amateur, US Amateur

In same year Harold Hilton (1911), R T Jones, Jr (1930), W Lawson Little (1934 and 1935), Bob Dickson (1967)
In different years Walter Travis, Jess Sweetser, Willie Turnesa, Dick Chapman, Harvie Ward, Deane Beman, Steve Melnyk, Marvin Giles III and Jay Sigel

US Open, US Amateur, US Masters

In same year None
In different years Arnold Palmer, Jack Nicklaus

US Open, US Amateur

In same year Charles Evans, Jr (1916), R T Jones, Jr (1930)
In different years Francis Ouimet, Jerome D Travers, R T Jones, Jr, John Goodman, W Lawson Little, Arnold Palmer, Gene Littler, Jack Nicklaus and Jerry Pate

British Open, British Amateur

In same year John Ball (1890), R T Jones, Jr (1930)
In different years Harold Hilton

US Open, USPGA

In same year Gene Sarazen (1922), Ben Hogan (1948), Jack Nicklaus (1980)
In different years Walter Hagen, Jim Barnes, Gene Sarazen, Tommy Armour, Olin Dutra, Byron Nelson, Ben Hogan, Gary Player, Jack Nicklaus, Julius Boros and Lee Trevino

British Open, USPGA

In same year Walter Hagen (1924)
In different years Jim Barnes, Jock Hutchison, Gene Sarazen, Walter Hagen, Tommy Armour, Densmore Shute, Sam Snead, Ben Hogan, Gary Player, Jack Nicklaus and Lee Trevino

US Open, US Masters

In same year Craig Wood (1941), Ben Hogan (1951 and 1953), Arnold Palmer (1960), Jack Nicklaus (1972)
In different years Gene Sarazen, Byron Nelson, Ralph Guldahl, Cary Middlecoff, Gary Player, Jack Nicklaus, Billy Casper, Tom Watson and Raymond Floyd

British Open, US Masters

In same year Ben Hogan (1953), Arnold Palmer (1962), Jack Nicklaus (1966), Gary Player (1974) and Tom Watson (1977)
In different years Gene Sarazen, Sam Snead, Arnold Palmer, Gary Player, Jack Nicklaus, Tom Watson and Severiano Ballesteros

USPGA, US Masters

In same year Sam Snead (1949), Jack Burke (1956), Jack Nicklaus (1963 and 1975)
In different years Gene Sarazen, Byron Nelson, Henry Picard, Sam Snead, Ben Hogan, Doug Ford, Gary Player, Jack Nicklaus and Raymond Floyd

US Amateur, US Masters

Arnold Palmer, Jack Nicklaus, Craig Stadler

Early stewards at a championship at Hoylake. They were known as the Rope Men. (Illustrated London News)

Jack Nicklaus whose championship winning span stretches from 1959 to 1986. (Allsport)

Jack William Nicklaus

b Columbus, Ohio, 21.1.1940

The staggering part about Jack Nicklaus's record is not so much the 20 major championships he has actually won, as the 20 others he so nearly won. Nobody, not even Harry Vardon, has matched the span of 25 years that has seen him not only at the top but actually winning as well.

From the moment that he defeated Arnold Palmer in a play-off in his first summer as a professional to the day in 1986 when he came home in 30 to capture his sixth Masters, he has preserved his game at a remarkable pitch.

This is a tribute to the technical excellence of his swing, to his bodily fitness and to the capacity to keep stoking up the desire to win. Quite what breeds the desire to win in champions of any sport, is never entirely clear, but the competitive urge is as vital a component of the make-up as a sound method. The confidence, caused by a string of successes, has undoubtedly led to more but not all stemmed from natural blessings.

Nicklaus has always paid meticulous attention to detail. Every year, he dissects the basic fundamentals of his swing. Every year, he plans his playing programme with greater care than generals prepare for battles. Nicklaus analyses courses and playing conditions with an intensity that has set new fashions. Nothing is left to chance.

Occasionally, one felt that the master tactician had played the percentages to an extent that eroded his supreme strokemaking powers. For all his triumphs, the sight of him storming along, guns blazing, was relatively rare. Often, there was no need for such last-minute heroics but in the last round of the 1986 Masters there most definitely was.

It would be too convenient to class it as the finest round he ever played. There are too many other contenders but his play for the last ten holes was well nigh perfect—a point Nicklaus himself, his sternest judge, later conceded.

Up until then, American golf had had little cheer for some time and perhaps was not prepared that it would be Nicklaus who would refuel interest so dramatically but it was not the first surprise that Nicklaus held up his sleeve; nor may it be the last.

It was as much as anything a tribute to the decision of Nicklaus some years ago to make strenuous efforts to look slimmer and trimmer. It is almost certain that at his earlier fighting weight, he would not have remained the threat he has but it was also a memorable reminder of how his game has stayed in shape as well.

His consistency has been a watchword. From 1962 to 1981 Nicklaus played 80 major championships. In only 20 of these did he finish outside the first ten; in only four did he fail to make the cut (the 1963 US Open, the 1967 Masters and the 1968 and 1978 USPGAs) and in no fewer than 42 was he in the first three.

In the 15 British Opens from 1966, he never finished worse than sixth. He has played 28 rounds under 70 (eleven more than anybody else) and he has been runner-up a record seven times. In addition, he has the highest number of rounds under 70 in the US Open, the record number of victories in the Masters and the highest number (14) of top five finishes.

Jack Nicklaus has been breaking records, in fact, ever since the Eisenhower Trophy in 1960 at Merion when he first dropped a hint of what was in store. Even making due allowance for the fact that the pins were positioned without the customary severity of an Open, 269 was an absurdly low score for a young amateur. The previous year he had made his debut in the Walker Cup at Muirfield and went home to win the US Amateur, a title he captured again in 1961 at Pebble Beach. Coincidentally, he won the US Open at Pebble Beach eleven years later—the only person to win the US Amateur and US Open on the same course. In 1960, he also set the lowest US Open aggregate by an amateur (282).

In retrospect, it seems inevitable that Nicklaus became a great golfer. In the foreword to Nicklaus's book, *The Greatest Game of All*, Bobby Jones recalled that as early as the age of 15 when Nicklaus first appeared in the US Amateur, 'it was not difficult to see that a new talent of the first magnitude had arrived'.

With the adoption of Jones as his hero, Nicklaus set out on his path to the top, encouraged by his father, Charlie Nicklaus, a keen golfer and qualified pharmacist; and was taught from the beginning by Jack Grout to whom he still turns when he has a technical problem.

During his developmental years, Nicklaus attended high school and college but by 1961 he was known as 'the amateur the pros fear' and, in view of the opportunities which professional golf had to offer, it was inevitable that he should take the decision to join its ranks.

It was inevitable, too, that Palmer's reign as the world's leading golfer should have been ended by Nicklaus. Not that this was universally welcome in America where Palmer's popularity knew no limits. Many resented the fact that Nicklaus, little more than a young college boy, could play so well. They did not think it right that he should topple their great hero so soon. So life was not always easy for Nicklaus as a result.

Luckily, however, he had a warm regard for Palmer and understood the situation perfectly. Equally, the hysteria of his followers which Palmer experienced must have been an embarrassment to him at times, but Nicklaus quickly made himself a model champion; a champion with less of the identifiable emotion that Palmer displayed, but one whose golf was indisputably supreme.

There had been many signs of his rising genius notably in the 1960 Open when he finished second to Palmer, two strokes behind. It was the highest finish by an amateur since Johnny Goodman won in 1933 but there was still an element of suddenness about the way he became champion two years later within such a short time of turning professional.

It was the best first tournament any professional could have won, but Nicklaus enjoyed phenomenal success wherever he went. The first of the eight years (a record) that he has finished as leading money-winner in the United States was 1964, and he has won tournaments regularly ever since despite rationing his appearances and concentrating on the major championships. To date, he has won 66 tournaments which puts him in second place in the United States behind Sam Snead on 84.

A year after winning the US Open, he won the Masters and the PGA championship. He won the Masters again in 1965, breaking all records with a total of 271, 9 strokes ahead of Palmer and Player; and he became the only person successfully to defend his title the following April.

This came only after a play-off with Tommy Jacobs and Gay Brewer, but it was the start of a summer which saw his first success in the British Open at Muirfield, the course for which he already had great affection and after which he called his own course Muirfield Village several years later.

After an inauspicious beginning in the 1962 British Open, when he made the cut only by a single stroke, he had a chance in 1963 and followed Tony Lema home at St Andrews in 1964. On the last day, Nicklaus had the lowest aggregate (134) of any last day but with the fairways narrow and the rough deep at Muirfield, he squeezed home with 1 stroke in hand.

Nicklaus had gone on record as saying that he was not a good 'fast course' player, but he was prepared to accept the course's essential demand for accuracy rather than length, taking an iron from many of the tees.

He squandered a big lead on the last 9 holes of the third round and dropped strokes at the 11th, 13th and 14th in the last round, but he managed the four 4s he needed to win, one of them a birdie.

His triumph completed victory in the four major championships, enabling him to join Gene Sarazen, Ben Hogan and Gary Player, but by 1971 he became the first person to win them all a second time and now he has won them all three times. He passed Bobby Jones's total of 13 major championships and, on the professional tour front, joined the million dollar 'Club' in 1970. Since then he has become the founder member of the two, three and four million dollar 'Club'.

Yet the impressive part of this recital of superlatives is the number of the individual records he holds. In the Masters, he is the most frequent winner, the youngest and the oldest winner, the winner by the biggest margin and has the highest number of top five finishes.

His 63 in 1980 equalled the lowest round in the history of the US Open championship and *en route* to victory by 2 strokes over Isao Aoki, he lowered his own record aggregate to 272 and set a record for the lowest first 36 holes and the 54 holes (with Aoki) although this was beaten at Merion a year later.

Nor was that an end to his record breaking for 1980. In August, he won the USPGA championship by 7 strokes and equalled Walter Hagen's tally of five victories set in the 1920s.

At Sandwich the following summer, he created a record of a different sort for him—a first round of 83. On the second day he produced a 66 and so maintained the British Open as the only major in which he has never once missed the cut. Alas, in 1985, also at Sandwich, his proud record ended.

In addition he has six victories to his name in the Australian Open and has been a member of six winning World Cup teams, but he has accomplished this huge catalogue of success without allowing it to dictate his whole life and without spoiling him as a person.

He has always given straight answers and the golf writers of the world have respected him for it but, early on, he could be a little abrasive. However, as the college boy image faded, he transformed his appearance and his weight and endeared himself to many by his good grace and generosity of mind.

Defeat can be harder to bear when somebody is as used to winning as he is but he accepts it calmly and philosophically and, at such moments, will continue interviews at length when some others grudge as much as a couple of minutes.

It is on these occasions that one is struck by his control, care, thoughtfulness and patience. But these are, after all, the same qualities that characterize his golf—the qualities that combine to make him unquestionably the best contemporary golfer and arguably the best that ever lived.

	British Open	*US Open*	*US Masters*	*USPGA*
1958	DNP	=41★		DNP
1959	DNP		F/Q★	DNP
1960	DNP	2★	=13★	DNP
1961	DNP	=4★	=7★	DNP
1962	=34	1	=15	=3
1963	3	F/Q	1	1
1964	2	=23	=2	=2
1965	=12	=32	1	=2
1966	1	3	1	=22
1967	2	1	F/Q	=3
1968	=2	2	=5	F/Q
1969	=6	=25	=24	=11
1970	1	=51	8	=6
1971	=5	2	=2	1
1972	2	1	1	=13
1973	4	=4	=3	1
1974	3	=10	=4	2
1975	=3	=7	1	1
1976	=2	=11	=3	=4
1977	2	=10	2	3
1978	1	=6	7	F/Q
1979	=2	=9	4	=65
1980	=4	1	=33	1
1981	=23	=6	=2	=4
1982	=10	2	=15	=16
1983	W/D	=43	=29	2
1984	=18	=21	=31	=25
1985	F/Q	F/Q	=6	=32
1986	=46	=8	1	=16
1987			=7	

United States Amateur champion 1959 and 1961.
DNP   Did not play.
F/Q   Failed to qualify for final 36 holes.
W/D   Withdrew.
=   Finished tied.
★   As Amateur.

DETAILED RECORDS

(Professional Years: 1962 to 1986 inclusive)

Official Tour Victories   71
Second Place or Ties   58
Third Place or Ties   36

Total Victories Around the World   89

Tops in Career Tour Average   70.61 strokes per round

Tops in Lowest Scoring Average
8 times (1964–65–71–72–73–74–75–76); runner-up 6 times

Top Money Winner
8 times (1964–65–67–71–72–73–75–76); runner-up 4 times

Tops in Career Official Tour Earnings
$4 912 295

Most Major Championships Titles
20 (Masters 6; PGA Championship 5; United States Open 4; British Open 3; US Amateur 2)

PGA Player-of-the-Year Award
5 times (1967–72–73–75–76)

Athlete-of-the-Decade Award
1970–79

Play-off Tour Record
Won 12 Lost 10

Holes in One   12

Lowest Tournament Records
all 62s—Ohio Kings Island Open, 7 October 1973 (3rd round), Sahara Invitational, 28 October 1967 (3rd round), Australian Dunlop Intl., 5 November 1971 (2nd round) (shot 59 in exhibition with three professionals 12 March 1973, at Palm Beach, Florida)

INTERNATIONAL AND OTHER VICTORIES
British Open (3): 1966–70–78 (runner-up 7 times)

Australian Open (6): 1964–68–71–75–76–78

World Series of Golf (5): 1962–63–67–70–76 (runner-up 6 times)

Ryder Cup: member of US teams that defeated Britain in 1971–73–75–77–81 and tied Britain 1969 (non-playing captain of winning 1983 US team)

World Match Play Championship: 1970

World Cup: winner of individual championship a record three times (1963–64–71) and six times a partner of US winning teams

MAJOR CHAMPIONSHIPS PERFORMANCES

SUMMARY:

Victories: 20	**Top three finish**: 48
Second place: 19	**Top ten finish**: 70
Third place: 9	

BREAKDOWN As a professional competing in 100 major championships, he has won 18, was second or tied for second 18 times, third or tied for third 9 times—to make it finishing 45 times in Top Three and 67 times in Top Ten.

As an amateur, he won the United States Amateur Championship twice and was runner-up in 1960 United States Open.

MILESTONES On 13 April 1986, he won the Masters for a record sixth time. Other Masters highlights: setting two Masters records on 11 April 1965, with the lowest total ever (271) and by the largest victory margin (9 strokes).

On 12 August 1973, he broke the record of the late Bobby Jones for major championships titles with 14 by winning the PGA Championship.

On 15 June 1980, he won the US Open for the fourth time with a record 272 at Baltusrol and later, on 10 August, won the PGA Championship for the fifth time by the largest margin ever at that Championship (7 strokes).

Titles Total
6 Masters; 5 PGA Championships; 4 United States Opens; 3 British Opens; 2 US Amateur Championships

CAREER TOUR STATISTICS

Year	Tour Appearances		Scoring Average	Tour Victories	2nd Place Finish	3rd Place Finish	Tour Winnings
1962	26		70.80	3	3	4	$61 868
1963	25		70.42	5	2	3	100 040
1964	26		69.96	4	6	3	113 284
1965	24		70.09	5	4	2	140 752
1966	19		70.58	3	3	3	111 419
1967	23		70.23	5	2	3	188 998
1968	22		69.97	2	3	1	155 285
1969	23		71.06	3	1	0	140 167
1970	19		70.75	2	3	2	142 149
1971	18	(25)	70.08	5	3	3	244 490
1972	19	(21)	70.23	7	3	0	320 542
1973	18	(22)	69.81	7	1	1	308 362
1974	18	(20)	70.06	2	3	0	238 178
1975	16	(20)	69.87	5	1	3	298 149
1976	16	(19)	70.17	2	2	1	266 438
1977	18	(21)	70.36	3	2	1	284 509
1978	15	(18)	71.07	3	2	0	256 672
1979	12	(13)	72.49	0	0	1	59 434
1980	13	(14)	70.86	2	1	0	172 386
1981	16	(18)	70.70	0	3	0	178 213
1982	15	(18)	70.90	1	3	2	232 645
1983	16	(18)	70.88	0	3	1	256 158
1984	13	(16)	70.75	1	2	1	272 595
1985	15	(17)	71.81	0	2	1	165 456
1986	15	(19)	71.56	1	0	0	226 015

(number beside 'Tour Appearances' represents overall total that year, eg British, Suntory, World Match Play Championship plus unofficial tour Chrysler)

Robert Tyre (Bobby) Jones, Jr

b Atlanta, Georgia, 17.3.1902
d Atlanta, 18.12.1971

The Impregnable Quadrilateral, so much nicer a term than the Grand Slam, is the most perfect achievement in golf. In the summer of 1930, Bobby Jones won the Open and Amateur championships of Britain and America.

Nowadays it is unthinkable for an amateur to win either Open and this is, therefore, a record that will almost certainly never be broken. It is the ultimate achievement and, though only 28 at the time, Jones understandably retired. For the previous eight years his consistency in the two Opens remains unsurpassed even by modern giants like Hogan and Nicklaus.

In his last nine US Opens, he was first four times and second four times. From 1923 to 1930, he was either US Open or Amateur champion although strangely he never won both in the same year until 1930. He won three of the four British Opens in which he took part and, after 1923, Walter Hagen, one of the leading golfers of the 1920s, only once finished above him in either championship.

Bobby Jones, Jr, who won 13 major championships in eight years. He exerted a profound and lasting influence on the game. (USGA)

In addition to winning the US Amateur a record five times, Jones was a finalist and semi-finalist twice and eventually succeeded in winning the British Amateur, a championship with its 18-hole matches which Jones always considered was the hardest of all to win.

In 36-hole matches, however, it was a different story. His successes in the Walker Cup and US Amateur were devastating. From 1923 to 1930, he lost only once over 36 holes—to George von Elm in the Amateur final of 1926.

At various other times, he defeated Chick Evans 7 and 6; von Elm 9 and 8; Roger Wethered 9 and 8, and 7 and 6; Cyril Tolley 12 and 11; Francis Ouimet 11 and 9; John Beck 14 and 13; and T P Perkins 13 and 12, and 10 and 9—both within 14 days.

No wonder Bernard Darwin wrote, 'Like the man in the song, many of Mr Jones's opponents are tired of living but feared of dying. However, their fears are rarely unduly protracted since they usually die very soon after lunch.'

In all, Jones won 13 major titles, a figure only beaten by Jack Nicklaus who, though not born until ten years after Jones retired, regarded Jones as his hero; but comparisons are worthless. Jones belonged to a leisured age when travel to Britain was a considerable undertaking. He played, too, with hickory-shafted clubs throughout his career but he had the style and technique to have played with a stair rod. He was as much loved in Britain as in America and did more than any overseas golfer to promote the importance of the British Open in the eyes of the world.

Although immensely considerate to others and later a model of behaviour, he often allowed youthful impetuosity to get the better of him if he failed to match his own high standards. It resulted in his tearing up his card in the third round of the 1921 Open at St Andrews and may have stemmed from the sort of frustration that the Old Course can invoke.

However, he made handsome amends, building up a genuine love of the Old course, extolling its virtues and when receiving the Freedom of the Burgh of St Andrews on 9 October 1958, paying it a unique compliment. He said he would choose St Andrews if he were allowed only one course in the world on which to play and added, 'I could take out of my life everything except my experiences at St Andrews and still have a rich, full life.'

Jones was only nine when he won the junior championship of his Club, East Lake, Atlanta, and was 14 when he won the Georgia State Amateur championship for the first time. A year later, he won the Southern Amateur and in 1919 was runner-up in the Canadian Open and US Amateur.

If Jones's father had not moved house from the city to the suburb of East Lake when the young Bobby was only five, he might not have taken to golf at all. His father cared little for sport but the fascination of looking through the gates of the East Lake Club had its effect. Jones clearly liked what he saw.

After being officially taken to the club by his mother, he was given the chance to try his hand and the game came easily to him. He needed few lessons but, like so many great players, he was a born imitator, basing his style on the professional at East Lake, Stewart Maiden, an emigrant Scot and friend to whom Jones always paid tribute. Without consciously trying Jones was a supreme stylist with a smooth, drowsy, rhythmic swing. His boyish good looks and sturdy, athletic build combined to give him a magnetic personality although it would be quite wrong to suggest that he did not suffer over his golf in the manner of humbler folk.

His great and trusted friend, O B Keeler, often wrote how Bobby could scarcely eat anything until a day's play was over; how, on occasions, he felt he could not even button his shirt collar for fear of the direst consequences; how he could lose a stone in weight during a championship and how he was capable of breaking down to the point of tears, not from any distress but from pure emotional overstrain.

Bernard Darwin recalled vividly, too, the close of the 1930 Open at Hoylake, the second leg of the Impregnable Quadrilateral. 'I was writing in the room where Bobby was waiting to see if he had won. He was utterly exhausted and had to hold his glass in two hands lest the good liquor be spilt. All he would say was that he would never, never do it again.'

Later that year he remained true to his word, but back in the days of his youth, his career had not yet reached full flower.

Jones played in his first US Open at the age of 18, finishing in a tie for eighth place. As so often happens with young players, too much was probably expected of him too soon and for seven years from the age of 15 he played in ten major championships without success. The 1921 British Open was one example and the British Amateur the same year another.

Then, in 1923, the Bobby Jones era really opened with victory in the US Open at Inwood, New York, after a play-off with Bobby Cruickshank. In the last round, Cruickshank had finished with a birdie, but in the play-off Jones won with 76 to 78, the 2-stroke difference coming at the 18th hole.

Jones was second for the next two years but won the US Amateur in those years and in 1926 returned to Britain, the first time since his unfortunate baptism at St Andrews. After beating Cyril Tolley 12 and 11 in the Walker Cup and losing in the fifth round of the Amateur, he decided to stay on for the Open.

The fact that he qualified safely is only half the story. In so doing, he scored his famous 66 on the Old course at Sunningdale which was described as being as near flawless as any round of golf could be. He was only bunkered once, holed one long putt and hit every green in the right number except one, ten of them with a 2-iron or wood.

It was an encouraging overture to the Open at Lytham where, despite taking 39 putts in his final round, he held off Al Watrous to win. That he did so owed everything to his famous recovery at the 17th when he found the green from the sandy wilderness on the left and Watrous, confident perhaps of clinching things at that hole, took 3 putts. Jones wore the mantle of champion naturally and easily, but at lunchtime on the final day he returned to his hotel, was not recognized by the gatekeeper on his return and had to pay to get back in. He was never one to make a scene.

The following year at St Andrews he opened with a 68, led all the way and won by 6 strokes, but his third victory in three appearances at Hoylake in 1930 was rather more a triumph of character. He was asked afterwards whether he had ever played worse so successfully; to which he answered no. In the third round, he lost 8 strokes to par in the first 3 holes and in the last round took 7 at the 8th. However, the great breakthrough had been the first leg of the Impregnable Quadrilateral, the British Amateur at St Andrews—the championship that had hitherto eluded him. No wonder, having secured his ambition, he said, 'There has been nothing in golf I wanted so much.'

Not that it was wholly straightforward. In a marvellous match in the fourth round, Cyril Tolley took him to the 19th watched by an estimated 12 000 spectators, and in the semi-final George Voigt was 2 up and 5 to play. 'I did not think Voigt was the kind of player who would toss away this sort of lead, and I was quite certain that I was not capable of the golf needed to wrest it away from him. All I could do was what I did, namely, resolve to swallow the medicine, whatever it might be, and to keep on trying as best I could.' Well, Voigt drove out of bounds at the 14th, made enough errors for Jones to take advantage and Jones swept to victory in the final by 7 and 6 against Roger Wethered.

Back in the United States the Open, played in fierce heat, was next at Interlachen CC, Minneapolis where Jones played his famous lily pad stroke. It happened in the second round and, according to Keeler, skidded on the surface of the lake at the 9th hole and covered the remaining 20 yd to the far side and safety. In the end, he had 2 strokes to spare despite a final round of 75.

That was the third trick of the Slam; the remaining act taking place at Merion where Keeler described him as 'incomparably brilliant and incredibly sloppy by turns'. The results, however, make that hard to understand. He led the qualifying rounds and then won five matches, his smallest margin being 5 and 4.

In the final, he beat E V Homans by 8 and 7, as convincing a way to complete golf's greatest feat as any that could be devised.

In between 1926 and 1930, he won the US Amateur in 1927 and 1928 and the Open of 1929. In the 1928 Open, he lost a play-off to Johnny Farrell and in 1927 unaccountably tied for eleventh. Otherwise, his consistency was phenomenal. Apart from 1927, he was nothing but second or first in his last nine US Opens.

Having taking the decision to retire in 1930, Jones was able to devote more time to his law practice in Atlanta. As well as being a superb golfer, he was undoubtedly the most highly educated man ever to have played the game successfully. He held degrees in engineering, literature and law, graduating at the Atlanta School of Technology and subsequently at Harvard.

After his death, a Bobby Jones Trust was set up offering scholarships to students in America and Britain. Jones's influence on golf remained—and a goodly and active influence it was.

Augusta National golf course was built under his guidance and the Masters tournament (first played in 1934) was his inspiration and later his memorial.

Jones was always in attendance with his wise counsel and kindly praise such as when Jack Nicklaus had his great year in 1965. 'He plays a game with which I am not familiar.'

There was nothing of the Muhammad Ali about Jones. His modesty and quietness were remarkable for a man of such talent, but those who saw and knew him in later life when a cruel affliction confined him to a wheelchair, will testify that his forbearance at such misfortune was his greatest triumph of all.

The best epitaph was that of Herbert Warren Wind, the great American writer. 'As a young man he was able to stand up to just about the best that life can offer, which is not easy, and later he stood up, with equal grace, to just about the worst.'

IMPREGNABLE QUADRILATERAL OR GRAND SLAM

This was the achievement of Bobby Jones in 1930 when, in the same summer, he won the Open and Amateur championships of Britain and the United States.
The sequence of victories was: British Amateur, British Open, US Open and US Amateur.
Details as follows:

British Amateur Championship at St Andrews

Round	Date	Opponent	Score
2	Monday, 26 May	S Roper (Wollaton Park)	3 and 2
3	Tuesday, 27 May	C Shankland (St George's Hill)	3 and 2
4	Wednesday, 28 May	Cyril J H Tolley (Royal & Ancient)	19th hole
5	Thursday, 29 May	G O Watt (Broughty)	7 and 6
6	Thursday, 29 May	H R Johnston (USA)	1 hole
7	Friday, 30 May	E W Fiddian (Stourbridge)	4 and 3
Semi-final	Friday, 30 May	G J Voigt (USA)	1 hole
Final	Saturday, 31 May	R H Wethered (Worplesdon)	7 and 6

British Open (Hoylake) 18, 19, 20 June

Name	Score				Total
R T Jones, USA	70	72	74	75	291
L Diegel, Agua Caliente, Mexico	74	73	71	75	293
Macdonald Smith, USA	70	77	75	71	293
F Robson, Cooden Beach	71	72	78	75	296
Horton Smith, Cragston, USA	72	73	78	73	296
A Compston, Coombe Hill	74	73	68	82	297
J Barnes, Pelham Manor, USA	71	77	72	77	297

US Open at Interlachen GC, Minneapolis
10, 11, 12 July

Name	Score				Total
R T Jones	71	73	68	75	287
Macdonald Smith	70	75	74	70	289
Horton Smith	72	70	76	74	292
Harry Cooper	72	72	73	76	293
John Golden	74	73	71	76	294
Tommy Armour	70	76	75	76	297

US Amateur Championship (Merion Cricket Club)
22–27 September

Having been medallist in the qualifying rounds with a score of 142, 1 stroke better than George von Elm (Rancho), Jones won the matchplay section as follows:

Round	Date	Holes	Opponent	Score
1	24 September	18	C Ross Somerville (Canada)	5 and 4
2	24 September	18	F G Hoblitzel (Canada)	5 and 4
3	25 September	36	Fay Coleman (California)	6 and 5
Semi-final	26 September	36	Jess W Sweetser (Siwanoy)	9 and 8
Final	27 September	36	Eugene V Homans (Englewood)	8 and 7

	US Open	British Open	US Amateur	British Amateur
1916	DNP	DNP	third round	DNP
1919	DNP	DNP	finalist	DNP
1920	=8	DNP	semi-final	DNP
1921	=5	Picked up in third round	third round	fourth round
1922	=2	DNP	semi-final	DNP
1923	1	DNP	second round	DNP
1924	2	DNP	winner	DNP
1925	2 (lost play-off)	DNP	winner	DNP
1926	1	1	finalist	sixth round
1927	=11	1	winner	DNP
1928	2 (lost play-off)	DNP	winner	DNP
1929	1	DNP	first round	DNP
1930	1	1	winner	winner

DNP Did not play.
= Finished tied.

1987 British Amateur championship Prestwick
P M Mayo, Newport (Gwent)
Semi-finals: *P M McEvoy beat R Claydon 4 and 3; Mayo beat L Mattiace at 20th.*
Final: *Mayo beat McEvoy 3 and 1.*

A total of 1407 players entered for the 1987 Open championship at Muirfield, only six short of the record set in 1986.

Walter Charles Hagen

b Rochester, New York, 21.12.1892
d Traverse City, Michigan, 5.10.1969

Walter Hagen was a joy to the headline writers and, more than anyone else, made golf front-page news. He did so as much by a flamboyant personality and fine disregard for convention as he did by a dashing approach to his game which was an ample reflection of the man himself.

His style of life set new standards for the professional golfer and he became the pioneer for many of the privileges which subsequent generations quickly took for granted. Nobody appreciated this more than his great contemporary, Gene Sarazen, who was never slow to acknowledge the debt to Hagen although Hagen himself was ever mindful of the opportunity to do good.

In 1920, when the Inverness Club in Toledo, Ohio became the first to open its doors to professionals at a US Open championship, Hagen was the first to raise a collection among his fellow players for a grandfather clock to be presented to the club. However, he could be just as quick to voice a protest.

In 1923, after finishing runner-up to Arthur Havers in the British Open, he declined to enter the clubhouse for the presentation ceremony because none of the professionals had been allowed to enter it during the week. Instead, while thanking officials for their courtesy, he invited spectators to the pub where he was staying.

For someone who entered golf earning 10 cents an hour as a caddie, he certainly did not acquire a taste for high living from his boyhood. His parents, of thrifty German stock, had to work hard to raise a family of five of which he was the only boy. His father made $18 a week as a blacksmith in the car shops of East Rochester and so the odd dollar from caddying came in very useful; but the urge to play could not be suppressed. He signed on as assistant at the Country Club of Rochester and quickly became a successful player—a player embarking on one of the most glamorous careers in the whole of professional sport.

Everyone knew Walter Hagen; everyone flocked to see him play. They admired his dashing style on the course and they were amused by the sometimes outrageous things that occupied him off it. But not all the countless stories of Hagen are true; nor was the image portrayed of him always accurate.

He drank only about half the drinks he accepted but he certainly never kept strict hours.

When told once that his opponent of the following day had been in bed for some time, he made the famous reply, 'Yeah, but he ain't sleeping.' The incident occurred in an Edinburgh night-club before the last day of the 1929 British Open at Muirfield where Hagen won. The opponent most feared to catch him, Leo Diegel, finished third.

There were other equally famous remarks, but all tended to emphasize the free and easy nature of a player

(1922) and the first American to win both the American and British titles.

His second British title was gained at Hoylake and he won for a third time at Sandwich in 1928. Although he only once finished in front of Bobby Jones's in Jones's last eight US Opens, his second victory had come in 1919, but his most notable supremacy was in the USPGA championship. By winning from 1924 to 1927, he scored 22 straight matches against America's best professionals.

This proved how he made his mark at both strokeplay and matchplay. He played in all the Ryder Cup matches until 1937 and, with Jones and Sarazen, helped to foster close ties between British and American golf. In addition, he won the French, Canadian and Belgian Opens but it was his fourth victory in the British Open at Muirfield that gave him as much pleasure as any.

He won by 6 strokes from a strong field including the American Ryder Cup team, never took more than 5 at any hole and received the trophy in 1928 from the Prince of Wales, who had watched him play his final round. It probably never occurred to Hagen that he should have received it from anyone else.

Walter Hagen, the first of the great golfing showmen. (USGA)

who realized that golf was not necessarily a tight-lipped, solemn game; and that everyone has to cultivate his own way of relaxing. He could turn up on the first tee at the last minute, break his concentration between shots by chatting nonchalantly to spectators and still give of his best.

He was the first golfing showman and perhaps the first to indulge in any form of gamesmanship. Even in defeat, he seldom did anything by halves. In 1928, he lost a challenge match over 72 holes by 18 and 17 to Archie Compston, but a few days later, he won the Open championship at Sandwich.

He also gained the reputation of being a marvellous putter, but that sort of compliment is frequently used to hide a lack of other golfing virtues. In Hagen's case, that was not so. Before the days of the Masters, he won two US Opens, four British Opens and five USPGA championships, four of them in succession. One could not win all those simply with a putter.

What is more, his career covered a wide span. He first won the US Open in 1914 and finished third 21 years later. However, the 1920s were his best years. He was the first American-born winner of the British Open

	US Open	British Open	Masters	USPGA
1913	=4			
1914	1			
1915	=10			
1916	7			
1919	1	NC		DNP
1920	11	=53		DNP
1921	=2	=6		1
1922	5	1		DNP
1923	=18	2		finalist
1924	=4	1		1
1925	=5	DNP		1
1926	7	=3		1
1927	6	DNP		1
1928	=4	1		quarter-final
1929	=19	1		quarter-final
1930	=17	DNP		DNP
1931	=7	DNP		DNP
1932	10	DNP		first round
1933	4	=22		DNP
1934	=58	DNP	=13	first round
1935	3	DNP	=15	DNP
1936	=33	DNP	=11	DNP
1937		=26		
1938		DNP		
1939		DNP	=33	

DNP Did not play.
NC No Championship.
= Finished tied.

Benjamin (Ben) William Hogan

b Dublin, Texas, 13.8.1912

Many golfers, like most actors, tend to linger for one more curtain call; but Ben Hogan was no sentimentalist. When he felt that he could no longer compete and win, he left the stage to others.

When the time comes, Jack Nicklaus will do the same, just as Bobby Jones did for slightly different reasons. Having conquered all worlds in 1930 at the age of 28, there were no more peaks for Jones to climb. The years of competition left their mark, too, although in Hogan's case, he survived a terrible car crash when his golf was in full bloom and was still able to play the lowest round in the Masters at 54.

He would never appear in public unless he could summon his best and certainly not for old times' sake. He was probably the finest shot-maker the game has ever known and preferred to be remembered as such. Gene Sarazen, whose knowledge of golfers is second to none, is emphatic about his rating of Hogan: 'nobody covered the flag like he did'.

His control from tee to green was legendary. More than any other player, he thought not of hitting the fairway, but which part of the fairway and where he should be to make the next shot simpler. This was the strategy, in fact, of an expert snooker player who is planning several shots ahead. He could shape the ball at will, fading it, drawing it, hitting it high or low.

'You felt', someone once said of Hogan, 'the ball had no option.'

Large crowds were no doubt a motivating force to him, but in an age when public image and cheap publicity is the concern of many professionals, Hogan spurned adulation. He could see nothing remarkable in a round of 68 or 69 and was a man of few words. For some years, it was frequently related that all he might say to his playing partners, during the course of a round was, 'You're away'. With Hogan, his golf did the talking.

He won the US Open four times, the Masters and PGA championship twice each and the British Open on his only appearance. In 14 consecutive Open championships up to 1960, and the same number of Masters, he was never outside the first ten, and 18 times was in the first four. Only Nicklaus can match that sort of consistency and then not in the US Open. But golf to Hogan was an intensely serious business and he practised with fantastic singlemindedness that later had a big influence on Gary Player.

Considering his tough boyhood and his introduction to golf through caddying, Hogan's fierce application was no surprise to his friends. Nor, indeed, was his reaction to playing again after the car accident, on the foggy morning of 2 February in 1949 in Texas, which left him with multiple injuries and a month in hospital. Many believe it was the same strong will that guided his golf,

Great contemporaries and rivals but seen here as partners in the Canada Cup 1956, Sam Snead and Ben Hogan. (BBC Hulton Picture Library)

so keeping him alive. Though hobbling badly, he made the trip to England later that year to captain the Ryder Cup team at Ganton, and in January 1950 filed an entry for the Los Angeles Open to see how he would stand up to it.

He stood up to it so well that he tied for first place with Sam Snead and, a month later, tied with Lloyd Mangrum and George Fazio for the US Open at Merion; and, despite wondering whether he would get round, he won the play-off.

Hogan's debut in the US Open was in 1936 when he failed to make the cut for the last 36 holes, and his first victory came in 1948 at the Riviera CC, Los Angeles. In between, his best finish was tied third in 1941, but his aggregate in 1948 (276) set a new record for the championship. It contained three rounds under 70, another record at that time.

His accident meant that he played none of the major championships in 1949, but he successfully defended his title in 1951 and, after finishing third in 1952, won again in his great year of 1953.

His victory in 1951 at Oakland Hills is remembered for his remark, 'I vowed I would bring this monster to its knees.' Probably because of the threat he posed to low scoring, the USGA began to doctor their Open courses but, though Hogan felt they had gone too far at Oakland Hills, he was determined to show there was a way to play it.

By now, his dedication was a by-word and from then on it was a regular sight for other professionals to congregate on the practice ground to watch him. His sessions were an education in themselves, but 1953 was a perfect example of how he transferred much of that mechnical precision to the course itself.

Hogan won the Masters for a second time with what he considers perhaps the best golf of his career. His total of 274 (70, 69, 66, 69) was a record which stood for twelve years, and he followed it by adding a fourth victory in the US Open, equalling the record of Bobby Jones and Willie Anderson.

By finishing at Oakmount with a par and two birdies, he won by 6 strokes from Sam Snead with the biggest margin since 1938. He led throughout—the first to do so for 42 years.

After his accident, Hogan was not keen on travelling, but he was persuaded to make the journey to Carnoustie for the British Open and never regretted it.

He was surprised to see how much people in Britain wanted him to win and even more surprised at the enormous size of the crowds. He would have been less happy with the informal nature of the stewarding; it was some years before it became the controlled art it is today.

As usual, Hogan's preparations were thorough. He arrived two weeks early to acquaint himself with the course and the small ball which he had never played; and though he was not entirely happy with his putting, he had each round lower than the one before (73, 71, 70, 68), and eventually won with one of the finest rounds ever played.

His victory gave him the unique distinction of winning the Masters and both Opens in the same summer and meant that he had emulated Gene Sarazen in winning the four major championships. Hogan rarely played in the PGA championship, decided by matchplay until 1958, and did not take part in it in 1953 because it clashed with the British Open—a tragedy.

The year 1953 would have been a good time for him to have retired, but golf was his life; ambition still burned within him and, most important of all, he felt he had not yet attained perfection. He would have liked to have won the US Open for a fifth time, but was thwarted more than once.

His most astonishing failure was in losing a play-off with the little-known Jack Fleck at the Olympic Club, San Francisco, in 1955. It was also the scene of Arnold Palmer's bewildering failure in 1966, although that is no consolation to either.

In 1956, Hogan needed two 4s to tie Cary Middlecoff, but missed from no more than a yard on the 71st green; and he had a chance again in 1960 at the age of 48. He was not helped by the fact that putting, particularly the holing out, had become a terrible affliction to him. He was not the first or the last, to confront these agonies and, while he overcame them for a period thanks to his superlative long game, they got the better even of Hogan.

There were other aches and pains; and a shoulder injury that required surgery, but he gave Augusta one last treat in 1967, going out in 30 on the Saturday and looking for a moment as though he might just turn back the years.

Altogether, Hogan won 62 tournaments on the US tour, one more than Palmer. He won all his three Ryder Cup games (two foursomes and one single) and won a famous victory for the United States in the Canada Cup at Wentworth with Sam Snead as his partner.

It made up in some measure for the fact that he never played a second time in the British Open, and he certainly put on a memorable show, his aggregate of 277 being the lowest.

He hit a variety of strokes all round the pin and might once have been out in 29, but he has done that sort of thing all his life. In the 1960 Open, in fact, he hit 34 consecutive greens in the right number on the final day only to go in the water on the last two holes. If golf were decided without the need to putt, Hogan would hardly ever have been beaten, but let us forget his putting and remember him as the man who has come nearer than anyone to reaching perfection in the part of the game that ordinary mortals find next to impossible.

	US Open	British Open	Masters	USPGA
1936	F/Q	DNP		
1937		DNP		
1938		DNP	=25	
1939		DNP	9	third round
1940	=5	DNP	=10	fourth round
1941	=3	DNP	4	fourth round
1942			2 (lost play-off)	third round
1946	=4	DNP	2	1
1947	=6	DNP	=4	first round
1948	1	DNP	6	1
1949	DNP	DNP	DNP	DNP
1950	1	DNP	=4	DNP
1951	1	DNP	1	DNP
1952	3	DNP	=7	DNP
1953	1	1	1	DNP
1954	=6	DNP	2 (lost play-off)	DNP
1955	2 (lost play-off)	DNP	2	DNP
1956	=2	DNP	=8	DNP
1957	DNP	DNP	F/Q	DNP
1958	=10	DNP	=14	DNP
1959	=8	DNP	=30	DNP
1960	=9	DNP	=6	F/Q
1961	=14	DNP	=32	DNP
1962			35	DNP
1963			DNP	DNP
1964			=9	=9
1965			=21	=15
1966	12	DNP	=13	DNP
1967			=10	DNP

DNP Did not play.
F/Q Failed to qualify.
=   Finished tied.

Tom Watson

b Kansas City, Missouri, 4.9.1949

James Braid took ten years to win five British Opens, Peter Thomson eleven, Harry Vardon 16 and J H Taylor 19. Tom Watson did it in nine.

Whether or not he goes on to equal or even beat Vardon's record of six victories, Watson's run of supremacy in the championship has never been matched. When one considers the scale of competition he faced compared to those in the earlier years of the century, it is even more remarkable. What is more, he won the Open at his first attempt, a distinction he shares with Ben Hogan and Tony Lema.

When he won his play-off with Jack Newton at Carnoustie in 1975, the prospect that the streets would subsequently be paved with gold seemed beyond the range of most crystal balls. In America, he had been dubbed as a man who could not win largely on account of surrendering one or two promising positions in the US Open. Although not a man given to vengeance, he must now smile at the absurdity of the accusations particularly as he effectively brought to an end, single-handed, the reign of Jack Nicklaus as the world's finest player.

He did this first of all with victory in the Masters in the same sort of direct conflict with Nicklaus that prompted his second British Open success later in the summer of 1977; and he followed up in 1982 by winning the US Open at Pebble Beach. Film of the chip he holed at the 17th in the final round, again to foil Nicklaus, quickly gained more reruns than *Gone with the Wind*.

Watson is very much a product of the US tour. He had no record as an amateur although, without impugning his professional dedication, it has always appeared that his less than intense approach would have made him well suited to the rich era of American amateur golf between the wars. He gives the impression of enjoying what he does rather than being a slave to his duty.

Watson was a college boy but not one with a golfing scholarship. His degree in psychology at Stanford was proof of his academic ability although, in view of the old saying that golf is 80 per cent mental, it was not a bad qualification for a professional golfer to have.

He signed on for the tour in 1971, earning just over $2000; yet he was never a sample of the production line. He was his own man. He had broad horizons. He likes links golf rather than pays lip service to it. Such a liking is fundamental to his successes. When he discovered the art of winning, he elevated himself to a rarefied plane with which only the great are familiar.

The confidence this gave him was shown in the boldness of his play. It was always his inclination to attack rather than defend but he achieved far more by way of consistency than his critics, a dwindling band in retreat, might concede.

He has been leading money winner in the States four times in a row, and five times in all; and, in a concen-

Tom Watson, a pensive moment for such a decisive champion. (Allsport)

trated period between 1975 and 1984, he had an outstanding record in the major championships. In something like 32 starts, he finished in the top six on 18 occasions.

The silver lining to perhaps his darkest cloud, defeat in the 1975 US Open where he suffered a collapse, turned out to be Byron Nelson who, recognizing the locker-room gloom that descended afterwards, had a consoling word in the form of an offer of help. Watson, no doubt flattered that it should have come from a man of such eminence, later accepted and between them they forged a formidable alliance. The Watson that emerged turned out to be technically more reliable and trusting in the critical moments in a touring pro's life when the swing must run smoothly and automatically.

Its greatest hour has come to be known as the Battle of Turnberry which, both statistically, dramatically, and in terms of casting, was the best any major championship has ever devised. The heir and the heir apparent played almost shot for shot for four days, Watson taking the lead for the first time only at the 70th hole. Nicklaus, for once, had to concede defeat but it is significant that he returned to St Andrews the following year and set the record straight.

Watson was by now into a rich seam of golf, becoming

champion golfer again three times in four years and being denied only by the iron will of Severiano Ballesteros at St Andrews in 1984. If there is a blot on the symmetry of Watson's achievements, it is that he never tasted the fruits of victory at the 'Home of Golf' but the win which meant as much to him as any was his triumph in the US Open in 1982.

Apart from anything else, it put him in the elite group, now a round half dozen, who have won the two Opens and the Masters. It is a place he occupies naturally and honourably. His scoring record speaks for itself but there is a lesson to be learned in the way he plays and conducts himself.

In a generation which seems to feel that deliberation and painstaking preparation is the key to success, his crisp decision-making is always refreshing. Even with the 2-iron which decided the 1983 Open at Birkdale, there was the minimum of fuss. Once he had taken his club and settled over the ball, the shot was instantly set in motion.

The tempo of the swing, too, is brisk but that does not mean he does not give deep thought to its mechanics. He seeks perfection and has come closer to it than most. Since he was at the height of his powers, no American professional has remotely threatened to command the scene or the respect that he and his supremacy held. He is a true champion in every sense.

	US Open	British Open	Masters	USPGA
1972	=22	DNP		
1973		DNP		
1974	=5	DNP		
1975	=9	1	=8	9
1976	7	F/Q	=33	=15
1977	7	1	1	=6
1978	=6	=14	=2	=2
1979	F/Q	=26	=2	=12
1980	=3	1	=12	=10
1981	=23	23	1	F/Q
1982	1	1	=5	=9
1983	2	1	=4	=47
1984	=11	=2	2	=39
1985	F/Q	=47	=10	=6
1986	=24	=35	=6	=16
1987	2		=7	

DNP Did not play.
F/Q Failed to qualify.
= Finished tied.

US Open 1987 Olympic Club, San Francisco

Scott Simpson	71	68	70	68	277
Tom Watson	72	65	71	70	278
Severiano Ballesteros	68	75	68	71	282
Bobby Wadkins	71	71	70	71	283
Bernhard Langer	69	69	73	72	283
Larry Mize	71	68	72	72	283
Curtis Strange	71	72	69	71	283
Ben Crenshaw	67	72	72	72	283

Gary Player

b Johannesburg, Transvaal, 1.11.1935

Gary Player was the first overseas professional to make a prolonged assault on the US tour and to become an outstanding champion. He was the first overseas winner of the Masters; the first US Open champion from overseas since 1920; he is the only non-American to have won the world's four major championships and one of only three born outside the United States to have won more than a million dollars on the professional circuit.

He has won the British Open in three different decades and is one of the best known and respected of all golfers. But not the least remarkable aspect of a remarkable story is that, when he first played in Britain, there were many who thought he did not have a chance. Player soon built up the knack of surprising everyone and has gone on surprising them.

Nobody without the necessary devotion and dedication would have contemplated the idea of going to Britain in 1955 in the first place. His small physique ('Jack Nicklaus was my size when he was twelve', Player often used to joke in later years) and a number of technical faults, were hardly the ideal credentials for the sort of life that shows no mercy. Player possessed a lion-sized will to learn, an insatiable capacity for practice, a rare zest for physical fitness and a limitless ambition.

Six years before he set out for England, he had not even taken up the game. Player's father, a mine captain, persuaded Gary to play with him one day. He soon became hooked and later took up his post as Assistant Professional to Jock Verwey whose daughter, Vivienne, he later married.

Player, whose mother died when he was eight, always enjoyed an outdoor life, like so many of his countrymen, and was in little doubt that, once he had decided to become a tournament golfer, he had to travel to England—the 'Mother country', as he described it in one of his books.

It was a big decision, but within a year or so of arriving in England and within four years of turning professional, he won the Dunlop tournament at Sunningdale in 1956 and soon set forth for his first taste of golf in America. If there were critics of his swing there, they were quietened, if not silenced, when he finished second to Tommy Bolt in the 1958 US Open at Southern Hills, Tulsa; but his first major championship success was back in Britain when he won the 1959 Open championship at Muirfield.

It was not a strong field by today's standards but Player, 8 strokes behind the leader at the start of the final day, had a steady downward progression of rounds (75, 71, 70, 68) and won by 2 strokes despite taking 6 at the 72nd hole.

It was the victory he was seeking and one which made him believe more strongly than ever that he could succeed in America. Although he had been a regular competitor in the British Open, he did not do as well again for some time but in two years he was Masters champion and soon to be compared with Arnold Palmer and Jack Nicklaus—the Big Three, as the American Press christened them.

Player's first victory at Augusta in 1961 could hardly have been more dramatic. On the final hole, he got down in 2 from the same bunker from which Palmer later took 4 more. Player won by a stroke from Palmer with 280, at a time when Palmer was at the very height of his powers. This was part of Player's graduation towards the Big Three although, in the public imagination at least, Player was the under-dog. That he was able to equal and sometimes dominate Palmer and Nicklaus underlined his ruthless self-discipline.

That same April, Nicklaus played in the Masters as an amateur but, far from his entrance on to the professional scene damping Player's hopes, it seemed to push him to new limits. In 1962, he won the USPGA championship in spite of recounting in *Grand Slam Golf*, how he was on the verge beforehand of 'quitting this ridiculous life'.

He had failed to qualify for the British Open at Troon where the ground was very hard and dry, but the sight of Aronimink and its softer, greener fairways inspired him to a 1-stroke victory and the third leg of the major championships. The US Open was the missing link and he had to wait until 1965 before making up an exalted trio with Gene Sarazen and Ben Hogan.

Player was thoroughly at home in America and it is some measure of his achievement that he completed his sequence of major championship victories in the space of six years. The pace of life was hot and it became hotter as Player's commitments grew with his success, but he never lost the urge to continue as a champion or the dedication needed to preserve his aim.

His record in the major championships lacks the consistency of Nicklaus, but he was forever popping up with a victory and, even today, can never be disregarded. After his US Open victory, he went until his second British Open in 1968 without another major success and he waited a further four years for his next, the 1972 USPGA.

However, he got something of a second wind, winning the Masters and the British Open in 1974 and then a third Masters in 1978. The US Open remains the only major title he has failed to win more than once.

One of his best performances was the 1974 British Open at Lytham when he was never behind in a championship which was the first to be played with the big ball. As it happened, conditions were windy almost throughout, but Player broke 70 twice—the only person to do so. He won by 4 strokes although he nearly lost his ball with his second shot at the 71st hole and ended up at the 72nd playing his third shot left-handed with a putter. The clubhouse wall prevented him from playing right-handed.

Gary Player seen playing in the first world matchplay championship at Wentworth against Ken Venturi, 1964 US Open champion. (Allsport)

	US Open	British Open	Masters	USPGA
1955		F/Q		
1956		4		
1957		24	=24	
1958	2	7	F/Q	
1959	=15	1	=8	
1960	=19	7	=6	
1961	=9	retired	1	=29
1962	=6	F/Q	2	1
1963	=8	=7	=5	=8
1964	=23	=8	=5	=13
1965	1	retired	=2	=33
1966	=15	=4	=28	=3
1967	=12	=3	=6	2
1968	=16	1	=7	=12
1969	=48	=23	=33	2
1970	=44	F/Q	3	=12
1971		=7	=6	=4
1972	=15	6	=10	1
1973	12	=14	DNP	=51
1974	=8	1	1	7
1975	=43	=32	=30	=33
1976	=23	=28	=28	=13
1977	=10	=22	=19	=31
1978	=6	=34	1	=26
1979	=2	=19	=17	=23
1980	F/Q	F/Q	=6	=26
1981	=26	F/Q	=15	
1982	F/Q	=42	=15	

DNP Did not play.
F/Q Failed to qualify.
= Finished tied.

In the next three years, he played all four major championships without once finishing in the first ten, but the 1978 Masters was yet another example of his resilience, his continued fitness and enduring ability. As in 1961, it needed some faltering by his principal rivals, whom he was able to watch after he had completed his final round, in order for Player to succeed.

At the age of 42, Player entered the last round 7 strokes behind the leader, Hubert Green, and around the final turn the Augusta crowd had not yet looked upon him as a possible winner; but he came home in 30, had 7 birdies in the last 10 holes and equalled Augusta's course record with 64. After that, he sat and waited as the chances of Tom Watson, Green and Rod Funseth came and went.

Nevertheless, the major events form only part of the Player story. Nobody has travelled further as a professional golfer in pursuit of success. There are a record seven victories in the Australian Open to consider as well as a record 13 in his own South African Open. In addition, he played some of his best golf in capturing the World Cup of 1965 for his country in partnership with Harold Henning and, within a week, he had won yet another victory with a fictional ring about it. This occurred in the world matchplay championship at Wentworth when he was 7 down to Tony Lema on the second tee of the afternoon round and beat him at the 37th. This is a championship in which Player invariably excels and the following year he was far too good for Jack Nicklaus in a final which Player won 6 and 4.

For someone who has led such a hectic life for 25 years, Player remains a marvel. His figure is still trim and his enthusiasm undiminished. In keeping with the modern fashion, he has now turned his main attention to the seniors' tour, but he has always loved spending time with his family and his busy programme is increasingly organized in order that he can do just that.

In his farm near Johannesburg with his string of horses, he has the perfect escape from a life, the better part of which has been spent in aeroplanes and hotel rooms.

When the time comes for him to quit the game, if ever he does, he will be well qualified to take on the full-time role of farmer; but he has repeatedly told press interviewers that he believes he can play better and his performance in winning the 1981 South African Open, his 13th, meant his victories spanned four decades. When you add to that millions of miles flying, some idea of his durability is evident. In terms of unquenchable spirit, fitness and application, Gary Player has had no peers.

Arnold Daniel Palmer

b Latrobe, Pennsylvania, 10.9.1929

History is full of examples of the right man in the right place at the right time. Golfing analogies are perhaps less plentiful but one shining example to the contrary is Arnold Palmer.

Whether he was the cause or the beneficiary of the golden era which launched professional golf in the early 1960s towards a promised land of untold and unsuspected riches, is hard to say. What is certain is that, without his influence, the change would have been longer delayed and nothing like as dramatic when it came.

Palmer made the world sit up and take notice of golf. Hitherto, interest had been confined to the enthusiastic ranks of members of private Clubs and to the even more enthusiastic band who found their pleasure on public courses.

Many great players of the past have had their following. Walter Hagen and Henry Cotton were the first to give the professional a recognized place in society. Hagen was golf's first showman but the arrival of Palmer, and the expansion of television, elevated the sport to dizzy heights. They went hand in hand.

Palmer was the answer to a producer's dream—tough, handsome, manly, articulate, devoid of pettiness and genuinely concerned to help others do their jobs. He never lost patience in the clamour for interviews.

Whether conscious of it or not, he personalized the image of the game to a degree unsurpassed. He maintained and polished up the standards of sportsmanship and behaviour that the game had handed down to him. However, it was the style, strength and character of his game which gave rise to the most passionate acclaim ever afforded any player.

Watching Palmer one never had any doubts about his golfing philosophy. The object of the exercise was to hit every shot with a ferocity that spared nothing, to attack from every quarter and, when the intricate mechanisms controlling the swing failed, to engage in a series of recovery shots that had to be seen to be believed.

Allied to all this was the belief that no putt was impossible. At his best, Palmer was as good a putter as Locke, calling on the subtleties of touch and feel that contrasted nicely with the more vigorous attributes of the longer shots.

In all departments, there was the accompaniment of grimaces, jubilant gestures and bodily contortions that became every bit as much an identifying mark. But herein lay the secret of his appeal. Those who followed felt they were part of the act. They shared the good and the bad.

Galleries can admire the clinical approach, the search for perfection that guided, say, Ben Hogan, but nobody had them roaring in the aisles like Palmer. Above all, he was human. In sporting folklore, he was a John Wayne who, as a national figure, became every bit as well known.

As the professionals of the 1920s owed an enormous debt to Walter Hagen, so their successors in the 1960s owed the same debt to Palmer, but despite being a fairly regular competitor at the age of 50, his major championship victories were confined to all too short a period.

To be precise, they were confined to the years between his first Masters victory in 1958 and his last in 1964, although he won the US Amateur in 1954, the first indication nationally that a rare talent was unfolding. This talent was based on a huge pair of hands and a good grip which his father, a worker in the Pennsylvania steelmills before becoming a professional, maintained were vital.

He inherited much of his father's strength, humour and respect for the game's traditions but nobody could have predicted the tumultuous years ahead. From the moment in 1958 that he won at Augusta with birdies on the last 2 holes when nothing else would have done, he was front-page news.

Having won the Masters and US Open in 1960, he went to St Andrews in the same summer to try and emulate Ben Hogan by winning the British Open at his first attempt. In Hogan's case, it was his only attempt.

For his part, Palmer started a great revival in the popularity of the British Open among overseas players and, although he was foiled in the Centenary Open by Kel Nagle, he finished as runner-up and won in 1961 and 1962. His finishes in his first three British Opens were, in fact, second, first, first—a record unmatched even by Young Tom Morris.

He concealed his disappointment admirably at not equalling Hogan's feat of winning three major championships of the world in the same year and returned to Birkdale in 1961 to win the British by a single stroke in a championship dogged for a day or two by stormy weather.

The temples may have greyed but it is still unmistakably Arnold Palmer. (USGA)

His playing of the first 6 holes of his second round in 3 under par is still regarded by him as perhaps the best golf of his life, but in 1962 at Troon he showed he could cope equally well with a fast-running seaside links. It was a year in which Gary Player failed to qualify and Nicklaus succeeded with only a stroke to spare.

These were not conditions which Palmer exactly relished, but he played the back 9 commandingly each day and beat Kel Nagle by 6 strokes and the rest of the field by 13. His total of 276 set a new record aggregate.

This was some consolation for Palmer who, a month previously, had lost the US Open in a play-off with Jack Nicklaus. In April, he had won a third Masters after a play-off with Player and Dow Finsterwald, but his defeat by Nicklaus was the first sign of the rising threat to his supremacy. Not that it blunted the devotion of Palmer's followers.

His bold putting, glove tucked into his hip pocket, could be deadly and undoubtedly helped him become leading money-winner in 1958–60–62–63. In 1963, he was the first player to top the $100 000 mark in a season and in the 1968 PGA championship, in which he was second, he became the first player to pass the million dollar mark.

	US Open	British Open	Masters	USPGA
1958	=23	DNP	1	
1959	=5	DNP	3	=14
1960	1	2	1	7
1961	=14	1	=2	=5
1962	2	1	1	=17
1963	=2	=26	=9	=40
1964	=5	DNP	1	=2
1965		=13	=2	=33
1966	2	=8	=4	=6
1967	2	DNP	4	=14
1968	59	=10	F/Q	=2
1969	=6	DNP	27	F/Q
1970	=54	12	36	=2
1971	=24	F/Q	=18	=18
1972	3	=7	=33	=16
1973	=4	=14	=24	F/Q
1974	=5	DNP	=11	=28
1975	=9	=16	=13	=33
1976	=50	=55	F/Q	=14
1977	=19	7	=24	=19
1978		=34	=37	F/Q
1979	=56	DNP	F/Q	F/Q
1980	63	F/Q	=24	=72
1981		=23	F/Q	
1982	F/Q	=27		

DNP Did not play.
F/Q Failed to qualify.
=   Finished tied.
In 1962, 63 and 66 he lost a play-off in US Open.
He was United States Amateur champion in 1954.

In the same way, however, that Sam Snead never won the US Open, the PGA title has always eluded Palmer; nevertheless he has three times been second, the last time in 1970. In all, he has won 61 tour events, one less than Hogan, and remained a real force until 1971 when he was third in the money list.

He won the Bob Hope Classic in 1973, a year in which he was 27th in the money list, but his last victory in a major championship was the 1964 Masters.

Happily, it was one of his most convincing. The Masters saw many of his best days; and rounds that year of 69, 68, 69, 70 gave him victory by 6 strokes over Nicklaus and Dave Marr. He was still then at the height of his powers, setting standards perceptibly higher than had existed before and forcing others to follow.

In addition, his good humour, friendliness and magnetic appeal made him an extremely marketable figure for whom Mark McCormack, a member of the same golf team at Wake Forest University, built up a vast financial empire which made people aware of how famous golfers had become. However, Palmer has never lost the urge to go on doing what he liked best—playing golf.

Despite trouble with a hip injury and the need to wear glasses for a time, he continued to draw crowds even when his chances of victory waned. He won the Spanish Open and the British PGA championship in 1975 in windy conditions at Sandwich which revived memories

of Birkdale in 1961; and he has become highly successful on the seniors' tour in America.

In the modern golfing world, there is a natural search for players to idolize and respect not only as masters of their craft but as the personification of what heroes should be. Nobody has fitted that bill better than Palmer.

THE GREAT TRIUMVIRATE
James Braid
b Earlsferry, Fife, 6.2.1870
d London, 27.11.1950
John Henry Taylor
b Northam, North Devon, 19.3.1871
d Northam, 10.2.1963
Harry Vardon
b Grouville, Jersey, 9.5.1870
d Totteridge, London, 20.3.1937

From 1894 until the outbreak of World War I in 1914 there were only five years in which the British Open championship was not won by one of the Great Triumvirate.

In that time, Harry Vardon won six times and J H Taylor and James Braid five times each. Three times they occupied the first three places and never once did one of them fail to finish in the first three. No major championship has ever been so dominated by three players over such a long period and they were the first to make the public conscious of golfing records.

Only Peter Thomson can rival them in terms of Open victories, but not even his tussle with Bobby Locke in the 1950s matched what was perhaps the most romantic period in golf.

Born within 13 months of one another the Triumvirate did more than anyone to establish professional golf as an honourable trade.

Without their example, the recognition of professionals at clubs may have taken even longer than it did. Taylor, in particular, was a natural speaker and a natural leader who was largely responsible for the founding of the PGA and the development of artisan golf; but it was their contribution to the playing side of the game that undoubtedly left the biggest mark.

Although John Ball and Harold Hilton had both won the Open championship as amateurs, J H Taylor's first victory in 1894 halted the supremacy of the Scots professionals. It took place, too, at Sandwich, the first time the Open ventured into England, and highlighted Taylor's almost revolutionary new style of hitting boldly up to the pin.

His swing and follow-through were a little curtailed and his stance rigidly flat-footed, but there was an abundance of defiance and determination about his golf that made him such a redoubtable bad-weather player.

When Taylor pulled down his cap, stuck out his chin and embedded his large boots in the ground, he could hit straight through the wind, especially with his trusty mashie. His last and best victory came in just such conditions at Hoylake in 1913. He won by 8 strokes, showing a control on the last day that nobody could match. He was the only player to break 80 in the third and fourth rounds and confirmed his oft-quoted saying that the best way to win is to win easily. Though a highly strung and emotional man, he was a stern competitor who, at the age of 53, had the lowest score in the 1924 Open, taking into account the qualifying rounds as well.

That was as creditable a performance as any in a career that blossomed after his first success in the Open in 1894. He defended his title with another victory at St Andrews in 1895, but lost it to Vardon the following year at Muirfield in a play-off—the first play-off since the championship was decided over four rounds.

Vardon had started the final day 6 strokes behind Taylor, but his ultimate victory was confirmation of his genius. In a career which saw him win his last Open 18 years after his first, he won a record six times. About the turn of the century when he went up and down the country, winning tournaments and breaking records, he raised the standards of those around him and had a great influence on methods of playing.

Until then, nobody had paid much attention to style, but suddenly people became aware that Vardon's upright swing was the essence of rhythm and grace. It was soon hailed as a perfect model for others to copy. Although he hit the ball a long way, he favoured light clubs and never carried more than ten.

Three of Vardon's six Opens were won after the advent of the rubber-cored ball, but it was with the gutty, before his serious illness in 1903, that he reigned supreme. Most of his success was attained in Britain, but he was also a pioneer of travel in days when it was long and laborious.

In 1900, he and Taylor finished first and second in the US Open at Chicago, the first time that either Open had been won by a traveller from overseas. Thirteen years later, he returned to Brookline for one of the most famous of all championships. It was the one in which he and Ted Ray lost a play-off to Francis Ouimet, an unknown local lad, who thus started the decline of British dominance.

Vardon's first tour of America took a lot out of him and it is said that he was never as brilliant again, although he was 44 years old when he won his last Open at Prestwick in 1914. After winning in 1903 with a total of 300, one of his proudest achievements, he contracted tuberculosis and had to go to a sanatorium for treatment but, by then, the third of the Triumvirate, James Braid, was in full swing.

The son of an Elie ploughman, he was a late starter compared to his great contemporaries. By the time he won his first Open in 1901, Taylor and Vardon had each won three times but, in a sudden golden era, Braid was the first of the three to win the championship five times.

In the space of ten years, he won at St Andrews and Muirfield twice and at Prestwick once. He never succeeded in England where he spent most of his life (first of all at the Army and Navy Stores in London, then at Romford and finally at Walton Heath) but, like Taylor and Vardon, he was seldom far away when not actually winning.

Until Jack Nicklaus finished second in 1979 for the seventh time, Taylor shared the title of champion runner-up with six, but Braid and Vardon were runners-up four times, Vardon once three years in succession.

Braid, who was said by Horace Hutchinson to drive with divine fury, was the winner of the first *News of the World* matchplay championship in 1903 and won money regularly in challenge and exhibition matches. In the 1904 Open at Sandwich, he played the last two rounds in a total of 140 strokes and was the first man to return a score under 70 in the championship. It came in his third round, Jack White, the winner, equalling it later in the day and Taylor, who finished third, beating it with 68.

Of the three, Braid's game was more liable to error, but his powers of recovery were immense, particularly in the now-familiar explosion shot from sand. It is just one more example of the way in which he, Taylor and Vardon set fashions over perhaps the most important 20 years in the whole history of championship golf.

	Harry Vardon	J H Taylor	James Braid
1894	=5	1	=10
1895	=9	1	DNP
1896	1	2	6
		(lost play-off)	
1897	6	=10	2
1898	1	4	11
1899	1	4	5
1900	2	1	3
1901	2	3	1
1902	=2	=6	=2
1903	1	=9	5
1904	5	=2	=2
1905	=9	=2	1
1906	3	2	1
1907	=7	2	=5
1908	=5	=7	1
1909	26	1	2
1910	=16	=14	1
1911	1	=5	=5
1912	2	=11	3
1913	=3	1	=18
1914	1	2	=10
1920	=14	12	=21
1921	=23	=26	=16
1922	=8	6	DNP
1924	DNP	5	=18

DNP Did not play.
=   Finished tied.

In addition, Vardon won the US Open in 1900 and was runner-up in 1913. He was also equal second when Ted Ray won in 1920. Taylor was second to Vardon in 1900.

Eugene (Gene) Sarazen

b Harrison, New York, 27.2.1902

Of all the great winners of the major championships down the years, Gene Sarazen was undoubtedly the smallest in stature. In some ways, he came into golf by accident, but his playing career spanned more than half a century and is among the most distinguished in the history of the game.

He is remembered for many things, but four feats of his must be recorded straightaway since they founded and preserved his reputation.

In the course of winning the British and American Opens in the same summer of 1932, he played 28 holes in 100 strokes at Fresh Meadow in the latter. Bobby Jones described it as 'the finest competitive exhibition on record'.

He became the first player to win all four major championships of the world, having been American champion for the first time at the age of 20; and he has to his credit two of the most famous single strokes ever played.

Caught off course. James Braid and Cecil Leitch instruct customers at Harrods on the finer points of putting in 1914. (BBC Hulton Picture Library)

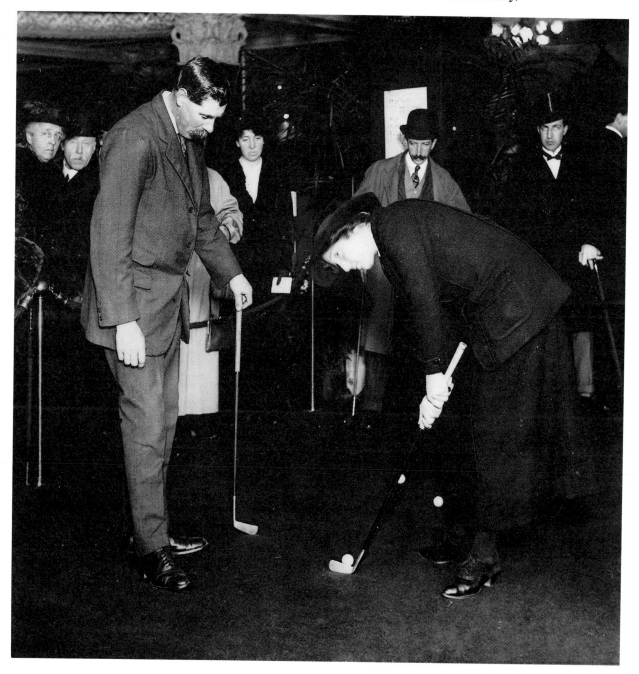

Gene Sarazen in natty attire. (USGA)

In only the second US Masters in 1935, he holed his second with a 4-wood at the 15th in the final round to turn a good chase into victory; and in the 1973 British Open at Troon, he holed in one at Troon's 8th, the celebrated Postage Stamp. To add piquancy to the tale, it was the 50th anniversary of his first appearance in the championship, also at Troon, and the shot was caught by the television cameras.

Sarazen was born in Harrison, New York, the son of a carpenter and christened Eugene Saraceni; the change of name came about because he felt he might be mistaken for a violinist. His father, who had studied for the priesthood back in Italy, was never in favour of his son becoming a golfer and it is possible that Gene might never have played at all if he had not contracted pleurisy while apprenticed to his father in Connecticut.

On medical advice, he found less strenuous work and, in the course of recuperation, tried his hand at golf. In a matter of months, he landed an assistant's post and before long he was Open champion. Having qualified for the championship in 1920 and 1921, his victory came at Skokie near Chicago where he was little known and spent the championship, so the story goes, sleeping in a dormitory of fellow professionals.

He practised extremely hard that week and had a premonition that he would win. He began with a 72 and 73 which put him in third place only to fall back with a moderate third round; but a 68, the first under 70 by a champion and the lowest last round until he beat it himself ten years later, gave him victory by a single stroke over John Black and Bobby Jones.

Golf has always been a full profession and a continuous business for Sarazen and, after the Open, he was inundated with invitations to take part in exhibition matches.

He won the PGA championship the same year and challenged Walter Hagen to a special match over 72 holes for the unofficial world championship. Not in the least daunted by the prospect, he beat 'The Haig' and then beat him again the following year at the 38th hole of the final of the PGA. They became good friends, dominated American professional golf for a number of years and, between them, put the professionals on the map, although Sarazen was always generous enough to give the lion's share of the credit to Hagen.

They became keen rivals and great contemporaries who, with Jones, set the tradition of supporting the British Open. Sarazen's first attempt in 1923 foundered even before he reached first base. He went to Troon, suitably hailed as the new star in the firmament, but failed to qualify in bad weather. With a humiliation that Hagen could understand after his experience in 1920, he vowed that he would be back even if he had to swim across the Atlantic.

As Herbert Warren Wind wrote of Hagen in *The Story of American Golf*, 'he had been press-agented as the golfer who would show British golf a thing or two' at Deal in 1920. 'Walter showed them four rounds in the eighties and finished a lurid fifty-fifth.'

Nobody doubted that Sarazen would be true to his word, but he had to wait until 1932 when the British Open was held at Prince's, Sandwich, for the first and only time. Accompanied by Daniels who had caddied for Hagen, Sarazen led from start to finish on a fast-running course, firmly obeying the advice of Daniels.

In 1928 over the fence at Royal St Georges, Sarazen took 7 on the 14th and lost to Hagen, but Daniels consoled him mightily by saying, 'I am going to win this championship for you if it is the last thing I do before I die.' Daniels kept his promise. Sarazen was never in danger and in the end had 5 strokes in hand over Macdonald Smith.

On the last day, in 1932, Daniels had been round the course early, checking the positions of the flags, showing that the modern propensity for pacing is nothing new but, in some ways, Sarazen's victory at Prince's was overshadowed by his second victory in the US Open a couple of weeks or so later.

In the previous months and years, he had not enjoyed the best of success and, for once in his life, he dabbled with technique.

He had always felt that his size had militated against him but, among other things, he experimented with the idea of a sand wedge with which he became a wizard; and, whether or not it was a big influence on his year of 1932, it gave him increased confidence.

Ironically, however, he started by playing cautiously and conservatively at Fresh Meadow in contrast to his normal approach of giving it everything he had. This seemed particularly misguided since the course encouraged players to attack from the tee and then to think about their second shots to well-bunkered greens.

With Sarazen's skill with his new bunker club, it seemed to justify further an attacking policy, but he decided otherwise and began with a 74 and a 76.

He persisted for a further 9 holes, but then was driven to return to his old ways. The results were as dramatic as could be. He played the last 28 holes in exactly 100 strokes, including a last round of 66. This was unheard of in those days and it remained the lowest last round by an American champion until Arnold Palmer returned 65 in 1960.

It was one of those almost fictional happenings that were such a feature of Sarazen's golfing life. His victory at the Masters and his hole in one at Troon are other examples, but 1932 marked the last of his victories in national championships although he came close more than once.

In his defence of the British Open at St Andrews in 1933, he finished 1 stroke away from a play-off with Densmore Shute and Craig Wood. Ironically, however, his trusty bunker club twice let him down. A lengthy argument with the Hill bunker cost him 6 at the short 11th in the second round and, in his final round, he failed to recover from Hell bunker on the 14th at his first attempt.

Sarazen also lost by 1 stroke to Olin Dutra in the US Open in 1934 at Merion, but he remained a regular competitor long after most of his contemporaries had retired. He could hold his own, too, and was instantly recognizable with his tanned, olive complexion and the knickers, or plus-fours, which became his trademark.

There have been better technicians and more elegant swingers but, rather like Gary Player some years later, Sarazen's consistent hitting, month after month and year after year, proved itself in the record books.

His nostalgic appearance in the British Open of 1973 was made possible by the exemption of all past Open champions, but Sarazen again stole the headlines on the first day by holing a punched 5-iron at the 8th. The following day, he holed a bunker shot for a 2 on the same hole and thereby set an incomparable record: an aggregate of 3 strokes for 1 hole in two days at the age of 71. Nine years later, aged 80, he accepted an invitation to Troon to play 9 holes as an exhibition on the last day of the Open but, in the end, he couldn't make it.

Sarazen has seen all the famous players from Vardon to Watson and has kept in touch with the game's development. He became an adviser in designing new courses and compered the popular film series, *Shell's Wonderful World of Golf*. He has introduced telecasts from the Masters and was made an Honorary Member of the Royal and Ancient Golf Club, but he will be best remembered as a champion golfer, an honest person and a man of charm and energy who is at home in all realms of society.

Known universally as 'The Squire', he has remained a popular figure for almost 60 years who, though not without his setbacks, knew how to win. In the words of someone summing up what he felt to be Sarazen's belief of himself after his first US Open victory, 'All men are created free and equal, and I am one shot better than the rest.'

	US Open	British Open	Masters	USPGA
1920	=30			DNP
1921	17			third round
1922	=1			1
1923	=16	F/Q		1
1924	=17	=41		first round
1925	=5	DNP		first round
1926	=3	DNP		second round
1927	3	DNP		third round
1928	=6	2		quarter final
1929	=3	=8		third round
1930	=28	DNP		finalist
1931	=4	=3		quarter final
1932	1	1		DNP
1933	=26	=3		1
1934	2	=21		second round
1935	=6	DNP	1	second round
1936	=28	=5	3	first round
1937	=10	DNP	24	second round
1938	10	=13		third round
1939	=47	5		first round
1940	2	=21		fourth round
1941	7			quarter final
1942		=29		
1946		DNP		
1947	=39	26		
1948		=23		
1949		=39		
1950		=10		
1951		=12		
1952		withdrew		
1953		=34		
1954		=52		
1955		withdrew		
1956		=49		
1963		49		

DNP Did not play.
F/Q Failed to qualify.
= Finished tied.

Keeping an eye on the performance of the early champions such as Walter Hagen and Gene Sarazen. A scoreboard on the wall of Royal St George's, Sandwich, 1928. (Illustrated London News)

One of Sam Snead's smaller galleries but his swing has been winning admirers for over 60 years. (USGA)

Samuel Jackson (Sam) Snead

b Hot Springs, Virginia, 27.5.1912

Only the Gods really know why Sam Snead never won the US Open. For a player who achieved every other distinction in over 40 years of regular, high-level competition, and was widely believed to possess the best swing in the world, it is a strange anomaly.

One possible explanation is that, since his approach to the game has been entirely intuitive, his tactical awareness was not always razor sharp in the crucial moments which decide major championships.

The other point is that, having come close to winning the Open once or twice in the early stages of a career which saw him beat his age (67) in the 1979 Quad Cities Open, he became haunted by the prospect of another chance of victory slipping away. Even the best golfers and the best methods are not immune to gnawing pressures.

In his first appearance in the US Open in 1937, he lost to Ralph Guldahl by 2 strokes and two years later took 8 on the 72nd hole at the Philadelphia CC, although he was unaware at the time that a 5 would have been enough.

In 1940, a last round of 81 destroyed the challenging position he held at lunchtime and in 1947 he missed from under a yard on the 18th green at St Louis to prolong a play-off with Lew Worsham. In 1949, he finished 1 stroke behind Cary Middlecoff; in 1953, he was second to Ben Hogan and sadly he never came as near again.

However, in every other respect, his record is incomparable especially in its durability. He won the Masters and USPGA titles three times each, the British Open once, and has scored no fewer than 84 victories on the US tour, and 135 in all. Three times he beat Ben Hogan, his great contemporary and rival, in play-offs; he was the first man to break 60 in a major event (at Greenbrier in 1959); and in official money, has earned over $620 000— a figure that would have been immeasurably more if he had been born 30 years later.

Snead was, in fact, raised in golfing terms at the Greenbrier Hotel course at White Sulphur Springs although he once said, 'none of us peckerwoods ever expected to get inside the gate, let alone out there with a club in our hands!' He was first a caddie and then a teaching professional, but he was astute enough, as his own golf developed, to win money from matches with members and guests.

As he wrote in his book *The Education of a Golfer*, 'My reputation for being so tight with money that I buried my winnings in tin cans in my backyard began about then, mostly due to my unwillingness to hang around clubhouse bars after tournaments and swap drink checks with the boys'; but his talents could not be checked and it was not long before he was one of the leading names on the tour.

It is an indication of the ever-growing wealth of the US tour that in the PGA's career money-winning list, he has already been passed by players of lesser ability who will certainly not be playing in the PGA championship in 40 years' time. But that is no disgrace. There will never be another Snead and nobody would dream of evaluating his success purely in monetary terms.

Nobody has brought to the game quite the same expression of power, grace and beauty. Nobody has hit more perfect shots and, even with the blemish of his failure to win the US Open, nobody could shortlist the ten best golfers of all time and omit the name of Sam Snead.

His swing, which owed little to practice or teaching, was based on a well-proportioned and extremely supple body. This made it possible for him to make an effortless, thorough and unhurried turn of hips and shoulders without detriment to control or balance. He could unleash tremendous power in his hands, but it was his sense of rhythm and timing which set him apart.

He did not devote the same effort of concentration that characterizes other champions; he did not have to. But he has gone on playing long after many others have given up, despite problems with his putting which he never allowed to be a deterrent to low scoring.

By adopting a side-saddle method, he overcame the problem remarkably well, finishing in the top ten in the US Open, Masters and PGA while in his mid-fifties. He also remains the oldest winner of a tournament on the PGA circuit (the 1965 Greater Greensboro Open when he was 52 years and 10 months); and he is the only player to beat his age in an official PGA event.

He did not play a great deal outside America and was an infrequent visitor to the British Isles. He once likened staying in Britain to 'camping out'. However, he added his name to the list of Open winners at St Andrews in 1946; took part in three Ryder Cup matches and is principally remembered for his play in two World Cups, one at Wentworth in 1956 and the second at Portmarnock in Eire four years later.

At Wentworth, he partnered Ben Hogan, and at Portmarnock, Arnold Palmer who was on his way to his first British Open. On both occasions the Americans won and, on both occasions, they attracted enormous crowds.

It is no wonder that Snead drew the crowds with such a classical swing. He has done so all his life, giving pleasure to millions and, at the same time, casting waves of envy that anyone could hit the ball so easily and elegantly. If Snead's skill could be transmitted and auctioned, the bidding would be never ending.

	US Open	British Open	Masters	USPGA
1937	2	=11	18	quarter final
1938	=38	DNP	=31	2 (runner-up)
1939	5	DNP	2	DNP
1940	=16	DNP	=7	2
1941	=13	DNP	=6	semi-final
1942		DNP	=7	1
1946	=19	1	=7	second round
1947	2 (lost play-off)	DNP	=22	second round
1948	5	DNP	=16	semi-final
1949	=2	DNP	1	1
1950	=12	DNP	3	second round
1951	=10	DNP	=8	1
1952	=10	DNP	1	first round
1953	2	DNP	=16	second round
1954	=11	DNP	1	semi-final
1955	=3	DNP	3	second round
1956	=24	DNP	=4	semi-final
1957	=8	DNP	2	quarter-final
1958		DNP	=13	3
1959	=8	DNP	=22	=8
1960	=19	DNP	=11	=3
1961	=17	DNP	=15	=27
1962	=38	=6	=15	=17
1963	=42		=3	=27
1964	=34		F/Q	DNP
1965	=24		F/Q	=6
1966			=42	=6
1967			=10	DNP
1968	=9		42	=30
1969			F/Q	=62
1970			=23	=12
1971			F/Q	=34
1972			=27	=4
1973			=29	=9
1974			=20	=3
1975			withdrew	F/Q
1976			F/Q	F/Q
1977			withdrew	=54
1978			F/Q	DNP
1979			F/Q	42

DNP Did not play.
F/Q Failed to qualify.
=   Finished tied.

Lee Trevino

b Dallas, Texas, 1.12.1939

Behind the scenes, Lee Trevino is quiet, almost subdued. In front of a microphone or a large gallery, he is an endless fount of banter, good humour and wise philosophy. It has been said many times, many ways, that he was just what the American tour needed at the end of the 1960s when it was in danger of taking itself too seriously.

In the wake of the Arnold Palmer era, it was also in danger of being totally monopolized by Jack Nicklaus. With a largely self-taught swing, Trevino leapt to fame by winning the 1968 US Open for which his wife had entered him and for almost twenty years has remained a leading figure in the game. His influence has been profound.

Trevino was an example of what the American people love, the boy from the wrong side of the tracks who became 'President'. Brought up in a maintenance shack in Dallas, Trevino's success brought a dramatic change of life; yet he adapted to it as naturally and as quickly as he visualized the right sort of pitch shot to be played in a critical moment in an important championship.

After all the hard times he knew, any form of prosperity could be said to have been a bonus but he has always been generous in thought and deed. Proof of the latter came when, after winning the 1968 Haiwaiian Open, he donated $10 000 to the family of his former room-mate, Ted Makalena who had been killed in a surfing accident.

At a time when the majority of American professionals were inclined to play down the talents of Severiano Ballesteros, Trevino came to his aid. Maybe it was the Mexican–Spanish connection that provided the bond.

But it was probably just as much recognition of the inventive genius which their golf shares and the fact that both chose the professional game as the best means of escape from the environment of the caddie shed in which they had been raised.

Incentive is a prime motivator but Trevino (and Ballesteros) made giant strides as soon as he realized that his game was good enough to chase the crock of gold at the end of the rainbow. Within four years, he was on top of the world, having won the US Open and British Open twice.

Just how exclusive a 'Club' he had joined can be seen from a list of the other 'members'—Hagen, Jones and Nicklaus. In 1972, he won the US, British and Canadian Opens within the space of about a month and this gave him access to membership of those who have won the British and US Opens in the same summer—Jones, Sarazen and Hogan.

In 1974, he added the PGA championship for the first time, leaving only the Masters to complete the professional's version of the grand slam although Augusta has never brought the best out in Trevino. He felt he could not fly the ball far enough to do well there.

Lee Trevino. Not one to let his golf do all the talking but one whose repartie is as entertaining as his play. (Benson and Hedges)

	US Open	British Open	Masters	USPGA
1966	=54	DNP	DNP	
1967	5	DNP	DNP	
1968	1	DNP	=40	=51
1969	F/Q	=34	=19	=48
1970	=8	=3	DNP	=26
1971	1	1	DNP	=13
1972	=4	1	=33	=11
1973	=4	=10	=43	=18
1974	F/Q	=31	DNP	1
1975	=29	=40	=10	=60
1976	DNP	DNP	=28	F/Q
1977	=27	4		=13
1978	=12	=29	=14	=7
1979	=19	=17	=12	=35
1980	=12	2	=25	7
1981	F/Q	=11		Disq
1982		=27		
1983	DNP	5	=20	=14
1984	=9	=14	=43	1
1985	F/Q	=20	=10	DNP
1986	=4	=59		=11
1987			F/Q	

DNP Did not play.
F/Q Failed to qualify.
Disq Disqualified.
=   Finished tied.

His failure to finish better than tenth bears him out, as does his liking for British links and the need, as he puts it, to 'bump and run'. The two types of golf are worlds apart but Trevino's greatest surprise has been his durability. Twenty years at the top is a long time.

It is an even longer time considering his physical battles of back problems and the terrible experience of being struck by lightning during the 1975 Western Open. The driving force has been his love of competition and the inborn ability to shape golf shots at will. Instrumental in this are the strength of his hands as his popular and highly entertaining golf clinics frequently indicate.

They enabled him to remain a regular tournament winner in the States, 1980 being a particularly good year for him but one of the finest victories of his career was his second PGA championship in 1984 at Shoal Creek, Alabama.

As he did in winning the 1968 US Open, he became the first player to return four rounds under 70. Rounds of 69, 68, 67, 69 gave him a total of 273, two strokes more than Bobby Nichols' tournament record but his total of 15 under par was a record.

The fact that Gary Player shared second place made it a triumph for the over-forties. Two years later, Nicklaus became the oldest winner of the Masters and Raymond Floyd the oldest winner of the US Open. In an age when so many young players are clamouring to show their worth, it is an unexpected trend but it is also a tribute to a vintage generation of which Trevino, Player and Nicklaus have been the undoubted leaders.

Byron Nelson

b Fort Worth, Texas, 4.2.1912

For a few years before, during and after World War II, Byron Nelson reigned supreme. Had it not been for the war, Nelson's name might have figured even higher in the ranks of the great. Having won the Masters, the US Open and the USPGA within the space of four years between 1937 and 1940, he was at his absolute peak at the outbreak of the war, from which he was excluded on account of haemophilia.

At that stage, he was a step ahead of Ben Hogan, a fellow Texan who became the greatest golfer of his generation but Nelson set records which neither Hogan nor anyone else, now or in the future, could ever hope to match.

In 1944, he won 13 of the 23 tournaments in which he played and the following season he won 18 tournaments, 11 of them in a row. He averaged 68.33 for 120 consecutive rounds and was never over par with any total in 30 events. In 1944, self-analysis of his golf revealed that his most common faults had been careless holing out and poor chipping. He worked at these to such effect that his average improved by a stroke.

These are astonishing statistics whether or not a golfer is playing in competition or friendly rounds, although it must be stressed that Nelson faced fairly stiff opposition. In 1945, Hogan and Snead were playing often enough to win eleven tournaments between them. Nelson played 113 events during the 1940s without missing a cut and in the 40 years since then nobody has come within a stroke of his average.

That is even more remarkable considering the improvement in the equipment and the condition of the courses but, though he won the French Open in 1955, he played little in the post-war period. He gained a considerable reputation as a coach (Tom Watson was perhaps the most notable to profit) and contributed to television commentaries.

His position as an elder statesman was lent weight by being Ryder Cup captain but, in the clamour of his tournament wins, his successes in the major championships must not be forgotten.

In the same year that he finished fifth in Cotton's Open at Carnoustie in 1937, he won the Masters at Augusta. He and Ralph Guldahl, in fact, were as responsible as any for the christening of part of the course as Amen Corner, for it was in 1937 that Nelson made up 6 strokes on Guldahl in 2 holes in the final round, the 12th and 13th. Nelson scored 2, 3 against Guldahl's 5, 6 to win by 2 but in 1942 it was even closer.

Nelson beat Hogan in a play-off, having, in 1939, won the US Open in a play-off with Craig Wood and Densmore Shute at the Philadelphia CC. In the first of his PGA titles, he defeated Snead in the final but for all the machine-like precision that Nelson's scoring suggests, he was an artist. He had a masterly touch with the driver, had command of flight in all his shots and possessed the authority in his large hands to shape any shot he wanted.

Byron Nelson, a man whose records on the US tour will never be equalled. (USGA)

	US Open	British Open	Masters	USPGA
1935	=32	DNP	=9	
1936		DNP	=13	
1937	=20	5	1	
1938	=5	DNP	5	
1939	1	DNP	7	
1940	=5	DNP	3	1
1941	=17	DNP	2	
1942		DNP	1	Finalist
1945	—	—	—	1
1946	=2	DNP	=7	
1947		DNP	=2	
1948		DNP	=8	
1949		DNP	=8	
1950		DNP	=4	
1951		DNP	=8	
1952		DNP	=24	

DNP Did not play.

Peter Thomson, MBE

b Melbourne, Australia, 23.8.1929

Peter Thomson's place in history will centre around his five victories in the British Open. On his first eight appearances, he won four (three of them in succession), was second three times and, on the other occasion, finished equal sixth.

He was the supreme master with the small ball on the fast links courses that traditionally house the Open, although in the last few years his success on the US seniors' tour indicates a liking for their courses as well. It has provided the perfect answer to those Americans who never perhaps appreciated his true potential but it was to Europe that he first turned his attentions—and there that he made his name. But it was long before the days of the European tour, although Thomson was still something of a pioneering force behind the idea. He turned professional in 1949 and, since there were hardly any tournaments in Australia in which to play, he had to focus his attentions on Britain in order to build up the experience which any young player needs.

However, he had the asset of one of the most orthodox and reliable of swings which he had moulded very much on his own and, even in days when prize money was hardly princely, started to make a good living.

As time progressed, he became the player who made the game appear remarkably easy. He obeyed the basic fundamentals of a good grip, a simple, natural stance and a lovely rhythmical balanced movement as he took the club back and swung it through.

Thomson had both a command of flight and the vision of the shot that was necessary. On seaside courses, this invariably involved knowing where to pitch the ball and calculating how much it would run. It may have owed more to chance than the air-routemindedness on which American professionals school themselves but Thomson made it look artistic and scientific.

Peter Thomson, the only golfer this century to have won the British Open three years in a row. (USGA)

His three victories in a row in the Open represent a feat that is unique in modern times although, again, his critics will maintain that the quality of the field he had to beat was relatively modest. Bobby Locke was his main rival. They monopolized the championship for seven years but Thomson's greatest triumph came in 1965 when his fifth victory, one short of Harry Vardon's record, was achieved against the might of Nicklaus, Palmer and Lema.

In more domestic tournaments, he weaved his spell of ascendancy in emphatic fashion, winning the match-play championship four times and the 1957 *Yorkshire Evening News* event at Sand Moor by 15 strokes.

Thomson also had a major hand in developing the Far East circuit and applied his acute mind to several aspects of the game. He wrote his own newspaper articles, was a regular commentator on television and wise counsellor to the affairs of the Australian PGA as well as helping several young Australian golfers.

Around 1981, he stood for election in the Victorian parliament and for many years before that was Chairman of the James McGrath Foundation in Victoria, which established Odyssey House in Melbourne as a place to help and to care for the problems of drug addicts.

No professional has ever had a greater diversity of interests but, having failed to be elected to the State parliament, Thomson found fruitful solace in the US seniors' tour where, in common with so many others, he has made more in a couple of years than in an entire career hitherto.

It led to the typical comment of his that for years as a young man he had prayed that he would become a better player. Now all he prayed for was that he wouldn't become any worse.

The 1959 and 1960 University Matches between Oxford and Cambridge at Royal Lytham produced six players (three on each side) who won the President's Putter a total of eleven times.

Young Tom Morris

b St Andrews, Fife, 20.4.1851
d St Andrews, 25.12.1875

Sooner or later most of the early championship records have been broken, but three which Young Tom Morris established are never likely to succumb. Making allowances for 1871 when there was no Open, owing to the fact that he had won the championship belt outright, he scored four successive victories; and, when he won his first title in 1868, he succeeded his father, Old Tom, as champion. In 1869, they finished first and second.

Young Tom was the man who put championship golf on the map and though he had only a handful of challengers, there is no telling how many other records he would have set if he had not died at the tragically early age of 24.

	US Open	British Open	Masters
1951	DNP	=6	
1952	DNP	2	
1953	=26	=2	
1954	DNP	1	=16
1955	DNP	1	=18
1956	=4	1	
1957	=22	2	5
1958	DNP	1	=23
1959	DNP	=23	
1960	DNP	=9	
1961	DNP	7	=19
1962	DNP	=6	
1963	DNP	5	
1964	DNP	=24	
1965	DNP	1	
1966	DNP	=8	
1967	DNP	=8	
1968	DNP	=24	
1969	DNP	=3	DNP Did not play.
1970	DNP	=9	= Finished tied.
1971	DNP	=9	
1972	DNP		
1977	DNP	=13	

His death came on Christmas Day 1875, only three months after that of his wife and newly born son. The tale, contradicted in the local St Andrews paper, was that he died of a broken heart. His memory is perpetuated by a plaque in St Andrews Cathedral which bears the inscription, 'Deeply regretted by numerous friends and all golfers, he thrice in succession won the championship belt and held it without rivalry and yet without envy, his many amiable qualities being no less acknowledged than his golfing achievements.'

Just how keen the rivalry was between father and son, is not recorded, but Old Tom once remarked in later years, 'I could cope wi' Allan [Robertson] mysel' but never wi' Tommy'; and nor could anyone else. At the age of 13, Young Tom won an exhibition match at Perth for a prize of £15; three years later, he won a professional tournament at Carnoustie, defeating Willie Park and Bob Andrew in a play-off, and in 1868 became the youngest Open champion.

Scores have inevitably improved over the years and it is no fairer to compare them than it is to measure success by the ever-increasing prize-money, but one achievement of Young Tom's is an undoubted measure of his ability.

In winning the 1870 Open by 12 strokes, only 1 stroke less than Old Tom's record-winning margin in 1862, he covered three rounds of Prestwick's 12-hole course in 149 strokes. It was a score never equalled even by Vardon, Taylor or Braid so long as the gutty ball was in use. Tom's last round of 49, 1 under fours, included a 3 at the 1st hole which measured considerably over 500 yd and gained him custody of the championship belt which was later presented to the Royal and Ancient Golf Club.

There was thus a gap of a year while the championship trophy, still played for today, was presented; in 1872, he won that, too. He beat Davie Strath by 3 strokes and once thereafter beat the better ball of Strath and Jamie Anderson. On another occasion, he backed himself to beat 83 round the Old course for a whole week, winning every time and then lowering his target to 81 and 80.

He had some detractors; for instance it was said that his swing lacked classic grace, but the power of his broad shoulders gave him the ability to squeeze the ball out of the bad lies that abounded in those days.

	British Open
1866	9
1867	4
1868	1
1869	1
1870	1
1871	NC
1872	1
1873	=3
1874	2

NC No Championship.
= Finished tied.

Severiano Ballesteros

b Santander, Spain, 9.4.1957

Fast disappearing are the days when the caddie yard could be depended on as professional golf's best source of recruitment. If social trends continue to accelerate, a fine heritage will soon come to an end but at least one of the last of the line has proved to be as great a recommendation to it as Ben Hogan, Lee Trevino and Walter Hagen.

The player who, more than anyone, convinced the world of the strength of the European golfers. Severiano Ballesteros. (Allsport)

It is easy to see that Ballesteros was as keen as they were to escape to a better life but to have moulded a swing of classic proportions more from instinct than instruction was indicative of a stroke of genius. He learned the game in fact, with a battered and borrowed 3-iron which became a multi-purpose club, capable of all manner of miracles, sneaking on to the course at Santander as early as the age of eight for a few holes when nobody was looking.

Like many blessed with youthful exuberance, he hit everything with full throttle, believing all things were possible and developing a liking for the spectacular. It was as well that nobody was around then to shackle or tame him although he may not have lacked for some brotherly help from Manuel or Baldovino who were both professionals.

When he first burst on to the golfing world outside Spain, Manuel was guide and interpreter but that 1976 Open championship at Royal Birkdale was convincing proof that a star was born. In his first major championship, Severiano tied with Jack Nicklaus for second place behind Johnny Miller and within three years was crowned as champion at Lytham.

Ballesteros was still inclined to hit the ball all over the place from the tee, a habit which prevented some American players from appreciating a player who would last but he had the answer for them by adding the Masters at Augusta the following April and has gone on surprising them ever since.

It is largely for this reason that he has always relished beating Americans but such a potent driving force stemmed as much from the knowledge that they were the leading players and he needed to beat them in order to stake his claim as the best player in the world.

This obsession was also the finest possible tribute to the European tour which had raised him and for whose welfare and good standing he did more than anybody. As experience grew apace, discretion replaced a little of the valour. Greater consistency from the tee relieved the strain on his powers of recovery which are based on a truly wonderful sense of touch, vision and sensitivity on all the pitching clubs, and with his putter.

He became the most prolific winner in Europe, established all sorts of money-winning records and was the architect of Europe's Ryder Cup victory in 1985 from a psychological standpoint if not as an actual slayer of dragons. His achievements impressed upon others that the Americans could be beaten; his own competitiveness raised their games significantly and established the kind of rivalry with Bernhard Langer that was a credit to both.

He repeated his victories in the British Open and the Masters although by the beginning of 1987, he had not cracked the US Open or the USPGA championships.

His failure so far will harden the need for patience, something which is out of keeping with a man itching to win everything he plays in. It means his story is far from complete, perhaps not even half-told. The prospect of what is to come makes for a bright future but his presence on the scene for over ten years has been the best single thing to have happened to the game in that time.

	US Open	British Open	Masters	USPGA
1976		=2		
1977		=15		DNP
1978	=16	=17	=18	DNP
1979	F/Q	1	=12	DNP
1980	Disq	=19	1	DNP
1981	=41	=39		=33
1982		=13	=2	13
1983	=4	=6	1	27
1984	=30	1	F/Q	5
1985	=5	=39	=2	=32
1986	=24	=6	4	F/Q
1987	3		3	

DNP Did not play.
F/Q Failed to qualify.
Disq Disqualified.
=   Finished tied.

Measuring a player's worth in world terms hinges on many factors and in 1986, Greg Norman more than came of age but from a census of informed opinion, Ballesteros is still head of the list and there are few indeed who do not anticipate that in the next ten years, he will join the immortals.

Raymond Floyd

b Fort Bragg, North Carolina, 4.9.1942

Raymond Floyd is one of the longest-serving professionals on the US tour still playing regularly. Only perhaps Jack Nicklaus has played longer but he has not played anything like as much as Floyd on what some call the 'weekly grind'.

There was a time when Floyd was as familiar a figure as the marshals and officials. In the last few years, he has confined his appearances to a couple of dozen or so tournaments a year but for a man who, since 1963, has only finished in the top ten of the money winners list on seven or eight occasions, he undoubtedly has flair for the spectacular.

Instead of being remembered as the journeyman pro, he features well in the parade of champions. By winning the US Open, Masters and the PGA (twice), he belongs to a select group consisting of Sarazen, Nelson, Hogan, Player and Nicklaus who have done the same. It is an achievement that speaks for itself.

What is more, his winning aggregate in the 1976 Masters (271) is a record he shares with Nicklaus; and, by his triumph in the 1986 US Open, he became the oldest winner. His PGA victories, 13 years apart, make a nice contrast, the first in the days of a flamboyant youth and the second in the days when he was recognized as the most solid of citizens.

In 1969 at Dayton, Ohio, the year of anti-apartheid demonstrations which affected Player and Nicklaus in the final round, he had a total of 276 but in 1972, a total of 272 was only one outside the record of Bobby Nichols.

Floyd's opening round of 63 at Southern Hills, Tulsa, was 'without a doubt the best round of golf I have ever played, anywhere, in my life' but, again, it was an example of the heights his game could attain. When he joined the tour in 1963, he played ten events without making the cut but then won the 11th, the St Petersburg Open; and in the 1969 American Golf Classic, he became the first person to shoot four sub-par rounds over the Firestone course.

In the 1976 Masters, he fired opening rounds of 65 and 66 to build up a lead of five and eventually won by eight. There has only been one more one-sided Masters but, even when running at its smoothest, his swing was never a thing of beauty.

One admired the results rather than the method of achieving them. Part of this is attributable to a well-built man having to compensate for his disproportionately short arms by using longer than standard clubs.

Raymond Floyd, one of the most consistent and respected of professionals in the last 20 years. (USGA)

This favours a short, stiffish swing but it was never seen to better effect than in the final 9 holes of the 1986 US Open at Shinnecock Hills. It embodied the very finest elements of Floyd, the technician and the competitor.

Of US Open champions, only Palmer, Nicklaus and Miller have shot lower in the last round, Floyd's 66, in which he came home in 32, being almost as good. In one way, it was perhaps even better. There are those who maintain that nerve is more valuable than experience but Floyd, who acknowledges his wife's stabilizing influence in his life, showed absolutely no sign that his nerves were fraying at the edges. Very much the opposite.

In July 1986 he went in search of the British Open title which would have been the trick which took his grand slam. It is a championship at which he has been a regular attender and in which he has finished second and third but, if Shinnecock should happen to be the final chapter in his major championship success, it was proof of how perseverance pays. Floyd took a leaf out of Gary Player's book.

Willie Anderson

b Scotland, 1878
d 1910

Willie Anderson belonged to the bygone age of Scottish professionals who went to the New World when golf began to spread faster than a prairie fire. It was in America rather than his homeland, therefore, that his golf took shape and it was certainly there that he developed champion's qualities.

His rise to capture four US Opens, a distinction he shares with Bobby Jones, Jack Nicklaus and Ben Hogan, has to be kept in the proper perspective. The biggest field he faced was 89 and one of his winning totals, 331 in 1901, is the highest in history. Nevertheless, his place in the records is secure and rightly so.

He was the hero that America needed at the time and he won again in 1903 at Baltusrol, his opening round of 73 being the lowest recorded to that point. He beat it himself the following year with a 72 in the final round at Glen View and he made it three victories in a row, his fourth in five years, by winning at Myopia in 1905.

This is a record that nobody has ever matched. However, Anderson, a dour, slim figure, suffered a long illness before his premature death in 1910 and that illness undoubtedly prevented further success by a player who, in keeping with that era, had a distinctively flat swing.

	US Open	British Open	Masters	USPGA
1966			=8	
1967	=38		=8	
1968	DNP		=7	=13
1969	=13	=34	F/Q	1
1970	=22	F/Q	F/Q	=8
1971	8		=13	F/Q
1972	F/Q		F/Q	=4
1973			54	=35
1974	=15		=22	=11
1975	=12	=23	=30	=10
1976	13	4	1	=2
1977	=47	8	=8	=40
1978	=12	=2	=16	=50
1979	F/Q	=36	=17	=62
1980	=47		=17	=17
1981	=37	=3	=8	=19
1982	=49	=15	=7	1
1983	=13	=14	=4	=20
1984	=52	F/Q	=15	13
1985	=23	DNP	=2	F/Q
1986	1	=16		
1987		F/Q		

DNP Did not play.
F/Q Failed to qualify.
= Finished tied.

	US Open				
1897	2	1903	1	1909	=4
1898	3	1904	1	1910	11
1899	5	1905	1		
1900	=11	1906	5		
1901	1	1907	15	=	
1902	=5	1908	4	Finished tied.	

Arthur D'Arcy (Bobby) Locke

b Germiston, South Africa, 20.11.1917
d 9.3.1987

Like Peter Thomson, with whom his name is inextricably linked where the British Open is concerned, Bobby Locke's reputation owed prime allegiance to Britain and Europe. He was Open champion on four occasions in a span of eight years and won countless other professional tournaments.

The secret of his scoring lay in his almost superhuman ability on and around the greens which disguised the fact that he might not be playing particularly well. Nobody went to watch Locke for the beauty of his swing. At times, he made one wonder just where he was aiming.

A highly individual closed stance gave rise to a long, full swing which less supple frames would have found impossible to engineer. The result was something between a draw and a hook but, however ungainly it may have appeared, Locke had it under complete control.

This was because his rhythm was always constant and he could rely upon an unhurried tempo never to rush things. He played with stately, unflustered command that became a watchword. The Americans christened him Muffin Face on account of his changeless expression but he gave them ample reason to remember him.

At Sam Snead's suggestion, Locke made lucrative raids on the American tour, winning six tournaments and finishing second twice in 1947. His successes continued and in 1950 he won the rich Tam O'Shanter and he was third twice and fourth twice in the US Open but, apart from the pleasure that any success brings, he was happier playing in Europe and back home in South Africa, where he took the South African Open title nine times.

Locke's year in Britain revolved around the Open in which he had first played as an amateur in 1936 at Hoylake. He was a distinguished bomber pilot in World War II but quickly got down to golf again afterwards and finished second equal to Sam Snead at St Andrews in 1946.

He did not play the next two years but he won at Sandwich in 1949 and successfully defended his title at Troon. It was a strange fact that in all four of his winning years, he had an opening round of 69 but by 1952, when he won again, Thomson had become a real threat to him. After Hogan's year when Thomson was equal 2nd and Locke 8th, Thomson denied him for three years on the trot but Locke's last victory came in 1957 although, on the final green, he replaced his ball incorrectly after marking it. However, the R and A took no action since he was three strokes ahead and the incident could not affect the outcome.

By now he was in his 40th year but, whilst normally that would have been a signal for the end of a career, the decision was soon to be taken for him. Three years later, a bad road accident kept him in hospital for several

months and, though he appeared in the Open through the special qualification extended to former champions, it undoubtedly meant that he was never the same again.

	British Open	US Open	Masters
1936	=8	DNP	DNP
1937	=17	DNP	DNP
1938	=10	DNP	DNP
1939	=9	DNP	DNP
1946	=2	DNP	DNP
1947		=3	=14
1948		4	=10
1949	1	=4	=13
1950	1		
1951	=6	3	
1952	1		=21
1953	8	=14	
1954	=2		
1955	4	5	
1956	F/Q		
1957	1		
1958	=16		
1959	=29		
1960			

DNP Did not play.
F/Q Failed to qualify.
= Finished tied.

Contrasting waistlines of Bobby Locke. Above before World War II in which he served as a distinguished bomber pilot and on the left on one of his last appearances in the Open championship. (USGA and Allsport)

The 25 Greatest Rounds

What constitutes greatness in a round of golf? The same might be asked about wine, books, loaves of bread, musical symphonies or bottles of perfume. The question is easier than the answer.

There is no such thing as the perfect round of golf. If there were, the solution to the quandary would be straightforward. In some games (Snooker, Darts) perfection can be measured, but the author's definition of a great round would be the nearest to perfection it would be reasonable to expect, weighing up the conditions, the course, the occasion and the opposition.

The great rounds which have been chosen here are rounds that, given these parameters, are perhaps those nobody else could have played. Nearly all contained blemishes, but that only serves to underline the tantalizing nature of the game.

Diagram of the 12-hole course at Prestwick, over which Young Tom Morris played one of golf's most famous rounds in 1870. (Prestwick GC)

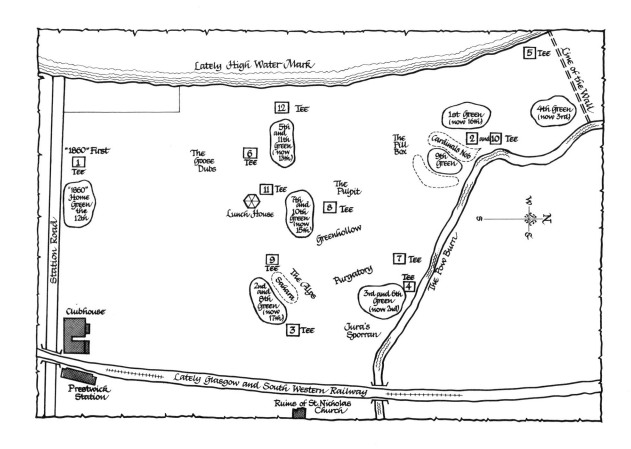

	Player	Event	Date	Venue	Score
1.	**Young Tom Morris**	Open championship	1870	Prestwick	47 for 12 holes
2.	**Francis Ouimet**	US Open play-off	1913	Brookline	72
3.	**George Duncan**	British Open	1922	Sandwich	69
4.	**Bobby Jones**	Open qualifying	1926	Sunningdale	66
5.	**Bobby Jones**	US Open	1930	Interlachen	68
6.	**Gene Sarazen**	US Open	1932	Fresh Meadow	28 holes in 100 strokes
7.	**Lawson Little**	British Amateur final	1934	Prestwick	66
8.	**Henry Cotton**	British Open	1934	Sandwich	65
9.	**Ben Hogan**	US Open	1951	Oakland Hills	67
10.	**Ben Hogan**	British Open	1953	Carnoustie	68
11.	**Arnold Palmer**	British Open	1961	Royal Birkdale	73
12.	**Jack Nicklaus**	US Masters	1965	Augusta	64
13.	**Catherine Lacoste**	US Women's Open	1967	White Sulphur Springs	70
14.	**Roberto de Vicenzo**	US Masters	1968	Augusta	66
15.	**Michael Bonallack**	English Amateur final	1968	Ganton	61
16.	**Tony Jacklin**	World matchplay championship	1972	Wentworth	63
17.	**Johnny Miller**	US Open	1973	Oakmont	63
18.	**Al Geiberger**	Memphis Classic	1977	Colonial CC	59
19.	**Tom Watson**	British Open	1977	Turnberry	65
20.	**Gary Player**	US Masters	1978	Augusta	64
21.	**David Graham**	US Open	1981	Merion	67
22.	**Tom Watson**	US Open	1982	Pebble Beach	70
23.	**Bernhard Langer**	Spanish Open	1984	El Saler	62
24.	**Jack Nicklaus**	US Masters	1986	Augusta	65
25.	**Greg Norman**	British Open	1986	Turnberry	63

Young Tom Morris

Event: Open Championship
Date: 1870
Venue: Prestwick
Score: First round, 47

The Open Championship was started very largely to find a champion golfer to succeed Allan Robertson who died in 1859. He was therefore an uncrowned king but there is no doubt that his mantle was very soon taken over by Young Tom who was the first player to make golf conscious of scores and records.

He is the only player in the Open's history to have won four titles in succession, but it was his victory in 1870 which had the added romance of making the championship belt his own by winning his third victory in succession.

It was in that year that he covered three rounds of Prestwick's 12-hole course in 149 or 2 over par. In those days that represented 2 strokes 'in excess of absolutely faultless play'.

It was a total never equalled while the championship was decided over 36 holes but the really stunning round was Young Tom's first. He went round in 47, or 2 under par. It was unquestionably the first great round of golf, well worthy of heading this section. It led to a winning margin of 12 strokes.

Details of the round are sketchy but the names and pars of the holes on a curiously criss-cross course make fascinating reading.

It will be seen that the highlight of the round was an opening albatross 3 on a bogey 6 plus a run of three 3s from the 6th. On the other hand, a finish of 4, 5 must have been a disappointment.

The man who made golf conscious of record breakers, Young Tom Morris. (Prestwick GC)

Hole	Name	Yards	Bogey	Score
1	Back of Cardinal	578	5	3
2	Alps	391	5	5
3	Tunnel (Red)	167	3	3
4	Stone Dyke	482	5	5
5	Sea He'therick	460	5	6
6	Tunnel (White)	350	4	3
7	Green Hollow	165	3	3
8	Station	162	3	3
9	Burn	298	5	4
10	Lunch House	290	4	3
11	Short	97	3	4
12	Home	359	4	5
Total		3799	49	47

Francis Ouimet

Event: US Open
Date: 20 September 1913
Venue: The Country Club, Brookline, Boston
Score: Play-off, 72

Nothing in the 70 or more years since Francis Ouimet won a play-off for the US Open has matched the story-book romance which surrounded his victory. It was the tale of the caddie boy from across the street who defeated two of the finest professionals in the world. It was the day that British supremacy ended and American supremacy began. It was David slaying Goliath.

The modern equivalent would be for a 20-year-old with no reputation behind him to topple Greg Norman and Severiano Ballesteros. Ouimet entered the championship as much as anything to get a closer look at Harry Vardon who was champion in 1900. That he did so, and more, merely added to the spice but, while some of the better known Americans failed to maintain a challenge to Vardon and Ted Ray, US Open champion in 1920, Ouimet needed an inspired finish to make the three-way play-off at all.

He had to play the last 4 holes of the final round in 1 under par to tie, a feat he accomplished with a 12-yard putt on the 17th for a birdie and a nasty one of a yard on the 18th.

Most people felt that Ouimet's nerve might let him down in the play-off and that the occasion might be too much for him. Vardon and Ray were redoubtable, experienced opponents whereas Ouimet was, by comparison, a raw recruit who had failed to qualify by one stroke in the US Amateur championships of 1910, 1911 and 1912.

He had, however, won the State Amateur of Massachusetts in 1913 and reached the second round in the US Amateur where he lost to the winner, Jerome Travers, earlier in the same month as the Open. It was not quite the sort of form that suggested an Open champion three weeks later but, if the play-off has been described as an anti-climax, it was because it was surprisingly one-sided, the biggest surprise being that Ouimet outscored the two professionals.

It had been raining for about 30 hours when ten o'clock came and the first 2 holes were halved. All three, in fact, reached the turn in 38 but Ouimet, who had perhaps been the steadiest of the three, apart from hitting his second at the 5th out of bounds, went ahead at the short 10th and stayed ahead. What is more, he never looked like cracking. He went two ahead at the 12th where he hit the green in two while Vardon and Ray missed it, Vardon left and Ray right; and though Vardon got a stroke back with a birdie at the 13th, disaster struck for the Englishmen over the last 4 holes.

Ray was the first victim with a 6 at the 15th, Vardon later falling foul of the 17th and 18th and so lightening the task for Ouimet. Ouimet gained 2 strokes on each, holing a beautiful putt for a 3 at the 17th, as he had done the evening before, and ending with a solid par 4. His inward half of 34 and round of 72 represented quite

remarkable golf and composure. His previous best round during the week was 74. He beat Vardon by 5 and Ray by 6, conquered the heavy conditions and wore the crown with the same grace and distinction that made him one of the most respected figures in the history of American golf—and the first overseas captain of the Royal and Ancient Golf Club of St Andrews.

Hole	Yards	Par	Score	Detail
1	430	4	5	D, 3W, Pitch, 2 putts
2		4	4	D, pitch, 2 putts
3	435	4	4	D, mid-iron, 2 putts
4			4	Wooden cleek, pitch, 2 putts
5	420	4	5	D, brassie (out of bounds), brassie, 2 putts
6		4	4	D, pitch, 2 putts
7		3	4	Mid-iron, chip, 2 putts
8		4	3	D, mashie, 1 putt (18 inches)
9	520	5	5	D, 3W, pitch, 2 putts
Out			38	
10	140	3	3	Mid-iron, 2 putts
11	390	4	4	D, mashie, 2 putts
12		4	4	D, mashie, 2 putts
13		4	4	D, pitch, 2 putts
14		5	5	D, brassie, pitch, 2 putts
15		4	4	D, mid-iron, 2 putts
16		3	3	Jigger, 2 putts
17	360	4	4	D, mashie, 1 putt
18			4	D, mashie, 2 putts
In			34	
Out			38	
Total			72	

Vardon Out 5, 4, 4, 4, 5, 3, 4, 4, 5 = 38
      In   4, 4, 5, 3, 5, 4, 3, 5, 6 = 39   Total 77

Ray Out 5, 4, 5, 4, 5, 4, 3, 3, 5 = 38
      In   4, 4, 5, 4, 5, 6, 4, 5, 3 = 40   Total 78

Photo. Sport and General.
MR. FRANCIS OUIMET,
The wonderful young Golfer who Won the American Open Championship.

Extract from the *Sport and General* magazine which, within about two weeks, carried news of Francis Ouimet's fairy tale victory in the US Open of 1913. (Illustrated London News)

Mr. Francis Ouimet, the golf prodigy of the United States, who defeated two of the most famous British professionals—Vardon and Ray—in the American Open Championship, is only twenty years of age. He is a French-Canadian, and has lived since childhood in a cottage near the course at Brookline, where the great match was played. He is a salesman in a golf store at Boston. Next year he hopes to play in the British Amateur Championship at Sandwich.

George Duncan

Event: British Open
Date: 1922
Venue: Royal St George's, Sandwich
Score: Fourth round, 69

Not all the greatest rounds have resulted in victory. Many represent the gallant challenge which failed. There seemed to be rather more in this category before the custom was established of sending the leaders out last on the final day.

When George Duncan won the first post-war Open at Deal in 1920, he had finished his third round before Abe Mitchell, the leader, had set out. What is more, he made up the 13 strokes by which he trailed Mitchell, in 18 holes; and so, two years later he was an obvious threat even though 6 strokes behind the reigning champion, Jock Hutchison, with a round to play.

Not that Duncan was the only contender. The chasing pack included the two old stalwarts, J H Taylor and Harry Vardon, Walter Hagen, the eventual champion, Jim Barnes, Charles and Ernest Whitcombe and Percy Alliss.

A 7 at the 4th proved the undoing of Hutchison but, in spite of a howling wind and the accompaniment of driving rain, Hagen gave the British crowds the first taste of his mastery. His 72 for a total of 300 was reckoned to be as good as anyone could have done in the conditions.

He had the advantage of hoisting his score early. When Duncan set off in pursuit, he may not even have had victory in mind but, with the roles reversed from two years earlier and requiring a 68 to tie, he came to the very threshold of another amazing triumph. He had the ability, when in the mood, of going for everything and bringing everything off.

James Braid once said of Duncan, 'I cannot make him out; he plays so fast that he looks as if he doesn't care, but I suppose it must be his way. He's the most extra-ordinary golfer I have ever seen'. Well, the dash, confidence and strength of his driving were most notable as he reached the turn in 34 over holes where the driving was far more daunting with less sophisticated equipment.

He took 3 putts on the old 8th with its sharp two-tier but when he started home with three 4s, the impossible was still just possible. Bernard Darwin obviously thought so, too. As he wrote many years later in *Golf Between Two Wars*, 'trudging the course, cursing my own conscience, I picked up Duncan and his partner by the 12th green and then I had my reward in 6 holes of delicious agony.

'Duncan had a handful of spectators with him and these were divided between joy and despair. They were full of joy over Duncan's astonishing play up to the flag and of despair because he could not crown these inspired approach shots by holing the putts'.

What really set his chances alight was a 3 on the 439 yards 13th with its green next door to Prince's. He had to be content with a 5 at the 14th which was well out of

The greens were rarely as slick as the locker room floor or as shiny as George Duncan's shoes but nobody had a reputation for playing more quickly. (BBC Hulton Picture Library)

range in two and though he missed a definite opportunity of a birdie at the 15th, where he hit a beautiful second shot, the 16th gave him exactly what he wanted—when he wanted it most.

A glorious shot with his favourite spoon nestled 4 yards from the pin and in went the putt. Now he needed two fours to tie, always a tall order at Sandwich but even more so when they need two wooden clubs.

Anyone comparing scores of 60 or 70 years ago with those of today will notice the big difference in the clubbing but Duncan was close enough to the 17th with two drivers to get his four and then laced another excellent drive down the 18th. Here, he was distracted by having to wait largely to control the crowds who had got wind of his deeds.

Information was harder to obtain in 1922 but eventually Duncan was ready, having debated about a spoon or a brassie for his second shot and opted for the latter. It was almost perfect but tailed away late in its flight into the little hollow on the left of the green which, ironically, became known as 'Duncan's Hollow'.

Understandably charged up, and seeing Hagen sitting behind the green looking suitably apprehensive, Duncan, choosing to play a little running shot with his mashie-iron, caught the ground fractionally behind the ball. It finished about 5 yards short of the hole and his putt to tie was short as well but it had been a famous chase which set a standard of scoring that was well ahead of its time. It was, in fact, only the third round under 70 in the Open and undoubtedly one of the finest bad weather rounds ever played.

THE ILLUSTRATED LONDON NEWS, JUNE 26, 1926.—1138

PERSONALITIES OF THE WEEK: PEOPLE IN THE PUBLIC EYE.

PHOTOGRAPHS BY LAFAYETTE, RUSSELL, VANDYK, ELLIOTT AND FRY, SPORT AND GENERAL, TOPICAL, AND CRISP (CAMBRIDGE).

A TRAGEDY OF MOTORING: THE LATE M. TORBEN DE BILLE.

SUED FOR ALLEGED LIBEL: EARL WINTERTON.

M.P. FOR 21 YEARS: THE LATE SIR SAMUEL ROBERTS, BT., OF SHEFFIELD.

A WELL-KNOWN COUNTY COURT JUDGE: THE LATE SIR EDWARD BRAY.

MOTHER OF THE LATE KING CONSTANTINE, AND FORMERLY REGENT OF GREECE: THE LATE QUEEN OLGA OF GREECE.

PERFORMER OF A REMARKABLE GOLFING FEAT AT SUNNINGDALE: MR. R. T. JONES (U.S.A.).

A FAMOUS INDIAN POET LECTURING IN ROME: SIR RABINDRANATH TAGORE.

THE PROFESSIONAL GOLF DUEL AT ST. GEORGE'S HILL: WALTER HAGEN (RIGHT) THE WINNER, AND ABE MITCHELL.

HEAD OF THE RIVER IN THE MAY RACES AT CAMBRIDGE FOR THE FIRST TIME SINCE 1872: THE LADY MARGARET (ST. JOHN'S COLLEGE) BOAT.

LEADING CANADIAN BUSINESS MEN ARRIVE AT WATERLOO: (L. TO R.) LORD SHAUGHNESSY, MR. E. W. BEATTY, SIR GEORGE McLAREN-BROWN, AND MESSRS. F. E. MEREDITH, W. R. MacINNES, AND W. S. C. MEREDITH.

Mr. Torben de Bille, Secretary of the Danish Legation, died on June 18 in Hounslow Hospital from injuries in a motor accident.——Earl Winterton, Under-Secretary for India, won the case brought against him by the widow of a British officer who died in India, for alleged libel in a letter written from the India Office.——Queen Olga of Greece was the widow of King George, and mother of King Constantine.——Sir Samuel Roberts was M.P. (Conservative) for the Ecclesall Division of Sheffield for twenty-one years.——Sir Edward Bray was appointed to the County Court Bench in 1905.——Mr. R. T. Jones, the American golfer, headed the list of competitors in the qualifying round of the Open Championship at Sunningdale with the remarkable score of 134 for the thirty-six holes.——Walter Hagen, the American professional, beat Abe Mitchell in a challenge match at St. George's Hill on June 19.—— In the May Races at Cambridge, Lady Margaret bumped First Trinity, and went Head of the River. The names of the crew (right to left in our photograph): are A. H. Galbraith (cox), R. B. T. Craggs (stroke), J. C. H. Booth, L. V. Bevan, R. L. C. Foottit, E. O. Connell, M. F. A. Keen, G. M. Simmons, and R. A. Symonds (bow).——Mr. E. W. Beatty, President of the C.P.R., met at Waterloo the other day a party of prominent Canadians. Our group includes Lord Shaughnessy, a Director of the C.P.R.; Mr. W. R. MacInnes, Vice-President; Sir George McLaren-Brown, European General Manager; and Mr. F. E. Meredith, Director of Canadian Pacific Steamships.

A variety of items made the news in June 1926 but none more worthy of acclaim than Bobby Jones's round of 66 in the Open championship qualifying rounds at Sunningdale. (Illustrated London News)

Bobby Jones

Event:	Open Championship
Date:	16 June 1926
Venue:	Sunningdale Old
Score:	Qualifying round, 66

Nowadays, a good tournament professional would regard a 66 round the Old course at Sunningdale as all part of a day's work. To some, it is no better than a couple under a realistic par. But, in 1926, it was a different story.

Golfers simply did not go round in 66. Up until then, the only rounds under 70 in the British Open had been the 69s of James Braid and Jack White (1904) and the 69s of George Duncan (1922) and Macdonald Smith (1925). In the US Open, the success rate was only marginally better but Jones was the outstanding golfer of the 1920s and it was entirely fitting that he should be the trend setter with regard to low scoring.

It was his second visit to Britain and, though it may seem strange 60 years later that he should have had to qualify at all, it was the fashion for many years. The year 1926 saw the experiment of advance qualifying in regions but the choice of Sunningdale evidently suited Jones well—coming as he had from the Walker Cup at St Andrews.

At the time, his first round of 66 was as near to perfection as anyone had seen. It certainly had perfect symmetry, 33 for each half and nothing but threes and fours. However, the truly remarkable part about it is that, with hickory shafted clubs and a ball that did not go anything like as far as its modern counterpart, Jones took wood for his second shot twice and a 2-iron no less than seven times. Even on the 3rd, 9th and 11th which many now think about driving, his seconds consisted of a firm push with a mashie or mashie niblick.

The other remarkable statistic is that the round contained 34 putts, the only single putts coming on the 5th for a birdie and on the short 13th where he saved his par after bunkering his tee shot with a mashie. It was the only green he missed in regulation.

O B Keeler, Jones's Boswell, described it as 'the finest round Bobby ever played'. It was not a hasty judgement either. It was included in *The Bobby Jones Story* which Grantland Rice compiled from the writings of Keeler who went on to say that Jones's card was 'played with a precision and freedom from error never attained before or after by the greatest precisionist of them all'.

Jones had picked up a new driver from Jack White, the Sunningdale professional, and obviously found inspiration from it. White christened it Jeannie Deans, the romantic heroine, and it served Jones for the rest of his playing career.

In the second round, Jones shot a 68 for a total of 134 although it caused him to reflect, erroneously, as it proved, that he had peaked too early. He went on to Lytham where he won the first of his three Open victories, the only ones in which he played.

It gave rise to his famous finish and the celebrated second shot which he hit on the 71st hole but it cannot have been easy after the euphoria of Sunningdale. Bernard Darwin, as usual, hit the most apt note about it by saying that 'the crowd had dispersed awestruck, realizing that they had witnessed something they had never seen before, and would never see again'.

Hole	Yards	Par	Score	Details
1	494	5	4	D, 3W, 2 putts
2	456	4	4	D, 2I, 2 putts
3	296	4	4	D, mashie, 2 putts
4	161	3	3	Mashie, 2 putts
5	417	4	3	D, 2-iron, 25 ft putt
6	418	4	4	D, 2I, 2 putts
7	434	4	4	D, 2I, 2 putts
8	172	3	3	Mashie, 2 putts
9	267	4	4	D, mashie niblick, 2 putts
Out	3115	35	33	
10	463	4	4	D, 2I, 2 putts
11	299	4	3	D, mashie, 2 ft putt
12	443	4	4	D, 2I, 2 putts
13	178	3	3	D, SI, 6 ft putt
14	503	5	4	D, brassie, 2 putts
15	226	3	3	Cleek, 2 putts
16	423	4	4	D, 2I, 2 putts
17	421	4	4	D, mashie, 2 putts
18	414	4	4	D, mashie, 2 putts
In	3370	35	33	
Out	3115	35	33	
Total	6485	70	66	

Bobby Jones

Event:	US Open
Date:	12 July 1930
Venue:	Interlachen
Score:	Third round, 68

So much of history is accepted by the generations that follow that it is sometimes difficult to conjure up the atmosphere that surrounded great achievements. America became very used to the triumphs of Bobby Jones but throughout the summer of 1930, one topic became uppermost: The Grand Slam.

By the time that the US Open moved on to Interlachen, Minneapolis, Jones had already captured the British Open for the third time but, more crucially, he had won his first British Amateur with its 18-hole matches in which even the best are vulnerable. It was hot, heavens hot, at Interlachen but Jones was clear about his goal and started confidently with rounds of 71–73 which left him two strokes off the pace set by Horton Smith; and just to keep Jones concentrating on his work, nearly all the big names were alongsides. Harry Cooper had the same score, Macdonald Smith, who had chased him home a month or so earlier at Hoylake, was on 145; Tommy Armour was on 146 and Walter Hagen, Johnny Farrell and Johnny Golden by no means out of the hunt.

After his lengthy trip to Britain, Jones was pleased to find his game working better than it had been over there, but there is no doubt that it reached its peak in the third round for which he was an early starter. Having reached the turn in 33, in spite of dropping a stroke at the 9th, he had a golden spell of 6 holes. Starting home, 4, 4, 4, 3, a run that included birdies at the 11th and long 12th, he came to the short 17th 6 under par needing a 3 and a 4 for a 66.

Such a score had rarely been contemplated before in a US Open and certainly never achieved. Jones had taken advantage of seven of Interlachen's holes being a drive and pitch, three times coming within a few inches of holing 100 yards pitches with his mashie-niblick.

The 17th was 262 yards, a long par 3 which nowadays would be a par 4. A 3 was asking a lot and Jones dropped one stroke here and another at the 402 yard 18th. It must have been a bitter disappointment but 68 was still a mighty round in the unique circumstances in which he found himself and news of it soon filtered back to his challengers.

Jones had a 5-stroke lead at lunchtime and it proved enough although he again messed up the 17th before finishing with a birdie and then found that Macdonald Smith chased him too hard for comfort. At Hoylake, he made up four of the 6 strokes by which he trailed Jones after 54 holes and at Interlachen, he retrieved 5 of the 7 strokes by which he trailed at the same stage.

After the celebrations, it was on to Merion and the US Amateur which posed the final leg of the Slam. Three down with one to go was an enviable state and Jones finished off in style. He led the medal stage and dismissed his opponents in match after match, his smallest victory being by 5 and 4.

It had been a triumphal march but the second half of the Slam was undoubtedly made easier by the important trick his marvellous 68 took at Interlachen.

Gene Sarazen

Event: US Open
Date: 25 June 1932
Venue: Fresh Meadow
Score: Fourth round, 66
          (but last 28 holes in 100 strokes)

In the same way that examples of modern racing cars go considerably faster than the now antique looking models which used to be familiar on pre-war circuits, scoring at golf keeps breaking new barriers. It is largely to do with the increased performance of the ball but, even today, the final rounds of 70 and 66 with which Gene Sarazen won his second US Open in 1932 are still a matter for envy and admiration.

No champion has yet beaten that total for the final 36 holes and only Ken Venturi, in 1964, has equalled it. What is more, both Sarazen's and Venturi's were put together when two rounds were played on the last day. So, what Bobby Jones called 'the finest competitive exhibition on record' is as true now as it was then.

This was very much Sarazen's year. He had won the

British Open for the first time at Prince's, Sandwich and therefore returned to Fresh Meadow, New York, in buoyant spirits, although his victory in Britain had taken a lot out of him.

It affected his preparation for the US Open which came up within a week of his return. He decided on a safety first approach in the opening rounds, mainly out of respect for the large sand traps which were the hallmark of the course's designer, A W Tillinghast.

The result of Sarazen's strategy were rounds of 74 and 76 which left him 5 strokes off the pace set by Phil Perkins, a former British Walker Cup player. Whilst this may not have been as good as Sarazen had hoped, there was plenty of trouble at Fresh Meadow and Sarazen saw no reason to alter his battle plan.

The first 8 holes of the third round brought an overall deterioration of 1 stroke and when he stood on the 9th tee, he needed par for 39 out. It was there and then that he vowed to throw defence overboard. From then on, it was a case of attack and be damned.

A 7-iron floated 12 feet from the flag at the 9th and down went the putt. The die was cast. More gusto went into his drives, he hit his irons right up to the flag as if the

Third Round

Hole	Yards	Par	Score	Details
9	143	3	2	
10	385	4	4	
11	413	4	4	
12	155	3	3	
13	448	4	4	
14	219	3	2	
15	424	4	3	
16	587	5	4	
17	373	4	4	
18	404	4	4	
Total	355	38	34	

Fourth Round

Hole	Yards	Par	Score	Details
1	437	4	4	D, 2I, 2 putts
2	395	4	5	D, second into bunker, SW, 2 putts
3	391	4	3	
4	188	3	2	2I, 12 ft, 1 putt
5	578	5	5	D, 3W, PW, 15 ft, 2 putts
6	428	4	3	D, 2I, 4 ft, 1 putt
7	412	4	4	D, 6I, 20 ft, 2 putts
8	435	4	4	D, 6I, 2 putts
9	143	3	2	7I, 15 ft, 1 putt
Out	3407	35	32	
10	385	4	4	D, 7I, 15 ft, 2 putts
11	413	4	4	D, 6I, 18 ft, 2 putts
12	155	3	3	Mashie (bunker), SW, 2 ft, 1 putt
13	448	4	4	D, 4I, 20 ft, 2 putts
14	219	3	3	3W, 16 ft, 2 putts
15	424	4	3	D, 7I, 10 ft, 1 putt
16	587	5	5	D, D, SW, 15 ft, 2 putts
17	373	4	4	D, SW, 10 ft, 2 putts
18	404	4	4	D, 7I (bunker), SW, 1 putt
In	3408	35	34	
Out	3407	35	32	
Total	6815	70	66	
Total, 28 holes		108	100	

Gene Sarazen, still taking the applause when past 80 but it never rang louder than in 1932 when he won the US Open by playing the last 28 holes in 100 strokes. (Allsport)

bunkers had disappeared in the night; and that meant he was in range for more birdies. In addition, his Calamity Jane putter, the only club which hitherto had served him well, responded to the challenge.

It dropped another putt for a 2 at the 14th and followed with two more birdies on the 15th and 16th. Two solid pars later and he was home in 32, round in 70, only 1 stroke off the lead and firmly wedded to the idea of continued attack.

Lunch included a couple of bottles of beer and a long chat with Bobby Jones who had retired in 1930. Sarazen drank a toast to Perkins, the leader, who was soon out in 35 in his last round. Sarazen felt he would need a 68 to win as he made for the tee. A drive into the rough and a second into a bunker contributed to a dropped stroke at the 2nd but Sarazen was undeterred. From there on, he was inspired.

Birdies at the 3rd and short 4th, the latter with a 2-iron, 9 feet from the flag, were just the reaction he needed and he negotiated the par-5 5th (578 yards) without any trace of mishap. The 6th, one of the danger holes, was not one Sarazen had played well. However, he launched a cracking drive that carried 220 yards over the pond, rifled another 2-iron 4 feet from the cup and sent down another confident putt.

Now, sustained by his deeds at Prince's, his thoughts were on winning. The 7th and 8th brought good pars, the 9th a second 2 of the round which took him out in 32. In the absence of the modern sophisticated scoring system, Sarazen was not sure of his position. He therefore stuck to his pre-round prediction about a 68 being good enough (which meant 36 home).

He needed all his skill with his sand wedge to save par at the short 12th, but the birdie he squeezed from the 15th gave just that little bit more breathing space; as it happened, his estimate of 68 was spot on but so was his own golf. With a 7 to tie Perkins and Bobby Cruickshank, he bunkered a 7-iron to the last but his recovery and subsequent putt were simply the final act in one of the most sustained pieces of low scoring the game has ever seen. He played the last 28 holes in 100 strokes.

Lawson Little

Event: British Amateur Championship
Date: June 1934
Venue: Prestwick
Score: Final, 66

Bernard Darwin once wrote of Lawson Little, 'I feel that the brush should be dipped in earthquake and eclipse to do justice to Lawson Little for here was a player for whom my too hard-worked epithet "formidable" is scarcely strong enough'.

Little is the only player ever to have won the British and American Amateur championships and to have successfully defended both the following year. When he turned professional, he won the US Open in 1940 but he perhaps was never more formidable than in 1934.

He arrived at Prestwick from St Andrews where, in the Walker Cup, he won his foursomes match against Cyril Tolley and Roger Wethered by 8 and 6 and then accounted for Tolley in the singles by 6 and 5. His passage through the week of the Amateur championship at Prestwick was relatively smooth although he had a close call in the semi-final. L G Garnett holed a long, curly putt to save the match on the 18th green—only to lose at the 19th.

However, the floodgates opened in the final against a West of Scotland player named Jimmy Wallace. Little

Lawson Little, the only player to win the US and British Amateur championships and defend them successfully. (USGA)

lived up to Darwin's description of being 'a bull in the long game and yet no dove could be gentler near the hole, so persuasive was his touch'. Wallace had been putting beautifully all week but he took three putts on the first green and Little was away. He reached the Cardinal (500 yards) with a drive and a brassie, added another 3 at the 6th and by now was 5 up.

Little bunkered his second shots at the 7th and 12th but made 5 in each case; otherwise, it was a mighty display. With 33 for each half, he went into lunch 12 up and, almost before many in a fine Scottish crowd had arrived to support their hero, was as relentless afterwards. For 5 holes he scored 3, 3, 4, 3, 3—victory came by 14 and 13, the largest in any Amateur final, and, as Darwin again wrote, there was 'nothing to do but laugh'. One interesting statistic, Little's score did not contain a 2 but in 23 holes he had 12 3s.

Hole	Yards	Score
1	339	4
2	166	3
3	505	3
4	378	4
5	201	3
6	363	3
7	433	5
8	436	4
9	463	4
Out	3284	33
10	474	4
11	190	3
12	503	5
13	461	4
14	376	3
15	329	4
16	288	3
17	383	4
18	283	3
In	3287	33
Out	3284	33
Total	6571	66

Henry Cotton

Event: Open Championship
Date: 28 June 1934
Venue: Royal St George's, Sandwich
Score: Second round, 65

Even at a distance of over 60 years, it is easy to appreciate how Cotton's 65 was entirely revolutionary. It raised the level of scoring so abruptly that people found it hard to believe.

Until 1934, the lowest score in the Open Championship proper had been the 67 of Walter Hagen in 1929 and, after that, a handful of 68s. An idea of how well Cotton's record lasted is related by the fact that it stood as the lowest individual round until 1977. Even more incredibly, his total of 132 (67, 65) for the first two rounds of the Open is still a record; and, in case it might be thought that the courses were much shorter in 1934, Royal St George's was only about 100 yards shorter than for the Open of 1985.

Offset against that must be the tremendous improvement in the performance of the ball. I remember Cotton telling me that in 1935, Alf Perry used the same ball morning and afternoon on the final day of the Open at Muirfield because he 'had got a good one'. Nevertheless, Cotton hit the ball vast distances. George Greenwood in the *Daily Telegraph* described Cotton's drive at the 2nd as 300 yards.

Nor could his brilliance be attributed to a hot putting round. Cotton had 28 putts in all, holing nothing above 12 feet, 'eloquent testimony to the extraordinary accuracy of his iron play'—again quoting Greenwood. The other intriguing statistic is that the round was comprised solely of 3s and 4s.

Although Cotton was not entirely happy with his game at the start of the week, he felt that his 66 in the first qualifying round was, from tee to green, better than his 65 two days later. In terms of great rounds, his final round of 71 at Carnoustie in 1937 and his 66 in the second round at Muirfield in 1948 are well worthy of consideration but, in 1934, he had not won the Open—and first victories are invariably the hardest.

Even allowing for a slightly rocky last round, however, Cotton made it look easy. Starting out in his second round in the fourth couple just before a quarter to ten, he rifled a drive down the first fairway, got the first of his birdies at the 2nd and added another on the old, blind 3rd where he hit the green. His putt for a 3 hung on the lip on the 4th and he was within inches of holing a little chip on the 5th for another 3.

The 8th (in those days a par 3 but now a par 4) was the crisis hole. Aptly named Hades, Cotton's tee shot plugged in the face of the huge bunker on the right. In establishing a stance at least a foot below the ball, he must have reflected the horrors that could have occurred if he had not got the ball out first time. In point of fact, he played a marvellous recovery and almost got his 3. It may have been his only blemish in terms of a stroke dropped but it must have seemed more like a birdie.

Out in 33, he played a mashie niblick with terrific backspin on the old 11th, a two-shotter over a ridge of dunes, and drove straight for the green on the 12th instead of observing the dogleg. A neat chip saved his four at the 13th but his finish was immense. He was home in two at the 14th, saw a fine 2-iron just slip off the green on the right of the 15th green and then ended with three 3s—something which had not been done before at Sandwich and probably not very often since.

On the 17th, he hit a spade mashie for his second shot 3 feet past the pin and on the 18th, launched a 2-iron straight at the flag and ran down the 7-foot putt that remained with a hickory-shafted Braid Mills putter and a method in which the elbows were prominent. In an attempt to 'mechanize' the operation, Cotton described it as putting with his shoulders but, as Bernard Darwin remarked, 'the machine worked and kept on working'.

In the end, Cotton won by 5 strokes from Sid Brews of South Africa but, equally important, ended the run of overseas victories that had lasted since Arthur Havers won in 1923.

Henry was a great advocate of strengthening the hands for golf. Here, he demonstrates a novel way. (**Illustrated London News**)

Hole	Yards	Bogey	Score	Details
1	441	5	4	D, Spade mashie, 2 putts
2	370	4	3	D, niblick, 12 ft, 1 putt
3	238	4	3	3W, 2 putts
4	460	5	4	D, 3W, 2 putts
5	451	5	4	D, 3I, chip, 1 putt
6	193	3	3	Spade mashie, 2 putts
7	493	5	4	D, 3W, chip, 1 putt
8	183	3	4	Spade mashie, bunker, 2 putts
9	396	4	4	D, mashie niblick, 2 putts
Out	3225	38	33	
10	380	4	4	D, mashie niblick, 2 putts
11	384	4	3	D, mashie niblick, 9 ft, 1 putt
12	343	4	4	D, bunker, 2 putts
13	443	5	4	D, 3I, chip, 3 ft, 1 putt
14	520	5	4	D, 3W, 2 putts
15	454	5	4	D, 2I, chip close, 1 putt
16	163	3	3	Mashie niblick, 2 putts
17	423	5	3	D, spade mashie, 3 ft, 1 putt
18	441	5	3	D, 2I, 7 ft, 1 putt
In	3551	40	32	
Out	3225	38	33	
Total	6776	78	65	

Ben Hogan

Event: US Open
Date: 16 June 1951
Venue: Oakland Hills
Score: Fourth round, 67

In his marvellous book, *The Story of American Golf*, Herbert Warren Wind stated that 'in later years, Hogan came to refer to his final 67 as the greatest round of his career'. For a man whose statements were always carefully considered, Hogan's remark is highly significant. He had played many that were numerically lower but this was the convincing proof (if proof were needed) that he could play better than any of his rivals.

It was the year that the Oakland Hills Club, in conjunction with the USGA, took the wraps off their modernized layout in which Robert Trent Jones had drastically reduced the freedom from the tee by closing down many defunct old traps, replacing them with new ones at 220 to 250 yards. These placed altogether greater demands on control. The hue and cry they provoked was deafening although the strategy is now more commonplace.

Hogan called it the 'toughest test' he played but made the point to the Press that it was not the 'finest test' he had played. That was his way of expressing disapproval of the new defences, but Hogan's supremacy lay as much in his management as in his technical skill and he combined the two to find the perfect answer.

Just how successful he was can be seen from the statistics. Apart from his 67, the final round of 69 by Clayton Heafner was the only other round under 70 in the entire three days. Up until the final day, only two players, Dave Douglas and Johnny Bulla, had equalled the par of 70 but, again quoting Herbert Warren Wind, Hogan claimed that his 'management' ability 'accounted for 80 per cent of his success'.

The policy of a great many that week was to resort to spoons and even irons off the tee but that presented problems when it came to negotiating the approaches to the greens. Hogan's policy was to rely far more on his driver although the rough was fierce and his opening round of 76, which left him tied for 41st place, was not the coup for which he had hoped. 'I made six mistakes and shot six over. You can't steal anything out there'.

However, it was a very much better round than the score suggests. He had gone into the championship happy with his game and, as he plotted his overthrow of the course, good driving was one sure rock on which he could depend. Where Hogan scored was in being able to channel and concentrate his irritation to bring forth his finest.

Even if a second round of 73 still left him 5 strokes behind the halfway leader, Bobby Locke, it took him out of the pack and left him ideally placed to challenge over the final 36 holes which were played in one day—as it happened, a gloriously sunny Saturday.

His disappointment in a third round of 71 that had promised much was his finish. A 6 at the 15th undid a lot

Ben Hogan, thought by his contemporaries to have come nearer to technical perfection than anyone. (USGA)

of the earlier good. Nevertheless, his 71 moved him within two strokes of Bobby Locke and Jimmy Demaret.

As he set out on the afternoon round which saw him through the turn in even par, 35, he was 'sullen with determination'. At the 10th, he hit one of his very best shots, a 2-iron to 5 feet on a hole measuring 448 yards and holed the putt. He went 2 under for the round by holing from 15 feet on the short 13th and, though he dropped a stroke at the 14th by hitting his second through the green, he conquered the 15th which had got the measure of him in the morning.

This time his drive carried over the central fairway bunker, a 6-iron settled 4 feet from the hole and he was back to 2 under. The 16th saw him miss a similar length putt for a birdie but, as if to prove the point he had been trying to show for two days, his finishing birdie was a typically defiant gesture.

He went for the carry over the angle of the dogleg, made it easily downwind, and then lofted a perfect 6-iron about 5 yards from the flag. There was only one way to finish after that and Hogan ended in style by adding a further birdie which made Locke's chase a forlorn one. It was a victory that gave Hogan a lot of pleasure particularly his last round which revealed all the qualities in a champion. There may have been criticism of the way the course had been set up but, at least, it had the virtue of summoning the best from the best player.

Hole	Yards	Par	Score	Details
1	446	4	4	
2	521	5	5	
3	202	3	3	
4	439	4	4	
5	442	4	4	
6	368	4	4	
7	408	4	4	
8	458	4	4	
9	216	3	3	
Out	3500	35	35	
10	448	4	3	D, 2I, 5 ft, 1 putt
11	420	4	4	
12	567	5	5	
13	173	3	2	6I, 15 ft, 1 putt
14	468	4	5	
15	392	4	3	D, 6I, 4 ft, 1 putt
16	405	4	4	
17	194	3	3	
18	459	4	3	D, 6I, 5 yd, 1 putt
In	3427	35	32	
Out	3500	35	35	
Total	6927	70	67	

Ben Hogan

Event: British Open
Date: 10 July 1953
Venue: Carnoustie
Score: Fourth round, 68

As long as golf is played, 1953 will always be remembered as Ben Hogan's year by the same token that 1930 was the year of Bobby Jones. In the space of about four months, Hogan became (and remains) the only golfer to have won the Masters, the US Open and the British Open in the same season. It was at the time when he was making something of a habit of winning the first two but his trip to Carnoustie for the British Open was uniquely special.

That he went to Scotland at all was largely in answer to the clamour that arose that he owed it to himself to have a crack at the oldest championship while his game was at its peak. The argument was based on the lines that the Open had served for years as the true measurement (in some cases, the final measurement) of an American's greatness. As Jones, Hagen and Sarazen had been the pioneers, Hogan must not decline the challenge—or so the argument continued.

Hogan needed some persuading. However, once his mind was made up, a decision that hinged on his winning the US Open, his preparation was as thorough as you would expect. It was his initiation to links golf and first impressions may have been a bit alarming. Carnoustie's fairways bore the scars of heavy play which a long dry spell had done nothing to disguise. The greens, too, were not as smooth or fast as he may have hoped and, during the four days of the championship, he was never really at home on them.

With the invaluable help of his celebrated caddie, Cecil Timms, he charted the course for over a week and adjusted to the use of the small ball which he reckoned went 25 yards further than a big ball—and further against the wind.

It seems strange now that Hogan had to subject himself to two qualifying rounds but, in those days it was a standard requirement; and, anyway, Hogan may have welcomed a little serious competition after so much serious practice. In the first round of the championship proper, a slightly disappointing finish left him on 73, 3 strokes behind Frank Stranahan. He then added a 71 and on the final morning a 70 left him tieing the lead with Roberto de Vicenzo on 224.

Vicenzo, or the gaucho, as Hogan called him, was perhaps the man he feared most—and not just because he shared the lead. Vicenzo started 3 or 4 holes ahead but, having munched his picnic lunch, Hogan promptly got down to business with four absolutely watertight 4s.

The 5th was one of the most crucial holes in providing Hogan with one of the breaks (and he had none up to then) that he sought and deserved. He missed the green with a 5-iron from a divot mark but, with one foot in the bunker on the right of the green and one on the bank, he chipped the ball cleanly as it sat up in the grass on the fringe of the sand. It was running a little strongly but it hit the hole and jumped in the air before disappearing. Even more crucially, it put him one ahead of Antonio Cerda and very much in the winning mood.

So many tales emanated from his playing of the 6th hole during the week that it became something of a legend. The problem posed were two bunkers on the right, out of bounds on the left, and only a narrow channel in between. There was an even narrower gap between the bunkers and the edge of the rough but Hogan nailed two drives on that line morning and afternoon and followed with two searing brassies.

The one in the afternoon Leonard Crawley told Timms was one of the greatest shots he ever saw. It finished on the fringe of the green, enabling Hogan to get his second birdie of the day. Hogan turned in 34 and with solid pars at the 10th, 11th and 12th and his second 2 in a few hours at the 13th, stretched his lead to three over Cerda.

He was not going to be caught now. Cerda fell back with a 5 at the 12th while de Vicenzo had posted a total of 284, but Hogan never let up and his finish was superb. He made an excellent 3 at the 16th and played the 17th and 18th as if the burn did not exist.

The Wee Ice Mon, as the Scots christened him on account of his lack of expression, signed off with a four at the 18th to the acclaim of all present who naturally sensed that they were witnessing a piece of history. There is no possible doubt that the right man won, improving as each round passed but the final word belonged to Bernard Darwin. 'If Hogan needed a 64 on his final round', he commented, 'you were quite certain he could have played a 64. Hogan gave you the distinct impression he was capable of getting whatever score he had to win.'

Hole	Yards	Par	Score	Details
1	406	4	4	D, 6I, 2 putts
2	464	4	4	D, 2I, 2 putts
3	348	4	4	3W, 9I, 2 putts
4	379	4	4	D, 4I, 2 putts
5	397	4	3	D, 5I, chipped in
6	524	5	4	D, 2W, chip, 1 putt
7	397	4	4	D, 5I, 2 putts
8	174	3	3	5I, 2 putts
9	421	4	4	D, 4I, chip, 1 putt
Out	3510	36	34	
10	453	4	4	D, 3I, 2 putts
11	372	4	4	D, 6I, chip from short, 1 putt
12	478	5	4	D, 3I, 2 putts
13	166	3	2	5I, 8 ft putt
14	488	5	5	D, 2I, PW, 2 putts
15	461	4	4	D, 4I, 2 putts
16	235	3	3	3W, 40 ft, 2 putts
17	453	4	4	3W, 3W, 2 putts
18	448	4	4	D, 5I, 2 putts
In	3554	36	34	
Out	3510	36	34	
Total	7064	72	68	

Arnold Palmer

Event: British Open
Date: 13 July 1961
Venue: Royal Birkdale
Score: Second round, 73

Great rounds can never be measured purely numerically. If they were, they would lose all value because the general level of scoring in all forms of golf has improved so rapidly that masses of dazzling scores can be misleading.

Players now reel off rounds in the mid- and low-sixties as easily as they might peel an apple. However, every now and then, weather conditions, the severity of the course or the opposition, introduce a new basis for judgement. These are the moments when the best rounds can only be played by the finest players.

Such a day came in 1961 when Arnold Palmer had come to Britain in search of the Open title that had eluded him so narrowly the previous year at St Andrews. After the first day's play had been completed with Palmer's 70, two strokes behind the scores of Kel Nagle, the holder, Dai Rees and Harold Henning, a storm of wind greeted the contestants on the second day. It was accompanied by intermittent rain and was a prelude to an even more unpleasant day on Friday when play was abandoned. Many tents were blown down and large parts of the Birkdale links were flooded.

Bad weather had become something of a habit at that time. The last round of the 1960 Open had to be rescheduled for Saturday and here, twelve months later, there

was the reality that, if another day were lost, the championship would be declared null and void. The Royal and Ancient actually issued a formal statement to the effect, no suggestion being given in those days of playing on a Sunday.

There are certain things which are unforgettable and the author reporting his first Open was one of those moments. Pat Ward-Thomas and he had played bridge with Palmer on that blank Friday afternoon and, though it was impressive how easily Palmer kept his mind on the cards, he also kept a watchful eye on the western sky.

He was worried that, if he had had to return home with no decision reached, he would have had an understandable job convincing other Americans to fit the Open into their programmes. What would have happened if the Saturday had also been washed out does not bear thinking about. Palmer's subsequent victory was vital to the Open but that is digression.

What made it possible was a spell of golf in the second round on Thursday, when the roaring, mighty wind was at its height, that Palmer maintained was the best of his life.

As he stood on the old, elevated first tee bedecked in several layers of sweater and a distinctive, dark cap, even he had a job keeping his balance. Horrendous stories had been circulating all day about the impossibility of the conditions but, by anchoring his feet, gripping the club as firmly as he dared without destroying all feel, and using his power to counteract the blast, he rode the whirlwind which, if anything, was fiercer in the afternoon when he was out.

He had five birdies in the first six holes against the old par system, which rated the 2nd (427 yards) a 5, when only three or four others reached the turn in less than 40. Not the least incredible part of the story was the fact that, over that opening stretch he had only 6 putts, since putting can be the hardest part of playing golf in a strong wind.

In a little more detail, even he could not get near the first green in two; he heaved might and mane to get two woods within 10 yards of the 2nd green, while he needed a 1-iron at the short 4th and a drive and a 6-iron on the 315 yard 5th.

Miraculously, he stopped his second within inches of the cup on the 3rd and manufactured a 4 on the fiendishly difficult 6th.

The round really should have ended there. Nobody could have maintained that standard and, by bunkering his tee shot at the short 7th (the easiest shot he had faced), and pulling his drive into the dunes on the 8th, he dropped his first strokes.

Still, 34 to the turn with only 11 putts was a minor miracle and it was no crime to drop another stroke at the 10th where he was unlucky to see his second in the crosswind run through the green. Apart from dropping a further stroke on the par 3 13th, he went resolutely on, picking up a birdie at the 14th. Even the breaking of 70 was just possible but on the 16th (now the 17th), he hit his second shot (not a bad one) into the bunker on the right of the green. It was lying very clean and he thinned his recovery slightly. He chipped back and took 2 putts for a 6. Or so everybody believed.

Alas, Palmer called a stroke on himself, his ball moving as he played it in the bunker. The 6 became a 7. Some might have said nothing. It was one of those moments when nobody else knew but his integrity was typical of the man, added to the worthiness of his triumph the following day and took absolutely nothing away from his 73 which laid the foundation for it. Nobody could argue that the best man won.

Hole	Yards	Par	Score	Detail
1	520	5	4	D, 3W, PW, 1 putt
2	427	5	4	D, 3W, PW, 1 putt
3	416	4	3	D, 5I, 1 putt (6 inches)
4	212	3	3	1I, chip, 1 putt
5	315	4	3	D, 6I, 1 putt
6	468	5	4	D, 3W, PW, 1 putt
7	158	3	4	7I, SW, 2 putts
8	434	4	5	D, 7I, PW, 2 putts
9	418	4	4	D, 4I, 2 putts
Out	3368	37	34	
10	390	4	5	D, 5I, chip, 1 putt
11	368	4	4	
12	452	4	4	
13	202	3	4	
14	517	5	4	
15	381	4	4	
16	510	5	7	
17	186	3	3	
18	470	5	4	
In	3476	37	39	
Out	3368	37	34	
Total	6844	74	73	

Golfers will do anything to help a putt. Arnold Palmer's attempt is more reminiscent of a chorus girl. (Allsport)

Jack Nicklaus

Event:	US Masters
Date:	April 1965
Venue:	Augusta
Score:	Third round, 64

When one has won 20 major championships as well as countless other events around the world, great rounds are as abundant as grains of sand in an hour glass. A month or so before he played his dramatic last round in the 1986 Masters, Jack Nicklaus nominated his three which, if pressed, would stand as the greatest in his mind although great players are understandably reluctant to make claims of their own.

He offered the third round in the 1965 Masters in which he scored 64; his final round of 66 in the 1972 British Open at Muirfield and his opening round of 63 in the 1980 US Open at Baltusrol. The author would unhesitatingly add his last round of 70 which enabled him to win his first British Open at Muirfield in 1966, but in 1965 nobody had had the temerity to reduce the winning aggregate at Augusta to 271 strokes, an act that prompted the now famous remark of Bobby Jones, 'He plays a game with which I am not familiar.'

In those days, too, Nicklaus had only just embarked upon his collection of major titles but there was about his golf then an increasing certainty that he would one day break all records. Of his 64 at Augusta in 1965, he wrote in his book, *The Greatest Game of All*, 'It is a round that I am very proud of' and then enlarging a little on detail, 'I am aware that I may forward the impression that the Augusta National is a short course. It is anything but. On this round, I got a lot of flight on my tee shots because the air was unusually light, and I got a lot of roll on them because the fairways were hard and dry. Also, I happened to have one of the best driving days of my life.'

The position at the start of the 3rd round was that Jack was level with Arnold Palmer and Gary Player on 138. The fact that it was these three who were at the head of affairs added to the spice but the greatness of the 64 which followed is that it virtually decided the tournament there and then.

It gave Nicklaus a 5-stroke advantage over Player and gave him the chance of establishing a new aggregate total, the previous best being Ben Hogan's 274 in 1953. Although winning was all that concerned Nicklaus on the final day, he set a new record of 271 and stretched the winning margin record to 9 strokes.

On a day when only two other players scored better than

69, and Tony Lema took 77, Nicklaus's round was composed of 8 birdies and 10 pars—and without a 5 on his card. He missed only two fairways but hit every green in regulation except the 17th where his 8-iron pitched on the green and screwed back off again.

His ability to reach three of the par-5s in two contributed to this absence of a five although he nearly made a botch of the 2nd after pushing his drive into the pines. He needed a 3-iron for his third shot and a 25-foot putt for his birdie.

It is funny how often great rounds blossom from a good break early on, but what also turned a good day into one to remember were the twos he plucked at the 4th, 6th and 16th. Added to a 3 at the 7th, he was out in 31 and on the inward half made scarcely a mistake of any kind. The big difference between 1965 and his final round 65 in 1986 was his putting on the back nine.

If he had shown the same hot streak on the greens that transformed the event in 1986, he would have broken 60 but it was an enchanted week, nevertheless, even if Nicklaus had arrived at Augusta the week before, hitting the ball all over the place and needing a tip from Deane Beman, his partner in one practice round, to get himself straightened out.

Many a champion has experienced the same in similar circumstances, but it is a mark of great champions to readjust and to allow the competitive atmosphere to bring the best out in them. Nobody was better at that than Nicklaus.

The master of the Masters, Jack Nicklaus. (Allsport)

Hole	Yards	Par	Score	Details
1	400	4	4	D, SW, 25 ft, 2 putts
2	555	5	4	D, chip from trees, 3I, 25 ft, 1 putt
3	355	4	4	D, PW, 8 ft, 2 putts
4	220	3	2	4I, 10 ft, 1 putt
5	450	4	4	D, 6I, 20 ft, 2 putts
6	190	3	2	6I, 20 ft, 1 putt
7	365	4	3	D, PW, 2 ft, 1 putt
8	530	5	4	D, 3I, 75 ft, 2 putts
9	420	4	4	D, PW, 20 ft, 2 putts
Out	3485	36	31	
10	470	4	4	D, 8I, 20 ft, 2 putts
11	445	4	4	D, 8I, 50 ft, 2 putts
12	155	3	3	8I, 4 ft, 2 putts
13	475	5	4	D, 5I, 45 ft, 2 putts
14	420	4	4	D, 7I, 25 ft, 2 putts
15	520	5	4	D, 5I, chip from back fringe (60 ft), 2 ft, 1 putt
16	190	3	2	6I, 14 ft, 1 putt
17	400	4	4	D, 8I, 30 ft, 2 putts
18	420	4	4	D, PW, 5 ft, 2 putts
In	3495	36	33	
Out	3485	36	31	
Total	6980	72	64	

Catherine Lacoste

Event: US Women's Open
Date: 30 June 1967
Venue: White Sulphur Springs
Score: Second round, 70

It took courage, skill and self-assurance for a 22-year-old amateur to challenge a field of world class professionals more than 3000 miles from home. It took a touch of genius to beat them.

Catherine Lacoste was certainly blessed with more than her measure of skill and confidence. You don't have to probe her family tree very far to discover where her champion's qualities originate. Her father, René Lacoste, tennis champion of Wimbledon and Forest Hills, was a player of exceptional talent while her mother, Thion de la Chaume, won the French Women's golf championship six times and the British once.

Catherine inherited the dash and flair of them both but her performance in going to White Sulphur Springs and sweeping the board so convincingly ranks as one of the most outstanding in post-war golf—men's or women's—amateur or professional. For the element of storybook romance it depicted it is unsurpassed.

It is a pleasant pursuit thinking of the great occasions one has missed and would like again to have the opportunity of seeing. Lacoste's victory comes high on the list, not just the four rounds but the build-up to them as well.

She arrived nine days in advance in order to become acclimatized to the course, climate and time change although one of the main reason for her success was undoubtedly her ability to find ways of taking her mind off the golf. She made friends with one particular family staying at the Cascades Inn in Hot Springs and never

Catherine Lacoste, the only amateur to have won the US Women's Open. (USGA)

had an idle moment. As she said later, she never spent a minute in her hotel room when she was not tired enough to go to sleep.

It showed, as Patty Berg observed that week, that golf is not the only thing in Lacoste's life. She was, in every sense, the true amateur but she was able to apply a fierce competitiveness to championships and to allow the occasion to bring forth the best in her. She once said, 'I need a high stake to produce the best scores'.

The stakes certainly could not have been higher over a 6191-yard course on which trees and water were a feature. Control was essential particularly in order to negotiate the ideal line to the greens flanked by severe slopes. She hit her iron shots as high as Jack Nicklaus which helped in getting near the pin on typically firm, fast greens but her driving and putting were equally bold.

She opened with a 71 which put her within 1 stroke of the leader, Sandra Haynie, but Haynie took 79 on the second day whereas Lacoste's 70 was 3 strokes better than anybody else's. That gives some idea of its greatness. It was a psychological body blow to deliver to the professionals and was the key to her ultimate success.

She hit the first 14 greens in regulation; indeed, her only regret can have been the 7 she took on the par-5 16th where she found the water. Nevertheless, her stunning play gave her a lead of five which a third round of 74 (40 out, 34 home) maintained.

In the final round, Lacoste bowed somewhat to the occasion. She let a lead of 7 dwindle to 1 but, as some present

saw it as a herald to total collapse, Lacoste unleashed the perfect answer.

She birdied the 71st hole and then played the last immaculately to finish on 294 (71, 70, 74, 79), two ahead of Beth Stone and Susie Maxwell. Two years later, she returned to pick up the US Women's Amateur in Texas, having in the meantime added the British Women's Amateur, but the US Women's Open was the real jewel in the crown.

Roberto de Vicenzo

Event: US Masters
Date: 14 April 1968
Venue: Augusta
Score: Fourth round, 66

It is a strange fact that, at a time of life when the game should be becoming more difficult, some players achieve the ambitions that have eluded them for years. Nobody tried longer or harder to win the British Open than Roberto de Vicenzo but, with everyone on the point of despair that he should ever succeed, there came that memorable afternoon in 1967 at Hoylake when he held off Nicklaus and Player to become the second oldest winner.

In view of all the implications, his final round of 70 must be ranked as one of the greatest in history. The previous summer, his second round of 66 in the Spanish Open at Sotogrande was a round which probably only Nicklaus could have matched, although the pressure on de Vicenzo was nothing like as intense as at Hoylake.

The burgeoning of a truly great player into a great champion was one of the happiest moments of the last 25 years. On the other hand, unquestionably the saddest moment came a few months later at Augusta where a careless oversight on the part of his playing partner and de Vicenzo himself deprived de Vicenzo of the chance of winning the Masters and thereby holding the two titles at the same time.

If one had not experienced the joy of Hoylake, there is no way one could have endured the agony of Augusta, but whatever the rules may say, and de Vicenzo never queried them, his final round of 65 that a slip of a pencil turned into a 66, was as good as any ever played. He passed one of the severest tests of heart, mind and skill that golf can devise.

He could be accused of no wrong on the course. His only failure was not to notice in a highly emotional atmosphere that the three all the world saw him get on television at the 17th had been marked down as a four. Nowadays, the various fail-safe methods that officials adopt in the recorders tent would almost certainly have averted the tragedy. For his part, de Vicenzo was no doubt still thinking more about the five that the 18th had just cost him than of checking his card; but nobody can deny him the technical and competitive triumph of his play that sunny Sunday—his 45th birthday.

In contrast to the sad end, the afternoon started ecstatically. A perfect 9-iron second shot to the 1st landed softly and spun gently into the hole; indeed, he had only 3 putts on the first 4 holes, all tap-ins.

His majestic driving, controlled pitching and, above all, his courage on the treacherous inward nine, conspired to give him the inspiration that can electrify his Latin temperament. In de Vicenzo's case, this was important because he is the most phlegmatic of Latins but, after being 4 under par for the first 3 holes and later turning in 31 to be one ahead of the field, he consolidated admirably.

He saved his par on the 10th with a neat explosion, missed an excellent birdie chance on the 11th, but capitalized on the 6-iron which nosed down 3 or 4 yards past the pin on the dangerous 12th. Two safe pars and a birdie over the water at the 15th made him 7 under. The crescendo was building up.

At exactly the same time as Bob Goalby hit a terrific second to the 15th, de Vicenzo matched him with a lovely high pitch to the 17th. Both putts, Goalby's for an eagle and de Vicenzo's for a birdie (in practice, if not in theory) went in simultaneously.

De Vicenzo could blame nobody except himself for the 5 he took at the 18th by pulling his second and spinning out with his 5-foot saving putt. They were two minor errors although nothing to the drama that followed as anxious officials began to run to and fro to Bobby Jones's bungalow to see if there was some way round the clerical error that was perpetrated.

Alas, there was none. As Jones said, 'Golf is a game where only the player can tell exactly what goes on; his word must be the final one'. However, if some good came out of 'evil', it was the example of de Vicenzo in accepting his fate with a shrug and a mild rebuke of himself. Nobody who knew him would have expected anything else.

Roberto de Vicenzo. Nobody could have accepted the heartbreak of the 1968 Masters as well as he did. (BBC Hulton Picture Library)

Michael Bonallack

Event: English Amateur Championship
          (Final against David Kelley)
Date: 27 July 1968
Venue: Ganton
Score: Final, 61

Scores in matchplay can never be official. Michael Bonallack's 61, therefore, was never regarded as a course record but it was still an incredible round of golf and, since every putt was holed out, it rightly takes its place in this exalted category.

Played when Bonallack was at the height of his powers, it was a well nigh flawless exhibition. He saved his 4 at the 7th with a good pitch to 8 feet and did the same at the 15th. On the 8th he missed his only holeable putt from about 8 feet. In all, he had 24 putts although he holed nothing outrageous. He owed far more to fine driving and controlled iron play.

It was the best round played by an amateur in the final of a national championship; indeed, it is a score no professional has matched in such a major event. Ganton has housed the Ryder Cup, two Amateur championships and several leading professionals tournaments, including the Dunlop Masters. The unfortunate victim was David Kelley who, nevertheless, was only about 1 over par for the 25 holes played—no mean achievement.

Hole	Yards	Par	Score	Details
1	400	4	2	D, 9I
2	555	5	4	D, 2I, 2 putts
3	355	4	3	D, PW, 1 ft
4	220	3	3	
5	450	4	4	
6	190	3	3	
7	365	4	4	
8	530	5	4	
9	420	4	4	
Out	3485	36	31	
10	470	4	4	D, 4I, SW, 4 ft, 1 putt
11	445	4	4	D, 4I, 9 ft, 2 putts
12	155	3	2	6I, 12 ft putt
13	475	5	5	D, 3I, SW
14	420	4	4	
15	520	5	4	D, 3I, SW, 10 ft, 1 putt
16	190	3	3	
17	400	4	4	D, PW, 3 ft putt
18	420	4	5	D, 4I, chip, 8 ft, 2 putts
In	3495	36	35	
Out	3485	36	31	
Total	6980	72	66	

He was 11 down at lunch, eventually losing by 12 and 11. The only time he had the honour was after winning the short 5th in the afternoon.

Hole	Yards	Par	Score	Details
1	380	4	3	Drive, 9-iron, 3 ft putt
2	427	4	3	Drive, 7-iron, 30 ft putt
3	335	4	3	4-iron, 8-iron, 2 ft putt
4	412	4	4	Drive, 6-iron, tiny chip, 3 ft putt
5	170	3	3	6-iron, 2 putts
6	457	4	4	Drive, 4-iron, 2 putts
7	440	4	4	Drive, 4-wood, pitch, 8 ft putt
8	420	4	4	Drive, 8-iron, 2 putts
9	500	5	4	Drive, 2-iron, chip and run, 3 ft putt
Out	3541	36	32	
10	173	3	2	6-iron, 24 ft putt
11	417	4	3	Drive, 9-iron, 18 ft putt
12	375	4	3	Drive, 9-iron, 12 ft putt
13	507	5	3	Drive, 3-wood, 21 ft putt
14	288	4	4	Drive, wedge, 2 putts
15	450	4	4	Drive, 5-iron, sand wedge, 15 ft putt
16	456	4	3	Drive, 5-iron, 18 ft putt
17	250	3	3	3-wood, 2 putts
18	448	4	4	Drive, 7-iron, 2 putts
In	3364	35	29	
Out	3541	36	32	
Total	6905	71	61	

Michael Bonallack seen here in his office at the Royal and Ancient Golf Club at St Andrews but in his playing days he was the most successful British amateur of this century. (Allsport)

Tony Jacklin

Event: World Matchplay Championship (Semi-final)
Date: 13 October 1972
Venue: Wentworth
Score: Semi-final (second round), 63

In keeping with two players who have won the British and US Open championships, Tony Jacklin and Lee Trevino have not been short of great rounds. One could number Jacklin's final round at Royal Lytham in 1969 and any of his rounds at Hazeltine in that category.

Similarly, Trevino had four rounds under 70 in winning the 1968 US Open; scored two 69s to tie Jack Nicklaus at Merion in 1971 and then closed him out with a 68 in the play-off. Equally memorable was a third round 66 at Muirfield in 1972 which, together with the end of his final round, deprived Jacklin of his second victory in the British Open.

It was a moment which still haunts the legion of Jacklin's supporters who had to witness his cruel fate, although it was nothing compared to what it did to Jacklin. He suffered more than once at Trevino's hands.

Meeting Trevino a few months later in the semi-final of the World Matchplay championship was therefore an ideal chance of revenge. In box office terms, it was the answer to a prayer and the match they put on certainly lived up to its star billing. Scheduled for 36 holes, it went every inch of the way but, in spite of going round in 63 in the afternoon, the lowest ever recorded in the championship, Jacklin suffered defeat at Trevino's hands once more.

Nevertheless, it was the perfect match and there is no doubt that the choice of it for this exalted section is a way of combining the wizardry of both. For all their distinguished achievements, they cannot often have played as well.

Trevino was the more consistent, going round in the morning in 67 to be 4 up, a lead he built up from the 11th. However, Jacklin's outward half of 29 in the afternoon contained the spark of brilliance that turned a fine match into a great one. In a championship series renowned for its spectacular scoring, it is still the lowest nine holes ever played—as is his 63 for a completed round.

Jacklin did not stage a recovery of the proportions of Gary Player against Tony Lema in 1965. Nobody could give Trevino a 7-up start but a deficit of four can seem a mighty gulf to bridge. Jacklin described his afternoon golf to Mark McCormack at the time as 'the best of my life'; and, of course, what made it much better as a match than Lema v Player was that both players showed peak form.

Jacklin determined at lunchtime to detach himself from Trevino's chat and it proved a rewarding tactic. After starting the second round by halving the first three holes in 4, 3, 4, Jacklin signalled to Trevino that he had a fight on his hands by hitting a towering 5-iron to 5 feet from the 4th hole and holing for an eagle—3 down.

Tony Jacklin, one of only three British golfers to have won the British and American Open championships. (Benson and Hedges)

Obeying the matchplay adage about hitting a short hole green when one has just won a hole, Jacklin went one better. A 6-iron plummeted within a yard of the cup at the 5th and the lead was cut to 2. As often happens when the pressure suddenly becomes acute, Trevino overhit his pitch to the 6th and another hole had gone. The 7th was halved in 4 but Jacklin squared with a 3 at the 8th and miraculously went one ahead with a 3 at the 9th.

Jacklin was a little unlucky to see his 1-iron run through the green at the short 10th and become entangled in a lady's skirt although there was nothing he could do about Trevino's 2 which put him level again. Still Jacklin replied positively with a 3 to win the 11th but so, too, did Trevino when it was his turn. An eagle at the par-5 12th maintained the pattern of 'anything you can do'. All square once more.

That was the end of the fireworks but not of the tension, the gallant chips and the crucial putts. The tempo of the match was not helped by having caught up the game in front at this stage. The missing of birdie putts on the 16th contributed to the suspense but the dangerous 17th saw two classic pitch shots. After Trevino had punched a little 8-iron to 6 feet, Jacklin, with a bit of help from the flag, stopped a wedge beside the hole.

Trevino's putt did more than keep the match all-square, it gave him that little edge in impetus that showed itself

at the 18th. Here, Jacklin, trying to fade a 3-wood, found it would not fade. He pitched well but Trevino hit a marvellous 3-wood to follow and, when Jacklin's putt slipped past, Trevino had 2 putts from 9 feet for a match that had everything.

Tommy Nakajima and Sandy Lyle produced a match of more ups and downs in 1986 but Trevino was 134 for the day, dropping only 3 strokes to par in 36 holes while Jacklin's better ball for the two rounds was 61.

First round
Trevino 4, 2, 4, 4, 3, 4, 3, 5, 3 = 32
Jacklin 4, 2, 5, 3, 3, 4, 5, 4, 4 = 34
Trevino 4, 3, 3, 4, 4, 4, 4, 5, 4 = 35
Jacklin 2, 5, c, 4, 3, 5, 4, 6, 5   —
c = conceded

Second round
Tony Jacklin

Hole	Yards	Par	Score	Details
1	476	5	4	D, 4I, 2 putts
2	157	3	3	7I, 2 putts
3	457	4	4	D, 3I, 2 putts
4	497	5	3	D, 5I, 4 ft, 1 putt
5	192	3	2	6I, 2 ft, 1 putt
6	347	4	3	1I, PW, 4 ft, 1 putt
7	403	4	4	1I, 7I, 15 ft, 2 putts
8	400	4	3	2I, 6I, 6 ft, 1 putt
9	460	4	3	D, 5I, 6 ft, 1 putt
Out	3389	36	29	
10	190	3	3	1I, chip, 1 putt
11	408	4	3	3W, 6I, 12 ft, 1 putt
12	480	5	4	D, 1I, chip, 4 ft, 1 putt
13	437	4	4	D, 5I, chip, 1 putt
14	183	3	3	4I, 25 ft, 2 putts
15	480	5	4	D, 3W, 2 putts from fringe
16	380	4	4	3W, 8I, 25 ft, 2 putts
17	555	5	4	D, 3W, pitch, 2 ft, 1 putt
18	495	5	5	D, 3W, chip, 10 ft, 2 putts
In	3608	38	34	
Out	3389	36	29	
Total	6997	74	63	

Trevino Second Round
4, 3, 4, 4, 3, 5, 4, 4, 4 = 35
2, 4, 3, 4, 3, 4, 4, 4, 4 = 32

Johnny Miller

Event: US Open
Date: 17 June 1973
Venue: Oakmont
Score: Fourth round, 63

Both Oakmont's and the United States Golf Association's policy for the presentation of a course for a modern US Open has been very much on the lines that rounds of 63 should be made difficult if not impossible. Oakmont's reputation was for years that it dispensed its favours grudgingly. For a start, it once had 220 bunkers raked in furrows 2 inches deep and 2 inches apart; and the greens were originally rolled with barrels of sand weighing a quarter of a ton each.

This was to give the greens a speed and firmness that became legend. Gauging pace was likened to putting down a marble staircase. So how did Miller catch Oakmont so unawares? The first reason is that the course was rendered unusually slow and holding by heavy rains on Saturday morning and some lighter rain on Sunday morning when Miller, at the start of play, was 3 over par and 6 shots behind the four co-leaders.

The other telling reason was Miller himself. It was the beginning of an enchanted spell of two or three years when he was as formidable a player as any in the world. His long flowing action was in full working order that day and it had the capacity of allowing shots to drop almost vertically onto the target. This was ideal in the circumstances but, even allowing for all that, 63 was still a remarkable score. Hitherto, the best last round by a US Open champion had been Arnold Palmer's 65 at Cherry Hills in 1960 and Jack Nicklaus's at Baltusrol in 1967.

Palmer was one of four tied for the 54-hole lead but Miller, out almost an hour ahead of them, was in the perfect position to launch an assault. He had no other option than to give it a go. Playing conservatively or defensively would get him nowhere. Most others would

Johnny Miller, a dashing, brilliant player at his best but never more dashing or brilliant than in the last round of the 1973 US Open. (Benson and Hedges)

have done the same in his spiked shoes, but the big difference between them and Miller was that Miller was able to sustain his challenge. The more meaningful the round became, the more he relished it.

He was off and running straightaway. A 5-iron settled 5 feet from the pin at the 1st and a 9-iron even closer at the 2nd. Another 5-iron found the middle of the green at the 3rd while, on the par-5 4th, he got up and down in 2 from a bunker.

Four birdies in a row brought him back to 1 under par for the championship and, more crucially, only 3 strokes off the leaders who had been watching the scoreboard from the putting green. If it had been anybody other than Miller who was beginning to work a miracle, they might not have been unduly worried but they knew how mighty Miller's best could be.

He allowed no respite. As news of his advance filtered across the Pennsylvania Turnpike and crowds rushed to join him, he had a period of consolidation. It was, after all, the US Open, and not even Miller could birdie every hole. His first blemish came in the form of 3 putts from 40 feet on the 8th but he then hit a glorious 2-iron to the par-5 9th and, with a birdie, turned in 32.

Once in the thick of the fight, Miller refused to back down although he was never reckless, relying on his big guns to maintain his momentum. His long game was superb. Another 3 birdies in a row from the 11th and the dream of being US Open champion, every American's dream, had really dawned.

His final birdie came on the 15th but his 3 solid finishing pars represented almost his finest golf of all. Closing holes lie strewn with punctured hopes.

His 63 meant he had broken the Open record for a single round by one stroke although those who held it, established it somewhat in isolation. Miller faced a long wait after giving the customary interviews but nobody would have changed places with him, certainly not those who faced an increasingly vain struggle to catch him.

Hole	Yards	Par	Score	Details
1	469	4	3	D, 5I, 5 ft, 1 putt
2	343	4	3	D, 9I, 6 inches, 1 putt
3	425	4	3	D, 5I, 25 ft, 1 putt
4	549	5	4	D, 3W, SI, 6 inches
5	379	4	4	D, 6I, 25 ft, 2 putts
6	195	3	3	3I, 25 ft, 2 putts
7	395	4	4	D, 9I, 6 ft, 2 putts
8	244	3	4	4W, 30 ft, 3 putts
9	480	5	4	D, 2I, 2 putts from 40 ft
Out	3479	36	32	
10	462	4	4	D, 5I, 30 ft, 2 putts
11	371	4	3	D, W, 14 ft, 1 putt
12	603	5	4	D in rough, 7I, 4I, 15 ft, 1 putt
13	185	3	3	4I, 5 ft, 1 putt
14	360	4	4	D, W, 12 ft, 2 putts
15	453	4	3	D, 4I, 10 ft, 1 putt
16	230	3	3	3W, 40 ft, 2 putts
17	322	4	4	1I, W, 10 ft, 2 putts
18	456	4	4	D, 7I, 20 ft, 2 putts
In	3442	35	31	
Out	3479	36	32	
Total	6921	71	63	

Al Geiberger. (Allsport)

Al Geiberger

Event: Danny Thomas Memphis Classic
Date: 10 June 1977
Venue: Colonial Country Club
Score: Second round, 59

Even allowing for all the modern golfing aids, breaking 60 still remains far more of a barrier than the 4-minute mile. Up until 1977, only a handful had weaved such magic. Among them, Sam Snead had a 59 at White Sulphur Springs and Gary Player returned a 59 in the Brazilian Open at Gavea, a relatively short course in Rio de Janeiro. Harry Weetman reduced his then home course of Croham Hurst to 58 in January 1956, while Homero Blancas notched a 55 while a student at the University of Houston on the 5002-yard Premier course at Longview, Texas, but there has been nothing before or since to come close to matching the 59 of Al Geiberger in the 1977 Memphis Classic.

It broke one of the longest lasting records on the PGA Tour, the previous best being the 60 set by Al Brosch in 1951. However, that was at Brackenridge Park, San Antonio where all sorts of records were set. Geiberger's was on a course measuring 7249 yards, the longest used on the US tour that year.

Although Geiberger was 1966 PGA champion, he had only won ten tournaments in a 17-year career. In 1977, he was in his 30th year but his play that day on a course flanked by trees and water, surpassed all else he has ever done. Since 1977, he has won only one other tournament but his 59 was 13 under par, containing, as it did, 11 birdies, 1 eagle and 6 pars.

Although Geiberger holed a 30-yard pitch at the 10th, his longest successful putt was 40 feet and he missed four of 20 feet or less. He did not reach any of the par 5s in two yet made a birdie on them all—testimony to his wedge play—but the impressive part was the manner in which he sustained his brilliance as the crescendo was reached.

He started out 7 behind the first round leader, Tom Storey, Geiberger's 1st hole being the normal 10th. This was in accordance with the PGA rule of using 2 tees. Apart from holing his longest putt on his 1st green, his opening was relatively modest. By the time he had played 5 holes, he was only 2 under—acceptable under normal circumstances but not in the context of a wonder round.

However, a 3-iron to 15 feet on the par-3 6th heralded the start of a run of 6 birdies interspersed with an eagle at the 10th. This made a dramatic transformation in his score and, having missed the tour record of 8 successive birdies and eagles, made him think in terms of breaking 60.

Two solid pars followed but the pot began to boil again with birdies at his 15th and 16th holes. Now he needed one more birdie. He had a chance on the 17th but on the 18th he made the perfect ending. A 9-iron floated 8 feet below the hole and, having urged himself not to leave the putt short on the understandable grounds that he might never get as near again, he stroked it home, the last of 23 putts in all.

It is incidental to this story, if no less commendable, that Geiberger went on to win with 273 (72, 59, 72, 70), 3 strokes better than Gary Player and Jerry McGee.

Geiberger naturally enough was front page news not least because the next score over 4 days apart from the 65 of Storey who tied 50th, and one by Raymond Floyd, was 67 but it also helped that, for once, it could not have happened to a nicer guy.

Hole	Yards	Par	Score	Details
1*	417	4	3	D, 6I, 40 ft, 1 putt
2	376	4	4	2I, 8I, 15 ft, 2 putts
3	218	3	2	4I, 14 ft, 1 putt
4	464	4	4	D, 7I, 30 ft, 2 putts
5	447	4	4	D, 7I, 8 ft, 2 putts
6	200	3	2	3I, 15 ft, 1 putt
7	512	5	4	D, 4W, chip 5 ft, 1 putt
8	433	4	3	D, 8I, 12 ft, 1 putt
9	548	5	4	D, 5I, PW, 12 ft, 1 putt
Out	3615	36	30	
10†	582	5	3	D, 3W, 30 yd pitch
11	414	4	3	D, PW, 18 ft, 1 putt
12	182	3	2	7I, 20 ft, 1 putt
13	423	4	4	D, PW, 13 ft, 2 putts
14	199	3	3	4I, 30 ft, 2 putts
15	388	4	3	3W, PW, 13 ft, 1 putt
16	564	5	4	D, 3W, PW, 9 ft, 1 putt
17	439	4	4	D, 5I, 20 ft, 2 putts
18	403	4	3	D, 9I, 8 ft, 1 putt
In	3594	36	29	
Out	3615	36	30	
Total	7249	72	59	

* Normal 10th.
† Normal 1st.

Tom Watson

Event: British Open
Date: 9 July 1977
Venue: Turnberry
Score: Fourth round, 65

This is a question of choosing between three 65s, two by Tom Watson and one by Jack Nicklaus. In passing, one would have to say that Nicklaus's last round of 66 was pretty good, too, in the circumstances. It had a slightly ragged finish which, at the end of a marvellous exhibition of thrilling strokemaking and exemplary competitiveness, made the difference between defeat and victory.

The struggle lasted two days in which the two finest players hit virtually stroke for stroke. No two golfers have so completely dominated a major championship; and certainly no two have backed it with such brilliant scoring. In terms of the British Open, the previous best total for the last two rounds had been Nicklaus's 66 and 68 at St Andrews in 1964 when, again, he finished second. Watson's two 65s shattered it.

The choice of Watson's final 65 at Turnberry was one which might be said to have hung by a thread, but there was nothing frail about his golf or the positive attitude that accompanied and inspired it. It was the second time in three months that he got the better of a head-to-head fight with Nicklaus. His victory at the Masters was an important step in establishing his candidature as successor to Nicklaus's crown but, in British eyes, his triumph at Turnberry was confirmation that he was more than just a fine player. He proved himself a fine champion.

Winning a second Open always sets a man apart and, with Watson, it paved the way to a glittering run of success, a unique run over the next few years. Each victory had its satisfying points but there was nothing to compare with his shoot-out with Nicklaus.

For the first two days, Nicklaus and Watson had been very much part of the pack but they climbed free on Friday and, though there were those who started the fourth round not without hope, they were soon left trailing.

Watson's final 65 was a round of four parts, a somewhat shaky start, another slightly shaky spell around the turn, his best play coming from the 4th to the 8th, and then in a lethal finishing burst. It must be remembered that conditions were fairly free-running and the greens were, as links greens should be, receptive to only the most truly hit shots.

Nicklaus made the first move on the last day, opening with 2 birdies and moving 3 ahead of Watson after four; Watson dropped a stroke at the 2nd where he pulled a 5-iron. Watson's reply, with a birdie at the 5th and others on the 7th and 8th, made amends but he hit a poor drive at the 9th, after a delay to reinforce the crowd marshals, and dropped one behind again with 34 to Nicklaus's 33. Nicklaus was then 9 ahead of anybody else.

The end of an epic encounter, Turnberry 1977. Jack Nicklaus congratulates Tom Watson with typical grace. (Allsport)

There is no doubt that, although Nicklaus played better for the next 3 holes, Watson won the championship over this stretch in spite of going further behind to Nicklaus's birdie at the 12th. Watson bunkered a 6-iron to the short 11th and had to work hard to save par here and at the 10th and 12th.

However, as he stood on the 13th tee, 2 behind, Nicklaus carried most of the impartial money. A fine wedge shot got one back at the 13th and a cruel putt from just off the 15th green brought them level.

A half in four followed on the 16th before Watson got his nose in front for the first time in two days on the par-5 17th. Watson's 3-iron was a fine shot which Nicklaus could not match; nor could he hole from about 4 feet after a well played chip.

Watson, with the honour, then rifled a 1-iron to the corner of the dogleg. Nicklaus, reaching for his driver, came off the shot. It finished on the edge of the gorse and heralded an amazing escape as he heaved an 8-iron to the front of the green and holed for a 3. All to no avail. Before Nicklaus had played his second, Watson had landed a 7-iron right beside the flag and, when the pandemonium subsided, knocked the putt firmly home. People left for home that night saying they would never see the like again.

Hole	Yards	Par	Score	Details
1	355	4	4	D, SW, 2 putts
2	428	4	5	D, 5I, SW, 2 putts
3	462	4	4	D, 7I, SW (bunker)
4	167	3	3	4I, 2 putts
5	411	4	3	D, 5I, 15 ft, 1 putt
6	222	3	3	3W, SW (bunker), 1 putt
7	528	5	4	D, D, 2 putts
8	427	4	3	D, 5I, 25 ft, 1 putt
9	455	4	5	D (rough), 1I, SW, 2 putts
Out	3455	35	34	
10	452	4	4	D, 2I, 2 putts
11	177	3	3	6I, SW (bunker), 1 putt
12	391	4	4	D, PW, 2 putts
13	411	4	2	D, PW, 12 ft, 1 putt
14	440	4	4	D, 4I, 2 putts
15	209	3	2	4I, 45 ft, 1 putt
16	409	4	4	D, PW, 2 putts
17	500	5	4	D, 3I, 2 putts
18	431	4	3	1I, 7I, 2 ft, 1 putt
In	3420	35	31	
Out	3455	35	34	
Total	6875	70	65	

Gary Player

Event:	US Masters
Date:	9 April 1978
Venue:	Augusta
Score:	Fourth round, 64

There is no such thing as a lost cause where Gary Player is concerned. His first victory in the 1959 British Open blossomed from the unpromising position of being 8 strokes behind the leader before the start of the final day and the epic nature of his recovery against Tony Lema in the 1965 World Matchplay championship is part of golfing legend.

On the 2nd tee of the afternoon round, he stood 7 down but, for the drama of a concerted charge over the back 9 at Augusta, Player's golf in 1978 came as the most glittering example of perhaps the oldest of golf's lessons—never give up. The bare bones are that he started the final round 7 strokes behind Hubert Green and had 7 birdies over the last 10 holes to win by a stroke. His 64 remains the lowest last round by a champion and it made him the oldest winner.

Jack Nicklaus took the age record off him in 1986 with a remarkably similar stretch of golf. He, too, came home in 30 with 6 birdies and an eagle in the last 10 holes, but he took one more to the turn than Player eight years earlier and dropped a stroke at the short 12th. That was the difference.

It was at the 12th that Player notched his 3rd birdie in 4 holes, having narrowly failed to chip in for a 3 at the 11th, but it was the 9th and 10th that got him going in the nick of time. On the 9th, he hit his 7-iron second within 12 ft and on the 10th, a 5-iron nosed down 25 ft from the cup on that big green.

When he was home in 2 at the 13th, he had drawn up to within 2 of the lead but he was by now launched on what

Teamwork—Gary Player and his caddie, 'Rabbit' in earnest consultation. (Allsport)

he later described as the most perfect spell of golf in his life and, though he has repeatedly told enrapt press rooms, 'I have never played better', this time there were no doubts.

Even now that he is a Senior, Player still retains a youthful countenance and, reminding everyone that in 1978 he was 42, perhaps has less significance than if it had been anyone else but he had, at the time, gone three years in America without a win of any sort and, even allowing for his pertinacity, his recovery must rank as a minor miracle.

It was his ninth major championship victory over a span of 19 years but it was not one gained by the other leading contenders suffering collapse. Tom Watson and Rod Funseth played fine last rounds, not without regret perhaps, but good and strong enough to let Player know that one slip could have been fatal.

Player's experience of recognizing his chance was certainly not surprising but his ability to sustain his challenge was truly remarkable. It is easy in runs such as he put together to see a missed putt as an error. If anyone can birdie 7 of the last 10 holes, why not all 10? Anyway, the birdies that got away were 11th, 14th and 17th—the latter one of Augusta's weaker holes—but not many have played the last 4 holes with 3 birdies and here lay the final key to his triumph.

So constantly was the leader board changing, it was not until his four at the 15th that Player could at last be said to have drawn level with the others who were still a few holes behind. After his round, in fact, Player had an awkward wait to see if anyone could catch him, but Player's birdie at the 16th was a huge bonus and that at the 18th positively manna from heaven.

A perfect second to about 15 ft left him one of the few straight putts on the 18th green but the delight as it disappeared meant there was scarcely a dry eye in the house. Severiano Ballesteros, his playing partner, was almost as excited as if he had won himself but he obviously learned a lot. Two years later, it was his turn to be invested with the green jacket.

Hole	Yards	Par	Score	Details
1	400	4	4	D, 9I, 25 ft, 2 putts
2	565	5	4	D, 3W, SW (bunker), 1 ft, 1 putt
3	360	4	4	3W, 8I, 8 ft, 2 putts
4	220	3	2	5I, 30 ft, 1 putt
5	450	4	4	D, 4I, chip, 1 ft, 1 putt
6	190	3	3	6I, 15 ft, 2 putts
7	365	4	5	3W (trees), second in bunker, SW, 5 ft, 2 putts
8	530	5	5	D, 3W, chip, 8 ft, 2 putts
9	440	4	4	D, 7I, 12 ft, 1 putt
Out	3520	36	34	
10	485	4	3	D, 5I, 25 ft, 1 putt
11	445	4	4	D, 4I, chip, 1 ft, 1 putt
12	155	3	2	7I, 15 ft, 1 putt
13	485	5	4	D, 4I, 12 ft, 2 putts
14	420	4	4	D, 8I, 8 ft, 2 putts
15	520	5	4	D, 3W, 50 ft, 2 putts
16	190	3	2	5I, 14 ft, 1 putt
17	400	4	4	D, 8I, 20 ft, 2 putts
18	420	4	3	3W, 6I, 15 ft, 1 putt
In	3520	36	30	
Out	3520	36	34	
Total	7040	72	64	

David Graham

Event: US Open
Date: 21 June 1981
Venue: Merion
Score: Fourth round, 67

For sheer execution and lack of error under the most demanding circumstances, David Graham's closing round of 67 in the 1981 US Open at Merion must rank as one of the finest ever played. He missed only one fairway, the 1st, where he got a birdie, and, whilst it is stretching the truth to say he hit every green in regulation, it is as near true as makes no difference.

He finished on the fringe of the three he missed but was able to putt on each of them—something harder to do in America than Britain. His putting round was steady

David Graham, the first Australian winner of the US Open, chases a putt home to give Australia victory in the 1986 Dunhill Cup at St Andrews. (Allsport)

rather than inspired. Altogether, he had 33, missing from inside 20 feet on nine occasions, but it was the solidity of his golf which was so marked.

He is not the easiest player to watch. His preparation for every shot is meticulously deliberate and the swing itself sculpted into the correct groove rather than free flowing, but one other thing impressed mightily on the final day of the Open when so many fall by the wayside. He recognized that he might not have another chance and therefore played his best precisely when it was needed.

At the beginning of the week when talk was about predicting the winner, the names of Nicklaus, Watson, Trevino and Bill Rogers featured more prominently. Graham's was mentioned among the respected group who had not so far won an Open but might one day. Merion's key to success lies in tactical control rather than length and here Graham showed himself something of a master.

In becoming the first Australian to win the US Open, he may, too, have been spurred on by the attention which Greg Norman received earlier in the week. After the first round, Graham was tied for third place; after two rounds, he had moved up to second, 1 stroke behind George Burns but, as he set out on Sunday, he was 3 behind Burns.

However, rounds of 68, 68, 70 were proof of consistent form to which he added the touch of brilliance in his final 67 which invariably separates champions from the pack. Birdies at the 1st and 2nd were just what were needed to light the competitive fire within and, when he caught Burns as early as the 4th, he became the most dangerous contender.

Three putts on the 5th by Graham were a setback in an outward half of 35, but Merion is often said to start at the 14th and, having drawn level with Burns again on the 10th, it was precisely there that Graham upheld the legend.

He also showed the champion's instinct on the 14th of knowing when to gamble. Reaching for his driver, he was able to hit the ball far enough from the tee to attack the flag with a lofted iron. In earlier rounds, he had played a 3-wood and 4-iron to the hole but his 7-iron was inch perfect. He holed the 6-foot putt for a birdie and added another from 10 feet on the 15th where he chose to play a 1-iron followed by an 8-iron.

With a cushion of two strokes, he had a little insurance as he came to the last 3 holes but he played those so superbly that nobody else had a chance. He dismissed the 16th with a 3-wood and 5-iron; hit a 2-iron 20 feet from the hole at the par-3 17th; and, at the 18th, fired a drive and a 4-iron to the heart of the green.

The 18th was reminiscent of Ben Hogan's drive and 2-iron in 1950, but Hogan needed his four to tie. Graham used his to consolidate a margin of 3 strokes and to confirm beyond any doubt that the Open had been won honestly and magnificently by the man who had played the best over the four days and, particularly when it mattered, over those last 5 holes.

Hole	Yards	Par	Score	Details
1	355	4	3	
2	535	5	4	
3	183	3	3	
4	600	5	5	
5	426	4	5	
6	420	4	4	
7	350	4	4	
8	360	4	4	
9	195	3	3	
Out	3424	36	35	
10	312	4	4	
11	370	4	4	
12	405	4	4	
13	129	3	3	
14	414	4	3	D, 7I, 6 ft, 1 putt
15	378	4	3	1I, 8I, 10 ft, 1 putt
16	430	4	4	3W, 5I, 10 ft, 2 putts
17	224	3	3	2I, 20 ft, 2 putts
18	458	4	4	D, 4I, 18 ft, 2 putts
In	3120	34	32	
Out	3424	36	35	
Total	6544	70	67	

Tom Watson

Event: US Open
Date: 20 June 1982
Venue: Pebble Beach
Score: Fourth round, 70

Tom Watson had said earlier in the week at Pebble Beach that one needs a little bit of magic to win the US Open. It can take the form of good fortune, divine guidance or, more likely, the ability to produce a master stroke when nothing less will do.

As Watson surveyed his little chip from the side of the 71st green, he was tied with Jack Nicklaus who had just parred the last 2 holes for a round of 69 and a total of 284. His was not the sort of shot you think about holing. From the kind of fringy rough they prepare for an Open, even the best professionals are happy just to get the ball close particularly when the ball is so difficult to hold on fast greens.

However, Watson was different. He did think about holing it. The odds against such a happening were enormous but it is amazing how often in golf the odds are turned upside down; and, if one had to pick anyone to perpetrate the miracle in question, Watson would have been the popular choice.

He is a wonderfully bold, decisive chipper yet with the ability to maintain a slow enough tempo really to throw the ball up. The key to it all is that the ball should land softly so that, even on a firm green surface, it can still be controlled. Watson opened the blade of his sand wedge and with a little cocking of the right wrist, sliced across and under the ball.

The result was perfect. It took two short bounces, began to roll like a good putt and took the break to the right to disappear into the hole. A normally restrained Watson, where displaying emotions is concerned, danced a delighted jig. At that moment, he knew he had won.

Watson played many lower rounds in championships but he had never won the US Open and he needed victory to determine whether he deserved to be considered an authentically great golfer or just one of unusual talent. No matter how it was achieved, his victory enabled him to graduate to the ranks of the authentically great under the greatest pressure imaginable. He faced the might of Pebble Beach and the challenge of Jack Nicklaus in the setting in which Nicklaus had won both the US Open and Amateur championships.

However, there had been other important developments towards Watson's state of mind. In his 3rd round, his game was more solid than on the first two days and it gave him the confidence on Sunday to hit every fairway except one with a power he has never bettered in an Open.

Pebble Beach is not an easy course on which to play safe and the comfort of driving well was invaluable. The first few holes are not the most celebrated part of the course and Watson had not played them very encouragingly. On the final day, he made a birdie from sand at the 2nd but missed a tiny putt for another birdie on the short 7th. Nevertheless, par of 36 to the turn was eminently satisfactory. The only worrying part was that, with the exception of the 2nd, his putting had been a little tentative.

He missed a good birdie putt on the 9th but after that they began to drop. Putts to save par are often said to be easier than those for birdies or eagles and his success from 25 feet on the 10th after missing the green with a 7-iron was the one that set him up.

He holed another for a birdie on the 11th and though he bunkered a 3-iron at the short 12th and took 4, he made a brute of a putt for a birdie four on the 14th.

By this time, Nicklaus had birdied 5 holes in a row and Watson needed his birdie at the 14th to go ahead again. It was down to Nicklaus, going for his fifth Open, and Watson, going for his first. It was the fourth of their great confrontations—all of which, as it happened, Watson won—but Watson suffered great anxiety at the 16th.

He drove into the new bunker and pitched his 3rd with a wedge to the back of the green. He required 2 putts just to stay level with Nicklaus and this was very much the range and type of first putt that was terribly difficult to

One of the most famous single shots in golf. Tom Watson holing his chip on the 71st hole of US Open, 1982, Pebble Beach. (Lawrence Levy/Yours in Sport)

get close. It is easy to understand therefore that Watson's effort to get it dead with a 10-foot borrow led him to state that it was the best pressure putt he ever made.

Although he had dropped a stroke, it turned out to be a winning bogey every bit as much as his oft-reshown chip at the 17th but, however uplifting the chip had been to his spirits, Pebble Beach's 18th is no pushover in any circumstances with the ocean always in play.

It was the only time in the round that Watson altered his game plan. A 3-wood and a 7-iron left him a 9-iron which settled 20 feet above the hole. It was a ticklish putt which Watson felt he had hit a little too hard, but it was Watson's day by now and another birdie meant he is the only US Open champion to have finished with two birdies.

As a boy, he used to say to himself when he came to the 17th, 'Okay, finish in one under par to beat Nicklaus in the US Open. Then, I would finish two over and say, you've a long way to go yet'. Maybe it was that fantasy that did the trick but it also showed the unmistakable magic of dreams.

Hole	Yards	Par	Score	Details
1	385	4	4	
2	507	5	4	D, 3I, SW, 1 putt
3	368	4	5	D, 9I, SW, 2 putts
4	325	4	4	
5	180	3	3	
6	515	5	5	
7	120	3	3	PW, 2 ft, 2 putts
8	425	4	4	
9	450	4	4	
Out	3302	36	36	
10	424	4	4	D, 7I, chip, 25 ft putt
11	382	4	3	D, PW, 22 ft putt
12	204	3	4	3I, 2W, 2 putts from 15 ft
13	393	4	4	D, PW, 2 putts from 15 ft
14	565	5	4	D, 5I, PW, 35 ft putt
15	395	4	4	D, PW, 2 putts from 12 ft
16	403	4	5	D, SW, SW, 2 putts from 50 ft
17	209	3	2	2I, SW from 32 ft
18	548	5	4	3W, 7I, 9I, 20 ft putt
In	3523	36	34	
Out	3302	36	36	
Total	6825	72	70	

Bernhard Langer

Event: Benson & Hedges Spanish Open
Date: 14 October 1984
Venue: El Saler, Valencia
Score: Fourth round, 62

Very occasionally, a round is so far and away superior to any other in a championship that it automatically places itself in an exalted bracket. Such a round was Bernhard Langer's final 62 at El Saler, one of the finest courses in Spain—the masterpiece of Xavier Arana.

After rounds of 73, 68 and 72 had left him 7 strokes behind the leader, he transformed the scene to win by two. On a course measuring over 7000 yards, he had 25

Bernhard Langer's 62 in the final round of the 1984 Benson and Hedges Spanish Open was one of the finest ever played on the European tour. (Benson and Hedges)

putts in a round which he said afterwards he had not thought possible. To put it in its proper perspective, the next best during the week was a closing 65 by the player who finished 6th. However, apart from Langer, there were only about 20 rounds under 70 in the entire week and only three better than 67.

So what was it that so suddenly brought Langer to life? Well, the first and most important thing is that Langer is a player who has these inspired spells. In 1984 alone, he had a memorable 64 (which included a 7) on the first day of the Dutch Open at Rosendaelsche; a 64 in the French Open at St Cloud, and won the Carrolls Irish Open at Royal Dublin with 267 (68, 66, 67, 66). In addition, he was second equal in the Open at St Andrews.

When in the mood, he has the relish to attack and go on attacking but no round on the European tour has ever transcended his 62 when one takes into account the conditions and the severity of the course.

It could also have stemmed from a reaction of having had money and valuables stolen from his hotel the previous day and for a fine of £100 for slow play. He must be the first winner of a major tournament to have been so penalized.

Anyway, his 62 contained 10 birdies in the first 15 holes, 9 in an 11-hole stretch from the 5th. He had 31 for each 9, opening the barrage with a putt of 10 feet for a birdie on the 2nd and from about 6 feet for another on the par-5 5th. He then had his one slight break by chipping in at the 6th but he added further birdies with medium range putts on the 7th and 9th.

Although he added two more birdies at the 10th and 11th with putts of around 5 yards, he had his one moment of scrambling on the short 12th where he bunkered his tee shot and had to hole from 10 feet to save his par. His response to that was 3 more successive birdies which raised the outside possibility of a score of 60 but, sensing victory at that point, he needed only 3 solid pars which he achieved without trouble.

As the last but one tournament of the European season, victory confirmed him as the leading money winner. Nobody could have achieved the goal in a grander manner.

Hole	Yards	Par	Score
1	438	4	4
2	399	4	3
3	530	5	5
4	191	3	3
5	530	5	4
6	454	4	3
7	372	4	3
8	372	4	4
9	159	3	2
Out	3445	36	31
10	410	4	3
11	569	5	4
12	208	3	3
13	355	4	3
14	421	4	3
15	569	5	4
16	432	4	4
17	213	3	3
18	470	4	4
In	3647	36	31
Out	3445	36	31
Total	7092	72	62

Jack Nicklaus

Event:	US Masters
Date:	13 April 1986
Venue:	Augusta
Score:	Fourth round, 66

For years after Jack Nicklaus's first appearance in the Masters as an amateur, Augusta took it for granted that he would be one of the most likely challengers. Even before the 1986 event, the 50th in all, he had more victories to his credit, more rounds under 70 and more finishes in the top five, than anybody else.

He is the only winner to have defended his title successfully and holds the record for the biggest margin of victory. Nicklaus is as much a part of the history of the Masters as George Washington is of the history of America but, by 1986, certain question marks had arisen as to whether Nicklaus's unique powers and unparalleled span as a competitor in important championships could stretch to one more victory.

Around three o'clock on Sunday, therefore, the major surprise was that it was Nicklaus who emerged as the saviour of American pride. At one stage it looked as if Ballesteros, Norman or Price would land yet another victory for the overseas players but as the final after-

Jack Nicklaus holing one of the many putts that led to his dramatic victory in the 1986 Masters. (Allsport)

noon developed, the biggest surprise was not that Nicklaus was cutting back his challengers but that he was doing so with as bold and adventurous a brand of golf as he had ever produced.

Although he naturally relied on those playing behind him to make mistakes, his mounting assault induced many of those mistakes with a spell of putting and precision iron play that would have made him envious in his younger years. Even Nicklaus could not explain the certainty of his holing out except that he had a newish putter and new putters can work wonders—even strange looking ones.

'At my age (46), I should have been incapable of even getting the putter back but the more nervous I got, the better I seemed to putt.' Nicklaus had predicted to one of his sons on the morning of the final round that he would need a 66 to tie and 65 to win, but it did not seem much of a prospect as he played the first 8 holes in even par. However he reduced the 9th to a drive and a wedge and, by holing from 10 feet, he set in motion a climax that was rousing even by Augusta's exacting standards.

There followed 2 more birdies on holes that have distinct dangers and then the only blemish, a 7-iron that missed the tiny 12th green, a chip from the back that was good rather than great and a sidehill putt of 6 feet that lacked the magic of the others.

It seemed then to be a costly lapse but Nicklaus, whose best in seven previous winter tournaments had been a tie for 39th place in Hawaii, quickly readjusted his sights and, as with many great rounds, used the setback as a spur. He played the 13th and 14th quite beautifully but it was the 15th and 16th that decided this day. A huge drive bounded over the ridge on the 15th and a four-iron followed, hit heavens high, that covered the flag.

The ball rolled 12 feet past the flag before his putt, aimed to borrow about a foot and a half from the left, caught the hole and toppled in. His 5-iron to the 16th that pulled up within about a yard of the cup was another inspired stroke and the ensuing 2 refuelled his charge but many, who have got the hard part behind them at Augusta, have faltered on the run-in. Not so Nicklaus.

Although he hooked his drive a little on the 17th, the first fairway he had missed since the 2nd, he floated a pitching-wedge within 12 feet and calmly stroked the ball home up the slope. There was nothing calm about the reception it produced and Nicklaus himself was no doubt bubbling nicely within but no champion has ever looked less flustered and, on a day when he turned back the clock, no lapse of nerve or temperament was going to betray him.

With his customary thought and awareness of the situation, he selected his 3-wood from the 18th tee, hit the shot he wanted and then fired a 5-iron about 45 feet from the flag which was sited in its usual last day position on the lower, left front of the hugely sloping green.

No putt is ever easy on those slopes, not even to a five-times Masters champion, but Nicklaus judged his to perfection, getting it to die 4 inches short of the hole. He tapped the ball in for a 65, a 4-round total of 279, 9 under par, and then waited as those behind him found the challenge just too much for them. Nicklaus had played the last 10 holes in 7 under par and deservedly found his sixth green jacket every bit as good to the touch as his previous five. What a comeback. What a man.

Hole	Yards	Par	Score	Details
1	400	4	4	D, PW, 2 putts
2	555	5	4	D, 4I, PW, 8 ft, 1 putt
3	360	4	4	1I, 9I, 2 putts
4	205	3	4	2I, 3 putts
5	435	4	4	D, 6I, 2 putts
6	180	3	3	6I, 2 putts
7	360	4	4	1I, 9I, 2 putts
8	535	5	5	D, 3W, PW, 2 putts
9	435	4	3	D, PW, 10 ft, 1 putt
Out	3465	36	35	
10	485	4	3	D, 4I, 25 ft, 1 putt
11	455	4	3	D, 8I, 20 ft, 1 putt
12	155	3	4	7I, chip, 6 ft, 2 putts
13	465	5	4	3W, 3I, 2 putts
14	405	4	4	3W, 9I, 2 putts
15	500	5	3	D, 4I, 12 ft, 1 putt
16	170	3	2	5I, 3 ft, 1 putt
17	400	4	3	D, PW, 10 ft, 1 putt
18	405	4	4	D, 5I, 45 ft, 2 putts
In	3440	36	30	
Out	3465	36	35	
Total	6905	72	65	

Greg Norman

Event: Open Championship
Date: 18 July 1986
Venue: Turnberry
Score: Second round, 63

It is seldom that one round transforms a championship in the way that Norman's second round 63 did at Turnberry. He was the dominant figure in world golf during 1986 but an opening 74 in rough conditions left him 4 strokes behind the leader.

Much had been said and written about the severity of the rough and the width of the fairways. After the bad conditions of the first day, the chorus intensified but Norman stood out as an almost lone voice that refused to be intimidated.

It was still his inclination to attack which he did from the start. On the two other occasions that a round of 63 had been returned in the Open, it was in favourable weather and the architect of each, Mark Hayes (1977) and Isao Aoki (1980), never came in sight of victory. With Norman it was different. It was a tactical and technical triumph, particularly as conditions on the second day were far from easy.

Norman dominated that day as he did the championship. His only anxious phase came late on Saturday when he was caught in a terrible squall of wind and rain, but on Friday he encountered no obstacles of any description.

Although comfortably the shortest of the par-4s, the 1st posed problems all week and Norman was pleased with his 4, but 3 birdies in a row from the 2nd set the tone, even though he followed with three putts on the 5th.

However, he made amends with an eagle at the 7th even if his 5-iron to the 8th came up short and he dropped another stroke.

Norman confounded the more conservative approach of others by taking his driver or a 3-wood from the tee whenever he could, presumably on the grounds that, if you are going to finish in the rough, the nearer you can get to the green the better.

His start for home was ideal, a 6-iron to 5 feet at the 10th and a 9-iron to one foot at the 11th setting up birdies that sent him shooting up the leader board. All eyes and thoughts were on him now but there was better to come. He dismissed the 14th, so formidable on the opening day that it yielded only one birdie, to a drive and 3-iron to a yard; a 4-iron floated down the wind on the 15th, an 8-iron on the 16th and a 5-iron on the long 17th.

Three birdies in 4 holes took him to 7 under par although there was an eagle putt on the 17th that got away. Even so, the 18th held no fears and a further birdie would have meant a 61. In 1977, the 18th cost Mark Hayes a 5 when he drove into a bunker. Norman avoided that trap, following a safe 2-iron from the tee with a 7-iron which came up a trifle short of the flag.

His mood by now was far from defensive and Norman gave his first putt every chance but, alas, he was perhaps a little too charged up. It finished four feet past, the return was wide and a new record for an individual round had gone.

Nevertheless, an indication of its greatness can be seen from the fact that the day's next best round was the 67 of Tommy Nakajima while only 14 others broke 70. Norman made a calculated decision which worked perfectly. Two days later came the reward of victory, his first in a major championship.

Hole	Yards	Par	Score	Details
1	350	4	4	4I, 8I, 18 ft, 2 putts
2	428	4	3	D, 8I to 18 ft
3	462	4	3	D, 6I to 5 ft
4	167	3	2	6I to 4 ft
5	441	4	5	D, 5I, 3 putts from 60 ft
6	222	3	3	3W, 2 putts from 40 ft
7	528	5	4	D, 1I to 20 ft
8	427	4	5	D, 5I, Pitch, 18 ft, 2 putts
9	455	4	4	D, 8I, Pitch, 3 ft putt
Out	3480	35	32	
10	452	4	3	3W, 6I, 5 ft
11	177	3	2	9I, 1 ft
12	448	4	4	D, 5I, 18 ft, 2 putts
13	411	4	4	3I, 8I, 18 ft, 2 putts
14	440	4	3	D, 3I, 3 ft
15	209	3	2	4I, 20 ft, 2 putts
16	409	4	3	2I, 8I, 8 ft
17	500	5	4	D, 5I, 18 ft, 2 putts
18	431	4	5	2I, 7I, 28 ft, 3 putts
In	3477	35	31	
Out	3480	35	32	
Total	6957	70	63	

Greg Norman, the worthy deed done. (Allsport)

The Four Major Championships

British Open

First played 1860

The oldest Open championship in the world was started by the Prestwick Club, Ayrshire, in October 1860 and, apart from 1871 and the war years, has been contested annually. There was no championship in 1871 because Young Tom Morris had won the previous three and had made the Open championship belt his own.

In 1872, a new trophy, a silver claret jug, was presented and the championship was then organized jointly by the Prestwick Club, the Royal and Ancient and the Honourable Company of Edinburgh Golfers. Until 1892, the championship was completed over 36 holes in one day. In 1892, it became 72 holes and the list of courses increased from three to include Royal St George's, Sandwich (1894) and Royal Liverpool, Hoylake (1897).

The Royal and Ancient took over full responsibility for running the Open in 1920 and have seen it develop steadily into the major competition that it is today.

A championship sketch, Muirfield 1892. (Illustrated London News)

In the 1920s, Bobby Jones, Walter Hagen and Gene Sarazen led the American invasion that gave it true international status and this has continued on and off ever since. Arnold Palmer revived the American interest in 1960, although Sam Snead won the championship in 1946 and Ben Hogan triumphed on his lone mission to Carnoustie in 1953.

Nowadays, the Open may be watched by over 130 000 spectators during the week and is seen by many millions on television all over the world. In the 17 years from 1970 to 1987, the total prize-money rose from £40 000 to £651 000.

It is traditional for the Open to be staged on a seaside links. As a result, the rota has always been limited. A total of only 14 courses have been used compared with over 40 for the American Open. Of the 14, three have only been used once, but modern needs dictate that more than just playing quality be taken into account. Such things as ease of crowd movement, car parking, hotel accommodation, access and the ability to house a vast tented village are vital considerations.

MILESTONES

1860 Birth of championship golf on Wednesday, 17 October at Prestwick.

Eight entries for first Open at Prestwick. Not strictly 'Open' as the field comprised all professionals. The death of Allan Robertson the previous year left the need to find a new top golfer, but it was not until 1861, after complaints from amateurs, that the championship was thrown open 'to all the world'.

One competitor took 21 for 1 hole, the highest ever recorded for a single hole.

Willie Park, Sr, was first champion with a score of 174 for three rounds of Prestwick's 12-hole course.

1862 Old Tom Morris's margin of victory: 13 strokes. This is a record which still stands.

1863 Prize-money instituted for the first time.

1865 Official score-cards introduced.

1868 Young Tom Morris succeeded his father as champion. At 17, he is still the youngest winner.

Young Tom also performed the first hole in one in championship golf at Prestwick's 8th hole.

1870 Young Tom Morris's third victory. In accordance with the rule, passed by the Prestwick Club in 1860, he won the championship belt outright.

Young Tom's total of 149 for three rounds of the Prestwick course was never equalled with the gutty ball.

1871 No championship while new trophy was found.

1872 The first championship for the silver trophy (a claret jug) that has been so envied by golfers. The permanent trophy presented by the Prestwick Club, the Royal and Ancient and the Honourable Company of Edinburgh Golfers. These three joined forces to manage the championship which was then played in rotation over the links of Prestwick, St Andrews and Musselburgh.

Young Tom won his fourth title in succession, an achievement never equalled.

1873 Record entry of 26 for St Andrews' first Open, the first, indeed, away from Prestwick.

1876 Total prize-money £20. First prize of £10 going to Bob Martin, but he tied for the title with David Strath and there was doubt over the procedure to be adopted as well as a call for

Strath's disqualification over a technicality. A decision was delayed, Strath refused to play-off and Martin was awarded the title.

1878 John Ball finished fifth at the age of 14.

1879 Jamie Anderson makes it three wins in a row at the age of 37. He was runner-up in 1873.

1880 Bob Ferguson deposed Jamie Anderson and began his run of three victories in a row. Ferguson, a former caddie at Musselburgh, accepted the post of greenkeeper when he withdrew from the competition scene.

1881 The year of the Great Storm, causing so few to complete the championship. The peaks of Arran were covered in snow and it was the day that 180 fishermen were lost around the coast of Scotland, 120 from the port of Eyemouth in Berwickshire.

1883 Play-off needed to deny Ferguson his fourth title in a row. In the first play-off which was actually held, Willie Fernie got home at the last hole. With the two golfers level, Fernie drove the green and holed a long 'steal' for a 2.

In the last round at Musselburgh, Ferguson finished with three 3s to tie and Fernie's total of 159 included a 10. This is the only time that a winner of a major championship has completed a hole in double figures.

1884 Until then, the winners had come from Prestwick, St Andrews, or Musselburgh. The new champion, Jack Simpson, was a Carnoustie man.

1885 Bob Martin's second win at St Andrews. He, James Braid, J H Taylor and Jack Nicklaus are the only players to have won twice at St Andrews. Record entry of 51.

1886 and 1888 Open won by 'artisan' golfers. David Brown, a slater by trade, in 1886 and by Jack Burns, a plasterer, in 1888.

1890 End of Scottish monopoly. First English winner and first amateur winner, John Ball.

1891 Prize-money total £28.50. First prize £10. Record entry of 82.

1892 Second amateur winner, Harold Horsfall Hilton.

First championship held at Muirfield which replaced Musselburgh as the home of the Honourable Company of Edinburgh Golfers.

Championship extended to 72 holes and two days, 36 holes each day.

Entry money imposed. Prize-money increased to £110.

1893 Atrociously wet first day. Harold Hilton took 10 at the Dyke hole.

1894 First championship to be held in England (Sandwich).

First victory by an English professional, J H Taylor.

First of 16 victories by the Triumvirate of Taylor, Harry Vardon and James Braid. Dawn of a new era.

Rotation of courses was fixed as follows: Prestwick, Sandwich, St Andrews, Muirfield, Hoylake.

1895 Old Tom Morris had first round of 107.

1896 First victory by Harry Vardon.

1897 First Open at Hoylake. Won for a second time by Harold Hilton, a local member.

Hilton, an amateur, received plate value at £40, James Braid taking the second prize of £20. It is of note that 70 years later, the Royal and Ancient's limit on the value of any prize for an amateur was £50.

1898 First Open to be won with four rounds under 80. Harry Vardon was the winner. Qualifying limit imposed after two rounds.

1899 Talk of a strike if the prize-money was not increased. Vardon, Park, Taylor and Braid against the idea, but during the championship the first prize was raised to £50.

1901 James Braid's first victory.

1902 Victory for Sandy Herd, the first with the new, revolutionary Haskell ball.

Herd was noted as the first club waggler at address.

1903 The brothers Harry and Tom Vardon finished first and second.

1904 First winning total under 300 and the first individual round under 70. Jack White won a notable championship at Sandwich with a score of 141 for the last two rounds, hoisting an aggregate of 296. His 141 was not beaten until 1935, but Braid and Taylor, tied on 297, also beat 300. Braid's aggregate for the final two rounds was one less than White's and his third round of 69 was the first to break 70 since the Open began. However, in a championship of low scores, Taylor had a last round of 68, a score which was not bettered for 30 years.

Until Braid's 69, James Sherlock's second-round 71 was an individual record.

1906 The Triumvirate of Braid, Taylor and Vardon finished first, second and third.

1907 Qualifying rounds first introduced. First overseas victor: Arnaud Massy of France.

1908 James Braid lowered Jack White's record aggregate by 5 strokes to 291. His 142 for the first two rounds was also a record.

1910 First round at St Andrews abandoned at 1.30 pm because of a thunderstorm. Only the leading 60 players were allowed to play the final two rounds.

Prize-money increased to £125. Golden Jubilee of championship. Braid's fifth victory.

1914 The year of Harry Vardon's record sixth victory.

Two qualifying rounds introduced, lowest 80 and ties going forward to the championship proper. First newsreel film made of Open.

1919 Management taken over by the Royal and Ancient Golf Club, but no championship until 1920.

1920 George Duncan, 13 strokes behind Abe Mitchell after 36 holes, won by 2 strokes from Sandy Herd. He made up the 13 strokes in the third round with a 71 to 84 at Deal. Duncan added a 72 in the afternoon while Mitchell finished fourth.

Duncan's score of 143 for the final 36 holes was the best since Jack White's 141 in 1904 and was not beaten until 1935. Total prize-money £225. First prize reached £100.

1921 The first time the Open trophy was taken to America. It was won at St Andrews by Jock Hutchison, a St Andrean based in America. In a play-off, he defeated Roger Wethered by 9 strokes.

In the first round, Hutchison holed in one at the 8th and was within an inch or two of another one at the 9th. However, successive holes in a total of 3 strokes is a major championship record.

In the third round Wethered, attempting to become the third amateur to win, was penalized one stroke for inadvertently stepping on his ball. Wethered, who began with a 78, had the lowest last day score of 143, including the penalty stroke. Three times, however, he took 5 at the 18th including the 72nd hole. Bobby Jones tore up his card at the 11th in the third round.

1922 Walter Hagen's first victory—the first by an American-born player. Starting the final round, 2 strokes behind the defending champion, Jock Hutchison, Hagen returned a 72, but tremendous golf by George Duncan nearly caught him. He came to the final hole, needing a 4 for a 68, but his second to the 18th at Sandwich missed the green, his pitch was short and he took 2 putts.

1923 Victory for Arthur Havers, the last by a British golfer, as it turned out, for eleven years.

First appearance of Gene Sarazen, the US champion, but he failed to qualify, being caught in a terrible storm.

1924 Hagen's second victory.

J H Taylor finished fifth at the age of 53. He had the lowest score for the six rounds including the qualifying rounds. Record entry of 277.

1925 Prestwick's last Open. Victory for Jim Barnes, but tragedy for Macdonald Smith before enormous crowds.

Macdonald Smith, facing his best chance to win an Open at last, and needing a 78 to do so, finished in 82.

1926 Having returned a 66 in one of his qualifying rounds at Sunningdale, by general consent as near flawless a round as

had been played, Bobby Jones won the first of his three Opens at Royal Lytham, making its debut as an Open course.

After two rounds of 72, Jones was 2 ahead of Al Watrous, but in the third round, Watrous (Jones's partner) had a 69 to Jones's 73. Jones, 2 behind with 5 holes left, was level with Watrous on the 17th tee, but he hooked into sandy ground off the tee. Watrous, on the green in 2, was well placed, but Jones played one of the famous strokes of history. His shot of 170 yd with a mashie iron finished inside Watrous's ball. Watrous took 3 putts to Jones's 2 and a par 4 at the 18th by Jones saw him home. Gate money introduced. Play held over three days.

1927 Jones again: having opened with a 68, his only round under 70 in any Open (qualifying rounds apart), his total of 285 set a new Open record. He led from the start.

Last appearance of John Ball, aged 65. He first played in 1878. All entrants played two qualifying rounds on the Monday and Tuesday, one on the championship course and one on an adjacent course. The leading 100 and ties qualified for the championship. One round was played on Wednesday and one on Thursday after which those 15 or more strokes off the lead were eliminated. The remainder played two rounds on Friday. Championship, therefore, extended to three days.

1928 and 1929 A double for Walter Hagen.

Trophy presented in 1928 by the Prince of Wales.

1930 Part two of the Grand Slam for Bobby Jones was at Hoylake, a sound victory in which he led for three rounds and edged out Leo Diegel and Macdonald Smith with a final 75. A Tingey, Jr, hit three shots out of bounds at the 1st hole. They were his shots to the green. The hole cost him 11.

1931 The first ever British Open held at Carnoustie. Watched by the Duke of Windor (then Prince of Wales) the Argentine player, Jose Jurado, had a chance to win. He needed a 75 in the fourth round, but took 77. A final 71 for Tommy Armour, born in Edinburgh, saw him home.

1932 Prince's only championship produced Gene Sarazen's only win. It was popular, deserved and impressive. He led from start to finish on ground that was fast and full running. It was a low-scoring championship and his total of 283 was the best recorded up until then. It was not beaten for 18 years.

Rules altered to allow 60 and ties on final day.

1933 After Britain had won the Ryder Cup, the Americans replied by having five in the first six at St Andrews. Sarazen looked as though he would defend his title successfully, but in the second round he took 6 at the short 11th to finish in 73 and on the last day tied, and failed, to carry Hell bunker when quite unnecessary. He was part of a triple tie for third place, one stroke behind Densmore Shute and Craig Wood. It was the first all-American play-off. Shute's rounds in the championship were 73, 73, 73, 73. Only champion with every round the same. At the first hole of the play-off which Shute won, Craig Wood played his second shot of the day out of the Swilcan Burn, but the stroke for which he is undoubtedly best remembered was a drive at the par-5 5th (530 yd). It finished in one of the bunkers in the face of the hill about 100 yd from the hole.

1934 Henry Cotton brought a new dawn for British golf. It was the first British victory for eleven years and Cotton celebrated in style. His second-round 65 remained the lowest round (or equal lowest) until 1977. His total of 132 for the first 36 holes has never been beaten and he led from start to finish.

Cotton led by 9 strokes at half-way and by 10 with one round to play. His fourth round was full of anxiety and his 79 spoiled a brilliant sequence, but he still had 5 strokes to spare over the South African, Sid Brews (the first Commonwealth golfer to do so well); and he equalled the record aggregate.

The entry was over 300 for the first time.

1935 A virtual unknown. Sam, Parks, won the US Open in 1935, and though Alf Perry was a golfer of proven worth, he was, nevertheless, a surprise winner at Muirfield.

One Scottish professional started 7, 10, 5, 10 and took 65 to reach the turn. He had another 10 at the 11th and retired at the 12th.

Muirfield's first clubhouse, 1892—the year of its first Open. (Illustrated London News)

1936 Reward for Alf Padgham after finishing second and third the previous two years. Before his final round, Padgham discovered that his clubs were locked in a local clubmaker's shop with his caddie nowhere to be seen. Padgham eventually smashed a window, rescued his clubs and hired a new caddie.

1937 Henry Cotton's triumph, often regarded as his greatest, over the American Ryder Cup team at Carnoustie.

Number of qualifiers increased to 140 and ties.

1938 Reg Whitcombe survived gales on the final day. Flags rent to tatters, exhibition tents blown down and Alf Padgham drove the 11th (380 yd). The Whitcombes were regular competitors but Reg's triumph, at the age of 40, was one which escaped his brothers, Ernest and Charles.

One player took 14 at the 12th, the third highest ever recorded in the Open for a single hole.

It was the last time that British players occupied the first three places.

Qualifiers reduced to 130 and the last day to a maximum of 40 players.

1939 Victory for Dick Burton, the last British golfer to win the Open at St Andrews. A third round of 77 lost him the lead but, needing a 72 to win, Burton holed for a 3 on the 18th to have 2 strokes to spare. Johnny Bulla, who finished two hours before Burton, was second.

1946 Sam Snead's only victory in either the US or British Opens. It was his second of only three appearances in the British Open. Johnny Bulla, another American, was second—as he was in 1939, also at St Andrews.

Total prize-money £1000.

German prisoners of war were employed to do some rough clearance before the championship.

1947 Fred Daly's victory at Hoylake included a third round of 78. Since then, no winner has had a round higher than 75.

1948 Play watched by King George VI. Third victory for Henry Cotton. No other Briton has won three victories in the last 60 years. Indeed, no other British player has won more than one.

1949 The beginning of the Locke/Thomson era. They won eight times in ten years. In 1949 at Sandwich, Locke defeated Harry Bradshaw in a play-off. It was a championship remembered for a drive of Bradshaw's finishing in a broken bottle at the 5th hole in the second round. It led to a change in the Rules of Golf but, at the time, he had to play the ball and bottle.

First prize £300.

1950 Locke lowered the record aggregate to 279 at Troon.

1951 Portrush's only Open and the last British victory for 18 years. Max Faulkner was champion.

Total prize-money £1700.

1952 Locke's third victory in four years, but Peter Thomson finished runner-up in his second Open.

1953 Ben Hogan's year. US Open and Masters champion, he added a third leg of the modern quadrilateral, the only player to perform the feat in the same year. His scores were 73, 71, 70, 68; the only other champions to have each round lower than the previous one are Jack White (1904), James Braid (1906) and Gary Player (1959).

First prize £500.

1954 Peter Thomson's first victory; also the first by an Australian and the first Open to be held at Birkdale.

Dai Rees, who came close on a number of occasions, finished joint second.

1955 £1000 first prize for the first time. First live coverage by BBC Television on 7 July.

Thomson's second victory; championship held at St Andrews.

1956 Thomson's third victory in three years, the only player to accomplish the feat in modern times. At Hoylake, he won by 3 strokes. Flory van Donck (Belgium), Roberto de Vicenzo (Argentina) and Gary Player (South Africa) were second, third and fourth.

1957 Championship transferred at late notice from Muirfield to St Andrews owing to petrol shortage during the Suez crisis. Locke won for the fourth time, but survived a technicality over the Rules. On the 72nd green, he marked his ball a putter's head length from the spot, but replaced it on the marker's spot, not a putter's head length away. He holed the short putt for a 3-stroke victory over Thomson. The likelihood is, therefore, that he could have stood a 2-stroke penalty.

It was the first year that leaders went out last in the final two rounds.

1958 Thomson's fourth victory in five years. Only Young Tom Morris can match this feat.

1959 Victory for Gary Player at Muirfield despite the highest first round by a champion for 30 years—a 75; and an agonizing wait after a 6 on the 72nd hole looked as though it might lose him the championship.

Player's 6 was the highest score by a champion at the last hole for many years.

Flory van Donck of Belgium finished second. Apart from Arnaud Massy who finished first in 1907 and second in 1911, van Donck's performances in 1956 and 1959 were the best by a continental professional until Ballesteros tied second in 1976. Total prize-money £5000.

1960 Centenary Open. Arnold Palmer's first appearance. He finished runner-up to Kel Nagle, the second Australian winner.

A violent storm washed out play on Friday afternoon. Final round played on Saturday.

Prize-money £7000. First prize £1250.

1961 Another Saturday finish owing to another storm washing out a day's play.

Arnold Palmer's supremacy confirmed by his victory. His play in the gale in the second round was considered among his finest. A plaque later erected on the old 15th hole to commemorate one particularly fine second shot.

Prize money £8500. First prize £1400.

Qualifiers reduced to a maximum of 120 and the 36-hole cut altered to allow a maximum of 50 for the final 36 holes.

1962 Palmer powered his way to a second victory on a course running freely. Set record aggregate of 276. Six-stroke victory, the biggest since Walter Hagen in 1929.

Jack Nicklaus's first appearance. He took 10 at the 11th. Made

The Prince of Wales examining the trophy before presenting it to Walter Hagen at Sandwich, 1928. (Illustrated London News)

ut on margin. His first round was 80.

Attendance 37 098 with many more thought to have got in along the seashore without paying. Crowd scenes led to much stricter crowd control.

1963 First victory in any major championship by a left-handed player. Bob Charles beat Phil Rodgers in a play-off, the last to be decided over 36 holes.

Qualifying rounds took place for first time ahead of the championship on neighbouring courses. System of exemptions introduced for the leading players.

The 36-hole cut admitted 45 and ties to the final 36 holes.

1964 Tony Lema won with a little more than a day's preparation. Five-stroke victory would have been greater but for Jack Nicklaus completing the last two rounds in 134 strokes—a record at the time. It was Lema's first British Open.

Announcement made that any future play-offs would be decided over 18 holes.

1965 Peter Thomson joined James Braid and J H Taylor by winning his fifth and best victory at Birkdale. It was the last year that two rounds were played on the last day (Friday) and he is the only person to have won two Opens at Birkdale.

He was 6 strokes behind Tony Lema, the defending champion, at the end of the first round, but won by 2 strokes.

Number of qualifiers for the championship (including those exempt) increased to 130.

Total prize-money up to £10 000.

1966 The first championship scheduled to end on a Saturday and the first victory for Jack Nicklaus on a course where the fairways were narrow and the rough knee high. David Thomas, with two 69s to finish, was runner-up for the second time.

It was Tony Lema's last championship. He was killed on 24 July 1966 in an air crash.

Attendance topped 40 000.

Thirty-six hole cut admitted 55 and ties. Play held over four days for the first time.

1967 Sentimental acclaim for the victory of Roberto de Vicenzo on what may prove to be Hoylake's last Open. Having been a loyal supporter of the Open, it was a popular and deserved triumph. Third in 1948 and 1949, second in 1950, third again in 1956 and third equal in 1960, there were those who believed that would be as close as he came, but he had final rounds of 67 and 70 and held off the strong golf of Jack Nicklaus.

1968 Gary Player's second victory in a generally high-scoring championship. His total of 289 was the highest for 21 years. Of the leading 30 players, only Casper and Nicklaus broke 70—only once. At 7252 yd, the course was the longest for an Open. Prize-money reached £15 000 with a first prize of £3000.

1969 British victory drought ended by the success of Tony Jacklin at Lytham. He ended the longest run in history without a British champion—18 years.

For the first time in ten years no American finished in the first five. The nationalities of the top five, being English, New Zealand, Argentine, Australian and Irish.

First prize of £4250 which is £3925 more than the previous British champion, Max Faulkner, received in 1951.

1970 Second all-American play-off; and it took place at St Andrews on a Sunday—an unprecedented step, Jack Nicklaus drove through the 18th green, chipped back and holed for a birdie to win by 1 stroke, but he might not have had the chance of a play-off. Doug Sanders, who had to pre-qualify, took 3 putts on the 18th green on the fourth afternoon. Nobody else who had had to pre-qualify has come as close to winning. It was the first play-off to be decided by a birdie. Hitherto, the play-offs were more one-sided.

Total prize-money £40 000.

Storm on first evening ended play early. Tony Jacklin, defending champion and out in 29, had to mark his ball for the night on the 14th hole and finish the next day.

His 29 was the lowest 9 holes at St Andrews as was Neil Coles's 65 for 18 holes.

1971 Lee Trevino's victory at Birkdale completed a unique treble. Within the space of about a month he captured the American, Canadian and British titles.

A final outward half of 31 left the Open at Trevino's mercy, but errors at the 10th and 14th were followed by a 7 at the 17th which might easily have been worse as his ball lodged in the dunes. Thoughts of breaking the aggregate record of 276 were gone, but his 278 gave him a stroke to spare over Lu Liang Huan of Formosa.

It was the first time that an Asian golfer had made such a mark. It was the 100th Open for which the prize-money was raised to £47 500.

Number of qualifiers increased to 150, including exempt players. Fifty-four-hole cut increased to 60 and ties.

1972 Lee Trevino again at Muirfield and definitely his week. He holed two chips and a bunker shot, the last chip on the 35th green for a 5 after seemingly having acknowledged defeat. Tony Jacklin promptly took 3 putts and Trevino recorded a total of 278, the first at Muirfield below 280.

Four qualifying courses used. Total prize-money £50 000.

1973 Tom Weiskopf led from start to finish, uncertain to begin with but helped later by still, damp conditions in which he excelled. His 276 tied the record set by Arnold Palmer, also at Troon in 1962. Gene Sarazen holed in one at the 8th in the first round. It was 50 years since he first played in the Open.

1974 From the moment he began 69, 68, Gary Player was a hot favourite. Of the others, only John Morgan had a round under 70. His 69 tied Player after 18 holes, but Player's halfway lead was 5 strokes and his 54-hole lead was 3.

Use of the large ball made compulsory.

1975 Another close play-off between Tom Watson and Jack Newton, but three or four others had chances of victory on Saturday, notably the South African, Bobby Cole. There was consistent low scoring, the like of which Carnoustie had not seen in an Open. Newton had a third round of 65.

1976 Johnny Miller won by 6 strokes but was given a long, hard tussle by the young Spaniard, Severiano Ballesteros, almost unknown in those days. Peter Dawson holed in one at the 4th, the first by a left-hander in the Open.

Britain's hottest summer of the century led to a part of the course catching fire on the first day.

Number of qualifying courses increased to five—Formby, West Lancashire, Southport and Ainsdale, Hesketh and Hillside.

1977 A championship of records galore for Turnberry's first. Tom Watson lowered the record aggregate by 8 strokes, Jack Nicklaus by 7.

Mark Hayes's second round of 63 was the lowest individual round in any Open.

Watson had the lowest last two rounds on record, the lowest aggregate for the first 54 holes and the lowest aggregate for the last 54 holes.

There were eleven scores of 66 or under. Those completing 72 holes had 40 rounds under 70 between them, 70 being Turnberry's par.

The first eight were all Americans.

The crowd total of 92 200 was a record for Scotland.

The top 20 all received four-figure prizes. Total prize-money £100 000.

Regional qualifying introduced, followed by standard qualifying over three courses.

1978 Jack Nicklaus's third victory and his second at St Andrews. For the second year running, his last two rounds were under 70. He accomplished the same feat in 1964, also at St Andrews. His total in 1978 was 2 lower than in 1970. Isao Aoki finished equal seventh, the highest placing ever by a Japanese golfer. First prize £12 500. Record attendance of 125 271.

1979 Victory for Severiano Ballesteros, the first by a Spaniard and the first by a professional from continental Europe since Arnaud Massy in 1907.

Lytham, therefore, kept its record that no American professional has won in seven Opens. Bobby Jones, an amateur, won there in 1926.

Gene Sarazen with his faithful caddie, 'Swankie' Daniels, Princes 1932. (Illustrated London News)

After equalling the course record of 65 in the second round, Ballesteros hit only two fairways with his driver on the last two days, but he finished on 283, the winner by 3 strokes. Ben Crenshaw was equal second for the second year running.

Jack Nicklaus second for a record seventh time. In his first round, Nicklaus holed in one at the 5th.

Hale Irwin, the US Open champion, was the 54-hole leader but, partnered by Ballesteros in the final round, finished sixth.

Bill Longmuir equalled the Lytham record with 65 on the first morning.

Prize-money totalled £155 000 and the attendance was 134 571—a record. The Open was estimated to cost £800 000 to stage.

1980 The British Open, the first officially scheduled to end on a Sunday, followed the US Open in providing a feast of record breaking. Isao Aoki had a third round of 63 to equal Mark Hayes's record for an individual round in 1977; and, in the same round, played in unusually easy conditions, Tom Watson and Hubert Green returned 64s. The day before, Horacio Carbonetti, an unknown Argentinian, set a new course record of 64.

Watson's 64 allowed him to break his own record score for 54 holes but, more importantly, it enabled him to make up 2 strokes on the overnight leader, Lee Trevino, and then establish a 4-stroke lead. On the last day, he was never likely to be caught and duly won his third victory, all in Scotland, by 4 strokes. He was only 3 strokes outside his own 72-hole aggregate of 268, and his 64 was the lowest round ever by a champion. In that third round, he came home in 30.

1981 A return to Sandwich after a gap of 32 years was a great success although the attendance was slightly down. However, the traffic flow was excellent and there was a greater feeling of spaciousness than at any other modern Open venues.

Bill Rogers won his first major victory by 4 strokes but there was a moment when, by taking 7 at the 7th in the final round, his lead was reduced to one. Bernhard Langer of Germany finished second, another sign of the growing number of good continental golfers.

The opening day was notable for Jack Nicklaus taking 83. In 1962, his first Open, he had a first round of 80 and a last round of 79; otherwise, his highest round was a 77 in 1965. However, he followed at Sandwich with a 66 and made the cut. Nevertheless, his finishing position of equal 23rd was his worst since 1962.

Two players in the same threesome were disqualified for failing to sign their cards after the second round.

Three players, Gordon Brand in the second round, Roger Chapman, an amateur, in the third and Sam Torrance in the fourth, holed in one at the 16th. It was the first time that there had been three holes in one at the same hole in any Open.

1982 Tom Watson's fourth victory, although it was not until late on the last day at Troon that people looked upon him as the winner. The first two and a half days or so were dominated by Bobby Clampett, a young American in his first Open who, after 5 holes of the third round, led by 7 strokes. He had opening rounds of 67 and 66, 1 stroke outside Henry Cotton's record for the first 36 holes. An 8 on the 6th in the third round where he visited three bunkers, was the start of his undoing but he still led after three rounds in spite of a 78.

As it turned out, his total for the second 36 holes was 23 strokes higher than for his first 36.

However, Nick Price had the best chance of victory thereafter but the task was beyond him. So, with a final round of 70, Watson snapped the title that nobody else seemed to want.

1983 Watson's fifth victory, his first in England, was sealed with a superb 2-iron to the 72nd green at Royal Birkdale. It gave him a total of 275, the lowest winning total apart from his own in 1977 and 1980. He beat Hale Irwin and Andy Bean by one stroke. Irwin, going to tap in a 2-inch putt on the 14th green in the third round, missed the ball, a lapse that cost him a stroke.

Craig Stadler set the pace on the opening day with a 64, the lowest first round on record.

The championship was the last to be conducted by Keith Mackenzie as Secretary of the Royal and Ancient GC.

1984 Severiano Ballesteros won again for the second time in five years, victory ending one of the most unsuccessful periods of his life. In a marvellous finish, he just got the better of Tom Watson and Bernhard Langer. He won by two strokes but, while he got a 3 at the 72nd hole, Watson hit his second shot against the wall at the 71st, the Road Hole, and took 5.

Ballesteros was the first St Andrews champion not to have at least one round that exceeded the par of 70. His rounds were 69, 68, 70, 69.

Friday's attendance of 34 897 was the highest for a single day in the history of the Open. The aggregate of 193 126 was also a record. More attended on the Friday than during the entire championship in 1964.

1985 Sandy Lyle's victory at Royal St George's was the first by a British golfer since Tony Jacklin in 1969. At the end of four days of unfriendly weather, birdies at the 14th and 15th in the final round gave him his chance and, though he took 5 at the 18th, his target was too much for David Graham and Bernhard Langer who were out last. In the end, Payne Stewart 'stole' second place with a final 68. Several others had their chances. Christy O'Connor Jr. monopolized the first day with a 64 which contained 7 consecutive birdies from the 4th.

Jack Nicklaus failed to qualify for the final two rounds for the first time since he made his first appearance at Troon in 1962.

1986 Turnberry's second Open turned out to be a case of Greg Norman all the way after a 74 on the first day which saw the strongest wind for the Open since 1961. The weather throughout was in distinct contrast to Turnberry's first Open in 1977 and, to make conditions harder, the rough was severe but Norman's 63 in the second round showed exactly what could be done.

From 4 shots behind, it shot him into a 2-stroke lead. A round that equalled the lowest individual round in the Open, it contained 8 birdies and an eagle as well as 3 putts on the last green. Having got caught in a nasty storm at the end of his third round, his lead was down to one but on Sunday he started well, holed a bunker shot on the 3rd and was never threatened.

For the first time, only one cut was made after 36 holes, the 54-hole cut was abolished. It was Norman's first major championship although he led in the 1986 Masters, US Open and US PGA as well at some stage.

Left: Alf Perry, Open champion 1935. (Illustrated London News)

The Illustrated SPORTING & DRAMATIC News

SATURDAY, MAY 18, 1929.
No. 2905.—Vol. CXXIII.
Registered for transmission in the United Kingdom.

PRICE ONE SHILLING.
Postage Rate: United Kingdom, 2d. Canada, 1½d.
Elsewhere abroad, 4½d.

Reginald Whitcombe, the professional of the Parkstone Club in Dorset, and youngest of the three golfing brothers, became Open champion of Great Britain in a phenomenal gale at Sandwich. It wrecked tents (left is exhibition stock being saved), blew balls past holes, put light-weight golfers at a disadvantage. Mr. Morrison describes play on this page

BAR

Above: Christy O'Connor, Jr, who broke the record for the Royal St George's course in the first round of the 1985 Open. (Benson and Hedges)

Top: After the gale was over—the Open champion emerged at Sandwich, 1938. (Illustrated London News)

Left: Walter Hagen, playing a left-handed shot from the wall when approaching the ninth hole on the last day of the Open championship at Muirfield. (Illustrated London News)

DETAILED RECORDS

Most victories
6, Harry Vardon, 1896–98–99–1903–11–14
5, James Braid, 1901–05–06–08–10; J H Taylor, 1894–95–
1900–09–13; Peter Thomson, 1954–55–56–58–65; Tom
Watson, 1975–77–80–82–83

Most times runner-up or joint runner-up
7, Jack Nicklaus, 1964–67–68–72–76–77–79
6, J H Taylor, 1896–1904–05–06–07–14

Oldest winner
Old Tom Morris, 46 years 99 days, 1867
Roberto de Vicenzo, 44 years 93 days, 1967

Youngest winner
Young Tom Morris, 17 years 5 months 8 days, 1868
Willie Auchterlonie, 21 years 24 days, 1893
Young Tom Morris, 21 years 5 months, 1872
Severiano Ballesteros, 22 years 3 months 12 days, 1979

Youngest and oldest competitor
John Ball, 14 years, 1878
Gene Sarazen, 71 years 4 months 13 days, 1973

Biggest margin of victory
13 strokes, Old Tom Morris, 1862
12 strokes, Young Tom Morris, 1870
 8 strokes, J H Taylor, 1900 and 1913; James Braid, 1908
 6 strokes, Bobby Jones, 1927; Walter Hagen, 1929; Arnold
Palmer, 1962; Johnny Miller, 1976

Lowest winning aggregates
268 (68, 70, 65, 65), Tom Watson, Turnberry, 1977
271 (68, 70, 64, 69), Tom Watson, Muirfield, 1980
275 (67, 68, 70, 70), Tom Watson, Royal Birkdale, 1983
276 (71, 69, 67, 69), Arnold Palmer, Troon, 1962
276 (68, 67, 71, 70), Tom Weiskopf, Troon, 1973
276 (72, 66, 67, 71), Bill Rogers, Sandwich, 1981
276 (69, 68, 70, 69), Severiano Ballesteros, St Andrews, 1984

Lowest aggregates by runner-up
269 (68, 70, 65, 66), Jack Nicklaus, Turnberry, 1977
275 (68, 67, 71, 69), Lee Trevino, Muirfield, 1980

Lowest aggregate by an amateur
283 (74, 70, 71, 68), Guy Wolstenholme, St Andrews, 1960

Lowest individual round by an amateur
66, Frank Stranahan, fourth round, Troon, 1950

Lowest individual round
63, Mark Hayes, second round, Turnberry, 1977;
Isao Aoki, third round, Muirfield, 1980;
Greg Norman, second round, Turnberry, 1986

Lowest first round
64, Craig Stadler, Royal Birkdale, 1983;
Christy O'Connor Jr, Royal St George's, 1985

Lowest second round
63, Mark Hayes, Turnberry, 1977;
Greg Norman, Turnberry, 1986

Lowest third round
63, Isao Aoki, Muirfield, 1980
64, Hubert Green and Tom Watson, Muirfield, 1980

Lowest fourth round
64, Graham Marsh, Royal Birkdale, 1983;
Severiano Ballesteros, Turnberry, 1986

Left-handed champion
Bob Charles, Royal Lytham, 1963

Bespectacled champions
None

Highest score on 72nd hole by a champion
6, Gary Player, Muirfield, 1959

First overseas winner
Arnaud Massy (France), 1907

First winner from America
Jock Hutchison, 1921

First American-born winner
Walter Hagen, 1922

Best placings on first three appearances
Arnold Palmer, 2nd, 1st, 1st, 1960–62

Play-offs
12, 1876 (tie but play-off never took place), 1883, 1889, 1896,
1911, 1921, 1933, 1949, 1958, 1963, 1970, 1975

By comparison, the US Open has had 27 play-offs in 29
fewer championships

Dazzling sequences
Bobby Jones played in only three Opens and won them all.
 Arnold Palmer's placings on his first three appearances
were 2nd, 1st, 1st

Lowest first 36 holes
132 (67, 65), Henry Cotton, Sandwich, 1934
133 (67, 66), Bobby Clampett, Royal Troon, 1982

Lowest second 36 holes
130 (65, 65), Tom Watson, Turnberry, 1977

Lowest first 54 holes
202 (68, 70, 64), Tom Watson, Muirfield, 1980
203 (68, 70, 65), Jack Nicklaus and Tom Watson, Turnberry,
1977

Lowest final 54 holes
200 (70, 65, 65), Tom Watson, Turnberry, 1977

Lowest 9 holes
28, Denis Durnian, first 9, Royal Birkdale, 1983
29, Peter Thomson and Tom Haliburton, first 9, Royal
Lytham, 1958; Tony Jacklin, first 9, St Andrews, 1970; Bill
Longmuir, first 9, Royal Lytham, 1979
30, Eric Brown, first 9, St Andrews, 1957; Eric Brown, second
9, Royal Lytham, 1958; Leopoldo Ruiz, first 9, Royal Lytham,
1958; Phil Rodgers, second 9, Muirfield, 1966; Jimmy
Kinsella, first 9, Royal Birkdale, 1971; Harry Bannerman,
first 9, Muirfield, 1972; Bert Yancey, first 9, Troon, 1973;
Christy O'Connor, Jr, first 9, Royal Birkdale, 1976; Arnold
Palmer, second 9, Turnberry, 1977; Jack Nicklaus, first 9,
Royal Lytham, 1979; Tom Watson, second 9, Muirfield, 1980;
Sam Torrance, first 9, St Andrews, 1984; Christy O'Connor,
Jr, first 9, Sandwich, 1985

Winner in three decades
J H Taylor, 1894, 1909, 1913
Harry Vardon, 1896, 1903, 1914
Gary Player, 1959, 1968, 1974

Biggest span between first and last victories
19 years, J H Taylor, 1894–1913
18 years, Harry Vardon, 1896–1914
15 years, Gary Player, 1959–74
14 years, Henry Cotton, 1934–48

Successive victories
4, Young Tom Morris, 1868–72. No championship in 1871
3, Jamie Anderson, 1877–79; Bob Ferguson, 1880–82; Peter
Thomson, 1954–56
2, Old Tom Morris, 1861–62; J H Taylor, 1894–95; Harry
Vardon, 1898–99; James Braid, 1905–06; Bobby Jones, 1926–
27; Walter Hagen, 1928–29; Bobby Locke, 1949–50; Arnold

Palmer, 1961–62; Lee Trevino, 1971–72; Tom Watson, 1982–83

Victories by amateurs
3, Bobby Jones, 1926–27–30
2, Harold Hilton, 1892–97
1, John Ball, 1890
Roger Wethered lost a play-off in 1921

Highest number of top three finishes
Jack Nicklaus 13: 1963–64–66–67–68–70–72–74–75–76–77–78–79
Harry Vardon 12: 1896–98–99–1900–01–02–03–06–11–12–13–14
J H Taylor 12: 1894–95–96–1900–01–04–05–06–07–09–13–14
James Braid 11: 1897–1900–01–02–04–05–06–08–09–10–12
Peter Thomson 8: 1952–53–54–55–56–57–58–65

Highest number of top six finishes
J H Taylor 18: 1894–95–96–98–99–1900–01–02–04–05–06–07–09–11–13–14–22–24
Jack Nicklaus 17: 1963–64–66–67–68–69–70–71–72–73–74–75–76–77–78–79–80
Harry Vardon 16
James Braid 16
Peter Thomson 12
Henry Cotton 9
Roberto de Vicenzo 9
Bobby Locke 8

Most consecutive top three finishes
Peter Thomson 7: 1952–58 (2nd, =2nd, 1st, 1st, 1st, 2nd, 1st).
In 1951 (his first Open) he finished =6th so in his first 8
Opens, he was never outside the top 6.
Jack Nicklaus 6: 1974–79
Harry Vardon 6: 1898–1903

Most consecutive top six finishes
Jack Nicklaus 15: 1966–80
James Braid 14: 1899–1912
Harry Vardon 9: 1896–1904

Highest number of rounds under 70
28, Jack Nicklaus
16, Tom Watson, Lee Trevino
15, Peter Thomson
13, Gary Player
12, Bobby Locke, Arnold Palmer, Severiano Ballesteros

First player to break 70
James Braid, 69, third round, Sandwich, 1904

First champion to break 70
Jack White, 69, fourth round, Sandwich, 1904

Outright leader after every round
Willie Auchterlonie, 1893; J H Taylor, 1894 and 1900; James Braid, 1908; Ted Ray, 1912; Bobby Jones, 1927; Gene Sarazen, 1932; Henry Cotton, 1934; Tom Weiskopf, 1973

Lowest round in a play-off
67, Bobby Locke, Sandwich, 1949
68, Peter Thomson, Royal Lytham, 1958; Bobby Locke, Sandwich, 1949

Record leads (since 1892)
After 18 holes:
4 strokes, James Braid, 1908; Bobby Jones, 1927; Henry Cotton, 1934; Christy O'Connor Jr, 1985
After 36 holes:
9 strokes, Henry Cotton, 1934
After 54 holes:
10 strokes, Henry Cotton, 1934
7 strokes, Tony Lema, 1964

6 strokes, James Braid, 1908
5 strokes, Arnold Palmer, 1962; Bill Rogers, 1981

Champions with each round lower than previous one
Jack White, 1904, Sandwich, 80, 75, 72, 69
James Braid, 1906, Muirfield, 77, 76, 74, 73
Ben Hogan, 1953, Carnoustie, 73, 71, 70, 68
Gary Player, 1959, Muirfield, 75, 71, 70, 68

Champion with four rounds the same
Densmore Shute, 1933, St Andrews, 73, 73, 73, 73 (excluding the play-off)

Biggest variation between rounds of a champion
14 strokes, Henry Cotton, 1934, second round 65, fourth round 79
11 strokes, Jack White, 1904, first round 80, fourth round 69; Greg Norman, 1986, first round 74, second round 63, third round 74

Biggest variation between two rounds
17 strokes, Jack Nicklaus, 1981, first round 83, second round 66; Ian Baker-Finch, 1986, first round 86, second round 69

Best comeback by champions
After 18 holes:
Harry Vardon, 1896, 11 strokes behind the leader
After 36 holes:
George Duncan, 1920, 13 strokes behind the leader
After 54 holes:
Jim Barnes, 1925, 5 strokes behind the leader

Champions with four rounds under 70
None
Arnold Palmer, 1962, Tom Watson, 1977 and 1980, and Severiano Ballesteros, 1984, had three rounds under 70
Of non-champions, Phil Rodgers, 1963, Jack Nicklaus, 1977, Lee Trevino, 1980, and Nick Faldo, 1984, had three rounds under 70

Best finishing round by a champion
65, Tom Watson, Turnberry, 1977
66, Johnny Miller, Royal Birkdale, 1976

Worst finishing round by a champion since 1920
79, Henry Cotton, Sandwich, 1934
78, Reg Whitcombe, Sandwich, 1938
77, Walter Hagen, Hoylake, 1924

Worst opening round by a champion since 1919
80, George Duncan, Deal, 1920 (he also had a second round of 80)
77, Walter Hagen, Hoylake, 1924

Best opening round by a champion
66, Peter Thomson, Royal Lytham, 1958
67, Henry Cotton, Sandwich, 1934; Tom Watson, Royal Birkdale, 1983

Champions with a 7 in final round
Bobby Jones, 1930 (8th Hoylake); Peter Thomson, 1955 (14th St Andrews); Bill Rogers, 1981 (7th Sandwich)

Biggest recovery in 18 holes by a champion
George Duncan, Deal, 1920, was 13 strokes behind the leader, Abe Mitchell, after 36 holes and level after 54

Most appearances on final day (since 1892)
30, J H Taylor
27, Harry Vardon, James Braid
26, Peter Thomson
24, Jack Nicklaus
23, Dai Rees
22, Henry Cotton

Championship with highest number of rounds under 70
68, Royal Birkdale, 1983

Championship since 1946 with the fewest rounds under 70

St Andrews, 1946; Hoylake, 1947; Portrush, 1951; Hoylake, 1956; Carnoustie, 1968. All had only two rounds under 70

Most holes in one

2, Charles H Ward, 8th, St Andrews, 1946; 13th, Muirfield, 1948

Most consecutive birdies

7, Christy O'Connor, Jr, Sandwich, 1985, first round holes 4–10 inclusive.

In 1983 Craig Stadler had 7 birdies in 9 holes from the 8th in his first round of 64. His score at Birkdale was 3, 3, 4, 4, 2, 4, 2, 4, 3

Lowest total for two consecutive holes

3, Jock Hutchison, St Andrews, 1921. He had a 1 at the 8th and a 2 at the 9th in his first round

Oldest player to hole in one

Gene Sarazen, 71 years 4 months, Troon, 1973

Champions who led after three rounds (1892–1986)

A total of 43 champions out of 83
Willie Auchterlonie, 1893; J H Taylor, 1894; Harry Vardon, 1899; J H Taylor, 1900; James Braid, 1901; Sandy Herd, 1902; Harry Vardon, 1903; James Braid, 1905; James Braid, 1908; J H Taylor, 1909; Harry Vardon, 1911; Ted Ray, 1912; J H Taylor, 1913; Arthur Havers, 1923; Bobby Jones, 1927; Walter Hagen, 1928; Walter Hagen, 1929; Gene Sarazen, 1932; Henry Cotton, 1934; Alf Perry, 1935; Reg Whitcombe, 1938; Henry Cotton, 1948; Max Faulkner, 1951; Peter Thomson, 1955; Peter Thomson, 1956; Bobby Locke, 1957; Peter Thomson, 1958; Kel Nagle, 1960; Arnold Palmer, 1961; Arnold Palmer, 1962; Bob Charles, 1963; Tony Lema, 1964; Peter Thomson, 1965; Roberto de Vicenzo, 1967; Tony Jacklin, 1969; Lee Trevino, 1971; Lee Trevino, 1972; Tom Weiskopf, 1973; Gary Player, 1974; Tom Watson, 1977; Tom Watson, 1980; Bill Rogers, 1981; Tom Watson, 1983; Greg Norman, 1986

Longest course

Carnoustie, 1968, 7252 yd

Courses used (1860–1986)

Prestwick, 24 (but not since 1925); St Andrews, 23; Muirfield, 12; Sandwich, 11; Hoylake, 10; Royal Lytham, 7; Musselburgh and Royal Birkdale, 6; Carnoustie, 5; Royal Troon, 5; Deal and Turnberry, 2; Royal Portrush and Prince's, 1

Lowest rounds on Open courses in an Open

Prestwick	69, Macdonald Smith, 1925
St Andrews	65, Neil Coles, 1970
Muirfield	63, Isao Aoki, 1980
Hoylake	67, Roberto de Vicenzo and Gary Player, 1967
Sandwich	64, Christy O'Connor, Jr, 1985
Royal Lytham and St Annes	65, Eric Brown and Leopoldo Ruiz, 1958; Christy O'Connor, Sr, 1969; Bill Longmuir and Severiano Ballesteros, 1979
Prince's	68, Arthur Havers, 1932
Royal Birkdale	64, Craig Stadler, 1983; Graham Marsh, 1983
Carnoustie	65, Jack Newton, 1975
Royal Troon	65, Jack Nicklaus, 1973
Turnberry	63, Mark Hayes, 1977; Greg Norman, 1986
Deal	71, George Duncan and Len Holland, 1920
Musselburgh	77, Willie Park, Jr, and Andrew Kirkaldy, 1889
Royal Portrush	68, Jimmy Adams, Charlie and Norman von Nida, 1951

Prize Money

Year	Total £	First Prize
1860	nil	nil
1863	10	nil
1864	16	6
1876	20	20
1889	22	8
1891	28.50	10
1892	110	(Amateur winner)
1893	100	30
1910	125	50
1920	225	75
1927	275	100
1930	400	100
1931	500	100
1946	1000	150
1949	1700	300
1953	2450	500
1954	3500	750
1955	3750	1000
1958	4850	1000
1959	5000	1000
1960	7000	1250
1961	8500	1400
1963	8500	1500
1965	10 000	1750
1966	15 000	2100

Year	Total £	First Prize
1968	20 000	3000
1969	30 000	4250
1970	40 000	5250
1971	45 000	5500
1972	50 000	5500
1975	75 000	7500
1977	100 000	10 000
1978	125 000	12 500
1979	155 000	15 500
1980	200 000	25 000
1981	200 000	25 000
1982	250 000	32 000
1983	300 000	40 000
1984	451 000	55 000
1985	530 000	65 000
1986	600 000	70 000
1987	651 000	75 000

Attendance

Year	Attendance
1962	37 098
1963	24 585
1964	35 954

Year	Attendance
1965	32 927
1966	40 182
1967	29 880
1968	51 819
1969	46 001
1970	81 593
1971	70 076
1972	84 746
1973	78 810
1974	92 796
1975	85 258
1976	92 021
1977	87 615
1978	125 271
1979	134 501
1980	131 610
1981	111 987
1982	133 299
1983	142 892
1984	193 126
1985	141 619
1986	134 203

The largest single day attendance was 39 755 on the Saturday of the 1984 championship.

RESULTS

*Amateur

1860 Prestwick
Willie Park, Musselburgh	174
Tom Morris Sr, Prestwick	176
Andrew Strath, St Andrews	180
Robert Andrew, Perth	191
George Brown, Blackheath	192
Charles Hunter, Prestwick St Nicholas	195

1861 Prestwick
Tom Morris Sr, Prestwick	163
Willie Park, Musselburgh	167
William Dow, Musselburgh	171
David Park, Musselburgh	172
Robert Andrew, Perth	175
Peter McEwan, Bruntsfield	178

1862 Prestwick
Tom Morris Sr, Prestwick	163
Willie Park, Musselburgh	176
Charles Hunter, Prestwick	178
William Dow, Musselburgh	181
*James Knight, Prestwick	186
*J F Johnston, Prestwick	208

1863 Prestwick
Willie Park, Musselburgh	168
Tom Morris Sr, Prestwick	170
David Park, Musselburgh	172
Andrew Strath, St Andrews	174
George Brown, St Andrews	176
Robert Andrew, Perth	178

1864 Prestwick
Tom Morris Sr, Prestwick	167
Andrew Strath, St Andrews	169
Robert Andrew, Perth	175
Willie Park, Musselburgh	177
William Dow, Musselburgh	181
William Strath, St Andrews	182

1865 Prestwick
Andrew Strath, St Andrews	162
Willie Park, Musselburgh	164
William Dow, Musselburgh	171
Robert Kirk, St Andrews	173
Tom Morris Sr, St Andrews	174
*William Doleman, Glasgow	178

1866 Prestwick
Willie Park, Musselburgh	169
David Park, Musselburgh	171
Robert Andrew, Perth	176
Tom Morris Sr, St Andrews	178
Robert Kirk, St Andrews	180
Andrew Smith, Prestwick	182
*William Doleman, Glasgow	182

1867 Prestwick
Tom Morris Sr, St Andrews	170
Willie Park, Musselburgh	172
Andrew Strath, St Andrews	174
Tom Morris Jr, St Andrews	175
Robert Kirk, St Andrews	177
William Doleman, Glasgow	178

1868 Prestwick
Tom Morris Jr, St Andrews	157
Robert Andrew, Perth	159

Willie Park, Musselburgh	162
Robert Kirk, St Andrews	171
John Allan, Westward Ho!	172
Tom Morris Sr, St Andrews	176

1869 Prestwick
Tom Morris Jr, St Andrews	154
Tom Morris Sr, St Andrews	157
*S Mure Fergusson, Royal and Ancient	165
Robert Kirk, St Andrews	168
David Strath, St Andrews	169
J Anderson, St Andrews	173

1870 Prestwick
Tom Morris Jr, St Andrews	149
Bob Kirk, Royal Blackheath	161
David Strath, St Andrews	161
Tom Morris Sr, St Andrews	162
*William Doleman, Musselburgh	171
Willie Park, Musselburgh	173

1871 No Competition

1872 Prestwick
Tom Morris Jr, St Andrews	166
David Strath, St Andrews	169
*William Doleman, Musselburgh	177
Tom Morris Sr, St Andrews	179
David Park, Musselburgh	179
Charlie Hunter, Prestwick	189

1873 St Andrews
Tom Kidd, St Andrews	179
Jamie Anderson, St Andrews	180
Tom Morris Jr, St Andrews	183
Bob Kirk, Royal Blackheath	183
David Strath, St Andrews	187
Walter Gourlay, St Andrews	188

1874 Musselburgh
Mungo Park, Musselburgh	159
Tom Morris Jr, St Andrews	161
George Paxton, Musselburgh	162
Bob Martin, St Andrews	164
Jamie Anderson, St Andrews	165
David Park, Musselburgh	166
W Thomson, Edinburgh	166

1875 Prestwick
Willie Park, Musselburgh	166
Bob Martin, St Andrews	168
Mungo Park, Musselburgh	171
Robert Ferguson, Musselburgh	172
James Rennie, St Andrews	177
David Strath, St Andrews	178

1876 St Andrews
Bob Martin, St Andrews	176
David Strath, North Berwick	176
(Martin was awarded the title when Strath refused to play-off)	
Willie Park, Musselburgh	183
Tom Morris Sr, St Andrews	185
W Thomson, Elie	185
Mungo Park, Musselburgh	185

1877 Musselburgh
Jamie Anderson, St Andrews	160
Bob Pringle, Musselburgh	162
Bob Ferguson, Musselburgh	164

William Cosegrove, Musselburgh	164
David Strath, North Berwick	166
William Brown, Musselburgh	166

1878 Prestwick
Jamie Anderson, St Andrews	157
Bob Kirk, St Andrews	159
J O F Morris, St Andrews	161
Bob Martin, St Andrews	165
John Ball, Hoylake	165
Willie Park, Musselburgh	166
William Cosegrove, Musselburgh	166

1879 St Andrews
Jamie Anderson, St Andrews	169
James Allan, Westward Ho!	172
Andrew Kirkaldy, St Andrews	172
George Paxton, Musselburgh	174
Tom Kidd, St Andrews	175
Bob Ferguson, Musselburgh	176

1880 Musselburgh
Bob Ferguson, Musselburgh	162
Peter Paxton, Musselburgh	167
Ned Cosgrove, Musselburgh	168
George Paxton, Musselburgh	169
Bob Pringle, Musselburgh	169
David Brown, Musselburgh	169

1881 Prestwick
Bob Ferguson, Musselburgh	170
Jamie Anderson, St Andrews	173
Ned Cosgrove, Musselburgh	177
Bob Martin, St Andrews	178
Tom Morris Sr, St Andrews	181
W Campbell, Musselburgh	181
Willie Park Jr, Musselburgh	181

1882 St Andrews
Bob Ferguson, Musselburgh	171
Willie Fernie, Dumfries	174
Jamie Anderson, St Andrews	175
John Kirkaldy, St Andrews	175
Bob Martin, St Andrews	175
*Fitz Boothby, St Andrews	175

1883 Musselburgh
Willie Fernie, Dumfries	159
Bob Ferguson, Musselburgh	159
(Fernie won play-off 158 to 159)	
W Brown, Musselburgh	160
Bob Pringle, Musselburgh	161
W Campbell, Musselburgh	163
George Paxton, Musselburgh	163

1884 Prestwick
Jack Simpson, Carnoustie	160
David Rollan, Elie	164
Willie Fernie, Felixstowe	164
Willie Campbell, Musselburgh	169
Willie Park Jr, Musselburgh	169
Ben Sayers, North Berwick	170

1885 St Andrews
Bob Martin, St Andrews	171
Archie Simpson, Carnoustie	172
David Ayton, St Andrews	173
Willie Fernie, Felixstowe	174
Willie Park Jr, Musselburgh	174
Bob Simpson, Carnoustie	174

1886 Musselburgh

David Brown, Musselburgh	157
Willie Campbell, Musselburgh	159
Ben Campbell, Musselburgh	160
Archie Simpson, Carnoustie	161
Willie Park Jr, Musselburgh	161
Thomas Gossett, Musselburgh	161
Bob Ferguson, Musselburgh	161

1887 Prestwick

Willie Park Jr, Musselburgh	161
Bob Martin, St Andrews	162
Willie Campbell, Prestwick	164
*Johnny Laidlay, Honourable Company	166
Ben Sayers, North Berwick	168
Archie Simpson, Carnoustie	168

1888 St Andrews

Jack Burns, Warwick	171
David Anderson Jr, St Andrews	172
Ben Sayers, North Berwick	172
Willie Campbell, Prestwick	174
*Leslie Balfour, Edinburgh	175
Andrew Kirkaldy, St Andrews	176
David Grant, North Berwick	176

Jim Barnes, born in Cornwall, but settled in America, won the US Open in 1921 and the British Open in 1925. (Illustrated London News)

*Amateur

1889 Musselburgh

Willie Park Jr, Musselburgh	155
Andrew Kirkaldy, St Andrews	155
(Play-off Park 158 to Kirkaldy 163)	
Ben Sayers, North Berwick	159
*Johnny Laidlay, Honourable Company	162
David Brown, Musselburgh	162
Willie Fernie, Troon	163

1890 Prestwick

*John Ball, Royal Liverpool	82 82 164
Willie Fernie, Troon	85 82 167
A Simpson, Carnoustie	85 82 167
Willie Park, Jr, Musselburgh	90 80 170
Andrew Kirkaldy, St Andrews	81 89 170
*Horace Hutchinson, Royal North Devon	87 85 172

1891 St Andrews

Hugh Kirkaldy, St Andrews	83 83 166
Willie Fernie, Troon	84 84 168
Andrew Kirkaldy, St Andrews	84 84 168
S Mure Fergusson, Royal and Ancient	86 84 170
W D More, Chester	84 87 171
Willie Park, Jr, Musselburgh	88 85 173

(From 1892 the competition was extended to 72 holes)

1892 Muirfield

*Harold Hilton, Royal Liverpool	78 81 72 74 305
*John Ball, Jr, Royal Liverpool	75 80 74 79 308
James Kirkaldy, St Andrews	77 83 73 75 308
Sandy Herd, Huddersfield	77 78 77 76 308
J Kay, Seaton Carew	82 78 74 78 312
Ben Sayers, North Berwick	80 76 81 75 312

1893 Prestwick

Willie Auchterlonie, St Andrews	78 81 81 82 322
*Johnny E Laidlay, Honourable Company	80 83 80 81 324
Sandy Herd, Huddersfield	82 81 78 84 325
Hugh Kirkaldy, St Andrews	83 79 82 82 326
Andrew Kirkaldy, St Andrews	85 82 82 77 326
J Kay, Seaton Carew	81 81 80 85 327
R Simpson, Carnoustie	81 81 80 85 327

1894 Sandwich

J H Taylor, Winchester	84 80 81 81 326
Douglas Rolland, Limpsfield	86 79 84 82 331
Andrew Kirkaldy, St Andrews	86 79 83 84 332
A Toogood, Eltham	84 85 82 82 333
Willie Fernie, Troon	84 84 86 80 334
Harry Vardon, Bury St Edmunds	86 86 82 80 334
Ben Sayers, North Berwick	85 81 84 84 334

1895 St Andrews

J H Taylor, Winchester	86 78 80 78 322
Sandy Herd, Huddersfield	82 77 82 85 326
Andrew Kirkaldy, St Andrews	81 83 84 84 332
G Pulford, Royal Liverpool	84 81 83 87 335
Archie Simpson, Aberdeen	88 85 78 85 336
Willie Fernie, Troon	86 79 86 86 337
David Brown, Malvern	81 89 83 84 337
David Anderson, Panmure	86 83 84 84 337

1896 Muirfield

Harry Vardon, Ganton	83 78 78 77 316
J H Taylor, Winchester	77 78 81 80 316
(Vardon won play-off 157 to 161)	
*Freddie G Tait, Black Watch	83 75 84 77 319
Willie Fernie, Troon	78 79 82 80 319
Sandy Herd, Huddersfield	72 84 79 85 320
James Braid, Romford	83 81 79 80 323

1897 Hoylake
*Harold H Hilton, Royal Liverpool	80	75	84	75	314
James Braid, Romford	80	74	82	79	315
*Freddie G Tait, Black Watch	79	79	80	79	317
G Pulford, Royal Liverpool	80	79	79	79	317
Sandy Herd, Huddersfield	78	81	79	80	318
Harry Vardon, Ganton	84	80	80	76	320

1898 Prestwick
Harry Vardon, Ganton	79	75	77	76	307
Willie Park, Musselburgh	76	75	78	79	308
*Harold H Hilton, Royal Liverpool	76	81	77	75	309
J H Taylor, Winchester	78	78	77	79	312
*Freddie G Tait, Black Watch	81	77	75	82	315
D Kinnell, Leven	80	77	79	80	316

1899 Sandwich
Harry Vardon, Ganton	76	76	81	77	310
Jack White, Seaford	79	79	82	75	315
Andrew Kirkaldy, St Andrews	81	79	82	77	319
J H Taylor, Mid-Surrey	77	76	83	84	320
James Braid, Romford	78	78	83	84	322
Willie Fernie, Troon	79	83	82	78	322

1900 St Andrews
J H Taylor, Mid-Surrey	79	77	78	75	309
Harry Vardon, Ganton	79	81	80	78	317
James Braid, Romford	82	81	80	79	322
Jack White, Seaford	80	81	82	80	323
Willie Auchterlonie, St Andrews	81	85	80	80	326
Willie Park, Jr, Musselburgh	80	83	81	84	328

1901 Muirfield
James Braid, Romford	79	76	74	80	309
Harry Vardon, Ganton	77	78	79	78	312
J H Taylor, Royal Mid-Surrey	79	83	74	77	313
*Harold H Hilton, Royal Liverpool	89	80	75	76	320
Sandy Herd, Huddersfield	87	81	81	76	325
Jack White, Seaford	82	82	80	82	326

1902 Hoylake
Sandy Herd, Huddersfield	77	76	73	81	307
Harry Vardon, South Herts	72	77	80	79	308
James Braid, Walton Heath	78	76	80	74	308
R Maxwell, Honourable Company	79	77	79	74	309
Tom Vardon, Ilkley	80	76	78	79	313
J H Taylor, Mid-Surrey	81	76	77	80	314
D Kinnell, Leven	78	80	79	77	314
*Harold Hilton, Royal Liverpool	79	76	81	78	314

1903 Prestwick
Harry Vardon, South Herts	73	77	72	78	300
Tom Vardon, Ilkley	76	81	75	74	306
Jack White, Sunningdale	77	78	74	79	308
Sandy Herd, Huddersfield	73	83	76	77	309
James Braid, Walton Heath	77	79	79	75	310
R Thompson, North Berwick	83	78	77	76	314
A H Scott, Elie	77	77	83	77	314

1904 Sandwich
Jack White, Sunningdale	80	75	72	69	296
James Braid, Walton Heath	77	80	69	71	297
J H Taylor, Mid-Surrey	77	78	74	68	297
Tom Vardon, Ilkley	77	77	75	72	301
Harry Vardon, South Herts	76	73	79	74	302
James Sherlock, Stoke Poges	83	71	78	77	309

1905 St Andrews
James Braid, Walton Heath	81	78	78	81	318
J H Taylor, Mid-Surrey	80	85	78	80	323
R Jones, Wimbledon	81	77	87	78	323
J Kinnell, Purley Downs	82	79	82	81	324
Arnaud Massy, Le Boulie	81	80	82	82	325
E Gray, Littlehampton	82	81	84	78	325

1906 Muirfield
James Braid, Walton Heath	77	76	74	73	300
J H Taylor, Mid-Surrey	77	72	75	80	304
Harry Vardon, South Herts	77	73	77	78	305
J Graham, Jr, Royal Liverpool	71	79	78	78	306
R Jones, Wimbledon Park	74	78	73	83	308
Arnaud Massy, La Boulie	76	80	76	78	310

1907 Hoylake
Arnaud Massy, La Boulie	76	81	78	77	312
J H Taylor, Mid-Surrey	79	79	76	80	314
Tom Vardon, Sandwich	81	81	80	75	317
G Pulford, Royal Liverpool	81	78	80	78	317
Ted Ray, Ganton	83	80	79	76	318
James Braid, Walton Heath	82	85	75	76	318

1908 Prestwick
James Braid, Walton Heath	70	72	77	72	291
Tom Ball, West Lancashire	76	73	76	74	299
Ted Ray, Ganton	79	71	75	76	301
Sandy Herd, Huddersfield	74	74	79	75	302
Harry Vardon, South Herts	79	78	74	75	306
D Kinnell, Prestwick St Nicholas	75	73	80	78	306

1909 Deal
J H Taylor, Mid-Surrey	74	73	74	74	295
James Braid, Walton Heath	79	73	73	74	299
Tom Ball, West Lancashire	74	75	76	76	301
C Johns, Southdown	72	76	79	75	302
T G Renouf, Manchester	76	78	76	73	303
Ted Ray, Ganton	77	76	76	75	304

1910 St Andrews
James Braid, Walton Heath	76	73	74	76	299
Sandy Herd, Huddersfield	78	74	75	76	303
George Duncan, Hanger Hill	73	77	71	83	304
Laurie Ayton, Bishops Stortford	78	76	75	77	306
Ted Ray, Ganton	76	77	74	81	308
W Smith, Mexico	77	71	80	80	308
J Robson, West Surrey	75	80	77	76	308

1911 Sandwich
Harry Vardon, South Herts	74	74	75	80	303
Arnaud Massy, St Jean de Lux	75	78	74	76	303
(Play-off; Massy conceded at the 35th hole)					
Harold Hilton, Royal Liverpool	76	74	78	76	304
Sandy Herd, Coombe Hill	77	73	76	78	304
Ted Ray, Ganton	76	72	79	78	305
James Braid, Walton Heath	78	75	74	78	305
J H Taylor, Mid-Surrey	72	76	78	79	305

1912 Muirfield
Ted Ray, Oxhey	71	73	76	75	295
Harry Vardon, South Herts	75	72	81	71	299
James Braid, Walton Heath	77	71	77	78	303
George Duncan, Hanger Hill	72	77	78	78	305
Laurie Ayton, Bishops Stortford	74	80	75	79	308
Sandy Herd, Coombe Hill	76	81	76	76	309

1913 Hoylake
J H Taylor, Mid-Surrey	73	75	77	79	304
Ted Ray, Oxhey	73	74	81	84	312
Harry Vardon, South Herts	79	75	79	80	313
M Moran, Dollymount	76	74	89	74	313
Johnny J McDermott, USA	75	80	77	83	315
T G Renouf, Manchester	75	78	84	78	315

1914 Prestwick
Harry Vardon, South Herts	73	77	78	78	306
J H Taylor, Mid-Surrey	74	78	74	83	309
H B Simpson, St Annes Old	77	80	78	75	310
Abe Mitchell, Sonning	76	78	79	79	312
Tom Williamson, Notts	75	79	79	79	312
R G Wilson, Croham Hurst	76	77	80	80	313

1920 Deal

George Duncan, Hanger Hill	80	80	71	72	303
Sandy Herd, Coombe Hill	72	81	77	75	305
Ted Ray, Oxhey	72	83	78	73	306
Abe Mitchell, North Foreland	74	73	84	76	307
Len Holland, Northampton	80	78	71	79	308
Jim Barnes, USA	79	74	77	79	309

1921 St Andrews

Jock Hutchison, USA	72	75	79	70	296
*Roger H Wethered, Royal and Ancient	78	75	72	71	296
(Hutchison won play-off 150 to 159)					
T Kerrigan, USA	74	80	72	72	298
Arthur G Havers, West Lancs	76	74	77	72	299
George Duncan, Hanger Hill	74	75	78	74	301

1922 Sandwich

Walter Hagen, USA	76	73	79	72	300
George Duncan, Hanger Hill	76	75	81	69	301
Jim Barnes, USA	75	76	77	73	301
Jock Hutchison, USA	79	74	73	76	302
Charles A Whitcombe, Dorchester	77	79	72	75	303
J H Taylor, Mid-Surrey	73	78	76	77	304

1923 Troon

Arthur G Havers, Coombe Hill	73	73	73	76	295
Walter Hagen, USA	76	71	74	75	296
Macdonald Smith, USA	80	73	69	75	297
Joe Kirkwood, Australia	72	79	69	78	298
Tom R Fernie, Turnberry	73	78	74	75	300
George Duncan, Hanger Hill	79	75	74	74	302
Charles A Whitcombe, Landsdowne	70	76	74	82	302

1924 Hoylake

Walter Hagen, USA	77	73	74	77	301
Ernest R Whitcombe, Came Down	77	70	77	78	302
Macdonald Smith, USA	76	74	77	77	304
F Ball, Langley Park	78	75	74	77	304
J H Taylor, Mid-Surrey	75	74	79	79	307
George Duncan, Hanger Hill	74	79	74	81	308
Aubrey Boomer, St Cloud, Paris	75	78	76	79	308

1925 Prestwick

Jim Barnes, USA	70	77	79	74	300
Archie Compston, North Manchester	76	75	75	75	301
Ted Ray, Oxhey	77	76	75	73	301
Macdonald Smith, USA	76	69	76	82	303
Abe Mitchell, Unattached	77	76	75	77	305

1926 Royal Lytham

*Bobby T Jones, Jr, USA	72	72	73	74	291
Al Watrous, USA	71	75	69	78	293
Walter Hagen, USA	68	77	74	76	295
George von Elm, USA	75	72	76	72	295
Abe Mitchell, Unattached	78	78	72	71	299
T Barber, Cavendish	77	73	78	71	299

1927 St Andrews

*Bobby T Jones, Jr, USA	68	72	73	72	285
Aubrey Boomer, St Cloud, Paris	76	70	73	72	291
Fred Robson, Cooden Beach	76	72	69	74	291
Joe Kirkwood, Australia	72	72	75	74	293
Ernest R Whitcombe, Bournemouth	74	73	73	73	293
Charles A Whitcombe, Crews Hill	74	76	71	75	296

1928 Sandwich

Walter Hagen, USA	75	73	72	72	292
Gene Sarazen, USA	72	76	73	73	294
Archie Compston, Unattached	75	74	73	73	295
Percy Alliss, Berlin	75	76	75	72	298
Fred Robson, Cooden Beach	79	73	73	73	298
Jose Jurado, Argentina	74	71	76	80	301
Aubrey Boomer, St Cloud, Paris	79	73	77	72	301
Jim Barnes, USA	81	73	76	71	301

1929 Muirfield

Walter Hagen, USA	75	67	75	75	292
John Farrell, USA	72	75	76	75	298
Leo Diegel, USA	71	69	82	77	299
Abe Mitchell, St Albans	72	72	78	78	300
Percy Alliss, Berlin	69	76	76	79	300
Bobby Cruickshank, USA	73	74	78	76	301

1930 Hoylake

*Bobby Jones, Jr, USA	70	72	74	75	291
Leo Diegel, USA	74	73	71	75	293
Macdonald Smith, USA	70	77	75	71	293
Fred Robson, Cooden Beach	71	72	78	75	296
Horton Smith, USA	72	73	78	73	296
Archie Compston, Coombe Hill	74	73	68	82	297
Jim Barnes, USA	71	77	72	77	297

1931 Carnoustie

Tommy D Armour, USA	73	75	77	71	296
Jose Jurado, Argentina	76	71	73	77	297
Percy Alliss, Berlin	74	78	73	73	298
Gene Sarazen, USA	74	76	75	73	298
Macdonald Smith, USA	75	77	71	76	299
John Farrell, USA	72	77	75	75	299

1932 Prince's

Gene Sarazen, USA	70	69	70	74	283
Macdonald Smith, USA	71	76	71	70	288
Arthur G Havers, Sandy Lodge	74	71	68	76	289
Charles A Whitcombe, Crews Hill	71	73	73	75	292
Percy Alliss, Beaconsfield	71	71	78	72	292
Alf H Padgham, Royal Ashdown Forest	76	72	74	70	292

1933 St Andrews

Densmore Shute, USA	73	73	73	73	292
Craig Wood, USA	77	72	68	75	292
Sid Easterbrook, Knowle	73	72	71	77	293
Gene Sarazen, USA	72	73	73	75	293
Leo Diegel, USA	75	70	71	77	293
Olin Dutra, USA	76	76	70	72	294

1934 Sandwich

Henry Cotton, Waterloo, Belgium	67	65	72	79	283
Sid F Brews, South Africa	76	71	70	71	288
Alf H Padgham, Sundridge Park	71	70	75	74	290
Macdonald Smith, USA	77	71	72	72	292
Joe Kirkwood, USA	74	69	71	78	292
Marcel Dallemagne, France	71	73	71	77	292

1935 Muirfield

Alf Perry, Leatherhead	69	75	67	72	283
Alf Padgham, Sundridge Park	70	72	74	71	287
Charles Whitcombe, Crews Hill	71	68	73	76	288
Bert Gad, Brand Hall	72	75	71	71	289
Lawson L Little, Presidio, USA	75	71	74	69	289
Henry Picard, Hershey, USA	72	73	72	75	292

1936 Hoylake

Alf H Padgham, Sundridge Park	73	72	71	71	287
Jimmy Adams, Romford	71	73	71	73	288
Henry Cotton, Waterloo, Belgium	73	72	70	74	289
Marcel Dallemagne, France	73	72	75	69	289
Percy Alliss, Leeds Municipal	74	72	74	71	291
T Green, Burnham Beeches	74	72	70	75	291
Gene Sarazen, USA	73	75	70	73	291

1937 Carnoustie

Henry Cotton, Ashridge	74	72	73	71	290
Reg A Whitcombe, Parkstone	72	70	74	76	292
Charles Lacey, USA	76	75	70	72	293
Charles A Whitcombe, Crews Hill	73	71	74	76	294
Byron Nelson, USA	75	76	71	74	296
Ed Dudley, USA	70	74	78	75	297

1938 Sandwich

Reg A Whitcombe, Parkstone	71	71	75	78	295
Jimmy Adams, Royal Liverpool	70	71	78	78	297
Henry Cotton, Ashridge	74	73	77	74	298
Alf H Padgham, Sundridge Park	74	72	75	82	303
Jack J Busson, Pannal	71	69	83	80	303
Dick Burton, Sale	71	69	78	85	303
Allan Dailey, Wanstead	73	72	80	78	303

1939 St Andrews

Dick Burton, Sale	70	72	77	71	290
Johnny Bulla, Chicago	77	71	71	73	292
Johnny Fallon, Huddersfield	71	73	71	79	294
Bill Shankland, Templenewsam	72	73	72	77	294
Alf Perry, Leatherhead	71	74	73	76	294
Reg A Whitcombe, Parkstone	71	75	74	74	294
Sam L King, Knole Park	74	72	75	73	294

1946 St Andrews

Sam Snead, USA	71	70	74	75	290
Bobby Locke, South Africa	69	74	75	76	294
Johnny Bulla, USA	71	72	72	79	294
Charlie H Ward, Little Aston	73	73	73	76	295
Henry Cotton, Royal Mid-Surrey	70	70	76	79	295
Dai J Rees, Hindhead	75	67	73	80	295
Norman von Nida, Australia	70	76	74	75	295

1947 Hoylake

Fred Daly, Balmoral, Belfast	73	70	78	72	293
Reg W Horne, Hendon	77	74	72	71	294
*Frank R Stranahan, USA	71	79	72	72	294
Bill Shankland, Templenewsam	76	74	75	70	295
Dick Burton, Coombe Hill	77	71	77	71	296
Charlie Ward, Little Aston	76	73	76	72	297
Sam L King, Wildernesse	75	72	77	73	297
Arthur Lees, Dore and Totley	75	74	72	76	297
Johnny Bulla, USA	80	72	74	71	297
Henry Cotton, Royal Mid-Surrey	69	78	74	76	297
Norman von Nida, Australia	74	76	71	76	297

1948 Muirfield

Henry Cotton, Royal Mid-Surrey	71	66	75	72	284
Fred Daly, Balmoral	72	71	73	73	289
Norman von Nida, Australia	71	72	76	71	290
Roberto de Vicenzo, Argentina	70	73	72	75	290
Jack Hargreaves, Sutton Coldfield	76	68	73	73	290
Charlie Ward, Little Aston	69	72	75	74	290

1949 Sandwich

Bobby Locke, South Africa	69	76	68	70	283
Harry Bradshaw, Kilcroney, Eire	68	77	68	70	283
(Locke won play-off 135 to 147; Locke's rounds were 67, 68)					
Roberto de Vicenzo, Argentina	68	75	73	69	285
Sam King, Knole Park	71	69	74	72	286
Charlie Ward, Little Aston	73	71	70	72	286
Arthur Lees, Dore and Totley	74	70	72	71	287
Max Faulkner, Royal Mid-Surrey	71	71	71	74	287

1950 Troon

Bobby Locke, South Africa	69	72	70	68	279
Roberto de Vicenzo, Argentina	72	71	68	70	281
Fred Daly, Balmoral, Belfast	75	72	69	66	282
Dai J Rees, South Herts	71	68	72	71	282
E Moore, South Africa	74	68	73	68	283
Max Faulkner, Royal Mid-Surrey	72	70	70	71	283

1951 Royal Portrush

Max Faulkner, Unattached	71	70	70	74	285
Tony Cerda, Argentina	74	72	71	70	287
Charlie Ward, Little Aston	75	73	74	68	290
Fred Daly, Balmoral	74	70	75	73	292
Jimmy Adams, Wentworth	68	77	75	72	292
Bobby Locke, South Africa	71	74	74	74	293
Bill Shankland, Templenewsam	73	76	72	72	293

Norman Sutton, Leigh	73	70	74	76	293
Harry Weetman, Croham Hurst	73	71	75	74	293
Peter W Thomson, Australia	70	75	73	75	293

1952 Royal Lytham

Bobby Locke, South Africa	69	71	74	73	287
Peter W Thomson, Australia	68	73	77	70	288
Fred Daly, Balmoral	67	69	77	76	289
Henry Cotton, Royal Mid-Surrey	75	74	74	71	294
Tony Cerda, Argentina	73	73	76	73	295
Sam L King, Knole Park	71	74	74	76	295

1953 Carnoustie

Ben Hogan, USA	73	71	70	68	282
*Frank R Stranahan, USA	70	74	73	69	286
Dai J Rees, South Herts	72	70	73	71	286
Peter W Thomson, Australia	72	72	71	71	286
Tony Cerda, Argentina	75	71	69	71	286
Roberto de Vicenzo, Argentina	72	71	71	73	287

1954 Royal Birkdale

Peter W Thomson, Australia	72	71	69	71	283
Sid S Scott, Carlisle City	76	67	69	72	284
Dai J Rees, South Herts	72	71	69	72	284
Bobby Locke, South Africa	74	71	69	70	284
Jimmy Adams, Royal Mid-Surrey	73	75	69	69	286
Tony Cerda, Argentina	71	71	73	71	286
J Turnesa, USA	72	72	71	71	286

1955 St Andrews

Peter W Thomson, Australia	71	68	70	72	281
Johny Fallon, Huddersfield	73	67	73	70	283
Frank Jowle, Edgbaston	70	71	69	74	284
Bobby Locke, South Africa	74	69	70	72	285
Tony Cerda, Argentina	73	71	71	71	286
Ken Bousfield, Coombe Hill	71	75	70	70	286
Harry Weetman, Croham Hurst	71	71	70	74	286
Bernard J Hunt, Hartsbourne	70	71	74	71	286
Flory van Donck, Belgium	71	72	71	72	286

1956 Hoylake

Peter W Thomson, Australia	70	70	72	74	286
Flory van Donck, Belgium	71	74	70	74	289
Roberto de Vicenzo, Mexico	71	70	79	70	290
Gary Player, South Africa	71	76	73	71	291
John Panton, Glenbervie	74	76	72	70	292
Henry Cotton, Temple	72	76	71	74	293
E Bertolino, Argentina	69	72	76	76	293

1957 St Andrews

Bobby Locke, South Africa	69	72	68	70	279
Peter W Thomson, Australia	73	69	70	70	282
Eric C Brown, Buchanan Castle	67	72	73	71	283
Angel Miguel, Spain	72	72	69	72	285
David C Thomas, Sudbury	72	74	70	70	286
Tom B Haliburton, Wentworth	72	73	68	73	286
*W Dick Smith, Prestwick	71	72	72	71	286
Flory van Donck, Belgium	72	68	74	72	286

1958 Royal Lytham

Peter W Thomson, Australia	66	72	67	73	278
David C Thomas, Sudbury	70	68	69	71	278
(Thomson won play-off 139 to 143)					
Eric C Brown, Buchanan Castle	73	70	65	71	279
Christy O'Connor, Killarney	67	68	73	71	279
Flory van Donck, Belgium	70	70	67	74	281
Leopoldo Ruiz, Argentina	71	65	72	73	281

1959 Muirfield

Gary Player, South Africa	75	71	70	68	284
Flory van Donck, Belgium	70	70	73	73	286
Fred Bullock, Prestwick St Ninians	68	70	74	74	286
Sid S Scott, Roehampton	73	70	73	71	287
Christy O'Connor, Royal Dublin	73	74	72	69	288

*Reid R Jack, Dullatur	71	75	68	74	288
Sam L King, Knole Park	70	74	68	76	288
John Panton, Glenbervie	72	72	71	73	288

1960 St Andrews

Kel D G Nagle, Australia	69	67	71	71	278
Arnold Palmer, USA	70	71	70	68	279
Bernard J Hunt, Hartsbourne	72	73	71	66	282
Harold R Henning, South Africa	72	72	69	69	282
Roberto de Vicenzo, Argentina	67	67	75	73	282
*Guy B Wolstenholme, Sunningdale	74	70	71	68	283

1961 Royal Birkdale

Arnold Palmer, USA	70	73	69	72	284
Dai J Rees, South Herts	68	74	71	72	285
Christy O'Connor, Royal Dublin	71	77	67	73	288
Neil C Coles, Coombe Hill	70	77	69	72	288
Eric C Brown, Unattached	73	76	70	70	289
Kel D G Nagle, Australia	68	75	75	71	289

1962 Troon

Arnold Palmer, USA	71	69	67	69	276
Kel D G Nagle, Australia	71	71	70	70	282
Brian Huggett, Romford	75	71	74	69	289
Phil Rodgers, USA	75	70	72	72	289
Bob Charles, NZ	75	70	70	75	290
Sam Snead, USA	76	73	72	71	292
Peter W Thomson, Australia	70	77	75	70	292

1963 Royal Lytham

Bob Charles, NZ	68	72	66	71	277
Phil Rodgers, USA	67	68	73	69	277
(Charles won play-off 140 to 148)					
Jack Nicklaus, USA	71	67	70	70	278
Kel D G Nagle, Australia	69	70	73	71	283
Peter W Thomson, Australia	67	69	71	78	285
Christy O'Connor, Royal Dublin	74	68	76	68	286

1964 St Andrews

Tony Lema, USA	73	68	68	70	279
Jack Nicklaus, USA	76	74	66	68	284
Roberto de Vicenzo, Argentina	76	72	70	67	285
Bernard J Hunt, Hartsbourne	73	74	70	70	287
Bruce Devlin, Australia	72	72	73	73	290
Christy O'Connor, Royal Dublin	71	73	74	73	291
Harry Weetman, Selsdon Park	72	71	75	73	291

1965 Royal Birkdale

Peter W Thomson, Australia	74	68	72	71	285
Christy O'Connor, Royal Dublin	69	73	74	71	287
Brian Huggett, Romford	73	68	76	70	287
Roberto de Vicenzo, Argentina	74	69	73	72	288
Kel D G Nagle, Australia	74	70	73	72	289
Tony Lema, USA	68	72	75	74	289
Bernard J Hunt, Hartsbourne	74	74	70	71	289

1966 Muirfield

Jack Nicklaus, USA	70	67	75	70	282
David C Thomas, Dunham Forest	72	73	69	69	283
Doug Sanders, USA	71	70	72	70	283
Gary Player, South Africa	72	74	71	69	286
Bruce Devlin, Australia	73	69	74	70	286
Kel D G Nagle, Australia	72	68	76	70	286
Phil Rodgers, USA	74	66	70	76	286

1967 Hoylake

Roberto de Vicenzo, Argentina	70	71	67	70	278
Jack Nicklaus, USA	71	69	71	69	280
Clive A Clark, Sunningdale	70	73	69	72	284
Gary Player, South Africa	72	71	67	74	284
Tony Jacklin, Potters Bar	73	69	73	70	285
Sebastian Miguel, Spain	72	74	68	72	286
Harold Henning, South Africa	74	70	71	71	286

1968 Carnoustie

Gary Player, South Africa	74	71	71	73	289
Jack Nicklaus, USA	76	69	73	73	291
Bob J Charles, NZ	72	72	71	76	291
Billy Casper, USA	72	68	74	78	292
Maurice Bembridge, Little Aston	71	75	73	74	293
Brian Barnes, Burnham & Berrow	70	74	80	71	295
Neil C Coles, Coombe Hill	75	76	71	73	295
Gay Brewer, USA	74	73	72	76	295

1969 Royal Lytham

Tony Jacklin, Potters Bar	68	70	70	72	280
Bob J Charles, NZ	66	69	75	72	282
Peter W Thomson, Australia	71	70	70	72	283
Roberto de Vicenzo, Argentina	72	73	66	72	283
Christy O'Connor, Royal Dublin	71	65	74	74	284
Jack Nicklaus, USA	75	70	68	72	285
Denis M Love, Jr, USA	70	73	71	71	285

1970 St Andrews

Jack Nicklaus, USA	68	69	73	73	283
Doug Sanders, USA	68	71	71	73	283
(Nicklaus won play-off 72 to 73)					
Harold Henning, South Africa	67	72	73	73	285
Lee Trevino, USA	68	68	72	77	285
Tony Jacklin, Potters Bar	67	70	73	76	286
Neil C Coles, Coombe Hill	65	74	72	76	287
Peter A Oosterhuis, Dulwich and Sydenham	73	69	69	76	287

1971 Royal Birkdale

Lee Trevino, USA	69	70	69	70	278
Lu Liang Huan, Taiwan	70	70	69	70	279
Tony Jacklin, Potters Bar	69	70	70	71	280
Craig de Foy, Coombe Hill	72	72	68	69	281
Jack Nicklaus, USA	71	71	72	69	283
Charles Coody, USA	74	71	70	68	283

1972 Muirfield

Lee Trevino, USA	71	70	66	71	278
Jack Nicklaus, USA	70	72	71	66	279
Tony Jacklin, Potters Bar	69	72	67	72	280
Doug Sanders, USA	71	71	69	70	281
Brian W Barnes, Fairway DR	71	72	69	71	283
Gary Player, South Africa	71	71	76	67	285

1973 Troon

Tom Weiskopf, USA	68	67	71	70	276
Neil C Coles, Holiday Inns	71	72	70	66	279
Johnny Miller, USA	70	68	69	72	279
Jack Nicklaus, USA	69	70	76	65	280
Bert Yancey, USA	69	69	73	70	281
Peter J Butler, Golf Domes	71	72	74	69	286

1974 Royal Lytham

Gary Player, South Africa	69	68	75	70	282
Peter Oosterhuis, Pacific Harbour	71	71	73	71	286
Jack Nicklaus, USA	74	72	70	71	287
Hubert M Green, USA	71	74	72	71	288
Danny Edwards, USA	70	73	76	73	292
Lu Liang Huan, Taiwan	72	72	75	73	292

1975 Carnoustie

Tom Watson, USA	71	67	69	72	279
Jack Newton, Australia	69	71	65	74	279
(Watson won play-off 71 to 72)					
Bobby Cole, South Africa	72	66	66	76	280
Jack Nicklaus, USA	69	71	68	72	280
Johnny Miller, USA	71	69	66	74	280
Graham Marsh, Australia	72	67	71	71	281

1976 Royal Birkdale

Johnny Miller, USA	72	68	73	66	279
Jack Nicklaus, USA	74	70	72	69	285
Severiano Ballesteros, Spain	69	69	73	74	285

Raymond Floyd, USA	76 67 73 70	286
Mark James, Burghley Park	76 72 74 66	288
Hubert Green, USA	72 70 78 68	288
Christy O'Connor, Jr, Shannon	69 73 75 71	288
Tom Kite, USA	70 74 73 71	288
Tommy A Horton, Royal Jersey	74 69 72 73	288

1977 Turnberry

Tom Watson, USA	68 70 65 65	268
Jack Nicklaus, USA	68 70 65 66	269
Hubert Green, USA	72 66 74 67	279
Lee Trevino, USA	68 70 72 70	280
Ben Crenshaw, USA	71 69 66 75	281
George Burns, USA	70 70 72 69	281

1978 St Andrews

Jack Nicklaus, USA	71 72 69 69	281
Simon Owen, NZ	70 75 67 71	283
Ben Crenshaw, USA	70 69 73 71	283
Raymond Floyd, USA	69 75 71 68	283
Tom Kite, USA	72 69 72 70	283
Peter Oosterhuis, GB	72 70 69 73	284

1979 Royal Lytham

Severiano Ballesteros, Spain	73 65 75 70	283
Jack Nicklaus, USA	72 69 73 72	286
Ben Crenshaw, USA	72 71 72 71	286
Mark James, Burghley Park	76 69 69 73	287
Rodger Davis, Australia	75 70 70 73	288
Hale Irwin, USA	68 68 75 78	289

1980 Muirfield

Tom Watson, USA	68 70 64 69	271
Lee Trevino, USA	68 67 71 69	275
Ben Crenshaw, USA	70 70 68 69	277
Jack Nicklaus, USA	73 67 71 69	280
Carl Mason, Unattached	72 69 70 69	280

1981 Sandwich

Bill Rogers, USA	72 66 67 71	276
Bernhard Langer, West Germany	73 67 70 70	280
Mark James, Otley	72 70 68 73	283
Raymond Floyd, USA	74 70 69 70	283
Sam Torrance, Caledonian Hotel	72 69 73 70	284
Bruce Leitzke, USA	76 69 71 69	285
Manuel Pinero, Spain	73 74 68 70	285

1982 Troon

Tom Watson, USA	69 71 74 70	284
Peter Oosterhuis, GB	74 67 74 70	285
Nick Price, South Africa	69 69 74 73	285
Nick Faldo, Glynwed Ltd	73 73 71 69	286
Des Smyth, EAL Tubes	70 69 74 73	286
Tom Purtzer, USA	76 66 75 69	286
Massy Kuramoto, Japan	71 73 71 71	286

1983 Royal Birkdale

Tom Watson, USA	67 68 70 70	275
Hale Irwin, USA	69 68 72 67	276
Andy Bean, USA	70 69 70 67	276
Graham Marsh, Australia	69 70 74 64	277
Lee Trevino, USA	69 66 73 70	278
Severiano Ballesteros, Spain	71 71 69 68	279
Harold Henning, South Africa	71 69 70 69	279

1984 St Andrews

Severiano Ballesteros, Spain	69 68 70 69	276
Bernhard Langer, West Germany	71 68 68 71	278
Tom Watson, USA	71 68 66 73	278
Fred Couples, USA	70 69 74 68	281
Lanny Wadkins, USA	70 69 73 69	281
Greg Norman, Australia	67 74 74 67	282
Nick Faldo, Glynwed Int.	69 68 76 69	282

1985 Sandwich

Sandy Lyle, Scotland	68 71 73 70	282
Payne Stewart, USA	70 75 70 68	283
Jose Rivero, Spain	74 72 70 68	284
Christy O'Connor Jr, Ireland	64 76 72 72	284
Mark O'Meara, USA	70 72 70 72	284
David Graham, Australia	68 71 70 75	284
Bernhard Langer, West Germany	72 69 68 75	284

1986 Turnberry

Greg Norman, Australia	74 63 74 69	280
Gordon J Brand, England	71 68 75 71	285
Bernhard Langer, West Germany	72 70 76 68	286
Ian Woosnam, Wales	70 74 70 72	286
Nick Faldo, England	71 70 76 70	287
Severiano Ballesteros, Spain	76 75 73 64	288
Gary Koch, USA	73 72 72 71	288

Historic return to Troon for Gene Sarazen, 1973. Here he chats to Fred Daly before the start of the round in which he holed in one at the 8th, The Postage Stamp. (Allsport)

US Open

First played 1895

The United States Open and the British Open championships are the two most important in the world. Although junior by 35 years and dominated in its early stages by the British professionals who settled in America, the US Open soon reached its exalted position because it is the title which American golfers covet most.

This is primarily for prestige, but increasingly because of the benefits which accrue from being champion. The championship has always been run by the United States Golf Association whose organization has kept pace with the development of championship golf. The modern entry of about 4500 has to be whittled down to more manageable proportions and then assembled at the appointed club where arrangements are made two or three years ahead.

The preparation of the course itself has become a matter of almost scientific detail: the fairways cut to the nearest millimetre; the rough grown to deter much in the way of a recovery and the greens geared to speed and treachery.

Frequently there are complaints that these things are overdone but, unlike the British Open which has been confined to 14 courses since 1860, the US Open has been housed at 47 clubs since 1895 when it was launched on a 9-hole course at Newport, Rhode Island.

It has been suggested that USGA develop a smaller rota of championship courses but, with such a big country, they rightly feel a responsibility to move it around and the idea has never really caught on. New courses of quality are always in the making and of the last fourteen US Opens four courses were played for the first time. These included the Atlanta Athletic Club in 1976, the first time the US Open had been held in the South.

So the mixture has become many of the old, traditional favourites and several new creations. It is a mixture that is readily acceptable, but there is a feeling that some over-preparation of courses has led to one or two surprising winners in recent years.

Right: Harry Vardon. (Dunhill Ltd)

Below: Francis Ouimet who caused such a stir by winning the 1913 US Open after a tie with the great English professionals, Harry Vardon and Ted Ray. (BBC Hulton Picture Library)

Harry Vardon

MILESTONES

1895 First Open held at Newport, Rhode Island, on 4 October, during the same week and on the same 9-hole course as the first United States Amateur championship. The championships were arranged for September but postponed because of a clash with the America's Cup yacht races.

There were five money prizes of $150, $100, $50, $25 and $10. Ten professionals and one amateur took part, the winner being Horace Rawlins, an English professional, with a score of 173 (91, 82).

1896 Second Open held at Shinnecock Hills on Long Island. Thirty-five players took part but it was again a sideshow to the US Amateur. The course measured only 4423 yd, the shortest in US Open history. Jim Foulis, a Scottish professional, became champion with 152 (78, 74). His 74 was not beaten for seven years and never with a gutty ball.

1898 The Open and Amateur championships were played separately and on different courses. The Open was also extended to 72 holes and won by Fred Herd at the Myopia Hunt Club, a 9-hole course in those days.

1899 Willie Smith's winning margin was 11 strokes, one which has never been equalled. Total purse increased to $650.

1900 The title went abroad for the first time although earlier winners had all been British. Harry Vardon beat J H Taylor by 2 strokes, his total of 313 including a stroke on the final green when he stabbed carelessly at the ball on a short putt and missed altogether.

1901 First play-off. Willie Anderson, the winner, and Alex Smith tied.

1902 The new champion, Laurie Auchterlonie, became the first man to break 80 in all four rounds. The feat was said to owe a lot to the new Haskell rubber-cored ball.

New record entry of 90, prize-money totalling $970.

1903 Willie Anderson became first man to win twice. His first round of 73 was a new low, but he needed another play-off before defeating David Brown with 82 to 84.

1904 Willie Anderson won twice in succession, his third win in all, but his first without a play-of. His 72 in the last round beat his own low round record.

1905 Willie Anderson set a record of three wins in a row, one which has never been equalled. His total of four victories was not equalled for 25 years, Bobby Jones's feat being later equalled by Ben Hogan and Jack Nicklaus.

1906 Anderson's run ended by Alex Smith whose total of 295 was the lowest to date in either the US Open or the British Open. The total purse was $900 and the first prize $300.

1908 Fred McLeod, only 108 lb, was the smallest winner ever. The championship marked the Myopia Hunt Club's last year as host.

1909 First round under 70. Dave Hunter had 68 in the opening round, Tom McNamara 69 in the second. George Sargent's 290 set record low aggregate.

1910 First three-way play-off, the participants being Alex Smith (the winner), Johnny McDermott and Smith's brother, Macdonald.

1911 Johnny McDermott became America's first home-bred champion.

1912 McDermott's second win. Tom McNamara had new final round record of 69 but McDermott was the first to be under par for the four rounds in total. Use of par adopted.

1913 The Open which changed the course of history. It ended British playing dominance. Story-book victory for Francis Ouimet, a 20-year-old coachman's son living across the street from the Country Club, Brookline. Ouimet defeated Harry Vardon and Ted Ray, the highly experienced English professionals, in a play-off. First victory by an amateur.

A total of 165 entries required the first qualifying round to be played. Half the field played two rounds on Tuesday and the other half two rounds on Wednesday, the low 32 and ties on each day making up the championship field on Thursday and Friday.

1914 Walter Hagen led every round and recorded his first victory at Midlothian CC. Chick Evans, needing 2 to tie on the last hole, hit the cup with his pitch and bounced out.

1915 Jerome Travers became the second amateur to win. He played the last 6 holes in 1 under par to beat Tom McNamara by one stroke.

1916 The crown taken over by another amateur, Chick Evans (1890–1979) the only time amateurs have won back to back. Evans was the third amateur winner in four years. His total of 286 meant he was the second man to beat par; it was a total which was not beaten for 20 years. Jock Hutchison's closing 68 bettered the low final round record. Evans won US Amateur three months later, the first man to win both titles the same year.

Prize-money increased to $1200 with $500 for leading professional.

1917–18 No championships.

1919 Hagen's second victory. He played the last 6 holes in 1 under 4s to tie Mike Brady and then beat him in a play-off, marked by several controversies over the Rules.

Willie Chisholm took 18 on the 185 yd 8th hole at Brae Burn in the first round.

Total prize-money $1745 with prizes for twenty players. Play extended to three days, one round on each of the first two days and two rounds on the final day.

1920 Second victory by an Englishman and the last for 50 years. Ted Ray was the winner, Harry Vardon playing the last 7 holes in a gale at Inverness in level fives having led by five. Ray remains oldest winner at 43.

Bobby Jones's first appearance at 18. Tied eighth.

Two-day playing format restored; record entry of 265. Also first time anywhere in a major championship that the professionals were allowed to use the full clubhouse facilities.

1921 The 25th championship won by Jim Barnes. Led after every round and won by 9 strokes. Trophy presented by President of the United States, Warren G Harding.

1922 Victory for Gene Sarazen, aged 20. Finished with a birdie for 68 and a 1-stroke victory. First winner to break 70 in last round.

Record entry of 323, the qualifying at the scene of the championship being extended to three days.

Gate money charged for the first time.

1923 Dawn of the Bobby Jones era. Victory after a play-off with Bobby Cruickshank. On the 72nd hole, Jones had a 6 and Cruickshank a birdie.

Record entry of 360.

1924 First elements of sectional qualifying introduced. Use of the steel-shafted putter allowed for first time. Victory for American-based Englishman Cyril Walker.

1925 Bobby Jones beaten in play-off by Willie Macfarlane; or rather after two play-offs, the first having ended even. Macfarlane, a Scotsman, representing Oak Ridge, was the first US Open champion who wore spectacles. His second round of 67 was a new low.

1926 Bobby Jones became first person to win British and US Opens in the same year.

Championship again extended to three days. Record entry of 694. Prize-money increased to $2145, the first 20 professionals winning money.

1927 Tommy Armour defeated Harry Cooper in a play-off, Armour holing a 10 ft birdie putt on the 72nd green and Cooper taking 3 putts.

Record entry of 898.

1928 Johnny Farrell defeated Bobby Jones in the first play-off over 36 holes. It was Jones's second play-off defeat in four years.

Entry over 1000 for the first time.

1929 Bobby Jones defeated Al Espinosa in a play-off despite having two 7s in his final round and then holing a 12 ft putt to tie.

Third play-off in a row.

Prize-money $5000, the leading professional prize $1000.

1930 Third leg of Bobby Jones's Grand Slam. His third-round 68 at Merion was his lowest in the Open and his total of 287 marking only the third time that par had been broken over four rounds. Entry of 1177 and the first championship to be played with the 1.62 in ball.

1931 Longest championship on record, a 72-hole play-off (36 holes twice) being necessary to separate Billy Burke, the winner, and George von Elm.

1932 Gene Sarazen added the US title to the British title he had won only a week or two previously. It was his second US victory but he played the last 28 holes in 100 strokes in order to do so. On the ninth tee of the third round, he was 7 strokes behind the leader.

His total of 286 equalled that set by Chick Evans in 1916, and his final round of 66 broke the individual record for any round by a winner.

1933 Victory for Johnny Goodman, the fifth and last by an amateur.

1934 The winner, Olin Dutra, made up an 8-stroke deficit over the last two rounds, a record matched by Arnold Palmer in 1960.

1935 Victory for unknown Sam Parks. None of the 20 leaders broke 75 in the final round at Oakmont.

1936 Final round of 67 gave Tony Manero a new record total of 282.

First appearance of Ben Hogan who failed to qualify for last 36 holes.

1937 Manero's record broken by Ralph Guldahl with 281. He beat Sam Snead, playing his first Open, by 2 strokes. In all, five players were under par for the four rounds.

1938 Guldahl became fourth player to win in successive years, but a new record for a single hole was also set. Ray Ainsley, who became a hero overnight, took 19 on the par-4 16th at Cherry

Ted Ray, the last British winner of the US Open until Tony Jacklin in 1970. Ray's victory in 1920 was some consolation for losing to Francis Ouimet in 1913. (Illustrated London News)

Hills in the second round. Most of these were taken in a swift-moving creek bordering the green. When finally he did get it out a little girl turned to her mother and said, 'Mummy, it must be dead now because the man has quit hitting at it.' Prize-money increased to $6000.

1939 Byron Nelson's year, but only after a three-way play-off and Sam Snead had come to the 72nd hole at the Philadelphia CC needing as it transpired later a par-5 to win. He took 8 and finished fifth but he was out early and might have adopted different tactics had he not been enthusiastic to set a hot pace. In the play-off, Densmore Shute was eliminated after 18 holes, but Nelson and Craig Wood, who both had 68s, had to play a second 18 holes, Nelson winning with a 70 to Wood's 73. At the 4th hole of the second play-off, Nelson holed a full 1 iron for an eagle 2.

1940 Gene Sarazen made a bid to win the title 18 years after his first victory, but he lost a play-off to Lawson Little.

Six players were disqualified for starting their final round ahead of their starting time in an attempt to beat an impending storm. One of them, Ed Oliver, made an 'unofficial' total of 287, the same as Little and Sarazen.

1941 Craig Wood won with 284. He considered withdrawing before the championship with a back injury which necessitated wearing a corset.

1942–45 No championships.

1946 Another three-way tie, war hero Lloyd Mangrum defeating Byron Nelson and Vic Ghezzi in a play-off. All three tied the first play-off with 72s but, surviving a thunderstorm, Mangrum, 3 behind Ghezzi and 2 behind Nelson with 6 holes left won with 72 to two 73s.

Prize-money increased to $8000. First prize $1500.

Billy Casper, US Open champion in 1959 and 1966. (Benson and Hedges)

1947 Victory for Lew Worsham, but another of Sam Snead's near misses. Having holed an 18-ft putt to earn a tie, he missed from less than a yard on the 18th green of the play-off after Worsham had interrupted him to ask for measurement. James B McHale, an amateur, set new low round record, a 65 in the third round.

Prize-money $10 000. First prize $2000.

1948 Ben Hogan's first victory with record score of 278. Record entry of 1411.

1949 Victory for Cary Middlecoff. Hogan unable to compete after his terrible car accident.

1950 Ben Hogan achieved a 'miracle' victory in the 50th championship. Still walking with great discomfort after his near-fatal accident, he tied with Lloyd Mangrum and George Fazio on 287 and won the play-off with a superb 69 to Mangrum's 73 and Fazio's 75. Trailing the play-off by one stroke with 3 holes to play, Mangrum was penalized 2 strokes for picking up his ball to blow off a fly.

Prize-money $15 000. First prize $4000. Every professional who completed 72 holes received $100.

1951 Back-to-back win for Ben Hogan at Oakland Hills. The presentation of the course and its remodelling were the subject of much controversy and only Hogan and Clayton Heafner broke the par of 70 in the last round, but Hogan's 67 is generally regarded as one of his greatest single rounds. He did the last 9 in 32 on a course of which he said, 'I vowed I'd bring this monster to its knees.'

Entry 1511.

1952 Won by Julius Boros who had been a professional for less than three years.

Entry 1688.

1953 Fourth victory for Ben Hogan, equalling the record of Willie Anderson and Bobby Jones. Led after every round, his 283 at Oakmont beating Sam Snead, runner-up for the fourth time, by 6 strokes. His four victories came in the space of only six years, a supremacy not matched by Jones. Hogan was the first to hold the lead throughout since 1921, and the margin was the widest for 15 years. However, there were only two rounds under 70, Hogan's first round and Snead's second.

Prize-money $20 400. First prize $5000.

1954 Amazing victory by Ed Furgol who shattered his left elbow, leaving his arm withered and crooked at the elbow. He scored 284, 1 stroke better than Gene Littler.

Open televised for the first time. Record entry of 1928; record crowd of 39 600 and record prize-money of $23 280 with a first prize of $6000.

1955 Ben Hogan's record-breaking fifth Open foiled by Jack Fleck, a municipal course professional from Iowa. Fleck made two birdies at the last 2 holes to tie Hogan and then, almost as incredibly, beat him in a play-off. One of the classic examples of David slaying Goliath.

Prize-money $30 000. First prize $7200.

1958 Entry of 2132 from which Tommy Bolt emerged as winner. Sam Snead failed to qualify for final 36 holes, the first time in 18 Opens.

1959 Billy Casper triumphed with a hot putting streak. Thunderstorms struck in the third round and the final round was postponed a day for the first time. Attendance 43 377; entry 2385. Prize-money $49 200. First prize $12 000.

1960 Arnold Palmer made a record comeback to win. Trailed by 7 strokes after 54 holes. Had 6 birdies in first 7 holes of final round. His 65 was the lowest ever (at the time) in the fourth round by a winner; his 30 for the first 9 tied the record held by James McHale.

Jack Nicklaus recorded the lowest aggregate (282) ever returned by an amateur. He finished second. Ben Hogan lost in what proved to be his last good chance of a fifth victory.

Art Wall set a qualifying record with 63, 65 (128) at Twin Hills CC, Oklahoma.

Entry 2453. Prize-money $60 720. First prize $14 400.

Gary Player, US Open champion in 1965, the first from outside America or Britain. He is pictured with Arnold Palmer, US Open champion in 1960. (Allsport)

1961 Gene Littler's victory at Oakand Hills made him the eighth player to win the US Open and US Amateur.

Ben Hogan failed to finish in first ten for first time since 1940. He did not play in 1949 and 1957. Four former champions: Boros, Middlecoff, Worsham and Furgol failed to make the 36-hole cut.

1962 Beginning of the professional reign of Jack Nicklaus. He beat Arnold Palmer at Oakmont in a play-off.

Attendance 62 300. Prize-money $73 800.

1963 Return to the Country Club, Brookline, for first time since 1913. Julius Boros won, defeating Arnold Palmer and Jacky Cupit in a play-off. Severe playing conditions, but Boros became oldest American to win, eleven years after his first victory.

Defending champion Jack Nicklaus failed to qualify and, for the first time, no amateur survived the 36-hole cut.

1964 Dramatic emergence from a dramatic slump by the winner, Ken Venturi, who survived a position of near exhaustion to win at Congressional CC, Washington, DC. It was the last year that two rounds were played on the final day. Six strokes behind after 36 holes, Venturi turned in a first half of 30 in a third round of 66. He needed a doctor's examination before continuing, but overhauled the 54-hole leader Tommy Jacobs and, walking with difficulty, parred the last 4 holes to finish four ahead of Jacobs. Jacobs had a second round of 64 which tied the lowest recorded at that time.

1965 Gary Player's victory after a tie with Kel Nagle, was the first by an overseas player since 1920. He was the first champion who was neither American nor British and he gave $25 000 of his $26 000 first prize to the USGA: $5000 for cancer relief work and $20 000 to promote junior golf.

Defending champion, Ken Venturi, with ailing hands, failed to qualify for the final 36 holes.

Attendance 72 052. Prize-money $123 890.

For the first time the 72 holes were spread over four days.

1966 Another dramatic finish at Olympic CC, San Francisco. Arnold Palmer, 7 strokes ahead of Billy Casper, was caught by Casper and beaten next day in a play-off.

A relatively unknown professional Rives McBee equalled the single-round scoring record with a second-round 64.

Prize-money $147 490.

1967 New Open scoring record of 275 by Jack Nicklaus at Baltusrol. It beat Hogan's 276 in 1948.

Attendance 88 414. Entry 2649.

1968 Lee Trevino played four rounds under par and equalled Nicklaus's aggregate of 275 by winning at Oak Hills CC, Rochester. First man to be under par in all four rounds, and in the 60s.

Bert Yancey tied the record of 135 for the first 36 holes. A third-round 70 for 205 broke the 54-hole record, but he was only 1 stroke better than Trevino who had a final 69 to win by 4 strokes.

Entry 3007. Prize-money $188 800.

1969 Orville Moody, until 1967 a sergeant in the Army, became champion at the Champions Club, Houston in only his second Open.

For the second time no amateur made the 36-hole cut.

Entry 3397. Prize-money $205 300.

1970 Tony Jacklin, the only player to beat par, became the first English winner since Ted Ray in 1920. He led after every round and his winning margin of 7 strokes was the biggest since Jim Barnes won by 9 in 1921.

The championship was notable for first rounds of 79, 80 and 81 by Arnold Palmer, Gary Player and Jack Nicklaus. Nicklaus's 81 being his worst Open round by 3 strokes. The week was also notable for the criticism of the course by runner-up Dave Hill who was later fined for his remarks.

Orville Moody failed to qualify for the final two rounds, the fifth defending champion in eight years to fail.

Hazeltine was the second longest course ever to house a USGA championship.

1971 Lee Trevino's second victory earned after a play-off in which Jack Nicklaus twice left shots in bunkers.

A 21-year-old amateur, Jim Simons, needed a birdie on the 72nd hole to tie Trevino and Nicklaus, but took 6, his total of 283 being 1 off Nicklaus's record aggregate for an amateur. His third-round 65, however, tied the record for the lowest individual round by an amateur.

Defending champion, Tony Jacklin, failed to make the cut, the sixth champion to fail in nine years.

It was Merion's 13th USGA event—a record.

1972 Jack Nicklaus won his third US Open, leading or tying for the lead throughout. It was Pebble Beach's first Open. Nicklaus won the 1961 US Amateur, also at Pebble Beach.

Only 48 of the 150 starters broke 80 on both the first two days and only 40 rounds beat the par of 72 by the 70 contestants who played all four rounds.

Jerry McGee holed in one at the 8th on the third day, the first hole in one in the Open since 1956. Bobby Mitchell repeated the feat at the same hole next day.

Entry 4196. Prize-money $202 400.

1973 Johnny Miller broke the record for the lowest individual round and the lowest finishing round. His 63 gave him a total of 279, the lowest in five Opens at Oakmont, and victory by 1 stroke. Miller, starting his last round an hour ahead of the leaders, made up 4 strokes on John Schlee and then went ahead.

It was Sam Snead's third Open at Oakmont and he played through his 27th Open, breaking a record he shared with Gene Sarazen.

Entry 3580. Prize-money $219 400.

1974 On a Winged Foot course which proved very difficult Hale Irwin, the second bespectacled champion, beat Forrest Fezler by 2 strokes.

Only 23 out of 150 players scored lower than 75 on the first day. Entry 3914. Prize-money $227 000.

1975 The 25th play-off in Open history brought victory for Lou Graham over John Mahaffey; a championship in which play in the second round was interrupted by an electrical storm.

Entry 4214. Attendance 97 345 plus 6246 for the play-off. Prize-money $235 700. First prize $40 000.

1976 A championship at the Atlanta Athletic Club, the first to be held in the South, in which four players had a chance of victory on the 72nd hole. Jerry Pate, who birdied the hole by hitting a 5 iron across water to 3 ft, was 1 stroke in front of John Mahaffey, Al Geiberger and Tom Weiskopf on the tee. His birdie was unanswerable as Mahaffey hit his second into the water and Weiskopf and Geiberger, having driven poorly, played short.

Attendance 113 084. Entry 4436.

1977 Hubert Green became champion at Southern Hills, Tulsa despite a threat to his life. This was conveyed to him by USGA officials during the last round, but he decided to play on and eventually holed from 3 ft to beat Lou Graham.

A record seven players tied the first-round lead. Twelve players were within 2 strokes of the lead as the last round began. Entry 4726. Prize-money $284 990.

1978 Andy North beat Dave Stockton and J C Snead by one stroke at Cherry Hills, but nobody beat par for the championship. North returned a 1 over par 285.

1979 Second victory for Hale Irwin. At Inverness, Toledo he won by 2 strokes with a final round of 75, the highest last round by a champion since 1949. Not since 1935 had there been anything higher, a 76.

Gary Player finished tied second with a final round of 68, his highest position since he won in 1965. Jack Nicklaus also finished with a 68, but only made the cut by 1 stroke. Tom Watson, the leading money-winner at the time, failed to make the cut.

Prize-money $330 400.

1980 A championship in which records galore were broken, beginning on the first day with Tom Weiskopf and Jack Nick-

aus equalling Johnny Miller's record of 63 for the lowest individual round in the Open. Nicklaus, in fact, missed from about a yard on the 18th green for a 62.

A second round of 71 lowered the aggregate for 36 holes and a further 70 lowered the 54-hole record, but it was a record shared by Isao Aoki of Japan who began with three 68s and chased Nicklaus hard in the last round.

A final 68 by Nicklaus gave him victory by 2 strokes and enabled him to break the record aggregate which he held jointly with Lee Trevino. He also joined Wille Anderson, Bobby Jones and Ben Hogan as the only four-time winners.

Aoki's second place was the best ever by an Asian golfer in the Open. Hubert Green's third round of 65 equalled the lowest third round and contained a record eight 3s in a row from the 9th.

Nicklaus's victory came 18 years after his first, a record span. It was the first time Nicklaus finished in the first six since 1973. Tom Watson holed in one on the famous 4th on the first morning. Severiano Ballesteros was disqualified for being late on the first tee on the second day and Aoki and Nicklaus played together in all four rounds.

Attendance at Baltusrol 102 000, the second largest in history.

1981 Victory for David Graham at Merion, the first by an Australian in the history of the event. He played the last 5 holes in 2 under par to come within 1 stroke of the record aggregate set by Jack Nicklaus the year before. He won by 3 strokes from Bill Rogers, who later in the year won the British Open, and George Burns who led for three rounds, setting the best total in history (203) for 54 holes. He was foiled by Graham's finish which was magnificent.

1982 Tom Watson's first US Open victory came at Pebble Beach thanks to one of the most celebrated single shots in golf. In the final round, and tied with Jack Nicklaus, he holed a chip from the edge of the green at the 17th for a 2. He then finished with a 4 for a total of 282, the first champion to finish with 2 birdies. It was Nicklaus's fourth time as runner-up.

There were 5255 entries.

1983 Larry Nelson played the last two rounds in 132, 10 under par and the lowest aggregate for the final 36 holes, to beat defending champion, Tom Watson, by 1 stroke at Oakmont. Nelson's total for the last two rounds was 16 strokes less than for his first two.

It was also a championship stretched to a fifth day by the weather. A storm forced play to be abandoned on Sunday as Watson was facing a 35-foot putt on the 14th and Nelson about to tee off on the par-3 16th. When play resumed on Monday morning, Nelson hit a 4-wood to the 16th green and holed a mammoth putt for a 2 to lead for the first time.

Nelson took 3 putts on the 18th green but Watson dropped a stroke on the 17th and could not make it up at the 18th.

Arnold Palmer, by competing in his 31st consecutive Open, equalled the record held by Gene Sarazen. It was his fourth Open at Oakmont—1953, 1962, 1973 and 1983.

1984 Drama over the closing holes at Winged Foot ended in the first tie since 1975. Greg Norman holed from 45 feet on the 72nd hole after hitting his second into the stand and getting a free drop but Fuzzy Zoeller, who had led by 3 strokes with 9 holes to play, played the last hole beautifully and thoroughly deserved both to be in a play-off and to win it. His good nature was never better shown than by his gesture of waving a white towel of surrender while he waited and watched Norman play the last hole of the last round. The play-off scores were 67 against 75.

1985 Andy North, champion in 1978, shot a final round of 74 to gain his second victory. It is a strange fact that, of his three victories as a professional, two have been in the US Open. He had a total of 279, one under par at Oakland Hills.

However, for much of the four days, Tze-Chung Chen from

Left: **Tony Jacklin, winner of the US Open in 1970 by 7 strokes. (Allsport)**

Taiwan looked as if he would become the first champion from the East. He made history on the first day by recording the first double eagle in the Open's history by holing his second shot on the par-5 2nd hole. It was quite a way to start. He broke the course record with a 65 and then added a 69 to tie the record aggregate at half-way in an Open.

With one round to play, he was still 2 strokes in the lead and after 56 holes he was 4 ahead but an 8 at the 5th where, amongst other things, he hit the ball twice, prompted his undoing.

Jack Nicklaus missed the cut, ending a run of 21 consecutive Opens in which he had played all four rounds.

1986 In a year in which Jack Nicklaus became the oldest winner of the Masters, Raymond Floyd became the oldest winner of the Open at Shinnecock Hills on Long Island, which was last the venue for the Open in 1896.

With an unusually large number of players with a chance of victory on the last day, Floyd finished with a 66 to win by two from Lanny Wadkins and Chip Beck who both closed with 65s. Lee Trevino was joint 4th, aged 46. Bad weather kept scoring high on the first day.

DETAILED RECORDS

Most victories

4, Willie Anderson, 1901–03–04–05
Bobby Jones, 1923–26–29–30
Ben Hogan, 1948–50–51–53
Jack Nicklaus, 1962–67–72–80
Nobody has won three times. 11 players have won twice

Most times runner-up or joint runner-up

4, Sam Snead, 1937–47–49–53
Bobby Jones, 1922–24–25–28
Arnold Palmer, 1962–63–66–67
Jack Nicklaus, 1960–68–71–82

Oldest winner

Raymond Floyd, 43 years 9 months 11 days, 1986
Ted Ray, 43 years 4 months 16 days, 1920
Julius Boros, 43 years 3 months 20 days, 1963
Ben Hogan, 40 years 10 months, 1953
Jack Nicklaus, 40 years 5 months 25 days, 1980

Youngest winner

John J McDermott, 19 years 10 months 14 days, 1911
Francis Ouimet, 20 years 4 months 11 days, 1913
Gene Sarazen, 20 years 4 months 16 days, 1922

Biggest margin of victory

11 strokes, Willie Smith, 1899
 9 strokes, Jim Barnes, 1921
 7 strokes, Fred Herd, 1898; Alex Smith, 1906;
Tony Jacklin, 1970

Lowest winning aggregate

272 (63, 71, 70, 68), Jack Nicklaus, Baltusrol, 1980
273 (68, 68, 70, 69), David Graham, Merion, 1981

Lowest aggregate by runner-up

274 (68, 68, 68, 70) Isao Aoki, Baltusrol, 1980

Lowest aggregate by an amateur

282 (71, 71, 69, 71), Jack Nicklaus, Cherry Hills, 1960

Lowest individual round

63, Johnny Miller, fourth round, Oakmont, 1973;
Tom Weiskopf, first round, Baltusrol, 1980;
Jack Nicklaus, first round, Baltusrol, 1980

Lowest individual round by an amateur

65, James B McHale, St Louis, 1947
65, Jim Simons, Merion, 1971

Lowest first round
63, Tom Weiskopf and Jack Nicklaus, Baltusrol, 1980

Lowest second round
64, Tommy Jacobs, Congressional CC, 1964;
Rives McBee, Olympic CC, 1966

Lowest third round
64, Ben Crenshaw, Merion, 1981

Lowest fourth round
63, Johnny Miller, Oakmont, 1973

Lowest first 36 holes
134 (63, 71) Jack Nicklaus, Baltusrol, 1980
134 (65, 69) Tze-Chung Chen, Oakland Hills, 1985

Lowest second 36 holes
132 (65, 67), Larry Nelson, Oakmont, 1983
136 (70, 66), Gene Sarazen, Fresh Meadow, 1932
136 (68, 68), Cary Middlecoff, Inverness, 1957
136 (66, 70), Ken Venturi, Congressional CC, 1964
136 (68, 68), Tom Weiskopf, Atlanta Athletic Club, 1976
136 (68, 68), Lou Graham, Southern Hills, 1977

Lowest first 54 holes
203 (69, 66, 68), George Burns III, Merion, 1981
203 (65, 69, 69), Tze-Chung Chen, Oakland Hills, 1985
204 (63, 71, 70), Jack Nicklaus, and (68, 68, 68), Isao Aoki, Baltusrol, 1980

Lowest final 54 holes
204 (67, 72, 65), Jack Nicklaus, Baltusrol, 1967

Lowest 9 holes
30, James B McHale, first 9, third round, St Louis, 1947; Arnold Palmer, first 9, fourth round, Cherry Hills, 1960; Ken Venturi, first 9, third round, Congressional CC, 1964; Steve Spray, second 9, fourth round, Oak Hill CC, 1968; Bob Charles, first 9, fourth round, Merion, 1971; Tom Shaw, first 9, first round, Merion, 1971; Raymond Floyd, first 9, first round, Baltusrol, 1980; George Burns, first 9, second round, Pebble Beach, 1982

Biggest span between first and last victories
18 years, Jack Nicklaus, 1962–80
11 years, Julius Boros, 1952–63

Successive victories
3, Willie Anderson, 1903–05
2, J J McDermott, 1911–12; Bobby Jones, 1929–30; Ralph Guldahl, 1937–38; Ben Hogan, 1950–51

Victories by amateurs
4, Bobby Jones, 1923–26–29–30
1, Francis Ouimet, 1913; Jerome D Travers, 1915; Chick Evans, 1916; John G Goodman, 1933

Winner of US Open and Amateur on the same course
Jack Nicklaus, Pebble Beach, Amateur (1961); Open (1972)

Most number of top three finishes
Jack Nicklaus 9: 1960–62–66–67–68–71–72–80–82
Ben Hogan 7: 1948–50–51–52–53–55–56
Gene Sarazen 7: 1922–26–27–29–32–34–40
Arnold Palmer 6: 1960–62–63–66–67–72
Willie Anderson 6: 1897–98–1901–03–04–05

Most number of top six finishes
Ben Hogan 12: 1940–41–46–47–48–50–51–52–53–54–55–56
Jack Nicklaus 11: 1960–61–62–66–67–68–71–72–73–78–80
Walter Hagen 11: 1913–14–19–21–22–24–25–27–28–33–35
Gene Sarazen 11: 1922–25–26–27–28–29–31–32–34–35–40
Arnold Palmer 11: 1959–60–62–63–64–66–67–69–72–73–74
Willie Anderson 11: 1897–98–99–1901–02–03–04–05–06–08–09

First player to break 70
Dave Hunter, 68, first round, Englewood, New Jersey, 1909; Tom McNamara, 69, second round, Englewood, New Jersey, 1909

Most consecutive appearances
31, Gene Sarazen and Arnold Palmer

Most rounds under 70
24, Jack Nicklaus
15, Arnold Palmer
14, Ben Hogan

Outright leader after every round
Walter Hagen, 1914; Jim Barnes, 1921; Ben Hogan, 1953; Tony Jacklin, 1970

Hot sequences
1922–30: Bobby Jones's finishes were =2nd, 1st, 2nd, 2nd, 1st, =11th, 2nd, 1st, 1st
In twelve successive appearances from 1940 to 1956 (he did not play in 1949), Ben Hogan's worst placing was tied for 6th place

Left-handed champions
None

Bespectacled champions
Willie Macfarlane, 1925; Hale Irwin, 1974–79

Unusual champions
Tommy Armour, 1927, lost an eye in World War I; Ed Furgol, 1954, had a withered left arm—the result of a childhood playground accident

Play-offs
26, 1901–03–08–10–11–13–19–23–25–27–28–29–31–39–40–46–47–50–55–57–62–63–65–66–71–75–84
By comparison, the British Open has produced only 12 play-offs in 115 championships

Lowest round in a play-off
68, Byron Nelson, 1939; Craig Wood, 1939; Lee Trevino, Merion, 1971
69, Lew Worsham, St Louis, 1947; Ben Hogan, Merion, 1950; Jack Fleck, Olympic CC, 1955; Billy Casper, Olympic CC, 1966

First American-born champion
Johnny McDermott, 1911

Record leads (since 1898)
After 18 holes:
5 strokes, Tommy Armour, 1933
After 36 holes:
5 strokes, Willie Anderson, 1903
After 54 holes:
7 strokes, Jim Barnes, 1921

Champions with each round lower than previous one
Ben Hogan, 1951, Oakland Hills, 76, 73, 71, 67

Champions with four rounds the same
None

Biggest variation between rounds of a champion
13 strokes, Johnny Miller, Oakmont, 1973, third round 76

Best finishing round by a champion
63, Johnny Miller, Oakmont, 1973
65, Arnold Palmer, Cherry Hills, 1960; Jack Nicklaus, Baltusrol, 1967

Worst finishing round by a champion since 1919
79, Bobby Jones, Winged Foot, 1929
(All-time worst: 84, Fred Herd, 1898)

Worst opening round by a champion since 1919
78, Walter Hagen, Brae Burn, 1919; Tommy Armour, Oakmont, 1927
(All-time worst: 91, Horace Rawlins, Newport, 1895; Worst since 1946: 76, Ben Hogan, Oakland Hills, 1951 and Jack Fleck, Olympic CC, 1955)

Best opening round by a champion
63, Jack Nicklaus, Baltusrol, 1980

Championship with highest number of rounds under 70
Southern Hills, 1977, 35 rounds

Championship since 1946 with fewest rounds under 70
Oakland Hills, 1951 and Oakmont, 1953, two rounds

Continuity of appearances
Gene Sarazen teed off in 31 successive Opens from 1920—a record. He also played right through 22 successive Opens from 1920 to 1941
Sam Snead played through 27 Opens between 1937 and 1973, a record

Champions who led outright after three rounds (1898–1986)
A total of 32 champions out of 86:
Fred Herd, 1898; Willie Smith, 1899; Harry Vardon, 1900; Laurie Auchterlonie, 1902; Willie Anderson, 1903; Alex Smith, 1906; Walter Hagen, 1914; Jerome Travers, 1915; Chick Evans, 1916; Jim Barnes, 1921; Bobby Jones, 1923; Willie Macfarlane, 1925; Bobby Jones, 1929; Bobby Jones, 1930; Johnny Goodman, 1933; Lawson Little, 1940; Craig Wood, 1941; Lew Worsham, 1947; Ben Hogan, 1948; Cary Middlecoff, 1949; Julius Boros, 1952; Ben Hogan, 1953; Ed Furgol, 1954; Cary Middlecoff, 1956; Tommy Bolt, 1958; Billy

Raymond Floyd enjoying a long awaited moment. US Open champion in 1986, the oldest at 43 years and 9 months. (Allsport)

Casper, 1959; Gary Player, 1965; Tony Jacklin, 1970; Jack Nicklaus, 1972; Hubert Green, 1977; Andy North, 1978; Hale Irwin, 1979

Longest course
Bellerive CC, St Louis, 1955, 7191 yd

Courses most often used (1895–1986)
Baltusrol, Oakmont, 6; Oakland Hills, 5; Winged Foot, Myopia Hunt, Inverness and Merion, 4

Lowest individual 18-hole score on Open courses since 1909

Merion	**64**, Lee Mackey, Jr, 1950; Ben Crenshaw, 1981
Oakmont	**63**, Johnny Miller, 1973
Atlanta Athletic	**67**, Michael Reid,* Butch Baird, 1976
Pebble Beach	**68**, Arnold Palmer, Lanny Wadkins, 1972
Medinah	**67**, Cary Middlecoff, 1949; Frank Beard, Tom Watson and Pat Fitzsimons, 1975
Winged Foot	**67**, Sam Snead, 1959; Hubert Green, 1974
Olympic	**64**, Rives McBee, 1966
Congressional	**64**, Tommy Jacobs, 1964
Southern Hills	**66**, Jerry McGee, Donald E Padgett II, 1977
Hazeltine National	**67**, Randy Wolff, Bob Charles, 1970

Houston | **66**, Bob Murphy, Bobby Mitchell, 1969
Oak Hill | **65**, John S Spray, 1968
Cherry Hills | **65**, Arnold Palmer, 1960
Baltusrol | **63**, Jack Nicklaus, Tom Weiskopf, 1980
Bellerive
Country Club, | **68**, Ray Floyd, Kel Nagle, 1965
Brookline | **69**, Arnold Palmer, Bob Gajda, Dow Finsterwald, 1963
Oakland Hills | **65**, Tze-Chung Chen, 1985
Inverness | **65**, Walter Burkemo, 1957
Northwood, Dallas | **68**, Julius Boros, Al Brosch, Johnny Bulla, 1952
Riviera, Los Angeles | **67**, Ben Hogan, Lew Worsham, 1948
St Louis | **65**, James McHale,* 1947
Canterbury, Ohio | **67**, Sam Snead, 1940; Chick Harbert, Chandler Harper, 1946
Colonial | **68**, Ben Hogan, 1941
Philadelphia CC | **66**, Clayton Heafner, 1939
North Shore, Illinois | **66**, Johnny Goodman,* Walter Hagen, 1933
Fresh Meadow | **66**, Gene Sarazen, 1932
Olympia Fields | **68**, Ed Dudley, 1928
Scioto | **68**, Bill Mehlhorn, Macdonald Smith, 1926
Worcester CC | **67**, Willie Macfarlane, 1925
Interlachen | **68**, Bobby Jones, 1930*
Inwood, New York | **70**, Jock Hutchison, 1923
Skokie, Illinois | **68**, Gene Sarazen, Walter Hagen, 1922
Columbia CC | **69**, Jim Barnes, Alfred Hackbarth, 1921
Brae Burn | **72**, Charles Hoffner, 1919
Minikhada | **68**, Jock Hutchison, 1916
Midlothian | **68**, Walter Hagen, 1914
CC of Buffalo | **69**, Tom McNamara, 1912
Chicago GC, Wheaton | **72**, John McDermott, Fred McLeod, 1911
Englewood, New Jersey | **68**, Dave Hunter, 1909
Philadelphia Cricket Club | **70**, Fred McLeod, 1910
Shinnecock Hills | **65**, Mark Calcavecchia, Chip Beck, Lanny Wadkins, 1986

*Amateur

PRIZE-MONEY

Year	Total $	First prize $
1926	2145	500
1929	5000	1000
1936	5000	1000
1940	6000	1000
1946	8000	1500
1953	20 400	5000
1958	35 000	8000
1960	60 720	14 400
1965	131 690	26 000
1970	203 500	30 000
1972	202 400	30 000
1974	227 700	35 000
1976	268 000	42 000
1977	284 990	45 000
1978	310 200	45 000
1979	330 400	50 000
1980	350 000	55 000
1981	361 730	55 000
1982	385 000	60 000
1983	506 184	72 000
1984	596 925	95 000
1985	654 756	103 000
1986	700 000	115 000

RESULTS

1895 Newport GC, Rhode Island
Horace Rawlins, Newport	45	46	41	41	173
Willie Dunn, Shinnecock Hills	43	46	44	42	175
James Foulis, Chicago	46	43	44	43	176
*A W Smith, Toronto	47	43	44	42	176
W F Davis, Newport	45	49	42	42	178
W Campbell, Brookline	41	48	42	48	179

1896 Shinnecock Hills GC, New York
James Foulis, Chicago		78	74	152
Horace Rawlins, Sadequada		79	76	155
G Douglas, Brookline		79	79	158
*A W Smith, Toronto		78	80	158
John Shippen, Shinnecock Hills		78	81	159
*H J Whigham, Onwentsia		82	77	159

1897 Chicago GC, Illinois
Joe Lloyd, Essex	83	79	162
Willie Anderson, Watch Hill	79	84	163
James Foulis, Chicago	80	88	168
Willie Dunn, New York	87	81	168
W T Hoare, Pittsburgh	82	87	169
A Ricketts, Albany	91	81	172
Bernard Nicholls, Lenox	87	85	172

1898 Myopia Hunt Club, Massachusetts
Fred Herd, Washington Park	84	85	75	84	328
Alex Smith, Washington Park	78	86	86	85	335
Willie Anderson, Baltusrol	81	82	87	86	336
Joe Lloyd, Essex County	87	80	86	86	339
Willie Smith, Shinnecock Hills	82	91	85	82	340
W V Hoare, Dayton	84	84	87	87	342

1899 Baltimore CC, Maryland
Willie Smith, Midlothian	77	82	79	77	315
George Low, Dyker Meadow	82	79	89	76	326
Val Fitzjohn, Otsego	85	80	79	82	326
W H Way, Detroit	80	85	80	81	326
Willie Anderson, New York	77	81	85	84	327
J Park, Essex County	88	80	75	85	328

1900 Chicago GC, Illinois
Harry Vardon, Ganton (England)	79	78	76	80	313
J H Taylor, Richmond (England)	76	82	79	78	315
David Bell, Midlothian	78	83	83	78	322
Laurie Auchterlonie, Glen View	84	82	80	81	327
Willie Smith, Midlothian	82	83	79	84	328
George Low, Dyker Meadow	84	80	85	82	331

1901 Myopia Hunt Club, Massachusetts
Willie Anderson, Pittsfield	84	83	83	81	331
Alex Smith, Washington Park	82	82	87	80	331
(Anderson won play-off 85 to 86)					
Willie Smith, Midlothian	84	86	82	81	333
Stewart Gardner, Garden City	86	82	81	85	334
Laurie Auchterlonie, Glen View	81	85	86	83	335
Bernard Nicholls, Boston	84	85	83	83	335

1902 Garden City GC, New York
Laurie Auchterlonie, Chicago	78	78	74	77	307
Stewart Gardner, Garden City	82	76	77	78	313
*Walter J Travis, Garden City	82	82	75	74	313
Willie Smith, Chicago	82	79	80	75	316
John Shippen, New York	83	81	75	79	318
Willie Anderson, Montclair	79	82	76	81	318

1903 Baltusrol GC, New Jersey
Willie Anderson, Apawamis	149	79	82	307
David Brown, Wollaston	156	75	76	307
(Anderson won play-off 82 to 84)				
Stewart Gardner, Garden City	154	82	79	315

Alex Smith, Nassau 154 81 81 316
Donald J Ross, Oakley 158 78 82 318
Jack Campbell, Brookline 159 83 77 319

1904 Glen View Club, Illinois
Willie Anderson, Apawamis 75 78 78 72 303
Gilbert Nicholls, St Louis 80 76 79 73 308
Fred Mackenzie, Onwentsia 76 79 74 80 309
Laurie Auchterlonie, Glen View 80 81 75 78 314
Bernard Nicholls, Elyria, Ohio 80 77 79 78 314
Robert Simpson, Riverside, Illinois 82 82 76 76 316
P F Barrett, Lambton, Ontario 78 79 79 80 316
Stewart Gardner, Garden City 75 76 80 85 316

1905 Myopia Hunt Club, Massachusetts
Willie Anderson, Apawamis 81 80 76 77 314
Alex Smith, Nassau 81 80 76 79 316
Peter Robertson, Oakmont 79 80 81 77 317
P F Barrett, Canada 81 80 77 79 317
Stewart Gardner, Garden City 78 78 85 77 318
Alex Campbell, The Country Club 82 76 80 81 319

1906 Onwentsia Club, Illinois
Alex Smith, Nassau 73 74 73 75 295
Willie Smith, Mexico 73 81 74 74 302
Laurie Auchterlonie, Glen View 76 78 75 76 305
James Maiden, Toledo 80 73 77 75 305
Willie Anderson, Onwentsia 73 76 74 84 307
Alec Ross, Brae Burn 76 79 75 80 310

1907 Philadelphia Cricket Club, Pennsylvania
Alec Ross, Brae Burn 76 74 76 76 302
Gilbert Nicholls, Woodland 80 73 72 79 304
Alex Campbell, The Country Club 78 74 78 75 305
John Hobens, Englewood 76 75 73 85 309
Peter Robertson, Oakmont 81 77 78 74 310
George Low, Baltusrol 78 76 79 77 310
Fred McLeod, Midlothian 79 77 79 75 310

1908 Myopia Hunt Club, Massachusetts
Fred McLeod, Midlothian 82 82 81 77 322
Willie Smith, Mexico 77 82 85 78 322
(McLeod won play-off 77 to 83)
Alex Smith, Nassau 80 83 83 81 327
Willie Anderson, Onwentsia 85 86 80 79 330
John Jones, Myopia 81 81 87 82 331
Jack Hobens, Englewood 86 81 85 81 333
Peter Robertson, Oakmont 89 84 77 83 333

1909 Englewood GC, New Jersey
George Sargent, Hyde Manor 75 72 72 71 290
Tom McNamara, Wollaston 73 69 75 77 294
Alex Smith, Wykagyl 76 73 74 72 295
Isaac Mackie, Fox Hills 77 75 74 73 299
Willie Anderson, St Louis 79 74 76 70 299
Jack Hobens, Englewood 75 78 72 74 299

1910 Philadelphia Cricket Club, Pennsylvania
Alex Smith, Wykagyl 73 73 79 73 298
John J McDermott, Merchantville 74 74 75 75 298
Macdonald Smith, Claremont 74 78 75 71 298
(Alex Smith won play-off 71 to 75 to 77)
Fred McLeod, St Louis 78 70 78 73 299
Tom McNamara, Boston 73 78 73 76 300
Gilbert Nicholls, Wilmington 73 75 77 75 300

1911 Chicago GC, Illinois
John McDermott, Atlantic City 81 72 75 79 307
Mike J Brady, Wollaston 76 77 79 75 307
George O Simpson, Wheaton 76 77 79 75 307
(McDermott won play-off 80 to 82 to 85)
Fred McLeod, St Louis 77 72 76 83 308
Gilbert Nicholls, Wilmington 76 78 74 81 309
Jock Hutchison, Allegheny 80 77 73 79 309

1912 Buffalo CC, New York
John J McDermott, Atlantic City 74 75 74 71 294
Tom McNamara, Boston 74 80 73 69 296
Alex Smith, Wykagyl 77 70 77 75 299
Mike J Brady, Wollaston 72 75 73 79 299
Alex Campbell, Brookline 74 77 80 71 302
George Sargent, Chevy Chase 72 78 76 77 303

1913 Brookline CC, Massachusetts
*Francis Ouimet, Woodland 77 74 74 79 304
Harry Vardon, England 75 72 78 79 304
Ted Ray, England 79 70 76 79 304
(Ouimet won play-off 72 to 77 to 78)
Walter Hagen, Rochester 73 78 76 80 307
Jim M Barnes, Tacoma 74 76 78 79 307
Macdonald Smith, Wykagyl 71 79 80 77 307
Louis Tellier, France 76 76 79 76 307

1914 Midlothian Country Club, Illinois
Walter C Hagen, Rochester 68 74 75 73 290
*Charles Evans, Jr, Edgewater 76 74 71 70 291
George Sargent, Chevy Chase 74 77 74 72 297
Fred McLeod, Columbia 78 73 75 71 297
*Francis Ouimet, Woodland 69 76 75 78 298
Mike J Brady, Wollaston 78 72 74 74 298
James A Donaldson, Glen View 72 79 74 73 298

1915 Baltusrol GC, New Jersey
*Jerome D Travers, Upper Montclair 148 73 76 297
Tom McNamara, Boston 149 74 75 298
Robert G MacDonald, Buffalo 149 73 78 300
Jim M Barnes, Whitemarsh Valley 146 76 79 301
Louis Tellier, Canoe Brook 146 76 79 301
Mike J Brady, Wollaston 147 75 80 302

1916 Minikahda Club, Minnesota
*Charles Evans, Jr, Edgewater 70 69 74 73 286
Jock Hutchison, Allegheny 73 75 72 68 288
Jim M Barnes, Whitemarsh Valley 71 74 71 74 290
Wilfrid Reid, Wilmington 70 72 79 72 293
Gilbert Nicholls, Great Neck 73 76 71 73 293
George Sargent, Interlachen 75 71 72 75 293

1919 Brae Burn CC, Massachusetts
Walter Hagen, Oakland Hills 78 73 75 75 301
Mike J Brady, Oakley 74 74 73 80 301
(Hagen won play-off 77 to 78)
Jock Hutchison, Glen View 78 76 76 76 306
Tom McNamara, New York 80 73 79 74 306
George McLean, Great Neck 81 75 76 76 308
Louis Tellier, Brae Burn 73 78 82 75 308

1920 Inverness Club, Ohio
Ted Ray, England 74 73 73 75 295
Harry Vardon, England 74 73 71 78 296
Jack Burke, Town and Country 75 77 72 72 296
Leo Diegel, Lake Shore 72 74 73 77 296
Jock Hutchison, Glen View 69 76 74 77 296
*Charles Evans, Jr, Edgewater 74 76 73 75 298
Jim M Barnes, Sunset Hills 76 70 76 76 298

1921 Columbia CC, Maryland
Jim M Barnes, Pelham 69 75 73 72 289
Walter Hagen, New York 79 73 72 74 298
Fred McLeod, Columbia 74 74 76 74 298
*Charles Evans, Jr, Edgewater 73 78 76 75 302
*Bobby T Jones, Jr, Atlanta 78 71 77 77 303
Emmett French, Youngstown 75 77 74 77 303
Alex Smith, Shennecossett 75 75 79 74 303

1922 Skokie CC, Illinois
Gene Sarazen, Highland, Pittsburgh 72 73 75 68 288
John L Black, Oakland, California 71 71 75 72 289
*Bobby T Jones, Jr, Atlanta 74 72 70 73 289
Bill E Mehlhorn, Shreveport 73 71 72 74 290

Walter Hagen, New York	68 77 74 72	291
George Duncan, England	76 73 75 72	296

1923 Inwood CC, New York

*Bobby T Jones, Jr, Atlanta	71 73 76 76	296
Bobby A Cruickshank, Shackamaxon	73 72 78 73	296
(Jones won play-off 76 to 78)		
Jock Hutchison, Glen View	70 72 82 78	302
Jack Forrester, Hollywood, New Jersey	75 73 77 78	303
Johnny J Farrell, Quaker Ridge	76 77 75 76	304
Francis Gallett, Port Washington	76 72 77 79	304
*W M Reekie, Upper Montclair	80 74 75 75	304

1924 Oakland Hills CC, Michigan

Cyril Walker, Englewood	74 74 74 75	297
*Bobby T Jones, Jr, Atlanta	74 73 75 78	300
Bill E Mehlhorn, Normandy, Missouri	72 75 76 78	301
Bobby A Cruickshank, Shackamaxon	77 72 76 78	303
Walter Hagen, New York	75 75 76 77	303
Macdonald Smith, San Francisco	78 72 77 76	303

1925 Worcester CC, Massachusetts

Willie Macfarlane, Oak Ridge	74 67 72 78	291
*Bobby T Jones, Jr, Atlanta	77 70 70 74	291
(Macfarlane won play-off 147 to 148)		
Johnny Farrell, Quaker Ridge	71 74 69 78	292
*Francis Ouimet, Woodland	70 73 73 76	292
Gene Sarazen, Fresh Meadow	72 72 75 74	293
Walter Hagen, Pasadena, Florida	72 76 71 74	293

1926 Scioto CC, Ohio

*Bobby T Jones, Jr, Atlanta	70 79 71 73	293
Joe Turnesa, Fairview	71 74 72 77	294
Bill E Mehlhorn, Chicago	68 75 76 78	297
Gene Sarazen, Fresh Meadow	78 77 72 70	297
Leo Diegel, Mountain View Farm	72 76 75 74	297
Johnny Farrell, Quaker Ridge	76 79 69 73	297

1927 Oakmont CC, Pennsylvania

Tommy Armour, Congressional	78 71 76 76	301
Harry Cooper, El Serreno	74 76 74 77	301
(Armour won play-off 76 to 79)		
Gene Sarazen, Fresh Meadow	74 74 80 74	302
Emmett French, Southern Pines	75 79 77 73	304
Bill E Mehlhorn, New York	75 77 80 73	305
Walter Hagen, Pasadena, Florida	77 73 76 81	307

1928 Olympia Fields CC, Illinois

Johnny Farrell, Quaker Ridge	77 74 71 72	294
*Bobby T Jones, Jr, Atlanta	73 71 73 77	294
(Farrell won play-off 143 to 144)		
Roland Hancock, Wilmington, North Carolina	74 77 72 72	295
Walter Hagen, New York City	75 72 73 76	296
*George von Elm, Tam O'Shanter	74 72 76 74	299
Joe Turnesa, Elmsford	74 77 74 74	299
Gene Sarazen, Fresh Meadow	78 76 73 72	299
Henry Ciuci, Mill River, Connecticut	70 77 72 80	299
Waldo W Crowder, Cleveland	74 74 76 75	299
Bill Leach, Overbrook	72 74 73 80	299
Macdonald Smith, Lakeville	75 77 75 72	299
Densmore Shute, Worthington, Ohio	75 73 79 72	299
Ed Dudley, Unattached	77 79 68 75	299

1929 Winged Foot CC, New York

*Bobby T Jones, Jr, Atlanta	69 75 71 79	294
Al Espinosa, Glencoe, Illinois	70 72 77 75	294
(Jones won play-off 141 to 164)		
Gene Sarazen, Fresh Meadow	71 71 76 78	296
Densmore Shute, Worthington, Ohio	73 71 76 76	296
Tommy Armour, Tam O'Shanter	74 71 76 76	297
*George von Elm, Tam O'Shanter	79 70 74 74	297

1930 Interlachen CC, Minnesota

*Bobby T Jones, Jr, Atlanta	71 73 68 75	287
Macdonald Smith, Lakeville	70 75 74 70	289
Horton Smith, Cragston	72 70 76 74	292
Harry Cooper, Glen Elyn, Illinois	72 72 73 76	293
Johnny Golden, Wee Burn	74 73 71 76	294
Tommy Armour, Tam O'Shanter	70 76 75 76	297

1931 Inverness Club, Ohio

Billy Burke, Round Hill	73 72 74 73	292
*George von Elm, Unattached	75 69 73 75	292
(Burke won play-offs 149/148 to 149/149)		
Leo Diegel, Mexico	75 73 74 72	294
Wiffy Cox, Brooklyn	75 74 74 73	296
Bill E Mehlhorn, Pinewald, New Jersey	77 73 75 71	296
Gene Sarazen, Lakeville	74 78 74 70	296

1932 Fresh Meadow CC, New York

Gene Sarazen, Lakeville	74 76 70 66	286
Bobby A Cruickshank, Willowbrook, New York	78 74 69 68	289
Phil Perkins, Unattached	76 69 74 70	289
Leo Diegel, Mexico	73 74 73 74	294
Wiffy Cox, Brooklyn	80 73 70 72	295
José Jurado, Argentina	74 71 75 76	296

1933 North Shore GC, Illinois

*Johnny Goodman, Omaha	75 66 70 76	287
Ralph Guldahl, St Louis	76 71 70 71	288
Craig Wood, Hollywood	73 74 71 72	290
Walter Hagen, Unattached	73 76 77 66	292
Tommy Armour, Medinah	68 75 76 73	292
Mortie Dutra, Red Run	75 73 72 74	294

1934 Merion Cricket Club, Pennsylvania

Olin Dutra, Brentwood, California	76 74 71 72	293
Gene Sarazen, New York City	73 72 73 76	294
Wiffy Cox, Dyker Beach, New York	71 75 74 75	295
Bobby Cruickshank, Virginia CC	71 71 77 76	295
Harry Cooper, Glen Oak, Illinois	76 74 74 71	295
Billy Burke, Cleveland	76 71 77 72	296
Macdonald Smith, Nashville	75 73 78 70	296

1935 Oakmont CC, Pennsylvania

Sam Parks, Jr, South Hills, Pennsylvania	77 73 73 76	299
Jimmy Thomson, Lakewood, California	73 73 77 78	301
Walter Hagen, Detroit	77 76 73 76	302
Densmore Shute, Chicago	78 73 76 76	303
Ray Mangrum, Los Angeles	76 76 72 79	303
Henry Picard, Hershey	79 78 70 79	306
Gene Sarazen, Brookfield, Connecticut	75 74 78 79	306
Alvin Krueger, Beloit, Wisconsin	71 77 78 80	306
Horton Smith, Oak Park, Illinois	73 79 79 75	306

1936 Baltusrol GC, New Jersey

Tony Manero, Sedgefield, North Carolina	73 69 73 67	282
Harry E Cooper, Glen Oak, Illinois	71 70 70 73	284
Clarence Clark, Forest Hill Field, New Jersey	69 75 71 72	287
Macdonald Smith, Glendale, California	73 73 72 70	288
Henry Picard, Hershey, Pennsylvania	70 71 74 74	289
Wiffy Cox, Kenwood, Maryland	74 74 69 72	289
Ky Laffoon, Northmoor, Illinois	71 74 70 74	289

1937 Oakland Hills CC, Michigan

Ralph Guldahl, Chicago	71 69 72 69	281
Sam Snead, Greenbrier	69 73 70 71	283
Bobby Cruickshank, Virginia CC	73 73 67 72	285
Harry E Cooper, Chicago	72 70 73 71	286
Ed Dudley, Philadelphia	70 70 71 76	287

Al Brosch, Bethpage State Park,
New York 74 73 68 73 288

1938 Cherry Hills Club, Colorado
Ralph Guldahl, Braidburn, New Jersey 74 70 71 69 284
Dick Metz, Mill Road Farm, Illinois 73 68 70 79 290
Harry Cooper, Chicopee 76 69 76 71 292
Tony Penna, Dayton, Ohio 78 72 74 68 292
Byron Nelson, Reading, Pennsylvania 77 71 74 72 294
Emery Zimmerman, Columbia
Edgewater, Oregon 72 71 73 78 294

1939 Philadelphia CC, Pennsylvania
Byron Nelson, Reading, Pennsylvania 72 73 71 68 284
Craig Wood, Winged Foot, New York 70 71 71 72 284
Densmore Shute, Huntington,
West Virginia 70 72 70 72 284
(Nelson won play-off 138 to 141, Shute
 eliminated)
Marvin (Bud) Ward, Spokane,
Washington 69 73 71 72 285
Sam Snead, Greenbrier 68 71 73 74 286
Johnny Bulla, Chicago 72 71 68 76 287

1940 Canterbury GC, Ohio
Lawson Little, Bretton Woods,
New Hampshire 72 69 73 73 287
Gene Sarazen, Brookfield Center,
Connecticut 71 74 70 72 287
(Little won play-off 70 to 73)
Horton Smith, Oak Park 69 72 78 69 288
Craig Wood, Winged Foot, New York 72 73 72 72 289
Ben Hogan, Century, New York 70 73 74 73 290
Ralph Guldahl, Chicago 73 71 76 70 290
Lloyd Mangrum, Oak Park 75 70 71 74 290
Byron Nelson, Inverness, Ohio 72 74 70 74 290

1941 Colonial Club, Texas
Craig Wood, Winged Foot, New York 73 71 70 70 284
Densmore Shute, Chicago 69 75 72 71 287
Johnny Bulla, Chicago 75 71 72 71 289
Ben Hogan, Hershey 74 77 68 70 289
Herman Barron, Fenway, New York 75 71 74 71 291
Paul Runyan, Metropolis, New York 73 72 71 75 291

1946 Canterbury GC, Ohio
Lloyd Mangrum, Los Angeles 74 70 68 72 284
Byron Nelson, Toledo, Ohio 71 71 69 73 284
Vic Ghezzi, Knoxville, Tennessee 71 69 72 72 284
(Mangrum won play-offs 72/72 to 72/73 to 72/73)
Herman Barron, Fenway, New York 72 72 72 69 285
Ben Hogan, Hershey 72 68 73 72 285
Jimmy Demaret, Houston 71 74 73 68 286
Porky Oliver, Jr, Wilmington, Delaware 71 71 74 70 286

1947 St Louis CC, Missouri
Lew Worsham, Oakmont 70 70 71 71 282
Sam Snead, Cascades, Virginia 72 70 70 70 282
(Worsham won play-off 60 to 70)
Bobby Locke, Vereeniging
(South Africa) 68 74 70 73 285
Porky Oliver, Jr, Wilmington, Delaware 73 70 71 71 285
*Marvin (Bud) Ward, Spokane,
Washington 69 72 73 73 287
Jim Ferrier, Chicago 71 70 74 74 289
Vic J Ghezzi, Victory Hills, Kansas 74 73 73 69 289
Leland Gibson, Blue Hills, Missouri 69 76 73 71 289
Ben Hogan, Hershey 70 75 70 74 289
Johnny Palmer, Badin 72 70 75 72 289
Paul Runyan, Annandale, California 71 74 72 72 289

1948 Riviera CC, California
Ben Hogan, Hershey 67 72 68 69 276
Jimmy Demaret, Houston 71 70 68 69 278

Jim Turnesa, Elmsford 71 69 70 70 280
Bobby Locke, Vereeniging
(South Africa) 70 69 73 70 282
Sam Snead, Greenbrier 69 69 73 72 283
Lew Worsham, Oakmont 67 74 71 73 285

1949 Medinah CC, Illinois
Cary Middlecoff, Colonial,
Tennessee 75 67 69 75 286
Clayton Heafner, Eastwood,
North Carolina 72 71 71 73 287
Sam Snead, Greenbrier 73 73 71 70 287
Jim Turnesa, Briar Hall, New York 78 69 70 72 289
Bobby Locke, Vereeniging
(South Africa) 74 71 73 71 289
Buck White, Greenwood, Mississippi 74 68 70 78 290
Dave Douglas, Newark, Delaware 74 73 70 73 290

1950 Merion GC, Pennsylvania
Ben Hogan, Hershey 72 69 72 74 287
Lloyd Mangrum, Tam O'Shanter 72 70 69 76 287
George Fazio, Woodmont, Maryland 73 72 72 70 287
(Hogan won play-off 69 to 73 to 75)
Dutch Harrison, St Andrews, Illinois 72 67 73 76 288
Joe Kirkwood, Jr, Kirkwood, California 71 74 74 70 289
Jim Ferrier, Chicago 71 69 74 75 289
Henry Ransom, St Andrews, Illinois 72 71 73 73 289

1951 Oakland Hills CC, Michigan
Ben Hogan, Hershey 76 73 71 67 287
Clayton Heafner, Eastwood,
North Carolina 72 75 73 69 289
Bobby Locke, Ohenimuri
(South Africa) 73 71 74 73 291
Lloyd Mangrum, Tam O'Shanter 75 74 74 70 293
Julius Boros, Mid Pines,
North Carolina 74 74 71 74 293
Al C Besselink, Hillcrest, Michigan 72 77 72 73 294
Paul Runyan, Annandale, California 73 74 72 75 294
Fred E Hawkins, El Paso, Texas 76 72 75 71 294
Dave Douglas, Newark, Delaware 75 70 75 74 294

1952 Northwood Club, Texas
Julius Boros, Mid Pines, North Carolina 71 71 68 71 281
Porky Oliver, Jr, Cog Hill, Illinois 71 72 70 72 285
Ben Hogan, Tamarisk, California 69 69 74 74 286
Johnny Bulla, Westmoreland,
Pennsylvania 73 68 73 73 287
George Fazio, Pine Valley,
New Jersey 71 69 75 75 290
Dick Metz, Maple City, Kansas 70 74 76 71 291

1953 Oakmont CC, Pennsylvania
Ben Hogan, Tamarisk, California 67 72 73 71 283
Sam Snead, Greenbrier, West
Virginia 72 69 72 76 289
Lloyd Mangrum, Tam O'Shanter 73 70 74 75 292
Peter Cooper, Century, New York 78 75 71 70 294
George Fazio, Pine Valley,
New Jersey 70 71 77 76 294
Jimmy Demaret, Concord, New York 71 76 71 76 294
Ted Kroll, New Hartford 76 71 74 74 295
Dick Metz, Maple City, Kansas 75 70 74 76 295

1954 Baltusrol GC, New Jersey
Ed Furgol, Westwood, Missouri 71 70 71 72 284
Gene Littler, Thunderbird, California 70 69 76 70 285
Dick Mayer, St Petersburg, Florida 72 71 70 73 286
Lloyd Mangrum, Tam O'Shanter 72 71 72 71 286
Bobby Locke, Ohenimuri CC
(South Africa) 74 70 74 70 288
Tommy Bolt, Memorial Park, Texas 72 72 73 72 289
Ben Hogan, Fort Worth, Texas 71 70 76 72 289
Shelly Mayfield, Sequin, Texas 73 75 72 69 289

Fred Haas, New Orleans	73 73 71 72	289
*Billy Joe Patton, Mimosa, North Carolina	69 76 71 73	289

1955 Olympic CC, California

Jack Fleck, Davenport Municipal, Iowa	76 69 75 67	287
Ben Hogan, Fort Worth, Texas	72 73 72 70	287
(Fleck won play-off 69 to 72)		
Sam Snead, Greenbrier, West Virginia	79 69 70 74	292
Tommy Bolt, Chattanooga	67 77 75 73	292
Julius Boros, Mid Pines, North Carolina	76 69 73 77	295
Bob R Rosburg, Palo Alto, California	78 74 67 76	295

1956 Oak Hill Country Club, New York

Cary Middlecoff, Riverlake, Texas	71 70 70 70	281
Julius Boros, Mid Pines, North Carolina	71 71 71 69	282
Ben Hogan, Fort Worth, Texas	72 68 72 70	282
Ed Furgol, Westwood, Missouri	71 70 73 71	285
Peter Thomson, Victoria (Australia)	70 69 75 71	285
Ted Kroll, Fort Lauderdale	72 70 70 73	285

1957 Inverness Club, Ohio

Dick Mayer, St Petersburg, Florida	70 68 74 70	282
Cary Middlecoff, Riverlake, Texas	71 75 68 68	282
(Mayer won play-off 72 to 79)		
Jimmy Demaret, Concord International, New York	68 73 70 72	283
Julius Boros, Mid Pines, North Carolina	69 75 70 70	284
Walter Burkemo, Franklin Hills, Michigan	74 73 72 65	284
Ken Venturi, California	69 71 75 71	286
Fred E Hawkins, El Paso, Texas	72 72 71 71	286

1958 Southern Hills, CC, Oklahoma

Tommy Bolt, Paradise, Florida	71 71 69 72	283
Gary Player, Killarney (South Africa)	75 68 73 71	287
Julius Boros, Mid Pines, North Carolina	71 75 72 71	289
Gene Littler, Singing Hills, California	74 73 67 76	290
Walter Burkemo, Franklin Hills, Michigan	75 74 70 72	291
Bob R Rosburg, Silverado, California	75 74 72 70	291

1959 Winged Foot GC, New York

Billy Casper, Jr, Apple Valley	71 68 69 74	282
Bob R Rosburg, Palo Alto, California	75 70 67 71	283
Claude Harmon, Winged Foot, New York	72 71 70 71	284
Mike Souchak, Grossinger, New York	71 70 72 71	284
Doug Ford, Paradise, Florida	72 69 72 73	286
Ernie Vossier, Midland, Texas	72 70 72 72	286
Arnold Palmer, Laurel Valley, Pennsylvania	71 69 72 74	286

1960 Cherry Hills CC, Colorado

Arnold Palmer, Laurel Valley, Pennsylvania	72 71 72 65	280
*Jack Nicklaus, Scioto, Ohio	71 71 69 71	282
Dutch Harrison, Old Warson, Missouri	74 70 70 69	283
Julius Boros, Mid Pines, North Carolina	73 69 68 73	283
Mike Souchak, Grossinger, New York	68 67 73 75	283
Ted Kroll, De Soto Lakes, Florida	72 69 75 67	283
Jack Fleck, El Caballero, California	70 70 72 71	283
Dow Finsterwald, Tequesta, Florida	71 69 70 73	283

1961 Oakland Hills CC, Michigan

Gene Littler, Singing Hills, California	73 68 72 68	281
Bob Goalby, Paradise, Florida	70 72 69 71	282
Doug Sanders, Ojai, California	72 67 71 72	282
Mike Souchak, Grossinger, New York	73 70 68 73	284
*Jack Nicklaus, Scioti, Ohio	75 69 70 70	284
Dow Finsterwald, Tequesta, Florida	72 71 71 72	286
Eric Monti, Hillcrest, California	74 67 72 73	286
Doug Ford, Tuckahoe, New York	72 69 71 74	286

1962 Oakmont CC, Pennsylvania

Jack Nicklaus, Tucson National, Arizona	72 70 72 69	283
Arnold D Palmer, Miami	71 68 73 71	283
(Nicklaus won play-off 71 to 74)		
Phil Rodgers, La Jolla, California	74 70 69 72	285
Bobby Nichols, Midland, Texas	70 72 70 73	285
Gay Brewer, Jr, Paradise, Florida	73 72 73 69	287
Tommy Jacobs, Bermuda Dunes, California	74 71 73 70	288
Gary Player, Ponte Vedra, Florida	71 71 72 74	288

1963 The Country Club, Brookline, Massachusetts

Julius Boros, Mid Pines, North Carolina	71 74 76 72	293
Jacky D Cupit, Mountain View, California	70 72 76 75	293
Arnold Palmer, Laurel Valley, Pennsylvania	73 69 77 74	293
(Boros won play-off 70 to 73 to 76)		
Paul Harney, Sunset Oaks, California	78 70 73 73	294
Billy Maxwell, Tropicana, Nevada	73 73 75 74	295
Bruce Crampton, Sydney (Australia)	74 72 75 74	295
Tony Lema, San Leandro, California	71 74 74 76	295

1964 Congressional CC, Washington, D.C.

Ken Venturi, Paradise, Florida	72 70 66 70	278
Tommy Jacobs, Bermuda Dunes, California	72 64 70 76	282
Bob J Charles, De Soto Lakes, Florida	72 72 71 68	283
Billy Casper, Mountain View, California	71 74 69 71	285
Gay Brewer, Jr, Dallas	76 69 73 68	286
Arnold Palmer, Laurel Valley, Pennsylvania	68 69 75 74	286

1965 Bellerive CC, Missouri

Gary Player, Johannesburg (South Africa)	70 70 71 71	282
Kel Nagle, Pymble (Australia)	68 73 72 69	282
(Player won play-off 71 to 74)		
Frank Beard, Seneca, Kentucky	74 69 70 71	284
Julius Boros, Mid Pines, North Carolina	72 75 70 70	287
Al Geiberger, Carlton Oaks, California	70 76 70 71	287
Raymond Floyd, St Andrews, Illinois	72 72 76 68	288
Bruce Devlin, Sydney (Australia)	72 73 72 71	288

1966 Olympic CC, California

Billy Casper, Jr, Peacock Gap, California	69 68 73 68	278
Arnold Palmer, Laurel Valley, Pennsylvania	71 66 70 71	278
(Casper won play-off 69 to 73)		
Jack Nicklaus, Scioto, Ohio	71 71 69 74	285
Tony Lema, Marco Island, Florida	71 74 70 71	286
Dave Marr, Goodyear, Arizona	71 74 68 73	286
Paul Rodgers, La Jolla, California	70 70 73 74	287

1967 Baltusrol GC, New Jersey

Jack Nicklaus, Scioto, Ohio	71 67 72 65	275
Arnold Palmer, Laurel Valley, Pennsylvania	69 68 73 69	279

Don January, Dallas 69 72 70 70 281
Billy Casper, Jr, Bonita, California 69 70 71 72 282
Lee Trevino, Horizon Hills, Texas 72 70 71 70 283
Bob Goalby, Tamarisk, California 72 71 70 71 284
Deane R Beman, Bethesda, Maryland 69 71 71 73 284
Gardner Dickinson, Jr, Lost Tree,
Florida 70 73 68 73 284

1968 Oak Hill CC, New York
Lee Trevino, Horizon Hills, Texas 69 68 69 69 275
Jack Nicklaus, Scioto, Ohio 72 70 70 67 279
Bert Yancey, Killearn, Florida 67 68 70 76 281
Bobby Nichols, Louisville, Kentucky 74 71 68 69 282
Don Bies, Seattle 70 70 75 69 284
Steve Spray, Cedar Rapids, Iowa 73 75 71 65 284

1969 Champions GC, Texas
Orville J Moody, Yukon, Oklahoma 71 70 68 72 281
Deane R Beman, Bethesda, Maryland 68 69 73 72 282
Al Geiberger, Santa Barbara, California 68 72 72 70 282
Bob R Rosburg, Westwood, Missouri 70 69 72 71 282
Bob Murphy, Jr, Bartow, Florida 66 72 74 71 283
Miller Barber, Woodlawn, Texas 67 71 68 78 284
Bruce Crampton, Bahama Reef 73 72 68 71 284
Arnold Palmer, Laurel Valley,
Pennsylvania 70 73 69 72 284

1970 Hazeltine GC, Minnesota
Tony Jacklin, The Cloisters, Georgia 71 70 70 70 281
Dave Hill, Evergreen, Colorado 75 69 71 73 288
Bob J Lunn, Haggin Oaks, California 77 72 70 70 289
Bob J Charles, Christchurch
(New Zealand) 76 71 75 67 289

Tom Watson, US Open champion 1982. (USGA)

Ken Still, Fircrest, Washington	78 71 71 71	291
Miller Barber, Woodlawn, Texas	75 75 72 70	292

1971 Merion GC, Pennsylvania

Lee Trevino, El Paso, Texas	70 72 69 69	280
Jack Nicklaus, Scioto, Ohio	69 72 68 71	280
(Trevino won play-off 68 to 71)		
Bob R Rosburg, French Lick, Indiana	71 72 70 69	282
Jim J Colbert, Jr, Prairie Creek, Arkansas	69 69 73 71	282
*Jim Simons, Butler, Pennsylvania	71 71 65 76	283
Johnny L Miller, San Francisco GC	70 73 70 70	283
George Archer, Gilroy, California	71 70 70 72	283

1972 Pebble Beach, California

Jack Nicklaus, Scioto, Ohio	71 73 72 74	290
Bruce Crampton, Australia	74 70 73 76	293
Arnold Palmer, Laurel Valley, Pennsylvania	77 68 73 76	294
Lee Trevino, El Paso, Texas	74 72 71 78	295
Homero Blancas, Houston, Texas	74 70 76 75	295
Kermit Zarley, Houston, Texas	71 73 73 79	296

1973 Oakmont CC, Pennsylvania

Johnny Miller, San Francisco GC	71 69 76 63	279
John Schlee, Preston Trails, Texas	73 70 67 70	280
Tom Weiskopf, Columbus, Ohio	73 69 69 70	281
Arnold Palmer, Laurel Valley, Pennsylvania	71 71 68 72	282
Lee Trevino, El Paso, Texas	70 72 70 70	282
Jack Nicklaus, Scioto, Ohio	71 69 74 68	282

1974 Winged Foot GC, New York

Hale Irwin, Boulder CC, California	73 70 71 73	287
Forest Fezler, Indian Wells CC, California	75 70 74 70	289
Lou Graham, Richland CC, Tennessee	71 75 74 70	290
Bert Yancey, Palm Aire CC, Florida	76 69 73 72	290
Arnold Palmer, Laurel Valley, Pennsylvania	73 70 73 76	292
Jim Colbert, Overland Park, Kansas	72 77 69 74	292
Tom Watson, Kansas City CC	73 71 69 79	292

1975 Medinah CC, Illinois

Lou Graham, Richland CC, Nashville	74 72 68 73	287
John D Mahaffey, Jr, Champions GC, Houston, Texas	73 71 72 71	287
(Graham won play-off 71 to 73)		
Bob Murphy, Delray Dunes, Florida	74 73 72 69	288
Hale Irwin, St Louis, Missouri	74 71 73 70	288
Ben Crenshaw, CC of Austin, Texas	70 68 76 74	288
Frank Beard, Hurstbourne CC	74 69 67 78	288

1976 Atlanta Athletic Club, Duluth, Georgia

Jerry Pate, Pensacola CC, Florida	71 69 69 68	277
Al Geiberger, Silver Lakes, California	70 69 71 69	279
Tom Weiskopf, Columbus, Ohio	73 70 68 68	279
Butch Baird, Miami Beach, Florida	71 71 71 67	280
John Mahaffey, Riverhill CC, Texas	70 68 69 73	280
Hubert Green, Bay Point CC, Florida	72 70 71 69	282

1977 Southern Hills CC, Tulsa, Oklahoma

Hubert M Green, Birmingham, Alabama	69 67 72 70	278
Lou Graham, Richland CC, Nashville	72 71 68 68	279
Tom Weiskopf, Columbus, Ohio	71 71 68 71	281
Tom Purtzer, Moon Valley CC, Arizona	69 69 72 72	282
Jay Haas, St Clair CC, Belleville	72 68 71 72	283
Gary Jacobson, Minnetonka	73 70 67 73	283

1978 Cherry Hills, Denver, Colorado

Andy North, Gainesville, Florida	70 70 71 74	285
Jesse C Snead, Hot Springs, Virginia	70 72 72 72	286
Dave Stockton, Westlake GC, California	71 73 70 72	286
Hale Irwin, St Louis, Missouri	69 74 75 70	288
Tom Weiskopf, Columbus, Ohio	77 73 70 68	288

1979 Inverness, Toledo, Ohio

Hale Irwin, St Louis, Missouri	74 68 67 75	284
Jerry Pate, Pensacola, Florida	71 74 69 72	286
Gary Player, South Africa	73 73 72 68	286
Larry Nelson, Kennesaw, Georgia	71 68 76 73	288
Bill Rogers, Texarkana, Texas	71 72 73 72	288
Tom Weiskopf, Columbus, Ohio	71 74 67 76	288

1980 Baltusrol GC, New Jersey

Jack Nicklaus, Muirfield Village GC, Dublin, Ohio	63 71 70 68	272
Isao Aoki, Golf Kikaku, Tokyo, Japan	68 68 68 70	274
Keith Fergus, Sugar Creek CC, Texas	66 70 70 70	276
Tom Watson, Kansas City, Missouri	71 68 67 70	276
Lon Hinkle, Carrollton, Texas	66 70 69 71	276
Mike Reid, Riverside CC, Provo, Utah	69 67 75 69	280
Mark Hayes, Oak Tree GC, Edmond	66 71 69 74	280

1981 Merion GC, Pennsylvania

David Graham, Preston Trail GC, Dallas, Texas	68 68 70 67	273
Bill Rogers, Northridge CC, Texas	70 68 69 69	276
George Burns III, Quail Ridge GC, Delray Beach, Florida	69 66 68 73	276
John Cook, Muirfield Village GC, Dublin, Ohio	68 70 71 70	279
John Schroeder, Delmar, California	71 68 69 71	279

1982 Pebble Beach, California

Tom Watson, Kansas City, Missouri	72 72 68 70	282
Jack Nicklaus, Muirfield Village GC, Dublin, Ohio	74 70 71 69	284
Bobby Clampett, Carmel Valley Ranch, California	71 73 72 70	286
Dan Pohl, Canadian Lakes CC, Michigan	72 74 72 70	286
Bill Rogers, Northridge CC, Texas	70 73 69 74	286

1983 Oakmont CC, Pennsylvania

Larry Nelson, Marietta, Georgia	75 73 65 67	280
Tom Watson, Kansas City, Missouri	72 70 70 69	281
Gil Morgan, Oak Tree GC, Edmond, Oklahoma	73 72 70 68	283
Severiano Ballesteros, Spain	69 74 69 74	286
Calvin Peete, Fort Myers, Florida	75 68 70 73	286
Hal Sutton, Shreveport, Louisiana	73 70 73 71	287

1984 Winged Foot GC, New York

Fuzzy Zoeller, New Albany, Indiana	71 66 69 70	276
Greg Norman, Bay Hill, Florida	70 68 69 70	276
(Zoeller won play-off 67 to 75)		
Curtis Strange, Kingsmill, Virginia	69 70 74 68	281
Johnny Miller, Boca West CC, Florida	74 68 69 69	282
Jim Thorpe, Buffalo, New York	68 71 70 73	282
Hale Irwin, St Louis, Missouri	68 68 69 79	284

1985 Oakland Hills CC, Michigan

Andy North, Vail/Beaver Creek, Colorado	70 65 70 74	279
Denis Watson, Plantation G&CC, Florida	72 65 73 70	280
Dave Barr, Canada	70 68 70 72	280
Tze-Chung Chen, Taiwan	65 69 69 77	280
Lanny Wadkins, Preston Trail GC, Texas	70 72 69 70	281
Payne Stewart, Lake Mary, Florida	70 70 71 70	281
Severiano Ballesteros, Spain	71 70 69 71	281

1986 Shinnecock Hills GC, New York

Raymond Floyd, Monte Carlo CC, Florida	75 68 70 66	279
Lanny Wadkins, Preston Trail GC, Texas	74 70 72 65	281
Chip Beck, Sea Palms, Georgia	75 73 68 65	281
Lee Trevino, El Paso, Texas	74 68 69 71	282
Hal Sutton, Shreveport, Louisiana	75 70 66 71	282
Payne Stewart, Lake Mary, Florida	76 68 69 70	283
Ben Crenshaw, CC of Austin, Texas	76 69 69 69	283

* Amateur

After comments about crowd behaviour at golf tournaments generally in recent years, it is worth including the message conveyed in the daily programme issued to spectators at the Masters at Augusta. It was written by the late Robert Tyre (Bobby) Jones.

'In golf, customs of etiquette and decorum are just as important as rules governing play. It is appropriate for spectators to applaud successful strokes in proportion to difficulty but excessive demonstrations by a player or his partisans are not proper because of the possible effect upon other competitors.

Most distressing to those who love the game of golf is the applauding or cheering of misplays or misfortunes of a player. Such occurrences have been rare at the Masters but we must eliminate them entirely if our patrons are to continue to merit the reputation as the most knowledgeable and considerate in the world.'

US Masters

First played 1934

This is the youngest of the world's four major championships. Unlike the other three (the British Open, the US Open and the USPGA), it is always played on the same course, the Augusta National in Georgia, and is an invitation-only tournament, invitations being based on a formula laid down in advance and reviewed from time to time.

Both the Augusta course and the Masters tournament were the brainchild of Bobby Jones whose influence always dominated the event even after his death. Although he retired as a player in 1930, he took part in the first tournament in 1934 because the Club was short of money and it needed someone to draw the local public.

Jones had invited some of his old rivals to what, by modern standards, was an informal gathering and he finished in a tie for 13th place. However, a start had been made and the following year it received maximum publicity from the famous double eagle at the 15th in the last round of the eventual winner, Gene Sarazen.

More recently, its fame has been spread by the televising of the event every April on a course, designed by Alister Mackenzie, which is spectacularly beautiful and always at its best in Masters week. Originally, it was a plantation that Baron Berckmans, a distinguished Belgian horticulturist, had developed into the South's first great nursery.

Another trend which the Masters set has been the advance booking of tickets and no admission on a casual daily basis. But the real difference between the Masters and the other major tournaments is the absence of advertising or any form of commercialism.

Nowadays, the field comprises the leading American professionals and amateurs together with a few selected overseas players who meet prescribed qualifications. For many years, the Masters was guided by Jones and Clifford Roberts and, since their deaths, it continues to be run from within the Club. It consists of 72 holes of strokeplay.

MILESTONES

1934 First tournament in which Horton Smith finished birdie, par to beat Craig Wood by 1 stroke. First hole in one by Ross Somerville the Canadian amateur. There have been nine since. Full list:
4th hole: None
6th hole: Leland Gibson (1954), Billy Joe Patton (1954), Charles Coody (1972)
12th hole: Claude Harmon (1947), William Hyndman III (1959)
16th hole: Ross Somerville (1934), Willie Goggin (1935), Ray Billows (1940), John Dawson (1949), Clive Clark (1968)
1935 One of golf's most famous strokes was played by Gene Sarazen at the par-5 15th hole in the last round. He holed a 220 yd 4-wood shot for a double eagle 2. Three behind Craig Wood on the 15th tee, he finished the last 3 holes in par, tied and won the play-off by 5 strokes. It was the only 36-hole play-off.
Frank Walsh took 12 on the 8th.
1936 Craig Wood shot 88 in the first round, 67 in the second. Horton Smith's second victory with a remarkable finish in extremely rainy conditions. He made up 6 strokes in the last two rounds on Harry Cooper; then went one ahead.
1937 Byron Nelson, the winner, picked up 6 strokes in the final round on Ralph Guldahl at the 12th and 13th. Nelson scored 2, 3 to Guldahl's 5, 6 and won by two. Nelson's first round 66 was the lowest to date.
1938 Henry Picard became the second winner by more than 1 stroke, winning by 2. A final 70 beat Ralph Guldahl and Harry Cooper who tied second on 287. Ben Hogan's first Masters.
1939 Sam Snead appeared to be the winner until Ralph Guldahl shot 33 on the back 9 to win by 1 stroke. In June of the same year, Snead took 8 on the final hole of the US Open at the Philadelphia Country Club.
1940 Two notable records. Jimmy Demaret won by 4 strokes, the biggest margin until 1948. In the first round, he covered the second 9 holes in 30 thus equalling the all-time record on a championship course. Lloyd Mangrum, who finished second, opened with a 64, the lowest score in any of the four major championships for many years. It was not matched at Augusta until 1965.
1941 Craig Wood's first major victory. The leader for three rounds, he was caught by Byron Nelson at the turn in the 4th, but came home in 34 to win by 3 strokes. Two months later, he also won the US Open.
1942 The first 18-hole play-off. In it, Byron Nelson gained 5 strokes on his fellow Texan Ben Hogan in a stretch of 11 holes although Hogan played them in one under par.
1946 Another chance for Hogan who took 3 putts on the 72nd green to finish runner-up for the second year running. A little earlier, Herman Keiser, the winner, also took 3 putts on the last green. Keiser had started the final round 5 strokes ahead of Hogan.
1947 Jimmy Demaret emulated Horton Smith and Byron Nelson as two-time winners of the Masters. Tied for the first-round lead with Nelson, he then went into the lead and stayed there. Gene Sarazen and George Fazio, first off in the final round, completed the course in 1 hr 57 min. Sarazen scored 70.
1948 Claude Harmon was better known as a club professional, but he won the Masters by 5 strokes and equalled the record

Billy Joe Patton, an amateur who led Sam Snead and Ben Hogan at the 12th hole in the final round of the 1954 Masters. He finished third. (USGA)

aggregate of 279. He covered the 6th, 7th and 8th in the final round in 2, 3, 3—4 under par.

1949 After high winds on the first two days, Sam Snead had two marvellous 67s to finish on 282. His total for the last two rounds was 14 strokes better than that for the first two rounds. They remained the best two finishing rounds until Jack Nicklaus scored 64, 69 in 1965.

In Snead's last round, he had more birdies (8) than pars (7).

1950 A 7-stroke swing on the last 6 holes enabled Jimmy Demaret to catch Jim Ferrier and beat him by 2 strokes. He thus became the first three-time winner.

Herman Barron took 11 on the par-3 16th.

1951 Having been close several times, Ben Hogan finally won with a final-round 68 for 280 and victory by 2 strokes over Skee Riegel who, in turn, was 4 ahead of those tied for third place. Dow Finsterwald took 11 on the par-3 12th.

1952 Sam Snead, who triumphed in high winds in 1949, did so again. This time, the winds came in the last two rounds. After gaining a 3-stroke lead at half-way (70, 67), Snead added a 77 and a 72 for a 4-stroke victory over Jack Burke, the only player to break 70 on the last day.

1953 Part one of Ben Hogan's *annus mirabilis*. He became the first player to have three rounds under 70 in the Masters, his last three rounds being 69, 66, 69 for a total of 274, a new low and victory by 5 strokes.

The Masters record book states Hogan's belief that his play at Augusta was the finest of his career.

There were 13 eagles on the 13th hole.

1954 The year in which the two best-known professionals, Sam Snead and Ben Hogan, contested a play-off, but were nearly defeated before they got there by a virtually unknown amateur playing his first Masters, Billy Joe Patton from North Carolina.

Patton led the field after 36 holes, was 5 strokes behind after 54 and lead again as late as the 12th hole in the final round, having been helped by holing in one at the 6th. However, a 7 at the 13th and a 6 at the 15th saved the professionals' pride. Patton finished 1 stroke behind Snead and Hogan. In the play-off Snead scored 70 to Hogan's 71.

Patton, who had a birdie on all four days at the par-4 9th, had a remarkable haul of prizes. Gold and silver cup for best amateur score; gold medal for best amateur score; crystal vase for being the low scorer in the first round; crystal cup for a hole in one and a gold money clip for winning the pre-tournament long driving contest.

1955 Record 7-stroke victory for Dr Cary Middlecoff who had a 65 in the second round which, though equalled by Frank Beard in 1968, was not bettered in any second round until 1979, when Miller Barber had a 64.

Ben Hogan and Sam Snead finished second and third.

1956 Jack Burke's winning score of 289 equalled the record highest, but he made up 8 strokes over the last 18 holes on the amateur Ken Venturi and beat him by one. Burke's final round was 71, Venturi's 80. Middlecoff, the holder, took 77 to finish third, 2 behind Burke. Gary Player's first Masters.

1957 A closing 66, the lowest final round at the time, brought victory for Doug Ford who holed out of a bunker at the 18th. He won by 3 strokes from Sam Snead who had started the last round 3 ahead.

1958 Arnold Palmer's first Masters victory. At 28, he was the youngest winner since Byron Nelson in 1937.

1959 Art Wall, the new champion, had 8 birdies in a final 66, 5 of them on the last 6 holes. He had started the final round 6 strokes behind Arnold Palmer, defending champion, and Canadian, Stan Leonard.

1960 Second of Arnold Palmer's victories. He led the field at the end of every round but in the final round he was 1 stroke behind Ken Venturi with 2 holes to play. Palmer birdied both to win by 1 stroke. It was the second time in five years that Venturi finished second.

George Bayer and Jack Fleck went round in 1 hr 52 min. Bayer scored 72 and Fleck 74.

1961 Gary Player, 25, became the first foreign winner of the Masters. He won by 1 stroke from the amateur Charles Coe and defending champion Arnold Palmer. In a dramatic finish, Player made a 4 from a bunker at the 18th; Palmer took 6 from the same bunker.

Coe's total of 281 is the lowest ever returned by an amateur at the Masters.

1962 Revenge for Palmer over Player in the first triple tie. In the play-off, Palmer scored 68 (the lowest in a play-off) to Player's 71 and Dow Finsterwald's 77. Palmer came home in 31.

1963 First victory for Jack Nicklaus, the youngest champion at 23. In rough weather, he won by 1 stroke from Tony Lema who was playing in his first Masters.

1964 Record fourth victory for Arnold Palmer in a span of only seven tournaments. He won by 6 strokes from Dave Marr and Jack Nicklaus, but it was his last victory in any of the world's four major championships.

The qualifying score was 148, equalled four times subsequently, but not bettered until 1979.

1965 Jack Nicklaus, second winner to have three rounds under 70, lowered the record aggregate to 271 and equalled Lloyd Mangrum's record individual round with a third-round 64.

Arnold Palmer and Gary Player tied second on 280, the only occasion on which the Big Three finished 1, 2, 3 in a major championship.

1966 Second triple tie but Jack Nicklaus (70) held off Tommy Jacobs (72) and Gay Brewer (78) in a play-off that only just beat darkness to become the first champion successfully to defend his title. It is one of the Masters' oddest records that he remains so.

Twelve amateurs made the cut. The qualifying was the highest,

153, although a record number of 64 qualified. The 10-stroke rule was invoked for the first time.

1967 Gay Brewer who had taken 5 at the 72nd the year before, defeated his playing partner Bobby Nichols in an exciting finish by 1 stroke.

Ben Hogan shot a third-round 66 at the age of 54, the lowest of the tournament.

Bobby Cole, 18, became the youngest player to survive the cut. He was still an amateur.

1968 The year Roberto de Vicenzo signed for a 4 on the 71st hole instead of a 3 and lost to Bob Goalby by 1 stroke.

Generally, the year of the best scores: 127 rounds of par or better were played during the four days compared with the next best of 94 in 1965.

During the final round, de Vicenzo, on his 45th birthday, played the first 3 holes in 4 under par, an all-time record. He began by holing his second at the par-4 1st hole, but little did anyone realize that the end would be so tragic.

1969 25 players led, or shared the lead, over the four days—a record—but George Archer (6 ft 6 in), the tallest champion, triumphed in the end. Billy Casper, the joint runner-up 2 strokes behind, went out in 40 in the final round.

1970 Compensation for the year before as Casper became the champion after a play-off with another Californian, Gene Littler.

1971 Charles Coody separated himself from some distinguished pursuers by playing the last 4 holes in 2 under par to become champion. After the 68th hole Johnny Miller had been 2 ahead of Coody and Jack Nicklaus. Coody's finish was in contrast to that in 1969 when he lost the title on the last 3 holes.

1972 Nicklaus joined Palmer as a four-time champion in a slightly disappointing Masters if there is such a thing. His total of 286 was the only one under par. Charles Coody, defending champion, holed in one at the 6th in the first round then took 7 at the par-4 7th.

1973 The Masters lost a day's play for the first time. Saturday was washed out by storms and the finish postponed until Monday when the first Georgian, Tommy Aaron, won the Green Jacket. In a close finish he won by 1 stroke from J C Snead.

At 24, Britain's Peter Oosterhuis became the youngest foreign player to lead the Masters at any point. He led after three rounds by 3 strokes, but he took a final 74 to finish in a triple tie for 3rd.

1974 Gary Player's second victory on a last day when six or seven others had a chance on the last 9 holes.

Sam Snead (61 years 1 month and 8 days) became the oldest player to make the cut.

Ralph Johnston became the first first-year player since Horton Smith in 1934 to complete four rounds of par or better.

Maurice Bembridge lowered the final round record with 64.

1975 Sometimes called the best Masters of all. Johnny Miller and Tom Weiskopf dominated the dramatic last day but could not prevent Jack Nicklaus from registering his record fifth victory. Weiskopf and Miller had chances of birdies at the 72nd hole to tie Nicklaus, but both failed. It was the fourth time Weiskopf finished second or joint second.

Hale Irwin had a final round of 64 to finish fourth, 5 strokes behind Weiskopf and Miller.

Miller had 6 birdies in a row from the 2nd in his record outward half of 30 in the third round.

1976 A championship dominated by Raymond Floyd. He led from start to finish; played the first 36 holes in a new record of 131 (65, 66); set another record for 54 holes (65, 66, 70), took an 8-stroke lead into the last round and equalled Jack Nicklaus's record aggregate of 271.

Floyd had a total of 21 birdies and 1 eagle.

1977 Tom Watson got the better of a terrific final day duel with Jack Nicklaus, who was playing just in front of him. A 67 for 276 gave Watson his second major championship victory, one he repeated in July over Nicklaus in the British Open.

Severiano Ballesteros, who celebrated his 20th birthday on the third day, became the youngest professional to take part in the Masters.

1978 Gary Player's third victory, 17 years after his first—a record span. Starting the last day 7 strokes behind the leader, Hubert Green, he had 7 birdies on the last 10 holes to win by 1 stroke. He came back in 30 to hoist a record last-round 64 by a winner.

Wally Armstrong finished equal 5th with 280, the lowest score ever by a player in his first Masters until Fuzzy Zoeller's win a year later.

Tsuneyuki Nakajima of Japan took 13 at the 13th. Three months later, he took 9 at the 17th in the British Open at St Andrews.

1979 Victory after the first sudden-death play-off in the Masters for Fuzzy Zoeller, the first player to win on his first Masters appearance (1934 and 1935 excluded). He beat Ed Sneed and Tom Watson with a birdie 3 at the 11th (the play-off started at the 10th) after all three had missed birdie chances at the 10th.

It was a Masters which Sneed lost. Having started poorly and then held his challenge together stoutly on the 11th, 12th, 13th, 14th and 15th, he dropped strokes on each of the last 3 holes. At the 18th, his 6 ft winning putt hung on the lip.

Jack Nicklaus maintained his incredible run of consistency, but overran the 17th green downwind in the final round and took 5.

Earlier in the tournament, Miller Barber had equalled the lowest score with a second round of 64. Owing to the edge of a

Roberto de Vicenzo, 1985 US Seniors' Open champion, who suffered such a cruel fate in finishing second in the 1968 Masters. (USGA)

tornado hitting Augusta, it was a round which began on Friday and ended on Saturday morning. The 36-hole cut was 145, the lowest ever.

First prize of $50 000.

1980 A Masters in which Severiano Ballesteros stole the show. Three strokes ahead after 36 holes and 7 ahead after 54, he was 10 strokes clear with 9 holes to play. Then 3 putts on the 10th, 5 at the par-3 12th and a 6 on the 13th gave Gibby Gilbert and Jack Newton a chance. It also meant that Ballesteros would not break the record winning margin, the record aggregate or become the first champion with four rounds under 70.

However, Ballesteros played the last 5 holes in 1 under par to become the youngest winner and the first European to win. With Jack Newton finishing equal 2nd, it was the first time two overseas players had finished so well. A third overseas player, David Graham, was 5th.

Tom Weiskopf took 13 on the par-3 12th in the first round and 7 on the same hole in the second round.

1981 Tom Watson's second victory, and once again it was Jack Nicklaus who chased him home. Nicklaus, in fact, held a fairly healthy halfway lead after a second round of 65—the lowest of the week. However, Nicklaus suffered the unusual experience of going from 4 ahead to 4 behind in the space of 12 holes of the third round. Nicklaus then played the 15th and 16th brilliantly and with Watson hitting his second with a wedge into the front bunker at the 17th and following with 3 putts, the two were level again.

Nicklaus fell one behind by taking 3 putts at the 18th and, though the last round had its ups and downs, Watson held his lead despite putting his second in the Creek at the 13th.

1982 Craig Stadler beat Dan Pohl at the first hole (the 10th) of a sudden-death play-off to take his first major title, having been 6 strokes ahead with 7 holes to play. Unseasonably cold weather and fast greens, allied to a storm which caused the first round to be completed on the second day, produced unusually high scores early on.

For only the second time in the history of the Masters, nobody was below par at the halfway stage; 1954 was the other occasion.

However, a third round of 67 took Stadler into a good lead and, though he faltered on the closing holes on Sunday, a par-4 at the 10th earned him the coveted Green Jacket. He won $64 000 and Pohl, in his first Masters, $39 000. Prior to coming to Augusta, Pohl had won only $6000 in 1982.

In the third round, Pohl had an unprecedented streak in which he played 4 holes (13th to 16th) in 6 under par. His sequence was eagle, eagle, birdie, birdie.

1983 Second victory in four years for Severiano Ballesteros. He won by 4 strokes from Ben Crenshaw and Tom Kite largely by a devastating start to his last round. In 4 holes, he went from 1 stroke behind to 3 in front. He started birdie, eagle, par, birdie, reached the turn in 31, 1 stroke outside Johnny Miller's record and was then 4 ahead. Thereafter, he was never in serious danger. Jack Nicklaus withdrew from the tournament with a back injury.

1984 One of the sentimental favourites, Ben Crenshaw, equal second the previous year, scored the victory, his first in a major championship, that meant so much to him. After bad weather had caused the third round to be completed on Sunday morning, Crenshaw, showing commendable control in his long game and an inspired touch with his putter, clinched victory by two strokes.

1985 The first German winner and the second winner from the Continent of Europe; Bernhard Langer was invested with the Green Jacket after third and fourth rounds of 68. After two rounds, he lay on 146, 6 strokes behind the joint leaders.

However, Curtis Strange, who finished joint 2nd, started with an 80. He then had an inspired spell of some 45 holes, moving into a four stroke lead with 9 holes to play. Then disaster struck.

1986 One of the great storybook results in the history of golf.

With an inward half of 30 and a final round of 65, Jack Nicklaus became the oldest winner of the Masters and boosted his own record by winning for a sixth time. His previous victory was in 1975.

It was a tournament that others lost as much as Nicklaus won but Nicklaus has rarely played better or more boldly than over the last 10 holes and it stretched his span of major championship victories. He won his first US Amateur in 1959 and his first US Open in 1962.

Nick Price lowered the individual round record on Saturday with a 63.

1987 Third sudden-death play-off in Masters history and a dramatic one it proved. Larry Mize chipped in on the second extra hole (11th) to register his second win in six years on the tour. Earlier he tied with the world's two best players, Norman and Ballesteros, on 285, the highest winning total since 1972. Ballesteros was eliminated on the first play-off hole by taking 3 putts.

Tom Weiskopf, the unluckiest player never to have won the Masters. He was runner-up four times.

DETAILED RECORDS

Most victories
6, Jack Nicklaus, 1963–65–66–72–75–86
4, Arnold Palmer, 1958–60–62–64

Most times runner-up or joint runner-up
4, Ben Hogan, 1942–46–54–55; Tom Weiskopf, 1969–72–74–75; Jack Nicklaus 1964–71–77–81

Oldest winners
Jack Nicklaus, 46 years 2 months 21 days, 1986
Gary Player, 42 years 5 months 9 days, 1978
Sam Snead, 41 years 11 months 15 days, 1954

Youngest winners
Severiano Ballesteros, 23 years 4 days, 1980
Jack Nicklaus, 23 years 2 months, 1963

Biggest margin of victory
9 strokes, Jack Nicklaus, 1965
8 strokes, Raymond Floyd, 1976
7 strokes, Cary Middlecoff, 1955

Lowest winning aggregate
271 (67, 71, 64, 69), Jack Nicklaus, 1965
271 (65, 66, 70, 70), Raymond Floyd, 1976

Highest winning aggregate
289 (72, 71, 75, 71), Jack Burke, Jr, 1956
289 (74, 73, 70, 72), Sam Snead, 1954

Lowest aggregate by runner-up
277 (75, 71, 65, 66), Johnny Miller, 1975
277 (69, 72, 66, 70), Tom Weiskopf, 1975

Lowest aggregate by an amateur
281 (72, 71, 69, 69), Charles Coe, 1961

Lowest individual round
63, Nick Price (33, 30), third round, 1986
64, Lloyd Mangrum (32, 32), first round, 1940; Jack Nicklaus (31, 33), third round, 1965; Maurice Bembridge (34, 30), fourth round, 1974; Hale Irwin (32, 32), fourth round, 1975; Gary Player (34, 30), fourth round, 1978; Miller Barber (31, 33), second round, 1979

Lowest first round
64, Lloyd Mangrum, 1940

Lowest second round
64, Miller Barber, 1979

Lowest third round
63, Nick Price, 1986

Lowest fourth round
64, Maurice Bembridge, 1974; Hale Irwin, 1975; Gary Player, 1978

Lowest first 36 holes
131 (65, 66), Raymond Floyd, 1976

Lowest middle 36 holes
133 (68, 65), Dow Finsterwald, 1962

Lowest final 36 holes
131 (65, 66), Johnny Miller, 1975

Lowest first 54 holes
201 (65, 66, 70), Raymond Floyd, 1976

Lowest final 54 holes
202 (71, 65, 66), Johnny Miller, 1976

Lowest 9 holes
30, second 9: Jimmy Demaret, 1940; Gene Littler, 1966; Ben Hogan, 1967; Miller Barber, 1970; Maurice Bembridge, 1974; Gary Player, 1978; Nick Price, 1986
30, first 9: Johnny Miller, 1975

Most rounds under 70
32, Jack Nicklaus

Champions with each round lower than previous one
Jack Nicklaus, 1986, 74, 71, 69, 65
In 1978 Gary Player had 72, 72, 69, 64

Biggest span between first and last victories
23 years, Jack Nicklaus, 1963–86
17 years, Gary Player, 1961–78. Player also won in 1974

Successive victories
2, Jack Nicklaus, 1965–66
Two defenders, Ben Hogan, 1954, and Gary Player, 1962, lost in a play-off

Victories by amateurs
None. Ken Venturi finished second in 1956; Frank Stranahan (1947) and Charles Coe (1961) tied for second. Billy Joe Patton finished third in 1954, 1 stroke behind Ben Hogan and Sam Snead, who tied. Patton led with 6 holes to play

Highest number of top five finishes
15, Jack Nicklaus
9, Sam Snead, Ben Hogan, Arnold Palmer

First player to break 70
Ed Dudley 69, second round, 1934

Outright leader after every round
Craig Wood, 1941; Arnold Palmer, 1960; Jack Nicklaus, 1972; Raymond Floyd, 1976

Led or tied for lead from start to finish
Horton Smith, 1934; Herman Keiser, 1946; Jimmy Demaret, 1947; Arnold Palmer, 1964; Severiano Ballesteros, 1980

Play-offs
1935–42–54–62–66–70–79–82

Lowest round in a play-off
68, Arnold Palmer, 1962. Sudden death introduced in 1979

Overseas winners
Gary Player, 1961–74–78; Severiano Ballesteros, 1980–83; Bernhard Langer, 1985

Record leads
After 18 holes: 5 strokes, Craig Wood, 1941
After 36 holes: 5 strokes, Herman Keiser, 1946; Jack Nicklaus, 1975; Raymond Floyd, 1976
After 54 holes: 8 strokes, Raymond Floyd, 1976

Biggest variation between rounds of a champion
10 strokes, Sam Snead, 1952, second round 67 third round 77
9 strokes, Byron Nelson, 1937, first round 66 third round 75
9 strokes, Arnold Palmer, 1962, second round 66 fourth round 75
9 strokes, Jack Nicklaus, 1986, first round 74 fourth round 65
In 1985, Curtis Strange, who finished joint second, had opening rounds of 80, 65.

Best comebacks by champions
After 18 holes: Jack Burke, 1956, and Gay Brewer, 1967, 6 strokes behind leader
After 36 holes: Jack Burke, 1956, 8 strokes behind the leader
After 54 holes: Jack Burke, 8 strokes behind the leader (made up 9 to win)

Champions with four rounds under 70
None. Ben Hogan, 1953; Gary Player, 1961; Arnold Palmer, 1964; Jack Nicklaus, 1965; Jack Nicklaus, 1975 and Severiano Ballesteros, 1980 had three rounds under 70

Best finishing round by a champion
64, Gary Player, 1978
65, Jack Nicklaus, 1986

Worst finishing round by a champion
75, Arnold Palmer, 1962 (after a play-off)

Best opening round by a champion
65, Raymond Floyd, 1976

Worst opening round by a champion
75, Craig Stadler, 1982

Winners at first attempt
Horton Smith, 1934; Gene Sarazen, 1935; Fuzzy (Frank Urban) Zoeller, 1979

Record number of appearances
39, Sam Snead, 1937–78

RESULTS

1934
Horton Smith   70 72 70 72 284
Craig Wood   71 74 69 71 285
Billy Burke   72 71 70 73 286
Paul Runyan   74 71 70 71 286

1935
Gene Sarazen   68 71 73 70 282
Craig Wood   69 72 68 73 282
(Sarazen won play-off 144 to 149)
Olin Dutra   70 70 70 74 284

1936
Horton Smith   74 71 68 72 285
Harry Cooper   70 69 71 76 286
Gene Sarazen   78 67 72 70 287

1937
Byron Nelson   66 72 75 70 283
Ralph Guldahl   69 72 68 76 285
Ed Dudley   70 71 71 74 286

1938
Henry Picard   71 72 72 70 285
Ralph Guldahl   73 70 73 71 287
Harry Cooper   68 77 71 71 287

1939
Ralph Guldahl   72 68 70 69 279
Sam Snead   70 70 72 68 280
Billy Burke   69 72 71 70 282
Lawson Little, Jr 72 72 68 70 282

1940
Jimmy Demaret   67 72 70 71 280
Lloyd Mangrum   64 75 71 74 284
Byron Nelson   69 72 74 70 285

1941
Craig Wood   66 71 71 72 280
Byron Nelson   71 69 73 70 283
Sam Byrd   73 70 68 74 285

1942
Byron Nelson   68 67 72 73 280
Ben Hogan   73 70 67 70 280
(Nelson won play-off 69 to 70)
Paul Runyan   67 73 72 71 283

1946
Herman Keiser   69 68 71 74 282
Ben Hogan   74 70 69 70 283
Bob Hamilton   75 69 71 72 287

1947
Jimmy Demaret   69 71 70 71 281
Byron Nelson   69 72 72 70 283
Frank Stranahan   73 72 70 68 283

1948
Claude Harmon   70 70 69 70 279
Cary Middlecoff   74 71 69 70 284
Chick Harbert   71 70 70 76 287

1949
Sam Snead   73 75 67 67 282
Johnny Bulla   74 73 69 69 285
Lloyd Mangrum   69 74 72 70 285

1950
Jimmy Demaret   70 72 72 69 283
Jim Ferrier   70 67 73 75 285
Sam Snead   71 74 70 72 287

1951
Ben Hogan   70 72 70 68 280
Skee Riegel   73 68 70 71 282
Lloyd Mangrum   69 74 70 73 286
Lew Worsham, Jr   71 71 72 72 286

1952
Sam Snead   70 67 77 72 286
Jack Burke, Jr   76 67 78 69 290
Al Besselink   70 76 71 74 291
Tommy Bolt   71 71 75 74 291
Jim Ferrier   72 70 77 72 291

1953
Ben Hogan   70 69 66 69 274
Porky Oliver, Jr 69 73 67 70 279
Lloyd Mangrum   74 68 71 69 282

1954
Sam Snead   74 73 70 72 289
Ben Hogan   72 73 69 75 289
(Snead won play-off 70 to 71)
Billy Joe Patton 70 74 75 71 290

1955
Cary Middlecoff   72 65 72 70 279
Ben Hogan   73 68 72 73 286
Sam Snead   72 71 74 70 287

1956
Jack Burke, Jr   72 71 75 71 289
Ken Venturi   66 69 75 80 290
Cary Middlecoff   67 72 75 77 291

1957
Doug Ford   72 73 72 66 283
Sam Snead   72 68 74 72 286
Jimmy Demaret   72 70 75 70 287

1958
Arnold Palmer   70 73 68 73 284
Doug Ford   74 71 70 70 285
Fred Hawkins   71 75 68 71 285

1959
Art Wall, Jr   73 74 71 66 284
Cary Middlecoff   74 71 68 72 285
Arnold Palmer   71 70 71 74 286

1960
Arnold Palmer   67 73 72 70 282
Ken Venturi   73 69 71 70 283
Dow Finsterwald   71 70 72 71 284

1961
Gary Player   69 68 69 74 280
Arnold Palmer   68 69 73 71 281
Charlie Coe   72 71 69 69 281

1962
Arnold Palmer   70 66 69 75 280
Gary Player   67 71 71 71 280
Dow Finsterwald   74 68 65 73 280
(Palmer won play-off 68 to 71 to 77)

1963
Jack Nicklaus   74 66 74 72 286
Tony Lema   74 69 74 70 287
Julius Boros   76 69 71 72 288
Sam Snead   70 73 74 71 288

1964
Arnold Palmer   69 68 69 70 276
Dave Marr   70 73 69 70 282

Jack Nicklaus   71 73 71 67 282

1965
Jack Nicklaus   67 71 64 69 271
Arnold Palmer   70 68 72 70 280
Gary Player   65 73 69 73 280

1966
Jack Nicklaus   68 76 72 72 288
Tommy Jacobs   75 71 70 72 288
Gay Brewer   74 72 72 70 288
(Nicklaus won play-off 70 to 72 to 78)

1967
Gay Brewer   73 68 72 67 280
Bobby Nichols   72 69 70 70 281
Bert Yancey   67 73 71 73 284

1968
Bob Goalby   70 70 71 66 277
Roberto de Vincenzo 69 73 70 66 278
Bert Yancey   71 71 72 65 279

1969
George Archer   67 73 69 72 281
Tom Weiskopf   71 71 69 71 282
George Knudson   70 73 69 70 282
Billy Casper   66 71 71 74 282

1970
Billy Casper   72 68 68 71 279
Gene Littler   69 70 70 70 279
(Casper won play-off 69 to 74)
Gary Player   74 68 68 70 280

1971
Charles Coody   66 73 70 70 279
Johnny Miller   72 73 68 68 281
Jack Nicklaus   70 71 68 72 281

1972
Jack Nicklaus   68 71 73 74 286
Tom Weiskopf   74 71 70 74 289
Bruce Crampton   72 75 69 73 289
Bobby Mitchell   73 72 71 73 289

1973
Tommy Aaron   68 73 74 68 283
Jesse C Snead   70 71 73 70 284
Peter Oosterhuis 73 70 68 74 285
Jim Jamieson   73 71 70 71 285
Jack Nicklaus   69 77 73 66 285

1974
Gary Player   71 71 66 70 278
Dave Stockton   71 66 70 73 280
Tom Weiskopf   71 69 70 70 280

1975
Jack Nicklaus   68 67 73 68 276
Johnny Miller   75 71 65 66 277
Tom Weiskopf   69 72 66 70 277

1976
Ray Floyd   65 66 70 70 271
Ben Crenshaw   70 70 72 67 279
Jack Nicklaus   67 69 73 73 282
Larry Ziegler   67 71 72 72 282

1977
Tom Watson   70 69 70 67 276
Jack Nicklaus   72 70 70 66 278
Tom Kite   70 73 70 67 280
Rik Massengale   70 73 67 70 280

RESULTS

1978
Gary Player	72 72 69 64 277
Rod Funseth	73 66 70 69 278
Hubert Green	72 69 65 72 278
Tom Watson	73 68 68 69 278

1979
Fuzzy Zoeller	70 71 69 70 280
Tom Watson	68 71 70 71 280
Ed Sneed	68 67 69 76 280

(Zoeller won play-off at 2nd extra hole)

1980
Severiano Ballesteros	66 69 68 72 275
Gibby Gilbert	70 74 68 67 279
Jack Newton	68 74 69 68 279

1981
Tom Watson	71 68 70 71 280

Jack Nicklaus	70 65 75 72 282
Johnny Miller	69 72 73 68 282

1982
Craig Stadler	75 69 67 73 284
Dan Pohl	75 75 67 67 284

(Stadler won play-off at 1st extra hole)
Severiano Ballesteros	73 73 68 71 285
Jerry Pate	74 73 67 71 285

1983
Severiano Ballesteros	68 70 73 69 280
Ben Crenshaw	76 70 70 68 284
Tom Kite	70 72 73 69 284

1984
Ben Crenshaw	67 72 70 68 277
Tom Watson	74 67 69 69 279
Gil Morgan	73 71 69 67 280

David Edwards	71 70 72 67 280

1985
Bernhard Langer	72 74 68 68 282
Curtis Strange	80 65 68 71 284
Severiano Ballesteros	72 71 71 70 284
Raymond Floyd	70 73 69 72 284

1986
Jack Nicklaus	74 71 69 65 279
Greg Norman	70 72 68 70 280
Tom Kite	71 68 72 70 281

1987
Larry Mize	70 72 72 71 285
Greg Norman	73 74 66 72 285
Severiano Ballesteros	73 71 70 71 285

(Mize won play-off on 2nd extra hole;
Ballesteros eliminated on 1st)

Larry Mize, the 1987 Masters winner after a play-off with Severiano Ballesteros and Greg Norman. (Allsport)

USPGA

First played 1916

The PGA championship is the oldest and most important of the events which make up the US professional tour. It has become known as one of the four championships comprising the modern Grand Slam, but is less publicized than the US and British Opens and the Masters.

This is because its emphasis is more domestic and entry to the championship as a player is based on qualification from events in America. Full membership of the American PGA is an essential. Life exemption from pre-qualifying for any PGA event is one of the benefits to the winner and it has now assumed a settled date in the calendar. For some time it was played opposite the British Open or in the week immediately following it. In 1953, Ben Hogan was prevented from playing in it after winning the Masters, US Open and British Open.

From the year of its inception until 1958, it was traditionally a matchplay event with a distinguished list of early champions including Jim Barnes, Walter Hagen, Gene Sarazen and Tommy Armour. Hagen won it five times, including four in a row. Starting in 1924, he won 22 consecutive matches against the best professional golfers in America.

As the modern dislike for matchplay among professionals grew in America, the championship fell victim to the supporters of strokeplay and the influence of television. Two rounds a day were also going out of fashion and in 1958 it became 72 holes of strokeplay just like all the other tournaments.

After Sam Snead won his third victory in 1951, nobody won more than once until Jack Nicklaus won his second victory in 1971, when the event was held in February, and Gary Player followed suit a year later. Nicklaus

later won thrice more, but it remains a championship which Arnold Palmer never won.

MILESTONES

1916 First title won by Jim Barnes, an Englishman from Lelant in Cornwall, later both British and American Open champion. He defeated Jock Hutchison, a 32-year-old Scotsman from St Andrews, by 1 hole. Both Barnes and Hutchison lived in America.

1919 Second title for Barnes. In the final, he beat another Scottish-born professional, Fred McLeod, by 6 and 5. McLeod was US Open champion in 1908.

1920 Jock Hutchison (runner-up in 1916) beat J Douglas Edgar by 1 hole in the final. Edgar, Canadian Open Champion in 1919 and 1920, was killed some months later.

1921 Walter Hagen became the first American-born champion and began a remarkable period of dominance with Gene Sarazen. Between them they won from 1921 to 1927. In the final, Hagen beat Jim Barnes 3 and 2.

1922 Hagen did not defend and in his absence Sarazen, later to become his great rival, beat Emmet French 4 and 3 in the final at Oakmont, Pennsylvania. He is the youngest winner of the title.

1923 The only final involving Sarazen and Hagen produced the first extra hole victory for Sarazen. He won on the 38th, his second title in a row.

1924 First of an historic run of four victories for Walter Hagen. He scored his second victory in a final against Jim Barnes.

1925 Hagen needed 39 holes to beat Al Watrous and 40 to shake off Leo Diegel but, starting his final at Olympia Fields with an eagle, he beat Bill Mehlhorn by 6 and 5.

1926 Hagen won for the third time in a row. Having accounted for Johnny Farrell by 6 and 5 in the semi-final, he beat Leo Diegel by 5 and 3. At the 1st hole after lunch, Diegel's ball finished under Hagen's parked car.

1927 Hagen's record run extended to a fourth successive victory at Cedar Crest CC, Dallas, although he was behind for most of the final against Joe Turnesa. He finally squared at the 29th and went ahead at the 31st.

1928 Hagen took his run of victorious matches to 22 before he lost in the third round, but Leo Diegel, finalist in 1926, crowned

Sam Snead, USPGA champion three times. (Allsport)

One of the early USPGA champions, Gene Sarazen with Jim Ferrier, the Australian who won in 1947. (Illustrated London News)

a great week at Five Farms, Baltimore. It was he who beat Hagen; he then beat Gene Sarazen 9 and 8 and finally defeated Al Espinosa 6 and 5.

1929 Second successive victory for Leo Diegel. He won the final against Johnny Farrell, US Open champion, by 6 and 4. However, Diegel was only 1 up after 27 holes. Twice, subsequently, Farrell, set a stymie, putted Diegel's ball into the hole.

1930 In a great final, Tommy Armour beat Gene Sarazen by 1 hole with a putt of 14 ft on the 36th green. Sarazen was 1 up after 9, Armour 1 up after 18 holes and the match all square after 27 holes.

1931 Tom Creavy, one-time caddie for Gene Sarazen and Johnny Farrell, scored a surprise victory, the second winner aged 20. On his way to the final Creavy beat Jock Collins, Peter O'Hara, Cyril Walker and Sarazen; in the final, he beat Densmore Shute by 2 and 1. Illness later curtailed his tournament career.

1932 Olin Dutra caused something of a surprise on his way to the final where he beat Frank Walsh. In the semi-final, Walsh beat Bobby Cruickshank who, in an earlier round, beat Al Watrous after being 9 down with 12 to play. On the 24th green, Watrous conceded a 6 ft putt for a half. In this same championship Johnny Golden beat Walter Hagen at the 43rd hole, the longest match in the history of the USPGA.

1933 Sarazen's third and last victory, eleven years after his first. He beat Willie Goggin by 5 and 4 in the final at Blue Mound CC, Milwaukee.

1934 Paul Runyan won the championship, beating his old teacher Craig Wood at the 38th, equalling the longest match played in the final.

1935 Johnny Revolta, a former caddie with the reputation of being a fine bunker player and putter, beat Tommy Armour by 5 and 4 to win the championship. In the final, he displayed a

phenomenal short game, having beaten Walter Hagen in the first round.

1936 Densmore Shute, though heavily out-hit, beat Jimmy Thomson in the final.

1937 Shute became the last man to win the PGA title twice in succession. He won an extra-hole final at the 37th after Harold 'Jug' McSpaden had missed a shortish putt to win on the 36th, but McSpaden had led a bit of a charmed life. He won at the 38th in the first round and at the 39th in the 4th.

1938 After a welter of low scoring, Paul Runyan recorded his second victory. His margin of 8 and 7 over Sam Snead was the biggest in a final. Runyan had a first round of 67 and a 5-up lead.

1939 One of Byron Nelson's few defeats at this time. Having looked likely to beat Henry Picard in the final at Pomonok CC, New York, he lost at the 37th.

1940 Nelson soon atoned for his defeat in the previous final. Snead, despite going 1 up on the 32nd, lost by 1 hole. It was his second losing final in three years.

1941 Three down on the 28th tee, Vic Ghezzi came from behind in the final against Byron Nelson at Cherry Hills. It was Nelson's third final in a row.

1942 Sam Snead's first national championship. At Seaview CC, Atlantic City, he beat Jim Turnesa in the final by 2 and 1. Turnesa's victims included Hogan, McSpaden and Nelson.

1944 Nelson's third defeat in the final in five years. Bob Hamilton, his surprising conqueror, halved the 36th with a birdie when 1 up.

1945 Byron Nelson's fifth final in six years produced a clear-cut victory over Sam Byrd by 4 and 3 at Morraine CC, Dayton, Ohio. It was one of the peaks of his career.

1946 At Portland GC, Oregon, Ben Hogan won his first PGA title, virtually deciding his final with Ed 'Porky' Oliver by covering the first 9 holes after lunch in 30. It took him from 3 down to 2 up.

1947 Deadly putting and the odd stroke of luck enabled Australian-born Jim Ferrier to beat Chick Harbert by 2 and 1 in the final at Plum Hollow CC, Detroit.

1948 In the year in which he won his first US Open, Ben Hogan won his second PGA. After some devastating scoring in the earlier rounds, he beat Mike Turnesa by 7 and 6 despite being heavily outdriven.

1949 Sam Snead scored his second victory on a course, the Hermitage, Richmond, Virginia in his own home territory. Well supported by the crowd, he beat Johnny Palmer in the final.

1950 Having beaten Lloyd Mangrum and Jimmy Demaret, Chandler Harper defeated Henry Williams by 4 and 3 in the final to record his only national success.

1951 Sam Snead followed Walter Hagen and Gene Sarazen by winning a third title; at 39, he was also the oldest winner at that time. In a one-sided final against Walter Burkemo at Oakmont, he won 5 of the first 6 holes.

1952 Jim Turnesa was also 39 when he won his title at the Big Spring CC, Louisville. Although the famous Turnesa family had many achievements—brother Joe was runner-up to Hagen in 1927—this was the best. In the final, Jim beat Chick Harbert having been 3 down at lunch.

1953 Walter Burkemo, beaten by Sam Snead in the final of 1951, won his greatest honour in golf in his home state of Michigan. He beat Felice Torza by 2 and 1 and completed an amazing recovery as Torza was 7 up at lunch. Burkemo had originally thought of becoming a professional boxer.
Six former champions fell in the first two rounds, a bad blow for those wedded to matchplay.

1954 Burkemo reached the final in defence of his title and won 3 of the first 4 holes but Chick Harbert, twice runner-up, was 8 under par for the remaining holes. He won 4 and 3.

1955 Doug Ford, noted for his great putting, scored a victory in the final over Cary Middlecoff at Meadowbrook CC.

1956 The penultimate championship to be decided by matchplay produced the biggest field, 128. The new champion was Jack Burke who, showing great touch with his putter throughout, came from behind in the semi-final and final. In the final, he beat Ted Kroll.

1957 The end of an era. The last major professional matchplay event in America. Held at Miami Valley GC, Daytona, Ohio, it saw Lionel Hebert crowned as champion. It was his first tournament victory. His victim in the final was Dow Finsterwald.

1958 As frequently happens, the runner-up one year becomes champion the next and Finsterwald maintained the tradition in the first PGA championship to be decided by strokeplay. At Llanerch CC, Pennsylvania, he was ahead with a 67 on the first day but behind with a round to play. However, he went out in 31 in the final round, returned another 67 and beat Billy Casper by 2 strokes.

1959 Bob Rosburg, a graduate at Stanford, achieved his most outstanding success at Minneapolis. Amazingly enough, nine players shared the first round lead on 69, but it was Rosburg's final round of 66 which settled things. It enabled him to beat Doug Sanders and Jerry Barber, 6 and 7 strokes more in the last round, by 1 stroke. Barber's 36-hole total of 134 (69, 65) has never been beaten in the PGA championship, nor has his 30 for the front 9 in his 65.

1960 The PGA is well known as the one major championship which Arnold Palmer never won. The year 1960 was as good a chance as he had. As the new Open champion, he opened with a 67, but he followed with 74 and 75 and the winner was Jay Hebert. He followed his brother, Lionel, champion in 1957.

1961 Jerry Barber rivalled Gene Sarazen as the smallest champion. At 5 ft 5 in and the wearer of spectacles, he was not long, but he was deadly on the greens, as he showed over the last three holes. He holed from 6, 12 and 20 yd at Olympia Fields to earn a play-off with Don January. This he won 67 to 68, was voted Player of the Year and captained the Ryder Cup team in England.

1962 Gary Player, having already won the British Open and the Masters, registered his third major victory at Aronimink. He defeated Bob Goalby by 1 stroke with Jack Nicklaus, the new Open champion playing in his first PGA, equal third.

1963 Nicklaus, though he failed to qualify in defence of his Open title, won the Masters and did not have to wait long to add a third major title. In fierce heat in Dallas, he started the final round 3 strokes behind Bruce Crampton who had a third round 65, but a final 68 gave him victory by 2 strokes from Dave Ragan. By his victory, Nicklaus joined the company of Ben Hogan, Gene Sarazen and Byron Nelson as winner of the US Open, Masters and PGA; and Nicklaus had been a professional for less than two years.

1964 Bobby Nichols's greatest hour. He started with a 64 at the Firestone CC, Akron, Ohio, and led after every round. He held off Arnold Palmer and Jack Nicklaus who were second and third but for Palmer, the only player to break 70 in all four rounds (68, 68, 69, 69), it was another disappointment. Nichols's total of 271 is the lowest recorded in any PGA championship.

1965 Victory for Dave Marr at Laurel Valley was the highlight of his career. Four even rounds (70, 69, 70, 71) gave him victory over Billy Casper and Jack Nicklaus by 2 strokes after he had driven into a bunker at the final hole but saved his 4. Arnold Palmer could not sustain a challenge on his own front door, but Nicklaus's share of second place meant that in his first four PGAs, he finished third, first, equal second and equal second.

1966 Al Geiberger recorded the biggest victory to date: 4 strokes from Dudley Wysong at Firestone CC. Wysong lost to Jack Nicklaus in the final of the 1961 US Amateur at Pebble Beach.

1967 Don January, the eventual winner, and Don Massengale tied with 281 at the Columbine CC, Denver. In 1961, January had lost a play-off to Jerry Barber and so was due a major win.

1968 The 50th championship produced the oldest winner in

Julius Boros, 48, and another close call for Arnold Palmer at the Pecan Valley CC, Texas. At the final hole, Boros got up and down in two from a long way to beat Palmer and Bob Charles by 1 stroke.

1969 Gary Player, the target of some unruly local demonstrators who broke on to the course, just failed to deny the new champion, Raymond Floyd at the NCR course, Dayton, Ohio. He took a 5-stroke lead into the last round, but it was whittled down to one in a close finish.

1970 Dave Stockton, having lifted himself with a third-round 66 to take a 3-stroke lead, ended with 73 for a 2-stroke victory. Bob Murphy finished with a 66 to share second place with Arnold Palmer. It was Palmer's third second-place finish. He never came as close again.

1971 The first championship to be held in February and the first to be housed on the PGA National course at Palm Beach Gardens, Florida. It was appropriate, therefore, that a near neighbour, Jack Nicklaus, should record his second PGA success when he had 2 strokes to spare over Billy Casper. His victory meant that he was the first player to win the US and British Opens, the PGA and the Masters twice.

1972 A championship won by a remarkable recovery stroke. At the 16th at Oakland Hills in the final round Gary Player, having dropped strokes at the 14th and 15th, pushed his drive, but hit a daring 9 iron over a host of trouble to within 4 ft of the flag. He holed for a birdie and went on to his second title.

1973 Remembered not as the best PGA championship, but the one in which Nicklaus won his 14th major victory and went ahead of Bobby Jones. At Canterbury GC, Cleveland, he won by 4 strokes from Bruce Crampton, thus equalling the biggest margin of victory since the championship moved to strokeplay.

1974 Gary Player had a 64 in his second round at Tanglewood GC, one off the PGA record set the following year, but in a week of heavy rain the new champion was Lee Trevino. Nicklaus was second and Bobby Cole of South Africa, who went into the lead at the start of the last round, was third. Trevino's win followed his victories in the US and British Opens.

1975 Jack Nicklaus crept within one of Walter Hagen's record with his fourth win. It was his 16th major victory, but he had to contend with a brilliant spell from Bruce Crampton. On the long and demanding Firestone CC South course, Crampton had a second-round 63. This is the lowest round ever played in the PGA and his total of 134 equalled that held by Jerry Barber for 36 holes.

However, playing together in the third round, Nicklaus had a 67 to Crampton's 75 and though Crampton finished strongly in the last round, nobody could catch Nicklaus.

1976 A championship in which thunderstorms made a Monday finish necessary, brought a second victory for Dave Stockton. His total of 281 at Congressional equalled the highest winning aggregate at that time, but Stockton had to get down in 2 from off the last green holing from 10 ft to prevent a play-off with Don January and Ray Floyd.

Gil Morgan's 36-hole total of 134 (66, 68) equalled the lowest in a PGA championship.

1977 Pebble Beach's first PGA seemed to be destined for Gene Littler. He led from the first round, was still 5 ahead with 9 holes to play and was only headed on the 3rd hole of the sudden-death play-off. Lanny Wadkins, having won no event for almost four years, had two eagles on the front 9 of the final round and profited when Littler dropped strokes on 5 of the first 6 holes on the back 9. Jack Nicklaus led after 15 holes, but he bogeyed the par-3 17th while Wadkins had a birdie at the par-5 18th. His score of 282 is the highest PGA-winning total.

Right: Bob Tway who holed out of a bunker on the final hole to win the 1986 championship from Greg Norman. (Allsport)

Having had to hole from 20 ft to stay in the play-off at the 1st hole, Wadkins won with a 4 to a 5 on the 3rd. It was the first time a sudden-death play-off had decided a major championship.

1978 A three-way tie resulting in the first major victory for John Mahaffey at Oakmont. It was the second sudden-death play-off in two years. Mahaffey won with a birdie on the 2nd extra hole from Tom Watson and Jerry Pate. Pate missed a short putt to win the championship on the 72nd hole, but Watson had been 4 ahead of Pate and 5 ahead of Mahaffey with 9 holes to play. However, after many setbacks, nobody begrudged Mahaffey his success.

1979 For the third year running, it needed a sudden-death play-off to decide the championship at Oakland Hills. David Graham and Ben Crenshaw were those involved and Graham holed from 6 yd and 10 ft on the first two sudden-death holes before winning on the 3rd with a 2 to a 4. He thus became the first Australian winner since Jim Ferrier in 1947, but there was drama on the 72nd hole. Needing a 4 for a 2-stroke victory which would have set a new 72-hole record aggregate and equalled the lowest single round in the USPGA (63), he took 6. His drive was way right, his second through the green and he needed 2 chips and 2 putts.

Crenshaw who was down in 2 from a bunker at the 17th and from the back of the 18th, got into a play-off but, after the British Open a few weeks previously, he again suffered a disappointment when in sight of his first major championship win. He was unluckily thwarted by Graham's 2 saving putts, but Graham's last round 65 was remarkable despite taking 6 at the last. His total of 272 (69, 68, 70, 65) earned first prize of $30 000. Sam Snead finished 40th on 288, level fours, at the age of 67. Crenshaw became only the second man to break 70 in all four rounds (69, 67, 69, 67). The first was Arnold Palmer at Columbus in 1964 (68, 68, 69, 69) but, like Crenshaw, he was second. Bobby Nichols (1964) won a record 271.

1980 After victory in the US Open, Jack Nicklaus won his fifth PGA title, breaking or equalling more records in the process. His 7-stroke victory was the biggest since the championship was decided by strokeplay and he equalled Walter Hagen's tally of five victories.

There had been changes to the Oak Hill course since the 1968 Open but they failed to limit Nicklaus's scoring powers. One stroke behind Gil Morgan at halfway, a third-round 66 gave him a 3-stroke lead and there was no holding him on the final day. First prize was $60 000 and the total purse $375 000.

1981 Larry Nelson's victory which also assured him of a place in the Ryder Cup team, was his first in a major championship but it was decisive enough. Second and third rounds of 66 gave him a lead of four going into the last round and he won by four. Lee Trevino was disqualified for not signing his card and Tom Watson failed to qualify.

1982 Raymond Floyd led all the way at Southern Hills, missing the record aggregate of 271 by taking a double bogey on the final hole. His second PGA title came by 3 strokes. His opening 63 was the lowest first round in the championship's history and equalled the low score for any round.

His second and third round totals also established PGA championship records. The previous lowest 54 hole total was held by himself.

1983 Hal Sutton followed up his victory in the Tournament Players championship by winning the PGA title at the Riviera CC, Los Angeles. His total of 274 beat Jack Nicklaus by one stroke. His total of 131 for the first two rounds broke the record set the previous year by Raymond Floyd.

1984 Turned out to be a triumph for the old-timers at Shoal Creek, Alabama. Lee Trevino won, aged 44, with a total of 273 and Gary Player, 48, was joint second. Trevino became the first player to win with all four rounds under 70. He holds the same record in the US Open.

1985 First PGA victory for Hubert Green in his 39th year at Cherry Hills. Two strokes behind defending champion, Lee Trevino after two rounds, Green moved 3 strokes clear after a third round of 70. A final 70 saw him home by no less than 8 strokes. Tze-Chung Chen, equal second in the US Open in June, finished third. Bad weather caused the first round to be completed on Friday. There was an hour's delay on the last afternoon.

1986 By holing a bunker shot on the 72nd hole, Bob Tway denied Greg Norman of victory at the Inverness Club, Toledo. Norman was 9 strokes ahead of Tway at halfway but Tway's third round 64, which set a new record, retrieved five of them. His last round of 70 to Norman's 76 was a fine effort although, as they played their second shots to the final hole, Norman seemed the more likely winner. The third round was washed out and play extended to Monday.

DETAILED RECORDS (to end of 1986)

Championship held by matchplay 1916 to 1957
Since 1958 held by strokeplay

Most victories
5, Walter Hagen, 1921–24–25–26–27; Jack Nicklaus, 1963–71–73–75–80
3, Gene Sarazen, 1922–23–33; Sam Snead, 1942–49–51

Most times runner-up or joint runner-up
4, Jack Nicklaus, 1964–65–74–83
3, Byron Nelson, 1939–41–44; Arnold Palmer, 1964–68–70; Billy Casper, 1958–65–71

Oldest winner
Julius Boros, 48 years 4 months 18 days, 1968
Lee Trevino, 44 years 8 months 19 days, 1984

Youngest winner
Gene Sarazen, 20 years 5 months 20 days, 1922
Tom Creavy, 20 years 7 months 11 days, 1931

Biggest margin of victory
Matchplay (final): 8 and 7, Paul Runyan beat Sam Snead, 1938
Strokeplay: 8 strokes, Hubert Green, 1985
　　　　　　 7 strokes, Jack Nicklaus, 1980

Lowest winning aggregate
271 (64, 71, 69, 67), Bobby Nichols, Columbus CC, Ohio, 1964
272 (69, 68, 70, 65), David Graham, Oakland Hills, 1979
272 (63, 69, 68, 72), Raymond Floyd, Southern Hills, 1982

Highest winning aggregate
282 (69, 71, 72, 70), Lanny Wadkins, Pebble Beach, 1977

Lowest individual round
63, Bruce Crampton, second round, Firestone CC, Akron, 1975
63, Raymond Floyd, first round, Southern Hills, 1982

Lowest first round
63, Raymond Floyd, Southern Hills, 1982

Lowest second round
63, Bruce Crampton, Firestone CC, Akron, 1975

Lowest third round
64, Bob Tway, Inverness, Toledo, 1986

Lowest fourth round
64, Jack Nicklaus, Columbus CC, Ohio, 1964

Lowest 36-hole total
131 (65, 66), Hal Sutton, Riviera CC, 1983
132 (63, 69), Raymond Floyd, Southern Hills, 1982

Lowest final 36-hole total
134 (68, 66), John Mahaffey, Oakmont, 1978
134 (64, 70), Bob Tway, Inverness, 1986

Lowest 54-hole total
200 (63, 69, 68), Raymond Floyd, Southern Hills, 1982

Lowest 9 holes
30, Art Wall, Jr, second 9, third round, Llanerch CC, 1958; Jerry Barber, first 9, second round, Minneapolis GC, 1959; Bob Rosburg, first 9, fourth round, Minneapolis GC, 1959; Jim Colbert, second 9, second round, Firestone CC, 1975

Biggest span between first and last victories
17 years, Jack Nicklaus, 1963–80

Successive victories
4, Walter Hagen, 1924–25–26–27
2, Jim Barnes, 1916–19; Gene Sarazen, 1922–23; Leo Diegel, 1928–29; Densmore Shute, 1936–37

Matchplay—most times in final
6, Walter Hagen, 1921–23–24–25–26–27
5, Sam Snead, 1938–40–42–49–51; Byron Nelson, 1939–40–41–44–45

Most consecutive finals
5, Walter Hagen, 1923–27

Most matches won
51, Gene Sarazen
42, Walter Hagen

Most consecutive matches won
22, Walter Hagen
14, Densmore Shute
13, Gene Sarazen

Longest final
38 holes: Gene Sarazen beat Walter Hagen, 1923; Paul Runyan beat Craig Wood, 1934; Vic Ghezzi beat Byron Nelson, 1941

Longest match
43 holes: Johnny Golden beat Walter Hagen, 1932

Best comeback
In a 36-hole match at Keller GC, St Paul, Minnesota, in 1932, Bobby Cruickshank beat Al Watrous at the 41st hole, having been 9 down with 12 holes to play. In the next round, Cruickshank lost to Frank Walsh who lost in the final to Olin Dutra.

Most extra hole matches in one championship
In 1937, Harold 'Jug' McSpaden won on the 38th in the first round, on the 39th in the fourth round and lost the final to Densmore Shute on the 37th.
In 1953, Dave Douglas won on the 20th in the first round, on the 19th in the second round and on the 37th in the third round. His opponents were Lew Worsham, Sam Snead and Jackson Bradley.

RESULTS

1916 Siwanoy CC, New York
Jim M Barnes beat Jock Hutchison 1 up

1919 Engineers CC, New York
Jim M Barnes beat Freddy McLeod 6 and 5

1920 Flossmoor CC, Illinois
Jock Hutchison beat J D Edgar 1 up

1921 Inwood CC, New York
Walter Hagen beat Jim M Barnes 3 and 2

1922 Oakmont CC, Pennsylvania
Gene Sarazen beat Emmet French 4 and 3

1923 Pelham CC, New York
Gene Sarazen beat Walter Hagen at 38th

1924 French Lick CC, Indiana
Walter Hagen beat Jim M Barnes 2 up

1925 Olympia Fields CC, Illinois
Walter Hagen beat Bill Mehlhorn 6 and 5

1926 Salisbury GC, New York
Walter Hagen beat Leo Diegel 5 and 3

1927 Cedar Crest CC, Texas
Walter Hagen beat Joe Turnesa 1 up

1928 Baltimore CC Five Farms, Maryland
Leo Diegel beat Al Espinosa 6 and 5

1929 Hillcrest CC, California
Leo Diegel beat John Farrell 6 and 4

1930 Fresh Meadow, New York
Tommy Armour beat Gene Sarazen 1 up

1931 Wannamoisett CC, Rhode Island
Tom Creavy beat Densmore Shute 2 and 1

1932 Keller GC, Minnesota
Olin Dutra beat Frank Walsh 4 and 3

1933 Blue Mound CC, Wisconsin
Gene Sarazen beat Willie Goggin 5 and 4

1934 Park CC, New York
Paul Runyan beat Craig Wood at 38th

1935 Twin Hills CC, Oklahoma
Johnny Revolta beat Tommy Armour 5 and 4

1936 Pinehurst CC, North Carolina
Densmore Shute beat Jimmy Thomson 3 and 2

1937 Pittsburgh CC, Pennsylvania
Densmore Shute beat Harold McSpaden at 37th

1938 Shawnee CC, Pennsylvania
Paul Runyan beat Sam Snead 8 and 7

1939 Pomonok CC, New York
Henry Picard beat Byron Nelson at 37th

1940 Hershey CC, Pennsylvania
Byron Nelson beat Sam Snead 1 up

1941 Cherry Hills CC, Colorado
Vic Ghezzi beat Byron Nelson at 38th

1942 Seaview CC, New Jersey
Sam Snead beat Jim Turnesa 2 and 1

1944 Manito G & CC, Washington
Bob Hamilton beat Byron Nelson 1 up

1945 Morraine CC, Ohio
Byron Nelson beat Sam Byrd 4 and 3

1946 Portland GC, Oregon
Ben Hogan beat Porky Oliver 6 and 4

1947 Plum Hollow CC, Michigan
Jim Ferrier beat Chick Harbert 2 and 1

1948 Norwood Hills CC, Missouri
Ben Hogan beat Mike Turnesa 7 and 6

1949 Hermitage CC, Virginia
Sam Snead beat John Palmer 3 and 2

1950 Scioto CC, Ohio
Chandler Harper beat Henry Williams Jr 4 and 3

1951 Oakmont CC, Pennsylvania
Sam Snead beat Walter Burkemo 7 and 6

1952 Big Spring CC, Kentucky
Jim Turnesa beat Chick Harbert 1 up

1953 Birmingham CC, Michigan
Walter Burkemo beat Felice Torza 2 and 1

1954 Keller GC, Minnesota
Chick Harbert beat Walter Burkemo 4 and 3

1955 Meadowbrook CC, Michigan
Doug Ford beat Cary Middlecoff 4 and 3

1956 Blue Hill CC, Massachusetts
Jack Burke beat Ted Kroll 3 and 2

1957 Miami Valley GC, Ohio
Lionel Hebert beat Dow Finsterwald 2 and 1

RESULTS

1958 Llanerch CC, Pennsylvania
(Decided by strokeplay hereafter)

Dow Finsterwald	67	72	70	67	276
Billy Casper	73	67	68	70	278
Sam Snead	73	67	67	73	280

1959 Minneapolis GC, Minnesota

Bob Rosburg	71	72	68	66	277
Jerry Barber	69	65	71	73	278
Doug Sanders	72	66	68	72	278

1960 Firestone CC, Ohio

Jay Hebert	72	67	72	70	281
Jim Ferrier	71	74	66	71	282
Sam Snead	68	73	70	72	283
Doug Sanders	70	71	69	73	283

1961 Olympia Fields CC, Illinois

Jerry Barber	69	67	71	70	277
Don January	72	66	67	72	277
(Barber won play-off 67 to 68)					
Doug Sanders	70	68	74	68	280

1962 Aronimink GC, Pennsylvania

Gary Player	72	67	69	70	278
Bob Goalby	69	72	71	67	279
Jack Nicklaus	71	74	69	67	281
George Bayer	69	70	71	71	281

1963 Dallas Athletic CC, Texas

Jack Nicklaus	69	73	69	68	279
Dave Ragan	75	70	67	69	281
Dow Finsterwald	72	72	66	72	282
Bruce Crampton	70	73	65	74	282

1964 Columbus CC, Ohio

Bobby Nichols	64	71	69	67	271
Arnold Palmer	68	68	69	69	274
Jack Nicklaus	67	73	70	64	274

1965 Laurel Valley GC, Pennsylvania

Dave Marr	70	69	70	71	280
Billy Casper	70	70	71	71	282
Jack Nicklaus	69	70	72	71	282

1966 Firestone CC, Ohio

Al Geiberger	68	72	68	72	280
Dudley Wysong	74	72	66	72	284
Billy Casper	73	73	70	70	286
Gene Littler	75	71	71	70	286
Gary Player	73	70	70	73	286

1967 Columbine CC, Colorado

Don January	71	72	70	68	281
Don Massengale	70	75	70	66	281
(January won play-off 69 to 71)					
Jack Nicklaus	67	75	69	71	282
Dan Sikes	69	70	70	73	282

1968 Pecan Valley CC, Texas

Julius Boros	71	71	70	69	281
Bob Charles	72	70	70	70	282
Arnold Palmer	71	69	72	70	282

1969 NCR GC, Dayton, Ohio

Ray Floyd	69	66	67	74	276
Gary Player	71	65	71	70	277
Bert Greene	71	68	68	71	278

1970 Southern Hills CC, Oklahoma

Dave Stockton	70	70	66	73	279
Bob Murphy	71	73	71	66	281
Arnold Palmer	70	72	69	70	281

1971 PGA National GC, Florida

Jack Nicklaus	69	69	70	73	281
Billy Casper	71	73	71	68	283
Tommy Bolt	72	74	69	69	284

1972 Oakland Hills GC, Michigan

Gary Player	71	71	67	72	281
Tommy Aaron	71	71	70	71	283
Jim Jamieson	69	72	72	70	283

1973 Canterbury Club, Ohio

Jack Nicklaus	72	68	68	69	277
Bruce Crampton	71	73	67	70	281
Mason Rudolph	69	70	70	73	282
Lanny Wadkins	73	69	71	69	282
Jesse C Snead	71	74	68	69	282

1974 Tanglewood GC, North Carolina

Lee Trevino	73	66	68	69	276
Jack Nicklaus	69	69	70	69	277
Bobby Cole	69	68	71	71	279
Hubert Green	68	68	73	70	279
Dave Hill	74	69	67	69	279
Sam Snead	69	71	71	68	279

1975 Firestone CC, Akron, Ohio

Jack Nicklaus	70	68	67	71	276
Bruce Crampton	71	63	75	69	278
Tom Weiskopf	70	71	70	68	279

1976 Congressional CC, Maryland

Dave Stockton	70	72	69	70	281
Raymond Floyd	72	68	71	71	282
Don January	70	69	71	72	282

1977 Pebble Beach, California

Lanny Wadkins	69	71	72	70	282
Gene Littler	67	69	70	76	282
(Wadkins won sudden-death play-off at 3rd hole)					
Jack Nicklaus	69	71	70	73	283

1978 Oakmont CC, Pennsylvania

John Mahaffey	75	67	68	66	276
Jerry Pate	72	70	66	68	276
Tom Watson	67	69	67	73	276

(Mahaffey won sudden-death play-off at 2nd hole)

1979 Oakland Hills, Michigan

David Graham	69	68	70	65	272
Ben Crenshaw	69	67	69	67	272
(Graham won sudden-death play-off at 3rd hole)					
Randy Caldwell	67	70	66	71	274

1980 Oak Hill CC, New York

Jack Nicklaus	70	69	66	69	274
Andy Bean	72	71	68	70	281
Lon Hinkle	70	69	69	75	283
Gil Morgan	68	70	73	72	283

1981 Atlanta Athletic Club, Georgia

Larry Nelson	70	66	66	71	273
Fuzzy Zoeller	70	68	68	71	277
Dan Pohl	69	67	73	69	278

1982 Southern Hills, Tulsa

Raymond Floyd	63	69	68	72	272
Lanny Wadkins	71	68	69	67	275
Fred Couples	67	71	72	66	276
Calvin Peete	69	70	68	69	276

1983 Riviera CC, Los Angeles

Hal Sutton	65	66	72	71	274
Jack Nicklaus	73	65	71	66	275
Peter Jacobsen	73	70	68	65	276

1984 Shoal Creek, Alabama

Lee Trevino	69	68	67	69	273
Lanny Wadkins	68	69	68	72	277
Gary Player	74	63	69	71	277

1985 Cherry Hills, Denver

Hubert Green	67	69	70	72	278
Lee Trevino	66	68	75	71	280
Andy Bean	71	70	72	68	281
Tze-Chung Chen	69	76	71	65	281

1986 Inverness, Toledo

Bob Tway	72	70	64	70	276
Greg Norman	65	68	69	76	278
Peter Jacobsen	68	70	70	71	279

The Major Open Championships

Australian Open

First played 1904

Most victories
7, Gary Player, 1958–62–63–65–69–70–74
6, Jack Nicklaus, 1964–68–71–75–76–78
5, Ivo Whitton, 1912–13–26–29–31

Oldest winner
Peter Thomson, 43 years, 1972

Youngest winner
Ivo Whitton, 19 years, 1912

Lowest aggregate
264 (62, 71, 62, 69), Gary Player, Kooyonga GC, Adelaide, 1965

Lowest individual round
62 (twice), Gary Player, Kooyonga GC, Adelaide, 1965

Biggest margin of victory
8 strokes, Jack Nicklaus, Royal Hobart, 1971
7 strokes, Gary Player, Royal Melbourne, 1968

Amateur winners
Hon Michael Scott, 1904–07; C Pearce, 1908; C Felstead, 1909; I Whitton, 1912–13–26–29–31; A Russell, 1924; M Ryan, 1932; J Ferrier, 1938–39; B Devlin, 1960

Biggest span between victories
19 years, Ivo Whitton, 1912–31

Prize money
1948, $500; 1978, $220 000; 1981, $150 000; 1986, $275 000

RESULTS

Year	Winner	Venue	Score
1904	*Hon Michael Scott	The Australian (Botany)	315
1905	D Soutar	Royal Melbourne	330
1906	Carnegie Clark	Royal Sydney	322
1907	*Hon Michael Scott	Royal Melbourne	318
1908	*Clyde Pearce	The Australian	311
1909	*C Felstead	Royal Melbourne	316
1910	Carnegie Clark	Royal Adelaide	306
1911	Carnegie Clark	Royal Sydney	321
1912	*Ivo Whitton	Royal Melbourne	321
1913	*Ivo Whitton	Royal Melbourne	302
1920	Joe Kirkwood	The Australian	290
1921	A Le Fevre	Royal Melbourne	295
1922	C Campbell	Royal Sydney	307
1923	T Howard	Royal Adelaide	301
1924	*A Russell	Royal Melbourne	303
1925	F Popplewell	The Australian	299
1926	*Ivo Whitton	Royal Adelaide	297
1927	R Stewart	Royal Melbourne	297
1928	F Popplewell	Royal Sydney	295
1929	*Ivo Whitton	Royal Adelaide	309
1930	F Eyre	Metropolitan	306
1931	*Ivo Whitton	The Australian	301
1932	*M J Ryan	Royal Adelaide	296
1933	M L Kelly	Royal Melbourne	302
1934	W J Bolger	Royal Sydney	283
1935	F McMahon	Royal Adelaide	293
1936	Gene Sarazen	Metropolitan	282
1937	G Naismith	The Australian	299
1938	*Jim Ferrier	Royal Adelaide	283
1939	*Jim Ferrier	Royal Melbourne	285
1946	Ossie Pickworth	Royal Sydney	289
1947	Ossie Pickworth	Royal Queensland	285
1948	Ossie Pickworth	Kingston Heath	289
1949	Eric Cremin	The Australian	287
1950	Norman von Nida	Kooyonga	286
1951	Peter Thomson	Metropolitan	283
1952	Norman von Nida	Lake Karrinyup	278
1953	Norman von Nida	Royal Melbourne	278
1954	Ossie Pickworth	Kooyonga	280
1955	Bobby Locke	Gailes	290
1956	Bruce Crampton	Royal Sydney	289
1957	Frank Phillips	Kingston Heath	287
1958	Gary Player	Kooyonga	271
1959	Kel Nagle	The Australian	284
1960	*Bruce Devlin	Lake Karrinyup	282
1961	Frank Phillips	Victoria	275
1962	Gary Player	Royal Adelaide	281
1963	Gary Player	Royal Melbourne	278
1964	Jack Nicklaus	The Lakes	287
1965	Gary Player	Kooyonga	264
1966	Arnold Palmer	Royal Queensland	276
1967	Peter Thomson	Commonwealth	281
1968	Jack Nicklaus	Laky Karrinyup	270
1969	Gary Player	Royal Sydney	288
1970	Gary Player	Kingston Heath	280
1971	Jack Nicklaus	Royal Hobart	269
1972	Peter Thomson	Kooyonga	281
1973	Jesse Snead	Royal Queensland	280
1974	Gary Player	Lake Karrinyup	279
1975	Jack Nicklaus	Australian	279
1976	Jack Nicklaus	Australian	286
1977	David Graham	Australian	284
1978	Jack Nicklaus	Australian	284
1979	Jack Newton	Metropolitan	288
1980	Greg Norman	The Lakes	284
1981	Bill Rogers	Victoria	282
1982	Bob Shearer	Australian	287
1983	Peter Fowler	Kingston Heath	285
1984	Tom Watson	Royal Melbourne	281
1985	Greg Norman (reduced to 3 rounds)	Royal Melbourne	212
1986	Rodger Davis	Metropolitan	278

* Denotes Amateur

Canadian Open

First played 1904

Most victories
4, Leo Diegel, 1924–25–28–29

Oldest winner
Kel Nagle, 43 years 6 months, Pinegrove, Quebec, 1964
Bob Murphy, 43 years 4 months 15 days, 1986

Youngest winner
Albert H Murray, 20 years 10 months, Montreal, 1908

Lowest 72-hole aggregate
263, John Palmer (USA), St Charles CC, Winnipeg, 1952

Lowest individual round
63, Jerry Pate (USA) fourth round, Windsor, Essex, 1976
64, Jack Nicklaus (USA) fourth round, Windsor, Essex, 1976

Amateur winner
Doug Sanders, Beaconsfield GC, Montreal, 1956

Biggest margin of victory
16 strokes, John Douglas Edgar, Hamilton, 1919.
He defeated Bobby Jones and Karl Keffer with a total of 278.
Edgar won again in 1920, but was killed in 1921, it was said in
a street gang fight in Atlanta before he could try for three in a
row

Brothers as champion
Charles and Albert Murray both won the title twice. Charles
in 1906 and 1911 and Albert, the elder by 7 years in 1908 and
1913

Sponsorship
Seagram's began sponsorship in 1936 with a purse of $3000. It
reached $25 000 in 1957; $100 000 in 1965 and in 1967; for one
year only, it went to $200 000 ($100 000 of which came from
the City of Montreal).
In 1971 Peter Jackson, a division of Imperial Tobacco, took
over at $150 000. By 1979, it was $350 000, both Peter Jackson
and the Royal Canadian Golf Association contributing to the
purse

RESULTS

Year	Winner	Venue	Score
1904	J H Oke	Montreal	156
1905	George Cumming	Toronto	146
1906	Charles R Murray	Ottawa	170
Increased to 72 holes from 1907			
1907	Percy Barrett	Toronto	300
1908	Albert Murray	Montreal	300
1909	Karl Keffer	Toronto	309
1910	D Kenny	Toronto	303
1911	Charles R Murray	Ottawa	314
1912	George Sargent	Toronto	299
1913	Albert Murray	Montreal	295
1914	Karl Keffer	Toronto	300
1919	J Douglas Edgar	Hamilton	278
1920	J Douglas Edgar	Ottawa	298
1921	William Trovinger	Toronto	293
1922	Al Watrous	Montreal	303
1923	Clarence Hackney	Toronto	295
1924	Leo Diegel	Montreal	285
1925	Leo Diegel	Toronto	295
1926	Macdonald Smith	Montreal	283
1927	Tommy Armour	Toronto	288
1928	Leo Diegel	Toronto	282
1929	Leo Diegel	Montreal	274
1930	Tommy Armour	Hamilton	277
1931	Walter Hagen	Toronto	292
1932	Harry Cooper	Ottawa	290
1933	Joe Kirkwood	Toronto	282
1934	Tommy Armour	Toronto	287
1935	G Kunes	Montreal	280
1936	Lawson Little	Toronto	271
1937	Harry Cooper	Toronto	285
1938	Sam Snead	Toronto	277
1939	Jug McSpaden	Saint John, New Brunswick	282
1940	Sam Snead	Toronto	281
1941	Sam Snead	Toronto	274
1942	Craig Wood	Toronto	275
1943–44	No championship		
1945	Byron Nelson	Toronto	280
1946	George Fazio	Montreal	278
1947	Bobby Locke	Toronto	268
1948	C Congdon	Vancouver, British Columbia	280
1949	Dutch Harrison	Toronto	271
1950	Jim Ferrier	Montreal	271
1951	Jim Ferrier	Toronto	273
1952	Johnny Palmer	Winnipeg	263
1953	Dave Douglas	Toronto	273
1954	Pat Fletcher	Vancouver	280
1955	Arnold Palmer	Toronto	265
1956	*Doug Sanders	Montreal	273
1957	George Bayer	Kitchener	271
1958	Wes Ellis, Jr	Edmonton	267
1959	Doug Ford	Montreal	276
1960	Art Wall	Toronto	269
1961	Jack Cupit	Winnipeg	270
1962	Ted Kroll	Montreal	278
1963	Doug Ford	Toronto	280
1964	Kel D G Nagle	Montreal	277
1965	Gene Littler	Toronto	273
1966	Don Massengale	Vancouver	280
1967	Billy Casper	Montreal	279
1968	Bob Charles	Toronto	274
1969	Tommy Aaron	Montreal	275
1970	Kermit Zarley	London, Ontario	279
1971	Lee Trevino	Montreal	275
1972	Gay Brewer	Ridgeway, Ontario	275
1973	Tom Weiskopf	Quebec	278
1974	Bobby Nichols	Mississauga, Toronto	270
1975	Tom Weiskopf	Royal Montreal	274
1976	Jerry Pate	Essex, Windsor	267
1977	Lee Trevino	Glen Abbey, Oakville, Ontario	280
1978	Bruce Lietzke	Glen Abbey, Oakville, Ontario	283
1979	Lee Trevino	Glen Abbey, Oakville, Ontario	281
1980	Bob Gilder	Royal Montreal	274
1981	Peter Oosterhuis	Glen Abbey, Oakville, Ontario	280
1982	Bruce Lietzke	Glen Abbey, Oakville, Ontario	277
1983	John Cook	Glen Abbey, Oakville, Ontario	277
1984	Greg Norman	Glen Abbey, Oakville, Ontario	278
1985	Curtis Strange	Glen Abbey, Oakville, Ontario	279
1986	Bob Murphy	Glen Abbey, Oakville, Ontario	280

* Denotes Amateur

One of the two or three most consistent professionals in 1986: Tommy Nakajima of Japan. (Allsport)

Left: Jill Thornhill, one of the heroines of Great Britain and Ireland's Curtis Cup victory in 1986 and Ladies' British Open Amateur champion, 1983. (John Bailey)

Below left: A large cup to keep clean but a small price to pay for winning the US Open. Raymond Floyd with his wife and daughter, Shinnecock Hills, 1986. (Allsport)

Below: Trisha Johnson, the first British or Irish Curtis Cup player ever to win two foursomes and two singles victories in one match. She did so at Prairie Dunes, Kansas, 1986. (John Bailey)

Above: A classic setting: Severiano Ballesteros playing from sand to the 18th green, Augusta National GC, during the 1986 US Masters. (Allsport)

Right: There are all sorts of ways of lining up a putt. Here, Ken Brown adopts the squatting on haunches method. (Benson and Hedges)

Left: no golfer can hide some feeling of anticipation at the thought of holing a putt, not least Severiano Ballesteros. (Benson and Hedges)

Below left: Two of the leading American women professionals: Betsy King and Amy Alcott. (USGA)

Right: Lee Trevino misses fewer fairways than almost anyone but this is one of the exceptions that proves the rule. (Allsport)

Left: Although the US Women's Open title has so far eluded her, Nancy Lopez has proved herself one of the best and most popular of the women professionals. (USGA)

Above: A unique experience for a British captain in the Curtis, Ryder or Walker Cup on American soil. Diane Bailey expressing feelings of delight in the aftermath of victory, August 1986. (John Bailey)

Below: Starting them young. Sandy Lyle's son, Stuart, inspecting the Open championship trophy with his father and mother, Christine. (Allsport)

Above: One of golf's greatest heroes, Arnold Palmer. (Allsport)

Left: Isao Aoki and caddie feeling the heat, 1984 USPGA championship. (Allsport)

Dinah Shore and the 1986 winner of the famous tournament bearing her name at Mission Hills, Pat Bradley. (Allsport)

Japanese Open

First played 1927

Most victories
6, Tomekichi Miyamoto, 1929–30–32–35–36–40

Oldest winner
Toichiro Toda, 49 years, 1963

Youngest winner
Severiano Ballesteros, 20 years 6 months, 1977

Lowest aggregate
277, Akira Yabe, Musashi CC, Toyooka, 1982

Overseas winners
Rin Man Fuku (Taiwan) 1938; En Toku Shun (Korea) 1941; Hang Chang Sang (Korea) 1972; Ben Arda (Philippines) 1973; Severiano Ballesteros (Spain) 1977–78; Kuo Chie Hsiung (Taiwan) 1979

First non-Asian winner
Severiano Ballesteros (Spain), 1977

Amateur winner
Rokuro Akahoshi, 309, Hodogaya, 1927

Total prize money
1987: 60 000 000 yen

RESULTS

Year	Winner	Venue	Score
1927	*R Akahoshi	Hodogaya	309
1928	R Asami	Tokyo	301
1929	T Miyamoto	Ibaraki	298
1930	T Miyamoto	Ibaraki	287
1931	R Asami	Hodogaya	281
1932	T Miyamoto	Ibaraki	298
1933	N Nakamura	Kasumigaseki	294
1934	No championship owing to typhoon disaster		
1935	T Miyamoto	Asaka	296
1936	T Miyamoto	Inagawa	293
1937	Chin Sei Sui	Sagami	284
1938	Rin Man Fuku	Fujisawa	294
1939	T Toda	Hirono	287
1940	T Miyamoto	Asaka	285
1941	En Toku Shun	Hodogaya	290
1942–49	No competition		
1950	Y Hayashi	Abiko	288
1951	Son Shi Kin	Inagawa	288
1952	T Makamura	Kawana	279
1953	Son Shi Kin	Takarazuka	291
1954	Y Hayashi	Tokyo	293
1955	K Ono	Hirono	291
1956	T Nakamura	Kasumigaseki	285
1957	H Kobari	Aichi	288
1958	T Nakamura	Takanodai	288
1959	Chen Ching-Po	Sagamihara	296
1960	H Kobari	Hirono	294
1961	K Hosoishi	Takanodai	289
1962	T Sugihara	Chiba	287
1963	T Toda	Yokkaichi	283
1964	H Sugimoto	Tokyo	288
1965	T Kitta	Miyoshi	284
1966	S Sato	Sodegaura	285
1967	T Kitta	Hirono	282
1968	T Kono	Sobu	284
1969	H Sugimoto	Ono	284
1970	M Kitta	Musashi	282
1971	Y Fujii	Aichi	282
1972	Hang Chang-sang	Iwai City	278
1973	B Arda	Osaka	278
1974	M Ozaki	Central	279
1975	T Murakami	Kasugai	278
1976	K Shimada	Central	288
1977	S Ballesteros	Narashino	284
1978	S Ballasteros	Yokohama	281
1979	Kuo Chie-Hsiung	Hino GC, Kyoto	285
1980	Katsuji Kikuchi	Sagamihara	296
1981	Yutaka Hagawa	Nihon Rhine	280
1982	A Yabe	Musashi	277
1983	I Aoki	Rokkokokusai	281
1984	K Uehara	Ranzan	283
1985	T Nakajima	Higashinagoya	285
1986	T Nakajima	Tozuka	284

* Denotes Amateur

New Zealand Open

First played 1907
No championships 1915–18 and 1940–45

Most victories
9, Peter Thomson (Australia) 1950–51–53–55–59–60–61–65–71
7, Kel Nagle (Australia) 1957–58–62–64–67–68–69; A J Shaw 1926–29–30–31–32–34–36

Oldest winner
Kel Nagle, 48 years 11 months, 1969

Youngest winner
Bob Charles, 18 years 7 months (then an amateur), 1954

Lowest aggregate
262, Rodger Davis (67, 62, 65, 68), The Grange GC, Auckland, 1986

Biggest margin of victory
18 strokes, A J Shaw, Manawatu GC, Palmerston North, 1930

Amateur winners
H W Berwick (Australia), 1956
R J Charles, 1954
A D S Duncan, 1907–10–11
R H Glading, 1946–47
J P Hornabrook, 1937–39
E M Macfarlane, 1925
S Morpeth, 1928

Lowest individual round
62, Rodger Davis, The Grange GC, Auckland, 1986

Consecutive victories
4, A J Shaw, 1929–30–31–32
3, E S Douglas, 1913–14–19; Peter Thomson, 1959–60–61; Kel Nagle, 1967–68–69
2, J A Clements, 1908–09; A D S Duncan, 1910–11; A Brooks, 1922–23; R H Glading, 1946–47; Peter Thomson, 1950–51; Kel Nagle, 1957–58

Unusual records
In 1930, Andy Shaw led by 15 strokes after 36 holes. He won by 18 strokes. His aggregate was 10 strokes better than the previous best. He achieved all this despite rain and strong winds. He was born near Troon, Scotland in 1898.
The first champion in 1907, A D S Duncan, finished leading amateur 28 years later at the age of 60.

In 1954, competing in his second championship, Bob Charles led after every round. Peter Thomson finished third, 4 months after winning his first British Open title.

B M Silk finished leading amateur in 1934 and did so again (for the fourth time) in 1963, aged 53.

Total prize money
1907: £25 for winner, £10 for runner-up or the two leading professionals
1953: $470
1958: $80
1963: $2000
1973: $16 000
1978: $50 000
1986: $120 000 (1st prize $21 600)
Sponsors: BP New Zealand Ltd (1969–82); Broadbank Corporation Ltd (1983–85); Nissan Mobil 1986

RESULTS

Year	Winner	Venue	Score
1907	*Mr A D S Duncan	Napier	159
1908	J A Clements	Otago	333
1909	J A Clements	Auckland	324
1910	*Mr A D S Duncan	Christchurch	295
1911	*Mr A D S Duncan	Wanganui	319
1912	J A Clements	Wellington	321
1913	E S Douglas	Otago	303
1914	E S Douglas	Auckland	313
1919	E S Douglas	Napier	327
1920	J H Kirkwood	Hamilton	304
1921	E S Douglas	Christchurch	302
1922	A Brooks	Manawatu	308
1923	A Brooks	Wanganui	312
1924	E J Moss	Auckland	301
1925	*E M Macfarlane	Christchurch	308
1926	A J Shaw	Miramar	307
1927	E J Moss	Hamilton	300
1928	*S Morpeth	Otago	303
1929	A J Shaw	Wanganui	299
1930	A J Shaw	Manawatu	284
1931	A J Shaw	Christchurch	287
1932	A J Shaw	Wellington	289
1933	E J Moss	Titirangi	300
1934	A J Shaw	Wanganui	288
1935	A Murray	Christchurch	286
1936	A J Shaw	New Plymouth	292
1937	*J P Hornabrook	Hamilton	299
1938	Bobby Locke	Otago	288
1939	*J P Hornabrook	Miramar	291
1946	*R H Glading	Manawatu	306
1947	*R H Glading	New Plymouth	291
1948	A Murray	Otago	294
1949	James Galloway	Hastings	283
1950	Peter Thomson	Christchurch	280
1951	Peter Thomson	Titirangi	288
1952	A Murray	Wanganui	293
1953	Peter Thomson	Otago	295
1954	*Bob Charles	Wellington	280
1955	Peter Thomson	Auckland	280
1956	*H W Berwick	Christchurch	292
1957	Kel Nagle	Manawatu	294
1958	Kel Nagle	Hamilton	278
1959	Peter Thomson	Paraparaumu	287
1960	Peter Thomson	Invercargill	281
1961	Peter Thomson	New Plymouth	267
1962	Kel Nagle	Titirangi	281
1963	Bruce Devlin	Wanganui	273
1964	Kel Nagle	Christchurch	266
1965	Peter Thomson	Auckland	278
1966	Bob Charles	Paraparaumu	273
1967	Kel Nagle	Hamilton	275
1968	Kel Nagle	Christchurch	272
1969	Kel Nagle	Wanganui	273
1970	Bob Charles	Auckland	271
1971	Peter Thomson	Dunedin	276
1972	Bill Dunk	Paraparaumu	279
1973	Bob Charles	Palmerston North	288
1974	Bob Gilder	Christchurch	283
1975	Bill Dunk	Hamilton	272
1976	Simon Owen	Wellington	284
1977	Bob Byman	Auckland	290
1978	Bob Shearer	Wanganui	277
1979	Stewart Ginn	Dunedin	278
1980	Buddy Allin	New Plymouth	274
1981	Bob Shearer	Wellington	285
1982	Terry Gale	Christchurch	284
1983	Ian Baker-Finch	Auckland	280
1984	Corey Pavin	Paraparaumu Beach	269
1985	Corey Pavin	Russley	277
1986	Rodger Davis	Auckland	262

* Denotes Amateur

South African Open

First played 1903

Most victories
13, Gary Player, 1956–60–65–66–67–68–69–72–75–76–77–79–81
9, Bobby Locke, 1935–37–38–39–40–46–50–51–55

Youngest winner
Bobby Locke, 17 years, 1935

Oldest winner
Sid Brews, 53 years, 1952

Lowest aggregate
272, Bobby Cole, Royal Johannesburg, 1974
272, Gary Player, Royal Johannesburg, 1981

Lowest individual round
63, Gary Player, Royal Johannesburg, 1977; Bobby Cole, Durban CC, 1980

Overseas winners
Tommy Horton (GB), 1970
Bob Charles (NZ), 1973
Charles Bolling (USA), 1983

Amateur winners (since 1930)
Bobby Locke, 1935 and 1937
C E Olander, 1936
R W Glennie, 1947
M Janks, 1948
J R Boyd, 1953
R C Taylor, 1954
A A Stewart, 1958
D Hutchinson, 1959

Total prize money
1978: R45 000
1981: R55 000
1986: R100 000
Since 1984, the Open has been sponsored by Southern Sun Hotels

Unusual records

At the age of 15 in 1977, Wayne Player, Gary Player's son, led the qualifying round with a 65. Then, at the 1st hole of the championship proper at Royal Johannesburg, he holed a 3-iron shot for an albatross 2

RESULTS

Year	Winner	Venue	Score
1903	L B Waters	Port Elizabeth	163
1904	L B Waters	Johannesburg	143
1905	A G Gray	Bloemfontein	—
1906	A G Gray	East London	151
1907	L B Waters	Kimberley	146
1908	George Fotheringham	Johannesburg	163
1909	John Fotheringham	Potchefstroom	306
1910	George Fotheringham	Wynberg	315
1911	George Fotheringham	Durban	301
1912	George Fotheringham	Potchefstroom	305
1913	*J A W Prentice	Kimberley	304
1914	George Fotheringham	Wynberg	299
1919	W H Horne	Durban	320
1920	L B Waters	Johannesburg	302
1921	J Brews	Port Elizabeth	316
1922	F Jangle	Port Alfred	310
1923	J Brews	Royal Cape	305
1924	B H Elkin	Durban	316
1925	Sid F Brews	Johannesburg	295
1926	J Brews	Port Elizabeth	301
1927	Sid F Brews	Maccauvlei	301
1928	J Brews	Durban	297
1929	A Tosh	Royal Cape	315
1930	Sid F Brews	East London	297
1931	Sid F Brews	Port Elizabeth	302
1932	C McIlvenny	Mowbray	304
1933	Sid F Brews	Maccauvlei	297
1934	Sid F Brews	Port Elizabeth	319
1935	*Bobby Locke	Johannesburg	296
1936	*C E Olander	Royal Cape	297
1937	*Bobby Locke	East London	288
1938	Bobby Locke	Maccauvlei	279
1939	Bobby Locke	Royal Durban	279
1940	Bobby Locke	Port Elizabeth	293
1946	Bobby Locke	Royal Johannesburg	285
1947	*R W Glennie	Mowbray, Cape Town	293
1948	*M Janks	East London	298
1949	Sid F Brews	Maccauvlei	291
1950	Bobby Locke	Durban	287
1951	Bobby Locke	Houghton	275
1952	Sid F Brews	Humewood	300
1953	*J R Boyd	Royal Cape	302
1954	*Reg C Taylor	East London	289
1955	Bobby Locke	Zwartkop	283
1956	Gary Player	Durban	286
1957	Harold Henning	Humewood	289
1958	*A A Stewart	Bloemfontein	281
1959	*Denis Hutchinson	Johannesburg	282
1960	Gary Player	Mowbray	288
1961	Retief Waltman	East London	289
1962	Harold R Henning	Johannesburg	285
1963	Retief Waltman	Durban	281
1964	Alan Henning	Bloemfontein	278
1965	Gary Player	Cape Town	273
1966	Gary Player	Johannesburg	274
1967	Gary Player	East London	279
1968	Gary Player	Houghton	278
1969	Gary Player	Durban	273

Year	Winner	Venue	Score
1970	Tommy Horton (Britain)	Royal Durban	285
1971	Simon Hobday	Mowbray, Cape Town	276
1972	Gary Player	Royal Johannesburg	274
1973	Bob Charles (NZ)	Durban	282
1974	Bobby Cole	Royal Johannesburg	272
1975	Gary Player	Mowbray, Cape Town	278
1976	Dale Hayes	Houghton	287
(with alteration in timing played twice in 1976)			
1976	Gary Player	Durban	280
1977	Gary Player	Royal Johannesburg	273
1978	Hugh Baiocchi	Mowbray	285
1979	Gary Player	Houghton	279
1980	Bobby Cole	Durban CC	279
1981	Gary Player	Royal Johannesburg	272
1982	With alteration in date, not played		
1983	Charles Bolling (USA)	Royal Cape	278
1984	Tony Johnstone	Houghton	274
1985	Gavin Levenson	Royal Durban	280
1986	David Frost	Royal Johannesburg	275
1987	Mark McNulty	Mowbray, Cape Town	278

* Denotes Amateur

John Bland of South Africa, a popular and regular visitor to Europe. (Benson and Hedges)

The Professionals

USPGA Tour

The tournament circuit—the tour—is a remarkable piece of organization. As long ago as 1899 there was a Western Open, but even in the 1920s when Gene Sarazen, Walter Hagen, Jim Barnes and Jock Hutchison were the main performers, there was little continuity.

Later, under the management of Bob Harlow and Fred Corcoran, the schedule grew with players like Ben Hogan, Sam Snead and Byron Nelson to adorn the shopwindow. Resorts, hotels and Chambers of Commerce soon realized the value of professional golf in promoting their interests, even if it did involve many players in a lot of travelling, it enabled them to follow the sun.

By 1938, there were 38 events and a purse of $158 000. By 1952, there was almost $500 000 to play for, but by the late fifties, the tour really took off.

Television brought the game to a new public; TV rights brought a huge increase in prize-money and a new generation of professionals, led by Arnold Palmer, entered a rich era. There was a tournament somewhere nearly every week. There was the establishment of the PGA School, stern rules about qualification and a satellite tour. In 1968, the tournament players separated from the PGA, formed their own organization known as the Tournament Players' Division and appointed Joe Dey as Commissioner.

Such rapid expansion brought its problems but, though the tournament schedule has been cut back to enable American players to play elsewhere at the end of the year, total prize-money in 1986 was almost $25½ million. Deane Beman is the Commissioner.

DETAILED RECORDS (to end of 1986)

Most victories during career (PGA TOUR co-sponsored and/or approved tournaments only):
84, Sam Snead
71, Jack Nicklaus
62, Ben Hogan
61, Arnold Palmer
54, Byron Nelson
51, Billy Casper

Most consecutive victories
11, Byron Nelson, from Miami Four Ball, 8–11 March 1945, through Canadian Open, 2–4 August 1945. Tournament site, dates, score, purse—Miami Four Ball, Miami Springs Course, Miami, Fla, 8–11 March, won 8–6, $1500; Charlotte Open, Myers Park Golf Club, Charlotte, NC, 16–19 March, 272,

$2000; Greensboro Open, Starmount Country Club, Greensboro, NC, 23–25 March, 271, $1000; Durham Open, Hope Valley Country Club, Durham, NC, 30 March–1 April, 276, $1000; Atlanta Open, Capital City Course, Atlanta, Ga, 5–8 April, 263, $2000; Montreal Open, Islemere Golf and Country Club, Montreal, Que, 7–10 June, 268, $2000; Philadelphia Inquirer Invitational, Llanerch Country Club, Phila, Pa, 14–17 June, 269, $3000; Chicago Victory National Open, Calumet Country Club, Chicago, Ill, 29 June–1 July, 275, $2000; PGA Championship, Moraine Country Club, Dayton, Ohio, 9–15 July, 4–3, $3750; Tam O'Shanter Open, Tam O'Shanter Country Club, Chicago, Ill, 26–29 July, 269, $10 000; Canadian Open, Thornhill Country Club, Toronto, Ont, 2–4 August, 280, $2000. Winnings for streak $30 250
NOTE: Nelson won a 12th event in Spring Lake, NJ, which is not accounted as official, as its $2500 purse was below the PGA $3000 minimum.
4, Jackie Burke, Jr, in 1952: From 14 February to 9 March—Texas Open, Houston Open, Baton Rouge Open, St Petersburg Open
3, Byron Nelson in 1944, 1945–46; Sam Snead in 1945; Ben Hogan in 1946; Bobby Locke in 1947; Jim Ferrier in 1951; Billy Casper in 1960; Arnold Palmer in 1960; 1962; Johnny Miller in 1974; Hubert Green in 1976; Gary Player in 1978

Most victories in a single event
8, Sam Snead, Greater Greensboro Open: 1938, 1946, 1949, 1950, 1955, 1956, 1960, and 1965
6, Jack Nicklaus, Masters: 1963, 1965, 1966, 1972, 1975 and 1986; Sam Snead, Miami Open: 1937, 1939, 1946, 1950, 1951, and 1955
5, Walter Hagen, PGA Championship: 1921, 1924, 1925, 1926, and 1927; Ben Hogan, Colonial NIT: 1946, 1947, 1952, 1953, and 1959; Arnold Palmer, Bob Hope Desert Classic: 1960, 1962, 1968, 1971, and 1973; Jack Nicklaus, Tournament of Champions: 1963, 1964, 1971, 1973, and 1977; Jack Nicklaus, PGA: 1963, 1971, 1973, 1975, and 1980; Walter Hagen, Western Open: 1916, 1921, 1926, 1927, 1932

Most consecutive victories in a single event
4, Walter Hagen, PGA Championship, 1924–27
3, Willie Anderson, US Open, 1903–05
3, Ralph Guldahl, Western Open, 1936–38
3, Gene Littler, Tournament of Champions, 1955–57
3, Billy Casper, Portland Open, 1959–61
3, Arnold Palmer, Texas Open, 1960–62, Phoenix Open, 1961–63
3, Jack Nicklaus, Disney World Golf Classic, 1971–73
3, Johnny Miller, Tucson Open, 1974–76
3, Tom Watson, Byron Nelson Classic, 1978–80

Most victories in a calendar year
18, Byron Nelson (1945)
13, Ben Hogan (1946)
11, Ben Hogan (1948)
10, Sam Snead (1950)
8, Byron Nelson (1944)
8, Lloyd Mangrum (1948)
8, Arnold Palmer (1960)
8, Johnny Miller (1974)
7, Sam Snead (1938)
7, Ben Hogan (1947)
7, Arnold Palmer (1962, 1963)
7, Jack Nicklaus (1972, 1973)

Most years between victories
1, Bob Murphy, Jackie Gleason-Inverarry Classic 1975 to Canadian Open 1986

Most consecutive years winning at least one tournament
7, Jack Nicklaus (1962–78), Arnold Palmer (1955–71)
6, Billy Casper (1956–71)

Most consecutive tournaments in the money
13, Byron Nelson, 1940s
105, Jack Nicklaus, November 1970 to September 1976
86, Hale Irwin, Tucson Open 1975 to end of 1978

Most consecutive rounds under 70
19, Byron Nelson, 1945

Leading money winner most often
8, Jack Nicklaus
5, Ben Hogan, Tom Watson
4, Arnold Palmer

Youngest winners
Johnny McDermott, 19 years and 10 months, 1911 US Open
Gene Sarazen, 20 years and 4 months, 1922 US Open
Horton Smith, 20 years and 5 months, 1928 Oklahoma City Open
Ray Floyd, 20 years and 6 months, 1963 St Petersburg Open
Seve Ballesteros, 20 years and 11 months, 1978 Greater Greensboro Open

Oldest winner
Sam Snead, 52 years and 10 months, 1965 Greater Greensboro Open

Widest winning margin
Strokes
16, Bobby Locke, 1948 Chicago Victory National Championship
14, Ben Hogan, 1945 Portland Invitational; Johnny Miller, 1975 Phoenix Open
13, Byron Nelson, 1945 Seattle Open
12, Arnold Palmer, 1962 Phoenix Open

Biggest span of years between first and last victory
29, by Sam Snead (1936–65)
24, by Jack Nicklaus (1962–86)
23, by Gene Littler (1954–77)
23, by Ray Floyd (1963–86)
22, by Art Wall (1953–75)

Lowest 72 hole total
257, (60–68–64–65) by Mike Souchak, at Brackenridge Park Golf Course, San Antonio, Tex, in 1955 Texas Open (27 under par)
259, (62–68–63–66) by Byron Nelson, at Broadmoor Golf Club, Seattle, Wash, in 1945 Seattle Open (21 under par)
259, (70–63–63–63) by Chandler Harper at Brackenridge Park Golf Course, San Antonio, Tex, in 1954 Texas Open (25 under par)
259, (63–64–66–66) by Tim Norris, at Wethersfield CC, Hartford, CT, in 1982 Sammy Davis Jr Greater Hartford Open (25 under par)

Lowest 90 hole total
333, (67–67–68–66–65) by Lanny Wadkins, at four courses, Palm Springs, CA, in the 1985 Bob Hope Classic (27 under par)
333, (66–68–64–69–66) by Craig Stadler, at four courses, Palm Springs, CA, in the 1985 Bob Hope Classic (27 under par)
333, (73–63–68–64–65) by Greg Norman, at three courses, Las Vegas, NV, in the 1986 Panasonic Las Vegas Invitational (27 under par)

Lowest 54 hole total
Opening rounds
191, (66–64–61) by Gay Brewer, at Pensacola CC, Pensacola, FL, in winning 1967 Pensacola Open
192, (60–68–64) by Mike Souchak, at Brackenridge Park Golf Course, San Antonio, Tex, in 1955 Texas Open
192, (64–63–65) by Bob Gilder, at Westchester CC, Harrison, NY, in 1982 Manufacturers Hanover Westchester Classic

Consecutive rounds
189, (63–63–63) by Chandler Harper in the last three rounds of the 1954 Texas Open at Brackenridge Park

Lowest 36 hole total
Opening rounds
126, (64–62) by Tommy Bolt, at Cavalier Yacht & Country Club, Virginia Beach, Va, in 1954 Virginia Beach Open

Consecutive rounds
125, (63–62) by Ron Streck in the last two rounds of the 1978 Texas Open at Oak Hills Country Club, San Antonia, Tex
126, (62–64) by Johnny Palmer in the last two rounds of the 1948 Tucson Open at El Rio Country Club, Tucson, Ariz
126, (63–63) by Sam Snead in the last two rounds of the 1950 Texas Open at Brackenridge
126, (63–63) by Chandler Harper in the middle rounds and last two rounds of the 1954 Texas Open at Brackenridge
126, (60–66) by Sam Snead in the middle rounds of the 1957 Dallas Open at Glen Lakes Country Club, Dallas, Tex
126, (61–65) by Jack Rule, Jr in the middle rounds of the 1963 St Paul Open at Keller Golf Club, St Paul, Minn
126, (63–63) by Mark Pfeil, in the middle rounds of the 1963 Texas Open at Oak Hills CC, San Antonio, Tex

Lowest 18 hole total
59, by Al Geiberger, at Colonial Country Club, Memphis, Tenn, in second round of 1977 Memphis Classic
60, by Al Brosch, at Brackenridge Park Golf Course, San Antonio, Tex, in third round of 1951 Texas Open
60, by Bill Nary, at El Paso Country Club, El Paso, Tex, in third round of 1952 El Paso Open
60, by Ted Kroll, at Brackenridge Park Golf Course, San Antonio, Tex, in third round of 1954 Texas Open
60, by Wally Ulrich, at Cavalier Yacht and Country Club, Virginia Beach, Va, in second round of 1954 Virginia Beach Open
60, by Tommy Bolt, at Wethersfield Country Club, Hartford, Conn, in second round of 1954 Insurance City Open
60, by Mike Souchak, at Brackenridge Park Golf Course, San Antonio, Tex, in first round of 1955 Texas Open
60, by Sam Snead, at Glen Lakes Country Club, Dallas, Tex, in second round of 1957 Dallas Open

Lowest 9 holes
27, by Mike Souchak, at Brackenridge Park Golf Course, San Antonio, Tex, on par-35 second nine of first round in 1955 Texas Open
27, by Andy North, at En-Joie Golf Club, Endicott, NY, on par 34 second nine of first round in 1975 BC Open

PUTTING RECORDS

Fewest putts, one round
18, Sam Trahan, at Whitemarsh Valley Country Club, in final round of 1979 IVB-Philadelphia Golf Classic
19, Bill Nary, at El Paso Country Club, El Paso, Tex, in third round of El Paso Open
19, Bob Rosburg, at Pensacola Country Club, Pensacola, Fla, in third round of 1959 Pensacola Open
19, Randy Glover, at Keller Golf Course, St Paul, Minn, in fourth round of 1965 St Paul Open

19, Deane Beman, at Mesa Verde Country Club, Costa Mesa, Calif, in first round of 1968 Haig Open

Fewest putts, four rounds
94, George Archer, in 1980 Sea Pines Heritage Classic at Harbour Town Golf Links, Hilton Head Island, SC
99, Steve Melnyk, in 1980 Sea Pines Heritage Classic at Harbour Town Golf Links, Hilton Head Island, SC
99, Bob Menne, in 1977 Tournament Players Championship at Sawgrass, Jacksonville, Fla

Fewest putts, 9 holes
8, Jim Colbert, at the Deerwood Club, Jacksonville, Fla, on front nine of last round in 1967 Greater Jacksonville Open
8, Sam Trahan, at Whitemarsh Valley Country Club, on the back nine of the last round in the 1979 IVB-Philadelphia Golf Classic

Most birdies in a row
8, Bob Goalby, at Pasadena Golf Club, St Petersburg, Fla, during fourth round of 1961 St Petersburg Open; Fuzzy Zoeller, at Oakwood Country Club, Coal Valley, Ill, during first round of 1976 Quad Cities Open

Best birdie-eagle streak
6 birdies and 1 eagle by Al Geiberger, at Colonial Country Club, Memphis, Tenn, during second round of 1977 Danny Thomas Memphis Classic

Best Vardon Trophy scoring average
69.23, Sam Snead in 1950 (6646 strokes, 96 rounds)
69.30, Ben Hogan in 1948 (5267 strokes, 76 rounds)
69.37, Sam Snead in 1949 (5064 strokes, 73 rounds)

PLAY-OFF RECORDS

Longest sudden death play-offs
Holes:
11, Cary Middlecoff and Lloyd Mangrum were declared co-winners by mutual agreement in the 1949 Motor City Open
8, Dick Hart defeated Phil Rodgers in the 1965 Azalea Open
8, Lee Elder defeated Lee Trevino in the 1978 Greater Milwaukee Open
8, Dave Barr defeated Woody Blackburn, Dan Halldorson, Frank Conner and Victor Regalado in the 1981 Quad Cities Open
8, Bob Gilder defeated Rex Caldwell, Johnny Miller and Mark O'Meara in the 1983 Phoenix Open

Most players in a sudden death play-off
5, 1981 Bing Crosby—John Cook defeated Hale Irwin, Bobby Clampett, Ben Crenshaw and Barney Thompson
5, 1981 Quad Cities Open—Dave Barr defeated Frank Conner, Woody Blackburn, Dan Halldorson and Victor Regalado
5, 1983 Kemper Open—Fred Couples defeated T C Chen, Barry Jaeckel, Gil Morgan and Scott Simpson

CAREER MONEY WINNERS

		Dollars	*No. of Seasons on Tour*
1	Jack Nicklaus	4 912 295	25
2	Tom Watson	4 085 279	16
3	Lee Trevino	3 264 291	21
4	Ray Floyd	3 249 460	24
5	Tom Kite	2 919 491	15
6	Hale Irwin	2 811 034	19
7	Lanny Wadkins	2 589 264	16
8	Andy Bean	2 484 032	11
9	Ben Crenshaw	2 336 891	14
10	Johnny Miller	2 267 789	18
11	Tom Weiskopf	2 222 066	22
12	John Mahaffey	2 217 256	16
13	Curtis Strange	2 189 548	10
14	Hubert Green	2 161 435	17
15	Bruce Lietzke	2 152 147	12
16	Craig Stadler	2 060 850	11
17	Calvin Peete	2 009 271	11
18	Fuzzy Zoeller	1 993 088	12
19	Arnold Palmer	1 891 020	31
20	Gil Morgan	1 884 989	14
21	Gary Player	1 795 994	29
22	George Archer	1 709 371	23
23	J C Snead	1 709 337	19
24	Hal Sutton	1 686 825	5
25	Billy Casper	1 686 458	26
26	Larry Nelson	1 672 371	13
27	David Graham	1 661 959	16
28	Miller Barber	1 602 408	20
29	Gene Littler	1 578 626	32
30	Bob Murphy	1 554 876	19
31	Jim Colbert	1 537 194	21
32	Jerry Pate	1 484 828	11
33	Wayne Levi	1 460 165	10
34	George Burns	1 405 319	11
35	Jay Haas	1 386 699	10
36	Bruce Crampton	1 374 294	19
37	Lou Graham	1 360 019	22
38	Bill Rogers	1 345 263	12
39	Payne Stewart	1 340 810	6
40	Jack Renner	1 336 256	10
41	Dan Pohl	1 270 905	9
42	Al Geiberger	1 256 548	27
43	Peter Jacobsen	1 247 965	10
44	Mark O'Meara	1 236 668	6
45	Roger Maltbie	1 231 077	12
46	Lon Hinkle	1 222 039	15
47	Scott Simpson	1 216 325	8
48	Dave Stockton	1 203 469	22
49	Charles Coody	1 201 994	20
50	Greg Norman	1 200 395	4

PAST LEADING MONEY-WINNERS

		Dollars
1934	Paul Runyan	6 767.00
1935	Johnny Revolta	9 543.00
1936	Horton Smith	7 682.00
1937	Harry Cooper	14 138.69
1938	Sam Snead	19 534.49
1939	Henry Picard	10 303.00
1940	Ben Hogan	10 655.00
1941	Ben Hogan	18 358.00
1942	Ben Hogan	13 143.00
1943	No Statistics Compiled	
1944	Byron Nelson (War Bonds)	37 967.69
1945	Byron Nelson (War Bonds)	63 335.66
1946	Ben Hogan	42 556.16
1947	Jimmy Demaret	27 936.83
1948	Ben Hogan	32 112.00
1949	Sam Snead	31 593.83
1950	Sam Snead	35 758.83
1951	Lloyd Mangrum	26 088.83
1952	Julius Boros	37 032.97
1953	Lew Worsham	34 002.00
1954	Bob Toski	65 819.81
1955	Julius Boros	63 121.55
1956	Ted Kroll	72 835.83
1957	Dick Mayer	65 835.00
1958	Arnold Palmer	42 607.50
1959	Art Wall	53 167.60
1960	Arnold Palmer	75 262.85
1961	Gary Player	64 540.45
1962	Arnold Palmer	81 448.33
1963	Arnold Palmer	128 230.00
1964	Jack Nicklaus	113 284.50
1965	Jack Nicklaus	140 752.14
1966	Billy Casper	121 944.92
1967	Jack Nicklaus	188 998.08
*1968	Billy Casper	205 168.67
1969	Frank Beard	164 707.11
1970	Lee Trevino	157 037.63
1971	Jack Nicklaus	244 490.50
1972	Jack Nicklaus	320 542.26
1973	Jack Nicklaus	308 362.10
1974	Johnny Miller	353 021.59
†1975	Jack Nicklaus	298 149.17
1976	Jack Nicklaus	266 438.57
1977	Tom Watson	310 653.16
1978	Tom Watson	362 428.93
1979	Tom Watson	462 636.00
1980	Tom Watson	530 808.33
1981	Tom Kite	375 698.84
1982	Craig Stadler	446 462.00
1983	Hal Sutton	426 668.00
1984	Tom Watson	476 260.00
1985	Curtis Strange	542 321.00
1986	Greg Norman	653 296.00

* Total money listed beginning in 1968 through 1974.
† Official money listed beginning in 1975.

GROWTH OF TOUR PURSES

Year	No. of Events	Total Purse Dollars
1938	38	158 000
1939	28	121 000
1940	27	117 000
1941	30	169 200
1942	21	116 650
1943	3	17 000
1944	22	150 500
1945	36	435 380
1946	37	411 533
1947	31	352 500
1948	34	427 000
1949	25	338 200
1950	33	459 950
1951	30	460 200
1952	32	498 016
1953	32	562 704
1954	26	600 819
1955	36	782 010
1956	36	847 070
1957	32	820 360
1958	39	1 005 800
1959	43	1 225 205
1960	41	1 335 242
1961	45	1 461 830
1962	49	1 790 320
1963	43	2 044 900
1964	41	2 301 063
1965	36	2 848 515
1966	36	3 704 445
1967	37	3 979 162
1968	45	5 077 600
1969	47	5 465 875
1970	55	6 751 523
1971	63	7 116 000
1972	71	7 596 749
1973	75	8 657 225
1974	57	8 165 941
1975	51	7 895 450
1976	49	9 157 522
1977	48	9 688 977
1978	48	10 337 332
1979	46	12 801 200
1980	45	13 371 786
1981	45	14 175 393
1982	46	15 089 576
1983	45	17 588 242
1984	46	21 251 382
1985	47	25 290 526
1986	46	25 442 242

MILLION DOLLAR CLUB

Name	Date/Event/Position	First Money	Time Elapsed Years	Months	Wins
Jack Nicklaus	25 January 1970 Bing Crosby 2nd	8 January 1962 Western Open T50-$33.33	8		30
(2nd million)	1 December 1973 Disney World Winner	25 January 1970 Bing Crosby 2nd-$11 840.83 towards 2nd million	3	11	21
(3rd million)	22 May 1977 Memorial Winner	1 December 1973 Disney World Winner-$12 068.09 towards 3rd million	3	5	12
(4th million)	6 February 1983 Bing Crosby Pro-Am 6th	22 May 1977 Memorial Winner-$45 000 towards 4th million	6	9	6
Tom Watson	7 May 1978 Byron Nelson Winner	24 October 1971 Kaiser Open Tied 28th-$1065	6	7	9
(2nd million)	25 May 1980 Memorial Tournament 2nd-$32 400	7 May 1978 Byron Nelson Classic Winner	2	1	13
(3rd million)	19 June 1983 US Open 2nd	25 May 1980 Memorial Tournament 2nd-$32 400	3	1	7
(4th million)	18 May 1986 Colonial NIT T3	19 June 1983 US Open 2nd	2	11	2
Lee Trevino	20 May 1973 Memphis Classic Tied 2nd	20 June 1966 US Open Tied 54th-$600.00	6	11	15
(2nd million)	24 June 1979 Canadian Open Winner	20 May 1973 Memphis Classic Tied 2nd-$16 187	6	1	7
(3rd million)	19 August 1984 PGA Championship Winner	24 June 1979 Canadian Open Winner-$63 000	5	2	5
Ray Floyd	17 July 1977 Pleasant Valley Winner	17 March 1963 St Petersburg Open Winner-$3500	14	4	10
(2nd million)	13 June 1982 Danny Thomas Memphis Winner	17 July 1977 Pleasant Valley Winner-$50 000	4	11	7
(3rd million)	15 June 1986 US Open Winner	13 June 1982 Memphis Winner	4		3
Tom Kite	8 March 1981 American Motors Inverrary Classic Winner	13 August 1972 Westchester Classic Tied 32nd-$1425	8	7	3
(2nd million)	11 March 1984 Doral-Eastern Open Winner	8 March 1981 Am Motors-Inverrary Winner-$54 000	3		3
Hale Irwin	5 September 1976 World Series of Golf 2nd	30 June 1968 Cleveland Open Tied 39th-$457.41	8	3	7
(2nd million)	14 March 1982 Honda Inverrary Classic Winner	5 September 1976 World Series of Golf 2nd-$50 000	5	6	7

MILLION DOLLAR CLUB

Name	Date/Event/Position	First Money	Time Elapsed Years	Months	Wins
Lanny Wadkins	12 October 1980 Pensacola Open Tied 10th	31 October 1971 Sahara Inv. Tied 9th-$3378	9	1	7
(2nd million)	27 January 1985 Los Angeles Open Winner	12 October 1980 Pensacola Open Tied 10th-$4150	4	3	7
Andy Bean	24 January 1970 Phoenix Open Tied 4th	7 March 1976 Citrus Open Tied 40th-$760	5	10	7
(2nd million)	26 January 1986 Phoenix T7	24 June 1982 Phoenix T4	4		2
Ben Crenshaw	23 March 1980 TPC 2nd	16 August 1973 USI Classic Tied 35th-$903	6	7	6
(2nd million)	15 June 1986 US Open T6	23 March 1980 TPC 2nd	6	3	4
Johnny Miller	8 February 1976 Bob Hope Classic Winner	11 May 1969 Texas Open Tied 23rd-$810.00	6	9	17
(2nd million)	1 April 1984 TPC Tied 29th	8 February 1976 Bob Hope Classic Winner-$36 000	8	2	5
Tom Weiskopf	25 August 1974 Westchester Classic 3rd	9 August 1964 Western Open Tied 30th-$487.50	10		9
(2nd million)	20 September 1981 LaJet Classic Winner	25 August 1974 Westchester Classic 3rd-$17 750	7	1	5
John Mahaffey	26 July 1981 Anheuser-Busch Classic Winner	9 January 1972 Glen Campbell-L.A. Open Tied 30th-$702	9	7	6
(2nd million)	30 May 1986 TPC Winner	26 July 1981 Anheuser-Busch Winner	4	8	3
Curtis Strange	28 March 1983 TPC Tied 8th	24 February 1977 Inverrary Tied 63-$443.75	6	1	4
(2nd million)	13 April 1986 Masters T21	28 March 1983 TPC T8	3	1	4
Hubert Green	26 March 1978 Heritage Winner	28 November 1970 Sea Pines Open Tied 13th-$540.00	7	4	14
(2nd million)	11 August 1985 PGA Winner	26 March 1978 Heritage Winner-$45 000	7	5	5
Bruce Lietzke	10 May 1981 Byron Nelson Classic Winner	5 July 1975 Greater Milwaukee Open Tied 50th-$299	5	10	8
(2nd million)	16 March 1986 Hertz Bay Hill T11	10 May 1981 Byron Nelson Winner	4	10	2
Craig Stadler	29 August 1982 World Series of Golf Winner	22 August 1976 Hartford Open Tied 50th-$520	6		7
(2nd million)	11 May 1986 Byron Nelson T4	29 August 1982 World Series Winner	3	8	1

Tournament Players Championship

This was introduced into the US Tour as a kind of fifth major championship. It has never quite lived up to that billing but it is regarded as one of the most important events. It now has a permanent home on the TPC's own course at Sawgrass designed by Pete Dye.

	Winner		Runner-up	Venue
1974	Jack Nicklaus	272	J C Snead	Atlanta CC
1975	Al Geiberger	270	Dave Stockton	Colonial CC
1976	Jack Nicklaus	269	J C Snead	Inverrary G and CC
1977	Mark Hayes	289	Mike McCullough	Sawgrass
1978	Jack Nicklaus	289	Lou Graham	Sawgrass
1979	Lanny Wadkins	283	Tom Watson	Sawgrass
1980	Lee Trevino	278	Ben Crenshaw	Sawgrass
1981	Raymond Floyd	285	Barry Jaeckel	
			Curtis Strange after play-off	
				Sawgrass
1982	Jerry Pate	280	Scott Simpson	
			Brad Bryant	TPC Sawgrass
1983	Hal Sutton	283	Bob Eastwood	TPC Sawgrass
1984	Fred Couples	277	Leo Trevino	TPC Sawgrass
1985	Calvin Peete	274	D A Weibring	TPC Sawgrass
1986	John Mahaffey	275	Larry Mize	TPC Sawgrass
1987	Sandy Lyle	274	Jeff Sluman after play-off	
				TPC Sawgrass

Nine Holes in 27 Strokes

The stretch of golf that, more than any, made people aware of the scoring capabilities of the post-war professionals was the 27 which Mike Souchak turned in for the inward half of his first round of the Texas Open at Brackenridge Park, San Antonio in 1955.

Brackenridge is not a long course and it was rather shot to pieces by players on the US Tour but Souchak showed what was possible and his 27 was not equalled in serious competition until Jose-Maria Canizares returned 27 (4, 3, 2, 3, 3, 3, 2, 3, 4) for 9 holes during the third round of the Swiss Open at Crans-sur-Sierre in 1978.

Souchak, a mighty hitter, was not tested for length by Brackenridge and on 5 holes on the back nine played a pitching wedge for his second shot. He had gone out in 33 but with his inward half of 27 returned a round of 60 to which he then added 68, 64, 65 for a total of 257. This is still the lowest aggregate for an official PGA event in the States.

Hole	Yards	Par	Score	Detail
10	180	3	2	6-iron, 14 ft
11	365	4	4	D, PW, 20 ft, 2 putts
12	375	4	4	D, PW, 25 ft, 2 putts
13	520	5	3	D, 3W, 5 ft
14	370	4	3	D, PW, 1 ft
15	385	4	3	D, PW, 8 ft
16	375	4	3	4W, 8I, 5 ft
17	360	4	3	D, PW, 12 ft
18	155	3	2	5I, 25 ft

Sony World Rankings 1986

A new system introduced for the first time in 1986 in an attempt to provide a world ranking of players although they may have played on a series of different circuits and continents. It is a system recognized by the Royal and Ancient GC for qualification for exemptions for the Open Championship.

In the first year, the interesting feature was that the first American, Bob Tway, finished 5th. He finished 4th in the American money list. However, 16 of the top 25 in the rankings were American.

Pos	Name	Circuit	Points
1	Greg Norman	ANZ*	1507
2	Bernhard Langer	Eur	1181
3	Severiano Ballesteros	Eur	1175
4	Tsuneyuki Nakajima	Jap	899
5	Andy Bean	USA	694
6	Bob Tway	USA	687
7	Hal Sutton	USA	674
8	Curtis Strange	USA	653
9	Payne Stewart	USA	652
10	Mark O'Meara	USA	639
11	Isao Aoki	Jap	624
12	Sandy Lyle	Eur	619
13	Calvin Peete	USA	614
14	Raymond Floyd	USA	612
15	Lanny Wadkins	USA	600
16	Tom Kite	USA	579
17	Rodger Davis	ANZ*	572
18	Tom Watson	USA	564
19	Corey Pavin	USA	539
20	Fuzzy Zoeller	USA	520
21	Mark McNulty	SA	480
22	Craig Stadler	USA	475
23	Masashi Ozaki	Jap	475
24	John Mahaffey	USA	469
25	Jack Nicklaus	USA	464

* ANZ = Australia/New Zealand

PGA European Tour

(Incorporating the continental championships, co-ordinated by the British PGA, beginning in 1972)

The professional tour in Britain and Europe is not as fortunate as its counterpart in America. Even allowing for the fact that the season is longer in Southern Europe, the weather limits the number of tournaments that are possible in a year. However, this works in its favour since players can make themselves available for other circuits in Japan, Australia, South Africa, New Zealand, Africa—and America. Nick Faldo, Severiano Ballesteros, Bernhard Langer and Sandy Lyle have all won in America.

The European season also continues to expand. In 1987, a new Moroccan Open was announced in March, the 1986 season having ended with the Portuguese Open at the end of October. This makes it a realistic alternative to the American tour and means that it is perfectly possible to earn a sizeable living without going near America. The prize money for 1987 reached a minimum of £7.25 million with 17 tournaments worth £200 000 or more compared with seven in 1986.

This is something new. For the first 30 years or so of its existence, the PGA, founded in 1901, looked after the interests of the club professional. There were tournaments, but most tournament players had a club job as well.

Things changed rapidly with the appointment as Secretary in 1933 of Commander Charles Roe. He realized the potential of the tournament side of golf and stoked the PGA into a far more active role.

In the 25 years that he was at the head of affairs, the tournament programme developed extensively but, ironically, it was after his retirement that the great golf boom occurred.

Nevertheless, under his training, the PGA was more ready than it would have been. It organized itself better, but it was not until the 1970s that the real impact was felt. Television was a major factor in encouraging sponsors and prize-money reflected their interest. Like the Americans, special qualification rules were introduced to sift out the enormous increase in professionals seeking to try their hand and in 1975 a Tournament Players' Division was formed quite separate from the rest of the PGA.

At the beginning of 1977, they became the European Players' Division, the European Opens and other events became part of the European tour; and in 1979 the Ryder Cup played America as a European team as distinct from a British one.

DETAILED RECORDS

Most victories (excluding British Open)
36, Severiano Ballesteros
27, Neil Coles (including two fourball victories with Bernard Hunt)
24, Christy O'Connor
22, Bernard Hunt (including two fourball victories with Neil Coles)
20, Dai Rees, Peter Thomson

Most consecutive victories
4, Alf Padgham, 1935 *News of the World* matchplay (Royal Mid-Surrey) 10–13 September. 1936 *Daily Mail* (Bramshot), total 284, 31 March–3 April. Silver King (Moor Park), total 280, 22–24 April. Dunlop Southport (Southport and Ainsdale) total 282, 4–8 May. Padgham was ninth in the next tournament but then won the Open at Hoylake, total 287, 22–26 June. In those days, there was only about one tournament per month
4, Severiano Ballesteros. 1986 Dunhill British Masters (Woburn) 5–8 June. Carrolls Irish Open (Portmarnock) 19–22 June. Johnnie Walker Monte Carlo Open (Mont Agel) 25–28 June. Peugeot French Open (La Boulie) 3–6 July. He did not play in the Jersey Open (La Moye) 12–15 June

Oldest winner
Sandy Herd, 58 years, *News of the World* matchplay championship, 1926

Youngest winner
Severiano Ballesteros, 19 years 3 months 27 days, Dutch Open, 1976
Paul Way, 19 years 4 months 24 days, Dutch Open, 1982
Nick Faldo, 20 years 10 months, Colgate PGA championship, 1978

Most victories in one season
7, Norman von Nida 1947. Dunlop Southport, *Star*, North British Harrogate, Lotus, Penfold (tied), *Yorkshire Evening News* (tied) and the Brand Lochryn
6, Severiano Ballesteros 1986. Dunhill British Masters, Carrolls Irish Open, Johnnie Walker Monte Carlo Open, Peugeot French Open, KLM Dutch Open and Lancome Trophy (tied)
5, Bernard Hunt, 1963. Dunlop Masters, Agfa Gevacolor, Swallow-Penfold, Carrolls and Smart Weston (36-hole event)

Winner of Harry Vardon Trophy most often
4, Peter Oosterhuis, 1971–72–73–74. Severiano Ballesteros, 1976–77–78–86
3, Bobby Locke, 1946–50–54, Bernard Hunt, 1958–60–65, Sandy Lyle, 1979–80–85

Most money in a single year
£259 275 Severiano Ballesteros, 1986
In 1963, when Neil Coles was leading money winner, he won £3742

Howard Clark, Whyte & Mackay PGA champion, 1985. (Whyte & Mackay Distillers Ltd)

Biggest margin of victory

15 strokes, Peter Thomson, *Yorkshire Evening News*, Sand Moor, 1957. Total 264 (65, 67, 64, 68)
12 strokes, Guy Wolstenholme, Jeyes, Royal Dublin, 1963
11 strokes, Tony Jacklin, Scandinavian Enterprise Open, Malmo, 1974
11 strokes, Dale Hayes, French Open, La Baule, 1978
11 strokes, Ken Brown, Glasgow Open, Haggs Castle, 1984
10 strokes, Greg Norman, French Open, St Cloud, 1980
Bernhard Langer won the Cacharel Under 25 tournament at Nimes in 1979 by 17 strokes

Lowest 72-hole totals

260 (64, 65, 66, 65), (24 under par), Kel Nagle, Irish Hospitals, Woodbrook, 1961
260 (67, 65, 61, 67), (16 under par), Mike Clayton, Timex Open, Biarritz, 1984
261 (63, 66, 66, 66), (27 under par), Jerry Anderson, Ebel European Masters, Crans-sur-Sierre, 1984
262, Percy Alliss, Italian Open, San Remo, 1936
262 (71, 63, 62, 66), Lu Liang Huan, French Open, Biarritz 1971
262 (66, 63, 66, 67), (26 under par), Bernard Hunt, Piccadilly strokeplay Wentworth (East), 1966
262 (64, 66, 66, 66), (26 under par), Jose-Maria Olazabal, Ebel European Masters, Crans-sur-Sierre, 1986
262 (14 under), Manuel Ballesteros, Timex Open, Biarritz, 1983
263, Flory Van Donck, Italian Open, San Remo, 1947
263, Hassan Hassanein, Italian Open, Villa d'Este, 1949
263, Severiano Ballesteros, Peugeot French Open, St Germain, 1985

Highest winning 72-hole score

306 (74, 79, 77, 76), Peter Butler, Schweppes PGA Closed Championship, Royal Birkdale, 1963

Fewest putts in 18 holes

22, Bill Large, Benson and Hedges Matchplay (Qualifying Round), Moor Park, 1972

Lowest 9-hole scores

27 (9 under), Jose-Maria Canizares, Swiss Open, Crans-sur-Sierre, 1978. Figures: 4, 3, 2, 3, 3, 3, 2, 3, 4. It was his third round and his total was 64
27 (7 under), Robert Lee, Johnnie Walker Monte Carlo Open, Mont Agel, 1985
28, John Panton, North British, Harrogate, 1952
28 (6 under), Bernard Hunt, Spalding, Worthing (Low course), 1953
28, Peter Mills, Bowmaker, Sunningdale Old, 1956
28 (8 under), Brian Barnes, Haig Whisky TPC, Dalmahoy, 1981
28 (6 under), Denis Durnian, Open Championship, first nine Royal Birkdale, 1983
28 (7 under), Gordon Brand, Carrolls Irish Open, Royal Dublin, 1985
28 (6 under), Mark McNulty, Johnnie Walker Monte Carlo Open, Mont Agel, 1986

Lowest 18-hole totals

60 (11 under), Baldovino Dassau, Swiss Open, Crans-sur-Sierre, 1978
61 (9 under), Tom Haliburton, Spalding, Worthing (Low course) 1952
61, Hugh Boyle, Senior Service, Dalmahoy (West), 1965
61, Tony Coop, Senior Service, Dalmahoy (West), 1965
61 (9 under), Peter Butler, Bowmaker, Sunningdale Old, 1967
61 (10 under), Peter Townsend, Swiss Open, Crans-sur-Sierre, 1971
61 (8 under), Mike Clayton, Timex Open, Biarritz, 1984
61 (8 under), Sam Torrance, Timex Open, Biarritz, 1984
61 (8 under), Robert Lee, Johnnie Walker Monte Carlo Open,

Jose-Maria Canizares who went out in 27 in the 1978 Swiss Open. (Benson and Hedges)

Mont Agel, 1985
61 (11 under), Roger Chapman, Ebel European Masters, Crans-sur-Sierre, 1985

Lowest 36-hole totals (First and second rounds unless stated)

125 (13 under) (2nd and 3rd rounds), Johnnie Walker Monte Carlo Open, Mont Agel, 1985
125 (13 under) (1st and 2nd rounds), Sam Torrance, French Open, Biarritz, 1971
126 (14 under), Tom Haliburton, Spalding, Worthing (Low course), 1952
126 (14 under) (3rd and 4th rounds), Nick Faldo, Lawrence Batley Classic, Bingley (St Ives), 1983
127 (15 under), Peter Alliss, Irish Hospitals, Woodbrook, 1961
127 (17 under), Sandy Lyle, Ebel European Masters, Swiss Open, Crans-sur-Sierre, 1983
128 (14 under), Mike McLean, Lawrence Batley Classic, Bingley (St Ives), 1983
128 (12 under), Ken Brown, Glasgow Open, Haggs Castle, 1984
128 (16 under) (3rd and 4th rounds), Ebel European Masters, Swiss Open, Crans-sur-Sierre, 1986
128 (16 under) (2nd and 3rd rounds), Ian Baker-Finch, Ebel European Masters, Swiss Open, Crans-sur-Sierre, 1986
128 (16 under) (2nd and 3rd rounds), Gordon Brand, Ebel European Masters, Swiss Open, Crans-sur-Sierre, 1986

Lowest 54-hole totals (1st three rounds unless stated)

193 (14 under), Mike Clayton, Timex Open, Biarritz, 1984
193 (14 under), Peter Teravainen, Timex Open, Biarritz, 1984
194 (16 under), John Lister, Gallaher Ulster Open, Shandon Park, 1970
194 (13 under), Sam Torrance, Johnnie Walker Monte Carlo Open, Mont Agel, 1985
194 (19 under), Severiano Ballesteros, Peugeot French Open, St Germain, 1985

MOST BIRDIES IN ONE ROUND

No.	Name	Tournament	Venue	Year
11	Baldovino Dassu	Swiss Open	Crans-sur-Sierre	1971
11	Jose-Maria Canizares	Ebel European Masters, Swiss Open	Crans-sur-Sierre	1986
10	Vicente Fernandez	Jersey Open	La Moye	1983
10	Sandy Lyle	Ebel European Masters, Swiss Open	Crans-sur-Sierre	1983
10	Peter Teravainen	Bob Hope British Classic	Moor Park	1983
10	Bernhard Langer	Benson & Hedges Spanish Open	El Saler	1984
10	Ian Woosnam	Benson & Hedges International	Fulford	1985
10	Christy O'Connor Jr	Open Golf Championship	Royal St George's	1985
10	Eamonn Darcy	Ebel European Masters, Swiss Open	Crans-sur-Sierre	1985
10	Gordon J. Brand	Ebel European Masters, Swiss Open	Crans-sur-Sierre	1986
9	Brian Waites	Bob Hope British Classic	RAC, Epsom	1980
9	Brian Waites	European Open	Hoylake	1981
9	John Bland	Haig Whisky TPC	Notts	1982
9	Jose-Maria Canizares	Lawrence Batley International	Bingley St Ives	1983
9	Eamonn Darcy	State Express Classic	The Belfry	1983
9	Ronan Rafferty	State Express Classic	The Belfry	1983
9	Michael King	Bob Hope British Classic	Moor Park	1983
9	Ian Woosnam	Ebel European Masters, Swiss Open	Crans-sur-Sierre	1984
9	Jerry Anderson	Lufthansa German Open	Frankfurt	1984
9	David Frost	Quinta do Lago Portuguese Open	Quinta do Lago	1984
9	Sandy Lyle	Scandinavian Enterprise Open	Sven Tumba CC	1984
9	Howard Clark	GSI Open	Le Touquet	1985
9	Severiano Ballesteros	Peugeot French Open	St German	1985
9	Sandy Lyle	Benson & Hedges International	Fulford	1985
9	Sam Torrance	Ebel European Masters, Swiss Open	Crans-sur-Sierre	1985
9	Sam Torrance	Lancome Trophy	St Nom-la-Breteche	1985
9	Tommy Armour III	Ebel European Masters, Swiss Open	Crans-sur-Sierre	1986
9	Ian Baker-Finch	Ebel European Masters, Swiss Open	Crans-sur-Sierre	1986
9	Derrick Cooper	Ebel European Masters, Swiss Open	Crans-sur-Sierre	1986
9	Wayne Westner	Dunhill British Masters	Woburn G & CC	1986
9	Rodger Davis	German Open	Hubbelrath	1986
9	Manuel Pinero	Quinta do Lago Portuguese Open	Quinto do Lago	1986

MOST BIRDIES AND EAGLES IN ONE ROUND

No.	Name	Tournament	Venue	Year
1E 9B	Eric Brown	Dunlop Masters	Notts	1957
1E 9B	Peter Townsend	Swiss Open	Crans-sur-Sierre	1971
1E 9B	Severiano Ballesteros	Italian Open	Molinetto	1985
1E 9B	Roger Chapman	Ebel European Masters, Swiss Open	Crans-sur-Sierre	1985
1E 8B	Jimmy Martin	Swallow Penfold	Stoneham	1961
1E 8B	Mark James	Haig Whisky TPC	Dalmahoy	1981
1E 8B	Hugh Baiocchi	Sanyo Open	El Prat	1983
1E 8B	Nick Faldo	Lawrence Batley International	Bingley St Ives	1983
1E 8B	Bernhard Langer	Carrolls Irish Open	The Royal Dublin	1983
1E 8B	Mark James	Tunisian Open	El Kantaoui	1984
1E 8B	Bernhard Langer	KLM Dutch Open	Rosendaelsche	1984
1E 8B	Wayne Grady	Lufthansa German Open	Frankfurt	1984
1E 8B	Jeff Hawkes	Sanyo Open	El Prat	1985
1E 8B	Howard Clark	Lancome Trophy	St Nom-la-Breteche	1985
1E 8B	Anders Forsbrand	Ebel European Masters, Swiss Open	Crans-sur-Sierre	1986
1E 8B	Greg Turner	Scandinavian Enterprise Open	Ullna	1986
1E 8B	Greg Norman	Open Golf Championship	Turnberry	1986
4E 4B	Gordon Brand Jr.	Jersey Open	La Moye	1986
3E 3B	Paul Carrigill	Lawrence Batley International	Bingley St Ives	1983
3E 3B	Jeff Hawkes	Panasonic European Open	Sunningdale	1984
2E 7B	Brian Barnes	Haig Whisky TPC	Dalmahoy	1981
2E 6B	Jerry Anderson	Ebel European Masters, Swiss Open	Crans-sur-Sierre	1984
2E 6B	Jose-Maria Canizares	Sanyo Open	El Prat	1985
2E 6B	Sam Torrance	Ebel European Masters, Swiss Open	Crans-sur-Sierre	1986
2E 5B	Garry Cullen	Carrolls Irish Open	The Royal Dublin	1983
2E 5B	Howard Clark	Whyte & Mackay PGA Champ	Wentworth	1984
2E 5B	Krister Kinell	St Mellion Timeshare TPC	St Mellion	1984
2E 5B	Lanny Wadkins	Ebel European Masters, Swiss Open	Crans-sur-Sierre	1984
2E 5B	Noel Ratcliffe	Panasonic European Open	Sunningdale	1984
2E 5B	Paul Way	*London Standard* 4 Stars Pro-Celeb	Moor Park	1986

LEADING PGA MONEY-WINNERS 1964–86

Year	Winner	£
1964	Neil Coles	7890
1965	Peter Thomson	7011
1966	Bruce Devlin	13 205
1967	Gay Brewer	20 235
1968	Gay Brewer	23 107
1969	Billy Casper	23 483
1970	Christy O'Connor	31 532
1971	Gary Player	11 281
1972	Bob Charles	18 538
1973	Tony Jacklin	24 839
1974	Peter Oosterhuis	32 127
1975	Dale Hayes	20 507
1976	Severiano Ballesteros	39 504
1977	Severiano Ballesteros	46 436
1978	Severiano Ballesteros	54 348
1979	Sandy Lyle	49 232
1980	Greg Norman	74 828
1981	Bernhard Langer	81 036
1982	Sandy Lyle	86 141
1983	Nick Faldo	140 761
1984	Bernhard Langer	160 883
1985	Sandy Lyle	199 020
1986	Severiano Ballesteros	259 275

EUROPEAN TOUR CAREER MONEY WINNINGS
(includes all prize money)

Pos.	Name & Country	Number of Seasons	Prize Money
1	Severiano Ballesteros (Spa)	13	£1 069 114
2	Sandy Lyle (Scot)	9	£739 333
3	Bernhard Langer (W. Ger)	11	£706 665
4	Greg Norman (Aus)	10	£646 686
5	Sam Torrance (Scot)	16	£602 244
6	Nick Faldo (Eng)	11	£556 528
7	Howard Clark (Eng)	13	£523 262
8	Jose-Maria Canizares (Spa)	16	£450 597
9	Ian Woosnam (Wal)	9	£425 170
10	Manuel Pinero (Spa)	16	£413 022
11	Graham Marsh (Aus)	17	£399 841
12	Mark James (Eng)	11	£396 273
13	Hugh Baiocchi (SA)	15	£358 435
14	Des Smyth (Ire)	13	£358 098
15	Bernard Gallacher (Scot)	19	£355 752
16	Neil Coles (Eng)	32	£348 953
17	Rodger Davis (Aus)	10	£326 315
18	Gordon Brand, Jr (Scot)	5	£323 249
19	Eamonn Darcy (Ire)	16	£323 196
20	Ken Brown (Scot)	12	£315 737
21	David Graham (Aus)	15	£299 471
22	Brian Barnes (Scot)	22	£295 384
23	Gordon J. Brand (Eng)	10	£292 384
24	Brian Waites (Eng)	23	£279 418
25	Antonio Garrido (Spa)	17	£271 016
26	Bob Charles (NZ)	27	£256 675
27	Christy O'Connor, Jr (Ire)	17	£255 773
28	John Bland (SA)	12	£254 812
29	Carl Mason (Eng)	13	£246 141
30	Vicente Fernandez (Arg)	15	£245 449

HARRY VARDON TROPHY

The Harry Vardon Trophy is awarded annually by the PGA to the leading player in the Order of Merit.

Year	Winner	Club/Country
1937	Charles Whitcombe	Crews Hill
1938	Henry Cotton	Royal Mid-Surrey
1939	Reg Whitcombe	Parkstone
1940–45	*in abeyance*	
1946	Bobby Locke	South Africa
1947	Norman von Nida	Australia
1948	Charlie Ward	Little Aston
1949	Charlie Ward	Little Aston
1950	Bobby Locke	South Africa
1951	John Panton	Glenbervie
1952	Harry Weetman	Croham Hurst
1953	Flory van Donck	Belgium
1954	Bobby Locke	South Africa
1955	Dai Rees	South Herts
1956	Harry Weetman	Croham Hurst
1957	Eric Brown	Buchanan Castle
1958	Bernard Hunt	Hartsbourne
1959	Dai Rees	South Herts
1960	Bernard Hunt	Hartsbourne
1961	Christy O'Connor	Royal Dublin
1962	Christy O'Connor	Royal Dublin
1963	Neil Coles	Coombe Hill
1964	Peter Alliss	Parkstone
1965	Bernard Hunt	Hartsbourne
1966	Peter Alliss	Parkstone
1967	Malcolm Gregson	Dyrham Park
1968	Brian Huggett	Betchworth Park
1969	Bernard Gallacher	Ifield
1970	Neil Coles	Coombe Hill
1971	Peter Oosterhuis	Dulwich & Sydenham
1972	Peter Oosterhuis	Pacific Harbour, Fiji
1973	Peter Oosterhuis	Pacific Harbour, Fiji
1974	Peter Oosterhuis	Pacific Harbour, Fiji
1975	Dale Hayes	St Pierre and South Africa
1976	Severiano Ballesteros	Spain
1977	Severiano Ballesteros	Spain
1978	Severiano Ballesteros	Spain
1979	Sandy Lyle	Hawkstone Park
1980	Sandy Lyle	Hawkstone Park
1981	Bernhard Langer	W Germany
1982	Greg Norman	Australia
1983	Nick Faldo	Glynwed Int (England)
1984	Bernhard Langer	West Germany
1985	Sandy Lyle	Ballantyne's Scotch Whisky (Scotland)
1986	Severiano Ballesteros	Spain

BRAID TAYLOR MEMORIAL MEDAL

This award is made to the PGA member, resident in Britain, who finishes highest in the Open Championship.

1966 David Thomas *2nd*
1967 Clive Clark *3rd*
1968 Maurice Bembridge *5th*
1969 Tony Jacklin *1st*
1970 Tony Jacklin *5th*
1971 Tony Jacklin *3rd*
1972 Tony Jacklin *3rd*
1973 Neil Coles *2nd*
1974 Peter Oosterhuis *2nd*

1975	Neil Coles		
	Peter Oosterhuis *7th*		
1976	Tommy Horton		
	Mark James		
	Christy O'Connor, Jr *5th*		
1977	Tommy Horton *9th*		
1978	Peter Oosterhuis *6th*		
1979	Mark James *4th*		
1980	Carl Mason *4th*		
1981	Mark James = *3rd*		
1982	Peter Oosterhuis *2nd*		
1983	Denis Durnian		
	Nick Faldo		
	Christy O'Connor, Jr *8th*		
1984	Nick Faldo *6th*		
1985	Sandy Lyle *1st*		
1986	Gordon Brand *2nd*		

THE TOOTING BEC CUP

Presented to the PGA in 1901, the Tooting Bec Cup is now awarded to the member, resident in Britain and Ireland, who returns the lowest round in the Open Championship.

Year	Winner	Venue	Score
1924	Ernest Whitcombe	Royal Liverpool	70
1925	Ted Ray	Prestwick	73
1926	Held in abeyance		
1927	Fred Robson	St Andrews	69
1928	Held in abeyance		
1929	Percy Alliss	Muirfield	69
1930	Archie Compston	Royal Liverpool	68
1931	Held in abeyance		
1932	Arthur Havers	Prince's	68
1933	Abe Mitchell	St Andrews	68
1934	William Davis	Royal St George's	68
1935	Alf Perry	Muirfield	67
1936	William Branch	Royal Liverpool	68
1937	Reg Whitcombe	Carnoustie	70
1938	Dick Burton	Royal St George's	69
	Jack Busson		
1946	Dai Rees	St Andrews	67
1947	Laurie Ayton	Royal Liverpool	69
	Henry Cotton		
1948	Henry Cotton	Muirfield	66
1949	Jimmy Adams	Royal St George's	67
	Ken Bousfield		
1950	Fred Daly	Troon	66
1951	Jimmy Adams	Royal Portrush	68
	Charlie Ward		
1952	Fred Daly	Royal Lytham	67
1953	Eric Lester	Carnoustie	70
	Dai Rees		
1954	Jack Hargreaves	Royal Birkdale	67
	Sid Scott		
1955	Johnny Fallon	St Andrews	67
1956	Dennis Smalldon	Royal Liverpool	68
1957	Laurie Ayton	St Andrews	67
	Eric Brown		
	Johnny Fallon		
1958	Eric Brown	Royal Lytham	65
1959	Peter Alliss	Muirfield	67
1960	Bernard Hunt	St Andrews	66
1961	Christy O'Connor	Royal Birkdale	67
1962	Sid Scott	Troon	68
1963	Tom Haliburton	Royal Lytham	68
	Christy O'Connor		

1964	Malcolm Gregson	St Andrews	67
	Bernard Hunt		
1965	Brian Huggett	Royal Birkdale	68
1966	Peter Butler	Muirfield	65
1967	Hugh Boyle	Royal Liverpool	68
	Lionel Platts		
1968	Brian Barnes	Carnoustie	70
	Gordon Cunningham		
1969	Christy O'Connor	Royal Lytham	65
1970	Neil Coles	St Andrews	65
1971	Peter Oosterhuis	Royal Birkdale	66
1972	Harry Bannerman	Muirfield	67
	Tony Jacklin		
	Guy Hunt		
1973	Neil Coles	Troon	66
1974	John Garner	Royal Lytham	69
	John Morgan		
	Peter Townsend		
1975	Maurice Bembridge	Carnoustie	67
	Neil Coles		
	Bernard Gallacher		
1976	Mark James	Royal Birkdale	66
1977	Tommy Horton	Turnberry	65
1978	Garry Cullen	St Andrews	67
1979	Bill Longmuir	Royal Lytham	65
1980	Ken Brown	Muirfield	68
	Eamonn Darcy		
	Bill McColl		
1981	Gordon Brand	Sandwich	65
1982	Sandy Lyle	Royal Troon	66
1983	Denis Durnian	Royal Birkdale	66
1984	Sam Torrance	St Andrews	66
1985	Christy O'Connor, Jr	Sandwich	64
1986	Gordon Brand	Turnberry	68

Safari Tour

DETAILED RECORDS

Lowest 72-hole total
255, Peter Tupling, Nigerian Open, Ikoyi, Lagos, 1981

Lowest 54 holes
191 (22 under), Peter Tupling, Nigerian Open, Ikoyi, Lagos, 1981

Lowest 36 holes
124 (18 under), Sandy Lyle, Nigerian Open, Ikoyi, Lagos, 1978

Lowest 18 holes
61 (10 under), Sandy Lyle, Nigerian Open, Ikoyi, Lagos, 1978
61 (10 under), Ian Woosnam, Nigerian Open, Ikoyi, Lagos, 1981

Japanese PGA Records

LEADING MONEY-WINNERS

Year	Winner	Yen
1973	Masashi Ozaki	43 814 000
1974	Masashi Ozaki	41 846 908
1975	Takashi Murakami	38 705 551
1976	Isao Aoki	40 985 801
1977	Masashi Ozaki	35 932 608
1978	Isao Aoki	62 987 200
1979	Isao Aoki	45 554 211

1980	Isao Aoki	60 532 660
1981	Isao Aoki	57 262 941
1982	Tsuneyuki Nakajima	68 220 640
1983	Tsuneyuki Nakajima	85 514 183
1984	Shinsaku Maeda	57 040 357
1985	Tsuneyuki Nakajima	101 609 333
1986	Tsuneyuki Nakajima	90 202 066

Career leading money winner (1973–86)
Isao Aoki 635 430 484

Most money in one year
101 609 333 Yen, 1985, Tsuneyuki Nakajima

Most tournaments in one year
10, Masashi Ozaki, 1972

Most overall victories
51, Teruo Sugihara

Biggest margin of victory
19 strokes, Akira Muraki, Japan PGA championship 1930, Takarazuka GC
13 strokes, Isao Aoki, KBC Augasta 1973, Fukuoka CC, Wajiro
13 strokes, Isao Aoki, Golf Japan Series 1979, Yomiuri CC and Tokyo Yomiuri CC

Lowest 72-hole aggregate
265 (23 under par), Masashi Ozaki, Setonaikai Circuit, 1971, Hiroshima CC, Hachihonmatsu
265 (23 under par), Chi-Hsiung Ko, Dunlop International, 1978, Ibaragi GC East
267 (23 under par), Tohru Nakamura, Golf Japan Series 1984, Yomiuri CC and Tokyo Yomiuri CC

Lowest 54-hole total
197 (19 under par), Tadashi Kitta, Kansia PGA championship, 1966, Genkai GC
197 (19 under par), Isao Aoki, Kanto PGA championship, 1972, Isogo GC
199 (19 under par), Tohru Nakamura, Golf Japan Series, 1984, Yomiuri CC and Tokyo Yomiuri CC

Lowest 36-hole total
127 (17 under par), Tsuneyuki Nakajima, East v West Golf Match, 1982, Asahigaoka CC

Lowest 18-hole total
61 (11 under par), Takashi Murakami, Kanto PGA championship, 1972, Isogo CC
61 (11 under par), Masahiro Kuramoto, Dunlop International, 1983, Ibaragi GC East
59 (11 under par), Tsutomu Irie, Kuzuha International, 1985, Kuzuha GC

Lowest 9-hole total
28 (8 under par), Isao Aoki, Kanto PGA championship, 1972, Isogo CC. First round, inward nine
28 (8 under par), Takashi Murakami, Kanto PGA championship, 1972, Isogo CC. Third round, inward nine
28 (8 under par), Shigeru Kawamata, Wakayama Open, 1985, Kunikihara GC. First round, inward nine

Ryder Cup

'The Ryder Cup is not only about winning, but also about goodwill. There is too little tradition left in the game as it is.'
Dave Marr
Captain US team 1981

MILESTONES

The Ryder Cup came into being slightly by chance. If Samuel Ryder, a boy from Manchester, had not persuaded his father, a seed merchant, to sell flower seeds in penny packets, he would never have moved south to start his own business at St Albans in Hertfordshire.

There, late in life, he took up golf under the skilled and watchful eye of Abe Mitchell and, whether at Mitchell's suggestion or not, presented a cup for competition between the professionals of America and Britain.

In an earlier unofficial match Britain won 13½–1½ at Wentworth, but in the first official match in 1927, five years after the start of the Walker Cup, Britain quickly learned the lesson about the formidable nature of American golfers.

1927 Britain, captained by Ted Ray, travelled to Worcester, Massachusetts where America, under Walter Hagen, captured the trophy 9½–2½. America won three of the four 36-hole foursomes and then took six of the singles. Charles Whitcombe won a notable half with Gene Sarazen while George Duncan won Britain's only single against Joe Turnesa, runner-up the same year to Hagen in the USPGA championship. It was Hagen's fourth victory in succession. In the Ryder Cup, Hagen won his foursome with Johnny Golden and his single against Arthur Havers.

1929 Immediate revenge for Britain at Moortown and defeat for Walter Hagen in the singles battle of the captains. He lost 10 and 8 to George Duncan, a victory that helped to turn the tables after America had again won the foursomes. It is the biggest 36-hole singles margin in the history of the event. The victory of Charles Whitcombe by 8 and 6 over Johnny Farrell, 1928 US Open champion, was followed by wins for Archie Compston, Aubrey Boomer and a youthful Henry Cotton.

1931 The Americans underlined their supremacy in their own country. At Scioto, Ohio, they lost only one foursome and two singles. They had five victories by 7 and 6 or more.

1933 One of the more famous matches which Britain won at Southport and Ainsdale, victory coming in the last match on the course. It was the most exciting finish to a team match seen up until then and one watched by enormous crowds. The British, captained by J H Taylor, went for a run on the sands at 6.30 each morning and underwent other forms of physical training unheard of before or since.

How much it contributed to their victory was never known but, for the first time, Britain gained a foursomes lead and hung on in the singles. Eventually, everything depended on Syd Easterbrook and Densmore Shute, the 1933 British Open champion. They came to the last all square. Easterbrook puttted almost dead for his four but Shute, characteristically for an American, knocked his winning putt past the hole and then, uncharacteristically for an American, missed the return.

Britain, without Henry Cotton who had gone to Brussels, had won but the match very nearly did not take place. Hagen did not keep the appointed meeting with Taylor to exchange orders beforehand—or a second appointed meeting. A third hour was named with Taylor issuing an ultimatum that, if Hagen defaulted again, he would call the match off and the world should know why. This time, Hagen kept his appointment and all was well.

1935 Under Hagen's captaincy of America for the fifth time, Britain never recovered from their defeat in the foursomes at Ridgewood, New Jersey. All they gained were two victories by 1 hole and two halves.

1937 History did not repeat itself at Southport and Ainsdale. The British pairing of Henry Cotton and Alf Padgham was very much a case of putting the two best eggs in the same basket. Byron Nelson and Ed Dudley cracked them and America never looked back. Cotton won his single, but the outstanding achievement was the victory of Dai Rees over Nelson. It was the first of many appearances by Rees, but the last as American Captain by Hagen.

1939 The match did not take place although the Americans picked a side.

1947 Britain went to Portland, Oregon, although the fact that the Ryder Cup was resumed so soon after the war owed a great deal to Robert Hudson, a Portland businessman who more or less financed the expedition and played host to the British.

The benevolence, however, was centred off the course. The Americans won the first eleven matches, a whitewash being prevented by Sam King winning the final single against Herman Keiser.

It was the biggest victory margin in the history of the event. Porky Oliver and Lew Worsham equalled the biggest 36-hole foursome win, by 10 and 9, in the history of the event.

1949 America, captained by Ben Hogan who was still recovering from his terrible car accident, lost the foursomes 3–1. However, they staged a typical comeback in the singles. Dutch Harrison set the example by leading off in the singles with five straight 3s against Max Faulkner and his victory was followed by five others. The match was played at Ganton and the score was 7–5.

1951 Another heavy defeat for the British who won only one foursome and one single, although both involved Arthur Lees. Played at Pinehurst, North Carolina, with Ben Hogan, Sam Snead (Captain), Jimmy Demaret and Lloyd Mangrum in the American side. All four won their singles. It was Demaret's sixth and last game.

The American side included Clayton Heafner whose son, Vance, played in the Walker Cup match in 1977. They are the only father and son to play in the Ryder and Walker Cup.

1953 One of the best matches of the series at Wentworth, the result hinging on the missing of two shortish putts by the youngest British players in the singles. It was, nevertheless, a fine recovery by the British to get that close. They lost the foursomes 3–1, but had the edge in the singles. Harry Weetman beat Sam Snead after being 4 down with 6 to play.

1955 The match ventured into the Californian desert for the first time. The margin of the American victory was 8–4, but it was closer than that scoreline suggests. Most notable for two victories by John Jacobs in his only Ryder Cup match.

1957 First British victory for 34 years and, as it proved, the last. At Lindrick before huge crowds, Britain came back after losing the foursomes 3–1. They won six singles by convincing margins and lost only one. Dai Rees who captained the side, won both his matches as did Ken Bousfield. It was the first time since 1933 that no American won twice. In 1933, Ed Dudley and Billy Burke won the only American point in the foursomes but did not play in the singles.

1959 The year in which the British party had a narrow escape when their plane met a storm while travelling from Los Angeles to Palm Desert. After that, the Americans won 8½–3½ but Eric Brown, the only British singles winner, preserved his 100 per cent singles record in his fourth and final match. He won all four singles and lost all four foursomes.

1961 Change to four series of 18-hole matches, foursomes the first day at Royal Lytham and singles the next. America, with Arnold Palmer in the team for the first time, won the foursomes 6–2, but there was only one point in the singles. It was also the first appearance of Billy Casper who set a record for the number of individual matches played. He was helped by the change of format.

1963 Introduction of fourballs, play being extended over three days. It was done to try and further interest in the matches in America, but served merely to emphasize American superiority. They won easily in Atlanta. Britain managed only one fourball victory out of eight.

1965 A closer match at Royal Birkdale although the day of fourballs ended in the dark. The first day of foursomes was halved, America winning the fourballs 4–2 and the singles 10–5. Peter Alliss won both his singles for Britain against Billy Casper and Ken Venturi.

1967 America's biggest win in Houston, 23½–8½, since the match was contested over six rounds. Britain scored no victories in the eight fourballs.

1969 After Tony Jacklin's victory in the Open championship earlier in the summer, the most exciting match of the whole series ended in a half.

The last day began with the scores even and ended the same way. Jacklin scored a 4 and 3 victory over Nicklaus on the last morning and was involved in the deciding game, again against Nicklaus, in the afternoon. Just ahead of them, Brian Huggett got a courageous half against Billy Casper. At the time that Huggett holed from 5 ft on the 18th, Jacklin holed a huge putt on the 17th to get back to square.

Huggett thought that his putt might be to win the whole contest, but not so. Jacklin and Nicklaus, all square with one to play, halved the 18th in 4, although Nicklaus generously conceded Jacklin's final putt of about two and a half feet after he had holed an awkward one himself.

To underline the closeness of the three days, 18 of the 32 matches finished on the 18th green. The teams became 12 a side.

1971 After the excitement of Birkdale, 1971 produced the best performance by a British side in America. This score was 18½–13½ at St Louis, the five-point difference coming in the fourballs in which the British rarely fare well. It was an encouraging match for some of the young British players including Peter Oosterhuis, Peter Townsend, Harry Bannerman, Bernard Gallacher, Maurice Bembridge and Brian Barnes. The final two days consisted of a foursome and fourball not a day of each.

1973 In the first match to be played in Scotland, Britain led at lunchtime on the second day at Muirfield, but America won the singles 11–5, although four were halved and six went to the 17th green or beyond.

1975 Played in Arnold Palmer country at Laurel Valley, Pennsylvania, America won 21–11, a result that was always assured after winning all four foursomes on the first morning. The singles were, for the most part, close and Brian Barnes beat Jack Nicklaus twice on the last day.

1977 At Royal Lytham, only 18 holes were played each day; it was an experiment that was not a success and not popular among the players. There were five foursomes on the first day, five fourballs on the second day and ten singles on the third. America led 7½–2½ after two days, but Hale Irwin, Tom Watson and Jack Nicklaus all lost their singles. Nicklaus's defeat meant that he had won only one of his last five singles in the Ryder Cup.

1979 For the first time, a European side was selected to play the Americans at the Greenbrier Club at White Sulphur Springs. Antonio Garrido and Severiano Ballesteros, British Open champion, won their places, although they only won one match. The form of play was altered yet again. There were two days when eight foursomes and eight fourballs were played, the final day being devoted to twelve singles matches. However, Gil Morgan and Mark James were not fit enough to play in the singles, it being agreed by the captains to call it a half to both sides. It was the first time this had happened.

The European team, captained by John Jacobs, came back well on the second day after trailing 5½–2½ on the first. They entered the final day trailing by one, but they lost the singles 8½–3½, although four matches which they lost finished on the last green.

For the Americans, captained by Billy Casper, Larry Nelson had a 100 per cent record from five games.

Tom Watson withdrew from the American side a few days before the match to be with his wife and newly born child. His place went to Mark Hayes.

Peter Oosterhuis's singles defeat by Hubert Green was his first in eight games.

Lee Elder became the first black golfer to take part in the Ryder Cup.

1981 After Europe had taken a one point lead at the end of the first day, the Americans exercised their dominance to win 18½–9½ at Walton Heath, the first time the Ryder Cup had been played in the South of England since 1953.

As has happened many times, the result was closer than the score suggests, but the outstanding player on either side was Larry Nelson who won all four of his matches—making his tally in two Ryder Cups nine out of nine.

Tom Kite, America's leading money winner for 1981, was 10 under par for his singles match against Sandy Lyle.

1983 The closest match since the tie in 1969 marked the shape of things to come. The United States won 14½–13½ at Palm Beach Gardens, Florida, but the final afternoon was desperately exciting and hinged on so little. The European lead on the first day (4½–3½) was wiped out on the second day. The United States won 4½–3½ which meant that all depended on the singles—only one of which was decided before the 17th.

1985 After all the years of waiting, the Europeans defeated the United States for the first time since 1957. On that occasion, it was a British and Irish team but there is no doubting the contribution of the Europeans (Bernhard Langer and four Spaniards) to the victory at the Belfry.

The Europeans got off to a poor start, losing three out of the four foursomes on the first morning. However, by lunch on the second day, they were level and by Saturday evening were ahead 9–7. It was an important psychological lift, for never did the Americans appear likely to recover.

The Europeans won 7½ of the 12 singles amid mounting scenes of jubilation and celebration.

DETAILED RECORDS

Most appearances
10, Christy O'Connor, Sr (Great Britain and Ireland), 1955–73
9, Sam Snead (US), 1937–59, excluding 1957. No matches were played in 1939 and 1941, but the United States picked a team and Snead's total includes these two occasions

Most consecutive appearances
10, Christy O'Connor, Sr

Biggest margin of victory in individual matches
Over 36 holes (1927–59)
Foursomes: **10 and 9**, Ed Oliver and Lew Worsham (United States), 1947. Walter Hagen and Densmore Shute (United States), 1931
Singles: **10 and 8**, George Duncan (Great Britain), 1929
Over 18 holes (from 1961)
Foursomes: **7 and 5**, Jose-Maria Canizares and Jose Rivero (Europe), 1985; Gil Morgan and Lanny Wadkins (United States), 1983; **6 and 5**, David Thomas and George Will (Great Britain and Ireland), 1965; Dave Marr and Arnold Palmer (United States), 1965; Bobby Nichols and Johnny Pott (United States), 1967; Jack Nicklaus and Arnold Palmer (United States), 1973
Singles: **7 and 6**, Miller Barber (United States), 1969; Lee Trevino (United States), 1971
Fourball: **7 and 6**, Tom Kite and Hale Irwin (United States), 1979; **7 and 5**, Lee Trevino and Jerry Pate (United States), 1981

Largest winning margin by team
36-hole matches, 1947: the United States won 11–1
18-hole matches (3 days), 1967: the United States won 23½–8½

Best team recovery
In 1957, Great Britain and Ireland lost the foursomes 3–1, but won the singles 6½–1½ for overall victory

Most consecutive team victories
7 by the United States, 1935–55

Course most often used
Britain: Southport and Ainsdale, Royal Lytham and Royal Birkdale, twice each
USA: No course has been used more than once

Oldest competitors
Britain: Ted Ray, 50 years 2 months 5 days, 1927
Christy O'Connor, Sr, 49 years 8 months 30 days, 1973
USA: Don January, 47 years 9 months 26 days, 1977
Julius Boros, 47 years 7 months 17 days, 1967

Youngest competitors
Britain: Nick Faldo, 20 years 1 month 28 days, 1977
Paul Way, 20 years 7 months 2 days, 1983
USA: Horton Smith, 21 years 4 days, 1929

Form of the match
1927–59: Two days, 36-hole matches, four foursomes, eight singles
1961: Two days, first day, two series 18-hole foursomes. Second day, two series 18-hole singles
1963–71: Three days, one day each of two series of 18-hole foursomes, fourballs and singles
1973–75: Three days, first two days, 18-hole foursomes and fourballs. Third day two series of singles
1977: Three days, first day, 18-hole foursomes; second day, 18-hole fourballs; third day 18-hole singles
1979–85: Three days, first two days, four foursomes and four fourballs, third day twelve singles

Teams winning all the foursomes or fourballs
1947: the United States won the foursomes 4–0
1963: the United States won the second series of foursomes 4–0
1975: the United States won the first series of foursomes 4–0
1967: the United States won the first series of fourballs 4–0
1971: the United States won the first series of fourballs 4–0

Teams winning all the singles
None, but in 1963 the United States won 7½ out of 8 in the second series of singles

The United States have won 21 matches, Great Britain and Ireland 4 and 1 halved

A total of 130 players have represented the United States, 99 have represented Great Britain and Ireland/Europe

Leo Diegel's eccentric putting method—so much the rage in the 1930s that Bernard Darwin wrote: I diegel, thou diegelest, he diegels, we all diegel. (Illustrated London News)

RESULTS

Year	Venue	Winners	Total	Great Britain and Ireland or Europe (from 1979) Total	Captains USA	Britain
1927	Worcester, Massachusetts	USA	9½	2½	Walter Hagen	Ted Ray
1929	Moortown, Leeds	Britain	5	7	Walter Hagen	George Duncan
1931	Scioto, Ohio	USA	9	3	Walter Hagen	Charles A Whitcombe
1933	Southport and Ainsdale, Lancashire	Britain	5½	6½	Walter Hagen	*J H Taylor
1935	Ridgewood, New Jersey	USA	9	3	Walter Hagen	Charles A Whitcombe
1937	Southport and Ainsdale, Lancashire	USA	8	4	*Walter Hagen	Charles A Whitcombe
1947	Portland, Oregon	USA	11	1	Ben Hogan	Henry Cotton
1949	Ganton, Scarborough, Yorkshire	USA	7	5	*Ben Hogan	*Charles A Whitcombe
1951	Pinehurst, North Carolina	USA	9½	2½	Sam Snead	*Arthur Lacey
1953	Wentworth, Surrey	USA	6½	5½	Lloyd Mangrum	*Henry Cotton
1955	Palm Springs, California	USA	8	4	Chick Harbert	Dai Rees
1957	Lindrick, Sheffield	Britain	4½	7½	Jack Burke	Dai Rees
1959	Palm Desert, California	USA	8½	3½	Sam Snead	Dai Rees
1961	Royal Lytham and St Annes, Lancashire	USA	14½	9½	Jerry Barber	Dai Rees
1963	Atlanta, Georgia	USA	23	9	Arnold Palmer	*Johnny Fallon
1965	Royal Birkdale, Lancashire	USA	19½	12½	*Byron Nelson	*Harry Weetman
1967	Houston, Texas	USA	23½	8½	*Ben Hogan	*Dai Rees
1969	Royal Birkdale, Lancashire	(tie)	16	16	*Sam Snead	*Eric C Brown
1971	St Louis, Missouri	USA	18½	13½	*Jay Hebert	*Eric C Brown
1973	Muirfield, East Lothian	USA	19	13	*Jack Burke	*Bernard J Hunt
1975	Laurel Valley, Pennsylvania	USA	21	11	*Arnold Palmer	*Bernard J Hunt
1977	Royal Lytham and St Annes, Lancashire	USA	12½	7½	*Dow Finsterwald	*Brian G C Huggett
1979	Greenbrier, White Sulphur Springs	USA	17	11	*Billy Casper	*John Jacobs
1981	Walton Heath, Surrey	USA	18½	9½	*Dave Marr	John Jacobs
1983	Palm Beach Gardens, Florida	USA	14½	13½	*Jack Nicklaus	*Tony Jacklin
1985	The Belfry, West Midlands	Europe	11½	16½	*Lee Trevino	*Tony Jacklin

* Non-playing captain

THE RYDER CUP 1927–1985
GREAT BRITAIN & IRELAND/EUROPE INDIVIDUAL RECORDS

Name	Years	Matches Played	Won	Lost	Halved	Percentage
Jimmy Adams	1939–47–49–51–53	7	2	5	0	28.57
Percy Alliss	1929–31–33–35–37	6	3	2	1	58.33
Peter Alliss	1953–57–59–61–63–65–67–69	30	10	15	5	41.66
Laurie Ayton	1949	0	0	0	0	—
Severiano Ballesteros	1979–83–85	15	6	6	3	55.00
Harry Bannerman	1971	5	2	2	1	50.00
Brian Barnes	1969–71–73–75–77–79	26	11	14	1	44.23
Maurice Bembridge	1969–71–73–75	16	5	8	3	40.62
Aubrey Boomer	1927–29	4	2	2	0	50.00
Ken Bousfield	1949–51–55–57–59–61	10	5	5	0	50.00
Hugh Boyle	1967	3	0	3	0	—
Harry Bradshaw	1953–55–57	5	2	2	1	50.00
Gordon Brand, Sr	1983	1	0	1	0	—
Eric Brown	1953–55–57–59	8	4	4	0	50.00
Ken Brown	1977–79–83–85	11	4	7	0	36.36
Stewart Burns	1929	0	0	0	0	—
Richard Burton	1935–37–39–49	5	2	3	0	40.00
Jack Busson	1935	2	0	2	0	—
Peter Butler	1965–69–71–73	14	3	9	2	28.57
Jose-Maria Canizares	1981–83–85	9	4	3	2	55.55
Alex Caygill	1969	1	0	0	1	50.00
Clive Clark	1973	1	0	1	0	—
Howard Clark	1977–81–85	7	3	3	1	50.00
Neil Coles	1961–63–65–67–69–71–73–77	40	12	21	7	38.75

Name	Years	Matches Played	Won	Lost	Halved	Percentage
Archie Compston	1927–29–31	6	1	4	1	25.00
Henry Cotton	1929–37–39–47	6	2	4	0	33.33
Bill Cox	1935–37	3	0	2	1	16.66
Allan Dailey	1933	0	0	0	0	—
Fred Daly	1947–49–51–53	8	3	4	1	43.75
Eamonn Darcy	1975–77–81	9	0	7	2	11.11
William Davies	1931–33	4	2	2	0	50.00
Peter Dawson	1977	3	1	2	0	33.33
Norman Drew	1959	1	0	0	1	50.00
George Duncan	1927–29–31	5	2	3	0	40.00
Syd Easterbrook	1931–33	3	2	1	0	66.66
Nick Faldo	1977–79–81–83–85	17	11	6	0	64.70
John Fallon	1955	1	1	0	0	100.00
Max Faulkner	1947–49–51–53–57	8	1	7	0	12.50
George Gadd	1927	0	0	0	0	—
Bernard Gallacher	1969–71–73–75–77–79–81–83	31	13	13	5	50.00
John Garner	1971–73	1	0	1	0	—
Antonio Garrido	1979	5	1	4	0	20.00
Eric Green	1947	0	0	0	0	—
Malcolm Gregson	1967	4	0	4	0	—
Tom Haliburton	1961–63	6	0	6	0	—
Jack Hargreaves	1951	0	0	0	0	—
Arthur Havers	1927–31–33	6	3	3	0	50.00
Jimmy Hitchcock	1965	3	0	3	0	—
Bert Hodson	1931	1	0	1	0	—
Reg Horne	1947	0	0	0	0	—
Tommy Horton	1975–77	8	1	6	1	18.75
Brian Huggett	1963–67–69–71–73–75	24	8	10	6	45.83
Bernard Hunt	1953–57–59–61–63–65–67–69	28	6	16	6	32.14
Geoffrey Hunt	1963	3	0	3	0	—
Guy Hunt	1975	3	0	2	1	16.66
Tony Jacklin	1967–69–71–73–75–77–79	35	13	14	8	48.57
John Jacobs	1955	2	2	0	0	100.00
Mark James	1977–79–81	10	2	7	1	25.00
Edward Jarman	1935	1	0	1	0	—
Herbert Jolly	1927	2	0	2	0	—
Michael King	1979	1	0	1	0	—
Sam King	1937–39–47–49	5	1	3	1	30.00
Arthur Lacey	1933–37	3	0	3	0	—
Bernhard Langer	1981–83–85	14	7	4	3	60.71
Arthur Lees	1947–49–51–55	8	4	4	0	50.00
Sandy Lyle	1979–81–83–85	14	4	8	2	35.71
Jimmy Martin	1965	1	0	1	0	—
Peter Mills	1957	1	1	0	0	100.00
Abe Mitchell	1929–31–33	6	4	2	0	66.66
Ralph Moffitt	1961	1	0	1	0	—
Christy O'Connor, Jr	1975	2	0	2	0	—
Christy O'Connor, Sr	1955–57–59–61–63–65–67–69–71–73	35	11	20	4	37.14
John O'Leary	1975	4	0	4	0	—
Peter Oosterhuis	1971–73–75–77–79–81	28	14	11	3	55.35
Alf Padgham	1933–35–37–39	6	0	6	0	—
John Panton	1951–53–61	5	0	5	0	—
Alf Perry	1933–35–37	4	0	3	1	12.50
Manuel Pinero	1981–85	9	6	3	0	66.66
Lionel Platts	1965	5	1	2	2	40.00
Eddie Polland	1973	2	0	2	0	—
Ted Ray	1927	2	0	2	0	—
Dai Rees	1937–39–47–49–51–53–55–57–59–61	18	7	10	1	41.66
Jose Rivero	1985	2	1	1	0	50.00
Fred Robson	1927–29–31	6	2	4	0	33.33
Syd Scott	1955	2	0	2	0	—
Des Smyth	1979–81	7	2	5	0	28.57
Dave Thomas	1959–63–65–67	18	3	10	5	30.55
Sam Torrance	1981–83–85	13	3	7	3	34.61
Peter Townsend	1969–71	11	3	8	0	27.27
Brian Waites	1983	4	1	3	0	25.00
Charles Ward	1947–49–51	6	1	5	0	16.66
Paul Way	1983–85	9	6	2	1	72.22
Harry Weetman	1951–53–55–57–59–61–63	15	2	11	2	20.00

Name	Years	Matches Played	Won	Lost	Halved	Percentage
Charles Whitcombe	1927–29–31–33–35–37–39	9	3	2	4	55.55
Ernest Whitcombe	1929–31–35	6	1	4	1	25.00
Reg Whitcombe	1935–39	1	0	1	0	—
George Will	1963–65–67	15	2	11	2	20.00
Norman Wood	1975	3	1	2	0	33.33
Ian Woosnam	1983–85	7	2	4	1	35.71

Britain named 8 of their 10 players for the 1939 match, but match not played because of World War II.

THE RYDER CUP 1927–1985
UNITED STATES INDIVIDUAL RECORDS

Name	Years	Matches Played	Won	Lost	Halved	Percentage
Tommy Aaron	1969–73	6	1	4	1	25.00
Skip Alexander	1949–51	2	1	1	0	50.00
Jerry Barber	1955–61	5	1	4	0	20.00
Miller Barber	1969–71	7	1	4	2	28.57
Herman Barron	1947	1	1	0	0	100.00
Andy Bean	1979	3	2	1	0	66.66
Frank Beard	1969–71	8	2	3	3	43.75
Homero Blancas	1973	4	2	1	1	62.50
Tommy Bolt	1955–57	4	3	1	0	75.00
Julius Boros	1959–63–65–67	16	9	3	4	68.75
Gay Brewer	1967–73	9	5	3	1	61.11
Billy Burke	1931–33	3	3	0	0	100.00
Jack Burke	1951–53–55–57–59	8	7	1	0	87.50
Walter Burkemo	1953	1	0	1	0	—
Billy Casper	1961–63–65–67–69–71–73–75	37	20	10	7	63.51
Bill Collins	1961	3	1	2	0	33.33
Charles Coody	1971	3	0	2	1	16.66
Wilfred Cox	1931	2	2	0	0	100.00
Ben Crenshaw	1981–83	6	3	2	1	58.33
Jimmy Demaret	1941–47–49–51	6	6	0	0	100.00
Gardner Dickinson	1967–71	10	9	1	0	90.00
Leo Diegel	1927–29–31–33	6	3	3	0	50.00
Dale Douglass	1969	2	0	2	0	—
Dave Douglas	1953	2	1	0	1	75.00
Ed Dudley	1929–33–37	4	3	1	0	75.00
Olin Dutra	1933–35	4	1	3	0	25.00
Lee Elder	1979	4	1	3	0	25.00
Al Espinosa	1927–29–31	4	2	1	1	62.50
Johnny Farrell	1927–29–31	6	3	2	1	58.33
Dow Finsterwald	1957–59–61–63	13	9	3	1	73.07
Ray Floyd	1969–75–77–81–83–85	23	7	13	3	36.95
Doug Ford	1955–57–59–61	9	4	4	1	50.00
Ed Furgol	1957	1	0	1	0	—
Marty Furgol	1955	1	0	1	0	—
Al Geiberger	1967–75	9	5	1	3	72.22
Vic Ghezzi	1939–41	0	0	0	0	—
Bob Gilder	1983	4	2	2	0	50.00
Bob Goalby	1963	5	3	1	1	70.00
Johnny Golden	1927–29	3	3	0	0	100.00
Lou Graham	1973–75–77	9	5	3	1	61.11
Hubert Green	1977–79–85	7	4	3	0	57.14
Ralph Guldahl	1937–39	2	2	0	0	100.00
Fred Haas, Jr	1953	1	0	1	0	—
Jay Haas	1983	4	2	1	1	62.50
Walter Hagen	1927–29–31–33–35	9	7	1	1	83.33
Bob Hamilton	1949	2	0	2	0	—
Chick Harbert	1949–55	2	2	0	0	100.00
Chandler Harper	1955	1	0	1	0	—
E J 'Dutch' Harrison	1947–49–51	3	2	1	0	66.66
Fred Hawkins	1957	2	1	1	0	50.00
Mark Hayes	1979	3	1	2	0	33.33

Name	Years	Matches Played	Won	Lost	Halved	Percentage
Clayton Heafner	1949–51	4	3	0	1	87.50
Jay Hebert	1959–61	4	2	1	1	62.50
Lionel Hebert	1957	1	0	1	0	—
Dave Hill	1969–73–77	9	6	3	0	66.66
Jimmy Hines	1939	0	0	0	0	—
Ben Hogan	1941–47–51	3	3	0	0	100.00
Hale Irwin	1975–77–79–81	16	11	4	1	71.87
Tommy Jacobs	1965	4	3	1	0	75.00
Peter Jacobsen	1985	3	1	2	0	33.33
Don January	1965–77	7	2	3	2	42.85
Herman Keiser	1947	1	0	1	0	—
Tom Kite	1979–81–83–85	15	8	4	3	63.33
Ted Kroll	1953–55–57	4	3	1	0	75.00
Ky Laffoon	1935	1	0	1	0	—
Tony Lema	1963–65	11	8	1	2	81.81
Bruce Lietzke	1981	3	0	2	1	16.66
Gene Littler	1961–63–65–67–69–71–75	27	14	5	8	66.66
John Mahaffey	1979	3	1	2	0	33.33
Harold McSpaden	1939–41	0	0	0	0	—
Jerry McGee	1977	2	1	1	0	50.00
Tony Manero	1937	2	1	1	0	50.00
Lloyd Mangrum	1941–47–49–51–53	8	6	2	0	75.00
Dave Marr	1965	6	4	2	0	66.66
Billy Maxwell	1963	4	4	0	0	100.00
Dick Mayer	1957	2	1	0	1	75.00
William Mehlhorn	1927	2	1	1	0	50.00
Dick Metz	1939	0	0	0	0	—
Cary Middlecoff	1953–55–59	6	2	3	1	41.66
Johnny Miller	1975–81	6	2	2	2	50.00
Gil Morgan	1979–83	6	1	2	3	41.66
Bob Murphy	1975	4	2	1	1	62.50
Byron Nelson	1937–39–41–47	4	3	1	0	75.00
Larry Nelson	1979–81	9	9	0	0	100.00
Bobby Nichols	1967	5	4	0	1	90.00
Jack Nicklaus	1969–71–73–75–77–81	28	17	8	3	66.07
Andy North	1985	3	0	3	0	—
Ed Oliver	1947–51–53	5	3	2	0	60.00
Mark O'Meara	1985	3	1	2	0	33.33
Arnold Palmer	1961–663–65–67–71–73	32	22	8	2	71.87
Johnny Palmer	1949	2	0	2	0	—
Sam Parks	1935	1	0	0	1	50.00
Jerry Pate	1981	4	2	2	0	50.00
Calvin Peete	1983–85	7	4	2	1	64.28
Henry Picard	1935–37–39	4	3	1	0	75.00
Johnny Pott	1963–65–67	7	5	2	0	71.42
Dave Ragan	1963	4	2	1	1	62.50
Henry Ransom	1951	1	0	1	0	—
Johnny Revolta	1935–37	3	2	1	0	66.66
Juan Rodriguez	1973	2	0	1	1	25.00
Bill Rogers	1981	4	1	2	1	37.50
Bob Rosburg	1959	2	2	0	0	100.00
Mason Rudolph	1971	3	1	1	1	50.00
Paul Runyan	1933–35–39	4	2	2	0	50.00
Doug Sanders	1967	5	2	3	0	40.00
Gene Sarazen	1927–29–31–33–35–37–41	12	7	2	3	70.83
Denny Shute	1931–33–37	6	2	2	2	50.00
Dan Sikes	1969	3	2	1	0	66.66
Horton Smith	1929–31–33–35–37–39–41	4	3	0	1	87.50
Jesse Snead	1971–73–75	11	9	2	0	81.81
Sam Snead	1937–39–41–47–49–51–53–55–59	13	10	2	1	80.76
Ed Sneed	1977	2	1	0	1	75.00
Mike Souchak	1959–61	6	5	1	0	83.33
Craig Stadler	1983–85	8	4	2	2	62.50
Ken Still	1969	3	1	2	0	33.33
Dave Stockton	1971–77	5	3	1	1	70.00
Curtis Strange	1983–85	7	3	3	1	50.00
Hal Sutton	1985	4	1	2	1	37.50
Lee Trevino	1969–71–73–75–79–81	30	17	7	6	66.66

Name	Years	Matches Played	Won	Lost	Halved	Percentage
Jim Turnesa	1953	1	1	0	0	100.00
Joe Turnesa	1927–29	4	1	2	1	37.50
Ken Venturi	1965	4	1	3	0	25.00
Lanny Wadkins	1977–79–83–85	17	12	4	1	73.52
Art Wall, Jr	1957–59–61	6	4	2	0	66.66
Al Watrous	1927–29	3	2	1	0	66.66
Tom Watson	1977–81–83	12	9	3	0	75.00
Tom Weiskopf	1973–75	10	7	2	1	75.00
Craig Wood	1931–33–35–41	4	1	3	0	25.00
Lew Worsham	1947	2	2	0	0	100.00
Fuzzy Zoeller	1979–83–85	10	1	8	1	15.00

The US named teams in 1939 and 1941, but matches not played because of World War II.

World Matchplay Championship

Since 1964, the World Matchplay Championship, sponsored first by Piccadilly then by Colgate and now by Suntory, has struck a blow for matchplay. In other parts of the professional golf-playing world, it has been a dwindling giant in its traditional form.

However, at Wentworth for the last 22 autumns, it has thrived in a way that has made the World Matchplay Championship probably the most popular and best attended event in Britain after the Open. This has been largely because of its distinguished cast which has been assembled under the direction of Mark McCormack but the basic nature of a match means that, with every game, more than just the result is at stake.

In a strokeplay event, pride is less dented if a player does not happen to win but, in a match, defeat can be full of regrets, frustration—even humiliation. The dislike of losing is what has led to so much memorable golf since 1964. It has been impossible to keep to the idea of inviting the winners of all the major championships but there has never been a bad year, rarely even a poor year. It has been said that, generally speaking, modern professionals and television companies hate matchplay. But the crowds love it and the BBC has had some of its finest televised moments when the leaves turn gold at Wentworth.

Originally the field was confined to eight players. In 1977 and 1978 they tried 16 players but now 12 start out, giving rise to four first round matches and four players receiving byes into the second round. Apart from a short experiment, when some early matches were over 18 holes, all matches have been over 36 holes.

DETAILED RECORDS

Most victories
5, Gary Player, 1965–66–68–71–73
4, Severiano Ballesteros, 1981–82–84–85
3, Greg Norman, 1980–83–86
2, Arnold Palmer, 1964–67; Hale Irwin, 1974–75

Most times runner-up
3, Sandy Lyle, 1980–82–86
2, Peter Thomson, 1965–67; Jack Nicklaus, 1966–71; Lee Trevino, 1970–72; Bernhard Langer, 1984–85

Oldest Winner
Gary Player, 37 years 11 months 12 days, 1973

Youngest Winner
Severiano Ballesteros, 24 years 6 months 2 days, 1981

Highest winning margin (in final)
6 and 5, Severiano Ballesteros beat Bernhard Langer, 1985

Highest winning margin (not in final)
11 and 9, Tom Watson beat Dale Hayes, first round, 1978
10 and 9, Gary Player beat Jean Garaialde, first round, 1968
10 and 8, Arnold Palmer beat Roberto de Vicenzo, first round, 1966

Longest final
40 holes, Gary Player beat Graham Marsh, 1973

Longest match (not in final)
40 holes, Isao Aoki beat Severiano Ballesteros, semi-final, 1979

Best single round
Tony Jacklin, 9 under par (63), 1972, second 18 of semi-final against Lee Trevino. Jacklin lost after going round in 63.

Best 9 holes
Outward: 29 (6 under par), Tony Jacklin, second 18 of semi-final, 1972. Score 4, 3, 4, 3, 2, 3, 4, 3, 3

Inward: 31 (6 under), Gary Player, first round v Ben Crenshaw, 1974. Score 2, 3, 4, 3, 2, 4, 4, 4, 5
31, David Graham, semi-final v Raymond Floyd, 1976. Score 2, 4, 3, 4, 2, 4, 4, 4, 4
31, Jose-Maria Olazabal, first round v Lanny Wadkins, 1986. Score 2, 4, 4, 4, 3, 3, 4, 4, 3.

Biggest 18-hole lead
10 up, Tom Watson led Dale Hayes, first round, 1978
10 up, Gary Player led Peter Thomson, first round, 1968

Successive threes
7 (5th to 11th), Gene Littler, 1969

Successive fours
11, Jack Nicklaus (7th to 17th), 1970

Successive birdies
6, Tom Watson (15th to 20th), 1978 v Dale Hayes
6, Sandy Lyle (2nd to 7th), second round v Tommy Nakajima, 1986, but his spell included an 8 at the 4th
5, Gary Player (10th to 14th), 1974 v Ben Crenshaw

Successive bogeys
5, Andy North (7th to 11th), 1978

Comebacks

Gary Player, 7 down after 19 holes, beat Tony Lema at the 37th, semi-final, 1965

Sandy Lyle, 6 down after 18 holes, beat Nick Faldo 2 and 1, first round, 1982

Consistency

In 1980, Sandy Lyle had nine 4s on the outward nine of his second 18 against George Burns, first round, 1980.

In the 1971 final, Gary Player and Jack Nicklaus began by halving the first 11 holes in 4, 3, 4, 4, 3, 4, 4, 4, 3, 4

BEST MATCH

Probably Sandy Lyle's second round match with Tommy Nakajima in 1986.

Nakajima went round in the morning in 65 and in the afternoon in 64 yet lost at the 38th hole. Between them they had 27 birdies and four eagles. As he stood on the 8th tee in the afternoon, Lyle was 4 up, needing two 4s to be out in 28 but he took 5 at the 8th and 9th, Nakajima took 4 holes in a row, three with birdies. By the 15th tee, Nakajima was 2 up, a position he held to the 17th tee, but Lyle finished 4, 3 to square the match and won at the second extra hole.

RESULTS

1964
Semi-finals: Arnold Palmer beat Gary Player 8 and 6. Neil Coles beat Bruce Devlin 2 and 1
Final: Palmer beat Coles 2 and 1

1965
Semi-finals: Gary Player beat Tony Lema at 37th. Peter Thomson beat Arnold Palmer 1 hole
Final: Player beat Thomson 3 and 2

1966
Semi-finals: Gary Player beat Arnold Palmer 2 and 1. Jack Nicklaus beat Billy Casper 2 and 1
Final: Player beat Nicklaus 6 and 4

1967
Semi-finals: Peter Thomson beat Gary Player 2 and 1. Arnold Palmer beat Billy Casper 3 and 2
Final: Palmer beat Thomson by 2 holes

1968
Semi-finals: Bob Charles beat Arnold Palmer 7 and 6. Gary Player beat Tony Jacklin at 37th
Final: Player beat Charles 1 hole

1969
Semi-finals: Gene Littler beat Gary Player 4 and 3. Bob Charles beat Tommy Aaron 9 and 7
Final: Charles beat Littler at 37th

1970
Semi-finals: Lee Trevino beat Dave Stockton 7 and 6. Jack Nicklaus beat Tony Jacklin 6 and 4
Final: Nicklaus beat Trevino 2 and 1

1971
Semi-finals: Jack Nicklaus beat Neil Coles 7 and 5. Gary Player beat Bob Charles 2 and 1
Final: Player beat Nicklaus 5 and 4

1972
Semi-finals: Tom Weiskopf beat Peter Oosterhuis 4 and 3. Lee Trevino beat Tony Jacklin 1 hole
Final: Weiskopf beat Trevino 4 and 3

1973
Semi-finals: Graham Marsh beat Tom Weiskopf 4 and 3. Gary Player beat Johnny Miller 3 and 2
Final: Player beat Marsh at 40th

1974
Semi-finals: Gary Player beat Jerry Heard 5 and 4. Hale Irwin beat Tony Jacklin 5 and 4
Final: Irwin beat Player 3 and 1

1975
Semi-finals: Hale Irwin beat Jack Newton 4 and 3. Al Geiberger beat Tom Watson 2 and 1
Final: Irwin beat Geiberger 4 and 2

1976
Semi-finals: David Graham beat Raymond Floyd 1 hole. Hale Irwin beat Gary Player 2 holes
Final: Graham beat Irwin at 38th

1977
Semi-finals: Graham Marsh beat Hale Irwin 7 and 6. Raymond Floyd beat Severiano Ballesteros 2 and 1
Final: Marsh beat Floyd 5 and 3

1978
Semi-finals: Simon Owen beat Graham Marsh 2 and 1. Isao Aoki beat Raymond Floyd 3 and 2
Final: Aoki beat Owen 3 and 2

1979
Semi-finals: Isao Aoki beat Severiano Ballesteros at 40th. Bill Rogers beat Fuzzy Zoeller 2 holes
Final: Rogers beat Aoki 1 hole

1980
Semi-finals: Greg Norman beat Bernard Gallacher 6 and 5. Sandy Lyle beat Peter Jacobsen 6 and 5
Final: Norman beat Lyle 1 hole

1981
Semi-finals: Severiano Ballesteros beat Bernhard Langer 5 and 4. Ben Crenshaw beat Bill Rogers 1 hole
Final: Ballesteros beat Crenshaw 1 hole

1982
Semi-finals: Severiano Ballesteros beat Lanny Wadkins 3 and 1. Sandy Lyle beat Tom Kite 8 and 7
Final: Ballesteros beat Lyle at 37th

1983
Semi-finals: Greg Norman beat Severiano Ballesteros 1 hole. Nick Faldo beat Bob Charles 6 and 5
Final: Norman beat Faldo 4 and 2

1984
Semi-finals: Bernhard Langer beat Greg Norman 2 and 1. Severiano Ballesteros beat Ben Crenshaw 9 and 8
Final: Ballesteros beat Langer 2 and 1

1985
Semi-finals: Severiano Ballesteros beat Andy North 4 and 2. Bernhard Langer beat Denis Watson 2 and 1
Final: Ballesteros beat Langer 6 and 5

1986
Semi-finals: Sandy Lyle beat Rodger Davis 2 and 1. Greg Norman beat Jack Nicklaus 1 hole
Final: Norman beat Lyle 2 and 1

The Asia Golf Circuit

Comprising the Hong Kong, Thailand, Indian, Malaysian, Korean, Singapore, Republic of China and Indonesian Opens, plus the Dunlop Japan International, played normally between February and April.

The foundation of what is today known as the Asia Golf Circuit was laid in 1959 when the late Eric Cremin, a former Australian Open champion, and the late Kim Hall, a Welsh International, then serving with the Royal Air Force, had the idea of running a small tournament for eight professionals who would be playing in the Philippines Open. In those days, the Philippines Open was the only truly 'open' event played in Southeast Asia.

As things turned out, Cremin and Hall managed to produce 24 professionals, including Kel Nagle, Bob Charles and Mr Lu, as he later became known. With these names and an offer of £1000 in prize money, Hall approached the Royal Hong Kong GC who accepted a proposal to run the first Hong Kong Open.

Together with the Philippines Open, the Far East Circuit was started and in 1961, Peter Thomson convinced the Singapore golfers to join in with the Singapore Open. The following year, the Malaysian Open followed suit while the Yomiuri Country Club in Tokyo staged the first Japan Invitational tournament.

India, the Republic of China (Taiwan) and Thailand came next and, with the inclusion of Korea in 1970 and Indonesia in 1974, the family circle was complete. The circuit became firmly established with ten tournaments, although the Philippines Open was unofficial for a year or two until 1987 when Brian Tennyson won the title from Chen Tze Ming. The other significant change is a closer liaison with the Japanese tour and its riches.

In 1961, Hall retired from the RAF and returned to Hong Kong to become co-ordinator of the circuit. He continued until 1968 when he handed over to Leonardo 'Skip' Guinto, then President of the Philippines Golf Association.

Guinto did much to build up prize money and in 1977 the first $100 000 event was reached. This was the Tokyo event whose sponsorship was taken over by the Sobhu Company.

In the early seventies, the minimum prize money for inclusion in the circuit, renamed the Asia Golf Circuit in 1970, was $15 000. This increased to $25 000 and in 1977 to $30 000. By 1985, the minimum was $100 000 with some up to $150 000. This has had the effect of increasing the strength of the fields which are drawn from Far East golfers, Australians and New Zealanders as well as a number of Americans who are not qualified to play the US circuit.

In 1979, 'Skip' Guinto died and Kim Hall returned as circuit director until his death but the success of the venture which Hall and Cremin envisaged, is well reflected by the thriving nature of the circuit and the number of fine players it has helped to foster.

The Japanese golfer, Isao Aoki, one of the most popular characters on not only the Asian golf circuit but worldwide. (Allsport)

Asia Circuit Winners 1962–1986

	Philippines	Hong Kong	Malaysia	Singapore	Indonesia
1962	Celestino Tugot (Ph) 284	Len Woodward (Aus) 271	Frank Phillips (Aus) 276	Brian Wilkes (SA) 283	
1963	Ben Arda (Ph) 289	Hsieh Yung-yo (Tai) 272	Bill Dunk (Aus) 276	Alan Brookes (SA) 276	
1964	Peter Thomson (Aus) 285	Hsieh Yung-yo (Tai) 269	Tomoo Ishii (Jap) 282	Ted Ball (Aus) 291	
1965	Lu Liang-huan (Tai) 288	Peter Thomson (Aus) 278	Tomoo Ishii (Jap) 282	Frank Phillips (Aus) 279	
1966	Luis Silverio (Ph) 287	Frank Phillips (Aus) 275	Harold Henning (SA) 278	Ross Newdick (NZ) 284	
1967	Hsu Sheng-san (Tai) 283	Peter Thomson (Aus) 273	Ireneo Legaspi (Ph) 286	Ben Arda (Ph) 282	
1968	Hsu Chi-san (Tai) 278	Randall Vines (Aus) 271	Kenji Hosoishi (Jap) 271	Hsieh Yung-yo (Tai) 275	
1969	Haruo Yasuda (Jap) 283	Teruo Sugihara (Jap) 274	Takaaki Kono (Jap) 280	Tomio Kamata (Jap) 278	
1970	Hsieh Yung-yo (Tai) 282	Isao Katsumata (Jap) 274	Ben Arda (Ph) 273	Hsieh Yung-yo (Tai) 276	
1971	Chen Chien-chung (Tai) 282	Orville Moody (US) 266	Takaaki Kono (Jap) 269	Haruo Yasuda (Jap) 277	
1972	Hideyo Sugimoto (Jap) 286	Walter Godfrey (NZ) 272	Takashi Murakami (Jap) 276	Takaaki Kono (Jap) 279	
1973	Kim Seung-hack (Kor) 289	Frank Phillips (Aus) 278	Hideyo Sugimoto (Jap) 277	Ben Arda (Ph) 284	
1974	Lu Liang-huan (Tai) 281	Lu Liang-huan (Tai) 280	Graham Marsh (Aus) 278	Eleuterio Nival (Ph) 275	Ben Arda (Ph) 28
1975	Kuo Chie-hsiung (Tai) 276	Hsieh Yung-yo (Tai) 288	Graham Marsh (Aus) 276	Yutaka Suzuki (Jap) 284	Hsu Sheng-san (Tai) 27
1976	Quintin Mancao (Ph) 281	Ho Ming-chung (Tai) 277	Hsu Sheng San (Tai) 279	Kesahiko Uchida (Jap) 273	Mya Aye (Bur) 27
1977	Hsieh Yung-yo (Tai) 281	Hsieh Min-nam (Tai) 280	Stewart Ginn (Aus) 276	Hsu Chi-san (Tai) 277	Gaylord Burrows (US) 28
1978	Lu Liang-huan (Tai) 278	Hsieh Yung-yo (Tai) 275	Brian Jones (Aus) 276	Terry Gale (Aus) 278	Kuo Chie-hsiung (Tai) 27
1979	Ben Arda (Ph) 286	Greg Norman (Aus) 273	Lu Hsi-chuen (Tai) 277	Lu Hsi-chuen (Tai) 280	Lu Hsi-chuen (Tai) 27
1980	Lu Hsi-chuen (Tai) 287	Kuo Chie-hsiung (Tai) 274	Mark McNulty (Zim) 270	Kurt Cox (US) 276	Lu Hsi-chuen (Tai) 26
1981	Tom Sieckman (US) 287	Chen Tze-ming (Tai) 279	Lu Hsi-chuen (Tai) 276	Mya Aye (Bur) 273	Payne Stewart (US) 28
1982	Hsieh Min-nam (Tai) 292	Kurt Cox (US) 276	Denny Hepler (US) 208	Hsu Sheng-san (Tai) 274	Eleuterio Nival (Ph) 28
1983	Lu Hsi-chuen (Tai) 277	Greg Norman (Aus) 134	Terry Gale (Aus) 279	Lu Chien-soon (Tai) 279	Robert Wrenn (US) 27
1984		Bill Brask (US) 268	Lu Chien-soon (Tai) 275	Tom Sieckman (US) 274	Terry Gale (Aus) 28
1985		Mark Aebli (US) 270	Terry Gale (Aus) 270	Chen Tze-ming (Tai) 274	Lu Chien-soon (Tai) 27
1986		Seichi Kanai (Jap) 285	Stewart Ginn (Aus) 276	Greg Turner (NZ) 271	Frankie Minoza (Ph) 27
1987	Brian Tennyson (US) 288	Ian Woosnam (GB) 275	Terry Gale (Aus) 280	Peter Fowler (Aus) 274	Wayne Smith (Aus) 27

Thailand		India		Taiwan		Korea		Dunlop Japan International		Champion
								Peter Thomson (Aus)	278	Peter Thomson (Aus)
								Doug Sanders (US)	289	Kel Nagle (Aus)
										Hsieh Yung-yo (Tai)
Hsieh Yung-yo (Tai)	283							Frank Phillips (Aus)	288	Hsieh Yung-yo (Tai)
Tadashi Kitta (Jap)	283			Lu Liang-huan (Tai)	281			Hugh Boyle (GB)	286	Lu Liang-huan (Tai)
Tomoo Ishii (Jap)	283			Hsieh Yung-yo (Tai)	277			Mitsutaka Kono (Jap)	282	Lu Liang-huan (Tai)
Randall Vines (Aus)	285			Hsieh Yung-yo (Tai)	282			Chen Ching-po (Tai)	283	Hsieh Yung-yo (Tai)
Hsieh Yung-yo (Tai)	277			Hideyo Sugimoto (Jap)	284			Guy Wolstenholme (GB)	288	Hsieh Yung-yo (Tai)
David Graham (Aus)	286	Chen Chien-chung (Tai)	279	Chang Chung-fa (Tai)	215	Hahn Chang-sang (Kor)	289	David Graham (Aus)	286	Ben Arda (Ph)
Lu Liang-huan (Tai)	278	Graham Marsh (Aus)	275	Chang Chung-fa (Tai)	286	Hahn Chang-sang (Kor)	281	Haruo Yasuda (Jap)	282	Hsieh Min-nam (Tai)
Hsieh Min-nam (Tai)	278	Brian Jones (Aus)	282	Haruo Yasuda (Jap)	284	Hahn Chang-sang (Kor)	276	Hsieh Min-nam (Tai)	279	Graham Marsh (Aus)
Graham Marsh (Aus)	286	Graham Marsh (Aus)	280	Eleuterio Nival (Ph)	283	Kim Seung-hack (Kor)	282	Shigeru Uchida (Jap)	279	Graham Marsh (Aus)
Yoshihiro Hitomi (Jap)	291	Kuo Chie-hsiung (Tai)	287	Kuo Chie-hsiung (Tai)	282	Cho Tae-woon (Kor)	286	Lu Liang-huan (Tai)	280	Kuo Chie-hsiung (Tai)
Howard Twitty (US)	285	Ted Ball (Aus)	282	Kuo Chie-hsiung (Tai)	277	Kuo Chie-hsiung (Tai)	284	Teruo Sugihara (Jap)	282	Hsieh Min-nam (Tai)
Ben Arda (Ph)	270	Peter Thomson (Aus)	288	Hsu Chi-san (Tai)	288	Kazunari Takahashi (Jap)	214	Ben Arda (Ph)	277	Hsu Sheng-san (Tai)
Norio Akitomi (Jap)	284	Brian Jones (Aus)	284	Hsieh Min-nam (Tai)	276	Ho Ming-chung (Tai)	285	Ben Arda (Ph)	282	Hsieh Min-nam (Tai)
Hsu Sheng-san (Tai)	280	Bill Brask (US)	284	Hsieh Yung-yo (Tai)	283	Kim Seung-hack (Kor)	277	Kuo Chie-hsiung (Tai)	265	Hsu Sheng-san (Tai)
Mike Krantz (US)	282	Gaylord Burrows (US)	284	Lu Liang-huan (Tai)	287	Shen Chung-shyan (Tai)	289	Hiroshi Ishii (Jap)	278	Lu Hsi-chuen (Tai)
Lu Hsi-chuen (Tai)	274	Kurt Cox (US)	286	Kuo Chie-hsiung (Tai)	277	Chen Tze-ming (Tai)	214	Masashi Ozaki (Jap)	277	Lu Hsi-chuen (Tai)
Tom Sieckman (US)	281	Payne Stewart (US)	284	Ho Ming-chung (Tai)	276	Chen Tze-ming (Tai)	285	Kosaku Shimada (Jap)	286	Lu Hsi-chuen (Tai)
Hsu Sheng-san (Tai)	281	Hsu Sheng-san (Tai)	277	Chen Tse-ming (Tai)	289	Kim Joo-heun (Kor)	285	Tsuneyuki Nakajima (Jap)	276	Hsu Sheng-san (Tai)
Chen Tze-ming (Tai)	283	Junichi Takahashi (Jap)	285	Lu Liang-huan (Tai)	295	Hiroshi Yamada (Jap)	212	Larry Nelson (US)	201	Lu Chien-soon (Tai)
Lu Chien-soon (Tai)	278	Rafael Alarcon (Mex)	279	John Jacobs (US)	218	Michael Clayton (Aus)	283	John Jacobs (US)	283	John Jacobs (US)
Bill Israelson (US)	273	Tony Grimes (US)	279	Lu Liang-huan (Tai)	282	Chen Tze-chung (Tai)	280	Chen Tze-chung (Tai)	277	Chen Tze-ming (Tai)
Ho Ming-chung (Tai)	288	Lu Hsi-chuen (Tai)	279	Lu Hsi-chuen (Tai)	212	Tsao Chien-teng (Tai)	280	Hideto Shigenobu (Jap)	281	Lu Hsi-chuen (Tai)
Chen Tze-ming (Tai)	272	Brian Tennyson (US)	280	Mark Aebli (US)	294	Chen Liang Hsi (Tai)	279	Isao Aoki (Jap)	277	Jim Hallet (US)

Courtesy: United Airlines

Lu Liang Huan, a frequent winner on the Asian circuit. (Benson and Hedges)

The Amateurs

British Amateur Championship

The oldest amateur championship in the world

MILESTONES

1885 First played 20 April to 23 April. Not recognized as the official start of the championship until much later. It was started by the Royal Liverpool Club as a 'tournament open to all amateur golfers' and the first champion at Hoylake was Allan F MacFie, a Scottish member of the home club.

However, it was unusual in that the tournament rules decreed that halved matches were not to be decided on an extra hole basis, but were simply replayed. Byes were not eliminated in the first round and, as there were 48 entries, three players reached the semi-final.

MacFie was the man in receipt of a bye into the final where he beat Horace Hutchinson by 7 and 6. If that part was fortunate, he also halved two matches in the fourth round with Walter M de Zoete (Blackheath) and was only successful in the third meeting.

He won on the last green, but was helped by a hole in one at the 13th, the first recorded in the event.

In the third round, John Ball beat his father by 4 and 2.

1886 After the highly successful start, the championship was officially instituted at St Andrews and won by Horace Hutchinson, runner-up at Hoylake. Straight matchplay. 44 entries but two disqualified as having at one time 'carried clubs' and therefore ranked as professional.

1887 Hutchinson won a second victory back at Hoylake against John Ball, the local player who was to become so famous. There were only 33 entries.

1887 to 1895 A period dominated by John Ball and Johnny Laidlay. They won the title alternately. Ball in 1888–90–92–94, and Laidlay in 1889–91. In addition, Laidlay was runner-up to Ball in 1888–90 and to Peter Anderson in 1893. Ball was runner-up in 1895. Ball won the Open in 1890 and shares the distinction with Bobby Jones of winning both the Open and Amateur titles in the same year.

In 1895, the winner was Leslie Balfour (afterwards Leslie Balfour Melville) who won his last three matches at the 19th hole. His opponents were William Grey, Laurie Auchterlonie and John Ball who all hit their second shots into the Swilcan Burn at St Andrews. It was the last time the final was played over 18 holes except for 1966—due to adverse weather conditions.

1896 Freddie Tait beat Harold Hilton at Sandwich in the first 36-hole final. It was Hilton's third defeat in the final. Tait was something of a bogeyman to Hilton and had earlier beaten Charles Hutchings, Johnny Laidlay, John Ball and Horace Hutchinson in succession.

1897 Something of a surprise win for Jack Allan, a medical student at Edinburgh University who never touched a club until 1891. At the time, he was the youngest winner and seemed destined for a fine career, but he died of lung disease the following year after taking up a medical appointment at Lasswade, near Edinburgh.

1898 A second victory for Freddie Tait who two years later was killed in the South African War. Reports of his victory at Hoylake say he was sadly out of form in the early rounds, saving himself with remarkable recovery play, but he was at his best in the final against S Mure-Fergusson.

1899 Entry of over 100 for the first time. John Ball scored his fifth win, this time against the defending champion, Freddie Tait, at Prestwick. He won at the 37th in Tait's last championship.

1900 Victory for Harold Hilton after three previous defeats in the final.

1901 Hilton conducted a successful defence of his title, the first to do so since 1887 and the last until Lawson Little in 1935.

1902 Both Charles Hutchings and Sidney Fry, the two finalists, used the new Haskell ball at Hoylake. Hutchings, the winner, was 53. The Hon Michael Scott, the oldest winner ever, was 54.

1903 First of two victories for Robert Maxwell. He won both at Muirfield where he was a member.

1904 Title taken overseas for the first time by Walter J Travis, an Australian-born resident of America, famous for his black cigars and centreshafted Schenectady putter. He beat James Robb, Harold Hilton, Horace Hutchinson and, in the final at Sandwich, Edward Blackwell.

1905 In a final remembered for consistent heavy rain A Gordon Barry defeated the Hon Osmund Scott by 3 and 2. It was felt that in these conditions Scott was at a considerable disadvantage with rubber grips. Two weeks later he had had them changed. Barry, 19, was a student at St Andrews University.

1906 James Robb, runner-up in 1897 and 1900, became champion at last.

1907 A record entry of 200 for the sixth victory of John Ball, apparently more interested in his garden and motor cycle since his last win.

1908 A Yorkshireman, E A Lassen caused a surprise by winning at Sandwich, but he proved his worth and reached the final again in 1911. An earlier round produced the longest match in the championship's history: C A Palmer beat Lionel Munn at the 28th.

1907, 1910 and 1912 The final chapters in the remarkable record of John Ball. At Westward Ho! in 1912, he completed his eighth victory, a record that will surely stand for ever. Michael Bonallack has come nearest to it with five successes. In 1912, Ball defeated Abe Mitchell, later a celebrated professional, in the final. The final lasted 38 holes, the second longest in the championship's history. They met in the 1910 semi-final when Ball also won. In 1912 Ball was 5 down and 7 to play in the fifth round.

In 1910 Ball scored the first double-figure victory in the final against C Aylmer.

1909 Of Robert Maxwell's second victory at Muirfield against Cecil Hutchison, the golf-course architect, Bernard Darwin wrote: 'They produced a never to be forgotten match by those who saw it. The golf was so faultless, the speed at which it was played so great, that they seemed to be playing not a championship final but one of the friendly, almost casual games which they had often played together on the links of the Lothians.'

1911 and 1913 Confirmation of Harold Hilton's skill in something of a revival. When he won at Prestwick in 1911, 20 years had passed since his first appearance in the final and ten since his previous victory. Hilton was also American champion in 1911.

1914 The champion, J L C Jenkins, was the player of the year who would no doubt have done greater things but for an injury in the war.

1920 In the first championship final for six years Cyril Tolley defeated Bob Gardner, twice American champion and the second American to reach the final of the British. At Muirfield, Tolley was 3 up and 4 to play in the final, but Gardner, at one time world record holder for the pole vault and US rackets doubles champion, won the 33rd, 34th and 36th. However, Tolley won the 37th with a superb 2, the old 1st hole at Muirfield being a short one.

1921 Willie Hunter, the son of the professional at Deal, won his championship over a burned-up course at Hoylake. He was a player of no great length but putted finely on very fast greens and handed a double-figure defeat in the final to Allan Graham. Earlier Graham beat Bobby Jones 6 and 5 with a queer brass putter. In the afternoon, he was still in such a daze, he had towards the end to ask his caddie to score. Later that year, Hunter beat Jones in the US Amateur. He then turned pro. Graham's father died the day before the final.

1922 At this time the amateur triumvirate of Tolley, Roger Wethered and Ernest Holderness were dominant. In 1922, Holderness, the epitome of steadiness, won his first title at Prestwick.

1923 Sandwiched between Holderness's two victories was one for Roger Wethered at Deal, two years after losing a play-off for the Open championship at St Andrews. Wethered played outstandingly in beating Robert Harris by 7 and 6 in the final.

1924 Holderness's second victory. In a very rainy final he beat Eustace Storey, then still an undergraduate at Cambridge.

1925 The second championship at Westward Ho! with the winner, Robert Harris, born in Dundee. Harris, however, runner-up to Harold Hilton in 1913 and Roger Wethered in 1923, was a redoubtable champion who, as a stockbroker in London, was an Anglo-Scot although he had learned his game at Carnoustie. He was also a pre-war golfer and was 43 when he won the championship, but his victory was thoroughly deserved. In the final, he defeated Kenneth Fradgley by 13 and 12, a severe margin which has only been exceeded by Lawson Little in 1934.

1926 A second American, Jess Sweetser, won the championship and so set a pattern of American victories in a Walker Cup year in Britain. It was not broken until 1963 when Michael Lunt won.

A quarter-mile runner at Yale, Sweetser swept through the hardest part of the draw and, as often happens, was rewarded with a relatively easy match in the final. He defeated an Edinburgh golfer, A F Simpson and became the second American (and the third person) to win both the British and American titles.

1927 A championship won by Dr William Tweddell, a deceptively good player who was born in Durham, qualified at Aberdeen University and played most of his golf in the Midlands. In the final, he beat Eustace Landale, a useful Hoylake player, by 7 and 6.

1928 T Phil Perkins, a product of the Midlands, followed his victory in the English championship the previous year, by winning the British, beating Roger Wethered 6 and 4 in the final at Prestwick. Later in the summer, Perkins played well in America, but he had what was described as a 'severe dose of the Bobby Jones's'.

In the Walker Cup match, Jones beat him 13 and 12 and in the final of the American Amateur at Brae Burn Jones won again, this time by 10 and 9.

He later turned professional and was joint runner-up in the US Open of 1932 won by Gene Sarazen; however, the US Amateur final was the first time the reigning British and American champions had met in a major final and, apart from Harold Hilton, Perkins is the only British golfer to have reached the final in both championships. Jack McLean reached the American final in 1936.

1929 Cyril Tolley's second victory, a little less spectacular than his first, but no more than his ability merited.

1930 Part of the legendary Grand Slam chapter of Bobby Jones. It was the first leg, but it was significant because it was always the championship which he found hardest to win; and, indeed it was the only one which he won just once.

Fittingly, it took place at St Andrews, scene of some of Jones's brightest and darkest moments, but even 1930 had its dark moments. He disliked 18-hole matches and had one or two close calls notably against George Voigt who was 2 up and 5 to play in their semi-final, and against Cyril Tolley in the second round. Jones won at the 19th.

In the final, Jones, with room to manoeuvre, beat Roger Wethered 7 and 6 and was never likely to be denied. It was the second defeat in the final for Wethered in three years.

1931 Surprise victory for Eric Martin Smith who, none the less, played and putted very consistently.

Some measure of the surprise at his success can be gauged by the telegram which he received on the morning of his final with John de Forest. From one who had played with him at Cambridge, it read, 'Quite ridiculous but keep at it.'

It was the last championship to be held at Westward Ho!

1932 John de Forest confirmed his full worth the following year by winning at Muirfield in a final with Eric Fiddian. It was the fourth time a player had reached the final one year and become champion the next. The final was played at a very slow pace partly because, at that time, de Forest was suffering from 'the waggling disease in its most exaggerated form'. In the semi-final de Forest beat Lionel Munn at the 26th hole, the longest semi-final on record.

1933 The year of the oldest winner on record, the Hon Michael Scott, at 54. He was a year older than Charles Hutchings who had won in 1902. Having just scrambled through his first-round match, Scott grew ever stronger. He beat the American George Dunlap in the semi-final and was too good for Dale Bourn in the final.

1934 Year of the biggest victory in the final: 14 and 13 by Lawson Little from Newport, Rhode Island over Jack Wallace. Wallace, a local West of Scotland golfer, was overwhelmed before many of his supporters could reach Prestwick.

However, he had plenty of excuse. Little, who had had one victory at the 19th, was round in 66 in the morning and after lunch played 4 of the remaining 5 holes of the match in 3 and the other in 4. Such scoring had never been approached in a final. In one round, J G Montgomery and his opponents hit 5 balls out of bounds at the 1st hole between them.

1935 Part two of Little's dominance, one which was not confined to the British championship. In 1934 and 1935, he won the British and American titles, a unique achievement.

However, in the final at Royal Lytham St Annes, he was given a terrific match by the 1927 champion, William Tweddell, who made up for being outgunned in the long game by his work round the greens. Three down and 10 to play, Tweddell took the match to the 36th green.

It was Lytham's first Amateur championship, but it was not at its best owing to a plague of leatherjackets.

1936 In the absence of Little who turned professional, Hector Thomson won for Scotland. It is a remarkable fact that since World War I, there have only been four Scottish champions: Thomson, Robert Harris in 1925, Alec Kyle in 1939 and Reid Jack in 1957. Thomson was the only one of these four to have won in Scotland.

In the final at St Andrews, Thomson beat Jim Ferrier by 2 holes. Ferrier was the first Australian to reach the final. Later, he turned professional, became an American citizen and won the USPGA championship. In the second round, J L Mitchell, later Captain of the Royal and Ancient, defeated Lionel Munn at the 26th hole. In 1908, Munn lost at the 28th, and in 1932 also at the 26th.

1937 Victory at Royal St George's for Robert Sweeny, an American who played much of his golf in Britain and Europe. He defeated Lionel Munn who knew Sandwich blindfold, by 3 and 2, but the championship marked the first appearance of a

John Ball, eight times winner of the British Amateur. Here seen at Sandwich, 1914. (BBC Hulton Picture Library)

17-year-old Irishman, James Bruen, who made a spectacular impact on amateur golf over a short period.

1938 A championship at Troon for the first time preceded the famous Walker Cup match at St Andrews. All the American team took part, however, and the winner was the ever-popular Charlie Yates of Atlanta whose opponent in the final was the Irishman Cecil Ewing.

1939 Alec Kyle's championship at Hoylake, the last before World War II. A Scotsman resident in Yorkshire, he won a delightful final against Tony Duncan played at a brisk pace. They took 2¼ hours for the first 18 holes, generally held to be a record.

It is the only final since 1914 played between two golfers from home countries who were not English. Duncan was the first Welsh finalist.

The other fact about this championship is that it was the first at which a running commentary for radio was tried. It was also the last.

1946 Deprived of championship glory during the war years, James Bruen from Cork made amends with victory over the 1937 champion, Robert Sweeny. The championship was Royal Birkdale's first, a course which has since become a regular venue for British championships and international matches. The Open followed in 1954.

1947 The first all-American final, Willie Turnesa adding the British crown to the American title he won in 1938. At Carnoustie, another new course on the Amateur championship list,

he defeated Dick Chapman by 3 and 2.

1948 Frank Stranahan, son of a millionaire and an obsessively devoted golfer, won the first of his two championships in three years. At Sandwich, he defeated Charlie Stowe, once a miner, in the final by 5 and 4. Stowe, one of the victorious British Walker Cup team in 1938, had lost the final of the English championship the previous year.

1949 The only championship to be played in the Republic of Ireland (Portmarnock) was won by Sam (or Max) McCready who was born in Belfast. He beat the 1947 champion, Willie Turnesa, 2 and 1 in the final.

1950 Frank Stranahan's second victory in the second all-American final although, as it happened, the first of three in a row. It was also the slowest on record, the first 18 holes taking 4½ hours at St Andrews. The match, however, turned out to be one sided with Stranahan beating Dick Chapman by 8 and 6. There was a record entry of 324, the first time that 300 had been exceeded.

1951 In his third final in five years, victory came at last for Dick Chapman. He is the only player to have won all the major amateur championships of the world, the American, British and Canadian. He also won the French, Italian and Portuguese titles.

In the first championship at Royal Porthcawl, he defeated Charlie Coe by 5 and 4.

1952 Prestwick's last major championship (the last Open was 1925), saw a third consecutive American winner and a third consecutive all-American final. In it, Harvie Ward beat Frank Stranahan by 6 and 5.

It was the second final between two players who subsequently became professionals. The others were 1938 (Hector Thomson

Peter McEvoy, back to back champion 1977 and 1978. (Allsport)

and Jim Ferrier), 1966 (Bobby Cole and Ronnie Shade), 1967 (Bob Dickson and Ron Cerrudo) and 1971 (Steve Melnyk and Jim Simons).

1953 The beginning of the Joe Carr era. His eventful and not unfortuitous win put an end to the run of American victories. His victory in the final at Hoylake against the defending champion, Harvie Ward, probably the most formidable amateur in the world at the time, was considered by many to be his best. Three up at lunch and all square after the 11th in the afternoon, Carr had the better of the closing holes but no champion ever had such a run of escapes in reaching the final. In his last three matches, he had to hole from 12 ft on the 18th to avoid defeat; hole again from the same distance the next morning when his opponent missed from 6 ft and in his semi-final with Cecil Beamish he was 2 down with 3 to play. Beamish then went out of bounds at the 16th and 19th, easy enough to do at Hoylake, and Carr was through.

1954 The bicentenary celebrations of the Royal and Ancient Golf Club brought the most international entry to the championship at Muirfield. Four different nationalities were represented in the semi-finals and the eventual champion was Doug Bachli, the first Australian to succeed. By a notable coincidence, the year also saw the first Australian winner of the British Open, Peter Thomson, who, even more remarkably, was a member of the same club as Bachli: the Victoria in Melbourne.

In the final, Bachli beat Bill Campbell, the popular and respected American, by 2 and 1. It was felt at the time that Campbell would win one day but, though he came again fairly regularly, he never did.

1955 Joe Conrad from Texas, played in the Walker Cup at St Andrews where he was one of only two Americans to lose his single; he then stayed on to win the championship at Lytham and came back in 1956 to finish leading amateur in the Open. At Lytham, he beat Alan Slater, a Yorkshireman, by 3 and 2 in the final.

1956 A year when the experiment of playing the quarter-finals, semi-finals and final over 36 holes was tried, produced a big surprise and the youngest winner.

John Beharrell, another Midlands golfer, won a month after his 18th birthday. On his way to the final, he beat Charles Lawrie, Ian Caldwell, Gene Andrews, Frank Deighton, Reid Jack and then Leslie Taylor, a local member of Troon. The margin was 5 and 4.

With the course playing easily, Beharrell hit very few poor shots and pitched and putted effortlessly. First appearance of Michael Bonallack.

1957 Formby's introduction to the list of championship courses confirmed the talent of Reid Jack who twice finished well up in the Open (1959 and 1960). It was a just and popular triumph. He defeated the American Staff Sergeant, Harold Ridgley, in the final. Ridgley spent many years serving in Britain in the US Air Force. He won his semi-final by 13 and 12. The championship was switched from Sandwich to a more central venue on account of the petrol strike.

1958 Only the semi-finals and final were played over 36 holes at St Andrews, but it did not stop a second victory for Joe Carr. Two years later, he might just possibly have won the Open on the same course had not the last round been washed out after he had started birdie, par.

In the final he beat Alan Thirlwell 3 and 2, one of the deciding strokes undoubtedly being a 4 iron on the 13th green out of Walkinshaw's bunker in the afternoon. Having just holed across the green for a 2 at the 12th, it enabled him to remain 2 up.

Michael Bonallack made his first real mark on the championship by reaching the semi-final, where he lost to Carr. Seeds (16) were introduced for the first time. Regional qualifying also introduced.

1959 Victory at Sandwich after the Walker Cup at Muirfield went not to the more experienced Americans, or to Jack Nicklaus who won the St George's Grand Challenge Cup, but to Deane Beman.

He accounted for Bill Hyndman in the first of Hyndman's three finals by 3 and 2, Hyndman having taken a lot out of himself the previous day in knocking out an obdurate American serviceman, Bob McGee at the 38th.

1960 The summit of Joe Carr's career. At Portrush, he stood 10 up on Bob Cochran on the 27th tee of the final. His third victory was the first time a British or Irish golfer had performed such a feat since Harold Hilton, more than half a century before.

Farewell championship appearance of James Bruen. He withdrew with a wrist injury during his first match. Semi-finals over 36 holes.

Like the Open (1951) Portrush has held only one Amateur championship.

1961 The emergence of Turnberry as a championship course and a new champion to match. Michael Bonallack scored the first of his five victories in the course of the next ten years. He began by defeating Jimmy Walker, a local Ayrshire golfer, by 6 and 4 in the final. The only time Bonallack had to play the 17th was on the morning of the final.

Only the final was 36 holes, the semi-finals reverting to 18. Regional qualifying abandoned.

1962 A surprising American winner in Richard Davies, a Californian; and a slightly surprising finalist in John Povall, only the second Welshman to survive that far until Duncan Evans won in 1980. The other was Tony Duncan in 1939, also at Hoylake.

1963 Historic victory for Michael Lunt. It was the first time since Sweetser set the pattern in 1926 that a British player won in a Walker Cup year at home.

His final opponent, however, was not an American, but John Blackwell, 48, Captain of Royal St George's and in 1966 Captain of the Royal and Ancient. The other two semi-finalists, Dr Ron Luceti and Ed Updegraff were both American although Luceti was not a Walker Cup player.

1964 The longest final on record. It took 39 holes for Gordon Clark to come from behind and beat Michael Lunt, so close to a successful defence of his title.

A long tradition was broken by the choice of Ganton for the championship. It was the first time it was played on other than a seaside links.

1965 Porthcawl's second championship and Michael Bonallack's second victory. The final against Clive Clark was a replica of the final of the English championship the following month; and the pattern was similar. In both events Bonallack was down at lunch although at Porthcawl he had been 6 down after 13 holes. His recovery is thus the best on record.

1966 The first final over 18 holes since 1895. A sea mist, common at Carnoustie, caused the loss of half a day and led to a revision of the programme. It also produced the first South African champion in Bobby Cole and the joint youngest at 18 years and 1 month exactly. He defeated Ronnie Shade 3 and 2 with half Scotland supporting Shade. Henri de Lamaze was the first Frenchman to reach the semi-final. He lost to Cole.

1967 Bob Dickson clinched the first leg of his double at Formby; he later went on to win the US Amateur also, the first man to win both in one year since Lawson Little. At Formby he beat fellow American Ron Cerrudo by 2 and 1 in what was undoubtedly the fastest final between two Americans, 2 hr 40 min for the first 18 holes.

1968 Two outstanding amateurs, Joe Carr and Michael Bonallack, met in the final at Troon although Carr was a little past his best. Bonallack won 7 and 6 and so began the first of three successive wins.

1969 In Hoylake's centenary year, Bonallack beat Bill Hyndman for his second successive title. It was his fourth victory, equalling Harold Hilton, a local man. Only John Ball, another Hoylake golfer, won more (8).

1970 More records for Michael Bonallack after his third win in a row at Newcastle, Co Down, the only time the championship

Garth McGimpsey earning the reward for winning the 1985 Amateur, an invitation to the Masters. (Allsport)

has been played there. He again beat Bill Hyndman in the only repeat final since 1890 and his three wins in a row is an outright record.

Hyndman also equalled a record of being most times runner-up (3 with Harold Hilton) but he had his chance. Two up after 13 holes and 1 up at lunch, he was in sight of becoming the oldest winner but, looking exhausted, as any man of 54 has a right to do, he lost 8 and 7.

1971 Another American monopoly in the championship at Carnoustie despite their Walker Cup defeat at St Andrews the previous week. Peter Moody prevented all four semi-finalists being American, but in the final Steve Melnyk beat Jim Simons who, inside a month, had come close to winning the US Open at Merion. He did so as an amateur but, like Melnyk, later turned professional.

1972 A surprising winner in Trevor Homer, another Midlander, who had never previously won even his county championship. However, he played extremely well all week and, in the first round of the final, completed Royal St George's in 69. He beat Alan Thirlwell by 4 and 3. It was 13 years since Thirlwell's other final. Only Horace Hutchinson (1885 to 1903) can claim such a span as runner-up.

1973 Richard Siderowf became the 16th American winner. At Porthcawl, he beat Peter Moody, semi-finalist in 1971, 5 and 3.

1974 Trevor Homer's second win in three years. At Muirfield, he defeated the American Walker Cup player Jim Gabrielsen

by 2 holes in the closest final for ten years. Homer won the 36t hole despite driving into a bunker and leaving it there, a unprecedented luxury for a champion.

1975 Snow marked the first day of the championship a Hoylake (2 June) but the final was played in shirtsleeves. Th weather caused a number of odd results but Vinny Giles was worthy champion. He became the sixth American since Worl War II to win both British and American titles. Two up at lunc on Mark James, he won 8 and 7. James, who played in th Walker Cup of 1975, was a member of the Ryder Cup team i 1977.

1976 Dick Siderowf's second championship and only the secon extra-hole final since 1920. At St Andrews, he beat John Davie at the 37th where Siderowf holed from 5 ft and Davies misse from 3½ ft. Davies lost the final of the English the same summe

1977 Ganton's second championship produced the sixth Mid land winner in Peter McEvoy. In the final, he beat Hugh Camp bell, 39, the first Scottish finalist for eleven years.

1978 McEvoy became only the fifth player successfully to de fend his title. The others were Hutchinson, Hilton, Little an Bonallack.

In Troon's centenary year (they became Royal Troon during th week), be beat Paul McKellar, a Walker Cup golfer from th West of Scotland, by 4 and 3 in a final which saw McKella drive the 1st green after lunch. It was a feat nobody coul remember happening before.

In their second-round match, Gordon Macdonald and A Liddl had played 19 holes when darkness beat them. They resumed a 7.30 am with Macdonald winning at the 25th. In point of time it is the longest match ever played in the championship.

1979 Peter McEvoy's three in a row bid ended. Two America finalists confirmed the pattern so prominent in Walker Cu years in Britain. Eight days after the match at Muirfield, Ja Sigel defeated Scott Hoch by 3 and 2 in the first Amateu championship to be played at Hillside, Royal Birkdale's neigh bour in Southport.

For the first time ever, no British player reached the semi-final The other semi-finalists were Tony Gresham of Australia an Doug Roxburgh of Canada.

A new qualification rule imposed by the Royal and Ancien greatly reduced the number of American entries. They wer required to have qualified for either the US Open or U. Amateur in any of the previous five years.

The championship cup, part of Sigel's luggage, was lost for day at London Airport. It was later found and sent on to Sigel.

1980 First Welsh champion appropriately enough on a Welsh course, Royal Porthcawl. In the final, Duncan Evans bea David Suddards of South Africa by 4 and 3.

Two South African semi-finalists, Suddards and D Lindsay Smith, for the first time. Arthur Pierse was the first Iris semi-finalist since Brian Hoey in 1970.

1981 A piece of history made at St Andrews with the victory o Philippe Ploujoux of France, the first continental winner of the oldest Amateur championship. He played steadily all week and was very much at home on the large greens.

For the third year in succession, no Englishman or Scotsman reached the semi-final but John Carr, son of Joe who won at S Andrews in 1958, was a semi-finalist in his first championship.

1982 Deal's first Amateur for 59 years produced the third youngest winner in Martin Thompson, 18, of Middlesborough, taking part in his first championship. In glorious weather, he had a hard road to the final, no victory coming before the 17th but he won the final by 4 and 3 against Andrew Stubbs of Leek Thompson was 5 under par for the 33 holes played.

In contrast to the previous year when all four semi-finalists came from overseas, all four semi-finalists were from Britain.

1983 The championship broke with tradition by introducing a 36-hole medal qualifying system, the leading 64 players going forward to matchplay over the Ailsa course at Turnberry. One round of qualifying was played over the neighbouring Arran course.

It was a week dominated by Phillip Parkin who, the previous week, had won two of his three matches in the Walker Cup at Hoylake. Parkin led the 288 qualifiers with a total of 140, won his first five matches without the alarm of a close finish and then outplayed Jim Holtgrieve in the final. It was the first time since 1963 in a Walker Cup year in Britain that a member of the American team failed to win the championship.

1984 Jose-Maria Olazabal became the first Spanish winner of the championship at Formby. It was the second time in four years that the winner came from Continental Europe. The other three semi-finalists were all British. Colin Montgomerie, the beaten finalist, and David Gilford went on to become Walker Cup players in 1985 while David Curry was to win the 1986 Amateur championship.

1985 The first Amateur to be played at Royal Dornoch in the centenary year of the championship, produced an impressive victory for Garth McGimpsey who became the second winner from Northern Ireland. After qualifying over Dornoch and Golspie with a total of 142, he reached the final without having to play beyond the 16th hole and beat Graham Homewood in the final by 8 and 7, a margin not exceeded for more than 50 years.

1986 David Curry, semi-finalist in 1984, won the championship in Royal Lytham and St Annes' centenary year. In the final he beat Geoff Birtwell, 41, a well known local golfer, by 11 and 9, the biggest margin for 52 years. The American entry included Jack Nicklaus, Jr.

Two early champions, A J T Allan (1897) and J Robb (1906) (right). Allan from Edinburgh University beat Robb in the final of 1897, the first over 36 holes. (Illustrated London News)

DETAILED RECORDS

Most victories
8, John Ball, 1888–90–92–94–99–1907–10–12
5, Michael Bonallack, 1961–65–68–69–70
4, Harold Hilton, 1900–01–11–13

Most times runner-up
3, Harold Hilton, 1891–92–96; William Hyndman III, 1959–69–70

Oldest winner
Hon Michael Scott, 54 years 9 months 8 days, 1933

Youngest winner
John Beharrell, 1956, and Bobby Cole, 1966; both 18 years 1 month to the day
Jose-Maria Olazabal, 1984, 18 years 4 months 4 days
Martin Thompson, 1982, 18 years 4 months 9 days

Oldest competitor
William Doleman, 73 years, 1910

Consecutive winners
3, Michael Bonallack, 1968–69–70
2, Horace Hutchinson, 1886–87; Harold Hilton, 1900–01; W Lawson Little, 1934–35; Peter McEvoy, 1977–78

Biggest span between first and last victories
24 years, John Ball, 1888–1912

First overseas winner
Walter Travis (USA), Sandwich, 1904

First winner from Continental Europe
Philippe Ploujoux (France), 1981

Longest final
39 holes: Gordon Clark beat Michael Lunt, Ganton, 1964

Longest match (18 holes)
C A Palmer beat Lionel Munn at the 28th, Sandwich, 1908

Biggest margin of victory
Final: **14 and 13,** W Lawson Little beat J Wallace, Prestwick, 1934
18 holes: **10 and 8;** Alexander Stuart beat John L Stewart, Prestwick, 1888; Captain E F Carter, Royal Portrush, beat F S Wheeler, USA, Muirfield, 1920

Most finals
10, John Ball
  7, Harold Hilton, three losing followed by four winning

Identical finals
1888 and 1890: John Ball beat John Laidlay
1969 and 1970: Michael Bonallack beat Bill Hyndman

First player to win the British Open and Amateur
John Ball, Amateur, 1888; Open, 1890

Players who have won the Amateur and Open
Same year: John Ball, 1890; Bobby Jones, 1930
Different years: Harold Hilton (Amateur 1900–01–11–13; Open 1892 and 1897)

Record entry
488, St Andrews, 1958

Most appearances
33, Harold Hilton (29 consecutively)
29, John Ball
27, Michael Bonallack (all consecutively), Alan Thirlwell
25, Bernard Darwin, Cyril Tolley

Courses most often used
Hoylake, 16
St Andrews, 15
Royal St George's, 11

Champion on the same course
John Ball, 3 times at Hoylake, twice at Prestwick

Brothers
In 1923 Willie Torrance beat Tony Torrance 4 and 2 in the fourth round

Father and Son
John Ball III beat his father John Ball, Jr in the third round in 1885

RESULTS

1885 Hoylake
A F MacFie, Royal Liverpool
Semi-finals: H G Hutchinson beat W J Ball 2 holes; MacFie a bye
Final: MacFie beat Hutchinson 7 and 6

1886 St Andrews
H G Hutchinson, Royal and Ancient
Semi-finals: Hutchinson beat C Chambers 5 and 3; H A Lamb beat J Ball, Sr 7 and 6
Final: Hutchinson beat Lamb 7 and 6

1887 Hoylake
H G Hutchinson, Royal and Ancient
Semi-finals: J Ball, Jr beat J G Tait 3 and 1; Hutchinson beat Ball, Sr 1 hole
Final: Hutchinson beat Ball 1 hole

1888 Prestwick
J Ball, Jr, Royal Liverpool
Semi-finals: J E Laidlay beat L M Balfour Melville 6 and 5; Ball beat A Stuart 4 and 3
Final: Ball beat Laidlay 5 and 4

1889 St Andrews
J E Laidlay, Hon Company
Semi-finals: Laidlay beat J Ball, Jr at 20th; L M Balfour Melville beat W S Wilson 5 and 4
Final: Laidlay beat Balfour Melville 2 and 1

1890 Hoylake
J Ball, Jr, Royal Liverpool
Semi-finals: Ball beat L M Balfour Melville 6 and 4; J E Laidlay beat D Leitch 1 hole
Final: Ball beat Laidlay 4 and 3

1891 St Andrews
J E Laidlay, Hon Company

Semi-finals: H H Hilton beat W Ballingall 6 and 4; Laidlay beat T Gilroy 5 and 4
Final: Laidlay beat Hilton at 20th

1892 Royal St George's
J Ball, Jr, Royal Liverpool
Semi-finals: H H Hilton beat J E Laidlay 5 and 4; Ball beat L M Balfour Melville 1 hole
Final: Ball beat Hilton 3 and 1

1893 Prestwick
P C Anderson, St Andrews University
Semi-finals: J E Laidlay beat F G Tait at 19th; Anderson beat S Mure Fergusson 2 holes
Final: Anderson beat Laidlay 1 hole

1894 Hoylake
J Ball, Jr, Royal Liverpool
Semi-finals: Ball beat J E Laidlay 5 and 3; S Mure Fergusson beat F G Tait 4 and 3
Final: Ball beat Mure Fergusson 1 hole

1895 St Andrews
L M Balfour Melville, Royal and Ancient
Semi-finals: J Ball, Jr beat F G Tait 5 and 3; Balfour Melville beat L Auchterlonie at 19th
Final: Balfour Melville beat Ball at 19th

1896 Royal St George's
F G Tait, Black Watch GC
Semi-finals: Tait beat H G Hutchinson 3 and 2; H H Hilton beat J H Graham 4 and 3
Final: Tait beat Hilton 8 and 7

1897 Muirfield (36-hole final introduced)
A J T Allan, Edinburgh University

Semi-finals: J Robb beat J L Low at 21st; Allan beat L M Balfour Melville 3 and 1
Final: Allan beat Robb 4 and 2

1898 Hoylake
F G Tait, Black Watch GC
Semi-finals: Tait beat J L Low at 22nd; S Mure Fergusson beat J Robb 1 hole
Final: Tait beat Mure Fergusson 7 and 5

1899 Prestwick
J Ball, Jr, Royal Liverpool
Semi-finals: Ball beat G C Whigham 8 and 7; F G Tait beat J M Williamson 3 and 1
Final: Ball beat Tait at 37th

1900 Royal St George's
H H Hilton, Royal Liverpool
Semi-finals: J Robb beat J A T Bramston 3 and 1; Hilton beat J Graham, Jr 7 and 5
Final: Hilton beat Robb 8 and 7

1901 St Andrews
H H Hilton, Royal Liverpool
Semi-finals: Hilton beat H G Hutchinson 2 and 1; J L Low beat J Graham, Jr 1 hole
Final: Hilton beat Low 1 hole

1902 Hoylake
C Hutchings, Royal Liverpool
Semi-finals: Hutchings beat J Robb 2 and 1; S H Fry bear R Maxwell 1 hole
Final: Hutchings beat Fry 1 hole

1903 Muirfield
R Maxwell, Tantallon
Semi-finals: Maxwell beat H W de Zoete at 19th; H G Hutchinson beat A McDonald 4 and 2
Final: Maxwell beat Hutchinson 7 and 5

1904 Royal St George's
W J Travis, USA
Semi-finals: E Blackwell beat
J E Laidlay 2 and 1; Travis beat
H G Hutchinson 4 and 2
Final: Travis beat Blackwell 4 and 3

1905 Prestwick
A G Barry, St Andrews University
Semi-finals: Barry beat J Graham, Jr 1
hole; Hon O Scott beat A R Aitken 2 and
1
Final: Barry beat Scott 3 and 2

1906 Hoylake
J Robb, Prestwick St Nicholas
Semi-finals: Rob beat H S Colt 3 and 2;
C C Lingen beat E A Smirke 1 hole
Final: Robb beat Lingen 4 and 3

1907 St Andrews
J Ball, Jr, Royal Liverpool
Semi-finals: C A Palmer beat R Harris 2
and 1; Ball beat G Campbell 2 and 1
Final: Ball beat Palmer 6 and 4

1908 Royal St George's
E A Lassen, Royal Lytham and St Annes
Semi-finals: H E Taylor beat J Graham,
Jr 4 and 3; Lassen beat C E Dick 2 and 1
Final: Lassen beat Taylor 7 and 6

1909 Muirfield
R Maxwell, Tantallon
Semi-finals: C K Hutchison beat
R Andrew 3 and 2; Maxwell beat
B Darwin 3 and 2
Final: Maxwell beat Hutchison 1 hole

1910 Hoylake
J Ball, Jr, Royal Liverpool
Semi-finals: C C Aylmer beat
H H Hilton 4 and 3; Ball beat A Mitchell
5 and 4
Final: Ball beat Aylmer 10 and 9

1911 Prestwick
H H Hilton, Royal Liverpool
Semi-finals: Hilton beat G Lockhart 4
and 3; E A Lassen beat L B Stevens 2
holes
Final: Hilton beat Lassen 4 and 3

1912 Westward Ho!
J Ball, Jr, Royal Liverpool
Semi-finals: A Mitchell beat
C B Macfarlane 4 and 3; Ball beat
A V Hambro 3 and 2
Final: Ball beat Mitchell at 38th

1913 St Andrews
H H Hilton, Royal Liverpool
Semi-finals: R Harris beat E P Kyle 3
and 2; Hilton beat C C Aylmer 1 hole
Final: Hilton beat Harris 6 and 5

1914 Royal St George's
J L C Jenkins, Troon
Semi-finals: C O Hezlet beat
R P Humphries 1 hole; Jenkins beat
E M Smith 2 and 1
Final: Jenkins beat Hezlet 3 and 2

1915–19 No Championship

1920 Muirfield
C J H Tolley, Rye

Semi-finals: R A Gardner beat Hon
M Scott 2 holes; Tolley beat G T Mellin 5
and 4
Final: Tolley beat Gardner at 37th

1921 Hoylake
W I Hunter, Walmer and Kingsdown
Semi-finals: A J Graham beat H S B
Tubbs; Hunter beat B Darwin 3 and 2
Final: Hunter beat Graham 12 and 11

1922 Prestwick
E W E Holderness, Walton Heath
Semi-finals: Holderness beat W I Hunter
2 and 1; J Caven beat R Scott, Jr 1 hole
Final: Holderness beat Caven 1 hole

1923 Deal
R H Wethered, Worplesdon
Semi-finals: Wethered beat F Ouimet 2
and 1; R Harris beat D Grant 5 and 4
Final: Wethered beat Harris 7 and 6

1924 St Andrews
E W E Holderness, Walton Heath
Semi-finals: E F Storey beat
R H Wethered 2 holes; Holderness beat
W A Murray 3 and 2
Final: Holderness beat Storey 3 and 2

1925 Westward Ho!
R Harris, Royal and Ancient
Semi-finals: Harris beat E N Layton 1
hole; K F Fradgley beat R H Hardman 2
holes
Final: Harris beat Fradgley 13 and 12

1926 Muirfield
J Sweetser, USA
Semi-finals: Sweetser beat Hon
W Brownlow at 21st; A F Simpson beat
A Jamieson, Jr 2 and 1
Final: Sweetser beat Simpson 6 and 5

1927 Hoylake
W Tweddell, Stourbridge
Semi-finals: Tweddell beat
R H Wethered 4 and 3; D E Landale beat
R H Jobson 1 hole
Final: Tweddell beat Landale 7 and 6

1928 Prestwick
T P Perkins, Castle Bromwich
Semi-finals: Perkins beat W Tulloch 6
and 5; R H Wethered beat E B Tipping 4
and 3
Final: Perkins beat Wethered 6 and 4

1929 Royal St George's
C J H Tolley, Rye
Semi-finals: Tolley beat R Hartley 1
hole; J N Smith beat J Dawson at 19th
Final: Tolley beat Smith 4 and 3

1930 St Andrews
R T Jones, Jr, USA
Semi-finals: Jones beat G J Voigt 1 hole;
R H Wethered beat L Hartley 2 and 1
Final: Jones beat Wethered 7 and 6

1931 Westward Ho!
E Martin Smith, Royal St George's
Semi-finals: J de Forest beat W Tulloch
1 hole; Martin Smith beat J D
MacCormack 1 hole
Final: Martin Smith beat de Forest 1
hole

1932 Muirfield
J de Forest, Addington
Semi-finals: de Forest beat L O M Munn
at 21st; E W Fiddian beat E A McRuvie 2
holes
Final: de Forest beat Fiddian 3 and 1

1933 Hoylake
Hon M Scott, Royal St George's
Semi-finals: Scott beat G T Dunlap, Jr 4
and 3; T A Bourn beat C J H Tolley at 20th
Final: Scott beat Bourn 4 and 3

1934 Prestwick
W Lawson Little, USA
Semi-finals: J Wallace beat G T Dunlap,
Jr 2 and 1; Lawson Little beat
L G Garnett at 19th
Final: Lawson Little beat Wallace 14
and 13

1935 Royal Lytham and St Annes
W Lawson Little, USA
Semi-finals: W Tweddell beat
T A Torrance 2 and 1; Lawson Little
beat R Sweeny, Jr 3 and 1
Final: Lawson Little beat Tweddell 1
hole

1936 St Andrews
H Thomson, Williamwood
Semi-finals: Thomson beat C Ewing 4
and 3; J Ferrier beat G A Hill 1 hole
Final: Thomson beat Ferrier 2 holes

1937 Royal St George's
R Sweeny, Jr, Royal and Ancient
Semi-finals: L O M Munn beat A de
Forest 4 and 3; Sweeny beat C Stowe 6
and 5
Final: Sweeny beat Munn 3 and 2

1938 Troon
C R Yates, USA
Semi-finals: C Ewing beat C Ross
Somerville 2 holes; Yates beat
H Thomson at 19th
Final: Yates beat Ewing 3 and 2

1939 Hoylake
A T Kyle, Sand Moor
Semi-finals: Kyle beat W E Holt, Jr 2
and 1; A A Duncan beat C Stowe 3 and 2
Final: Kyle beat Duncan 2 and 1

1940–45 No Championship

1946 Royal Birkdale
J Bruen, Cork
Semi-finals: Bruen beat H E Walker 3
and 2; R Sweeny, Jr beat G H Micklem 5
and 3
Final: Bruen beat Sweeny 4 and 3

1947 Carnoustie
W P Turnesa, USA
Semi-finals: Turnesa beat J G Campbell
4 and 3; R D Chapman beat
S L McKinlay 2 holes
Final: Turnesa beat Chapman 3 and 2

1948 Royal St George's
F R Stranahan, USA
Semi-finals: Stranahan beat
D H R Martin 3 and 1; C Stowe beat
W P Turnesa 1 hole
Final: Stranahan beat Stowe 5 and 4

1949 Portmarnock
S M McCready, Sunningdale
Semi-finals: W P Turnesa beat
E P Millward 1 hole; McCready beat
K G Thom at 20th
Final: McCready beat Turnesa 2 and 1

1950 St Andrews
F R Stranahan, USA
Semi-finals: R D Chapman beat
J B McHale 1 hole; Stranahan beat
C J H Tolley 4 and 3
Final: Stranahan beat Chapman 8 and 6

1951 Royal Porthcawl
R D Chapman, USA
Semi-finals: C R Coe beat A D Evans 4
and 2; Chapman beat J B Carr 4 and 3
Final: Chapman beat Coe 5 and 4

1952 Prestwick
E Harvie Ward, USA
Semi-finals: Harvie Ward beat J B Carr
2 and 1; F R Stranahan beat J R Cater 2
holes
Final: Harvie Ward beat Stranahan 7
and 5

1953 Hoylake
J B Carr, Sutton
Semi-finals: Carr beat C H Beamish at
19th; E Harvie Ward beat A H Perowne
6 and 5
Final: Carr beat Harvie Ward 2 holes

1954 Muirfield
D W Bachli, Australia
Semi-finals: W C Campbell beat
J B Carr 3 and 2; Bachli beat W A Slark
3 and 2
Final: Bachli beat Campbell 2 and 1

1955 Royal Lytham and St Annes
J W Conrad, USA
Semi-finals: A Slater beat A H Perowne
3 and 2; Conrad beat P F Scrutton 5 and
4
Final: Conrad beat Slater 3 and 2

1956 Troon (Quarter-finals, semi-finals
and final played over 36 holes in 1956–
57)
J C Beharrell, Little Aston
Semi-finals: Beharrell beat R Reid Jack
2 and 1; L G Taylor beat G G Henderson
6 and 5
Final: Beharrell beat Taylor 5 and 4

1957 Formby
R Reid Jack, Dullatur
Semi-finals: Reid Jack beat A F Bussell
3 and 2; H B Ridgley beat A Walker 13
and 12
Final: Reid Jack beat Ridgley 2 and 1

1958 St Andrews (Semi-finals and final
only played over 36 holes)
J B Carr, Sutton
Semi-finals: Carr beat M F Bonallack 4
and 3; A Thirlwell beat T Holland 4 and
3
Final: Carr beat Thirlwell 3 and 2

1959 Royal St George's (Semi-finals
and final played over 36 holes)
D Beman, USA

Semi-finals: W Hyndman III beat
B Magee at 38th; Beman beat
G B Wolstenholme 5 and 4
Final: Beman beat Hyndman 3 and 2

1960 Royal Portrush
J B Carr, Sutton
Semi-finals: Carr beat J Walker 2 holes;
B Cochran beat G Huddy 3 and 2
Final: Carr beat Cochran 8 and 7

1961 Turnberry
M F Bonallack, Thorpe Hall
Semi-finals: J Walker beat R L Morrow
1 hole; Bonallack beat M J Christmas 3
and 2
Final: Bonallack beat Walker 6 and 4

1962 Hoylake
R D Davies, USA
Semi-finals: J D Povall beat
B H G Chapman 1 hole; Davies beat
R Foster 3 and 2
Final: Davies beat Povall 1 hole

1963 St Andrews
M S R Lunt, Moseley
Semi-finals: Lunt beat E Updegraff 1
hole; J G Blackwell beat R Luceti 3 and 2
Final: Lunt beat Blackwell 2 and 1

1964 Ganton
G J Clark, Whitley Bay
Semi-finals: M S R Lunt beat J Hall 4
and 3; Clark beat M J Christmas 2 holes
Final: Clark beat Lunt at 39th

1965 Royal Porthcawl
M F Bonallack, Thorpe Hall
Semi-finals: Bonallack beat R Foster 1
hole; C A Clark beat M J Christmas 1
hole
Final: Bonallack beat Clarke 2 and 1

1966 Carnoustie
R Cole, South Africa
Semi-finals: R D B M Shade beat
G B Cosh 2 and 1; Cole beat H de Lamaze
2 and 1
Final: Cole beat Shade 3 and 2 (Final
played over 18 holes)

1967 Formby
R B Dickson, USA
Semi-finals: Dickson beat G J Clark 4
and 3; R Cerrudo beat M Fleckman at
19th
Final: Dickson beat Cerrudo 2 and 1

1968 Troon
M F Bonallack, Thorpe Hall
Semi-finals: J B Carr beat R L Glading 3
and 1; Bonallack beat G C Marks 3 and 2
Final: Bonallack beat Carr 7 and 6

1969 Hoylake
M F Bonallack, Thorpe Hall
Semi-finals: Bonallack beat
W C Davidson 4 and 3; W Hyndman III
beat D Hayes 3 and 2
Final: Bonallack beat Hyndman 3 and 2

1970 Royal County Down
M F Bonallack, Thorpe Hall
Semi-finals: Bonallack beat B Critchley
2 and 1; W Hyndman III beat T B C Hoey

2 holes
Final: Bonallack beat Hyndman 8 and 7

1971 Carnoustie
S Melnyk, USA
Semi-finals: J Simons beat T Kite 1 hole;
Melnyk beat P H Moody 4 and 3
Final: Melnyk beat Simons 3 and 2

1972 Royal St George's
T W B Homer, Walsall
Semi-finals: A Thirlwell beat
M F Bonallack 2 and 1; Homer beat
R Revell 4 and 3
Final: Homer beat Thirlwell 4 and 3

1973 Royal Porthcawl
R Siderowf, USA
Semi-finals: Siderowf beat H Ashby 6
and 5; P H Moody beat H K Clark 3 and 2
Final: Siderowf beat Moody 5 and 3

1974 Muirfield
T W B Homer, Walsall
Semi-finals: J Gabrielsen beat M A
Poxon 5 and 4; Homer beat H B Stuart 1
hole
Final: Homer beat Gabrielsen 2 holes

1975 Hoylake
M M Giles III, USA
Semi-finals: Giles beat R Siderowf at
21st; M James beat G C Marks 3 and 2
Final: Giles beat James 8 and 7

1976 St Andrews
R Siderowf, USA
Semi-finals: J C Davies beat I Carslaw 1
hole; Siderowf beat A Brodie 2 and 1
Final: Siderowf beat Davies at 37th

1977 Ganton
P M McEvoy, Copt Heath
Semi-finals: H M Campbell beat
M F Bonallack at 24th; McEvoy beat
P J McKellar 2 and 1
Final: McEvoy beat Campbell 5 and 4

1978 Royal Troon
P M McEvoy, Copt Heath
Semi-finals: McEvoy beat D R Suddards
4 and 3; P M McKellar beat J C Davies 3
and 2
Final: McEvoy beat McKellar 4 and 3

1979 Hillside
Jay Sigel, USA
Semi-finals: S Hoch beat A Y Gresham 3
and 2; Sigel beat D Roxburgh 6 and 5
Final: Sigel beat S Hoch 3 and 2

1980 Royal Porthcawl
D Evans, Leek
Semi-finals: Evans beat A D Pierse 2
and 1; D R Suddards beat D Lindsay-
Smith 2 and 1
Final: Evans beat Suddards 4 and 3

1981 St Andrews
P Ploujoux, France
Semi-finals: Ploujoux beat J Carr 2 and
1; J Hirsch beat A Y Gresham 2 and 1
Final: Ploujoux beat Hirsch 4 and 2

1982 Deal
M S Thompson, Middlesbrough
Semi-finals: A K Stubbs beat A P Parkin

4 and 2; Thompson beat P J Hedges 3 and 1
Final: Thompson beat Stubbs 4 and 3

1983 Turnberry
A P Parkin, Newton
Semi-finals: Parkin beat S D Keppler 2 and 1; J Holtgrieve beat P Deeble 7 and 5
Final: Parkin beat Holtgrieve 5 and 4

1984 Formby
J-M Olazabal, Spain
Semi-finals: C Montgomerie beat D Curry 5 and 4; Olazabal beat D Gilford 1 hole
Final: Olazabal beat Montgomerie 5 and 4

1985 Royal Dornoch
G McGimpsey, Bangor (Northern Ireland)
Semi-finals: McGimpsey beat P Hall 3 and 2; G Homewood beat D James 5 and 4
Final: McGimpsey beat Homewood 8 and 7

1986 Royal Lytham and St Annes
D Curry, Prudhoe
Semi-finals: S G Birtwell beat B Shields 1 hole; Curry beat P M McEvoy at 19th
Final: Curry beat Birtwell 11 and 9

Cyril Tolley playing from the road, Walker Cup, St Andrews, May 1923. (BBC Hulton Picture Library)

US Amateur Championship

**Matchplay 1895–1964 and after 1972
Strokeplay 1965–72**

MILESTONES

1895 First champion, Charles Blair Macdonald at Newport, Rhode Island. No qualifying.
1896 Qualifying introduced, H J Whigham being medallist (87, 77) and matchplay champion. Whigham, an Oxford man, learned his golf in England.
1898 A field of 120 brought a new method of 36 holes qualifying for 32 places.
1900 Victory for Walter J Travis, an Australian who took to the game at 35.
1901 Travis made a successful defence of his title using the new Haskell ball. The death of President McKinley led to the championship being postponed a week.
1902 Eighteen-holes qualifying for 64 places. The winner was Louis James, 19 years and 10 months old.
1903 Walter Travis's third and last victory; 128 players allowed to compete, all at matchplay.
1904 Fifty-four holes qualifying for 32 places.
1905 Thirty-six holes qualifying for 32 places. An all-Chicago final, H Chandler Egan defeating D E Sawyer 6 and 5.
1907 First of four triumphs for Jerome D Travers and first appearance of Charles 'Chick' Evans, Jr.
1909 Robert A Gardner became the youngest winner at 19 years and 5 months and remains so.
1911 Title won by the Englishman, Harold Hilton. Having been 6 up on Fred Herreshoff in the final, he eventually won at the

37th. At that hole Hilton's second shot with a spoon got a lucky break.
1912 Jerome Travers, last in the qualifying, went on to win his fourth victory, a record he shares with Bobby Jones.
1914 Travers again reached the final but was beaten by Francis Ouimet who the previous year had scored his legendary win in the US Open.
1916 Momentous year at Merion. Charles 'Chick' Evans became the first man to win the US Open and US Amateur in the same year. He won the Open in June and added the Amateur by defeating defending champion, Robert A Gardner in the final. It was momentous for another reason; the first appearance, aged 14, of Bobby Jones who won two rounds.
1919 When the championship was resumed after the war, S Davidson Heron, playing on his own course, Oakmont, was four under 4s in beating Bobby Jones in the final by 5 and 4. The entry reached 150.
1920 A huge increase in the entry to 235 forced the use of two courses for the qualifying. The record entry stood for eleven years. Evans beat Ouimet for the title. Cyril Tolley and several other British players failed to qualify.
1921 Championship held west of the Mississippi for the first time.
1922 Triumph for Jess Sweetser at 20. He defeated defending champion, Jesse P Guilford, Willie Hunter, Bobby Jones and Charles Evans, Jr, in the final. Jones's defeat by 8 and 7 was the biggest he suffered in the US Amateur. Admission charge levied for the first time.
1924 Beginning of the Jones era and his first victory at Merion. In the semi-final he beat Ouimet 11 and 10 and in the final he accounted for George von Elm.
1925 Jones's second victory. He beat Watts Gunn, his friend and protégé in the final. It was the only time two finalists represented the same club, Atlanta Athletic Club's East Lake course.
There were 16 qualifiers with all matches at 36 holes, but it was unpopular.
1926 Reversion to the old system of 36 holes qualifying for 32 places. Jones thwarted by George von Elm from achieving

three victories in a row.

1927 Number three for Jones. Victory in the final against Charles Evans, Jr.

1928 For the first time, the United States champion met the British champion in the final. Jones beat Phil Perkins 10 and 9.

1929 First championship on the Pacific coast. Bobby Jones beaten in the first round for the only time. His conqueror was Johnny Goodman, a future champion who was then beaten by another future champion, Lawson Little.

1930 One of the most historic championships of all time. The ultimate in achievement: the Grand Slam for Bobby Jones. The dream came true on Merion's 11th green when he beat Eugene Homans by 8 and 7. It was Jones's last championship.

Records of a different kind were set by Maurice McCarthy. He played 10 extra holes before beating George von Elm in the second round. This followed a 19-hole match with Watts Gunn and a play-off match, all in one day. He made a hole in one to make a place in the play-off for the qualifying.

1931 Francis Ouimet won again after a 17-year gap, a record. He defeated Jack Westland who, 21 years later, won the title himself. That gap of 21 years between finals is also a record. Sectional qualifying for an entry of 583 was played at 20 different locations.

1932 Ross Somerville took the title to Canada for the first time.

1933 The champion, George Dunlap, was among the twelve players who played off for the last eight places in the championship.

1934 New format with no qualifying at the course, but 36-hole semi-finals and final produced Lawson Little as champion. He emulated Jones by winning the British and American titles in the same year.

1935 The double for Lawson Little both as American and British champion, the only time it has ever been done.
Entry of 945.

1936 Following the Walker Cup match at Pine Valley, Jack McLean lost the final at Garden City to Johnny Fischer. Fischer, 1 down and 3 to play against the British player, saved the 34th with a dead stymie and won on the 37th.

1937 Championship held in Pacific Northwest for the first time. Qualifying held at the course in addition to sectional qualifying to determine the 64 matchplayers. The champion was Johnny Goodman who won the US Open in 1933.

1938 Willie Turnesa, one of seven brothers, won at Oakmont despite being in bunkers on 13 of the 29 holes of the final.

1942–45 No championships.

1946 After regional qualifying, 150 played for 64 places. New qualifying record for Skee Riegel with 136 (69, 67).

1947 In order to accommodate a larger field, qualifying on the site was abandoned and 210 admitted to matchplay.

1948 Entry of 1220, the largest to date. After ten years, Willie Turnesa won again, beating Ray Billows in the final. It was Billows's third final.

1949 Two of the best-known names in post-war American amateur golf, Charles Coe and Harvie Ward contested a memorable fifth-round match, Coe, 3 down with 5 to play, winning at the 19th. He then went on to inflict upon Rufus King the largest defeat, 11 and 10, in any final.

1950 Having had the shortest the previous year, 1950 produced the longest on record. In it, Sam Urzetta, a former caddie, defeated Frank Stranahan at the 39th hole.

1951 A record field of 1416. Billy Maxwell outlasted all the Walker Cup team, only Charles Coe surviving as far as the last 8.

1952 In keeping with a record-breaking period of three or four years, Jack Westland, finalist in 1931, became the oldest winner of the championship at 47. He beat Al Mengert in the first all-Northwest final, Westland from Everett, Washington, and Mengert from Spokane, Washington.

The championship was preceded by the first match between America, Canada and Mexico.

1953 Gene Littler became champion while serving in the US Navy. In the final, Dale Morey squared the final with birdies at the 34th and 35th, but Littler closed him out with a birdie at the 36th. Littler, 23, turned professional a few months later.

1954 The year of another US Open champion-to-be, Arnold Palmer. In an excellent final he beat Robert Sweeny on the 36th green. Like Littler the previous year, Palmer turned professional shortly afterwards.

For the first time the fairways were roped off.

1955 Some compensation for previous disappointments awaited Harvie Ward, British Amateur champion in 1952. A morning round of 66 in the final enabled him to lunch 8 up on Bill Hyndman who eventually went down 9 and 8.

Entry of 1493. Hillman Robbins set a sectional qualifying scoring record with 132 (66, 66) at Memphis.

1956 Ward became the sixth player to defend his title successfully. Two down in the final to Charles 'Chuck' Kocsis, he was 5 under par for the last 13 holes. He was 11 under par for the entire week.

Entry of 1600.

1957 Before the championship, Harvie Ward was adjudged by the USGA to have forfeited his amateur status and was not, therefore, eligible for a second defence of his title. In a year in which both British and American Walker Cup teams took part, the title was won by Hillman Robbins who beat Dr Frank Taylor by 5 and 4. Both played in the Walker Cup and the other two semi-finalists, Mason Rudolph and Rex Baxter, were also members of the American team. The most successful British player was Alan Thirlwell, beaten in the 5th round.

1958 Charles Coe won his second title when he defeated Tommy Aaron, later to play for his country as an amateur and a professional, by 5 and 4 over the Lake course of the Olympic Club, San Francisco.

Scott Verplank (1984) (USGA)

Harvie Ward returned and reached the 5th round. Nearly all the members of the Americas Cup matches took part.

George Boutell, aged 14, was in the field along with Dick and Dixie Chapman, the first father and son pair since 1950.

1959 In his second championship, Jack Nicklaus became the second youngest champion after a captivating final with Charles Coe, the defending champion.

Coe completed the morning round in 69 to be 2 up but, having twice squared the match Nicklaus, all square on the 36th tee, sank an 8 ft putt for a winning birdie. Both had played in the Walker Cup match in Britain earlier in the summer. One of the semi-finalists, Gene Andrews, was 46 years old.

Entry 1696—a record.

1960 Deane Beman, one of the new young players in the Walker Cup match the previous year, became the ninth player to win both British and American titles. He defeated Bill Hyndman in the British and at St Louis CC, he beat Robert Gardner 6 and 4.

Charles Lewis of Little Rock, Arkansas, playing in his first Amateur, accounted for Jack Nicklaus, the defending champion, in the fourth round. In the third round, Nicklaus was 7 under par for 13 holes.

Entry 1737—another record.

1961 Jack Nicklaus made a triumphant farewell in his last Amateur. He was 20 under par for the holes he played at Pebble Beach, was rarely extended and won his final against Dudley Wysong 8 and 6. He became the 14th player to win the title at least twice.

William C Campbell set a new qualifying record 131 (67, 64) at the Guyan Golf and Country Club, West Virginia.

1962 On Pinehurst's famous No 2 course measuring 7051 yd, the longest for any USGA event, Labron Harris beat Downing Gray on the 36th hole of the final after being 5 down at lunch.

Charles Evans, Jr, made his record 50th appearance in the championship and President Eisenhower was a spectator on the final afternoon.

1963 A second victory for Deane Beman. At the Wakonda Club, Iowa, he won his final against R H Sikes, the 1961 and 1962 Public Links champion by 2 and 1. For the second year running the champion had to come from behind in the final. Beman was 3 down after 14 holes.

1964 Years of trying at last bore fruit for William C Campbell. A semi-finalist in 1949 who reached the fifth round on five other occasions, he defeated Ed Tutwiler by 1 hole in the final. These two had met many times in West Virginia, Tutwiler winning six out of seven times.

A revision was made in the format: 150 players played two rounds on the championship course before the leading 64 advanced to matchplay.

1965 A major change from matchplay to medal play was made for this championship held at Southern Hills. After 72 holes, the winner was Robert Murphy, later a successful professional who beat Bob Dickson by 1 stroke with a total of 291. However, Dickson suffered the grave misfortune of a 4-stroke penalty for carrying a 15th club for the first 2 holes of the second round. To make matters worse, the club was not his and he did not use it although he was leading after 70 holes. He went 1 over par at each of the last holes.

Charles Coe, the 54-hole leader, finished with an 80 to be 6 strokes behind Murphy.

1966 Gary Cowan became the second Canadian and the first foreign winner since 1932. He won after a play-off at Merion with Deane Beman who finished his fourth round with a 6. Ron Cerrudo might have tied with Beman and Cowan but missed a tiny putt on the last green.

The championship was televised nationally for the first time.

1967 Bob Dickson made up for his disappointment in 1965 by winning at Broadmoor a month or two after winning the British championship. Lawson Little was the last to achieve this feat and Bobby Jones the only other. Dickson won with a par 4 after missing the fairway on the 72nd hole and obtaining a free drop away from a television cable. He played back on to the

Sam Randolph (1985) (USGA)

fairway, hit his third shot to 7 ft and holed the putt. Two rounds were played on the last day because heavy rain caused a day to be lost earlier in the week.

1968 Bruce Fleisher became the fourth youngest winner in his first championship. He scored 284 at Scioto and edged out Vinny Giles who had a final round of 65.

The entry was 2057—a record at the time.

1969 In a championship at Oakmont in which there were only four rounds under par and only six which equalled it, Steve Melnyk won by 5 strokes with a total of 286. This was convincing enough, but it was hard on Vinny Giles who finished runner-up for the third year in succession.

The entry increased to 2142.

1970 In a close finish, Lanny Wadkins just got the better of Tom Kite. His total of 279 was the lowest for eight years during which the championship was decided by strokeplay.

1971 Canadian Gary Cowan won his second title with a dramatic finish at the Wilmington Country Club. One shot ahead of Eddie Pearce playing the 72nd hole, he drove into deep rough and was in some danger of dropping a stroke, but his 9 iron recovery finished in the hole for an eagle 2. This made his winning margin a rather more comfortable 3 strokes. Entry 2327.

1972 Deserved triumph for Vinny Giles at the Charlotte CC, North Carolina, when he beat Mark Hayes and Ben Crenshaw by 3 strokes. It was the last championship to be decided by strokeplay; in the eight years of this form, the only champions to remain as amateurs were Giles and Gary Cowan who did not defend his title.

1973 With matchplay restored, Craig Stadler defeated David Strawn at Inverness. Vinny Giles, having played in the Walker

Cup, reached the semi-final in defence of his title where he lost to Stadler. In the other semi-final, Strawn beat William C Campbell, playing in his 30th championship at the age of 50.

1974 Jerry Pate won the championship at Ridgewood, New Jersey, two years before he added the US Open at Atlanta Athletic Club. He beat John Grace 2 and 1 in the final after being 3 down after 20 holes. It was the first time that Pate qualified for the championship.
Entry 2420.

1975 Fred Ridley defeated Keith Fergus in the final but Ridley's best performances were in beating Curtis Strange and Andy Bean on the way.

1976 In the final at Bel-Air CC, Bill Sander beat C Parker Moore by 8 and 6, the biggest victory margin since 1961.
Entry 2681.

1977 John Fought defeated Doug Fischesser by 9 and 8 in the final at Aronimink, the largest margin of victory since 1955. He won the last 4 holes of the morning round and the 1st hole after lunch to go 7 up.
In his 34th championship, Bill Campbell won his 52nd match over all.

1978 John Cook won the championship at Plainfield CC, New Jersey, with consistently good play. He beat Scott Hoch by 5 and 4 in the final but, for the first time, both semi-finals went to extra holes. Cook beat Michael Peck and Hoch beat Bob Clampett, both at the 20th.

1979 Cook was deposed as champion by Mark O'Meara, 22, the California State champion. O'Meara was persuaded to play by Cook and stayed during the championship at the Cook's condominium at the course. No champion has won back to back since Harvie Ward in 1956, but Cook started favourite in the final. He survived a long day on Friday, defeating Lennie Clements at the 8th extra hole and then accounting for Gary Hallberg. In the final, O'Meara lunched 4 up with a round of 70 and was 8 up after 26 holes.

1980 Hal Sutton completed a memorable week at the Country Club of North Carolina by beating Bob Lewis, a former professional, by 9 and 8 in the 36-hole final. Sutton was 4 under par for the match, making an overall total of 12 under par for 145 holes, strokeplay and matchplay. Using the format introduced in 1979, 282 players took part after sectional qualifying, 36 holes of strokeplay determining the leading 64 for matchplay. Pinehurst No 2 was the other course used for the strokeplay. William C Campbell made his 36th appearance, a record only surpassed by Chick Evans. The USGA accepted a record 4008 entries, overtaking the previous best of 3916 the year before.

1981 One of the great sentimental victories, Nathaniel Crosby, son of Bing, winning at the Olympic Club, San Francisco, only a few miles from the Crosby home at Hillsborough. He had a few close calls in the matchplay section but showed a remarkable flair for producing the right shot or holing the crucial putt when needed. He beat Brian Lindley at the 37th, the first final to go to extra holes since 1950. Crosby had been 3 down and 7 to play.

1982 At his 16th attempt, Jay Sigel won his first title at The Country Club. At 38, he was the oldest winner since William C Campbell in 1964. He also became the 13th player to win the US and the British Amateur championship. In the final, he defeated David Tolley of Roanoke, Virginia by 8 and 7. Apart from the previous year when Nathaniel Crosby won by 1 hole, it maintained the trend of one-sided finals. The five margins prior to 1981 were 8 and 6, 9 and 8, 5 and 4, 8 and 7, and 9 and 8.

1983 Jay Sigel, the outstanding American amateur of the past few years, struck again at the North Shore CC, Glenview, Illinois. By defeating Chris Perry in the final by 8 and 7, he became the first back to back winner since Harvie Ward in 1955–56 and the eighth in all. The entry was 3553. Perry had three victories at the 19th hole on his way to the final.

1984 The championship produced outstanding finalists at Oak Tree, Oklahoma. Scott Verplank, who in 1985 won a professional tournament as an amateur on the US tour, defeated Sam Randolph who succeeded him as champion. Jay Sigel, cham-

pion in 1982 and 1983, was beaten in the first round.

1985 Sam Randolph of Santa Barbara, California, went from the Walker Cup at Pine Valley to take the championship at Montclair, New Jersey. He had a close first round match but did not again have to play the 18th hole on his way to the final. In the final, he beat Peter Persons, a graduate of the University of Georgia, on the final green. Randolph lunched 1 up but neither was able to get more than 1 up.

1986 Buddy Alexander, son of 'Skip' Alexander, an American Ryder Cup golfer, won the 86th Amateur by means of some marvellous golf in the final at Shoal Creek, Alabama. A reinstated amateur (the first to win) and golf coach at Louisiana State University, he beat Chris Kite by 5 and 3. He was reinstated only a month before the championship. In the morning Alexander, 2 down at the turn, finished the round 2 up and was 12 under par when the match ended on the 33rd green.

A dinner was held prior to the championship at which twelve former champions were present. They were Charlie Coe (1949 and 1958), Jack Nicklaus (1959 and 1961), Bill Campbell (1964), Deane Beman (1960 and 1963), Labron Harris (1962), Vinny Giles (1972), Steve Melnyk (1969), Lanny Wadkins (1970), Jerry Pate (1974), Fred Ridley (1975), Hal Sutton (1980) and Jay Sigel (1982 and 1983).

DETAILED RECORDS

Most victories
5, Bobby Jones, 1924–25–27–28–30
4, Jerome D Travers, 1907–08–12–13
3, Walter J Travis, 1900–01–03

Most times runner-up or joint runner-up
3, Chick Evans, 1912–22–27; Ray Billows, 1937–39–48; Marvin Giles III, 1967–68–69

Oldest winner
Jack Westland, 47 years 8 months 9 days, 1952

Youngest winner
Robert A Gardner, 19 years 5 months, 1909
Jack Nicklaus, 19 years 8 months 29 days, 1959
Nathaniel Crosby, 19 years 10 months 8 days, 1981

Consecutive winners
2, Walter Travis, 1900–01; H Chandler Egan, 1904–05; Jerome D Travers, 1907–08, and 1912–13; Bobby Jones, 1924–25, and 1927–28; W Lawson Little, 1934–35; E Harvie Ward, 1955–56; J Sigel, 1982–83

Biggest span between first and last victories
17 years, Francis Ouimet, 1914–31

Biggest span between finals
21 years, Jack Westland, 1931–52

Overseas winners
Harold Hilton (England), 1911; C Ross Somerville (Canada), 1932; Gary Cowan (Canada), 1966 and 1971

Longest final
39 holes: Sam Urzetta beat Frank Stranahan, Minneapolis GC, 1950

Longest match (18 holes)
28 holes; Maurice McCarthy beat George von Elm, Merion, 1930

Most finals
7, Bobby Jones
5, Jerome D Travers and Chick Evans

Identical finals
None

Nathaniel Crosby (1981) (USGA)

Most appearances
50, Chick Evans, Jr
37, William C Campbell

Most golf in one day
63 holes, Maurice McCarthy, Jr, Merion, 1930. In the second qualifying round, he came to the 17th needing two birdies or an eagle to tie for the last qualifying place. He made a hole in one at the 17th to get the tie. Next morning, he won the play-off match lasting 16 holes, followed by a 19-hole match with Watts Gunn and in the afternoon beat George von Elm at the 28th, the longest 18-hole match ever played in the championship.

First player to win the US Amateur and US Open
Francis Ouimet, Open 1913; Amateur, 1914

First player to win US Amateur and US Open the same year
Chick Evans, Jr, 1916, followed by Bobby Jones, 1930

Other amateur winners of both events
Jerome D Travers and John Goodman

Record entry
4008, Country Club of North Carolina, 1980

Youngest qualifier
Bobby Jones, 14 years 5½ months, 1916
George Boutell, 1958, 14 years 9 months

Strokeplay—biggest margin of victory
5 strokes, Steve Melnyk, Oakmont, 1969

Lowest aggregate
279 (67, 73, 69, 70), Lanny Wadkins, Waverley CC, Oregon, 1970

Lowest individual round
65, Marvin Giles III, Scioto CC, 1968; Kurt Cos, Waverley CC, Oregon, 1970

Courses most often used
The Country Club, Brookline, 5
Garden City (NY), Merion, Oakmont, Chicago GC, 4

Champion twice on same course
Bobby Jones, Merion, 1924 and 1930; Jerome Travers, Garden City, 1908 and 1913

Father and son combination in same year
There have been several examples of father and son playing in the same championship but in 1971 William Hyndman III played with two sons, William Hyndman IV and Thomas Hyndman, in the same championship.

RESULTS

1895 Newport, Rhode Island
C B Macdonald, Chicago
Semi-finals: Macdonald beat C Claxton 8 and 7; C E Sands beat F I Amory 3 and 2
Final: Macdonald beat Sands 12 and 11

1896 Shinnecock Hills, New York
H J Whigham, Onwentsia
Semi-finals: Whigham beat A M Coats 8 and 6; J G Thorp beat H P Toler 4 and 3
Final: Whigham beat Thorp 8 and 7

1897 Chicago, Illinois
H J Whigham, Onwentsia
Semi-finals: Whigham beat F S Douglas 6 and 5; W R Betts beat C B Macdonald 1 up
Final: Whigham beat Betts 8 and 6

1898 Morris County, New Jersey
F S Douglas, Fairfield
Semi-finals: Douglas beat W J Travis 8 and 6; W B Smith beat C B Macdonald 2 and 1
Final: Douglas beat Smith 5 and 3

1899 Onwentsia, Illinois
H M Harriman, Meadow Brook
Semi-finals: F S Douglas beat W J Travis 2 and 1; Harriman beat C B Macdonald 6 and 5
Final: Harriman beat Douglas 3 and 2

1900 Garden City, New York
W J Travis, Garden City
Semi-finals: Travis beat A G Lockwood 11 and 10; F S Douglas beat H M Harriman 4 and 3
Final: Travis beat Douglas 2 up

1901 Atlantic City, New Jersey
W J Travis, Garden City
Semi-finals: W E Egan beat C H Seeley 11 and 10; Travis beat F S Douglas at 38th
Final: Travis beat Egan 5 and 4

1902 Glen View, Illinois
L N James, Glen View
Semi-finals: E M Byers beat D P Fredericks 4 and 3; James beat F O Reinhart 2 and 1
Final: James beat Byers 4 and 2

1903 Nassau, New York
W J Travis, Garden City
Semi-finals: Travis beat F O Reinhart 5 and 4; E M Byers beat B Smith 5 and 4
Final: Travis beat Byers 5 and 4

1904 Baltusrol, New Jersey
H C Egan, Exmoor
Semi-finals: F Herreshoff beat W T West 6 and 5; Egan beat D P Fredericks 2 and 1
Final: Egan beat Herreshoff 8 and 6

1905 Chicago, Illinois
H C Egan, Exmoor
Semi-finals: D E Sawyer beat H C Fownes 2 up; Egan beat H Weber 7 and 5
Final: Egan beat Sawyer 6 and 5

1906 Englewood, New Jersey
E M Byers, Allegheny
Semi-finals: G S Lyon beat E Knowles 5 and 4; Byers beat W J Travis 4 and 3
Final: Byers beat Lyon 2 up

1907 Euclid, Ohio
J D Travers, Montclair
Semi-finals: Travers beat E M Byers 6 and 5; A Graham beat H C Fownes 4 and 3
Final: Travers beat Graham 6 and 5

1908 Garden City, New York
J D Travers, Montclair
Semi-finals: Travers beat W J Travis 2 up; M Behr beat F Herreshoff 37th
Final: Travers beat Behr 8 and 7

1909 Chicago, Illinois
R A Gardner, Hinsdale
Semi-finals: H C Egan beat C Evans 1 up; Gardner beat M E Phelps 2 up
Final: Gardner beat Egan 4 and 3

1910 The Country Club, Brookline, Massachusetts
W C Fownes, Jr, Oakmont
Semi-finals: Fownes beat C Evans 1 up; W K Wood beat W R Tukerman 2 up
Final: Fownes beat Wood 4 and 3

1911 Apawamis, New York
H H Hilton, Royal Liverpool
Semi-finals: Hilton beat C W Inslee 8 and 6; F Herreshoff beat C Evans 3 and 2
Final: Hilton beat Herreshoff 37th

1912 Chicago, Illinois
J D Travers, Upper Montclair
Semi-finals: Travers beat H K Kerr 7 and 5; C Evans beat W K Wood 4 and 3
Final: Travers beat Evans 7 and 6

1913 Garden City, New York
J D Travers, Upper Montclair
Semi-finals: J G Anderson beat C Evans 2 and 1; Travers beat F Herreshoff 5 and 4
Final: Travers beat Anderson 5 and 4

1914 Ekwanok, Vermont
F D Ouimet, Woodland
Semi-finals: J D Travers beat W J Travis 5 and 3; Ouimet beat W C Fownes 1 up
Final: Ouimet beat Travers 6 and 5

1915 Detroit CC, Michigan
R A Gardner, Hinsdsale
Semi-finals: Gardner beat M Marston 37th; J G Anderson beat S Sherman 2 and 1
Final: Gardner beat Anderson 5 and 4

1916 Merion, Pennsylvania
C Evans, Edgewater
Semi-finals: R A Gardner beat J P Guilford 4 and 3; Evans beat D C Corkran 3 and 2
Final: Evans beat Gardner 4 and 3

1919 Oakmont, Pennsylvania
S D Herron, Oakmont
Semi-finals: R T Jones, Jr beat W C Fownes 5 and 3; Herron beat J W Platt 7 and 6
Final: Herron beat Jones 5 and 4

1920 Engineers, New York
C Evans, Jr, Edgewater
Semi-finals: Evans beat E P Allis 10 and 8; F Ouimet beat R T Jones, Jr 6 and 5
Final: Evans beat Ouimet 7 and 6

1921 St Louis CC, Missouri
J P Guilford, Woodland
Semi-finals: Guilford beat C Evans, Jr 5 and 4; R A Gardner beat W I Hunter 6 and 5
Final: Guilford beat Gardner 7 and 6

1922 The Country Club, Brookline, Massachusetts
J W Sweetser, Siwanoy
Semi-finals: Sweetser beat R T Jones, Jr, 8 and 7; C Evans, Jr beat R E Knepper 11 and 9
Final: Sweetser beat Evans 3 and 2

1923 Flossmoor, Illinois
M R Marston, Pine Valley
Semi-finals: J W Sweetser beat R A Gardner 8 and 7; Marston beat F Ouimet 3 and 2
Final: Marston beat Sweetser at 38th

1924 Merion, Pennsylvania
R T Jones, Jr, Atlanta
Semi-finals: Jones beat F Ouimet 11 and 10; G von Elm beat M R Marston 7 and 6
Final: Jones beat von Elm 9 and 8

1925 Oakmont, Pennsylvania
R T Jones, Jr, Atlanta
Semi-finals: W Gunn beat R A Jones 5 and 3; Jones beat G von Elm 7 and 6
Final: Jones beat Gunn 8 and 7

1926 Baltusrol, New Jersey
G von Elm, Rancho
Semi-finals: Von Elm beat G Dawson 11 and 10; R T Jones beat F Ouimet 5 and 4
Final: Von Elm beat Jones 2 and 1

1927 Minikahda Club, Minnesota
R T Jones, Jr, Atlanta
Semi-finals: C Evans, Jr beat R Mackenzie at 37th; Jones beat F Ouimet 11 and 10
Final: Jones beat Evans 8 and 7

1928 Brae Burn CC, Massachusetts
R T Jones, Jr, Atlanta
Semi-finals: T P Perkins beat G J Voigt 6 and 4; Jones beat P Finlay 13 and 12
Final: Jones beat Perkins 10 and 9

1929 Del Monte CC, California
H R Johnston, White Bear
Semi-finals: O F Willing beat H C Egan 4 and 3; Johnston beat F Ouimet 6 and 5
Final: Johnston beat Willing 4 and 3

1930 Merion, Pennsylvania
R T Jones, Jr, Atlanta
Semi-finals: E V Homans beat C H Seaver 1 hole; Jones beat J W Sweetser 9 and 8
Final: Jones beat Homans 8 and 7

1931 Beverly CC, Illinois
F Ouimet, Woodland
Semi-finals: Ouimet beat B Howell 2 and 1; J Westland beat
M J McCarthy, Jr 3 and 2
Final: Ouimet beat Westland 6 and 5

1932 Baltimore CC, Maryland
C Ross Somerville, London (Canada)
Semi-finals: Somerville beat J P Guilford 7 and 6; J Goodman
beat F Ouimet 4 and 2
Final: Somerville beat Goodman 2 and 1

1933 Kenwood CC, Ohio
G T Dunlap, Pomonok
Semi-finals: M R Marston beat J Munger 6 and 5; Dunlap beat
W Lawson Little 4 and 3
Final: Dunlap beat Marston 6 and 5

1934 The Country Club, Brookline, Massachusetts
W Lawson Little, Jr, Presidio
Semi-finals: D Goldman beat Reynolds Smith 4 and 2; Lawson
Little beat D Armstrong 4 and 3
Final: Lawson Little beat Goldman 8 and 7

1935 The Country Club, Cleveland, Ohio
W Lawson Little, Jr, Presidio
Semi-finals: Lawson Little beat J Goodman 4 and 3; W Emery
beat J P Lynch 4 and 3
Final: Lawson Little beat Emery 4 and 2

1936 Garden City GC, New York
J W Fischer, Highland
Semi-finals: Fischer beat J Goodman 2 and 1; J McLean beat
G J Voigt 8 and 7
Final: Fischer beat McLean at 37th

1937 Alderwood CC, Oregon
J W Goodman, Omaha
Semi-finals: R Billows beat J W Fischer 6 and 5; Goodman
beat M Ward 1 hole
Final: Goodman beat Billows 2 holes

1938 Oakmont CC, Pennsylvania
W P Turnesa, Briar Hills
Semi-finals: B P Abbott beat R D Chapman 5 and 4; Turnesa
beat E C Kingsley 4 and 3
Final: Turnesa beat Abbott 8 and 7

1939 North Shore CC, Illinois
M Ward, Spokane
Semi-finals: R Billows beat D Schumacher 6 and 5; Ward beat
A L Doering 2 and 1
Final: Ward beat Billows 7 and 5

1940 Winged Foot GC, New York
R D Chapman, Winged Foot
Semi-finals: Chapman beat W Wehrle 3 and 2; W McCullogh
beat R Billows 5 and 3
Final: Chapman beat McCullogh 11 and 9

1941 Omaha Field, Nebraska
M Ward, Spokane
Semi-finals: Ward beat R H Riegel 9 and 8; B P Abbott beat
T Bishop 1 hole
Final: Ward beat Abbott 4 and 3

1946 Baltusrol GC, New Jersey
S E Bishop, Norfolk
Semi-finals: S L Quick beat A F Kammer, Jr 3 and 1; Bishop
beat R W Willits 10 and 9
Final: Bishop beat Quick at 37th

1947 Pebble Beach GL, California
R H Riegel, California
Semi-finals: J W Dawson beat J H Selby 5 and 4; Riegel beat
F Torza 2 and 1
Final: Riegel beat Dawson 2 and 1

1948 Memphis CC, Tennessee
W P Turnesa, Knollwood
Semi-finals: R E Billows beat C R Coe 6 and 5; Turnesa beat
E Dahlbender 8 and 6
Final: Turnesa beat Billows 2 and 1

1949 Oak Hill CC, New York
C R Coe, Oklahoma City
Semi-finals: R King beat W P Turnesa 2 and 1; Coe beat
W C Campbell 8 and 7
Final: Coe beat King 11 and 10

1950 Minneapolis GC, Minnesota
S Urzetta, Irondequoit
Semi-finals: Urzetta beat R W Knowles, Jr 6 and 5;
F R Stranahan beat J P Ward 1 hole
Final: Urzetta beat Stranahan at the 39th

1951 Saucon Valley CC, Pennsylvania
B Maxwell, Odessa
Semi-finals: J F Gagliardi beat K T Jacobs, Jr 6 and 5;
Maxwell beat J C Benson 10 and 9
Final: Maxwell beat Gagliardi 4 and 3

1952 Seattle GC, Washington
J Westland, Everett
Semi-finals: A Mengert beat D Cherry 3 and 2; Westland beat
W C Mawhinney 5 and 4
Final: Westland beat Mengert 3 and 2

1953 Oklahoma City CC, Oklahoma
G Littler, La Jolla
Semi-finals: D Morey beat D Albert 5 and 4; Littler beat
B Cudd 10 and 8
Final: Littler beat Morey 1 hole

1954 Detroit CC, Michigan
A D Palmer, Pine Ridge
Semi-finals: Palmer beat E L Meister at the 39th; R Sweeny
beat T N Lenczyk 5 and 4
Final: Palmer beat Sweeny 1 hole

1955 Virginia CC, Virginia
E H Ward, San Francisco
Semi-finals: W Hyndman III beat H Robbins 4 and 3; Ward
beat W A Booe 4 and 2
Final: Ward beat Hyndman 9 and 8

1956 Knollwood Club, Illinois
E H Ward, San Francisco
Semi-finals: C Kocsis beat G J Magee 4 and 2; Ward beat
J Campbell 2 and 1
Final: Ward beat Kocsis 5 and 4

1957 The Country Club, Brookline, Massachusetts
H Robbins, Colonial
Semi-finals: F M Taylor beat E M Rudolph 5 and 4; Robbins
beat R Baxter, Jr 2 holes
Final: Robbins beat Taylor 5 and 4

1958 Olympic CC, California
C R Coe, Oklahoma City
Semi-finals: Coe beat R T McManus 3 and 2; T D Aaron beat
D Foote 10 and 9
Final: Coe beat Aaron 5 and 4

1959 Broadmoor GC, Colorado
J W Nicklaus, Scioto
Semi-finals: C R Coe beat D Wysong 6 and 4; Nicklaus beat
G Andrews 1 hole
Final: Nicklaus beat Coe 1 hole

1960 St Louis CC, Minnesota
D R Beman, Bethesda
Semi-finals: R W Gardner beat C F Lewis 2 and 1; Beman beat
J Farquhar 5 and 4
Final: Beman beat Gardner 6 and 4

1961 Pebble Beach GL, California
J W Nicklaus, Scioto
Semi-finals: H D Wysong beat J B Carr 2 holes; Nicklaus beat
M C Methvin 9 and 8
Final: Nicklaus beat Wysong 8 and 6

1962 Pinehurst CC, North Carolina
L E Harris, Jr, Oakwood
Semi-finals: Harris beat W J Paton 3 and 1; Downing Gray
beat C Coody 3 and 2
Final: Harris beat Gray 1 hole

1963 Wakonda, Iowa
D R Beman, Bethesda
Semi-finals: Beman beat G W Archer 5 and 4; R H Sikes beat
C R Coe 2 and 1
Final: Beman beat Sikes 2 and 1

1964 Canterbury GC, Ohio
W C Campbell, Guyan
Semi-finals: Campbell beat J M Hopkins 3 and 1; E Tutwiler
beat D Eichelberger 3 and 2
Final: Campbell beat Tutwiler 1 hole

Stroke play introduced

1965 Southern Hills CC, Oklahoma

R J Murphy, Jr, Long Palm	73	69	76	73	291
R B Dickson, Muskogee	71	75	72	74	292
D C Allen, Rochester CC	70	74	76	73	293
C Sanudo, Carlton Oaks	71	76	72	74	293

1966 Merion GC, Pennsylvania

G Cowan, West Mount (Canada)	74	72	72	67	285
D R Beman, Bethesda	71	67	76	71	285

(Cowan won play-off 75 to 76)

J W Lewis, Florence CC	73	69	75	69	286
R Cerrudo, California GC	70	75	70	71	286
A Downing Gray, Pensacola	74	72	68	72	286

1967 Broadmoor GC (West), Colorado

R B Dickson, McAlester	71	71	74	69	285
M M Giles III, Boonsboro	76	69	72	69	286
R Cerrudo, California GC	75	73	73	68	289
A D Gray, Pensacola	75	72	70	73	290

1968 Scioto CC, Ohio

B Fleisher, Miami CC	73	70	71	70	284
M M Giles III, Boonsboro	75	72	73	65	285
J Bohmann, Chaparral	74	73	74	67	288
H M Green, Birmingham CC	72	71	73	73	289

1969 Oakmont CC, Pennsylvania

S N Melnyk, Brunswick	70	73	73	70	286
M M Giles III, Boonsboro	72	75	72	72	291
A L Miller, Pensacola	77	69	73	74	293
R I Zender, Evanston	75	78	72	70	295

1970 Waverley CC, Oregon

L Wadkins, Meadowbrook	67	73	69	70	279
T Kite, Jr, Austin CC	69	67	71	73	280
G Cowan, West Mount (Canada)	69	70	73	72	284
J R Gabrielsen, Peachtree	75	67	69	73	284
J B Simons, Butler	69	72	69	74	284

1971 Wilmington CC, Delaware

G Cowan, West Mount (Canada)	70	71	69	70	280
E Pearce, Temple Terrace	70	69	73	71	283
M M Giles III, Virginia CC	74	73	68	69	284
J C McLean, Rainier	72	67	73	73	285

1972 Charlotte CC, North Carolina

M M Giles III, Virginia CC	73	68	72	72	285
M S Hayes, Twin Hills	73	72	69	74	288
B Crenshaw, Austin	71	75	71	71	288
M R West III, Columbia	73	71	73	72	289

Reverted to Matchplay

1973 Inverness, Illinois
C Stadler, La Jolla
Semi-finals: D Strawn beat W C Campbell 6 and 5; C Stadler
beat M M Giles III 3 and 1
Final: Stadler beat Strawn 6 and 5

1974 Ridgewood CC, New Jersey
J Pate, Pensacola CC
Semi-finals: J P Grace beat G Koch 2 and 1; Pate beat
C Strange 3 and 1
Final: Pate beat Grace 2 and 1

1975 CC of Virginia, Richmond, Virginia
Fred S Ridley, Winter Haven, Florida
Semi-finals: Ridley beat Andy Bean 2 and 1; Keith Fergus
beat Henri de Lozier 3 and 2
Final: Ridley beat Fergus 2 holes

1976 Bel-Air CC, Los Angeles, California
Bill Sander, Kenmore, Washington
Semi-finals: C Parker Moore, Jr, beat Stan K M Souza at 19th;
Sander beat James T Mason 8 and 7
Final: Sander beat Parker Moore 8 and 6

1977 Aronimink GC, Newtown Square, Pennsylvania
John Fought, Portland, Oregon
Semi-finals: Doug H Fischesser beat Ralph L Landrum 1 hole;
Fought beat Jay Sigel 2 holes
Final: Fought beat Fischesser 9 and 8

1978 Plainfield CC, New Jersey
John Cook, Upper Arlington, Ohio
Semi-finals: Cook beat Michael Peck at 20th hole; Scott Hoch
beat Bob Clampett at 20th hole
Final: Cook beat Hoch 5 and 4

1979 Canterbury GC, Cleveland, Ohio
Mark O'Meara, Mission Viejo CC, California
Semi-finals: O'Meara beat Joe Rassett 3 and 1; J Cook beat
Cecil Ingram 5 and 3
Final: O'Meara beat Cook 8 and 7

1980 CC of North Carolina
Hal Sutton, Shreveport, Louisiana
Semi-finals: Sutton beat J Holtgrieve 3 and 2; Lewis beat
D von Tacky 4 and 2
Final: Sutton beat Lewis 9 and 8

1981 Olympic Club, California
Nathaniel Crosby, JDM. CC, Palm Beach Gardens, Florida
Semi-finals: B Lindley beat B Lewis 3 and 2; Crosby beat
W Wood 1 hole
Final: Crosby beat Lindley at 37th

1982 The Country Club, Brookline
Jay Sigel, Berwyn, Pennsylvania
Semi-finals: Sigel beat Bob Lewis, Jr, 3 and 2; D Tolley beat
R Fehr 1 hole
Final: Sigel beat Tolley 8 and 7

1983 North Shore CC, Glenview, Illinois
Jay Sigel, Berwyn, Pennsylvania
Semi-finals: Sigel beat C Burroughs 3 and 2; C Perry beat
C Pierce at the 19th
Final: Sigel beat Perry 8 and 7

1984 Oak Tree GC, Edmond, Oklahoma
Scott Verplank, Dallas, Texas
Semi-finals: Verplank beat R Sonnier 1 hole; S Randolph beat
J Haas 7 and 5
Final: Verplank beat Randolph 4 and 3

1985 Montclair GC, New Jersey
Sam Randolph, Santa Barbara, California
Semi-finals: Randolph beat J Kay, Jr, 4 and 3; P Persons beat
C Drury 3 and 1
Final: Randolph beat Persons 1 hole

1986 Shoal Creek, Birmingham, Alabama
Buddy Alexander, Baton Rouge, Louisiana
Semi-finals: Alexander beat B Lewis, Jr, 5 and 4; C Kite beat
B Montgomery 2 and 1
Final: Alexander beat Kite 5 and 3

Walker Cup

MILESTONES

The Walker Cup was 'born' in the years after World War I when the leading British and American amateur golfers were seeking to win each other's championships. In addition, the USGA were invited to confer with the Royal and Ancient Golf Club over the rules and among the American delegation was George Herbert Walker of the National Golf Links of America on Long Island, USGA President in 1920.

On his return from St Andrews, the possibility of international team matches was discussed by the USGA executive committee and the idea so appealed to Mr Walker that he submitted a plan and offered to present an International Challenge Trophy. When the news was published, the newspapers called it the Walker Cup and the name stuck.

In 1921, the USGA invited all countries to send teams to compete for the Trophy, but none accepted. Desperate for competition, Mr William C Fownes, Jr who had twice assembled teams to play against Canada, rounded up a third team and this time took it to Hoylake, England where, in an informal match, they defeated a British team by 9 matches to 3 on the day before the Amateur championship.

The members of this informal American team were Charles Evans, Jr, William Fownes, Jesse Guilford, Paul Hunter, Bobby Jones, Francis Ouimet, J Wood Platt and Frederick J Wright, Jr. They were opposed by Cyril Tolley, J L C Jenkins, J Gordon Simpson, Ernest Holderness, Roger Wethered, R H de Montmorency, C C Aylmer and Tommy Armour who, five years later, played for America against Britain in the forerunner to the Ryder Cup.

If there had been any doubts that the Americans might not provide adequate opposition, they soon vanished and there have been none since. The following spring, the Royal and Ancient sent a team to compete for the Walker Cup in the United States. The match was held every two years after 1924 and is played alternately in Britain and America.

1922 Played at the National Golf Links, it proved most notable for the fact that Bernard Darwin, sent to cover the match for *The Times*, was called into replace the British Captain, Robert Harris, who fell ill, and won his single.

In the first single, Hooman's match with Sweetser went to extra holes before anyone could stop them. Hooman won at the 37th and the result stood, but it is the only match ever to have played an extra hole. Ever since, halved matches have stood.

1923 A return match was soon settled at St Andrews in which the British side fared very much better. They won three of the four foursomes and led in most of the singles at one point, but the first of many disappointments for British teams followed. The Americans made a remarkable recovery and won the match 6–5 with one match halved. Ouimet halved after being 2 down and 3 to play to Wethered; George Rotan, 6 down after 14, won 11 of the next 12 holes and Frederick Wright won the 34th, 35th and 36th holes to beat Holderness.

1924 A comfortable victory for the Americans at the Garden City Golf Club by 9–3, although the biggest of their wins was 4

and 3. It was felt that an annual match was too much and thereafter the sides agreed to meet in alternate years.

1926 Another narrow victory for the Americans at Muirfield, the highlight being the 12 and 11 victory of Bobby Jones over Cyril Tolley. Jess Sweetser began the long sequence of victories in the Amateur championship in Walker Cup years in Britain.

1928 A heavy defeat (11–1) for Britain and the beginning of a lean period. Bobby Jones beat Phil Perkins at the Chicago Golf Club by 13 and 12, the biggest margin in the history of the Walker Cup. Tony Torrance won Britain's lone point, a 1-hole victory over Chick Evans.

1930 At Royal St George's, Sandwich, the United States won 10–2. In his Grand Slam year, Bobby Jones beat Roger Wethered 9 and 8 and preserved his 100 per cent record in his fifth and last single, but the most notable victory was that of Donald K Moe. He was 7 down with 13 to play but won with a birdie on the last hole. He was round in 67.

1932 Francis Ouimet took over the captaincy from Bobby Jones, appropriately enough on his own course, the Country Club, Brookline where he had won the US Open in 1913. He was captain until 1949 although in a non-playing role after 1934.

The British had the brothers, Rex and Lister Hartley playing together in the first foursome, but they won only one match, that in which Leonard Crawley defeated George Voigt. Crawley also dented the Walker Cup with an overstrong second at the 18th in the morning, the Cup being on display.

1934 The Americans won their eighth successive victory at St Andrews. Michael Scott became the oldest participant at 56, but the British won only one foursome and one single. The singles winner was Tony Torrance who won three and halved one of his last four singles.

1936 The first and only time that Britain failed to win a match. It meant that they had only won two foursomes and four singles in the five matches from 1928. At Pine Valley, a complete whitewash was avoided by 2 half points in the foursomes. In the fourth foursome, Alec Hill and Cecil Ewing were 7 down to George Voigt and Harry Givan with 11 holes to play. They squared on the 35th and the Americans had to hole an awkward putt on the 36th to gain a half.

1938 In two years, Britain went from their worst result to their best. Prior to the Walker Cup, Charlie Yates had won the Amateur championship at Troon but at St Andrews, amid scenes of wild delight, Britain won the foursomes 2½–1½ and the singles 5–3. It was only the second time that Britain had won a series of singles and they were not to do so again until 1963.

1947 Because of post-war conditions, a two-year gap resulted and the Americans agreed to come to Britain although it was Britain's turn to go to America. St Andrews was once again the venue but this time there was a comfortable American victory. But Ward was the only survivor of 1938 in the American team; Leonard Crawley, Alec Kyle and Cecil Ewing for Britain and Ireland. The match, however, saw the introduction of several outstanding players: Joe Carr, Ronnie White, Frank Stranahan and Dick Chapman.

1949 A one-sided contest at Winged Foot, but encouragement for Britain in the golf of Ronnie White who won both his foursome (with Joe Carr) and single.

1951 Britain led in three foursomes and were square in the fourth after 18 holes on the first day, but they failed to win any of them. The best they could manage was two halves.

This was one of many disappointments over the years but in the singles, Ronnie White, playing on his home course, Royal Birkdale, beat Charlie Coe, Joe Carr beat Frank Stranahan and Alec Kyle beat Willie Turnesa.

1953 Notable for the incident on the first morning when James Jackson, paired with Gene Littler, discovered that he was carrying 16 clubs. In those days, the penalty was disqualification, but the British, captained by Tony Duncan, refused to accept victory in that way. The penalty was therefore modified to the loss of 2 holes. As the incident occurred on the 2nd hole, America, having lost the 1st at Kittansett, were 3 down on the fourth tee where the match resumed. Jackson and Littler were still 3 down at the turn, but they lunched 2 up and went on to win 3 and 2.

The outstanding single was that in which Ronnie White, 3 down after 30 holes, beat Dick Chapman by 1 hole. He had 3 birdies in the last 6 holes and so won his fourth successive single—a British record. John Morgan won both his matches for Britain.

1955 Back at St Andrews, America won all four foursomes and six of the eight singles; even Ronnie White suffered his first defeat for Britain in the singles. The American Captain, Bill Campbell, did not play himself although he was one of their best players and had reached the final of the British Amateur at Muirfield the previous summer.

1957 One of the best British sides and one of the best matches at Minikhada, but still a victory (8½–3½) for America. However, Charlie Coe, the American Captain, commented at the presentation that he thought during the afternoon the Walker Cup was half-way back across the Atlantic!

He referred to the moment when three crucial singles were all square with 6, 5, and 2 holes to play, but America won them all. The best recovery was that of Billy Joe Patton, 5 down at lunch, who was round in 68 in the afternoon to beat Reid Jack, British champion, on the last green.

1959 Another big disappointment for the British side at Muirfield. They lost all four foursomes, but the Americans, who included the young Jack Nicklaus, fielded what many regard as their best team ever.

1961 The matches were held for the first time on the west coast, at Seattle where the Americans equalled their record victory margin (11–1) in 1928. Martin Christmas, the youngest member of the British side, was their only winner.

1963 A change in the form of the match took place at Turnberry, 18-hole matches being introduced for the first time. Foursomes and singles were played each day and at the end of the first day, Britain led 7½–4½. They lost the foursomes and then won only their second series of singles since the matches began. However, despite promising to win at least two of the second series of foursomes, they lost them all—the 16th hole proving enormously costly. Suitably reprieved, America then won five singles in the afternoon.

1965 The only halved match in the history of the series, America making a dramatic recovery on the last afternoon and then Clive Clark having to hole from 30 ft to prevent a British defeat. Britain had a lead of five matches going into the last afternoon at Five Farms, Baltimore, but America made an historic rally.

1967 Not even the cold May weather at Royal St George's, Sandwich, could deter the Americans. They had the match well won on the first day and though Britain won three foursomes on the second morning, there were no dramatic recoveries, as there had been in Baltimore. Bill Campbell won four matches for America. Last match for Joe Carr who was picked for a record ten teams.

1969 A fine, close match at Milwaukee Country Club, Britain staging an effective rally after America had won the first day 8–4. On the second day, America won only three matches, but they held on to win 10–8 with six halved.

1971 A second victory for Great Britain and Ireland at St Andrews, the scene of their first in 1938. It was the 50th anniversary of the first informal match in 1921 and was made possible by their winning six of the final afternoon's singles. They lost the second series of foursomes 2½–1½ to go 2 points behind, but they got the better of six close singles, two on the 17th green and four on the last green. The deciding point was supplied by David Marsh who hit a 3 iron to the famous 17th to go dormie 1 on Bill Hyndman.

The British and Irish side included Roddy Carr, son of Joe. It is the only instance of a father and son winning Walker Cup honours.

1973 A good defence of the Cup by Britain at the Country Club, Brookline. Having managed only a half on the first morning, they won five singles, but again on Saturday the foursomes were their undoing. They went down 14–10 without winning one foursome match. It was the last appearance of Michael Bonallack whose 25 individual matches is a record.

1975 Steady control for the Americans at St Andrews, the eighth time the match has been played over the Old course. They were four points clear on the first day, shared the second series of foursomes and won the final singles 5½–2½.

1977 Great Britain and Ireland travelled to Shinnecock Hills with obvious hopes of victory, but they were destroyed on the first day by a new, young American side who led 9–3 at the end of it. Only Dick Siderowf had played in a previous match. Britain did better on the second day, but it was too late.

1979 Another young American side went to Muirfield although it was not at full strength owing to a clash with the National Collegiate championship which deprived them of Bob Clampett, Garry Hallberg and John Cook. It was a close match, America gaining a 1 point lead on the first day and preserving it on the second morning.

Britain made the better start in the last series of singles and, at one stage, were down in only one. However, in the end, they won only one.

America won by the margin of 15½–8½.

1981 A Californian venue for the first time, Cypress Point, provided a fine match in which the Americans won 15–9. However, there were several notable performances by the British and Irish who won the second series of foursomes 3–1. This gave interest to the last afternoon but America produced unbeatable golf.

Ronan Rafferty and Philip Walton won both their foursomes, the first all-Irish pair to win a point in the history of the Walker Cup. On the first morning, they finished their match by holing two chip shots. Roger Chapman won three matches out of four including both singles.

1983 The result hung very much in the balance on the final afternoon. The teams were tied 8–8 at lunch on the second day at Hoylake which was hosting the matches for the first time. However, having begun the better in the deciding singles, Great Britain and Ireland lost 5½–2½, although Andrew Oldcorn set a record by becoming the first British and Irish player to win four matches. Jay Sigel was the first playing captain of America since Charlie Coe in 1959.

1985 Fifty years after hosting its first Walker Cup match, Pine Valley witnessed a fine, close contest—maintaining the pattern of the previous two. The turning point came on the second morning when the United States won the foursomes 3½–½ after ending the first day level. However, Great Britain and Ireland took the second series of singles 4½–3½ and there was no doubting the sense of relief the Americans felt by their victory. In the final matches, John Hawksworth defeated the American Captain and Pine Valley champion, Jay Sigel.

DETAILED RECORDS

Most appearances
10, Joe Carr (for Great Britain and Ireland). In addition he was Captain in 1965 but did not play.

Most consecutive appearances
9, Joe Carr, 1947–63

8, Francis Ouimet 1922–34. In addition, he was Captain in 1934–36–38–47–49. Michael Bonallack, 1959–73. He was a member of the 1957 side, but did not play.

Biggest margin of victory in individual matches
Over 36 holes (1922–61)

Foursomes: **9 and 8**, E Harvie Ward and Jack Westland, 1953;

Billy Joe Patton and Charles Coe, 1959, both for the United States
Singles: **13 and 12**, Bobby Jones, 1928
Over 18 holes
Foursomes: **7 and 5**, Marvin Giles and Gary Koch (United States), 1973; **7 and 6**, Bob Lewis and Jim Holtgrieve (United States), 1983
Singles: **9 and 7**, Scott Hoch 1979; **8 and 7**, Douglas Clarke 1979; **7 and 6**, Scott Simpson 1977 (all United States)

Largest winning margin by team
11–1, United States, 1928 and 1961

Outstanding individual records
William C Campbell won seven singles, halved one and never lost. He also won six foursomes, lost three and halved one. Bobby Jones won all his five singles matches and four of his five foursomes.

Best team recovery
The United States trailed by 3–1 after the foursomes in 1923, but won 6–5. In 1963 they trailed 6–3 after the first day and won 12–8. In 1965 they were 8–3 down on the first day and 10–5 down at lunch on the second day; and earned a halved match.

Brothers
In 1932, Rex and Lister Hartley played in the British side and were paired together in the foursomes.
Willie and Tony Torrance both played in the British side, Willie in the first match in 1922 and Tony on five occasions.

Father and Son
Joe and Roddy Carr are the only instance of father and son having played in the Walker Cup although Vance Heafner who played for America in 1977 is the son of Clayton Heafner who played in American Ryder Cup teams of 1949 and 1951.

Most consecutive team victories
9, United States 1922–36, 1947–63

Courses most often used
Britain: St Andrews, 8
America: The Country Club, Brookline, 2

Oldest competitor
Hon Michael Scott (Great Britain and Ireland) 56 years, 1934

Youngest competitor
Ronan Rafferty (Great Britain and Ireland) 17 years 8 months 15 days, 1981
Peter Baker (Great Britain and Ireland) 17 years 10 months 14 days, 1985
James Bruen (Great Britain and Ireland) 18 years 25 days, 1938
John Langley (Great Britain and Ireland) 18 years 4 months 7 days, 1936
Peter Oosterhuis (Great Britain and Ireland) 19 years 2 weeks, 1967

Team winning all the foursomes
United States: 1928–32–55–59–61. They also won the second series of foursomes in 1963.
Great Britain and Ireland won 4–0 in the first series of foursomes in 1971

Team winning all the singles
None, but the United States won 7½ out of 8 in 1936 at Pine Valley.

Form of the match
Foursomes and singles. From 1922 until 1961, there were four foursomes matches and eight singles—all played over 36 holes.
From 1963, one series of foursomes and one series of singles have taken place each day, all the matches being over 18 holes.

In all cases, halved matches count; the exception was in 1922 when Hooman and Sweetser played 37 holes before anyone could rectify the mistake. The result, victory for Hooman, was allowed to stand.

Unusual facts
In 1930, Jack Stout of Britain was 7 up with 13 holes to play on Donald Moe. However, when Moe had completed the second 18 in 67 at Sandwich, he had recovered to win on the last green.
In 1936, George Voigt and Harry Givan were 7 up with 11 holes to play in their foursomes match at Pine Valley. However, the British pair Alec Hill and Cecil Ewing squared on the 35th and halved the match—the Americans holing an awkward putt on the last green.
In 1971, Cecil Ewing and Frank Pennink, both members of Britain's first winning side in 1938, were selectors on the occasion of Britain and Ireland's second victory.
Up to and including 1979, the United States have won 25 matches, Great Britain and Ireland two, with one halved.

Open champions of either Britain or America who have taken part
Francis Ouimet, Robert T Jones, Johnny Goodman, Lawson Little, Gene Littler, Ken Venturi, Jack Nicklaus, Bill Rogers, Jerry Pate, Sandy Lyle.

Success at his 16th attempt for Jay Sigel, 1982. He won again in 1983. (USGA)

RESULTS

Year	Venue	Winners	US Total	Great Britain and Ireland Total	USA	Captains Britain
1922	National Links, Long Island, New York	USA	8	4	William C Fownes, Jr	Robert Harris
1923	St Andrews, Scotland	USA	6½	5½	Robert A Gardner	Robert Harris
1924	Garden City, New York	USA	9	3	Robert A Gardner	Cyril J H Tolley
1926	St Andrews, Scotland	USA	6½	5½	Robert A Gardner	Robert Harris
1928	Chicago GC, Wheaton, Illinois	USA	11	1	Robert T Jones, Jr	Dr William Tweddell
1930	Royal St George's, Sandwich	USA	10	2	Robert T Jones, Jr	Roger H Wethered
1932	Brookline, Massachusetts	USA	9½	2½	Francis D Ouimet	Tony A Torrance
1934	St Andrews, Scotland	USA	9½	2½	Francis D Ouimet	Hon Michael Scott
1936	Pine Valley, New Jersey	USA	10½	1½	*Francis D Ouimet	Dr William Tweddell
1938	St Andrews, Scotland	GB & I	4½	7½	*Francis D Ouimet	John B Beck
1947	St Andrews, Scotland	USA	8	4	*Francis D Ouimet	John B Beck
1949	Winged Foot, New York	USA	10	2	*Francis D Ouimet	Percy B 'Laddie' Lucas
1951	Royal Birkdale, Lancashire	USA	7½	4½	*William P Turnesa	Raymond Oppenheimer
1953	Kittansett Club, Massachusetts	USA	9	3	*Charles R Yates	Lt-Col Tony Duncan
1955	St Andrews, Scotland	USA	10	2	*William C Campbell	*G Alec Hill
1957	Minikhada Club, Minnesota	USA	8½	3½	*Charles R Coe	*Gerald H Micklem
1959	Muirfield, Scotland	USA	9	3	Charles R Coe	*Gerald H Micklem
1961	Seattle, Washington	USA	11	1	*Jack Westland	*Charles D Lawrie
1963	Ailsa Course, Turnberry, Scotland	USA	14	10	*Richard S Tufts	*Charles D Lawrie
1965	Baltimore, Maryland	(tie)	12	12	*John W Fischer	*Joe B Carr
1967	Royal St George's, Sandwich	USA	15	9	*Jess W Sweetser	Joe B Carr
1969	Milwaukee, Wisconsin	USA	13	11	*Billy Joe Patton	Michael Bonallack
1971	St Andrews, Scotland	GB & I	11	13	*John M Winters, Jr	Michael Bonallack
1973	Brookline, Massachusetts	USA	14	10	*Jess W Sweetser	Dr David Marsh
1975	St Andrews, Scotland	USA	15½	8½	*Dr Ed R Updegraff	*Dr David Marsh
1977	Shinnecock Hills, New York	USA	16	8	*Lou W Oehmig	*Sandy C Saddler
1979	Muirfield, Scotland	USA	15½	8½	*Richard Siderowf	*Rodney Foster
1981	Cypress Point, California	USA	15	9	*Jim Gabrielsen	*Rodney Foster
1983	Royal Liverpool, Lancashire	USA	13½	10½	Jay Sigel	*Charlie Green
1985	Pine Valley, New Jersey	USA	13	11	Jay Sigel	*Charlie Green
1987	Sunningdale, England	USA	16½	7½	Fred Ridley	Geoffrey Marks

*Non-playing captain

A total of 147 players have represented Great Britain and Ireland, 140 the United States.

PLAYERS—GREAT BRITAIN AND IRELAND
A total of 149 players have represented GB/I, 140 the USA

Name	Played	Won	Lost	Halved	Percentage
M F Attenborough (1967)	2	0	2	0	–
C C Aylmer (1922)	2	1	1	0	50.00
P Baker (1985)	3	2	1	0	66.66
J B Beck (1928)	1	0	1	0	–
P J Benka (1969)	4	2	1	1	62.5
H G Bentley (1936–38)	3	0	1	2	33.33
D A Blair (1955–61)	4	1	3	0	25.00
C Bloice (1985)	3	0	2	1	16.66
M F Bonallack (1957–59–61–63–65–67–69–71–73)	25	8	14	3	38.00
G Brand of Scotland (1979)	3	0	3	0	–
O C Bristowe (1924)	1	0	1	0	–
A Brodie (1977–79)	8	5	2	1	68.75
A Brooks (1969)	3	2	0	1	83.3
Hon W G E Brownlow (1926)	2	0	2	0	–
J Bruen (1938–49–51)	5	0	4	1	10.00
J Buckley (1979)	1	0	1	0	–
J Burke (1932)	2	0	1	1	25.00
A Bussell (1957)	2	1	1	0	50.00

Name	Played	Won	Lost	Halved	Percentage
I Caldwell (1951–55)	4	1	2	1	37.50
W Campbell (1930)	2	0	2	0	–
J B Carr (1947–49–51–53–55–57–59–61–63–65–67)	20	5	14	1	27.50
R Carr (1971)	4	3	0	1	87.50
D Carrick (1983)	2	0	2	0	–
I Carslaw (1979)	3	1	1	1	50.00
R Cater (1955)	1	0	1	0	–
J Caven (1922)	2	0	2	0	–
B H G Chapman (1961)	1	0	1	0	–
R Chapman (1981)	4	3	1	0	75.00
M J Christmas (1961–63)	3	1	2	0	33.33
C A Clark (1965)	4	2	0	2	75.00
G J Clark (1965)	1	0	1	0	–
H K Clark (1973)	3	1	1	1	50.00
G B Cosh (1965)	4	3	1	0	75.00
T Craddock (1967–69)	6	2	3	1	41.60
L G Crawley (1930–32–38–47)	6	3	3	0	50.00
B Critchley (1969)	4	1	1	2	50.00
C R Dalgleish (1981)	3	1	2	0	33.33
B Darwin (1922)	2	1	1	0	50.00
J C Davies (1973–75–77–79)	13	3	8	2	30.76
P Deeble (1977–81)	5	1	4	0	20.00
F W G Deighton (1957)	2	0	2	0	–
J de Forest (1932)	1	0	1	0	–
N V Drew (1953)	1	0	1	0	–
J M Dykes (1936)	2	0	1	1	25.00
C Ewing (1936–38–47–49–51)	9	1	6	2	22.22
G R D Eyles (1975)	4	2	2	0	50.00
E Fiddian (1932–34)	4	0	4	0	–
R Foster (1965–67–69–71–73)	17	2	13	2	17.60
D W Frame (1961)	1	0	1	0	–
D Gilford (1985)	1	0	1	0	–
G Godwin (1979–81)	7	2	4	1	35.71
C W Green (1963–69–71–73–75)	17	4	10	3	32.35
R Hardman (1928)	1	0	1	0	–
R Harris (1923–26)	4	1	3	0	25.00
L Hartley (1932)	2	0	2	0	–
R Hartley (1930–32)	4	0	4	0	–
J Hawksworth (1985)	4	2	1	1	62.50
P J Hedges (1973–75)	5	0	2	3	30.00
C Hezlet (1924–26–28)	6	0	5	1	8.30
G A Hill (1936)	2	0	1	1	25.00
E W E Holderness (1923–26–30)	6	2	4	0	33.33
T W B Homer (1973)	3	0	3	0	–
C V L Hooman (1922–23)	3	1	2	0	33.33
W L Hope (1923–24–28)	5	1	4	0	20.00
G Huddy (1961)	1	0	1	0	–
I C Hutcheon (1975–77–79–81)	15	5	8	2	40.00
R Reid Jack (1957–59)	4	2	2	0	50.00
A Jamieson, Jr (1926)	2	1	1	0	50.00
M James (1975)	4	3	1	0	75.00
M J Kelley (1977–79)	7	3	3	1	50.00
S D Keppler (1983)	3	0	2	1	16.66
M G King (1973)	4	1	2	1	37.50
A Kyle (1938–47–51)	5	2	3	0	40.00
D H Kyle (1924)	1	0	1	0	–
J D A Langley (1936–51–53)	5	0	4	1	10.00
M E Lewis (1983)	1	0	1	0	–
P B Lucas (1936–47)	2	1	1	0	50.00
M S R Lunt (1961–63–65)	9	2	6	1	27.77
A W B Lyle (1977)	3	0	3	0	–
Dr A R MacCallum (1928)	1	0	1	0	–
J S Macdonald (1971)	1	1	1	1	50.00
G Macgregor (1971–75–83–85)	12	5	6	1	45.83
R C Macgregor (1953)	1	0	1	0	–
W W MacKenzie (1922–23)	3	1	2	0	33.33
J F D Madeley (1963)	3	0	2	1	16.66
L Mann (1983)	4	2	1	1	62.50
B Marchbank (1979)	4	2	2	0	50.00

Name	Played	Won	Lost	Halved	Percentage
G C Marks (1971–73)	6	2	4	0	33.33
Dr D M Marsh (1959–71)	3	2	1	0	66.66
P Mayo (1985)	2	0	1	1	25.00
S M McCready (1949–51)	3	0	3	0	–
P M McEvoy (1977–79–81–85)	14	3	10	1	25.00
J McLean (1934–36)	4	1	3	0	25.00
G McGimpsey (1985)	4	1	2	1	37.50
P M McKellar (1977)	1	0	1	0	–
S L McKinlay (1934)	2	0	2	0	–
E McRuvie (1932–34)	4	1	2	1	37.50
G H Micklem (1947–49–53–55)	6	1	5	0	16.66
D J Millensted (1967)	2	1	1	0	50.00
E B Millward (1955)	2	0	2	0	–
W T Milne (1973)	4	2	2	0	50.00
C S Montgomerie (1985)	4	0	3	1	12.50
J L Morgan (1951–53–55)	6	2	4	0	33.33
P Mulcare (1975)	3	2	1	0	66.66
G H Murray (1977)	2	1	1	0	50.00
S W T Murray (1963)	4	2	2	0	50.00
W A Murray (1923–24)	4	1	3	0	25.00
A Oldcorn (1983)	4	4	0	0	100.00
P Oosterhuis (1967)	4	1	2	1	37.50
P Parkin (1983)	3	2	1	0	66.66
J J F Pennink (1938)	2	1	1	0	50.00
T P Perkins (1928)	2	0	2	0	–
A H Perowne (1949–53–59)	4	0	4	0	–
G B Peters (1936–38)	4	2	1	1	62.50
A Pierse (1983)	3	0	2	1	16.66
A K Pirie (1967)	3	0	2	1	16.66
R Rafferty (1981)	4	2	2	0	50.00
A S Saddler (1963–65–67)	10	3	5	2	40.00
Hon M Scott (1924–34)	4	2	2	0	50.00
R Scott (1924)	1	1	0	0	100.00
P F Scrutton (1957)	2	0	2	0	–
D N Sewell (1957)	2	1	1	0	50.00
R D B M Shade (1963–65–67)	12	5	6	1	45.80
D B Sheahan (1963)	4	2	2	0	50.00
A E Shepperson (1959)	2	1	1	0	50.00
W D Smith (1959)	1	0	1	0	–
J N Smith (1930)	2	0	2	0	–
S Stephen (1985)	4	2	1	1	62.50
E F Storey (1924–26–28)	6	1	5	0	16.66
J A Stout (1930–32)	4	0	3	1	12.50
C Stowe (1938–47)	4	2	2	0	50.00
H B Stuart (1973–75–77)	10	4	6	0	40.00
K G Thom (1949)	2	0	2	0	–
H Thomson (1936–38)	4	2	2	0	50.00
M Thompson (1983)	3	1	2	0	33.33
C J H Tolley (1922–23–24–26–30)	10	4	6	0	40.00
T A Torrance (1924–28–30–32–34)	9	3	5	1	38.88
W B Torrance (1922)	2	0	2	0	–
P M P Townsend (1965)	4	3	1	0	75.00
P L Tupling (1969)	2	1	1	0	50.00
Dr W Tweddell (1928)	2	0	2	0	–
J Walker (1959)	2	0	2	0	–
P Walton (1981)	4	3	1	0	75.00
P Way (1981)	4	2	2	0	50.00
R H Wethered (1922–23–26–30–34)	9	5	3	1	61.11
R J White (1947–49–51–53–55)	10	6	3	1	66.66
John Wilson (1923)	2	2	0	0	100.00
J C Wilson (1947–53)	4	0	4	0	–
G B Wolstenholme (1957–59)	4	1	2	1	37.50

PLAYERS—UNITED STATES OF AMERICA

Name	Played	Won	Lost	Halved	Percentage
T Aaron (1959)	2	1	1	0	50.00
D C Allen (1965–67)	6	0	4	2	16.66
E Andrews (1961)	1	1	0	0	100.00
D Ballenger (1973)	1	1	0	0	100.00
R Baxter (1957)	2	2	0	0	100.00
D Beman (1959–61–63)	11	7	2	2	72.72
R Billows (1938–49)	4	2	2	0	50.00
S Bishop (1947–49)	3	2	1	0	66.66
A S Blum (1957)	1	0	1	0	–
J Bohmann (1969)	2	1	1	0	50.00
C Burroughs (1985)	3	1	2	0	33.33
A E Campbell (1936)	2	2	0	0	100.00
J Campbell (1957)	1	0	1	0	–
W C Campbell (1951–53–55–57–65–67–71–75)	18	11	4	3	69.44
R D Chapman (1947–51–53)	5	3	2	0	60.00
D Cherry (1953–55–61)	5	5	0	0	100.00
D Clarke (1979)	3	2	0	1	83.33
R Cochran (1961)	1	1	0	0	100.00
C R Coe (1949–51–53–59–61–63)	13	7	4	2	61.53
J Conrad (1955)	2	1	1	0	50.00
B Cudd (1955)	2	2	0	0	100.00
R D Davies (1963)	2	0	2	0	–
J W Dawson (1949)	2	2	0	0	100.00
G T Dunlap, Jr (1932–34)	4	3	1	0	75.00
D Edwards (1973)	4	4	0	0	100.00
H C Egan (1934)	1	1	0	0	100.00
D Eichelberger (1965)	3	1	2	0	33.33
J Ellis (1973)	3	2	1	0	66.66
W Emery (1936)	2	1	0	1	75.00
C Evans, Jr (1922–24–28)	5	3	2	0	60.00
J Farquhar (1971)	3	1	2	0	33.33
J Fischer (1934–36–38)	4	3	0	1	87.50
D Fischesser (1979)	3	1	2	0	33.33
M Fleckman (1967)	2	0	2	0	–
B Fleisher (1969)	4	0	3	1	12.50
J Fought (1977)	4	4	0	0	100.00
W C Fownes (1922–24)	3	1	2	0	33.33
J Gabrielsen (1971)	3	1	2	0	33.33
Robert A Gardner (1922–24–26)	6	5	1	0	83.33
R W Gardner (1961–63)	5	4	0	1	90.00
M Giles III (1969–71–73–75)	15	8	2	5	70.00
H L Givan (1936)	1	0	0	1	50.00
J Goodman (1934–36–38)	6	4	2	0	66.66
M Gove (1979)	3	2	1	0	66.66
J Grace (1975)	3	2	1	0	66.66
A Downing Gray (1963–65–67)	12	5	6	1	45.83
J P Guildford (1922–24–26)	6	4	2	0	66.66
W Gunn (1926–28)	4	4	0	0	100.00
F Haas (1938)	2	0	2	0	–
Jay Haas (1975)	3	3	0	0	100.00
Jerry Haas (1985)	3	1	2	0	33.33
G Hallberg (1977)	3	1	2	0	33.33
L Harris (1963)	4	3	1	0	75.00
V Heafner (1977)	3	3	0	0	100.00
S D Herron (1923)	2	0	2	0	–
S Hoch (1979)	4	4	0	0	100.00
J Holtgrieve (1979–81–83)	10	6	4	0	60.00
J M Hopkins (1965)	3	0	2	1	16.66
W Howell (1932)	1	1	0	0	100.00
W Hyndman III (1959–61–69–71)	8	5	2	1	68.75
J Inman (1969)	2	2	0	0	100.00
J G Jackson (1953–55)	3	3	0	0	100.00
H R Johnston (1923–24–28–30)	6	5	1	0	83.33
R T Jones (1922–24–26–28–30)	10	9	1	0	90.00
A F Kammer, Jr (1947)	2	1	1	0	50.00
M Killian (1973)	3	1	2	0	33.33

Name	Played	Won	Lost	Halved	Percentage
T Kite (1971)	4	2	1	1	62.50
R W Knowles (1951)	1	1	0	0	100.00
G Koch (1973–75)	7	4	1	2	71.42
C R Kocsis (1938–49–57)	5	2	2	1	50.00
W Lawson Little (1934)	2	2	0	0	100.00
J Lewis (1967)	4	3	1	0	75.00
R Lewis (1981–83–85)	10	6	4	0	60.00
G Littler (1953)	2	2	0	0	100.00
D Love III (1985)	3	2	0	1	83.33
M R Marston (1922–23–24)	6	4	2	0	66.66
R R MacKenzie (1926–28–30)	6	5	1	0	83.33
M J McCarthy, Jr (1932)	1	1	0	0	100.00
B N McCormick (1949)	1	1	0	0	100.00
J B McHale, Jr (1949–51)	3	2	0	1	83.33
S Melnyk (1969–71)	7	3	3	1	50.00
A Miller (1969–71)	8	4	4	0	50.00
L Miller (1977)	4	4	0	0	100.00
D K Moe (1930–32)	3	3	0	0	100.00
G Moody (1979)	3	1	2	0	33.33
G T Moreland (1932–34)	4	4	0	0	100.00
D Morey (1955–65)	4	1	3	0	25.00
J F Neville (1923)	1	0	1	0	–
J W Nicklaus (1959–61)	4	4	0	0	100.00
F Ouimet (1922–24–26–28–30–32–34)	15	8	5	2	60.00
H D Paddock, Jr (1951)	1	0	0	1	50.00
J K Pate (1975)	4	0	4	0	–
W J Patton (1955–57–59–63–65)	14	11	3	0	78.57
M Peck (1977)	3	1	1	1	50.00
M Pfeil (1973)	4	2	1	1	62.50
M Podolak (1985)	2	1	0	1	75.00
S L Quick (1947)	2	1	1	0	50.00
S Randolph (1985)	4	2	1	1	62.50
R H (Skee) Riegel (1947–49)	4	4	0	0	100.00
F Ridley (1977)	3	2	1	0	66.66
H Robbins (1957)	2	0	1	1	25.00
W Rogers (1973)	2	1	1	0	50.00
G V Rotan (1923)	2	1	1	0	50.00
E Mason Rudolph (1957)	2	1	0	1	75.00
W Sander (1977)	3	0	3	0	–
C H Seaver (1932)	2	2	0	0	100.00
R Siderowf (1969–73–75–77)	14	4	9	1	32.14
J Sigel (1977–79–81–83–85)	19	11	5	3	65.78
R H Sikes (1963)	3	1	2	0	33.33
J Simons (1971)	2	0	2	0	–
S Simpson (1977)	3	3	0	0	100.00
C B Smith (1961–63)	2	0	1	1	25.00
Reynolds Smith (1936–38)	4	2	2	0	50.00
R Sonnier (1985)	3	0	2	1	16.66
C Stadler (1975)	3	3	0	0	100.00
F Stranahan (1947–49–51)	6	3	2	1	58.33
C Strange (1975)	4	3	0	1	87.50
H Sutton (1981)					
J Sweetser (1922–23–24–26–28–32)	12	7	4	1	62.50
Dr F Taylor (1957–59)	3	3	0	0	100.00
W P Turnesa (1947–49–51)	6	3	3	0	50.00
E Tutwiler (1965–67)	6	5	1	0	83.33
Dr E Updegraff (1963–65–69)	7	3	3	1	50.00
S Urzetta (1951–53)	4	4	0	0	100.00
K Venturi (1953)	2	2	0	0	100.00
S Verplank (1985)	4	3	0	1	87.50
G Voigt (1930–32–36)	5	2	2	1	50.00
G von Elm (1926–28–30)	6	4	1	1	75.00
L Wadkins (1969–71)	7	3	4	0	42.85
D Waldorf (1985)	3	1	2	0	33.33
E Harvie Ward (1953–55)	4	4	0	0	100.00
M H (Bud) Ward (1938–47)	4	2	2	0	50.00
M West (1973)	3	2	1	0	66.66
J Westland (1932–34–53)	5	3	0	2	80.00
W Wettlaufer (1959)	2	2	0	0	100.00

Name	Played	Won	Lost	Halved	Percentage
E White (1936)	2	2	0	0	100.00
Dr O F Willing (1923–24–30)	4	4	0	0	100.00
F J Wright (1923)	1	1	0	0	100.00
C R Yates (1936–38)	4	3	0	1	87.50
R L Yost (1955)	2	2	0	0	100.00

Bud Alexander (1986).
(USGA)

World Amateur Team Championship

EISENHOWER TROPHY

The idea for this championship was put by the United States Golf Association to the Royal and Ancient Golf Club in March 1958. It was agreed that the two governing bodies should join forces in running the event which was first played in October 1958 and has since been held every other year. A handsome trophy was presented bearing the name of President Eisenhower and the inscription, 'To foster friendship and sportsmanship among the Peoples of the World'.

The form of the tournament is strokeplay for teams of four, the best three scores to count for the four rounds played. The lowest aggregate of the four daily totals constitutes the winner.

1958 Played appropriately at St Andrews, the first championship was one of the best and certainly the closest. It produced a tie (the only tie so far) between Australia and the United States with Great Britain and Ireland 1 stroke behind in third place. It is the only time that 1 stroke has divided three teams. Australia set the target of 918 thanks largely to Bruce Devlin, later such a well-known professional. In the first round, all four Australians took over 80 and they finished 17 strokes behind Britain.

On the last day, the United States, captained by Bobby Jones, looked out of it but Bill Hyndman had a 72, the lowest of all the fourth-round scores. He even had a 3 at the 17th to force the tie. In the play-off, the Australians, with Devlin again leading the way, won by 2 strokes with a total of 222.

1960 The championship in which the Americans set all sorts of records at Merion which may never be broken. Led by Jack Nicklaus whose four rounds of 66, 67, 68, 68 for an 11 under par 269 is easily a record, they won by 42 strokes—another record. Yet a further record was their team total of 834. No other championship has ever been so completely dominated by one team.

Thirty-two teams took part, three more than in 1958.

1962 At the Fuji Golf Course, Kawana, Japan, the United States gained their second title. Deane Beman was the only survivor of Merion (Jack Nicklaus had turned professional, winning the US Open in 1962) but they held off Canada for whom Gary Cowan was the star. He won the individual title with 280. In the final round, after Billy Joe Patton had opened with an 81, Beman had 66, Richard Sikes 69 and Labron Harris 70. They had started the last round 2 behind Canada. Great Britain and Ireland were third for the third time.

1964 In rainy and blustery weather, Great Britain and Ireland won their first victory at Olgiata, Rome. Again Canada were the runners-up and on the last afternoon, Keith Alexander caused a terrible fright among the British and Irish by almost completing a miracle. Needing 5 birdies to tie the British total of 895, he got 4 of them, but bunkered his second to the 18th and took 5.

The lowest individual score was 294 by Hsieh Min Nan of the Republic of China. It was the first example of the strength of players from that country.

1966 Australia won their second victory at the Club de Golf, Mexico in Mexico City. Having built a good lead on the first day, they eventually won by 2 strokes from the United States. There were only four rounds under 70: one by Kevin Hartley of Australia in the first round, one by Deane Beman in the final round for America and two by Ronnie Shade of Great Britain and Ireland whose total of 283 was the lowest of all.

1968 On the composite course of Royal Melbourne, the United States had a great battle with Great Britain and Ireland who began the last round with a 7-stroke lead. At one point in the final round, Britain led by 11 strokes, but the United States made up the deficit. On the final hole, Ronnie Shade missed from 6 ft and Dick Siderowf holed from a yard to give America a 1-stroke victory.

Michael Bonallack and Vinny Giles had the lowest individual totals, Bonallack's third-round 66 equalling the championship record previously held by Jack Nicklaus.

1970 At the Club de la Puerta de Hierro in Madrid, the United States successfully defended their title despite Tom Kite being ill on the last day and unable to play. By then, however, their victory was not in doubt. Over the four days, a 74 was their highest score; and on the first two days, the 73s of Vinny Giles did not count to the team total. They eventually won by 15 strokes from New Zealand.

Victor Regalado of Mexico had the best individual score—280.

1972 Third successive victory for the United States, but they did it the hard way at the Olivos Golf Club in Buenos Aires. They were 9 behind after the first round, 7 behind after the second round and 3 strokes back with 18 holes to play. A 68 in the last round by Ben Crenshaw led the way to a 5-stroke victory over Australia. Crenshaw had a third round of 69. Tony Gresham of Australia had the lowest individual total.

Spain finished fourth, Argentina fifth and Japan ninth.

1974 A late switch of venue from Royal Selangor in Kuala Lumpur to the Cajuiles Golf Club, La Romana in the Dominican Republic brought the fourth successive victory for the United States and their sixth in nine championships. A fine new but difficult course posed many problems and the winning score of 888 was the highest since 1964.

However, America led after every round and finished 10 strokes ahead of Japan with Brazil third. The best score of the week was 70.

1976 Second victory for Great Britain and Ireland who were never behind at Penina, Portugal. They led by 2 strokes after the third round, but it needed an outstanding round under enormous pressure by Ian Hutcheon to see them through. His 71 gave them 2 strokes to spare over Japan, second for the second time in a row, and Australia.

The United States finished fifth, their worst placing since the championship began in 1958.

1978 The United States, 9 strokes ahead after the first round and 11 ahead after the second round, had their victory won long before the final day in Fiji. They took a 17-stroke lead into the last round, winning eventually by 13 strokes from Canada. Bob Clampett had the lowest score of the entire championship (287) but Doug Roxburgh of Canada was only 2 strokes worse, he and Clampett having the only rounds under 70. Clampett's came on the first day, Roxburgh's on his last.

1980 A triumph at Pinehurst, North Carolina for the United States and particularly Hal Sutton, their reigning Amateur champion. They led throughout and won by 27 strokes to record their 8th victory. It was the second largest winning margin ever. Sutton recorded a four-round total of 276, only 7 strokes outside Jack Nicklaus's record.

Thirty-nine countries took part, beating the 38 countries which played in 1976. South Africa were second on 875, nine strokes better than the Republic of China.

1982 A third win in a row for the United States in Lausanne, their ninth in all. They led from start to finish, although they were hard pressed on the last afternoon and were indebted to 68 posted in the morning by Nathaniel Crosby. Sweden and Japan ran them close at one stage, eventually finishing 5 strokes adrift in joint second place.

1984 First victory by an oriental country in the oriental setting of Hong Kong. Japan ended a run of three victories by the United States, beating them into second place with a total of 870. The Philippines took third place, one ahead of Great Britain and Ireland.

1986 Canada won for the first time at Lagunita CC near Caracas in Venezuela. They defeated the United States by 3 strokes, 838–841 thanks largely to the play of Mark Brewer. He had scores of 70, 69, 69, 69, for a total of 277. However, the low individual was Eduardo Herrera of Colombia. China were third and Sweden fourth.

DETAILED RECORDS

Most victories
9, United States
2, Great Britain and Ireland
2, Australia
1, Japan, Canada

Lowest winning aggregate
834, United States, at Merion 1960

Highest winning score
918, Australia (after play-off with the United States) at St Andrews, 1958

Lowest individual round
66, Jack Nicklaus, 1960; Ronnie Shade and Deane Beman, 1962; Michael Bonallack, 1968

Lowest individual aggregate
269 (66, 67, 68, 68) Jack Nicklaus, Merion, 1960

Lowest individual first round
66, Jack Nicklaus, Merion, 1960

Lowest individual second round
66, Ronnie Shade (Great Britain and Ireland) Fuji GC, Kawana, Japan, 1962

Lowest individual third round
66, Michael Bonallack (Great Britain and Ireland) Royal Melbourne, 1968

Lowest individual fourth round
66, Deane Beman (United States) Merion, 1960; Juan Estrada (Mexico) Kawana, Japan, 1962

Largest lead, 18 holes
9 strokes, United States, Merion, 1960

Largest lead, 36 holes
20 strokes, United States, Merion, 1960

Largest lead, 54 holes
38 strokes, United States, Merion, 1960

Largest margin of victory
42 strokes, United States, Merion, 1960

Smallest margin of victory
Australia and the United States tied in 1958

Smallest lead, 18 holes
Great Britain and Ireland, and South Africa were tied at 219 in 1976

Smallest lead, 36 holes
Great Britain and Ireland, and South Africa were tied at 443 in 1976

Smallest lead, 54 holes
1 stroke, South Africa, 1966

Most teams to compete
39, Pinehurst, North Carolina, 1980; Lagunita, Venezuela, 1986

Most individual appearances
11, Alexis Godillot (France) 1964–66–68–70–72–74–76–80–82–84–86

Lowest individual score not counted by team
69, Deane Beman, Merion, first round, 1960

Lowest 9-hole score
31, William Hyndman III, Merion, 1960

Play-off
1958, Australia and the United States; Australia won 222 to 224

Oldest competitors
W J Gibb (Malaya) was 58 in 1958
I S Malik (India) was 57 in 1960

Fathers and sons
I S Malik and A S Malik both played for India in 1958 and 1960. In 1960, Visconde de Pereira Machado was in the same Portuguese team as his son, Nuno Alberto de Brito e Cunha

Brothers
In 1982, Neil and Derek James played for South Africa

RESULTS

1958 St Andrews, Scotland 8–11 and 13 October
Australia 918 (Doug Bachli, Peter Toogood, Bruce Devlin, Robert Stevens)
United States 918 (Charles Coe, Bill Hyndman, Billy Joe Patton, Frank Taylor)
Play-off Australia 222; United States 224
1960 Merion Golf Club, Ardmore, Pennsylvania 28 September–1 October
United States 834 (Deane Beman, Jack Nicklaus, Bill Hyndman, Robert Gardner)
1962 Fuji GC, Kawana, Japan 10–13 October
United States 854 (Deane Beman, Labron Harris, Billy Joe Patton, Richard Sikes)
1964 Olgiata Golf Club, Rome 7–10 October
Great Britain and Ireland 895 (Michael Bonallack, Rodney Foster, Michael Lunt, Ronnie Shade)
1966 Mexico Golf Club, Mexico City 27–30 October
Australia 877 (Harry Berwick, Philip Billings, Kevin Donohoe, Kevin Hartley)
1968 Royal Melbourne Golf Club, Australia 9–12 October
United States 868 (Bruce Fleisher, Vinny Giles, Jack Lewis, Dick Siderowf)
1970 Real Club de la Puerta de Hierro, Madrid 23–26 September
United States 854 (Vinny Giles, Tom Kite, Allen Miller, Lanny Wadkins)
1972 Olivos Golf Club, Buenos Aires 18–21 October
United States 865 (Ben Crenshaw, Vinny Giles, Mark Hayes, Marty West)
1974 Campo de Golf Cajuiles, Dominica 30 October–2 November
United States 888 (George Burns, Gary Koch, Jerry Pate, Curtis Strange)
1976 Penina Golf Club, Algarve, Portugal 13–16 October
Great Britain and Ireland 892 (John Davies, Ian Hutcheon, Michael Kelley, Steve Martin)
1978 Pacific Harbour, Fiji 18–21 October
United States 873 (Bob Clampett, John Cook, Scott Hoch, Jay Sigel)
1980 Pinehurst No 2, North Carolina 8–11 October
United States 848 (Jim Holtgrieve, Jay Sigel, Hal Sutton, Robert Tway)
1982 Lausanne, Switzerland 15–18 September
United States 859 (Nathaniel Crosby, Jim Holtgrieve, Bob Lewis, Jay Sigel)

1984 Royal Hong Kong 7–10 November
Japan 870 (Kazuhiko Kato, Noriaki Kimura, Kiyotako Oie, Tetsuo Sekato)
1986 Lagunita, Venezuela 22–25 October
Canada 838 (Mark Brewer, Brent Franklin, Jack Kay, Warren Sye)

Home Internationals

This is the series, started in 1932, in which England, Scotland, Ireland and Wales meet to play each other every year. They now compete for the Raymond Trophy, donated by Raymond Oppenheimer.

The first official international was that between England and Scotland in 1903 when only singles were played. This form continued until 1912, when five foursomes were introduced at Westward Ho! The first recorded match between Wales and Ireland was played in 1913.

England and Scotland continued their match, organized by the Royal and Ancient GC until 1932, when the international week began. It now comes under the auspices of the Council of National Golf Unions. Between 1922 and 1932, Ireland also played matches with Wales, England and Scotland.

Each match in the Home Internationals comprises five foursomes and ten singles. The records that follow deal only with the series since 1932 although they should be interpreted in the knowledge that all four countries play other countries as well, including the European Team championship. As with Test cricket or international rugby, there are far more matches played now than in pre-war and early post-war days.

MATCH RESULTS

1932—Troon
Scotland bt England	8–7
Scotland bt Ireland	11½–4½
Scotland bt Wales	9–6
England bt Ireland	12–3
England bt Wales	11½–3½
Ireland bt Wales	9½–5½

1933—Newcastle Co. Down
Scotland bt England	9½–5½
Scotland bt Ireland	9–6
Scotland bt Wales	11–4
England bt Ireland	9½–5½
England bt Wales	9–6
Ireland bt Wales	11–4

1934—Porthcawl
Scotland bt England	10–5
Scotland bt Ireland	10½–4½
Scotland bt Wales	9½–5½
Ireland bt Wales	10–5
Ireland bt England	12–3
England bt Wales	10–5

1935—Lytham St Annes
Scotland bt Wales	10½–4½
Scotland bt England	12½–2½
England bt Ireland	8½–6½
England bt Wales	10½–4½
Ireland bt Scotland	9–6
Ireland bt Wales	10½–4½

1936—Prestwick
Scotland bt Wales	9½–5½
Scotland bt Ireland	8–7
Scotland bt England	8–7
England bt Ireland	13–2
England bt Wales	12–3
Ireland bt Wales	11–4

1937—Portmarnock
Scotland bt Ireland	9½–5½
Scotland bt England	9–6
Scotland ½ with Wales	7½ each
England bt Ireland	8–7
England bt Wales	8½–6½
Ireland bt Wales	9–6

1938—Porthcawl
England bt Ireland	10–5
England bt Wales	10½–4½
England bt Scotland	8½–6½
Scotland bt Wales	8½–6½
Scotland bt Ireland	9½–5½
Ireland bt Wales	9–6

1947—Hoylake
England bt Wales	14–1
England bt Ireland	9–6
England bt Scotland	8–7
Scotland bt Ireland	10–5
Scotland bt Wales	11–4
Ireland bt Wales	12–3

1948—Muirfield
England bt Scotland	10½–4½
England bt Wales	8½–6½
England bt Ireland	8–7
Ireland bt Scotland	10½–4½
Ireland bt Wales	12½–2½
Scotland bt Wales	11–4

1949—Portmarnock
England bt Ireland	8–7
England bt Wales	10–5
England bt Scotland	10–5
Ireland bt Wales	10½–4½
Ireland bt Scotland	10½–4½
Wales bt Scotland	8½–6½

1950—Harlech
Ireland bt Wales	10–5
Ireland ½ with Scotland	7½ each
Ireland bt England	8½–6½
Scotland bt England	9–6
Scotland ½ with Wales	7½ each
England bt Wales	10–5

1951—Lytham St Annes
Ireland bt Scotland	8½–6½
Ireland bt England	8–7
Scotland bt Wales	8–7
Scotland bt England	8–7
Wales bt Ireland	9½–5½
England bt Wales	10–5

1952—Troon
(for Raymond Trophy presented 1952)
Scotland bt Wales	10–5
Scotland bt England	9–6
Scotland bt Ireland	9½–5½
England bt Wales	9–6
Ireland ½ with England	7½ each
Ireland ½ with Wales	7½ each

1953—Killarney
Scotland bt Wales	10–5
Scotland bt England	8½–6½
Scotland ½ with Ireland	7½ each
Ireland bt England	9–6
England bt Wales	9–6
Wales bt Ireland	8½–6½

1954—Porthcawl
England bt Wales	12–3
England bt Scotland	9–6
England bt Ireland	8½–6½
Ireland bt Scotland	9–6
Scotland bt Wales	9–6
Wales bt Ireland	8–7

1955—Birkdale
Ireland bt Scotland	9–6
Ireland bt Wales	9–6
Ireland ½ with England	7½ each
Scotland bt Wales	8–7
Scotland bt England	8–7
England bt Wales	9½–5½

1956—Muirfield
Scotland bt Wales	10½–4½
Scotland bt Ireland	8–7
Scotland bt England	9½–5½
England bt Ireland	11–4
England bt Wales	10½–4½
Wales bt Ireland	9–6

1957—Newcastle, Co. Down
England bt Scotland	12–3
England bt Wales	9–6
England bt Ireland	10½–4½
Scotland bt Ireland	13–2
Scotland bt Wales	10–5

Wales bt Ireland — 8½–6½

1958—Porthcawl
England bt Ireland — 9–6
England bt Wales — 11½–3½
England bt Scotland — 8–7
Scotland bt Ireland — 8½–6½
Scotland bt Wales — 10½–4½
Wales bt Ireland — 8–7

1959—Lytham St Annes
England bt Scotland — 10–5
Ireland bt Wales — 8–7
Scotland bt Wales — 10–5
Ireland bt England — 8½–6½
Scotland bt Ireland — 8½–6½
England bt Wales — 11½–3½

1960—Turnberry
Scotland ½ with England — 7½ each
Scotland bt Wales — 9–6
England bt Ireland — 8–7
England bt Wales — 11½–3½
Ireland bt Wales — 12–3
Ireland bt Scotland — 8–7

1961—Portmarnock
Scotland bt England — 12½–2½
Scotland bt Ireland — 11½–3½
Scotland bt Wales — 8–7
Ireland bt Wales — 11–4
Ireland bt England — 8–7
Wales bt England — 12–3

1962—Porthcawl
Scotland bt England — 9–6
Scotland bt Wales — 9–6
England bt Ireland — 8½–6½
England bt Wales — 11½–3½
Ireland bt Scotland — 8–7
Ireland bt Wales — 10½–4½

1963—Lytham St Annes
Scotland bt England — 10½–4½
Scotland bt Wales — 10½–4½
England bt Ireland — 8½–6½
England bt Wales — 9–6
Ireland bt Scotland — 10–5
Ireland bt Wales — 11–4

1964—Carnoustie
England bt Wales — 12½–2½
England bt Ireland — 8½–6½
England bt Scotland — 8–7
Ireland bt Scotland — 8–7
Ireland bt Wales — 10–5
Scotland bt Wales — 12½–2½

1965—Portrush
England bt Wales — 8–7
England bt Scotland — 11½–3½
England bt Ireland — 8½–6½
Ireland bt Wales — 10½–4½
Ireland bt Scotland — 9½–5½
Scotland bt Wales — 9–6

1966—Porthcawl
England bt Scotland — 8–7
England bt Ireland — 12½–2½
England bt Wales — 8–7
Ireland bt Scotland — 10½–4½
Ireland bt Wales — 9–6
Scotland bt Wales — 8–7

1967—Ganton
Scotland bt England — 8–7

Scotland bt Ireland — 8½–6½
Scotland bt Wales — 8–7
England bt Ireland — 10½–4½
England bt Wales — 10½–4½
Ireland bt Wales — 8½–6½

1968—Gullane
England bt Scotland — 9½–5½
England bt Ireland — 12–3
England bt Wales — 11–4
Scotland bt Ireland — 8–7
Scotland bt Wales — 9–6
Ireland bt Wales — 9–6

1969—Killarney
England bt Scotland — 10½–4½
England ½ with Ireland — 7½ each
England bt Wales — 11–4
Scotland bt Ireland — 9½–5½
Wales bt Scotland — 8–7
Ireland bt Wales — 8–7

1970—Porthcawl
Scotland bt Ireland — 10–5
Scotland bt Wales — 10–5
Scotland bt England — 10–5
Ireland bt Wales — 8–7
Ireland ½ with England — 7½ each
Wales bt England — 8½–6½

1971—Formby
Scotland bt England — 8–7
Scotland bt Ireland — 8½–6½
Scotland bt Wales — 12–3
England bt Ireland — 12–3
England bt Wales — 8½–6½
Ireland bt Wales — 9½–5½

1972—Troon
Scotland ½ with England — 7½ each
Scotland bt Ireland — 8½–6½
Scotland bt Wales — 10½–4½
England bt Ireland — 8–7
England bt Wales — 10½–4½
Ireland bt Wales — 12–3

1973—Lytham St Annes
England bt Scotland — 9–6
England bt Ireland — 10½–4½
England bt Wales — 9½–5½
Scotland bt Ireland — 9½–5½
Scotland ½ with Wales — 7½ each
Ireland bt Wales — 10½–4½

1974—Harlech
England bt Scotland — 10½–4½
England bt Ireland — 11–4
England ½ with Wales — 7½ each
Scotland bt Ireland — 9–6
Scotland bt Wales — 9–6
Ireland bt Wales — 8–7

1975—Portmarnock
Scotland bt England — 9½–5½
Scotland bt Ireland — 10½–4½
Scotland bt Wales — 13–2
England bt Ireland — 10½–4½
England bt Wales — 11–4
Ireland bt Wales — 9–6

1976—Muirfield
Scotland bt England — 10–5
Scotland bt Ireland — 10–5
Scotland bt Wales — 9–6

England bt Ireland — 10½–4½
England bt Wales — 10–5
Ireland bt Wales — 8–7

1977—Hillside
England bt Scotland — 8–7
England bt Wales — 9–6
England bt Ireland — 8½–6½
Scotland bt Wales — 10–5
Scotland bt Ireland — 11½–3½
Wales bt Ireland — 9–6

1978—Ashburnham
England bt Wales — 8½–6½
England bt Scotland — 9–6
England bt Ireland — 8½–6½
Wales bt Scotland — 8–7
Scotland bt Ireland — 9–6
Ireland bt Wales — 8–7

1979—Cancelled
In place of the Home International Matches
Scotland bt England — 17–13 at Troon and
Wales bt Ireland — 17–15 at Porthcawl

1980—Dornoch
England ½ with Ireland — 7½ each
England bt Wales — 10–5
England bt Scotland — 11–4
Ireland ½ with Wales — 7½ each
Ireland bt Scotland — 9–6
Wales ½ with Scotland — 7½ each

1981—Woodhall Spa
Scotland bt Ireland — 9–6
Scotland bt England — 11½–3½
Scotland bt Wales — 9½–5½
Ireland bt England — 8–7
Ireland bt Wales — 10½–4½
Wales ½ with England — 7½ each

1982—Porthcawl
Scotland bt England — 8–7
Scotland bt Wales — 9½–5½
England bt Ireland — 8½–6½
England bt Wales — 8–7
Ireland bt Scotland — 8–7
Ireland ½ with Wales — 7½ each

1983—Portmarnock
Ireland bt Scotland — 9½–5½
Ireland ½ with England — 7½ each
Ireland bt Wales — 10–5
Scotland bt England — 8½–6½
Scotland bt Wales — 8–7
England bt Wales — 9–6

1984—Troon
Ireland ½ with Wales — 7½ each
England bt Scotland — 8–7
Scotland bt Ireland — 10–5
England bt Wales — 12½–2½
Scotland bt Wales — 7–3
Ireland bt England — 6–4
(Foursomes of third series of matches cancelled due to torrential rain)

1985—Formby
England bt Wales — 11–4
England bt Scotland — 8–7
England bt Ireland — 8½–6½
Wales bt Scotland — 8–7
Wales bt Ireland — 9½–5½
Ireland bt Scotland — 11½–3½

1986—Harlech

Scotland bt England	9½–5½
Scotland bt Ireland	10½–4½
Scotland bt Wales	10–5
Ireland ½ with Wales	7½ each
England bt Wales	9–6
Ireland bt England	8–7

Total England 20 wins, Scotland 17, Ireland 3, 6 ties.

INDIVIDUAL RECORDS

Players winning six matches in a single year.
England: 1932, R Straker. 1936, F Francis. 1959, A E Shepperson. 1967, P A Oosterhuis. 1973, T W B Homer. 1982, S D Keppler. 1985 P M McEvoy
Ireland: 1948, J B Carr. 1950, S M McCready. 1959, J F D Madeley. 1962, W A Kelleher. 1981, A D Pierse
Scotland: 1935, J McLean. 1952, J R Cater. 1956, A F Bussell. 1964, C W Green. 1970, C W Green. 1981, C R Dalgleish. 1981, I A Carslaw
Wales: 1952, J L Morgan. 1956, Colonel A A Duncan

Most appearances

England	*Played*	*Won*	*Lost*	*Halved*	*Percentage*
M F Bonallack (57–74)	131	79	37	15	66.03
P McEvoy (76–86)	100	72	20	8	76.00
D M Marsh (56–72)	75	40	28	7	58.00
R Foster (63–73)	86	53	25	8	66.27
L G Crawley (31–55)	71	43	22	6	64.78
P Deeble (75–85)	67	33	24	10	56.71
A Thirlwell (51–64)	70	41	22	7	63.57

Ireland	*Played*	*Won*	*Lost*	*Halved*	*Percentage*
J B Carr (47–68)	157	92	53	12	62.42
C Ewing (34–58)	92	44	39	9	52.71
T Craddock (55–71)	91	46	39	6	53.84
A D Pierse (76–86)	90	39	39	12	50.00
G McGimpsey (78–86)	76	43	26	7	61.18
J Burke (32–49)	74	34	26	14	55.40

Scotland	*Played*	*Won*	*Lost*	*Halved*	*Percentage*
C W Green (61–79)	118	77	28	13	70.76
G Macgregor (69–86)	118	61	42	15	58.05
I C Hutcheon (71–80)	75	45	24	6	64.00
A K Pine (66–75)	64	35	20	9	61.71
Allan Brodie (70–80)	63	29	26	8	52.38
R D B M Shade (57–68)	62	40	17	5	68.54
R R Jack (50–61)	60	29	24	7	54.16

Wales (Home International results only)

	Played	*Won*	*Lost*	*Halved*	*Percentage*
W I Tucker (49–75)	147	53	71	23	44.00
H C Squirrell (55–75)	117	42	65	10	40.00
J K D Povall (60–77)	106	44	54	8	45.00
Col A A Duncan (33–59)	100	37	46	17	45.50
D McLean (68–86)	100	29	61	10	34.00
J L Morgan (48–64)	95	39	51	5	43.50
A D Evans (31–61)	92	28	48	17	40.00
E N Davies (59–74)	92	36	47	9	44.00

Getting the priorities right. (Arthur Guinness Son & Company (Park Royal) Limited)

Women's Golf

Ladies' British Open Amateur Championship

DETAILED RECORDS

Most victories
4, Cecil Leitch, 1914–20–21–26. She won one victory in each of the four home countries; Joyce Wethered (later Lady Heathcoat-Amory), 1922–24–25–29
3, Lady Margaret Scott, 1893–94–95; May Hezlet, 1899–1902–07; Enid Wilson, 1931–32–33; Jessie Valentine (née Anderson), 1937–55–58

Oldest winner
Belle Robertson, 45 years 1 month 26 days, 1981
Jessie Valentine, 43 years 3 months, 1958
Anne Sander, 42 years 9 months, 1980

Youngest winner
May Hezlet, 17 years 1 week, 1899
Marnie McGuire, 17 years 3 months 23 days, 1986
Michelle Walker, 18 years 6 months 9 days, 1971

Biggest margin of victory in final
36 holes: **9 and 7**, Joyce Wethered beat Cecil Leitch, Prince's, 1922
18 holes: Pre 1913: **7 and 5**, Miss L Thomson beat Miss G C Neville, Yarmouth, 1898
Post 1964: **6 and 5**, Angela Uzielli beat Vanessa Marvin, Hillside, 1977

Longest final
39 holes, Moira Paterson beat Frances Stephens, Troon, 1952

Most finals
6, Cecil Leitch, 1914–20–21–22–25–26

Most times runner-up
3, Philomena Garvey (1946–53–60), Belle Robertson (née McCorkindale) 1959–65–70

Biggest span between first and last finals
22 years, Belle Robertson, 1959–81

Shortest 18-hole match
Ruth Porter beat Mrs A McCoy 10 and 8, first round, Royal Portrush, 1963

Longest 18-hole match
26 holes, Miss C Gerber (South Africa) beat Julia Greenhalgh, St Andrews, 1975

Consecutive winners
3, Lady Margaret Scott, 1893–94–95; Cecil Leitch, 1914–20–21; no championship 1915–19; Enid Wilson, 1931–32–33
2, Joyce Wethered, 1924–25; Marley Spearman, 1961–62; Elizabeth Chadwick, 1966–67; Michelle Walker, 1971–72

Longest span between victories
21 years, Jessie Valentine, 1937–58

Family records
In 1907, May Hezlet beat her sister, Florence Hezlet in the final. In 1897, Edith Orr beat her sister

First overseas winner
Mlle Thion de la Chaume (France), 1927

First American winner
Mildred 'Babe' Zaharias, 1947; Glenna Collett reached the finals of 1929 and 1930

Repeat finals
1893–94, Lady Margaret Scott beat Isette Pearson

1922 and 1925, Joyce Wethered beat Cecil Leitch; in 1921, Cecil Leitch beat Joyce Wethered

Club hosting most championships
7 each, Royal County Down (Northern Ireland) Newcastle, and Royal Portrush (Northern Ireland)

Winners of British and American championships
Dorothy Campbell, Gladys Ravenscroft, Pam Barton, 'Babe' Zaharias, Louise Suggs, Marlene Stewart, Barbara McIntire, Catherine Lacoste, Carol Semple, Anne Sander

Winners the same year
Dorothy Campbell, 1909; Pam Barton, 1936; Catherine Lacoste, 1969

First winner of the championship, Lady Margaret Scott, 1893. (Illustrated London News)

Captain Adair Presenting the Gold Medal to Lady Margaret Scott.

Fore.

Lady Scott Driving from first Tee.

Lady Scott.

The Himalayas. The finish of the Championship

Sketches of the 1895 championship. (Illustrated London News)

RESULTS

Year	*Winner*	*Runner-up*	*Venue*	*By*
1893	Lady Margaret Scott	Isette Pearson	St Annes	7 and 5
1894	Lady Margaret Scott	Isette Pearson	Littlestone	3 and 2
1895	Lady Margaret Scott	Miss E Lythgoe	Portrush	3 and 2
1896	Amy Pascoe	Miss L Thomson	Hoylake	3 and 2
1897	Edith C Orr	Miss Orr	Gullane	4 and 2
1898	Miss L Thomson	Miss E C Neville	Yarmouth	7 and 5
1899	May Hezlet	Miss Magill	Newcastle, Co Down	2 and 1
1900	Rhona Adair	Miss E C Neville	Westward Ho!	6 and 5
1901	Miss Graham	Rhona Adair	Aberdovey	3 and 1
1902	May Hezlet	Miss E C Neville	Deal	19th hole
1903	Rhona Adair	Miss F Walker-Leigh	Portrush	4 and 3
1904	Lottie Dod	May Hezlet	Troon	1 hole
1905	Miss B Thompson	Miss M E Stuart	Cromer	3 and 2
1906	Mrs Kennion	Miss B Thompson	Burnham	4 and 3
1907	May Hezlet	Florence Hezlet	Newcastle, Co Down	2 and 1
1908	Miss M Titterton	Dorothy Campbell	St Andrews	19th hole
1909	Dorothy Campbell	Florence Hezlet	Birkdale	4 and 3
1910	Miss Grant Suttie	Miss L Moore	Westward Ho!	6 and 4
1911	Dorothy Campbell	Violet Hezlet	Portrush	3 and 2
1912	Gladys Ravenscroft	Miss S Temple	Turnberry	3 and 2
1913	Muriel Dodd	Miss Chubb	St Annes	8 and 6
1914	Cecil Leitch	Gladys Ravenscroft	Hunstanton	2 and 1
1915–18	No Championship owing to World War I			
1919	Should have been played at Burnham in October, but abandoned owing to Railway Strike			
1920	Cecil Leitch	Molly Griffiths	Newcastle, Co Down	7 and 6
1921	Cecil Leitch	Joyce Wethered	Turnberry	4 and 3
1922	Joyce Wethered	Cecil Leitch	Prince's, Sandwich	9 and 7
1923	Doris Chambers	Miss A Macbeth	Burnham, Somerset	2 holes
1924	Joyce Wethered	Mrs Cautley	Portrush	7 and 6
1925	Joyce Wethered	Cecil Leitch	Troon	37th hole
1926	Cecil Leitch	Mrs Garon	Harlech	8 and 7
1927	Miss Thion de la Chaume (France)	Miss Pearson	Newcastle, Co Down	5 and 4
1928	Nanette Le Blan (France)	Miss S Marshall	Hunstanton	3 and 2
1929	Joyce Wethered	Glenna Collett (USA)	St Andrews	3 and 1
1930	Diana Fishwick	Glenna Collett (USA)	Formby	4 and 3
1931	Enid Wilson	Wanda Morgan	Portmarnock	7 and 6
1932	Enid Wilson	Miss C P R Montgomery	Saunton	7 and 6
1933	Enid Wilson	Miss D Plumpton	Gleneagles	5 and 4
1934	Helen Holm	Pam Barton	Royal Porthcawl	6 and 5
1935	Wanda Morgan	Pam Barton	Newcastle, Co Down	3 and 2
1936	Pam Barton	Miss B Newell	Southport and Ainsdale	5 and 3
1937	Jessie Anderson	Doris Park	Turnberry	6 and 4
1938	Helen Holm	Elsie Corlett	Burnham	4 and 3
1939	Pam Barton	Mrs T Marks	Portrush	2 and 1
1940–45	No Championship owing to World War II			
1946	Jean Hetherington	Philomena Garvey	Hunstanton	1 hole
1947	Babe Zaharias (USA)	Jacqueline Gordon	Gullane	5 and 4
1948	Louise Suggs (USA)	Jean Donald	Royal Lytham	1 hole
1949	Frances Stephens	Val Reddan	Harlech	5 and 4
1950	Vicomtesse de Saint Sauveur (France)	Jessie Valentine	Newcastle, Co Down	3 and 2
1951	Mrs P G MacCann	Frances Stephens	Broadstone	4 and 3
1952	Moira Paterson	Frances Stephens	Troon	39th hole
1953	Marlene Stewart	Philomena Garvey	Porthcawl	7 and 6
1954	Frances Stephens	Elizabeth Price	Ganton	4 and 3
1955	Jessie Valentine	Barbara Romack (USA)	Portrush	7 and 6
1956	Margaret Smith	Mary P Janssen	Sunningdale	8 and 7
1957	Philomena Garvey	Jessie Valentine	Gleneagles	4 and 3
1958	Jessie Valentine	Elizabeth Price	Hunstanton	1 hole
1959	Elizabeth Price	Belle McCorkindale	Ascot	37th hole
1960	Barbara McIntire (USA)	Philomena Garvey	Harlech	4 and 2
1961	Marley Spearman	Diane Robb	Carnoustie	7 and 6
1962	Marley Spearman	Angela Bonallack	Royal Birkdale	1 hole
1963	Brigitte Varangot (France)	Philomena Garvey	Newcastle, Co Down	3 and 1
1964	Carol Sorenson (USA)	Bridget Jackson	Prince's, Sandwich	37th hole
1965	Brigitte Varangot (France)	Belle Robertson	St Andrews	4 and 3
1966	Elizabeth Chadwick	Vivien Saunders	Ganton	3 and 2

1967	Elizabeth Chadwick	Mary Everard	Harlech	1 hole
1968	Brigitte Varangot (France)	Claudine Rubin (France)	Walton Heath	20th hole
1969	Catherine Lacoste (France)	Ann Irvin	Portrush	1 hole
1970	Dinah Oxley	Belle Robertson	Gullane	1 hole
1971	Michelle Walker	Beverley Huke	Alwoodley	3 and 1
1972	Michelle Walker	Claudine Rubin (France)	Hunstanton	2 holes
1973	Ann Irvin	Michelle Walker	Carnoustie	3 and 2
1974	Carol Semple (USA)	Angela Bonallack	Royal Porthcawl	2 and 1
1975	Nancy Syms (USA)	Suzanne Cadden	St Andrews	3 and 2
1976	Cathy Panton	Alison Sheard (S Africa)	Silloth	1 hole
1977	Angela Uzielli	Vanessa Marvin	Hillside	6 and 5
1978	Edwina Kennedy (Australia)	Julia Greenhalgh	Notts	1 hole
1979	Maureen Madill	Jane Lock (Australia)	Nairn	2 and 1
1980	Anne Sander (USA)	Liv Wollin (Sweden)	Woodhall Spa	3 and 1
1981	Belle Robertson	Wilma Aitken	Caernarvonshire	20th hole
1982	Kitrina Douglas	Gillian Stewart	Walton Heath	4 and 2
1983	Jill Thornhill	Regine Lautens (Swi)	Silloth	4 and 2
1984	Jody Rosenthal (USA)	Julie Brown	Royal Troon	4 and 3
1985	Lilian Behan	Claire Waite	Ganton	1 hole
1986	Marnie McGuire (NZ)	Louise Briers (Aus)	West Sussex	2 and 1
1987	Janet Collingham	Susan Shapcott	Harlech	19th hole

From 1893 to 1912, the final was played over 18 holes. From 1913 to 1964, the final was played over 36 holes. In 1965, the final should have been played over 36 holes but bad weather earlier in the week caused it to be 18 holes and in 1966 it reverted to 18 holes on a permanent basis.

Henry Cotton with his hands full playing against four redoubtable champions: Enid Wilson, Joyce Wethered (Lady Heathcoat-Amory), Madame Lacoste and Pam Barton; Maylands, Essex 1938. (BBC Hulton Picture Library)

Glenna Collett Vare

In an age when successful women golfers are lured by the professional circuit, Glenna Collett's six victories in the US Women's Amateur championship are no more likely to be matched than Bobby Jones's Grand Slam.

Throughout the 1920s and early 30s, she was the outstanding player in America although Virginia van Wie won three times in succession and Glenna was twice runner-up, once to van Wie. However, Glenna Vare, as she had then become, won again in 1935, beating Patty Berg in the final.

As well as capturing the imagination of galleries by her skill, she was popular away from the course but her attempts to win the British were twice thwarted by Joyce Wethered, once in an epic final, and then by Diana Fishwick in the final of 1930.

Joanne Gunderson Carner

An amateur who stood comparison with Glenna Collett Vare and Babe Zaharias, JoAnne Carner then embarked upon a wonderfully successful professional career which shows no sign of waning.

She turned professional in 1970 after winning the US Women's Amateur five times and, within a year, had added the US Women's Open. She won again in 1976 but her best year was 1974 and though her game is based on an obvious inclination to attack, she has retained a remarkable consistency.

Joyce Wethered (Lady Heathcoat-Amory)

Thought by Bobby Jones to be the best golfer, man or woman, he had seen—a view nobody could possibly contradict. Certainly, she and Jones were the best players of their generation—perhaps of all time.

They had other things in common, too. They combined style, ease and elegance in their play and managed, while concentrating fiercely, to act as the most gracious and courteous opponents. However, it was their achievements which stood them apart.

Joyce Wethered won the Ladies' British Open Amateur championship four times and was runner-up on another occasion; she dominated the English championship, winning it five times in a row, and won the Worplesdon mixed foursomes which, in those days, attracted the best amateurs, eight times with seven different partners.

Yet, having achieved supremacy, she withdrew from the competitive scene for three years but returned to win the 1929 British final against Glenna Collett who had been 5 up after 11 holes.

Glenna Collett was the leading American woman golfer of that era and the match was inevitably seen as a comparison of strength but the other quality Joyce Wethered had in common with Jones was an innate modesty and, as a result, an unawareness of just how good she was.

Though most pictures show her on her toes at impact, she had perfect balance and once told Leonard Crawley: 'On the rare occasions that I am playing my best, I feel nobody could push me off my right heel at the top of the swing and, at the other end, I feel nobody could push me off my left foot.' You cannot define balance better than that.

Lady Margaret Scott

The first lady champion and an outstanding one in her own right. She won the first three British championships (1893–95) and only once, the semi-final of 1895, was she ever in danger of defeat. She came from a great golfing family, her three brothers, Michael, Osmund and Denys, were all fine players but she gave up the game after her third win. She became Lady Margaret Hamilton-Russell on her marriage.

Cecilia Leitch

Cecil Leitch, one of five daughters of a Cumberland doctor, was a multiple champion of Britain, England, France and Canada but it was her rivalry with Joyce Wethered, ten years her junior, which made women's golf front page news for the first time.

Altogether, she won four British and two English titles. In the four finals she played against Joyce Wethered, Cecil Leitch won only one, the British of 1921, but their match at Troon in 1925 was one of the best and most famous in women's history which lasted 37 holes.

Enid Wilson

Apart from Joyce Wethered, Enid Wilson was regarded as the best British player to grow up between the two wars. She won three successive victories in the British championship (1931–33) and two, by commanding margins, in the English.

She played in the first Curtis Cup match in 1932 but, after an early retirement, became well known as a writer and respected authority on the game.

Pam Barton

Pam Barton's career, tragically ended by her death in a plane crash in 1943, was short but highly distinguished. At the age of 19, she won the British and American championships within the space of a few weeks in the summer of 1936, the first player to do so since Dorothy Campbell in 1909. She won the British again in 1939 and seemed destined for many more successes.

May Hezlet

May Hezlet, the youngest winner of both Irish and British women's championships, belonged to a remarkable golfing family. May, Florence and Violet played in the first three of the singles order for Ireland and their brother, Charles, played in three Walker Cup matches. However, May was the outstanding champion although in four finals, three Irish and one British, May was opposed by Florence. Her first victory in the Irish came a few days before her 17th birthday and her first in the British a few days after.

Jessie Valentine

The last three-time winner of the Ladies' British Open championship, Jessie Valentine won her first title in 1937, the year after she had holed a fine putt on the last green to win her Curtis Cup single and halve the entire contest.

In a notable post-war era which included Frances Smith, Jean Donald, Elizabeth Price, Jeanne Bisgood and Philomena Garvey, Jessie Valentine confirmed her competitive qualities by winning the British twice more and the Scottish championship a total of six times. Noted for control rather than power, she became the first woman to be recognized for her services to the game, receiving the MBE in 1959.

Catherine Lacoste

Catherine Lacoste, the finest woman golfer from the continent of Europe, holds a special place in the history of the game. She is the only amateur to have won the US Women's Open and belongs to the distinguished handful of players who have won the British and American Amateur championships.

She inherited her sporting talents from her parents. Few women have matched her power, particularly with a 1 iron, and there is no doubt that she could have made a highly successful professional. Her victory in the US Women's Open was an acute embarrassment to the American professionals but it was an achievement matched by her winning the Amateur titles of Britain and America in the same summer of 1969; she is the last player to have done this.

Anne Quast
(later Decker, later Welts, later Sander)

One of the American amateurs who resisted the temptation to turn professional, Anne Sander was an outstanding champion whose reign was spread over four decades. She won the first of three American titles in 1958 and surprised and delighted everyone by winning the British in 1980 when she had virtually given up hope of so doing.

She reached the quarter-finals of the American in 1955 as a girl of 17 but her greatest performance was winning the national title in 1961. She was 9 under par for the week at Tacoma, lost only 6 holes and set a record winning margin in the final by defeating Phyllis Preuss by 14 and 13.

US Women's Amateur Championship

DETAILED RECORDS

Most victories
6, Glenna Collett Vare, 1922–25–28–29–30–35
5, JoAnne Gunderson Carner, 1957–60–62–66–68
3, Beatrix Hoyt; Margaret Curtis; Dorothy Campbell Hurd; Alexa Stirling; Virginia van Wie; Anne Quast (later Decker, later Welts, later Sander)

Oldest winner
Dorothy Campbell Hurd, 41 years 4 months, 1924

Youngest winner
Laura Baugh, 16 years 2 months 21 days, 1971
Beatrix Hoyt, 16 years 3 months 4 days, 1896
Peggy Conley reached the 1963 final at 16 years 2 months 2 weeks, and Roberta Albers reached the semi-final in 1961 aged 14 years 8 months

Biggest margin of victory in final
14 and 13, Anne Quast beat Phyllis Preuss at Tacoma in 1961. Anne Quast was 12 up at lunch—also a record

Longest final
41 holes, JoAnne Gunderson Carner beat Marlene Stewart Streit in 1966 at Sewickley Heights, Pennsylvania. This was the longest final in any USGA competition.
In 1954, the second 18 holes of the final was halted by storms and played on Sunday. It thus took 29 hours 15 minutes to complete

Most times in the final
8, Glenna Collett Vare

Most times runner-up
3, Mrs William A Gavin, 1915–19–22; Alexa Stirling, 1921–23–25; Anne Quast, 1965–68–73

Longest 18-hole match
27 holes, Mae Murray beat Fay Crocker in the fourth round at East Lake, Atlanta in 1950
27 holes, Denise Hermida (USA) beat Carole Caldwell (GB) in the first round at Plymouth Meeting, Pennsylvania in 1978

Consecutive winners
3, Beatrix Hoyt, 1896–97–98; Alexa Stirling, 1916–19–20 (no championship in 1917–18); Glenna Collett Vare, 1928–29–30; Virginia van Wie, 1932–33–34; Juli Simpson Inkster, 1980–81–82
2, Genevieve Hecker, 1901–02; Dorothy Campbell, 1909–10; Margaret Curtis, 1911–12; Betty Jameson, 1939–40

Family records
In 1907, the final was contested by the sisters Margaret Curtis and Harriot Curtis. Margaret won 7 and 6, succeeding Harriot as champion. In 1962, Jean Trainor defeated her daughter Anne Trainor by 4 and 3 in the fourth round

First to win American and British championships
Dorothy Campbell (later Dorothy Hurd), 1909

First American to win American and British championships
Mildred 'Babe' Didrikson Zaharias, 1946 and 1947

Overseas winners
Dorothy Campbell; Gladys Ravenscroft; Pam Barton; Marlene Stewart; Catherine Lacoste

Winner of British and American championships the same year
Catherine Lacoste, 1969; Pam Barton, 1936; Dorothy Campbell, 1909

Longest span between victories
15 years, Dorothy Campbell, 1909–24

Club hosting most championships
4 times, Merion, Pennsylvania

Winners of British and American championships
'Babe' Zaharias; Gladys Ravenscroft; Pam Barton; Louise Suggs; Dorothy Campbell; Barbara McIntire; Marlene Stewart; Catherine Lacoste; Carol Semple; Anne Sander

Winners of British, American and Canadian championships
Marlene Stewart and Dorothy Campbell Hurd

Repeat finals
1928 and 1930, Glenna Collett Vare beat Virginia van Wie

Largest entry
329, in 1985

Foreign-born champions
Dorothy Campbell 1909–10–24; Gladys Ravenscroft (England) 1913; Pam Barton (England) 1936; Marlene Stewart (Canada) 1956; Catherine Lacoste (France) 1969; Cathy Sherk (Canada) 1978; Michiko Hattori (Japan) 1985

Sisters in final
Margaret Curtis beat her sister, Harriot Curtis, 7 and 6 in 1907. They were the donors of the Curtis Cup

Glenna Collett Vare and Joyce Wethered (Lady Heathcoat-Amory) playing in the Ladies British Open Amateur championship final at St Andrews, 1929. (BBC Hulton Picture Library)

RESULTS

Year	Winner	Runner-up	Venue	Score
1895	Mrs C S Brown	Miss N C Sargeant	Meadow Brook	132
Matchplay				*By*
1896	Beatrix Hoyt	Mrs Arthur Turnure	Morris County	2 and 1
1897	Beatrix Hoyt	Miss N C Sargeant	Essex CC	5 and 4
1898	Beatrix Hoyt	Maude Wetmore	Ardsley Club	5 and 3
1899	Ruth Underhill	Mrs Caleb Fox	Philadelphia CC	2 and 1
1900	Frances Griscom	Margaret Curtis	Shinnecock Hills	6 and 5
1901	Genevieve Hecker	Lucy Herron	Baltusrol	5 and 3
1902	Genevieve Hecker	Louisa Wells	The Country Club	4 and 3
1903	Bessie Anthony	Miss J A Carpenter	Chicago GC	7 and 6
1904	Georgianna Bishop	Mrs E F Sanford	Merion	5 and 3
1905	Pauline Mackay	Margaret Curtis	Morris County CC	1 hole
1906	Harriot Curtis	Mary Adams	Brae Burn CC	2 and 1
1907	Margaret Curtis	Harriot Curtis	Midlothian CC	7 and 6
1908	Catherine Harley	Mrs Polhemus	Chevy Chase Club	6 and 5
1909	Dorothy Campbell	Mrs R H Barlow	Merion	3 and 2
1910	Dorothy Campbell	Mrs G M Martin	Homewood CC	2 and 1
1911	Margaret Curtis	Lillian Hyde	Baltusrol	5 and 3
1912	Margaret Curtis	Mrs R H Barlow	Essex CC	3 and 2

1913	Gladys Ravenscroft	Marion Hollins	Wilmington CC	2 holes
1914	Mrs Arnold Jackson	Elaine Rosenthal	Glen Cove	1 hole
1915	Mrs C H Vanderbeck	Mrs W A Gavin	Onwentsia Club	3 and 2
1916	Alexa Stirling	Mildred Caverly	Belmont Springs CC	2 and 1
1917–18	No Championship—World War I			
1919	Alexa Stirling	Mrs W A Gavin	Shawnee CC	6 and 5
1920	Alexa Stirling	Dorothy Hurd Campbell	Mayfield CC	5 and 4
1921	Marion Hollins	Alexa Stirling	Hollywood GC	5 and 4
1922	Glenna Collett	Mrs W A Gavin	Greenbrier GC	5 and 4
1923	Edith Cummings	Alexa Stirling	Westchester-Biltmore CC	3 and 2
1924	Dorothy Campbell Hurd	Mary Browne	Rhode Island CC	7 and 6
1925	Glenna Collett	Alexa Fraser Stirling	St Louis CC	9 and 8
1926	Helen Stetson	Mrs W D Goss, Jr	Merion	3 and 1
1927	Miriam Burns Horn	Maureen Orcutt	Cherry Valley Club	5 and 4
1928	Glenna Collett	Virginia van Wie	Hot Springs	13 and 12
1929	Glenna Collett	Leona Pressier	Oakland Hills CC	4 and 3
1930	Glenna Collett	Virginia van Wie	Los Angeles CC	6 and 5
1931	Helen Hicks	Glenna Collett Vare	CC of Buffalo	2 and 1
1932	Virginia van Wie	Glenna Collett Vare	Salem CC	10 and 8
1933	Virginia van Wie	Helen Hicks	Exmoor CC	4 and 3
1934	Virginia van Wie	Dorothy Traung	Whitemarsh Valley CC	2 and 1
1935	Glenna Collett Vare	Patty Berg	Interlachen CC	3 and 2
1936	Pamela Barton	Maureen Orcutt	Canoe Brook CC	4 and 3
1937	Mrs Julius A Page	Patty Berg	Memphis CC	7 and 6
1938	Patty Berg	Mrs Julius A Page	Westmoreland CC	6 and 5
1939	Betty Jameson	Dorothy Kirby	Wee Burn Club	3 and 2
1940	Betty Jameson	Jane Cothran	Del Monte G and CC	6 and 5
1941	Elizabeth Hicks Newell	Helen Sigel	The Country Club	5 and 3
1942–45	No Championship—World War II			
1946	Mildred Zaharias	Clara Sherman	Southern Hills	11 and 9
1947	Louise Suggs	Dorothy Kirby	Franklin Hills CC	2 holes
1948	Grace Lenczyk	Helen Sigel	Del Monte G and CC	4 and 3
1949	Dorothy Germain Porter	Dorothy Kielty	Merion	3 and 2
1950	Beverly Hanson	Mae Murray	Atlanta AC, East Lake	6 and 4
1951	Dorothy Kirby	Claire Doran	Town and CC, St Paul	2 and 1
1952	Jacqueline Pung	Shirley McFedters	Waverley CC	2 and 1
1953	Mary Lena Faulk	Polly Riley	Rhode Island CC	3 and 2
1954	Barbara Romack	Mickey Wright	Allegheny CC	4 and 2
1955	Patricia Lesser	Jane Nelson	Myers Park CC	7 and 6
1956	Marlene Stewart	JoAnne Gunderson	Meridian Hills CC	2 and 1
1957	JoAnne Gunderson	Anne Casey Johnstone	Del Paso CC	8 and 6
1958	Anne Quast	Barbara Romack	Wee Burn CC	3 and 2
1959	Barbara McIntire	Joanne Goodwin	Congressional CC	4 and 3
1960	JoAnne Gunderson	Jean Ashley	Tulsa CC	6 and 5
1961	Anne Quast	Phyllis Preuss	Tacoma G and CC	14 and 13
1962	JoAnne Gunderson	Ann Baker	CC of Rochester	9 and 8
1963	Anne Quast	Peggy Conley	Tacoma GC	2 and 1
1964	Barbara McIntire	JoAnne Gunderson	Prairie Dunes CC	3 and 2
1965	Jean Ashley	Anne Quast	Lakewood CC	5 and 4
1966	JoAnne Gunderson Carner	Marlene Stewart Streit	Sewickley Heights GC	41st hole
1967	Mary Lou Dill	Jean Ashley	Annandale GC	5 and 4
1968	JoAnne Gunderson Carner	Anne Quast	Birmingham CC	5 and 4
1969	Catherine Lacoste	Shelley Hamlin	Las Colinas CC	3 and 2
1970	Martha Wilkinson	Cynthia Hill	Wee Burn CC	3 and 2
1971	Laura Baugh	Beth Barry	Atlanta CC	1 hole
1972	Mary Anne Budke	Cynthia Hill	St Louis CC	5 and 4
1973	Carol Semple	Anne Quast	CC of Rochester	1 hole
1974	Cynthia Hill	Carol Semple	Broadmoor GC, Seattle	5 and 4
1975	Beth Daniel	Donna Horton	Brae Burn CC	3 and 2
1976	Donna Horton	Marianne Bretton	Del Paso CC	2 and 1
1977	Beth Daniel	Cathy Sherk	Cincinatti CC	3 and 1
1978	Cathy Sherk	Judith Oliver	Sunnybrook GC	4 and 3
1979	Carolyn Hill	Patty Sheehan	Memphis CC	7 and 6
(Hereafter the final was decided over 18 holes)				
1980	Juli Inkster	Patti Rizzo	Prairie Dunes	2 holes
1981	Juli Inkster	Lindy Goggin	Waverley CC	1 hole
1982	Juli Inkster	Cathy Hanlon	Broadmoor, Colorado Springs	4 and 3
1983	Joanne Pacillo	Sally Quinlan	Canoe Brook CC	2 and 1
1984	Deb Richard	Kimberly Williams	Broadmoor CC, Seattle	1 hole
1985	Michiko Hattori	Cheryl Stacy	Fox Chapel CC, Pittsburgh	5 and 4
1986	Kay Cockerill	Kathleen McCarthy	Pasatiempo GC, California	9 and 7

Pam Barton, ladies' champion on both sides of the Atlantic. (Illustrated London News)

The victorious Great Britain and Ireland side at Prairie Dunes, 1986. They were the first British and Irish side to win the Curtis, Walker or Ryder Cups on American soil. Back row from left: Lillian Behan, Belle Robertson, Mary McKenna, Patricia Johnson, Karen Davies and Claire Hourihane. Front row from left: Jill Thornhill, Diane Bailey (captain), Elsie Brown (vice-captain), Vicki Thomas. (John Bailey)

Curtis Cup

MILESTONES

An international match, involving the Curtis sisters Harriot and Margaret, was first played at Cromer, Norfolk, in 1905, but it was not until 1932 that the Cup bearing their name became the trophy for competition between America and Great Britain. In 1931, the USGA undertook to finance the American team while British arrangements were in the hands of the Ladies' Golf Union.

1932 The first match at Wentworth set a trend of American superiority that other matches followed. The British, with victories by the formidable trio of Joyce Wethered, Enid Wilson and Diana Fishwick, won the singles 3½–2½, but a clean sweep by the Americans in the foursomes was the decisive factor. In the foursomes Glenna Collett Vare and Mrs Hill beat Wethered and Wanda Morgan by 1 hole, but in the singles Wethered beat Vare 6 and 4. They were incomparably the best players of their time. It was the only time that Wethered took part in the Curtis Cup.

1934 Chevy Chase Club, Chevy Chase, Maryland, was chosen for the first match on American soil and the British made a

promising start by sharing the foursomes. The foursomes were played in a severe rainstorm, but the weather improved the next day when America won five of the six singles. Mrs J B Walker was the lone British winner. Mrs L D Cheney beat Pam Barton who, two years later, won the British and American Women's championship the same summer.

1936 The year of the first tie. At Gleneagles, the foursomes were again shared, but the real excitement came in the singles. Two last-green victories by Charlotte Glutting and Maureen Orcutt for America were countered by Helen Holm and Marjorie Ross Garon for Britain. Glenna Collett Vare had won the top match for America and so all depended on Mrs L D Cheney and Jessie Anderson (later Jessie Valentine), a 21-year-old who was born just down the road in Perth. In the first of a record seven appearances in the Curtis Cup, she became the British heroine, holing a putt of 20 ft on the last green to win her match and tie the whole contest.

1938 At the Essex Country Club, Massachusetts, a very British-sounding name, the British had high hopes of their first victory after winning the foursomes 2½–½, but they won only one single. The deciding match was between Nan Baird and Charlotte Glutting who won the last 3 holes for a 1-hole victory.

1948 After a gap of ten years because of World War II, the Americans resumed with a victory at Royal Birkdale. A newcomer, Jean Donald, won both her matches for Britain, but after her singles win and a half at the top from Philomena Garvey against Louise Suggs, who won the last 2 holes, America won the remaining four matches.

1950 Britain's defeat by 7½–1½ at the Country Club of Buffalo was the largest margin to date. There was never any doubt about the result, but there was encouragement for the British in the first appearance of Frances Stephens. She won her foursome with Elizabeth Price and halved the leading single with Dorothy Germain Porter.

1952 An historic first victory for Britain at the Honourable Company of Edinburgh Golfers, Muirfield, a club with no lady members and no provision for them. In cold blustery conditions, Britain won the foursomes by the odd match but they suffered a shock before winning three of the singles through Frances Stephens, Jeanne Bisgood and Elizabeth Price. Jean Donald, 5 up and 11 to play, lost on the 18th to Dorothy Kirby but, by then, Elizabeth Price had control of the bottom match with Grace DeMoss.

1954 Britain lost the Cup at Merion by losing all three foursomes by wide margins. However, they showed their strength by sharing the singles. In the top match, Frances Stephens beat Mary Lena Faulk by 1 hole. Mary Lena Faulk squared with a 2 at the 35th but Frances Stephens holed from 6 yd on the 36th for victory.

1956 Great Britain confirmed their strength throughout the fifties by winning again, this time at Prince's, Sandwich, scene of Gene Sarazen's Open championship victory. They lost the foursomes 2–1, but they had three commanding victories in the singles; Mrs George Valentine beat Patricia Lesser 6 and 4, Angela Ward (later Mrs Michael Bonallack) won her first Curtis Cup on a course where she was a member by 4 and 3 against Mary Ann Downey; and Elizabeth Price beat Jane Nelson 7 and 6.

This left Frances Stephens Smith and Polly Riley in the deciding match, both players being undefeated in singles matches. Polly Riley squared on the 32nd and again on the 34th but, after a half at the 35th, Mrs Smith won the 36th.

1958 The second halved match of the series occurred at Brae Burn Country Club, Massachusetts. It was the first time that any British team in Walker, Ryder or Curtis Cup had avoided defeat in America, a feat which only the 1965 Walker Cup equalled subsequently.

As holders, the British side retained the Cup. They won the foursomes 2–1, but America had a slight edge in the singles. In the end, the whole match depended, as in 1956, on the match between Frances Smith and Polly Riley, this time playing in the last match. Mrs Smith, 1 up playing the 18th, won the hole to win by 2 holes.

1960 At Lindrick, Yorkshire, scene of Britain's Ryder Cup victory in 1957, America won the Curtis Cup for the first time since 1954. They held onto it until 1986. The Americans won the foursomes 2–1 and there was none of the excitement of the previous three matches. The Americans won 4½ singles.

Mrs Frances Stephens Smith's remarkable Curtis Cup career ended after the foursomes. She did not play in the singles in which she was unbeaten in five matches.

1962 A British team, with five new names in its midst, suffered their worst defeat, 8–1 at Broadmoor Golf Club, Colorado Springs. They lost all three foursomes and only Mrs Alistair Frearson won her single. She beat Judy Bell 8 and 7.

1964 A change to 18-hole matches produced a fine contest at Royal Porthcawl. Peggy Conley, 17, was the youngest competitor in the Curtis Cup at the time and she played a decisive part at the end of a close match.

After the first three singles on the last afternoon, the teams were level but Peggy Conley, Barbara Fay White and Carol Sorenson, who went on to win the British Women's championship, beat Bridget Jackson, Angela Bonallack and Ruth Porter to settle things for America. Mrs Marley Spearman halved both singles and won both foursomes with Angela Bonallack for the British side.

1966 A big victory by 13–5 for the Americans at Virginia Hot Springs. All the Americans had previous Curtis Cup experience compared to three of the British. On the second day, the British won only two matches.

Mary McKenna who has played more times in the Curtis Cup than anybody else. (John Bailey)

1968 As in 1964, the result hung in the balance for a long time on the second day of the match held at Royal County Down, Newcastle, Northern Ireland. It was the first time that the Curtis, Walker or Ryder Cup had been held on the other side of the Irish Sea; it was a huge success in two days of glorious weather.

Ann Irvin was the outstanding British player, but once again the last three American victories in the singles made the difference between the teams.

1970 Back at Brae Burn, Massachusetts, the Americans won 11½–6½, but the British began by winning the first foursomes series. However, they got only two points from the next nine matches which made all the difference.

1972 A match at Western Gailes, Ayrshire, notable for the play of the two young champions, Michelle Walker and Laura Baugh. The single between the two was halved; Walker won the foursome in which they were both involved, but they won their other matches, Walker dropping only that one half point in two days.

Overall, it was a match which swung in the Americans' favour on the first afternoon. They had lost the foursomes in the morning, but won the singles 4½–1½. The second day's play was halved.

1974 For the first time, the match was held on America's west coast at the San Francisco Golf Club. After the first morning's play was halved, the Americans gained and maintained a steady advantage. They won 13–5 with Mrs Anne Sander who played her first Curtis Cup match in 1958, winning all her three matches.

1976 An $11\frac{1}{2}$–$6\frac{1}{2}$ victory for the United States was never seriously in doubt after they led $6\frac{1}{2}$–$2\frac{1}{2}$ on the first day at Royal Lytham St Annes. The American side included Nancy Lopez who, though winning her matches, played only twice.

1978 Britain made an encouraging start on the first morning at Apawamis, New York. They won the foursomes $2\frac{1}{2}$–$\frac{1}{2}$, but thereafter were disappointing. They finished the first day behind at 5–4 and then lost all the second day's foursomes.

1980 A one-sided match at St Pierre, Chepstow, after the first morning. The Americans ran away on Friday afternoon and Saturday morning to win 13–5. The new British Professional tour had its effect upon the strength of the British. Jane Connachan was the youngest to take part in any Curtis Cup.

1982 A special gathering was arranged for the 50th anniversary of the first Curtis Cup match. Altogether 47 former players attended, including four of the original 1932 teams—Glenna Collett Vare, Maureen Orcutt, Dorothy Higbie and Enid Wilson.

The match itself was one-sided and decided by lunch on the second day. The final tally was $14\frac{1}{2}$–$3\frac{1}{2}$ to the United States— the largest margin in the history of the event.

1984 A return to Muirfield, Home of the Honourable Company of Edinburgh Golfers where Great Britain and Ireland won in 1952, produced one of the finest matches. After the United States' record win in 1982, this was the closest since the tied match in 1958.

Great Britain and Ireland had a putt that would have tied this match, although it was not known for certain at the time. The first timers to the British and Irish team did particularly well. The final aggregate was $9\frac{1}{2}$–$8\frac{1}{2}$.

1986 Glorious victory for Great Britain and Ireland at Prairie Dunes, Kansas. It was their first for 30 years, only their third in all and easily the biggest. In every way, the Americans, without any previous Curtis Cuppers in their team, were outplayed. Needing only half a point for overall victory from the second series of singles, Patricia Johnson supplied it immediately. She became the first British and Irish player to win all four matches but every member of the team contributed something. Mary McKenna set a record by her ninth appearance while her foursomes partner, Belle Robertson, at 50, became the oldest to play in the Curtis Cup. The final tally was 13–5.

For the first time since the first match in 1932, the American side did not include one player who had played in a previous Curtis Cup.

DETAILED RECORDS 1932–86

Most appearances
9, Mary McKenna (GB and I)
7, Jessie Valentine (GB and I); Belle Robertson (GB and I)
6, Philomena Garvey (GB and I); Elizabeth Price (GB and I); Frances Smith (GB and I); Angela Bonallack (GB and I); Polly Riley (USA); Barbara McIntire (USA); Anne Quast Sander (USA)

Consecutive appearances
9, Mary McKenna
6, Elizabeth Price; Frances Smith; Angela Bonallack and Polly Riley

Biggest margin of victory (Team)
Over 36 hole matches: By USA, 1962, 8–1
By GB and I, 1952 and 1956, 5–4
Over 18 hole matches: By USA, 1982, $14\frac{1}{2}$–$3\frac{1}{2}$
By GB and I, 1986, 13–5

Biggest margin of victory
Over 36 holes (1932–62)
Foursomes: **8 and 7**, Jean Ashley and Lee Johnstone (USA) beat Diane Frearson and Ruth Porter, 1962

Belle Robertson, the oldest player ever to take part in the Curtis Cup, 1986. (John Bailey)

Singles: **9 and 8**, Margaret 'Wiffi' Smith (USA) beat Philomena Garvey 1956; Polly Riley (USA) beat Elizabeth Price, 1954
8 and 7, Judy Bell (USA) beat Belle McCorkindale (later Robertson), 1960; Diane Frearson beat Judy Bell, 1962
Over 18 holes (from 1964 onwards)
Foursomes: **8 and 7**, Carol Sorenson and Barbara Fay White (USA) beat Bridget Jackson and Susan Armitage, 1964
7 and 6, Jill Thornhill and Lilian Behan (GB and I) beat Kandi Kessler and Cindy Shreyer, 1986
Singles: **7 and 6**, Kathy Baker (USA) beat Belle Robertson, 1982; Juli Inkster (USA) beat Kitrina Douglas, 1982

Ties There have been two tied matches, 1936 and 1958

Best comebacks
In 1938, United States won $5\frac{1}{2}$–$3\frac{1}{2}$ after trailing $2\frac{1}{2}$–$\frac{1}{2}$ in the foursomes
In 1956, Great Britain and Ireland won 5–4 after losing the foursomes 2–1

Teams winning all the foursomes
In 1932, 1954, 1964, 1978 (second series) and 1980 (second series) all won by the United States.
In 1986 (first series) by Great Britain and Ireland

Teams winning all the singles
None, but the United States won $5\frac{1}{2}$ out of 6 in 1950

Most consecutive victories
13, United States 1960–84

Youngest competitor
Jane Connachan, 16 years 3 months 12 days, 1980

Oldest competitor
Belle Robertson, 50 years 3 months 20 days, 1986

RESULTS

Year	Venue	Winners	US Total	Great Britain and Ireland Total	Captains USA	Britain
1932	Wentworth GC, Surrey, England	USA	5½	3½	Marion Hollins	Joyce Wethered
1934	Chevy Chase Club, Maryland	USA	6½	2½	Glenna Collett Vare	Doris Chambers
1936	King's Course, Gleneagles, Scotland	(tie)	4½	4½	Glenna Collett Vare	Doris Chambers
1938	Essex CC, Massachusetts	USA	5½	3½	Frances Stebbins	Kathleen Wallace-Williamson
1948	Royal Birkdale, Lancashire England	USA	6½	2½	Glenna Collett Vare	Doris Chambers
1950	Buffalo CC, New York	USA	7½	1½	Glenna Collett Vare	Diana Critchley
1952	Links of the Honourable Company of Edinburgh Golfers, Muirfield, Scotland	Britain	4	5	Aneila Goldthwaite	Lady Katherine Cairns
1954	Merion GC (East course), Pennsylvania	USA	6	3	Edith Flippin	Dorothy 'Baba' Beck
1956	Prince's GC, Sandwich, England	Britain	4	5	Edith Flippin	Zara Bolton
1958	Brae Burn GC, Massachusetts	(tie)	4½	4½	Virginia Dennehy	Daisy Ferguson
1960	Lindrick GC, Yorkshire, England	USA	6½	2½	Mildred Prunaret	Maureen Garrett
1962	Broadmoor GC, Colorado Springs	USA	8	1	Polly Riley	Frances Smith
1964	Royal Porthcawl GC, Wales	USA	10½	7½	Helen Hawes	Elsie Corlett
1966	Cascades Course, Hot Springs, Virginia	USA	13	5	Dorothy Porter	Zara Bolton
1968	Royal County Down GC, Newcastle, Northern Ireland	USA	10½	7½	Evelyn Monsted	Zara Bolton
1970	Brae Burn GC, Massachusetts	USA	11½	6½	Carol Cudone	Jeanne Bisgood
1972	Western Gailes, Scotland	USA	10	8	Jean Crawford	Frances Smith
1974	San Francisco GC, California	USA	13	5	Allison Choate	Belle Robertson
1976	Royal Lytham and St Annes, Lancashire	USA	11½	6½	Barbara McIntire	Belle Robertson
1978	Apawamis, New York	USA	12	6	Helen Sigel Wilson	Carol Comboy
1980	St Pierre, Chepstow, England	USA	13	5	Nancy Syms	Carol Comboy
1982	Denver CC, Colorado	USA	14½	3½	Scott L (Betty) Probasco	Maire O'Donnel
1984	Links of the Honourable Company of Edinburgh Golfers, Muirfield, Scotland	USA	9½	8½	Phyllis (Tish) Preuss	Diane Bailey
1986	Prairie Dunes, Hutchinson, Kansas	GB and I	5	13	Judy Bell	Diane Bailey

PLAYERS—UNITED STATES OF AMERICA

A total of 97 players have represented the United States; 84 have represented GB and I

Name	Played	Won	Lost	Halved	Percentage
Roberta Albers (1968)	2	1	0	1	75.00
Danielle Ammacapane (1986)	3	0	3	0	—
Jean Ashley (1962–64–68)	8	6	2	0	75.00
Kathy Baker (1982)	4	3	0	1	87.50
Barbara Barrow (1976)	2	1	0	1	75.00
Beth Barry (1972–74)	4	2	1	1	62.50
Jean Bastunchury (later Mrs Booth) (1970–72–74)	12	9	3	0	75.00
Laura Baugh (1972)	4	2	1	1	62.50
Judy Bell (1960–62)	2	1	1	0	50.00
Amy Benz (1982)	3	2	1	0	66.66
Patty Berg (1936–38)	4	1	2	1	37.50
Mary Budke (1974)	3	2	1	0	66.66
Lori Castillo (1980)	3	2	1	0	66.66
Mrs L D Cheney (1932–34–36)	6	5	1	0	83.33
Glenna Collett (later Mrs Vare) (1932–36–38–48)	7	4	2	1	64.28
Peggy Conley (1964–68)	6	3	1	2	66.66

Name	Played	Won	Lost	Halved	Percentage
Patricia Cornett (1978)	2	1	0	1	75.00
Clifford Ann Creed (1962)	2	2	0	0	100.00
Mrs Philip Cudone (1956)	1	1	0	0	100.00
Beth Daniel (1976–78)	8	7	1	0	87.50
Mary Lou Dill (1968)	3	1	1	1	50.00
Claire Doran (1952–54)	4	4	0	0	100.00
Grace de Moss (later Mrs Smith) (1952–54)	3	1	2	0	33.33
Mary Ann Downey (1956)	2	1	1	0	50.00
Mrs Paul Dye (1970)	2	1	0	1	75.00
Judy Eller (1960)	2	2	0	0	100.00
Heather Farr (1984)	3	2	1	0	66.66
Jane Fassinger (1970)	1	0	1	0	—
Mary Lena Faulk (1954)	2	1	1	0	50.00
Kim Gardner (1986)	3	1	1	1	50.00
Charlotte Glutting (1934–36)	4	2	1	1	62.50
Brenda Goldsmith (1978–80)	4	2	2	0	50.00
Mrs Frank Goldthwaite (1934)	1	0	1	0	—
Joanne Goodwin (1960)	2	1	1	0	50.00
JoAnne Gunderson (1958–60–62–64)	10	6	3	1	66.66
Mary Hafeman (1980)	2	1	0	1	75.00
Nancy Hager (1970)	2	1	1	0	50.00
Shelley Hamlin (1968–70)	8	3	3	2	50.00
Penny Hammel (1984)	3	1	1	1	50.00
Cathy Hanlon (1982)	3	2	1	0	66.66
Beverly Hanson (1950)	2	2	0	0	100.00
Kathryn Hemphill (1938)	1	0	0	1	50.00
Helen Hicks (1932)	2	1	1	0	50.00
Carolyn Hill (1978)	3	0	1	2	33.33
Cynthia Hill (1970–74–76–78)	13	5	5	3	50.00
Mrs O S Hill (1932–34–36)	6	2	3	1	41.66
Donna Horton (1976)	2	2	0	0	100.00
Dana Howe (1984)	3	1	1	1	50.00
Juli Inkster (1982)	4	4	0	0	100.00
Mrs Ann Casey Johnstone (1958–60–62)	4	3	1	0	75.00
Kandi Kessler (1986)	3	1	1	1	50.00
Dorothy Kielty (1948–50)	4	4	0	0	100.00
Dorothy Kirby (1948–50–52–54)	7	4	3	0	57.14
Peggy Kirk (1950)	2	1	1	0	50.00
Bonnie Lauer (1974)	4	2	2	0	50.00
Grace Lenczyk (1948–50)	3	2	1	0	66.66
Patricia Lesser (1954–56)	3	2	1	0	66.66
Marjorie Lindsay (1952)	2	1	1	0	50.00
Nancy Lopez (1976)	2	2	0	0	100.00
Deborah Massey (1974–76)	5	5	0	0	100.00
Kathleen McCarthy (1986)	3	0	2	1	16.66
Mrs M McDougall (1982)	2	2	0	0	100.00
Barbara McIntire (1958–60–62–64–66–72)	16	6	6	4	50.00
Marion Miley (1938)	2	1	0	1	75.00
Dottie Mochrie (1986)	3	0	2	1	16.66
Terri Moody (1980)	2	1	0	1	75.00
Mae Murray (1952)	1	0	1	0	—
Jane Nelson (1956)	1	0	1	0	—
Judith Oliver (1978–80–82)	8	5	1	2	75.00
Maureen Orcutt (1932–34–36–38)	8	5	3	0	62.50
Patricia O'Sullivan (1952)	1	0	1	0	—
Joanne Pacillo (1984)	3	1	1	1	50.00
Mrs Julius Page (1938–48)	4	3	1	0	75.00
Dorothy Germain Porter (1950)	2	1	0	1	75.00
Phyllis Preuss (1962–64–66–68–70)	15	10	4	1	70.00
Anne Quast (later Mrs Welts, Mrs Decker, Mrs Sander) (1958–60–62–66–68–74–84)	20	9	7	4	55.00
Polly Riley (1948–50–52–54–56–58)	10	5	5	0	50.00
Lucile Robinson (1934)	1	0	1	0	—
Barbara Romack (1954–56–58)	5	3	2	0	60.00
Judy Rosenthal (1984)	3	2	0	1	83.33
Nancy Roth (later Mrs Syms) (1964–66–76)	9	3	5	1	38.88
Carol Semple (1974–76–80–82)	14	8	4	2	64.28
Lesley Shannon (1986)	3	0	2	1	16.66
Patty Sheehan (1980)	4	4	0	0	100.00

Name	Played	Won	Lost	Halved	Percentage
Cindy Shreyer (1986)	3	1	2	0	33.33
Helen Sigel (1950)	1	0	1	0	—
Lancy Smith (1972–78–80–82–84)	17	7	5	5	55.00
Margaret Smith (1956)	2	2	0	0	100.00
Carol Sorenson (later Mrs Flenniken) (1964–66)	8	6	1	1	81.25
Hollis Stacy (1972)	2	0	1	1	25.00
Louise Suggs (1948)	2	0	1	1	25.00
Mrs Noreen Uihlein (1978)	3	1	1	1	50.00
Virginia Van Wie (1932–34)	4	3	0	1	87.50
Barbara Fay White (later Mrs Boddie) (1964–66)	8	7	0	1	93.75
Mary Anne Widman (1984)	3	2	1	0	66.66
Martha Wilkinson (later Mrs Kirouac) (1970–72)	8	5	3	0	62.50
Helen Sigel Wilson (1966)	1	0	1	0	—
Joyce Ziske (1954)	1	0	1	0	—

Anne Sander.
(USGA)

PLAYERS—GREAT BRITAIN AND IRELAND

Name	Played	Won	Lost	Halved	Percentage
Wilma Aitken (1982)	2	0	2	0	—
Jessie Anderson (1936–38–50–52–54–56–58)	11	2	9	0	18.18
Veronica Anstey (1956)	1	0	1	0	—
Susan Armitage (1964–66)	6	0	5	1	8.33
N. Baird (1938)	1	0	1	0	—
Pam Barton (1934–36)	4	0	3	1	12.50
Lilian Behan (1986)	4	3	1	0	75.00
Jeanne Bisgood (1950–52–54)	4	1	3	0	25.00
Zara Bolton (1948)	2	0	2	0	—
Angela Bonallack (1956–58–60–62–64–66)	15	6	8	1	43.33
Sally Bonallack (1962)	1	0	1	0	—
Ita Burke (1966)	3	2	1	0	66.66
Suzanne Cadden (1976)	4	0	4	0	—
Carole Caldwell (1978–80)	5	1	3	1	30.00
Elizabeth Chadwick (1966)	4	1	3	0	25.00
Jane Connachan (1980–82)	5	0	5	0	—
Elsie Corlett (1932–38)	3	1	2	0	33.33
Karen Davies (1986)	4	2	0	2	75.00
Laura Davies (1984)	2	1	1	0	50.00
Jean Donald (1948–50–52)	6	3	3	0	50.00
Kitrina Douglas (1982)	4	0	3	1	12.50
Mary Everard (1970–72–74–78)	15	6	7	2	46.66
Diana Fishwick (1932–34)	3	1	2	0	33.33
Marjorie Fowler (1966)	1	0	1	0	—
Diane Frearson (Mrs Bailey) (1962–72)	5	2	2	1	50.00
Philomena Garvey (1948–50–52–54–56–60)	11	2	8	1	22.72
Jacqueline Gordon (1948)	2	1	1	0	50.00
Molly Gourlay (1932–34)	4	0	2	2	33.33
Julia Greenhalgh (1964–70–74–76–78)	17	6	7	4	47.05
Penny Grice (1984)	4	2	1	1	62.50
Joan Hastings (1966)	2	0	1	1	25.00
Helen Holm (1936–38–48)	5	3	2	0	60.00
Claire Hourihane (1984–86)	5	2	2	1	50.00
Ann Howard (1968)	2	0	2	0	—
Beverley Huke (1972)	2	0	2	0	—
Ann Irvin (1962–68–70–76)	12	4	7	1	37.50
Bridget Jackson (1958–64–68)	8	1	6	1	18.75
Patricia Johnson (1986)	4	4	0	0	100.00
Joan Lawrence (1964)	2	0	2	0	—
Jennifer Lee-Smith (1974–76)	3	0	3	0	—
Carol Le Feuvre (1974)	3	0	3	0	—
Maureen Madill (1980)	4	0	3	1	12.50
Vanessa Marvin (1978)	3	1	2	0	33.33
Mary McKenna (1970–72–74–76–78–80–82–84–86)	30	10	16	4	40.00
Linda Moore (1980)	3	1	1	1	50.00
Wanda Morgan (1932–34–36)	6	0	5	1	8.33
Claire Nesbitt (1980)	3	0	1	2	33.33
Beverley New (1984)	4	1	3	0	25.00
Dinah Oxley (1968–70–72–76)	11	3	6	2	36.36
Doris Park (1932)	1	0	1	0	—
Moira Paterson (1952)	2	1	1	0	50.00
Marjorie Peel (1954)	1	0	1	0	—
Tegwen Perkins (1974–76–78–80)	14	4	8	2	35.71
Kathryn Phillips (1972)	2	1	1	0	50.00
Margaret Pickard (1968–70)	5	2	3	0	40.00
Diana Plumpton (1934)	2	1	1	0	50.00
Ruth Porter (1960–62–64)	6	3	3	0	50.00
Elizabeth Price (1950–52–54–56–58–60)	12	7	4	1	62.50
Val Reddan (1948)	1	0	1	0	—
Jean Roberts (1962)	1	0	1	0	—
Belle Robertson (née McCorkindale) (1960–66–68–70–72–82–86)	24	5	12	7	35.41
Janette Robertson (1954–56–58–60)	8	3	5	0	37.50
Maureen Ruttle (Mrs Garrett) (1948)	2	0	2	0	—
Vivien Saunders (1968)	4	1	2	1	37.50

Name	Played	Won	Lost	Halved	Percentage
Frances Smith (née Stephens) (1950–52–54–56–58–60)	11	7	3	1	68.18
Jane Soulsby (1982)	4	1	2	1	37.50
Marley Spearman (1962–64)	6	2	2	2	50.00
Anne Stant (1976)	1	1	1	1	—
Gillian Stewart (1980–82)	4	1	3	0	25.00
Vicki Thomas (1984–86)	4	2	1	1	41.66
Muriel Thomson (1978)	3	2	1	0	66.66
Jill Thornhill (1984–86)	8	4	1	3	68.75
Clarrie Tiernan (1938)	2	2	0	0	100.00
Pam Tredinnick (1966–68)	4	0	3	1	12.50
Angela Uzielli (1978)	1	0	1	0	—
Mrs George Valentine (see Jessie Anderson)					
Sheila Vaughan (1962–64)	4	1	2	1	37.50
Phyllis Wade (1938)	1	0	0	1	50.00
Claire Waite (1984)	4	2	2	0	50.00
Mrs J B Walker (1934–36–38)	6	2	3	1	41.66
Maureen Walker (1974)	4	2	2	0	50.00
Michelle Walker (1972)	4	3	0	1	87.50
Mrs J B Watson (1932)	1	0	1	0	—
Joyce Wethered (1932)	2	1	1	0	50.00
Enid Wilson (1932)	2	1	1	0	50.00

Laura Davies, leading European money winner in her first two seasons, 1985 and 1986. (Allsport)

Women's World Amateur Team Championship

For the Espirito Santo Trophy

MILESTONES

The championship was instituted by the French Golf Federation on a suggestion of the United States Golf Association. The inaugural event was held at the Saint-Germain Club in Paris in October 1964. Each team consists of three players, the two best each day making up the team's score. The sum of the four daily totals decides the winner.

1964 Appropriately, the first championship was won by France, the host country who, at that time, had three of the best players in the world, Claudine Cros, Catherine Lacoste and Brigitte Varangot.

They had a close duel with the United States who led by only 1 stroke after 54 holes. Lacoste had a final round of 73 and Cros 74, but the issue was decided when the American, Barbara McIntire, played the last 2 holes in 3 over par. France won by 1 stroke with a total of 588.

1966 A comfortable victory in Mexico City for the Americans despite losing the services of Mrs JoAnne Gunderson Carner. She was replaced by 17-year-old Shelley Hamlin who, after failing to count in the first two rounds, finished with two 72s, the best last 36-hole score by any player. The Americans won by 9 strokes from Canada and 17 from France, the holders.

1968 In a championship of high scoring, the United States won for the second time at the Victoria Golf Club, near Melbourne. After three rounds, America and Australia were level on 463, 1 ahead of France, but America won by 5 strokes.

1970 America won a desperate victory over France by a single stroke at the Club de Campo in Madrid. They had trailed after three rounds by 2 strokes but, with Martha Wilkinson, the US champion, paired with Catherine Lacoste, there were fluctuations in plenty before America squeezed home. The individual title was won by the South African, Sally Little.

1972 The United States won for the fourth time in a row at the Hindu Country Club, Buenos Aires. They won by 4 strokes from France who were 18 strokes behind America at the halfway. Then Claudine Rubin and Brigitte Varangot had a 68 and a 71 to make up 14 strokes. Good finishing rounds of 72 and 73 by Laura Baugh and Jane Bastanchury Booth, whose 68 in the first round equalled the lowest round ever in the championship, saw America home.

1974 The United States made it five victories in a row at the Campo de Golf, Cajuiles, Dominica, beating South Africa and Great Britain and Ireland into second place by a record 16 strokes. It was none the less, the highest winning total—620. America were close to disaster on the first day—or so it seemed. Deborah Massey almost withdrew after 9 holes, having been heavily medicated, but in the end her score of 84 counted, because Carol Semple committed a breach of the rules and was disqualified. Cynthia Hill had 76, the lowest first round and one of the few under 80. They were only a stroke behind Italy and never looked back.

The lowest score of the championship was a 71 by Catherine Lacoste de Prado of France in the last round. The first six teams had only 25 rounds under 80 out of a possible 72.

1976 The United States yet again at Vilamoura, Portugal. They were never headed and steadily built up the record-winning margin of 17 strokes, 1 more than the previous championship. Nancy Lopez, whose 72 in the first round was the lowest of all the four days, had the best aggregate of all—297. France, the only other country to have won, were second for the third time.

1978 First victory for Australia and the first time that the United States have finished outside the first two. They were tied fourth.

At Pacific Harbour, Fiji, Australia won by a single stroke in a desperate finish with Canada who started the final round 6 strokes behind. France had a good last day to finish third on 602, 6 strokes behind the winners.

1980 United States claimed revenge on Australia over Pinehurst No 2 although at halfway the two countries were level. In the third round, the United States returned 74s from Carol Semple and Juli Inkster to take a 3-stroke lead and on the final day Semple and Inkster shot 71 and 73 respectively, the lowest daily total of the week. This made their winning margin 7 strokes. The third member of the American team, Patti Rizzo had the lowest individual total, 294 (73–70–75–76). There were a record 28 team entries. It was the first time the Espirito Santo Trophy had been contested in the United States.

1982 A new aggregate record of 579 for four rounds was posted by the winners, the United States in Geneva. The team of Amy Benz, Kathy Baker and Juli Inkster led throughout, their final margin over New Zealand being 17 strokes.

1984 United States scored their ninth victory in Hong Kong, defeating France by 12 strokes with a total of 585. Deb Richard, the new US women's champion headed the individual list with 295 (75, 75, 70, 75). France maintained their fine record in the event. They have won once, been second four times and third four times.

1986 United States' run of three successive victories was brought to an end in Venezuela. Two months or so after losing the Curtis Cup, they finished third behind Spain, and runners-up, France. Spain's victory showed that it is not just their men who are successful in world class company.

DETAILED RECORDS

Most victories
9, United States
1, France
1, Australia
1, Spain

Lowest aggregate total
579, United States, 1982

Highest winning total
620, United States, 1974

Lowest individual round
68, Jane Bastanchury Booth, Marlene Stewart and Claudine Cros Rubin, all in 1972

Lowest individual aggregate
289 (74, 71, 70, 74) Marlene Stewart, Mexico City CC, 1966

Lowest individual first round
68, Marlene Stewart and Jane Bastanchury Booth, Hindu CC, Buenos Aires, 1972

Lowest individual second round
70, Patti Rizzo (USA) and Marta Figueras-Dotti (Spain), 1980

Lowest individual third round
68, Claudine Cros Rubin, Hindu CC, Buenos Aires, 1972

Lowest individual fourth round
70, Juli Inkster, 1982
71, Claudine Cros Rubin and Isa Goldschmid, Hindu CC, Buenos Aires, 1972
71, Catherine Lacoste de Prado, Campo de Golf, Cajuiles, Dominican Republic, 1974

71, Carol Semple and Marie Laure de Lorenzi, Pinehurst No 2, 1980

Largest lead after 18 holes
5 strokes, United States, 1972 and 1982

Largest lead after 36 holes
13 strokes, United States, 1972

Largest lead after 54 holes
11 strokes, United States, 1984

Largest margin of victory
17 strokes, United States, 1976 and 1982

Smallest lead after 18 holes
1 stroke, France in 1964, United States in 1966, Italy in 1974, Great Britain and Ireland in 1978, and Australia in 1980

Smallest lead after 36 holes
United States and Australia were tied after 36 holes, 1980

Smallest lead after 54 holes
United States and Australia tied in 1968

Smallest margin of victory
1 stroke, France in 1964, the United States in 1970 and Australia in 1978

Youngest competitors
Maria de la Guardia and Silvia Corrie, both of the Dominican Republic, were both only 14 years old in 1974

Most sub-par rounds in one championship
14 in 1980 and 1984

RESULTS

Espirito Santo Trophy
1964 Saint-Germain GC, Paris 1–4 October
France 588 (Claudine Cros, Catherine Lacoste, Brigitte Varangot)
1966 Mexico City Country Club 20–23 October
United States 580 (Marjorie Boddie, Shelley Hamlin, Anne Welts)
1968 Victoria GC, Nr Melbourne, Australia 2–5 October
United States 616 (Jane Bastanchury, Shelley Hamlin, Anne Welts)
1970 Club de Campo, Madrid 30 September–3 October
United States 598 (Jane Bastanchury, Cynthia Hill, Martha Wilkinson)
1972 Hindu CC, Buenos Aires 11–14 October
United States 583 (Laura Baugh, Jane Bastanchury Booth, Mary Anne Budke)
1974 Campo de Golf, Cajuiles, Dominica 22–25 October
United States 620 (Cynthia Hill, Deborah Massey, Carol Semple)
1976 Vilamoura GC, Algarve, Portugal 6–9 October
United States 605 (Donna Horton, Nancy Lopez, Deborah Massey)
1978 Pacific Harbour, Fiji 10–13 October
Australia 596 (Lindy Goggin, Edwina Kennedy, Jane Lock)
1980 Pinehurst No 2, North Carolina, USA 1–4 October
United States 588 (Juli Inkster, Patti Rizzo, Carol Semple)
1982 Geneva GC, Switzerland 8–11 September
United States 579 (Kathy Baker, Amy Benz, Juli Inkster)
1984 Royal Hong Kong GC, 30 October–2 November
United States 585 (Heather Farr, Deb Richard, Jody Rosenthal)
1986 Lagunita CC, Venezuela 14–17 October
Spain 580 (Macarena Campomanes, Mary Carmen Navarro, Maria Orueta)

Mickey Wright

In any argument about the greatest woman golfer of all time, the name of Mickey Wright would be on the shortest of short lists. Her scoring, unparalleled in women's golf, set new standards but it also brought her victory after victory.

Altogether she scored 82 victories on the LPGA circuit and was one of those primarily responsible for the expansion of the tour but she holds other records. In 1961, she won ten tournaments, four of them in a row, and she shares with Betsy Rawls the highest number (4) of victories in the US Women's Open.

Daughter of an attorney, she turned professional after losing the final of the US Women's Amateur to Barbara Romack in 1954 and quickly established her supremacy. In addition to her four Open wins, she won the LPGA championship four times and holds the record for the lowest 18 holes on the tour—62.

Mildred 'Babe' Zaharias

A legendary name in women's golf and in the field of athletics where she won two gold medals and one silver in the 1932 Olympic Games.

She took up golf relatively late but soon earned the reputation as the longest hitter the game had seen at that time, although she possessed all the control in the short game as well.

The war hindered her career but she won US Women's Amateur in 1946, became the first American to win the British the following year and promptly reverted to the professional status she was forced to acquire in 1935.

Her strong sense of publicity and her spectacular play were a godsend to the women's tour and she was the star of the show. She won more than 30 events including three US Opens, but her most famous victory was in 1954 less than a year after a major operation for cancer.

She won by a record 12 strokes, added a further four events as well as two more in 1955 but a year later cancer had claimed another victim and one of the great figures was lost.

Patty Berg and Louise Suggs

With Babe Zaharias, the pioneers of the women's tour; Berg, a teenage prodigy and a great personality, was a tireless tournament player and giver of clinics. Louise Suggs, who won four tournaments in her first two years as a professional, was the first woman to be elected to the LPGA Hall of Fame, and, like Berg, won both US Amateur and Open championships.

In ten years (1976–86), the prize money on the PGA European Tour rose from £0.85 million to £5.4 million.

Kathy Whitworth

One of the great names of women's professional golf. She has been the model of consistency since she joined the LPGA in 1958, although the US Women's Open has eluded her. However, her principal fame lies in her record number of victories on tour—a record for the men's and women's tours.

In 1982, she caught the previous women's record holder, Mickey Wright on 82 wins; since then, she has taken her tally to 88. In 1981, she became the first woman to win over $1 million. She was elected to the LPGA Hall of Fame in 1975.

Nancy Lopez

Having graduated to the LPGA tour after playing in the 1976 Curtis Cup match, she made an immediate impact on the professional world. In her first full season, she won nine tournaments, including five in a row. She has now won 34 events and by the end of 1985 had won over $1½ million. However, she played only four tournaments in 1986. Her lowest individual round was 64 in the 1981 Dinah Shore.

She has been leading money winner three times. In 1985, she won close on $1½ million.

Pat Bradley

One of the most consistent lady professionals in history, she had her finest season in 1986. She was leading money winner with a record for any season of $492 021. Of the 27 tournaments she played, she won 5. This brought her total of victories to 21. She has won over $100 000 in each of the last nine years and in 1986 went to the head of the career money leaders with over 2 million dollars.

Laura Davies

Since turning professional at the end of 1984, Laura Davies headed the money list on each of her first two seasons as a professional. What is more, her powerful game has made her the most notable attraction since the women's tour began. She can hit the ball further than most men without any apparent effort. Her best performance was in winning the Ladies' British Open championship at Royal Birkdale in October 1986. She beat several good Americans with a score of 283 (71, 73, 69, 70).

Cecil Leitch playing at Frinton, 1913. (Hulton Picture Library)

US Ladies' Professional Golf Association

DETAILED RECORDS

Most victories
88, Kathy Whitworth
82, Mickey Wright
55, Betsy Rawls
50, Louise Suggs

Oldest winner
JoAnne Carner, 46 years 5 months 9 days, 1985 Safeco Classic

Youngest winner
Marlene Hagge, 18 years 14 days, 1952 Sarasota Open

Most consecutive victories in tournaments participated
5, Nancy Lopez, 1978
4, Mickey Wright, 1962 and 1963; Kathy Whitworth, 1969

Most victories in one calendar year
13, Mickey Wright, 1963

Most official money in one calendar year
$492 021, Pat Bradley, 1986

Biggest margin of victory
14 strokes, Louise Suggs, USGA Women's Open, 1949
14 strokes, Cindy Mackey, Mastercard International Pro-Am, 1986
12 strokes, Betsy Rawls, St Louis Women's Open, 1954
12 strokes, Mickey Wright, Memphis Women's Open, 1960
12 strokes, Kathy Whitworth, Milwaukee Jaycee Open, 1956

Lowest 72-hole total
268 (65, 67, 69, 66), Nancy Lopez, Willow Creek GC, NC, Henredon Classic, 1985

Lowest 54-hole total
198 (65, 69, 64), Jan Stephenson, Bent Tree CC, Dallas, Mary Kay Classic, 1981

Lowest 36-hole total
129 (64, 65), Judy Dickinson, Pasadena Yacht and CC, Florida, S and H Golf Classic, 1985

Lowest 18 holes
62 (30–32), Mickey Wright, Hogan Park GC, Texas, Tall City Open, 1964
62 (32–30), Vicki Fergon, Almaden G and CC, San Jose Classic, 1984

Lowest 9 holes
28, Mary Beth Zimmerman, Rail GC, Illinois, Rail Charity Golf Classic, 1984
28, Pat Bradley, Green Gables GC, Denver, 1984 Columbia Savings Classic
28, Muffin Spencer-Devlin, Knollwood GC, NY, 1985 Mastercard International Pro-Am

Leading money winner most often
8, Kathy Whitworth

Most official money by a rookie in a year
$217 424, Juli Inkster (August 1983 to July 1984)

Most consecutive holes without a bogey
55, Tatsuko Ohsako, 1982 American Express Sun City Classic. Record is unofficial

Most eagles in one round
3, Alice Ritzman, Colgate European Open, Sunningdale, 1979

Most holes-in-one in one tournament
2, Jo Ann Washam, second and fourth rounds, Women's Kemper Open, Mesa Vedre CC; the 16th and 17th holes

Fewest putts in one round
17, Joan Joyce, Brookfield West G and CC, Georgia, third round, 1982 Lady Michelob

Most birdies in one round
11, Vicki Fergon, Almadaen G and CC, second round San Hose Classic, 1984. She finished in 62, 11 under par.
10, Nancy Lopez, Bent Tree CC, Dallas, Mary Kay Classic, 1979

Most consecutive birdies
8, Mary Beth Zimmerman, Rail GC, Illinois, Rail Charity Classic, 1984. She finished in 64 (36–28)—8 under par

Most top ten finishes in one year
25, Judy Rankin, 1973

Most rounds under 70 in one calendar year
27, Pat Bradley, 1986

Lowest scoring average for season
70, 73, Nancy Lopez, 1985

Quickest first victory
Amy Alcott, 1975 in her third tournament

Fastest round
1 hr 35 min 33 sec Lynn Adams and Catherine Duggan, final round 1984 Sarasota Classic. Adams shot 78 and Duggan 72

Youngest to earn a million dollars prize money
Beth Daniel, 27 years 9 months 15 days

Most sub-par holes in one tournament
25, Nancy Lopez, 1985 Henredon Classic (66, 67, 69, 66)

Amy Alcott who broke Jerilyn Britz's record of a US Women's Open 9 stroke victory in 1980. (Allsport)

CAREER MONEY LEADERS

Rank	Player	Total $
1	Pat Bradley	2 286 218.03
2	JoAnne Carner	2 013 991.63
3	Amy Alcott	1 806 648.14
4	Nancy Lopez	1 711 078.83
5	Kathy Whitworth	1 666 762.01
6	Donna Caponi	1 339 444.73
7	Patty Sheehan	1 309 962.84
8	Beth Daniel	1 301 110.65
9	Jane Blalock	1 288 300.62
10	Jan Stephenson	1 265 443.00
11	Hollis Stacy	1 151 766.99
12	Betsy King	1 098 219.59
13	Sandra Palmer	1 074 823.86
14	Sally Little	1 056 107.80
15	Sandra Haynie	990 970.57
16	Judy Rankin	887 600.44
17	Ayako Okamoto	767 597.85
18	Sandra Post	746 714.76
19	Alice Miller	733 528.72
20	Judy Dickinson	670 749.92
21	Juli Inkster	623 665.23
22	Jo Ann Washam	613 896.04
23	Debbie Massey	594 772.13
24	Donna White	567 854.08
25	Kathy Postlewait	557 154.27
26	Debbie Austin	532 972.75
27	Carol Mann	506 666.46
28	Sandra Spuzich	503 428.03
29	Silvia Bertolaccini	489 279.46
30	Janet Coles	489 192.33
31	Penny Pulz	487 769.66
32	Chris Johnson	465 175.50
33	Marlene Hagge	460 895.92
34	Laura Baugh	449 640.17
35	Bonnie Lauer	434 136.27
36	Lori Garbacz	429 733.13
37	Cathy Morse	414 909.08
38	Dot Germain	403 881.83
39	Janet Anderson	401 216.84
40	Jerilyn Britz	400 306.51
41	Jane Geddes	397 663.34
42	Pat Meyers	397 488.88
43	Muffin Spencer Devlin	388 416.85
44	Dale Eggeling	384 838.12
45	Vicki Fergon	372 760.59
46	Patti Rizzo	370 186.75
47	Jo Ann Prentice	369 812.87
48	Mickey Wright	368 770.01
49	Shelley Hamlin	367 726.02
50	Val Skinner	350 056.75
51	Mary Beth Zimmerman	347 705.29
52	Alice Ritzman	345 625.32
53	Mary Mills	341 193.83
54	Joyce Kazmierski	330 761.89
55	Becky Pearson	328 664.01
56	Beth Solomon	327 625.06
57	Myra Blackwelder	323 809.82
58	Laurie Rinker	315 506.29
59	Vicki Tabor	311 472.52
60	Cindy Hill	304 434.05
61	Betsy Rawls	302 664.00
62	Marilynn Smith	296 258.03
63	Betty Burfeindt	287 742.81
64	Rosie Jones	287 321.97
65	Susie McAllister	286 085.88
66	Clifford Ann Creed	281 608.49
67	Barbara Moxness	271 511.25
68	Murle Breer	263 474.37
69	Kathy McMullen	263 437.49
70	Susie Berning	251 373.74

CAREER WINS

	Player	Wins	Years
1	Kathy Whitworth	88	28
2	Mickey Wright	82	30
3	Betsy Rawls	55	34
4	Louise Suggs	50	37
5	Sandra Haynie	42	26
6	JoAnne Carner	42	17
7	Patty Berg	41	36
8	Carol Mann	38	24
9	Nancy Lopez	34	10
10	Babe Zaharias	31	7
11	Jane Blalock	29	18
12	Judy Rankin	26	25
13	Amy Alcott	26	12
14	Marlene Hagge	25	37

MOST VICTORIES IN A SEASON

1948	Patty Berg	3
	Babe Zaharias	
1949	Patty Berg	3
	Louise Suggs	
1950	Babe Zaharias	6
1951	Babe Zaharias	7
1952	Betsy Rawls	6
	Louise Suggs	
1953	Louise Suggs	8
1954	Louise Suggs	5
	Babe Zaharias	
1955	Patty Berg	6
1956	Marlene Hagge	8
1957	Patty Berg	5
	Betsy Rawls	
1958	Mickey Wright	5
1959	Betsy Rawls	10
1960	Mickey Wright	6
1961	Mickey Wright	10
1962	Mickey Wright	10
1963	Mickey Wright	13
1964	Mickey Wright	11
1965	Kathy Whitworth	8
1966	Kathy Whitworth	9
1967	Kathy Whitworth	8
1968	Kathy Whitworth	10
	Carol Mann	
1969	Carol Mann	8
1970	Shirley Englehorn	4
1971	Kathy Whitworth	5
1972	Kathy Whitworth	5
	Jane Blalock	
1973	Kathy Whitworth	7
1974	JoAnne Carner	6
	Sandra Haynie	
1975	Carol Mann	4
	Sandra Haynie	
1976	Judy Rankin	6
1977	Judy Rankin	5
	Debbie Austin	
1978	Nancy Lopez	9
1979	Nancy Lopez	8
1980	JoAnne Carner	5
	Donna Caponi	
1981	Donna Caponi	5
1982	JoAnne Carner	5
	Beth Daniel	
1983	Pat Bradley	4
	Patty Sheehan	
1984	Patty Sheehan	4
	Amy Alcott	
1985	Nancy Lopez	5
1986	Pat Bradley	5

ANNUAL PURSES

Year	Prize Money $	Events
1950	45 000	9
1951	70 000	14
1952	150 000	21
1953	120 000	24
1954	105 000	21
1955	135 000	27
1956	140 000	26
1957	147 830	26
1958	158 600	25
1959	202 500	26
1960	186 700	25
1961	288 750	24
1962	338 450	32
1963	345 300	34
1964	351 000	33
1965	356 316	33
1966	509 500	37
1967	435 250	32
1968	550 185	34
1969	597 290	29
1970	435 040	21
1971	558 550	21
1972	988 400	30
1973	1 471 000	36
1974	1 752 500	35
1975	1 742 000	33
1976	2 527 000	32
1977	3 058 000	35
1978	3 925 000	37
1979	4 400 000	38
1980	5 150 000	40
1981	5 800 000	40
1982	6 400 000	38
1983	7 000 000	36
1984	8 000 000	38
1985	9 000 000	38
1986	10 000 000	36
1987	11 000 000	36
Total	88 440 161	1153

Kathy Whitworth, holder of the record for the most victories on the US Women's tour. (USGA)

LEADING MONEY-WINNERS (1948–1986)

Year	Player	Amount $
1948	Babe Zaharias	3400.00*
1949	Babe Zaharias	4650.00*
1950	Babe Zaharias	14 800.00*
1951	Babe Zaharias	15 087.00*
1952	Betsy Rawls	14 505.00
1953	Louise Suggs	19 816.25
1954	Patty Berg	16 011.00
1955	Patty Berg	16 492.34
1956	Marlene Hagge	20 235.50
1957	Patty Berg	16 272.00
1958	Beverly Hanson	12 639.55
1959	Betsy Rawls	26 744.39
1960	Louise Suggs	16 892.12
1961	Mickey Wright	22 236.21
1962	Mickey Wright	21 641.99
1963	Mickey Wright	31 269.50
1964	Mickey Wright	29 800.00
1965	Kathy Whitworth	28 658.00
1966	Kathy Whitworth	33 517.50
1967	Kathy Whitworth	32 937.50
1968	Kathy Whitworth	48 379.50
1969	Carol Mann	49 152.50
1970	Kathy Whitworth	30 235.01
1971	Kathy Whitworth	41 181.75
1972	Kathy Whitworth	65 063.99
1973	Kathy Whitworth	82 864.25
1974	JoAnne Carner	87 094.04
1975	Sandra Palmer	76 374.51
1976	Judy T Rankin	150 734.28
1977	Judy T Rankin	122 890.44
1978	Nancy Lopez	189 813.83
1979	Nancy Lopez	197 488.61
1980	Beth Daniel	231 000.42
1981	Beth Daniel	206 977.66
1982	JoAnne Carner	310 399.75
1983	JoAnne Carner	291 404.25
1984	Betsy King	266 771.00
1985	Nancy Lopez	416 472.50
1986	Pat Bradley	492 021.00

*Approximate figure

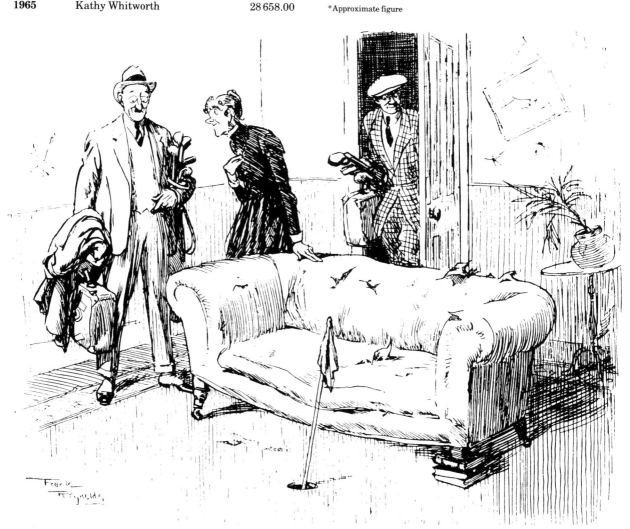

HOLIDAY GOLF

Landlady (showing apartments in the vicinity of famous links). 'OH, YOU'LL BE QUITE COMFORTABLE HERE, SIR; YOU SEE, WE'RE USED TO GOLFERS.' (Punch)

MILLION DOLLAR CLUB

Kathy Whitworth was the first player to earn a million dollars in prize money on the tour. She reached that landmark on 26 July 1981. Since then, 13 others have reached that goal, although the regularity with which it is now being achieved reflects the rapid increase in prize money in the last few years. This is reflected by the fact that Mickey Wright, the second most successful player in the tour's history, earned $368 770.01 between 1955 and 1980. Juli Inkster has won almost twice that amount in 3½ seasons.

Name	*Date/Event/Position*	*First Money*	*Wins*
Kathy Whitworth	26 July 1981 US Women's Open 3rd, $9000	8 July 1959 Fort Wayne Classic T7, $192.50	81
JoAnne Carner	30 August 1981 Columbia Savings Winner $22 500	15 February 1970 Burdine's Invitational T36, $305	31
(2nd million)	10 August 1986 Henredon Classic 2nd, $21 275	7 September 1981 Rail Charity Classic 1st, $18 750	11
Donna Caponi	30 August 1981 Columbia Savings T24, $1410	25 April 1965 Betsy Rawls, Peach Blossom Open T21, $102.50	24
Pat Bradley	3 April 1983 Nabisco Dinah Shore T15, $5292.40	3 February 1974 Burdine's Invitational T23, $246	10
(2nd million)	18 May 1986 Chrysler-Plymouth Classic T11, $3425	10 April 1983 J&B Scotch Pro-Am T30, $1313	11
Nancy Lopez	3 April 1983 Nabisco Dinah Shore T6, $12 294.50	6 August 1977 Colgate European Open 2nd, $9750	26
Amy Alcott	22 May 1983 Chrysler-Plymouth 3rd, $8750	2 February 1975 Burdine's Invitational T31, $230	17
Jane Blalock	17 July 1983 McDonald's Kids T25, $3220	25 May 1969 Bluegrass Invitational T15, $272	27
Beth Daniel	29 July 1984 du Maurier T6, $9281	18 February 1979 Elizabeth Arden T7, $3050	13
Jan Stephenson	24 March 1985 GNA Classic Winner, $37 500	7 July 1974 Niagara Iron 26th, $255	12
Hollis Stacy	7 April 1985 Nabisco Dinah Shore T13, $5605	21 July 1974 US Women's Open T14, $998.75	17
Patty Sheehan	5 May 1985 Moss Creek T2, $12 750	3 August 1980 West Virginia Classic T41, $420	14
Sally Little	10 November 1985 Mazda Japan T18, $3192	26 September 1971 Lincoln-Mercury Open T11, $610	14
Sandra Palmer	29 June 1986 Mayflower Classic 1st, $52 500	28 June 1964 Wademar Open T11, $230	21
Betsy King	10 August 1986 Henredon Classic 1st, $34 500	14 August 1977 Long Island Charity Classic T15, $1490	7

US Women's Open

A championship started in 1946 and adopted by the United States Golf Association in 1953, it is the leading championship in women's golf. Unlike all the others, there is no sponsorship, but the popularity of women's golf has grown out of all recognition in recent years and in 1979, the Open was watched by crowds averaging 12 000 for the last three days.

The championship is decided by 72 holes of strokeplay and is one of the very few occasions when amateurs and professionals compete together.

MILESTONES

1946 The first Women's Open produced one of the most famous players as winner. Patty Berg headed the qualifying field with 73, 72 for 145 at Spokane, Washington. In the matchplay section, she then beat Betty Jameson 5 and 4 in the final.

1947 Adoption of 72 holes of strokeplay. Betty Jameson, the previous year's runner-up, came back to win at Starmount Forest CC, Greensboro, North Carolina. She won by 6 strokes with a total of 295. Two amateurs were second.

1948 The great Mildred Zaharias, the 'Babe', triumphed with an even-par total of 300 at Atlantic City CC, New Jersey. In bad weather, she won by 8 strokes.

1949 Under the guidance of the Ladies' Professional Golf Association, Louise Suggs beat 'Babe' Zaharias by 14 strokes to register a total of 291—a record at that time.

1950 At the Rolling Hills CC, Wichita, Kansas, Mildred Zaharias wasted no time in equalling Louise Suggs's record of 291. She won by 9 strokes from the amateur Betsy Rawls, now Tournament Director of the LPGA.

1951 Betsy Rawls, now a professional, won the title at Druid Hills GC, Atlanta. Her score was 293, five better than Louise Suggs.

1952 Louise Suggs became champion for the second time with a record-breaking aggregate of 284 (70, 69, 70, 75) at the Bala GC, Philadelphia. Marilynn Smith set a low individual round record with 67 in the second round, but Marlene Bauer and Betty Jameson were joint runners-up on 291.

1953 A total of 37 entrants of whom 17 were professionals competed for the first championship to be run, at the request of the LPGA, by the USGA. It took place at the Country Club of Rochester, New York, and was won by Betsy Rawls after a play-off with Jacqueline Pung of Honolulu. Their 72-hole score was 302, Rawls winning the 18-hole play-off with 71 to 77.

1954 In a manner akin to Ben Hogan winning the US Men's Open after his terrible car crash, 'Babe' Zaharias ran away with the Women's championship at the Tam O'Shanter CC just over a year after her serious cancer operation. She won by 12 strokes from Betty Hicks, a victory which confirmed her as the leading American woman golfer of her time. It was her last appearance in the Open.

Mickey Wright, later one of the most famous names herself, was fourth and the leading amateur.

1955 Fay Crocker of Montevideo, Uruguay, became the first foreign winner at the Wichita CC, Kansas. In high winds, she led after every round and won by 4 strokes with a total of 299. 'Babe' Zaharias was unable to defend owing to another operation just before the event.

1956 Kathy Cornelius defeated Barbara McIntire, later to become US Women's Amateur champion, after they had tied on

302 at Northland CC, Minnesota. 'Babe' Zaharias was too ill to take part and died later in the year.

1957 Betsy Rawls won her third title at Winged Foot with a total of 299 without it actually being the lowest score. That was the 298 of Jacqueline Pung. However, she signed and returned the card as kept by her marker on which the 6 she had taken at the 4th hole was shown as a 5. The total was correct, but Jacqueline Pung was disqualified since a player is solely responsible for his or her score at each hole. If the mistake had been in the addition, it would not have mattered.

It was a tragedy even worse than that befalling Roberto de Vicenzo at the 1968 Masters who was not disqualified—simply prevented by his error from taking part in a play-off. The members of Winged Foot promptly raised a collection for Jacqueline Pung which reached over $3000 and exceeded the first prize of $1800 which she lost. Total prize-money was $7200. Competitors were asked to wear skirts not shorts in order to conform with a club rule.

1958 Start of a great burst of victories by Mickey Wright. She won three times in four years and four times in seven years. Her first success at Forest Lake CC, Michigan, was by 5 strokes after she had led throughout. A total of 290 left her 5 strokes clear of Louise Suggs. It was a new record total for championships under the USGA's direction. At 23, she was also the youngest winner to date. The leading amateur was Anne Quast, 20.

1959 Mickey Wright lowered her record total to 287 and Louise Suggs again followed her home, this time only 2 strokes behind. To maintain the uniformity, Anne Quast was again leading amateur, her 299 being the first by an amateur under 300. At Churchill Valley CC near Pittsburgh, Mickey Wright sought advice on the telephone for her putting troubles from Paul Runyan.

1960 Betsy Rawls became the first four-time winner with a score of 292 at Worcester CC, Massachusetts. This Club housed the men's Open in 1925 and became the first to complete the double. Mickey Wright led for three rounds before posting a final 82. Joyce Ziske was second, 1 stroke behind Rawls. Judy Torluemke, 15, finished leading amateur.

1961 Mickey Wright's third victory and one of her best over the Lower course at Baltusrol. The course measured 6372 yd and Wright's controlled power was seen to excellent advantage. She played the final 36 holes in 141 strokes and won by 6 strokes from Betsy Rawls with a total of 293.

1962 High scores and a surprising winner at the Dunes Golf and Beach Club, Myrtle Beach, South Carolina. Murle MacKenzie Lindstrom made up 5 strokes in the last round to win with 301. It was her first professional victory and she won by 2 strokes from Ruth Jessen and JoAnn Prentice. Her prize was $1800.

In contrast to the previous year, Mickey Wright scored 158 for the final 36 holes. The weather was bad throughout.

1963 Another winner, Mary Mills, scoring her first success in professional golf. Having set a record of 141 for the first two rounds, she won by 3 strokes with a total of 289 at Kenwood Country Club, Cincinnati. Mickey Wright did not play.

Prize-money totalled $9000 and the event was televised locally for the first time.

1964 Wright won her fourth title under USGA direction at her old home club, the San Diego CC, California, after a play-off with Ruth Jessen. They had tied on 290, but at the 72nd hole, Wright got down in 2 from a bunker whereas Jessen hit a wood to 3 ft and made a birdie. In the play-off, Wright had 70 against 72.

1965 Carol Mann, 6 ft 3 in tall, came back to win at Atlantic City CC, New Jersey, after an opening round of 78 which put her 7 strokes behind the leader, Cathy Cornelius. Cornelius had a closing round of 69 to finish on 292, 2 strokes behind Mann who had second and third rounds of 70.

Mickey Wright was unable to defend her title, but Catherine Lacoste was second amateur, 8 strokes behind Mrs Helen Sigel

Wilson whose 296 set an amateur record.

The last two rounds were played over two days and the final round was televised nationally for the first time.

1966 Sandra Spuzich, 29, became yet another to celebrate her first professional victory in the national Open. At Hazeltine CC, Chaska, she defeated defending champion Carol Mann by 1 stroke with 297. The lowest round of the championship was an opening 71 by Mickey Wright.

1967 A famous victory by Catherine Lacoste of France at the Cascades course in Hot Springs, Virginia. She became the first amateur to win the title after leading at the half-way stage by 5 strokes. She preserved this lead in the third round and increased her lead to 7 at one point, but her play deteriorated and, in the end, she had only a couple of strokes to spare from Susie Maxwell and Beth Stone. At one stage, Louise Suggs, 9 behind after 54 holes, had made up 8 of them.

1968 A triumph from start to finish for Susie Maxwell Berning who married only seven weeks before the championship began at Moselem Springs, Pennsylvania. She won by 3 strokes from Mickey Wright with a total of 289, her 71 equalling the lowest last round by a champion. However, Wright's 68 was the lowest last round by any player.

There was a record entry of 104; first prize was $5000.

1969 Another first professional victory in the Open. Donna Caponi held off the challenge of Peggy Wilson to win by 1 stroke at the Scenic Hills CC, Pensacola, Florida.

She took the lead late on and was delayed 15 minutes by an electric storm as she waited to play the 18th. After taking shelter in the clubhouse, she then got a birdie for a round of 69, the best by a champion.

1970 Donna Caponi joined Mickey Wright as the only champion at that time to successfully defend her title. In so doing she also equalled Wright's record score of 287. At Muskogee CC, Oklahoma, she was almost caught by Sandra Haynie and Sandra Spuzich after being 4 ahead with a record 54-hole total of 210.

1971 A commanding win for JoAnne Carner at the Kahkwa Club, Pennsylvania. She led after every round and won by 7 strokes from Kathy Whitworth with a total of 288. She thus became the fourth player to have won the US Women's Amateur and Open championships; she won her last Amateur title in 1968.

Three amateurs finished in the first ten.

Prize-money totalled $34 450.

1972 Susie Berning joined a select group of six who have won the Open at least twice. At Winged Foot, New York, she won with a score of 299, 1 stroke ahead of Judy Rankin, Pam Barnett and Kathy Ahern. However, after an opening 79, she did not look the likely champion. The defending champion JoAnne Carner also began with a 79, but despite the heavy rains that made 70 the best round of the week, Susie Berning's final round of 71 saw her home. In that round, she had a 2 at the 17th to Pam Barnett's 4.

Marilynn Smith finished 72 holes in her 20th consecutive Open—a record. Nine amateurs from the entry of 176 also completed 72 holes although the USGA set a limit of 150 competitors. Prize-money exceeded $38 000 with the winner claiming $6000—both records.

1973 Susie Berning successfully defended her title and so became only the third player to win the Open three times. At Rochester, New York, she won by 5 strokes from Shelley Hamlin and Gloria Ehret with a total of 290.

Marilynn Smith played through her 21st consecutive Open and the amateur Cynthia Hill set a new record with a first round of 68.

1974 Sandra Haynie of Texas had birdies on the last 2 holes of La Grange CC, Illinois, to win by a single stroke from Carol Mann and Beth Stone. JoAnne Carner who led the field by 2 strokes with 9 holes to play, tied for 4th place on 297, 2 strokes behind Haynie.

Prize-money totalled $40 000.

1975 There were only two sub-par rounds all week in the 23rd championship at Atlantic City CC. One of these was a third round of 71 by Sandra Palmer who added a final par round of 72 to win by 4 strokes on 295. Among those who tied for 2nd place was Nancy Lopez, then still an amateur. It was the best finish by an amateur since Catherine Lacoste won in 1967.

1976 JoAnne Carner, champion in 1971, denied Sandra Palmer a successful defence of her title. After they had tied on 292, 8 over par, at Rolling Green GC, Pennsylvania, Carner won the play-off with 76 to 78, further indication of the difficulty of the course. It was the first play-off since 1964.

Miss Nancy Porter made a hole-in-one on the 16th (135 yd) in the second round. It was only the fourth in the history of the championship, but two of the four have been by Nancy Porter. Sectional qualifying was necessary for the first time. The entry reached 205.

1977 Hollis Stacy, 23, had a creditable victory at Hazeltine National GC, Chaska, Minnesota, scene of Tony Jacklin's US Open victory in 1970. She led after all four rounds and won by 2 strokes with a total of 292. Nancy Lopez and JoAnne Carner were 2nd and 3rd. All three were former Girls' Junior champions. It was Lopez's first tournament as a professional. Prize-money totalled a record $75 000.

1978 Hollis Stacy joined the band of those who have successfully defended their titles. She is also the youngest to win twice. It was her fifth USGA title; she won three consecutive Girls' titles.

Sally Little set a new individual round record with 65.

1979 Jerilyn Britz chose a good moment to win her first tournament as a professional. She captured the 27th Women's Open at Brooklawn CC, Connecticut, by 2 strokes from Debbie Massey and Sandra Palmer. Her total of 284 (70, 70, 75, 69) was 3 strokes lower than any returned by a winner since the USGA took over the running of the event. Louise Suggs won with 284 in 1952, but the Bala course measured only 5460 yd compared with 6010 yd at Brooklawn.

Jerilyn Britz, who did not turn professional until she was 30 in 1973, left a position as a teacher of physical education at New Mexico State University to try her hand on the golf tour. Twenty-third in the money list in 1978, she led the 1979 LPGA championship with 7 holes to play, but it was obviously good experience.

Susie Berning's second-round 66 was the second lowest in the championship's history. Sally Little set the record in 1978.

1980 A championship dominated by Amy Alcott, 24 of Santa Monica, California. In a temperature of over 100 degrees at Richland CC, Nashville, Tennessee, she broke the 72-hole aggregate by 4 strokes. She also set a record for the lowest first (208) and last (210) 54 holes and equalled the lowest last 36 holes, 140, by Mickey Wright in 1959.

She was 8 strokes ahead after three rounds and 10 ahead with 1 hole to play. She dropped a stroke at the 18th and won by 9. There were 337 entries and the prize-money was a record $140 000.

1981 In a thrilling finish, Pat Bradley beat Beth Daniel by 1 stroke at La Grange CC, Illinois, breaking Amy Alcott's 72-hole aggregate record, set the year before, by 1 stroke. Bradley achieved her first victory in the championship with third and fourth rounds of 68 and 66. This lowered by 6 strokes the record total for the final 36 holes held by Mickey Wright since 1959 and equalled in 1980 by Amy Alcott.

1982 Janet Alex, the only player to finish under par, joined the ranks of those whose first victory as a professional came in the US Women's Open. Her total was 283, a comfortable 6 strokes clear of the first four-way tie for second place. JoAnne Carner led by 3 at halfway and Beth Daniel by 1 after 54 holes but Alex beat them all in the final round with a marvellous 68.

1983 Jan Stephenson won a high scoring Open in sweltering heat at the Cedar Ridge CC, Tulsa, with a total of 290. Daily temperatures were over 100 degrees. Stephenson's first round 72 included the holing of a 6-iron shot for an eagle 2 on the 11th but it was not until the third day that Stephenson took over the lead. In her fourth round of 74, she could afford bogeys at the 17th and 18th to win by one. Defending champion Janet Alex (now Mrs Anderson) shot a first round 82 and missed the cut. Pat Bradley, with a hole-in-one at the 6th, went out in 31 in her third round to equal the Open's 9-hole record set by Judy Bell in 1964.

1984 Hollis Stacy completed a hat-trick of wins by winning at Salem CC, Peabody, Massachusetts by 1 stroke from Rosie Jones with a total of 290. Three strokes behind with a round to play, Stacy ended with a 69, the lowest score of the four days. She is only the fifth player to have won three titles.

1985 Kathy Baker, a member of the 1982 Curtis Cup and World Amateur teams, scored her first victory as a professional with a score of 280 at Baltusrol, New Jersey. She defeated Judy Clark by 3 strokes. Clark matched the Open record for an individual round with her 65 on Saturday. There were 626 entries.

1986 This was the championship that had almost everything: Monsoon weather; a train on the nearby track that burst into flames; an earth tremor on Saturday morning (4.2 on the Richter Scale); a play-off and finally a worthy champion in Jane Geddes. For the third time in five years, it was the champion's first victory as a professional.

She had tied with Sally Little on 287, closing with a 69 to Little's 70, but won the play-off, the first since 1976, with 71 to 73.

DETAILED RECORDS

Most victories
4, Mickey Wright, 1958–59–61–64; Betsy Rawls, 1951–53–57–60
3, 'Babe' Zaharias, 1948–50–54; Susie Berning, 1968–72–73; Hollis Stacy, 1977–78–84

Oldest winner
Fay Crocker, 40 years 11 months, 1955

Youngest winner
Catherine Lacoste, 22 years and 5 days, 1967
Hollis Stacy, 23 years 4 months 8 days, 1977

Biggest margin of victory
14 strokes, Louise Suggs, 1949
12 strokes, Mildred 'Babe' Didrikson Zaharias, 1954

Lowest winning aggregate (after 1953)
279, Pat Bradley, La Grange CC, 1981
280, Amy Alcott, Richland CC, 1980; Kathy Baker, Baltusrol, 1985

Lowest aggregate by runner-up
280, Beth Daniel, La Grange CC, 1981

Most times runner-up
4, Louise Suggs, 1955–58–59–63

Lowest single round
65, Sally Little, fourth round, Indianapolis CC, 1978; Judy Clark, third round, Baltusrol, 1985
66, Susie Maxwell Berning, second round, Brooklawn CC, 1979; Pat Bradley, fourth round, La Grange, 1981

Lowest first round
68, Cynthia Hill, Rochester CC, New York, 1973; Kathy Ahern, La Grange, Illinois, 1974; Donna Young, Indianapolis CC, 1978

Lowest second round
66, Susie Maxwell Berning, Brooklawn CC, 1979

Lowest third round
65, Judy Clark, Baltusrol, 1985

Lowest fourth round
65, Sally Little, Indianapolis CC, 1978

Lowest first 36 holes
139, Donna Caponi and Carol Mann, Muskogee CC, 1970; Kathy Whitworth and Bonnie Lauer, La Grange CC, 1981; JoAnne Carner, Del Paso CC, 1982

Lowest last 36 holes
134, Pat Bradley, La Grange CC, 1981

Lowest first 54 holes
208, Amy Alcott, 1980

Lowest last 54 holes
208, Pat Bradley, 1981

Lowest last round by a champion
66, Pat Bradley, 1981
68, Janet Alex, 1982

Lowest 9 holes
31, Judy Bell, 1964 and Pat Bradley, 1983

Highest winning score
302, Betsy Rawls and Jacqueline Pung, Rochester CC, 1953 and Kathy Cornelius and Barbara McIntire, Northland CC, 1956

Largest span between victories
9 years, Betsy Rawls, 1951–60

Consecutive winners
27, Mickey Wright, 1958–59; Donna Caponi, 1969–70; Susie Maxwell Berning, 1972–73; Hollis Stacy, 1977–78

Amateur winner
Catherine Lacoste, 1967. Barbara McIntire lost a play-off to Kathy Cornelius in 1956

Overseas winners
Fay Crocker, 1955; Catherine Lacoste, 1967; Jan Stephenson, 1983

Play-offs
6, 1947–52–53–56–64–76

Poorest start by champion
79, Susie Maxwell Berning, 1972

Poorest finish by champion
79, Kathy Cornelius, 1956; Catherine Lacoste, 1967

Youngest leading amateur winner
Judy Torluemke was 15 years, 1960

Best comebacks by champions
After 18 holes: Susie Maxwell Berning in 1972 and Carol Mann in 1965 were 7 strokes behind
After 36 holes: in 1953, Betsy Rawls was 9 behind
After 54 holes: in 1962, Murle Lindstrom and in 1969, Donna Caponi were 5 behind
In 1956, Barbara McIntire made up 8 strokes in the last round to tie Kathy Cornelius but lost the play-off

Leaders' fate
Up until 1981, a player who has led after 18 holes has won 13 of the 29 Opens. A player who has led after 36 holes has won 14 times. A player who has led after 54 holes has won 21 times.

Most top ten finishes
14, Louise Suggs
13, Mickey Wright, Kathy Whitworth
10, JoAnne Carner
 9, Donna Caponi, Sandra Haynie

Prize Money

	Total $	First Prize
1965	17 780	
1981	148 670	22 000
1982	175 000	27 000
1983	200 000	32 780
1984	225 000	36 000
1985	250 000	41 975
1986	300 000	50 000

RESULTS

Year	Winner	Venue	Score
1946	Patty Berg beat Betty Jameson 5 and 4	Spokane, Washington	
1947	Betty Jameson	Starmount Forest CC	295*
1948	Mildred Zaharias	Atlantic City CC	300
1949	Louise Suggs	Prince Georges G and CC	291
1950	Mildred Zaharias	Rolling Hills CC	291
1951	Betsy Rawls	Druid Hills GC	293
1952	Louise Suggs	Bala GC	284*
	Taken over by USGA		
1953	Betsy Rawls	CC of Rochester	302*
1954	Mildred Zaharias	Salem CC	291
1955	Fay Crocker	Wichita CC	299
1956	Kathy Cornelius	Northland CC	302*
1957	Betsy Rawls	Winged Foot	299
1958	Mickey Wright	Forest Lake CC	290
1959	Mickey Wright	Churchill Valley CC	287
1960	Betsy Rawls	Worcester CC	292
1961	Mickey Wright	Baltusrol GC (Lower)	293
1962	Murle Lindstrom	Dunes Golf and Beach Club	301
1963	Mary Mills	Kenwood CC	289
1964	Mickey Wright	San Diego CC	290*
1965	Carol Mann	Atlantic City CC	290
1966	Sandra Spuzich	Hazeltine National GC	297
1967	Catherine Lacoste	Hot Springs, Virginia	294
1968	Susie Berning	Moselem Springs GC	289
1969	Donna Caponi	Scenic Hills CC	294
1970	Donna Caponi	Muskogee CC	287
1971	JoAnne Carner	Kahkwa Club	288
1972	Susie Berning	Winged Foot	299
1973	Susie Berning	CC of Rochester	290
1974	Sandra Haynie	La Grange CC	295
1975	Sandra Palmer	Atlantic City CC	295
1976	JoAnne Carner	Rolling Green GC	292*
1977	Hollis Stacy	Hazeltine National	292
1978	Hollis Stacy	Indianapolis CC	289
1979	Jerilyn Britz	Brooklawn CC	284
1980	Amy Alcott	Richland CC	280
1981	Pat Bradley	La Grange CC	279
1982	Janet Alex	Del Paso CC	283
1983	Jan Stephenson	Cedar Ridge CC	290
1984	Hollis Stacy	Salem CC	290
1985	Kathy Baker	Baltusrol	280
1986	Jane Geddes	NCR CC, Dayton	287*

*After play-off

SCENE—*Country Police Court*

Magistrate. " My boy, do you fully realise the nature of an oath ? "

Boy. " Well, I oughter, considerin' the times I've caddied for yer ! " (Punch)

WPGA Tour (1979–86)

DETAILED RECORDS

Most victories
12, Cathy Panton, Dale Reid
 9, Muriel Thomson
 8, Jenny Lee Smith
 7, Beverly Huke
 6, Michelle Walker
 5, Laura Davies, Debbie Dowling

Most wins in one year
4, Laura Davies (1986)
3, Christine Langford (1979)
  Alison Sheard (1979)
  Muriel Thomson (1980)
  Jenny Lee Smith (1981)
  Cathy Panton (1983)
  Dale Reid (1983)

Youngest winner
Liselotte Neumann, 19 years 97 days, 1984 Hoganas Open, Molle GC, Sweden
Christine Lyle (née Trew), 20 years 76 days, 1980 Carlsberg Tournament, Sand Moor, Leeds
Jane Connachan, 20 years 174 days, 1984 Colt Cars Jersey Open, Royal Jersey

Oldest winner
Kathy Whitworth, 45 years 17 days, 1984 Smirnoff Ladies' Irish Open, Clandeboye

Career Money Leaders

	Year joined tour	£
Dale Reid	1979	106 597
Muriel Thomson	1979	85 693
Cathy Panton	1979	62 048
Debbie Dowling	1981	60 725
Beverly Huke	1979	59 932
Laura Davies	1985	59 236
Kitrina Douglas	1984	52 857
Liselotte Neumann	1985	51 064
Jenny Lee Smith	1979	50 997
Jane Forrest	1979	49 706
Peggy Conley	1984	45 979
Jane Connachan	1984	44 868
Maxine Burton	1979	43 415
Gillian Stewart	1985	41 992

Leading Money Winners
1979	Alison Sheard	£4965
1980	Muriel Thomson	8008
1981	Jenny Lee Smith	13 519
1982	Jenny Lee Smith	12 551
1983	Beverly Huke	9226
1984	Dale Reid	28 239
1985	Laura Davies	21 736
1986	Laura Davies	37 500

Order of Merit Winners
1979	Catherine Panton
1980	Muriel Thomson
1981	Jenny Lee Smith
1982	Jenny Lee Smith
1983	Muriel Thomson
1984	Dale Reid
1985	Laura Davies
1986	Laura Davies

Most official money won in a rookie year
1984	Kitrina Douglas	£19 900
1985	Laura Davies	£21 736

Lowest stroke average
1983	Beverly Huke	74.96 (1.96 over par)
1984	Dale Reid	73.01 (1.01 over par)
1985	Beverly Huke	72.37 (0.17 under par)
1986	Laura Davies	72.09 (0.71 under par)

Biggest winning margin
11 strokes, Ayako Okamota, 1984 Hitachi Ladies' British Open, Woburn
 9 strokes, Penny Grice Whittaker, 1986 Belgian Ladies' Open, Royal Waterloo
 8 strokes, Sarah Levaque, 1981 United Friendly Tournament, Manor House Hotel, Moretonhampstead
 8 strokes, Dale Reid, 1984 J S Bloor Eastleigh Classic, Fleming Park

Lowest winning aggregate
268, Laura Davies, 1986 Greater Manchester Tournament, Haigh Hall
274, Debbie Dowling, 1986 Laing Ladies' Classic, Stoke Poges
278, Kitrina Douglas, 1986 Mitsubishi Colt Cars Jersey Open, Royal Jersey

In 1984, Dale Reid won the J S Bloor Eastleigh Classic at Fleming Park with 254 (61, 64, 63, 66) but the course measured only 4436 yards.

Lowest 54-hole total
200, Laura Davies, 1986 Great Manchester Tournament, Haigh Hall
204, Debbie Dowling, 1986 Laing Ladies' Classic, Stoke Poges
205, Debbie Dowling, 1985 Bowring Birmingham Ladies' Classic, Pype Hayes

Lowest 36-hole total
133, Laura Davies, 1986 Greater Manchester Tournament, Haigh Hall
135, Penny Grice Whittaker, 1986 Belgian Ladies' Open, Royal Waterloo
135, Debbie Dowling, 1986 Laing Ladies' Classic, Stoke Poges

Lowest individual rounds
63, Laura Davies, 1986 Greater Manchester Tournament, Haigh Hall
64, Alison Sheard, 1986 Greater Manchester Tournament, Haigh Hall
65, Corinne Dibnah, 1986 Laing Ladies' Classic, Stoke Poges
65, Penny Grice Whittaker, 1986 Belgian Ladies' Open, Royal Waterloo
65, Penny Grice, 1985 Bowring Birmingham Ladies' Classic, Pype Hayes
65, Federica Dassu and Debbie Dowling, 1986 Mitsubishi Colt Cars Jersey Open, Royal Jersey

Lowest 9 holes
30, Susan Moon, 1979 European Open, Valbonne
30, Joanna Smurthwaite, 1983 Woodhall Hills Tournament, Woodhall Hills
30, Karstin Ehrnlund, 1984 McEwan's Lager Manchester Classic, Heaton Park
30, Kim Bauer, 1984 United Friendly Tournament, Hill Barn, Worthing
30, Alison Nicholas, UBM Classic, Arcot Hall
30, Penny Grice Whittaker, 1986 Belgian Ladies' Open, Royal Waterloo

Most consecutive birdies
6, Michelle Walker, 1984 Baume and Mercier Ladies' International Classic, Lilley Brook, Cheltenham
6, Federica Dassu, 1985 Ulster Volkswagen Classic, Belvoir Park

Most birdies in one round

10, Laura Davies, 1986 Greater Manchester Tournament, Haigh Hall

9, Alison Sheard, 1986 Greater Manchester Tournament, Haigh Hall

9, Beverly New, 1986 Ladies' British Open, Royal Birkdale

9, Michelle Walker, 1984 Baume and Mercier Ladies' International Classic, Lilley Brook

9, Federica Dassu, 1985 Ulster Volkswagen Classic, Belvoir Park

9, Maxine Burton, 1983 White Horse Whisky Challenge, Selsdon Park

First Player. 'MY WIFE THREATENS TO LEAVE ME IF I DON'T CHUCK GOLF.'
Second Player. 'THAT SOUNDS SERIOUS.'
First Player. 'IT *IS* SERIOUS. I SHALL MISS HER.' (Punch)

Great Golfing Achievements

Record Dimensions

Note—these records are taken from the *Guinness Book of Records*

Origins

Although a stained glass window in Gloucester Cathedral, dating from 1350, portrays a golfer-like figure, the earliest mention of golf occurs in a prohibiting law passed by the Scottish Parliament in March 1457 under which 'goff be utterly cryit doune and not usit'. The Romans had a cognate game called *paganica* which may have been carried to Britain before AD 400. The Chinese Nationalist Golf Association claim the game is of Chinese origin ('*Ch'ui Wan*—the ball hitting game') in the 3rd century BC. There were official ordinances prohibiting a ball game with clubs in Belgium and Holland from 1360. Gutta percha balls succeeded feather balls in 1848 and by 1902 were in turn succeeded by rubber-cored balls, invented in 1899 by Coburn Haskell (USA). Steel shafts were authorized in the USA in 1925 and in Britain in 1929

Club

Oldest The oldest club of which there is written evidence is the Gentlemen Golfers (now the Honourable Company of Edinburgh Golfers) formed in March 1744—ten years prior to the institution of the Royal and Ancient Club of St Andrews, Fife. However, the Royal Burgess Golfing Society of Edinburgh claim to have been founded in 1735.

Course

Highest The highest golf course in the world is the Tuctu Golf Club in Morococha, Peru, which is 14 335 ft above sea-level at its lowest point. Golf has, however, been played in Tibet at an altitude of over 16 000 ft.

The highest golf course in Great Britain is one of 9 holes at Leadhills, Strathclyde, 1500 ft above sea-level.

Longest hole

The longest hole in the world is the 7th hole (par-7) of the Sano Course, Satsuki GC, Japan, which measures 909 yd. In August 1927 the 6th hole at Prescott Country Club in Arkansas, USA, measured 838 yd. The longest hole on a championship course in Great Britain is the sixth at Troon, Strathclyde, which stretches 577 yd.

Largest green

Probably the largest green in the world is that of the par-6 695 yd 5th hole at International GC, Bolton, Massachusetts, USA, with an area greater than 28 000 ft.

Biggest bunker

The world's biggest bunker (called a trap in the USA) is Hell's Half Acre on the 585 yd hole of the Pine Valley course, Clementon, New Jersey, USA, built in 1912 and generally regarded as the world's most trying course.

Longest course

The world's longest course is the par-77 8325 yd International GC, (*see also above*), from the 'Tiger' tees, remodelled in 1969 by Robert Trent Jones. Floyd Satterlee Rood used the United States as a course, when he played from the Pacific surf to the Atlantic surf from 14 September 1963 to 3 October 1964 in 114 737 strokes. He lost 3511 balls on the 3397.7 mile trail.

Longest drives

In long-driving contests 330 yd is rarely surpassed at sea-level. In officially regulated long driving contests over level ground the greatest distance recorded is 392 yd by William Thomas 'Tommie' Campbell (Foxrock Golf Club) at Dun Laoghaire, Co. Dublin, in July 1964.

On an airport runway Liam Higgins (Ireland) drove a Spalding Top Flite ball 579.8 m at Baldonnel military airport, Dublin, Ireland on 25 September 1984. The greatest recorded drive on an ordinary course is one of 515 yd by Michael Hoke Austin of Los Angeles, California, USA, in the US National Seniors Open Championship at Las Vegas, Nevada, on 25 September 1974. Austin, 6 ft 2 in tall and weighing 210 lb drove the ball to within a yard of the green on the par-4 450 yd 5th hole of the Winterwood Course and it rolled 65 yd past the flagstick. He was aided by an estimated 35 mph tailwind.

A drive of 2640 yd across ice was achieved by an Australian meteorologist named Nils Lied at Mawson Base, Antarctica, in 1962. Arthur Lynskey claimed a drive of 200 yd horizontal and 2 miles vertical off Pikes Peak, Colorado (14 110 ft) on 28 June 1968. On the moon the energy expended on a mundane 300 yd drive would achieve, craters permitting, a distance of 1 mile.

Longest putt

The longest recorded holed putt in a major tournament was one of 86 ft on the vast 13th green at the Augusta National, Georgia by Cary Middlecoff (USA) in the 1955 Masters' Tournament. Robert Tyre 'Bobby' Jones, Jr (1902–71) was reputed to have holed a putt in excess of 100 ft at the fifth green in the first round of the 1927 Open at St Andrews. Bob Cook (USA) sunk a putt measured at 140 ft 2¾ in on the 18th at St Andrew's in the International Fourball Pro Am Tournament on 1 October 1976.

SCORING RECORDS

Lowest 9 holes and 18 holes

Men At least four players are recorded to have played a long course (over 6000 yd) in a score of 58, most recently Monte Carlo Money (USA) (b. 3 December 1954) the par-72, 6607 yd Las Vegas Municipal GC, Nevada, USA on 11 March 1981. The lowest recorded score on a long course in Britain is 58 by Harry Weetman (1920–72) the British Ryder Cup golfer, for the 6171 yd Croham Hurst Course, Croydon, Surrey, on 30 January 1956. Alfred Edward Smith (1903–85) achieved an 18-hole score of 55 (15 under bogey 70) on his home course on 1 January 1936. The course measured 4248 yd. The detail was 4, 2, 3, 4, 2, 4, 3, 4, 3 = 29 out, and 2, 3, 3, 3, 3, 2, 5, 4, 1 = 26 in.

Nine holes in 25 (4, 3, 3, 2, 3, 3, 1, 4, 2) was recorded by A J 'Bill'

Burke in a round in 57 (32 + 25) on the 6389 yd par-71 Normandie course St Louis Missouri, USA on 20 May 1970. The tournament record is 27 by Mike Souchak (USA) for the second nine (par-35) first round of the 1955 Texas Open (*see 72 holes*), Andy North (USA) second nine (par-34), first round, 1975 BC Open at En-Joie GC, Endicott, NY, Jose Maria Canizares (Spain), first nine, third round, in the 1978 Swiss Open on the 6811 yd Crans-Sur course and by Robert Lee (GB) first nine, first round, in the Monte Carlo Open on the 6249 yd Mont Agel course on 28 June 1985.

The United States PGA tournament record for 18 holes is 59 (30 + 29) by Al Geiberger in the second round of the Danny Thomas Classic, on the 72-par 7249 yd Colonial GC course, Memphis, Tennessee on 10 June 1977. Three golfers have recorded 59 over 18 holes in non-PGA tournaments: Samuel Jackson Snead in the third round of the Sam Snead Festival at White Sulphur Springs, West Virginia, USA on 16 May 1959; Gary Player (South Africa) in the second round of the Brazilian Open in Rio de Janeiro on 29 November 1974, and David Jagger (GB) in a Pro-Am tournament prior to the 1973 Nigerian Open at Ikoyi Golf Club, Lagos.

Lowest 18 holes

Women The lowest recorded score on an 18-hole course (over 6000 yd) for a woman is 62 (30 + 32) by Mary 'Mickey' Kathryn Wright (USA) on the Hogan Park Course (par-71, 6286 yd) at Midland, Texas, USA, in November 1964. Wanda Morgan recorded a score of 60 (31 + 29) on the Westgate and Birchington Golf Club course, Kent, over 18 holes (5002 yd) on 11 July 1929.

Lowest 18 holes

Great Britain The lowest score recorded in a first class professional tournament on a course of more than 6000 yd in Great Britain is 61 (29 + 32), by Thomas Bruce Haliburton (1915–75) of Wentworth GC in the Spalding Tournament at Worthing, West Sussex, in June 1952, and 61 (32 + 29) by Peter J Butler in the Bowmaker Tournament on the Old Course at Sunningdale, Berkshire, on 4 July 1967.

Lowest 36 holes

The record for 36 holes is 122 (59 + 63) by Sam Snead in the 1959 Sam Snead Festival on 16–17 May 1959. Horton Smith (1908–1963), twice US Masters Champion, scored 121 (63 + 58) on a short course on 21 December 1928 (*see 72 holes*). The lowest score by a British golfer has been 124 (61 + 63) by Alexander Walter Barr 'Sandy' Lyle (b. 9 February 1958) in the Nigerian Open at the 6024 yd (par-71) Ikoyi Golf Club, Lagos in 1978.

Lowest 72 holes

The lowest recorded score on a first-class course is 255 (29 under par) by Leonard Peter Tupling (GB) in the Nigerian Open at Ikoyi Golf Club, Lagos in February 1981, made up of 63, 66, 62 and 64 (average 63.75 per round).

The lowest 72 holes in a US professional event is 257 (60, 68, 64, 65) by Mike Souchak in the 1955 Texas Open at San Antonio.

The lowest 72 holes in an Open championship in Europe is 262 (67, 66, 66, 63) by Percy Alliss (GB) (1897–1975) in the 1932 Italian Open at San Remo, and by Lu Liang Huan (Taiwan) in the 1971 French Open at Biarritz. Kelvin D G Nagle of Australia shot 261 in the Hong Kong Open in 1961. The lowest for four rounds in a British first class tournament is 262 (66, 63, 66 and 67) by Bernard Hunt in the Piccadilly tournament on the par-68 6184 yd Wentworth East Course, Virginia Water, Surrey on 4–5 October 1966. Horton Smith scored 245 (63, 58, 61 and 63) for 72 holes on the 4700 yd course (par-64) at Catalina Country Club, California, USA, to win the Catalina Open on 21–23 December 1928.

World one-club record

Thad Daber (USA), with a 6-iron played the 6037 yd Lochmore GC, Cary, N. Carolina, USA in 73 on 10 November 1985 to win the world one-club championship.

Highest score

It is recorded that Chevalier von Cittern went round 18 holes in 316, averaging 17.55 per hole, at Biarritz, France in 1888. Steven Ward took 222 strokes for the 6212 yd Pecos Course, Reeves County, Texas, USA, on 18 June 1976—but he was only aged 3 years 286 days.

Most shots for one hole

A woman player in the qualifying round of the Shawnee Invitational for Ladies at Shawnee-on-Delaware, Pennsylvania, USA, in c 1912, took 166 strokes for the short 130 yd 16th hole. Her tee shot went into the Binniekill River and the ball floated. She put out in a boat with her exemplary but statistically minded husband at the oars. She eventually beached the ball 1½ miles downstream but was not yet out of the wood. She had to play through one on the home run. In a competition at Peacehaven, Sussex, England in 1890, A J Lewis had 156 putts on one green without holing out.

The highest score for a single hole in the British Open is 21 by a player in the inaugural meeting at Prestwick in 1860. Double figures have been recorded on the card of the winner only once, when Willie Fernie (1851–1924) scored a ten at Musselburgh, Lothian, in 1883. Ray Ainsley of Ojai, California, took 19 strokes for the par-4 16th hole during the second round of the US Open at Cherry Hills Country Club, Denver, Colorado, on 10 June 1938. Most of the strokes were used in trying to extricate the ball from a brook. Hans Merell of Mogadore, Ohio, took 19 strokes on the par-3 16th (222 yd) during the third round of the Bing Crosby National Tournament at Cypress Point Club, Del Monte, California, USA, on 17 January 1959.

Rounds fastest

Individual With such variations in lengths of courses, speed records, even for rounds under par, are of little comparative value. Rick Baker completed 18 holes (6142 yd) in 25 min 48.47 sec at Surfer's Paradise, Queensland, Australia on 4 September 1982, but this test permitted the striking of the ball whilst still moving. The record for a still ball is 28.09 min by Gary Shane Wright at Tewantin-Noosa Golf Club, Queensland (18 holes, 6039 yd) on 9 December 1980. Roger Sanders set a British record of 31 min 50 sec at East Berkshire Golf Club, Berkshire on 11 May 1986.

Round fastest

Team Seventy-seven players completed the 18-hole 6502 yd Kern City course, California, USA in 10 min 30 sec on 24 August 1984 using only one ball. They scored 80!

Rounds slowest

The slowest stroke play tournament round was one of 6 hr 45 min taken by South Africa in the first round of the 1972 World Cup at the Royal Melbourne GC, Australia. This was a four-ball medal round, everything holed out.

Most rounds

The greatest number of rounds played on foot in 24 hr is 22 rounds and 5 holes (401 holes) by Ian Colston, 35, at Bendigo GC, Victoria (par-73, 6061 yd) on 27–28 November 1971. The British record is 360 holes by Antony J. Clark at Childwall GC, Liverpool on 18 July 1983. Using golf carts for transport Charles Stock played 702 holes in 24 hr at an average 72.12 per round at Boston Hills Country Club, Hudson, Ohio, USA on 7–8 July 1985. Terry Zachary played 391 holes in 12 hours on the 6706 yd course at Connaught Golf Club, Alberta, Canada on 16 June 1986. The most holes played on foot in a week (168 hr) is 1128 by Steve Hylton at the Mason Rudolph Golf Club (6060 yd), Clarkesville, Tennessee, USA, from 25–31 August 1980.

Throwing the golf ball

The lowest recorded score for throwing a golf ball round 18 holes (over 6000 yd) is 82 by Joe Flynn (USA), 21, at the 6228 yd Port Royal Course, Bermuda, on 27 March 1975.

Longest span
Jacqueline Ann Mercer (née Smith) won her first South African title at Humewood GC, Port Elizabeth in 1948, and her fourth at Port Elizabeth GC on 4 May 1979, 31 years later.

Most club championships
Bernard Charles Cusack has won a record total of 34 Club championships, including 33 consecutively, at the Narembeen GC, Western Australia, between 1943 and 1982. The women's record is 31 by Molly St John Pratt at the Stanthorpe GC, Queensland, Australia from 1931 to 1979, and also by 67 year old Helen Gray at Todmorden GC, Lancashire between 1951 and 1985. The record for consecutive wins is 22 (1959–80) by Patricia Mary Shepherd at Turriff GC, Aberdeenshire, Scotland.

Record tie
The longest delayed result in any National Open Championship occurred in the 1931 US Open at Toledo, Ohio. George von Elm (1901–61) and Billy Burke (1902–72) tied at 292, then tied the first replay at 149. Burke won the second replay by a single stroke after 72 extra holes.

Largest tournament
The Volkswagen Grand Prix Open Amateur Championship in the United Kingdom attracted a record 321 779 (206 820 men and 114 958 women) competitors in 1984.

HOLES IN ONE

Longest
The longest straight hole ever holed in one shot is the tenth (447 yd) at Miracle Hills Golf Club, Omaha, Nebraska, USA by Robert Mitera on 7 October 1965. Mitera stood 5 ft 6 in tall and weighed 165 lb (11 st 11 lb). He was a two handicap player who normally drove 245 yd. A 50 mph gust carried his shot over a 290 yd drop-off. The longest 'dog-leg' hole achieved in one is the 480 yd fifth at Hope Country Club, Arkansas by L Bruce on 15 November 1962. The women's record is 393 yd by Marie Robie on the first hole of the Furnace Brook Golf Club, Wollaston, Massachusetts, USA, on 4 September 1949. The longest hole in one performed in the British Isles is the 7th (par-4, 393 yd) at West Lancashire GC by Peter Richard Parkinson on 6 June 1972.

Most
The greatest number of holes-in-one in a career is 68 by Harry Lee Bonner from 1967 to 1985, most at his home 9-hole course of Las Gallinas, San Rafael, California, USA. The British record is 31 by Charles T Chevalier of Heaton Moor Golf Club, Stockport, Greater Manchester between 20 June 1918 and 1970.

The most holes-in-one in a year is 28 by Scott Palmer from 5 June 1983 to 31 May 1984, all on par-3 or par-4 holes between 130 yd and 350 yd in length at Ballboa Park, San Diego, California, USA.

Consecutive
There are at least 16 cases of 'aces' being achieved in two consecutive holes, of which the greatest was Norman L Manley's unique 'double albatross' on the par-4 330 yd seventh and par-4 290 yd eighth holes on the Del Valle Country Club Course, Saugus, California, on 2 September 1964. The first woman to record consecutive 'aces' was Sue Prell, on the 13th and 14th holes at Chatswood Golf Club, Sydney, Australia on 29 May 1977.

The closest to achieving 3 consecutive holes-in-one was the late Dr Joseph Boydstone on the 3rd, 4th and 9th at Bakersfield GC,

California, USA, on 10 October 1962 and the Rev Harold Snider who aced the 8th, 13th and 14th holes of the par-3 Ironwood course, Arizona, USA on 9 June 1976.

The only instance of two consecutive holes-in-one being performed in a major competition was during the Martini professional tournament at Royal Norwich on 11 June 1971. Bob Hudson, then a 25-year-old professional at Hendon, London, holed-in-one at the 11th (195 yd) and the 12th (311 yd). He finished ninth in the tournament.

Youngest and oldest
The youngest golfer recorded to have shot a hole-in-one was Coby Orr (5 years) of Littleton, Colorado on the 103 yd 5th at the Riverside Golf Course, San Antonio, Texas in 1975. The oldest golfers to have performed this feat are: (men) 99 yr 244 days Otto Bucher (Switzerland) on the 130 yd 12th at La Manga GC, Spain on 13 January 1985; (women) 96 yr Erna Ross on the 112 yd 17th at The Everglades Club, Palm Beach, Florida, USA on 25 May 1986. The British record was set by Samuel Richard Walker at the 156 yd 8th at West Hove GC, E. Sussex at the age of 92 yr 169 days on 23 June 1984.

The oldest player to score his age is C Arthur Thompson of Victoria, British Columbia, Canada, who scored 103 on the Uplands course of 6215 yd aged 103 in 1973.

Bobby Jones Award

The award is made annually by the United States Golf Association in recognition of 'distinguished sportsmanship'. The criterion of 'sportsmanship' can be difficult to define but the USGA has in mind 'the demonstration of personal qualities esteemed in sport: fair play, self-control and perhaps self-denial; generosity of spirit towards the game as a whole, and the manner of playing or behaving so as to show respect for the game and the people in it'.

RECIPIENTS

1955	Francis D Ouimet	1972	Michael Bonallack
1956	William C Campbell	1973	Gene A Littler
1957	Mrs Mildred D	1974	Byron Nelson
	Zaharias	1975	Jack Nicklaus
1958	Miss Margaret Curtis	1976	Ben Hogan
1959	Findlay S Douglas	1977	Joseph C Dey, Jr
1960	Charles Evans, Jr	1978	Bing Crosby and Bob
1961	Joseph B Carr		Hope
1962	Horton Smith	1979	Tom Kite, Jr
1963	Miss Patty Berg	1980	Charles R Yates
1964	Charles R Coe	1981	Mrs JoAnne
1965	Mrs Glenna Collett		Gunderson Carner
	Vare	1982	William J Patton
1966	Gary Player	1983	Mrs Maureen Ruttle
1967	Richard S Tufts		Garret
1968	Robert R Dickson	1984	R Jay Sigel
1969	Gerald H Micklem	1985	Fuzzy Zoeller
1970	Roberto de Vicenzo	1986	Jess W Sweetser
1971	Arnold Palmer	1987	Tom Watson

The only person to have lost two finals of the British Boys' championship later became Open champion—Sandy Lyle.

Family Connections

FAMOUS GOLFERS WITH RELATIVES DISTINGUISHED IN OTHER SPORTS

René Lacoste, the champion French tennis-player, has a wife and daughter who are champion golfers. His wife, as Simone Thion de la Chaume, became the first French-woman to win the British Women's championship in 1927. In addition, she won the Open championship of France four times. She also won the French Women's Close championship six times in a row (1925–30).

Her daughter, Catherine, is the only overseas golfer to win the US Women's Open (1967); she also won the US (1969) and British (1969) Women's Amateur championships, and several French titles.

Graham Marsh, winner of many professional tournaments all round the world, is the brother of Rodney, the Australian Test cricketer. Rodney made more Test dismissals than any other Australian wicket-keeper, reaching the 200 mark in the 1979/80 series against England.

John Lister, the New Zealander who won a tournament in 1976 on the US professional tour, and has been a consistent player there, has a brother Tom who played rugby for the New Zealand All Blacks in 1968–71.

John Schroeder, a successful American touring professional, is the son of Ted Schroeder, the Wimbledon Lawn Tennis champion in 1949.

Frank Pennink's father Karel played soccer for Holland. Pennink, a Walker Cup player, was twice English Amateur champion.

Both the father and brother of **J Morton 'Morty' Dykes** (a Walker Cup player in 1936 and Scottish Amateur champion in 1951), played rugby football for Scotland. Morty Dykes himself was a reserve for Scotland at rugby football on 17 occasions.

Charles Dennehy, son of Virginia Dennehy, American Curtis Cup Captain in 1948, was a member of the American Olympic Equestrian team.

Cecil Beamish, the Irish international golfer and semi-finalist in the 1953 Amateur championship at Hoylake, had two brothers, George and Charles, who played rugby for Ireland. For many years, in fact, George held the record number of caps for Ireland (25). Cecil would probably have played rugby for Ireland had it not been for World War II but he, George, Charles and his other brother, Victor, killed in the Battle of Britain, played rugby for the Royal Air Force. Cecil, RAF champion at golf many times, reached the rank of Air Vice Marshal as a dentist.

Greg Turner, who won the 1986 Scandinavian Enterprises Open, the Singapore Open and finished 25th in the European Order of Merit in his first season, is brother of Glenn Turner, one of the most famous of all New Zealand cricketers.

A characteristic shot of Harry Vardon with pipe, the first great stylist. (Illustrated London News)

FAMILY ACHIEVEMENTS IN IMPORTANT COMPETITIONS

FATHER AND SON

Willie Park, Sr (1860–63–66–75) and **Willie Park, Jr** (1889), both won the British Open championship.

The other father and son winners of the Open were **Old Tom Morris** (1861–62–64–67) and **Young Tom Morris** (1868–69–70–72)—the only occasion of son succeeding father as a major Open champion.

Percy Alliss and his son, **Peter**, both played for Great Britain in the Ryder Cup. Percy played three times and Peter eight. They are the only father and son on either side to have done this. Percy's best finish in the Open was equal third in 1931, Peter's eighth in 1969. He was equal eighth in 1954, 1961 and 1962.

Joe Carr and his sons, **Roddy** and **John**, have all played for Ireland; and Joe and Roddy in the Walker Cup. Both are unparalleled achievements.

Joe also established the record number of appearances for Ireland between 1947 and 1969 and in the Walker Cup between 1947 and 1967.

In 1981, John Carr reached the semi-final of the Amateur championship at St Andrews and later, the same summer, played in the Home Internationals under his father's non-playing captaincy.

Clayton Heafner played for the American Ryder Cup teams of 1949 and 1951; his son, **Vance**, played for the 1977 American Walker Cup team and, like his father, was unbeaten. He later turned professional.

Stanley Lunt and his son, **Michael**, both won the English Amateur championship, Stanley in 1934 and Michael in 1966. In addition, Michael won the British Amateur in 1963 and was runner-up a year later. He was also runner-up to Michael Bonallack in the English final of 1962.

Gary Player's son, **Wayne**, played for South Africa in the World Amateur team championship at Pinehurst in 1980. He later turned professional.

In the first British Amateur championship at Hoylake in 1885, **John Ball** defeated his father, also **John**, by 4 and 2 in the third round. It is the only instance in the championship of father and son playing against each other.

Harry Vardon, winner of the British Open more times than anyone else, had a younger brother, **Tom**, who finished second to Harry in the 1903 Open championship at Prestwick.

Jack Nicklaus, Jr won the 1985 North and South Amateur in America and played in the 1986 British Amateur before turning professional. His first appearance as a professional in Europe was in the Lancome Trophy in Paris. In the qualifying rounds of the 1986 US Amateur, 17-year-old Gary Nicklaus shot 79–73 to miss qualifying for the matchplay by 3 strokes. The championship was played at Shoal Creek, Alabama, a course designed by Jack Nicklaus.

Buddy Alexander, golf coach at Louisiana State University, won the 1986 US Amateur championship at Shoal Creek. He is the son of Skip Alexander, who won two PGA events in 1948, was fifth in the money list the same year and played for the United States in the Ryder Cup of 1949 and 1951.

Apart from the Lunts and the Carrs, two other fathers and sons have represented their countries in the Home Internationals: **Teddy** and **Michael Dawson** for Scotland; **James** and **Peter Flaherty** for Ireland.

Two fathers and sons have played for their countries in the same World Amateur team championship for the Eisenhower Trophy. In 1958 and 1960, **I S Malik** and **A S Malik** played for India; and the **Visconde de Pereira Machado** and **Nuno Alberto de Brito e Cunha** for Portugal.

In 1986, Mr Mark Parry, 56, and his son, Phillip, holed-in-one with consecutive shots at the 13th hole of the Warren Club, Dawlish, Devon. The hole is 134 yards long.

C Legh Winser, who died in Australia in December 1983 aged 99, went round Barwon Heads, Victoria in 76 strokes when he was 88.

The most famous golfing father and son partnership in South America is **Mario** and **Jaimé Gonzales**. Mario, equal eleventh in the 1948 British Open, has been a regular winner of the Brazilian Open. His son, Jaimé won the Brazilian Amateur championship four times before turning professional.

In 1952, the final of the Swiss Amateur championship was contested by **Antoine** and **André Barras**, father and son, the son winning.

Sandy Lyle, Sam Torrance and **Gordon Brand, Jr**, are all sons of leading Club professionals who are also well known teachers.

Davis Love III, Walker Cup player for America in 1985 at Pine Valley and now a professional on the US Tour, is the son of **Davis Love II** who finished equal 6th with Jack Nicklaus in the 1969 British Open at Royal Lytham and St Annes.

Antonio Cerda, whose father of the same name was a contemporary of Roberto de Vicenzo in Argentina before moving to Mexico, gained his card on the US Tour in 1975 after a fine record as an amateur. In 1967, he was Mexican and Costa Rican Amateur champion. As a professional, his best finish on the tour was tied 6th in the 1986 Los Angeles Open. His father finished 2nd, equal 5th and equal 2nd in the British Opens of 1951, 52 and 53.

GRANDSON

Tommy Armour III, who finished 50th in the 1986 European Order of Merit, is the grandson of Tommy Armour, winner of the British Open (1931) and US Open (1927).

BROTHERS

In 1963, the brothers, **Bernard** and **Geoffrey Hunt** played for Great Britain and Ireland in the Ryder Cup in Atlanta. In 1953, they contested the final of the British Assistants' championship at Hartsbourne. Bernard won 2 and 1.

Willie and **Tony Torrance** played Walker Cup golf for Great Britain. Willie in 1922 and Tony in 1924–28–30–32 and 34.

In 1932, the brothers **Rex** and **Lister Hartley** played for Great Britain in the Walker Cup match. They were paired together in the top foursome, but were beaten 7 and 6 by Jess Sweetser and George Voigt.

The brothers **Jay** and **Lionel Hebert** both played for the United States in the Ryder Cup, Lionel in 1957 and Jay in 1959 and 1961. They have also both won the USPGA championship, Lionel in 1957 and Jay in 1960.

In 1910, **Alex Smith** defeated his brother, **Macdonald**, in a play-off for the title in the US Open, which he had previously won in 1906. His victory followed that of another brother, **Willie**, in 1899. In 1906, Alex was first and Willie second.

Charles, **Ernest** and **Reg Whitcombe** all played in the Ryder Cup. In 1935, Charles and Ernest were paired together in the foursomes. Reg Whitcombe was British Open champion in 1938.

The seven **Turnesa** brothers (sons of the greenkeeper at Fairview CC) were equally famous. Six of them were professionals.

Joe Turnesa, runner-up to Walter Hagen (beaten 1 hole) in the USPGA championship of 1927, played in the Ryder Cup match of 1927 and 1929.

Jim Turnesa, the sixth son, won the USPGA championship in 1952 which earned him a place in the Ryder Cup of 1953; and **Willie**, the youngest, won the US Amateur championship in 1938 and again in 1948. He also won the British Amateur in 1947 and played in the Walker Cup, 1947–49–51.

The Spanish professionals, **Angel** and **Sebastian Miguel** were leading players in Europe for a number of years before the European circuit was established. Both won the Spanish Open championship, Angel twice and Sebastian three times, in 1961, Angel succeeding Sebastian for the title.

In the 1958 World Cup competition in Mexico City, they were runners-up together for Spain and, additionally, in partnership with Ramón Sota, they each finished second—Sebastian in 1963 and Angel in 1965.

Harry and **Arnold Bentley** both won the English Amateur championship, the only brothers to achieve the feat. Harry won in 1936, the year in which he played in the Walker Cup at Pine Valley and halved his single, the only British success in the singles. He also played in the winning British team two years later. Arnold won the English title in 1939.

Alistair and **Walter McLeod**, and **Andrew** and **Allan Brodie** are brothers who played for Scotland in the Home International series. The McLeods played in the same team, the Brodies missed by a year. **Tony** and **George Duncan** played together in the Welsh teams of 1952–59. **Roddy** and **John Carr**, sons of Joe, represented Ireland, but not in the same team.

In 1954, **Peter Toogood** won the final of the Australian Amateur championship with his brother, **John**, runner-up. Two years later, they finished first and third in the Tasmanian Open. In second place was their father Alfred.

More recently, **Severiano** and **Manuel Ballesteros** have succeeded the Miguels as the leading Spanish golfing brothers. Severiano, the best player ever to come out of Spain, has few peers and Manuel, though naturally overshadowed, is a good player in his own right. He has featured prominently in many European events, winning the 1983 Timex Open in Biarritz. Incidentally, they are nephews of Ramón Sota.

In America, **Lanny** and **Bobby Wadkins** are the most notable golfing brothers. Lanny, a Walker and Ryder Cup player, was USPGA champion in 1977 and third in the money list; Bobby, the younger by about 20 months, has yet to win a big tournament in the States, but won the first European Open in London in October 1978.

The **Wilkes brothers**, **Trevor** and **Brian** of South Africa, were both successful tournament professionals in the late fifties and early sixties.

Arthur Lacey, Ryder Cup captain in 1951, was the brother of **Charles** who finished third in the 1937 British Open championship at Carnoustie behind Reg Whitcombe and Henry Cotton.

Count John de Bendern, British Amateur champion in 1932 when he was **John de Forest**, had a brother **Alexis**, who reached the semi-final of the British Amateur in 1937.

Harold, **Alan** and **Graham Henning** were all successful tournament professionals in South Africa, Harold and Alan both winning the South African Open. A fourth brother, **Brian**, was chairman of the South African PGA.

Danny and **David Edwards** have both won tournaments on the US Tour. Danny, the elder by five years and a Walker Cup player in 1973, has won five and

Jose-Maria Olazabal, the only player to have won the British Amateur, Boys and Youths championships. (Allsport)

Jose-Maria Olazabal of Spain is the only golfer ever to have won the British Amateur (1984), the British Youths (1985) and the British Boys (1983) championships. In the autumn of 1985, he finished first in the European Tour qualifying school and in 1986 was second in the money winnings and Order of Merit on the tour itself.

David two. One of these was the 1980 Walt Disney World National Team championship with his brother. In the 1987 Bob Hope Desert Classic, David opened with a 61.

Taiwan's most famous golfing brothers are **T C** and **T M Chen**. Both played on the national amateur team before turning professional. In an open tournament in Malaysia, T M, playing as an amateur, beat the low professional by 13 strokes.

In 1985, T C or Tze-Chung Chen, broke several records before finishing joint second one stroke behind the winner. He also led the Masters briefly in 1986 on the second day but T M, Tze-Ming Chen, his elder brother, is a leading player on the Asian/Japanese tours. He won the 1983 Dunlop Phoenix in Japan, defeating Tom Watson in a play-off. He is a wizard of the short game.

In 1984, he qualified for the World Series at Firestone CC and had T C as his caddie. In Taiwan, they live in Taipei.

In February 1987, **Chen Tze Chung** won the Los Angeles Open after a play-off with Ben Crenshaw. He became only the second Asian golfer to win a tour event in America. By coincidence, his brother Chen Tze Ming just failed to win the Philippines Open the same weekend, taking a double bogey at the final hole to lose to Brian Tennyson.

Neil and **Derek James** both played for South Africa in their four-man team in the 1982 World Amateur team championship in Lausanne, Switzerland.

As celebrated in their way as the Turnesa family are the **Bessners** from Germany. There were seven sons of Josef Bessner, a greenkeeper and gardener at Golf Club Bad Kissingen in Bavaria. He then succeeded as professional.

All his sons, Ludwig, Willi, Georg, Franz, Paul, Hans and Hermann became professionals. Franz and Georg became German professional champions, Georg later representing Germany six times (1953–58) in the World (Canada) Cup.

All seven brothers appeared once in the same competition at Berlin-Wannsee in 1933. They took five of the seven prizes.

The four **Doleman** brothers, **William, Alexander, John** and **Frank** were distinguished figures in the last century. The best players were William and Alexander who finished fifth and equal ninth in the Open championship of 1870. William, who took part in his last Amateur championship in 1910, aged 73, was third in the 1872 Open.

Total entries for the USGA run championships broke all records in 1986. The 24 830 entries exceeded the 23 789 in 1985. In the past ten years, the entries accepted for USGA championships have increased more than 70 per cent. The respective figures were: US Open 5410, US Amateur 4069, Women's Open 704, Women's Amateur 387, Senior Amateur 1362, Senior Open 1225, Junior Amateur 2320, Girls' Junior 193, Women's Public Links 1085, Men's Public Links 5427, Senior Women's Amateur 137 and Mid-Amateur 2511.

BROTHERS IN LAW

Jerry Pate and **Bruce Lietzke** were members of the 1981 US Ryder Cup team. Lietzke is married to Pate's sister.

SIBLINGS

Undoubtedly the most famous brother and sister combination was **Roger** and **Joyce Wethered** (later Lady Heathcoat-Amory). Joyce won the British Women's championship four times (1922–24–25–29) and the English five times in a row (1920–24). Roger, British Amateur champion in 1923, tied for the British Open championship in 1921.

The Wethereds and the **Bonallacks** (**Michael** and **Sally**) were the only brothers and sisters to have played for Britain in the Walker and Curtis Cup, until the Moodys, Griff and Terri for America in 1979–80.

However, Charles Hezlet played in the Walker Cup and his sister, May, was British Women's champion on three occasions before the Curtis Cup started.

In 1906, the brothers, the **Hon Denys Scott** and the **Hon Osmund Scott** contested the final of the second Italian Open Amateur championship. Denys won 4 and 3. Their brother, the **Hon Michael Scott**, won the British Amateur of 1933, the oldest to do so, and played in the Walker Cup. Osmund was beaten in the 1905 final of the British Amateur by A G Barry.

Their sister, **Lady Margaret Scott**, won the first three British Women's championships (1893–95) and, to complete a remarkable golfing family, Osmund's son, **Kenneth Scott**, played for England in 1937 and 1938 while an undergraduate at Oxford University. Alas, he was killed in the war.

Claudine and **Patrick Cros**, brother and sister, were both champions of France in the same years, 1964 and 1965. She also won the French Women's Open on two occasions and Patrick the Men's Open, once. Claudine's older brother, **Jean Pierre Cros**, was French Close champion in 1959.

Franco Bevione and his sister, **Isa Goldschmid Bevione**, were national amateur champions of Italy; Franco 13 times (between 1946 and 1971) and Isa ten times (between 1952 and 1969). Franco was Italian Open Amateur champion three times.

Equally well known in Italy are **Baldovino Dassu** and his sister, **Federica**, lady champion of Italy in 1976. Baldovino, Professional and Amateur champion of Italy, won the Dunlop Masters in 1976.

In the United States, the best-known brother and sister in professional golf are **Raymond** and **Marlene Floyd**. Raymond, US Masters and USPGA champion, has been one of the leading players for a number of years. Marlene, though not as successful as her brother, is making her mark on the LPGA tour.

Sam Torrance. (Benson and Hedges)

Another brother and sister combination on the PGA and LPGA tours is **Jack** and **Jane Renner**. Jack won the 1979 West Chester Classic.

Jack Graham, semi-finalist in the British Amateur championship on four occasions, was brother of **Molly Graham**, British Women's champion in 1901. Their cousin **Allan Graham** was runner-up in the British Amateur in 1921. They were all Hoylake players and Allan's son, **John**, was captain of the Royal Liverpool GC, Hoylake, in 1956.

Monika Möller Blaubach and **Peter Möller** won the German Men's and Women's International Amateur championship in the same year (1962) on their own home course at Hamburg-Falkenstein. Monika won the national amateur on three occasions and Peter once. Peter played for Germany on 26 occasions between 1959 and 1966 and was a member of the Continent of Europe team against Great Britain and Ireland in 1962. Monika was a member of the German women's team on 29 occasions and played three times for the Continent in the Vagliano Trophy. Their mother, **Vera Möller**, was national amateur champion of Germany in 1953 and played for her country eleven times.

Marietta Gutermann-Burghartz and her brother **Jost Burghartz** both won their respective National Amateur titles of Germany in 1963 on the same course, Hannover GC. Marietta won the national title a total of ten times and the International Amateur championship of Germany on four occasions. She represented the Continent in the Vagliano Trophy four times. Jost played for Germany 16 times.

SISTERS

In 1897, **Edith Orr** defeated her sister in the final of the British Women's championship at Gullane. A third sister reached the fourth round.

It is said that when their father discovered that there had been betting on the outcome of the final involving his two daughters, he did not allow them to compete subsequently. They lived nearby in North Berwick.

The other instance of sisters in a British final was in 1907 when **May Hezlet** defeated **Florence Hezlet**. They also contested the Irish finals of 1905, 1906 and 1908. May Hezlet won those also.

May is the youngest winner of the British championship. She was 16 when she won the Irish for the first time; the following week she won the British on the same course, County Down, and celebrated her 17th birthday during the week-end between the two events. In 1905 Florence, May and Violet Hezler played first, second and third in the order for the Irish Ladies' team.

In June 1986, David Smith, a 21-handicapper from Swindon, Wiltshire, took 13 shots on the 1st hole at Marlborough GC and then at the 157-yard 2nd hole, holed-in-one.

In the same year that the Hezlet sisters contested the final of the British (1907) the **Curtis** sisters, **Margaret** and **Harriot** contested the final of the US Women's Amateur. Margaret won 7 and 6, the other remarkable record being that she succeeded Harriot as champion.

Pam and **Mervyn Barton** were both English internationals. Mervyn, later Mrs Sutherland Pilch, was an England player, but Pam was the champion. She won the British and American Women's championships in the same year, 1936.

Donna Caponi Young, twice US Women's Open champion, has a sister, **Janet Caponi LePera**, who also competes on the LPGA tour.

Mandy Rawlins, 17, played her sister, **Mrs Vicki Thomas**, 27, in the 1982 final of the Welsh women's championship.

Both have won the Welsh Ladies championship at least twice and have played together in several Welsh teams. Vicki Thomas was a member of the 1984 and 1986 Curtis Cup teams.

HUSBAND AND WIFE

John Beharrell, the 1956 British Amateur champion, is married to **Veronica Anstey**, Curtis Cup player in 1956.

Peter and **Pam Benka** played for Britain, Peter in the 1969 Walker Cup and Pam (née Tredinnick) in the Curtis Cup matches of 1966 and 1968.

Another Walker Cup and Curtis Cup husband and wife combination is **Carole** and **Ian Caldwell**. Ian, English champion in 1961, played in the Walker Cup in 1951 and 1955. Carole was a member of the Curtis Cup teams of 1978 and 1980.

Janette Robertson, Curtis Cup golfer on four occasions, married **Innes Wright**, Scottish international from 1958 to 1961. Their daughter, Pamela, has also played for Scotland and been a reserve for the Curtis Cup, thus creating a unique treble.

Tony Slark, English international and semi-finalist in the Amateur championship in 1954, is married to **Ruth Porter**, former English women's champion and Curtis Cup player.

Michael and **Angela Bonallack** were both English champions who played in the Walker and Curtis Cup respectively. Angela's sister (née Ward) was formerly English Girl champion. Michael's sister (Mrs Sally Barber) was a Curtis Cup player and his brother, Tony, an Essex county player.

John and 'Baba' **Beck** were Captain of the Walker Cup and Curtis Cup.

Yan le Quellec was 1933 French Amateur champion and his wife, **Yvonne**, the 1948 French Women's champion. Their nephew is Alexis Godillot, a famous French golfer.

Angela and Michael Bonallack. (Allsport)

Sandy Lyle's wife, **Christine** (formerly Trew), played on the women's professional in Britain after a promising career as an amateur. She was reinstated in 1985. She was a former British Youth swimming international.

Alice, the wife of **Pete Dye**, the well known American golf course architect, played in the American Curtis Cup team of 1970.

Ramon Taya, a former Spanish Amateur champion, is married to **Marie Laure de Lorenzi Taya**, a French girl who is regarded as one of the best and most stylish players in Europe. Both she and her husband have played for the Continent of Europe in the Vagliano and St Andrews Trophy matches with Great Britain and Ireland.

Gaetan and **Cecilia Mourgue d'Algue** are champions of their respective countries. Gaetan was French Open and Close Amateur champion at least twice. Cecilia, born in Sweden, has been champion of Sweden and France as well as a semi-finalist in the British Women's championship. She has played for Sweden and France in the Espirito Santo Trophy.

Jeannette and **Jürgen Weghmann** are both German internationals. Jeannette (née Edye) was International Amateur champion in 1972, playing 27 times for Germany between 1968 and 1977. Jürgen was national amateur champion in 1968 and was a member of the Continental side of 1968 which played against Great Britain and Ireland.

FATHER AND DAUGHTER

One of the most famous father and daughter combinations is **André Vagliano**, French Amateur champion in 1925, and **Lally Segard** (formerly the Vicomtesse de Saint Sauveur). She is one of the most celebrated of all Europe's lady golfers, many times champion of France and also British Women's champion in 1950.

John Panton's daughter, **Cathy**, was British Women's Amateur champion in 1976. After heading the LPGA Order of Merit in the first season of the women's professional tour in Britain, she quickly became one of its best players. John Panton, one of the best known Scottish professionals, played in the Ryder Cup three times and was the 1956 *News of the World* matchplay champion at Hoylake.

In 1981, the United States Golf Association launched the Mid-Amateur championship. It is a championship for men 25 years of age and over. The winners include Jim Holtgrieve and Jay Sigel (twice).

In 1986, the final pre-qualifying events for places at the PGA European Tour School were concluded with a play-off lasting almost 18 hours. When ten players were called to the tee to compete for one play-off spot at El Saler, Valencia, a thunderstorm forced play to be suspended overnight. When they tried again next morning, another thunderstorm delayed play for 3 hours.

MOTHER AND DAUGHTER/MOTHER AND SON

Diana Critchley (née Fishwick), British Women's champion in 1932, English champion in 1932 and Curtis Cup player in 1932 and 1934, is mother of **Bruce Critchley**. He was an England international, a Walker Cup player and semi-finalist in the 1970 Amateur championship at Royal County Down. Nowadays, he is better known as a television commentator on golf. His father, Brig. Gen. A C Critchley, a scratch golfer, was founder of the Greyhound Racing Association with Charles Munn.

Lieselotte Strenger was International Amateur champion of Germany and national Amateur champion five times. Her victories covered a span of 1934–1961. Her son, **Christian**, was also national and international amateur champion of his country and represented the Continent of Europe in the St Andrews Trophy twice.

Madame **Rene Lacoste** and **Catherine** are the most distinguished golfing mother and daughter. Both have won the British Women's Open Amateur championship, Madame Lacoste the first overseas player to do so (1927). Catherine, however, won the British, French and US Amateur championships. The highlight of a glittering career was the US Women's Open title in which she defeated the leading professionals. She is the only amateur ever to have won. She did so in 1967.

In 1962, **Jean Trainor** defeated her daughter, **Anne**, by 4 and 3 in the second round of the US Women's Amateur championship at the Rochester CC.

Erika Sellschopp was a pre-war German international champion and a member of the German team. Her son, **Erik**, was international and national Amateur champion, appeared regularly between 1966 and 1978 in German teams and was twice a member of the Continent side in the St Andrews Trophy against Great Britain and Ireland.

Angela Uzielli, British Women's Open Amateur champion in 1977 and a Curtis Cup player, is the daughter of **Peggy Carrick** who played for England in 1939 and has been Norfolk champion ten times. Angela's husband, John, is a former county golfer and winner of the President's Putter.

Kay Cornelius, who, at 14, became the youngest winner of the US Girls' Junior championship in 1981, is the daughter of **Kathy Cornelius**. Kathy, Southern Amateur champion in 1952, turned professional the following year and won seven victories on the LPGA Tour.

Sue Hedges, runner-up in the English Women's championship in 1979, is the sister-in-law of **Peter Hedges**, the British Walker Cup player. Her husband, **David**, is also a low-handicap golfer.

Gary Player's brother-in-law is **Bobby Verwey**, a leading South African tournament professional.

Dave Marr, USPGA champion in 1965, is a cousin of **Jack Burke**, champion in 1956.

Jay Haas, a winner of the US professional tour and a former Walker Cup player, is a nephew of **Bob Goalby**, the 1968 US Masters champion.

Sam Snead and his nephew, **Jesse C Snead**, played for the United States in the Ryder Cup, Sam on seven occasions and Jesse on three.

Christy O'Connor, Sr, and his nephew, **Christy O'Connor, Jr**, played in the Ryder Cup. Christy, Sr, on a record ten occasions and Christy, Jr, in 1975.

Lu Liang Huan, familiarly known as 'Mr Lu' is the uncle of **Lu Hsieh Chuen** or 'Master Lu'. 'Mr Lu' was runner-up in the British Open of 1971 and like his nephew has won many events in the Far East.

Alexis Godillot, one of the most famous French amateurs, is the nephew of **Yan** and **Yvonne le Quellec**. Yan was French champion in 1933, Yvonne in 1948 and Godillot on four occasions. Godillot has also played many times for the continent of Europe against Great Britain and Ireland.

FAMILY

As a family, the achievements of the Duncans are unique. **John Duncan** was Welsh champion in 1905 and 1909, and runner-up in 1920. His wife was Welsh Women's champion in 1922–27–28 and his sister, **Blanche**, was champion in 1906–07–08–09–12; she was also runner-up in 1905.

His brother, **J Hugh Duncan**, was semi-finalist in 1908 and 1909; he just missed meeting John in the final. With Blanche winning the Ladies' championship in 1909, it was quite a year for the Duncans but family traditions were carried on faithfully by John's two sons, **Tony** and **George**.

Tony was Welsh champion in 1938–48–52–54, and runner-up in 1933. In addition, he reached the final of the British Amateur at Hoylake in 1939 and was Captain of the British Walker Cup team in 1953.

George's best year in the Welsh championship was 1956 when he lost a notable semi-final to Iestyn Tucker, but he played for Great Britain against Europe the same year and represented Wales many times.

A third brother, **John**, who was killed in the war, was a low-handicap golfer. **Derek**, son of Hugh, was equally good while **Michael Ivor Jones**, son of Blanche Duncan, won the British Seniors' championship in 1974.

In addition to **Willie Park, Jr** who won the Open championship, like his father, **Willie Park, Sr**, **Mungo Park**, brother of Willie, Sr, was Open champion in 1874. Although a little in the shadow of his brother and nephew, he might have been even better if he had not been a sailor.

To complete the Park family, Willie Park, Jr, had a daughter, **Doris Park** (Mrs Aylmer Porter) who had a good record in ladies' international and championship golf.

J Lara Sousa e Mello, who has played for the continent of Europe against Britain, has been Portuguese champion four times. His mother **Maria** has also won the

Women's championship (1953) while his father **José de Sousa e Mello** has represented his country in international competition.

In 1968, **Michael Bonallack** won the English Amateur championship in the same year that his sister, **Sally**, was English Women's champion. His wife, **Angela**, was twice English Women's champion (1958–63) and twice reached the final of the British Women's championship (1962–74). In one of these years (1962), Michael was English champion. To complete the family's achievements, Angela's sister, **Shirley Ward**, won the English Girls' championship in 1964 while Michael's brother Tony was an Essex county player.

Versatility

GOLFERS WITH OTHER SPORTING DISTINCTIONS

Leslie Balfour Melville, 1895 British Amateur champion, played rugby and cricket for Scotland. He was also Scottish long jump, tennis and billiards champion.

'Babe' Zaharias, one of the most famous of women golfers, won two gold medals at the 1932 Olympic Games in Los Angeles. They were for the javelin and high hurdles. In each, she broke the existing world record. She was also second in the high jump.

As a golfer, she won the British and American Amateur championships and the American Women's Open three times.

Bob Falkenburg, Wimbledon tennis champion in 1948, was Brazilian Amateur golf champion three times (1959–60–61) and a regular competitor for a time in the British Amateur championship.

Leonard Crawley, English Amateur champion in 1931 and a Walker Cup player, played county cricket in England for Worcestershire and Essex; he scored nine first-class hundreds. He also toured the West Indies with the MCC in 1925. At lawn tennis he won the North of England doubles championship with his uncle, was a fine rackets player and won a gold medal at skating. He was arguably the best all-round sportsman of all time.

In 1984, J Davis of Kings Norton, Birmingham, holed-in-one on a 174-yard par-3 hole. In receipt of 2 strokes in a stableford competition, he scored six points. The only way a player could score more points would be to be in receipt of 2 strokes and hole in one on a par-4 hole.

In 1954, the Victoria GC, Melbourne produced the first Australian winner of the British Open, Peter Thomson, and the first Australian winner of the British Amateur, Doug Bachli.

However, in 1952, the Houghton GC, Johannesburg, supplied the winners of the South African Open (Sid Brews), the South African Amateur (Mickey Janks) and the South African Women's (Mrs Reggie Green).

George 'Pete' Bostwick, an American who won the 1964 French Amateur championship, was also the world champion at real tennis (1969–72).

Charlotte Dod, British Ladies' champion in 1904, was a fine all-round athlete. She won the women's singles at Wimbledon five times; was an international hockey-player, a champion skater, a skilful archer (silver in the 1908 Olympics), fine billiards player and noteworthy member of the Alpine Club.

George Lyon did not take up golf until he was 38 yet, within two years, he had won the first of eight Canadian Amateur championships and was a versatile athlete. He excelled at cricket, baseball, tennis, football, curling and rowing. As a cricketer, he established the Canadian batting record of 238 not out.

In the 1904 Olympic Games, he won the golfing medal for Canada and at the dinner following the competition, walked the length of the dining-room on his hands.

Robert A Gardner, twice US Amateur champion and runner-up in the British Amateur in 1920 to Cyril Tolley, was a fine all-round athlete. At one time, he held the world record for the pole vault and, in addition, won the American double rackets championship. He was the first to vault over the then magic height of 13 ft in winning the IC4A title on 1 June 1912. However his record only lasted seven days.

Ellsworth Vines, the famous American tennis star who won Wimbledon (1932) and Forest Hills (1931–32), later turned professional at golf and was good enough to become one of America's top 15 players.

In 1924, **Mary Kimball Browne** reached the final of the US Women's Amateur championship in the same year in which she reached the semi-final of the American Women's tennis championship at Forest Hills.

George Roberts played in the Home International golf matches for Scotland in 1937 and 1938 and also received five caps for Scotland at rugby football in 1938 and 1939.

Sam Roberts was a dual international for Wales at golf and hockey.

George Crosbie, who played international golf for Ireland, was also an Olympic yachtsman.

Yvonne le Quellec, French ladies' golf champion in 1948, was French champion at a total of five sports. The other four are hockey, tennis, skating and curling.

Eric Dalton, the South African Test cricketer who scored two hundreds against England, later became South African Amateur champion at golf in 1950 and played for his country in the first Commonwealth tournament at St Andrews in 1954. He took to golf as a result of breaking his jaw during a South African cricket tour of Australia. During his convalescence, he played golf nearly every day for a month with Ivo Whitton, the great Australian amateur. He progressed so well that at the end he had a handicap of four.

A man who claimed the wickets of Wyatt and Hammond in the first South African victory over England, he was also a fine bowls player, a hard man to beat at tennis and table tennis, an accomplished pianist and a fine baritone singer.

A few years ago, **Jack Nicklaus**, fishing off the Australian coast, caught the fourth largest blue marlin ever taken. It weighed 1358 lb.

Ted Dexter, a regular participant in major amateur golf events in Britain and winner of the 1983 and 1985 President's Putter at Rye, played 43 consecutive Test Matches for England and 62 in all. He was also captain and scored eight Test centuries.

Philippe Washer of Belgium was a Davis Cup tennis-player for many years. In addition, he played golf for his country.

Sven Tumba played golf and ice hockey for Sweden and was capped once as centre-forward for the Swedish national soccer side.

Sune Malmstrom played in the Swedish Davis Cup tennis team and for his country at golf. He was Swedish matchplay champion in 1932–36–38.

Jess Sweetser, former British and American Amateur champion was a distinguished quarter-miler during his days at Yale. He was timed at a shade over 50 sec. Sweetser won the US Amateur in 1922 and the British in 1926.

Alfred J Evans, runner-up in the 1932 and 1935 President's Putters and a participant in major championships, played cricket for England in one Test match against Australia in 1921. He also earned fame for his escapes from German prison camps in World War I when he served in the Royal Flying Corps.

Norman Stewart Mitchell-Innes, Captain of Oxford University at golf, also played one Test match for England at cricket while still an undergraduate.

Sidney Fry, runner-up in the British Amateur championship of 1902 was eight times English National Amateur champion in billiards between 1893 and 1925. In 1925, he was 57 years old. In 1899, he set a new championship record break of 168.

He was also English National Amateur snooker champion. He was the first man to win both billiards and snooker championships, which he won in the same year, 1919.

Althea Gibson became a regular competitor on the American LPGA tour after retiring as a distinguished lawn tennis champion, winner of Forest Hills and Wimbledon, both 1957–58.

Tom Crow, Australian Amateur champion in 1961 and an international golfer, was also a leading player of

---

Jeff Burn, the Shropshire and Herefordshire Vice-Captain, returned a 10 under par gross 60 in the monthly medal of the Shrewsbury Golf Club in September 1986. Burn, aged 32, returned his score on a course measuring 6212 yards without any incredible putting. He had 26 putts in all, the longest being 25 feet. He missed three of around 8 feet. His figures were 3, 3, 4, 4, 4, 2, 4, 3, 3, Out 30. 4, 4, 4, 2, 3, 4, 3, 3, 3. In 30. Total 60.

On 20 May 1984, Charlie Law, aged 84, went round his home course of Hayston, near Glasgow in 75 strokes.

Australian Rules football and a State class cricketer.

Bill Shankland, professional at Potters Bar, England, when Tony Jacklin joined him as assistant, played Rugby League for Australia.

Freddie Tait, twice British Amateur champion (1896 and 1898), was an expert rifle-shot and a first-class rugby player and cricketer. He was killed in the Boer War.

John Jacobs, British Ryder Cup player and Captain, and a well-known teacher in many countries, is also a keen fisherman. In 1978, he caught the most valuable salmon ever landed on the River Avon in Dorset. It weighed 27 lb and was sold to a local hotel for £130.

John S F Morrison, an England golfer in 1930, played football for the Corinthians and Sunderland. He also captained Cambridge University at cricket and represented Somerset. Later, he became a well-known golf course architect.

Winnie Wooldridge (née Shaw), the British Wightman Cup tennis player, reached the semi-final of the Scottish Women's golf championship in 1980. She is scratch at Wentworth, where she also coaches tennis.

Dr Reginald H B Bettington, Australian Amateur champion in 1932, was a cricketer of great note. A leg-spin bowler and attacking batsman, he was the first Australian to captain Oxford University in 1923. He won other Blues at golf and rugby; played cricket for the Gentlemen, Middlesex and was later captain of New South Wales in the year he won the NSW golf championship.

Charles Victor Lisle Hooman, who played in the first Walker Cup match and won the only game in the entire series which went to extra holes, also won a cricket Blue at Oxford, 1909–10. He helped Kent to win the County Championship and played for the Gentlemen in the same year that he played golf for England.

FAMOUS GOLFERS WITH DISTINCTIONS IN OTHER WALKS OF LIFE

Jack Westland, US Amateur champion in 1952 and runner-up in 1931, served as a US Congressman.

Bill Campbell, 1964 US Amateur champion and a member of several American Walker Cup teams, has served as a member of the West Virginia State legislature. He is also a qualified pilot. He took over the office of President of the United States Golf Association in January 1982.

Gene Littler, US Amateur champion in 1953 and US Open champion in 1961, makes a hobby of collecting vintage cars—especially Rolls Royces.

He also made a marvellous recovery from a cancer operation in spring 1972.

Raymond Oppenheimer, British Walker Cup Captain (1951) and an English International, is the world's leading breeder of bull terriers and a world authority on the breed.

William Whitelaw, Home Secretary in the Rt Hon Mrs Thatcher's 1979 Government, is a former Captain of the Royal and Ancient Golf Club (1969) and a former Cambridge Blue.

Percy Belgrave 'Laddie' Lucas, a Walker Cup player and Captain, was a distinguished fighter pilot in World War II. He later became a Member of Parliament and Chairman of the Greyhound Racing Association.

Henry Longhurst, the well-known British writer, television commentator and former German Amateur champion, served for a time as a Member of Parliament when Winston Churchill was Prime Minister.

Tom Blackwell, Captain of the Royal and Ancient Golf Club in 1963/64, was later twice Deputy Senior Steward of the Jockey Club.

Bing Crosby was a good enough golfer to have started 3, 3, in a British Amateur championship at St Andrews. He is also one of only two players to have holed in one at the famous 16th at Cypress Point, California. The shoot involves a carry of some 180 yd across the edge of the Pacific Ocean.

He died suddenly on 14 October 1977, after playing a round of golf in Madrid. His son **Nathaniel** who won the 1981 US Amateur championship continues to run the Bing Crosby tournament held in California in January.

Robin Cater, a Walker Cup player for Britain in 1955, later became Chairman of the Distillers' Company. In 1986, he was elected Captain of the Royal and Ancient GC.

Bobby Locke, four times British Open champion, flew as a bomber pilot with the South African Airforce during World War II.

Bernard Darwin, twice a semi-finalist in the British Amateur championship and winner of his Walker Cup single, when he was called in to replace the sick British captain, was an incomparable writer on golf. Grandson of Charles Darwin, he practised law on leaving Cambridge but decided on a life writing about golf. He was described by Herbert Asquith as 'the greatest living essayist in the English language' and was said by another eminent critic to be 'one of the six best essayists since Charles Lamb'. He was also a great authority on the works of Dickens.

Arnold Palmer and **Jerilyn Britz**, the 1979 US Women's Open champion, are qualified pilots.

Peter Thomson stood as Liberal candidate for Prahran in the Victoria State government election, Australia, in 1982. He is also Chairman of the James McGrath Foundation which established Odyssey House in Melbourne which helps and cares for the problems of drug addicts.

During the 1939–45 war, some of the most important military decisions were taken in the concrete corridors that ran below Wentworth. It was the headquarters of GHQ Home Forces. The underground fortress extended from the clubhouse, beneath the practice ground and half-way up Wentworth West Drive.

Golden age of golf course architecture

For the first two hundred years or so of the game, golf courses simply evolved. Golfers adapted to the natural shapes and contours, particularly on terrain known as linksland. Then, in the latter half of the nineteenth century, man himself began to take a hand although, in the opinion of Tom Simpson, the early architects 'failed to reproduce any of the features of the courses on which they had been bred and born'.

Their efforts bore the artificial look of flat, unimaginatively shaped platform greens. The 'architects' were largely greenkeepers and professionals who relied pretty much on their instinct, drew no plans and incorporated features (often unsuitable) as they found them. Their work involved little construction and invariably depended on local turf which, inland, was hardly perfect for the purpose.

However, it was probably the courses' lack of aesthetic appeal which prompted an approach whereby golf course architecture became a recognized art—a career to which such as Harry Colt and Alister Mackenzie, turned after qualifying as solicitor and doctor respectively. Apart from what may be termed an eye for land, they realized that successful course building incorporated elements of botany, soil chemistry, drainage, civil engineering, agronomy and surveying.

The popularity of the game spread rapidly between 1890 and 1930 and, though the seaside was still regarded as the traditional setting, they took it to provincial towns and cities. The glories of the heathland to the south and west of London convinced them that inland golf could no longer be deemed to be second best. So, slowly at first, but quickly gathering pace, a golden era was born.

The best known architects, who only had simple machinery at their disposal, were Willie Park, Jr, Harry Colt, Herbert Fowler, Alister Mackenzie, MD, J F Abercromby, C H Alison, James Braid, C K Hutchison and Tom Simpson. However, golf was growing apace by this time in America and elsewhere and the names that later came to be revered were Charles Blair Macdonald, the Dunns, Donald Ross and A W Tillinghast together with

Mackenzie to whom goes the credit for Cypress Point and Augusta. But there were one or two individuals who confined their activity to just one great course. Such men were George Crump (Pine Valley), Jack Neville (Pebble Beach) and Hugh Wilson (Merion).

All these men might be classed as the founders of golf course architecture which is part intuition, part knowledge and part judgment backed up by the technical subjects mentioned. They placed the emphasis on strategic design which put the onus on the player to think. They ensured this by clever bunkering of fairways, use of existing natural features and by making green design an art in itself.

They angled, tilted, raised and sculpted greens to give the advantage to the player who was correctly placed from the tee; and they created interesting levels that added spice to the putting. They encouraged boldness and created spectacular holes which, hitherto, might have been thought of as impossible.

They had to adjust their sights as hickory became replaced by steel shafts, a battle that has been carried into the present day by the continued improvement in the distance the ball can be hit and by the miracles of recovery which the wedge and sand wedge have wrought.

Nowadays, the profession has yielded to the machine. All sorts of successful courses have popped up in all sorts of places on land whose natural origins was jungle, swamp, desert, hill or refuse tip. Terrifying sums of money are lent to make it all possible but it still remains an exercise in blending courses with the surroundings, of creating new, sympathetic, landscapes as well as testing and giving pleasure to the legions of golfers who try their hand.

Golf courses have a great air of permanence as the following list of the work of some of the early architects (now dead) illustrates. It is not intended as a complete list and the courses mentioned only constitute a random selection of the courses they designed or extensively remodelled.

John Frederick Abercromby (1861–1935): Addington, Coombe Hill, Cowdray Park, Knole Park, Manor House Hotel (Moretonhampstead), West Kent, Worplesdon and Haagsche (Holland).

Charles Hugh Alison (1882–1952): Sunningdale and Wentworth (with Colt), Longniddry, Real Santander (Spain), Huntingdale (Australia), Bryanston (Johannesburg) and Fuji, Hirona, Kawana and Tokyo (Japan).

James Braid (1870–1950): Hankley Common, North Hants (Fleet), Luffenham Heath, St Enodoc, Thorpeness, Wildernesse, Blairgowrie, Boat of Garten, Brora, and the Singapore Island GC (Bukit Timah in 1924).

Harry Shrapland Colt (1869–1951): Eden (St Andrews) Blackmoor, Denham, Brokenhurst, Northamptonshire County, Moor Park, Sandy Lodge, Stoke Poges, Rye, St George's Hill, Burhill, Camberley Heath, Sunningdale (alterations and additions), Little Aston, Frankfurter and Hamburger (Germany), Southerndown, Royal Waterloo and Royal Zoute (Belgium); also, helped in finishing Pine Valley.

The 1993 Walker Cup match will be held at Chicago Golf Club, one of five charter members when the USGA was formed in 1894. It was the site of the US Open and US Amateur in 1897, two of nine USGA championships held there. The Walker Cup was staged there in 1928 when America had a ten-point margin of victory.

The venues for the next five US Open championships are as follows: 1988, The Country Club, Brookline. 1989, Oak Hill CC, Rochester, NY. 1990, Medinah CC, Chicago. 1991, Hazeltine National GC, Chaska, Minnesota. 1992, Pebble Beach, California.

 The first and only time that Chaska has been used previously resulted in victory for Tony Jacklin.

William Herbert Fowler (1856–1941): Beau Desert, The Berkshire (Red and Blue), Delamere Forest, Saunton, Walton Heath, West Surrey, Cruden Bay, Blackwell and RAC.

Alister Mackenzie, MD (1870–1934): Cypress Point, Augusta, Royal Melbourne, Pasatiempo (California), Alwoodley, Castletown (Isle of Man), Moortown, Fulford, Heretaunga (New Zealand), Jockey Club (Buenos Aires).

Willie Park, Jr (1864–1925): Atlantic City, Maidstone (Long Island NY), Vienna GC (Austria), Aldeburgh, Berkhamsted, Hollinwell, Huntercombe, Temple, Luffness, Sunningdale (Old).

Donald James Ross (1872–1948): Broadmoor, Seminole, East Lake, Bob O'Link CC, Cedar Rapids, Shawnee CC, Chevy Chase, Oakland Hills, Englewood CC, Montclair GC, Oak Hill, Siwanoy, Pinehurst, Pine Needles, Inverness (Toledo), Scioto, Aronimink, Myrtle Beach, and CC of Havana and Havana Biltmore (Cuba).

Philip MacKenzie Ross (1890–1974): Royal Guernsey, Turnberry (Ailsa), Pyle and Kentig, Castletown (Isle of Man), Southerness, Estoril, GC d'Hardelot, Royal Golf Club des Fagnes (Spain), and Club de Campo de Malaga.

Tom Simpson (1877–1964): Royal Antwerp, Royal GC des Fagnes, Spa (Belgium), Hardelot, Hossegor, Chiberta (Biarritz), Club du Lys Chantilly, Carlow GC (Ireland).

Albert Warren Tillinghast (1874–1942): Baltusrol, Fresh Meadow, Winged Foot, Brook Hollow, Indian Hills, Quaker Ridge, Newport (RI), Knollwood.

Charles Blair Macdonald (1856–1939): Chicago GC (Wheaton), St Louis CC, National Golf Links of America (Long Island), Greenbriar, Mid-Ocean (Bermuda).

Miscellaneous

In February 1983, Isao Aoki became the first Japanese golfer to win a tournament on the US Tour. He triumphed in the Hawaiian Open by holing an 80-yard pitch for an eagle 3 at the 539-yard 18th. He won by 1 stroke from Jack Renner.

On 12 February 1984, Lynn Adams and Catherine Duggan played the last round of the Sarasota Classic at Bent Tree Golf and Racquet Club in 1 hr 35 min 33 sec on a course measuring 6124 yards. Duggan scored 72 and Adams 78. This is an LPGA record.

In 1986, the Chinese Open Amateur championship was restored after a gap of 38 years. It was won by 40-year-old Michael Evans of California, who was the only player to break 300 at Chung Shan Hot Spring GC, the course designed by Arnold Palmer. His four round total was 296 (76, 72, 76, 72).

In 1986, Arnold Palmer scored a hole-in-one twice at the same hole on consecutive days. The hole in question was the 187-yard 3rd hole at the New Tournament Players Club at Avenel outside Washington. He used a 5-iron in each case. They came on the first and second days of the Pro-Am in the Senior PGA Tour's inaugural Chrysler Cup. The odds against such a happening were put at 9 000 000 to 1.

Victory for Nancy Lopez at the Sarasota Classic, the second event on the 1987 LPGA Tour schedule, proved to be the passing of a significant milestone in her outstanding professional golf career. Now the holder of 35 LPGA tournament titles, she was inducted into the prestigious LPGA Hall of Fame in July 1987 when she reached ten years of membership with the Association.

David Graham, US Open champion in 1981, shares with Arnaud Massy, British Open champion in 1907, the distinction of starting to play golf left-handed and converting to right-handed.

Paul Azinger, who finished 29th in the US money winners' list in 1986, won his first tour event in January 1987, the Phoenix Open. By contrast, the following week's tournament, the AT and T National Pro-Am, brought victory to Johnny Miller, three months short of his 40th birthday. It was Miller's 23rd victory on the tour but his first since the Honda-Inverrary Classic in March 1983.

Greg Norman was voted Australia's sportsman of the year for 1986. Such polls are common throughout the world but golf winners are rare. He was also elected BBC Overseas Sports Personality for 1986.

In 1928, Colonel Duggie Lyall Grant and Major Phil Hulls played 100 holes in a day at Royal Wimbledon with a relay of caddies and food laid on.

They played 26 holes in 2 hr 35 min before breakfast. They then played two further 18-holes, the first in 1 hr 45 min and the second in 1 hr 40 min, followed by lunch. After lunch, they played a further round in 1 hr 50 min and a final 20 holes in 2 hr 5 min. The total of 100 holes took 9 hr 55 min.

At the Chester saleroom of Phillips Fine Art Auctioneers on 23 January 1987, a world record price was reached for a mint condition Gourlay feather ball from the mid-19th century. It fetched £4500. Also included in the sale were four small pamphlets—among the earliest publications on the game. One, 'Historical Gossip' made £11 200.

INDEX

Major entries are indicated by **bold** type; illustrations are indicated by *italics*: colour plates by *col*.

The names in these tables have not been included in this index; pp. 149–51 Ryder Cup, individual records; pp. 164–7 British Amateur Championship results; pp. 171–5 US Amateur Championship results; pp. 178–83 Walker Cup players; p. 185 World Amateur Team Championship results; pp. 191–2 Ladies British Open Amateur Championship; pp. 195–6 US Women's Amateur Championship results; pp. 201–5 Curtis Cup players.